20th SIGMORPHON Workshop on Computational Research in Phonetics, Phonology, and Morphology (SIGMORPHON 2023)

Toronto, Canada
14 July 2023

ISBN: 978-1-7138-8180-3

Printed from e-media with permission by:

Curran Associates, Inc.
57 Morehouse Lane
Red Hook, NY 12571

Some format issues inherent in the e-media version may also appear in this print version.

Printed with permission by Curran Associates, Inc. (2024)

Association for Computational Linguistics
209 N. Eighth Street
Stroudsburg, Pennsylvania 18360

Phone: 1-570-476-8006
Fax: 1-570-476-0860

acl@aclweb.org

Additional copies of this publication are available from:

Curran Associates, Inc.
57 Morehouse Lane
Red Hook, NY 12571 USA
Phone: 845-758-0400
Fax: 845-758-2633
Email: curran@proceedings.com
Web: www.proceedings.com

ACL 2023

The 20th SIGMORPHON Workshop on Computational Research in Phonetics, Phonology, and Morphology (SIGMORPHON 2023)

July 14, 2023

Order copies of this and other ACL proceedings from:

Association for Computational Linguistics (ACL)
209 N. Eighth Street
Stroudsburg, PA 18360
USA
Tel: +1-570-476-8006
Fax: +1-570-476-0860
acl@aclweb.org

Introduction

eWelcome to the 20th SIGMORPHON Workshop on Computational Research in Phonetics, Phonology, and Morphology, to be held on July 14, 2023 as part of ACL in Toronto. The workshop aims to bring together researchers interested in applying computational techniques to problems in morphology, phonology, and phonetics. Our program this year highlights the ongoing investigations into how neural models process phonology and morphology, as well as the development of finite-state models for low-resource languages with complex morphology.

We received 22 submissions, and after a competitive reviewing process, we accepted 12, for an acceptance rate of 54.5%. The workshop is very happy to present two invited talks this year. Carmen Saldana, from the University of Zürich, and CUNY's Kyle Gorman presented talks at this year's workshop.

This year also marks the seventh iteration of the SIGMORPHON Shared Task. We hosted two Shared Tasks this year:
The UniMorph Shared Task on Typologically Diverse and Acquisition-Inspired Morphological Inflection Generation continued SIGMORPHON's tradition of shared tasks that investigate inflectional patterns. The task had two parts. The first part invited participants to build models that predict an inflected form from either a lemma, or other inflected form, as well as desired properties of the output. The second part investigates the cognitive plausibility of inflectional forms - namely, the task asks users to train a classification model that determines the phonological constraints that lead to generalization patterns in Korean; the final part investigates child-like errors made by inflectional systems.

The Shared Task on Interlinear glossing challenges participants to automate the process of glossing morphological processes in lower-resource languages - a task that is essential in language documentation. In the open track, participants train a model that produces a morphologically-specified gloss from the original source sentence, a canonically-segmented representation, and optionally, a second language translation. In the closed track, the segmented representation is absent.

We also present the results from the 2022 Shared Task on Cross-Lingual and Low-Resource Grapheme-Phoneme prediction. Due to time constraints with last year's proceedings, we were unable to publish the results. We apologize to the organizers and participants, who have had to wait a year to see their work in print.

We are grateful to the program committee for their careful and thoughtful reviews of the papers submitted this year. Likewise, we are thankful to the shared task organizers for their hard work in preparing the shared tasks. We are looking forward to a workshop covering a wide range of topics, and we hope for lively discussions.

Garrett Nicolai, Eleanor Chodroff, Çagri Çöltekin, and Fred Mailhot, workshop organization team.

Organizing Committee

Co-Chair

Garrett Nicolai, University of British Columbia
Eleanor Chodroff, University of York
Çagri Çöltekin, University of Tübingen
Fred Mailhot, Dialpad, Inc.

SIGMORPHON Officers

President: Garrett Nicolai, University of British Columbia
Secretary: Miikka Silfverberg, University of British Columbia
At Large: Eleanor Chodroff, University of York
At Large: Çağrı Çöltekin, University of Tübingen
At Large: Fred Mailhot, Dialpad, Inc.

Program Committee

Program Committee

Khuyagbaatar Batsuren, National University of Mongolia
Gasper Begus, University of California, Berkeley
Canaan Breiss, UCLA
Basilio Calderone, Université Toulouse Jean Jaurès & CNRS
Daniel Dakota, Indiana University
Aniello De Santo, University of Utah
Indranil Dutta, Jadavpur University
Jason Eisner, Johns Hopkins University + Microsoft Corporation
Micha Elsner, The Ohio State University
Michael Ginn, University of Colorado
Omer Goldman, Bar Ilan University
Nizar Habash, New York University Abu Dhabi
Nabil Hathout, CLLE, CNRS & Universite de Toulouse
Mathilde Hutin, Université Paris-Saclay, CNRS, LIMSI
Cassandra L. Jacobs, University at Buffalo
Adam Jardine, Rutgers University
Jordan Kodner, Stony Brook University
Sandra Kübler, Indiana University
Giorgio Magri, Centre National de la Recherche Scientifique
Rob Malouf, San Diego State University
Connor Mayer, UCLA
Sarah Moeller, University of Colorado
Kemal Oflazer, Carnegie Mellon University
Jeff Parker, Brigham Young University
Jelena Prokic, Leiden University
Jonathan Rawski, San Jose State University
Brian Roark, Google Inc.
Maria Ryskina, Massachusetts Institute of Technology
Miikka Silfverberg, University of British Columbia
Kairit Sirts, University of Tartu
Caitlin Smith, University of North Carolina at Chapel Hill
Morgan Sonderegger, McGill University
Kenneth Steimel, Educational Testing Service
Ekaterina Vylomova, University of Melbourne
Adam Wiemerslage, University of Colorado Boulder
Adina Williams, Meta Platforms, Inc.
Colin Wilson, Johns Hopkins University
Changbing Yang, University of British Columbia
Kristine Yu, University of Massachusetts Amherst

Keynote Talk: Cross-linguistic recurrent patterns in morphology mirror human cognition

Carmen Saldana
University of Zürich
2023-07-14 08:30:00 –

Abstract: A foundational goal of language science is to detect and define the set of constraints that explain cross-linguistic recurrent patterns (i.e., typological universals) in terms of fundamental shared features of human cognition. In this talk, I will present a series of Artificial Language Learning experimental studies which test a hypothesised link between biases in language learning and morphological universals in typology both at the syntagmatic (i.e., morpheme order) and paradigmatic levels (e.g., structure of inflectional paradigms). I will focus in particular on two types of universals in inflectional morphology: (1) affixes with stronger structural relationships to the word stem tend to appear linearly closer to it, and (2) different categories with the same identity (be it the same word form, or the same word structure) in morphological paradigms tend to be semantically similar. The results from the studies I will present provide evidence in favour of a shared typological and learning bias towards compositional transparency and locality in morpheme order, and a bias towards partitions of morphological paradigms that reflect semantic relatedness. In light of these results, I will argue that cross-linguistic recurrent morphological patterns mirror to some extend universal features of human cognition.

Bio: Carmen Saldana is currently a postdoctoral fellow in the Department of Comparative Language Science at the University of Zurich. Her research focuses on investigating the cognitive biases and processes that shape the current cross-linguistic distributions of morphosyntactic features and their evolution. Her work specifically contributes to the understanding of the relationship between individuals' cognitive biases at play during language learning and use and universal tendencies in morpheme order and paradigmatic morphological structure. She carries out her research within a comprehensive interdisciplinary framework combining methods from linguistic theory, quantitative typology and experimental linguistics.

Keynote Talk: Deep Phonology Features in Computational Phonology

Kyle Gorman
City University of New York
2023-07-14 13:00:00 –

Abstract: The linguist Ray Jackendoff considers "the discovery of distinctive features . . . to be a scientific achievement on the order of the discovery and verification of the periodic table in chemistry." Despite this, quite a bit of work in phonology—whether formal or computational—works with extensional sets of indivisible segments rather than the intensional, internally-structured definitions derived from distinctive features. In this talk I will first present philosophical and empirical arguments that phonological patterns are defined intensionally: segments are bundles of features and processes are defined in terms of "natural classes", or conjunctions of feature specifications. Then, I will argue against the received wisdom—both in formal and computational phonology—that phonological patterns should be specified "minimally", in terms of the fewest possible features consistent with the observed data. I show that feature minimization has undesirable cognitive and computational properties. In contrast, feature maximization—which, under the intensional view, is equivalent to set intersection—is empirically adequate and free of the problems that plague feature minimization.

Bio: Kyle Gorman is a professor of linguistics at the Graduate Center, City University of New York, and director of the master's program in computational linguistics. He is also a software engineer at Google LLC. Along with his collaborators, he is the author of Finite-State Text Processing and of award-winning papers at ACL 2019 and WNUT 6.

Table of Contents

Program

Friday, July 14, 2023

08:25 - 08:30 *Opening Remarks*

08:30 - 09:30 *Invited Talk:Carmen Saldana*

09:30 - 10:30 *Morning Session:Morphology*

Evaluating Cross Lingual Transfer for Morphological Analysis: a Case Study of Indian Languages
Siddhesh Pawar, Pushpak Bhattacharyya and Partha Talukdar

Joint Learning Model for Low-Resource Agglutinative Language Morphological Tagging
Gulinigeer Abudouwaili, Kahaerjiang Abiderexiti, Nian Yi and Aishan Wumaier

Generalized Glossing Guidelines: An Explicit, Human- and Machine-Readable, Item-and-Process Convention for Morphological Annotation
David R. Mortensen, Ela Gulsen, Taiqi He, Nathaniel Robinson, Jonathan Amith, Lindia Tjuatja and Lori Levin

Lightweight morpheme labeling in context: Using structured linguistic representations to support linguistic analysis for the language documentation context
Bhargav Shandilya and Alexis Palmer

10:30 - 11:00 *Morning Break*

11:00 - 12:00 *Post-break Session:Phonology and Phonetics*

Investigating Phoneme Similarity with Artificially Accented Speech
Margot Masson and Julie Carson-berndsen

Improving Automated Prediction of English Lexical Blends Through the Use of Observable Linguistic Features
Jarem Saunders

Colexifications for Bootstrapping Cross-lingual Datasets: The Case of Phonology, Concreteness, and Affectiveness
Yiyi Chen and Johannes Bjerva

Character alignment methods for dialect-to-standard normalization
Yves Scherrer

Friday, July 14, 2023 (continued)

12:00 - 13:00 *Lunch*

13:00 - 14:00 *Invited Talk:Kyle Gorman*

14:00 - 14:30 *ACL Findings Session*

AxomiyaBERTa:A Phonologically-aware Transformer Model for Assamese
Abhijnan Nath, Sheikh Mannan and Nikhil Krishnaswamy

Do Transformer Models do Phonology like a Linguist?
Saliha Muradoğlu and Mans Hulden

14:30 - 15:30 *Glossing Shared Task*

15:30 - 16:00 *Afternoon Break*

16:00 - 17:00 *Inflection Shared Task*

Friday, July 14, 2023 (continued)

17:00 - 18:00 *Afternoon Session:Multilinguality and Language Resources*

Multilingual Sequence-to-Sequence Models for Hebrew NLP
Matan Eyal, Hila Noga, Roee Aharoni, Idan Szpektor and Reut Tsarfaty

Translating a low-resource language using GPT-3 and a human-readable dictionary
Micha Elsner and Jordan Needle

Revisiting and Amending Central Kurdish Data on UniMorph 4.0
Sina Ahmadi and Aso Mahmudi

Jambu: A historical linguistic database for South Asian languages
Aryaman Arora, Adam Farris, Samopriya Basu and Suresh Kolichala

Translating a low-resource language using GPT-3 and a human-readable dictionary

Micha Elsner and **Jordan Needle**
Department of Linguistics
The Ohio State University
Columbus, Ohio
{elsner.14,needle.6}@osu.edu

Abstract

We investigate how well words in the polysynthetic language Inuktitut can be translated by combining dictionary definitions, without use of a neural machine translation model trained on parallel text. Such a translation system would allow natural language technology to benefit from resources designed for community use in a language revitalization or education program, rather than requiring a separate parallel corpus. We show that the text-to-text generation capabilities of GPT-3 allow it to perform this task with BLEU scores of up to 18.5. We investigate prompting GPT-3 to provide multiple translations, which can help slightly, and providing it with grammar information, which is mostly ineffective. Finally, we test GPT-3's ability to derive morpheme definitions from whole-word translations, but find this process is prone to errors including hallucinations.

1 Introduction

In low-resource language communities, resource creation efforts are restricted by the limited time community members can contribute— and this problem is worsened when effort must be divided between development of community-facing resources and those targeted at machines. Language revitalization and pedagogy programs need dictionaries (especially those which incorporate tools for morphological analysis and flexible search) and grammar lessons, while machine translation systems need large corpora. If community-facing resources could be used within machine learning systems to compensate for the limited availability of text, community efforts could serve both pedagogical and technological goals at the same time. But while this has occasionally been attempted, techniques for doing so are still not effective enough to serve as standard methods.

One reason why community-facing resources like bilingual dictionaries have not been widely used in applications like low-resource translation is that understanding definitions can require sophisticated tools for natural language understanding. Recent advances in large language model technology (LLMs) provide a promising candidate for such a toolset, at least for definitions written in high-resource languages. In this paper, we investigate methods for using a representative LLM, GPT-3, to translate multi-morphemic words in Inuktitut using dictionary definitions for the morphemes. In addition, we measure GPT-3's capacity to perform the reverse task of inferring the dictionary definition of a morpheme given a decomposed word in which it occurs.

Inuktitut is a polysynthetic language in which words can be very long and morphologically complex. As such, it is representative of a number of languages of the Americas for which natural language processing tasks have historically been difficult due to limited resources and typological differences from better-resourced languages (Mager et al., 2018a). Computational tools are an important part of education or revitalization efforts for American languages, including Inuktitut (Ngoc Le and Sadat, 2020).

We show that GPT-3 can stitch together English dictionary definitions to produce reasonable translations of many Inuktitut words. We investigate two further questions: methods for dealing with morphemes with multiple definitions, and the extent to which performance can be improved by priming GPT-3 with some grammatical information. We envision our system as one component of an interactive dictionary/translation system, in which a human learner or non-native speaker asks for possible analyses of a morphologically complex form and is given both a morph-by-morph gloss and some possible translations into fluent English. This kind of system might help to bridge the gap between a conventional dictionary, which is incapable of interactively translating morphologically complex words into fluent English, and full-scale neural ma-

Proceedings of the 20th SIGMORPHON workshop on Computational Research in Phonetics, Phonology, and Morphology, pages 1–13
July 14, 2023

chine translation (NMT), which is data-hungry and non-transparent. We further see possibilities for suggesting new dictionary definitions which can be curated by native speakers. Finally, we believe it holds some potential as a stepping stone towards larger-scale NMT applications by providing simple examples for use in a curriculum learning paradigm (Platanios et al., 2019; Liang et al., 2021, among others).

2 Related work

The use of bilingual dictionary entries in neural machine translation was pioneered by Luong et al. (2015), who augment an English/French MT system with mechanisms for aligning rare words across languages, then copying material from definitions to translate them. This work makes several key assumptions about the benefits dictionary definitions can provide. In particular, it assumes a relatively capable NMT system already exists. Because of this, the main contribution of the dictionary is to provide lexical equivalents for rare items. In most cases, these are content words, and their definitions, once known, are easily integrated into the translated sentence (Dinu et al., 2019; Zhang et al., 2021). Pham et al. (2018); Niehues (2021) are among the earliest to provide dictionary information as augmented input rather than via a custom architecture (thus moving toward a zero-shot method), but still requires the NMT system to be trained to use definitions.

Our work follows from recent approaches which use LLMs rather than purpose-built NMT systems. The ability of LLMs to translate some high-resource language pairs in a prompt-based zero or few-shot setting is established by Brown et al. (2020). Some other recent papers attempt to augment LLMs with information derived from dictionaries or phrase tables. Sun et al. (2022) translates full sentences, using hints from a phrase aligner (Dou and Neubig, 2021). Their approach also emphasizes the monolingual text-to-text generation capacity of LLMs, but uses aligned phrases rather than dictionary definitions intended for human readers. The closest point of comparison to our work is Ghazvininejad et al. (2023), which improves translation performance by augmenting few-shot prompts with dictionary translations for a few selected words. Unlike our setting, where the baseline NMT system performs poorly, their languages are selected so that the baseline NMT model performs reasonably without augmentation (10-30% BLEU).

In contrast to these approaches, we assume a setting in which common morphs, including functional as well as content items, must be translated with the aid of the dictionary. While this is an artificial constraint in the case of Inuktitut, which does have enough parallel text to train an NMT system, it is the case for other low-resource polysynthetic languages of the Americas which lack parallel corpora large enough to train any NMT system. Even where data is more plentiful, dictionary definitions are potentially helpful for translating functional items in polysynthetic languages because these languages can have very large paradigms with very unbalanced attestations in corpora. Inuktitut has a polypersonal agreement system in which subject and object person and number are both marked on verbs; some subject-object markers rarely appear in written corpora due to discourse constraints (for example, dual subjects). Other morphosemantic distinctions (such as dual number, evidentiality, intensifiers and applicatives) which are common in American languages but rare in European ones, are translated in very different ways across contexts, leading MT systems to misalign them due to limited data (Mager et al., 2018b).

In this setting, dictionary definitions may be patched together in relatively complex ways. First, composing the definitions is more difficult than simple concatenation: *takujara* "I see him/her" is made up of *taku* "see" and *jara* "I ... him/her" (1SG>3SG). Second, Inuktitut uses derivational processes to express terms which have independent content words in English. *qukiut* "gun" is made up of *qukit* "shoot" and the instrumental marker *ut*. While a literal translation would produce "an instrument for shooting", the leap to paraphrase this expression as "gun" requires a deeper representation of English semantics. Thus, while previous systems could use dictionary material mainly by copying, our task setting emphasizes text-to-text generation.

Related tasks which use language modeling to patch together fragments of target-language structure include bag-to-sequence word ordering (Hasler et al., 2017) and dependency linearization (Mille et al., 2020). Generating fluent text from grammatical element annotations is also similar to generating translations from glosses (Zhang and Duh, 2021; Garera and Yarowsky, 2008), although, despite recent interest in glosses (e.g. Moeller and Hulden, 2021), this task is also comparatively understudied.

Inuktitut itself is one of the best-resourced indigenous American languages, with a large parallel corpus collected from the Nunavut Parliamentary Hansards (Joanis et al., 2020); their baseline NMT system yields an IU→EN BLEU score of 35.0. This dataset was used as a challenge for the Workshop on Machine Translation in 2020 (Barrault et al., 2020). Scores remained low compared to better-resourced languages— the system rated highest by humans reports a BLEU score of only 29.1 on test (Zhang et al., 2020). As stated, we use Inuktitut as a potential model for less-resourced polysynthetic languages where even this level of NMT performance is not available.

In addition to assuming access to a dictionary, we also assume access to a system which provides canonical morphological segmentations (based on Farley (2012) and further described in Section 3), so that a complex word can be decomposed into parts whose lexical entries can be accessed. Such systems (Wiemerslage et al., 2022) can be developed with access to substantially less data than NMT systems. They may be created using finite-state toolkits (Park et al., 2021) or supervised learning from relatively small annotated datasets (Mager et al., 2020; Liu et al., 2021), potentially incorporating active learning (Grönroos et al., 2016).

Segmentation of Inuktitut is easier than translation— Uqailaut (Farley, 2012) is a widely used finite-state system for canonical segmentation of Inuktitut. Micher (2017) describes an improved segmenter with neural disambiguation; Roest et al. (2020) conduct more recent experiments on segmentation using Transformer networks. While our assumption that a segmentation system is available constitutes a weakness of our method, we hope that future work can continue to reduce the resource burden of developing such systems and can also tie their development more closely to community-facing resources such as grammar texts.

3 Data and metrics

We extract a lexicon of Inuktitut morphemes and their definitions from the Uqausiit dictionary (`uqausiit.ca`) created by Inuit Uqausinginnik Taiguusiliuqtiit, an Inuit language authority funded by the Nunavut Legislature. Uqausiit also provides example phrases with English translations and hand-annotated partial morphological decompositions. We extract all single-word example phrases with a multi-morphemic partial decomposition for development and testing of our translation systems. Tables 1, 2 and 3 show statistics of the Uqausiit datasets used in this paper.

Whole words	Count	With seg.
Dev.	50	22
Test	448	219

Table 1: Statistics of the translation data from Uqausiit.

Target morpheme	Instances	Unique
Root	219	89
Functional	218	130

Table 2: Statistics of the definition prediction data from Uqausiit.

Morphemes	Count
Root	2782
Grammatical	1524
Variable	157
Total	4462

Table 3: Statistics of the Uqausiit morpheme dictionary.

Because our aim is primarily to evaluate the potential of LLMs to operate on dictionary definitions, rather than to evaluate algorithms for segmentation, we use a fixed canonical morphological segmentation for each word in our dataset. These are provided by a partial oracle which is implementationally simple to create. We run the Uqailaut FST segmenter (Farley, 2012), which produces a set of candidate analyses. We then intersect these analyses with the partial decomposition of the phrase from Uqausiit. If one or more analyses match, we select the first one and return it. If Uqailaut cannot analyze the word, or produces no analyses matching the partial decomposition, we do not use the word. (Many of these errors result from orthographic or dialectal variation beyond the scope of Uqailaut's design, as noted by Mallon (2000).)

For instance, *sikujuittuq* "an area of the ocean where ice does not form" has the Uqausiit partial segmentation *siku-juit*, without the final *tuq*. Uqailaut produces 6 candidate segmentations, which vary as to the analysis of the medial *juitt* sequence; of these, we select *siku-juit-juq* since this matches the provided partial segmentation. (The resulting segmentation may still contain an incorrect element which is not part of the partial decomposition; we have no way to measure how often this occurs, but did not find cases in development.)

We also create datasets for creating dictionary definitions, for both root and functional morphemes. In each case, we use a whole word with its translation as the prompt, and query the definition of one of the component morphemes. We assume the root morpheme is the first one in the word; for functional morphemes, we select a later one at random. We create instances for all 219 segmentable words in the test set.[1] Some of these instances ask for a definition of the same query morpheme (but with different whole-word prompts); there are 89 unique root types and 130 unique functional types in the dataset. Where a query morpheme has multiple possible definitions, we refer to Uqausiit and the whole-word definition to select the correct one as a reference.

We evaluate translations against the English references using Sacrebleu (Post, 2018) and BLEURT (Sellam et al., 2020)[2]. In some cases, we ask the system to produce multiple candidate translations. We anticipate a human user of the dictionary considering the context in which they encountered the phrase they are looking up and picking the best one; this may be especially helpful in cases where the phrase is actually ambiguous in its translation, since otherwise there is no way to pick between candidate meanings. For these, we evaluate BLEURT in two ways: the **average** performance is the expected score of each response against the reference, and reflects the user's experience if they are looking up a word for which they have no useful context. The **oracle** score is the best score of any response, and reflects the user's experience if they can always pick the correct translation given the context in which they heard the target word.

Because Sacrebleu produces a global precision score over the whole corpus, we evaluate the expected Sacrebleu in multiple-translation cases by sampling one translation from the set of proposals for each word; we average across five samples. We produce an **oracle** Sacrebleu score by collating the translations of each word with the highest BLEURT score and evaluating them as a group.

[1]One functional item had no listed definition and was discarded.

[2]Using the recommended BLEURT-20 checkpoint.

The Inuktitut word saviggirunnaqtutit is made up of the following parts:
savik: (1) metal; steel; iron (2) snow-knife; or, to be fitted with a metal point (harpoon; spear)
ggiq: to bring someone or something along, as in "Don't bring your gun along."
runnaq: to be able to perform a certain action, as in "Could you find that out if he/she arrived"
tutit: you, as in "you sleep"
In English, saviggirunnaqtutit means roughly:

Figure 1: An example prompt for the **definition+example** case.

4 Single-word translation

All our experiments use the OpenAI API to access the GPT-3 model TEXT-DAVINCI-003, which was the largest GPT-3 available until the release of GPT-3.5-TURBO in March 2023. We do not experiment with models tuned for chat using reinforcement learning, nor with smaller but more efficient LLMs such as T5. Because the goal of this work is to generate translations, rather than to measure the acceptability of pre-existing translations, we sample strings from the model rather than measuring their probability (Hu and Levy, 2023); we use the standard text completion API with temperature .7 and 128 maximum tokens.

To translate an Inuktitut word into an English phrase, we look up every morph in the canonical segmentation and obtain their dictionary definitions. We then produce one or more prompts for the GPT-3 system. Figure 1 shows a sample prompt for the **Definition+example** method; examples of the other prompts are given in Appendix A.

Concatenate: As a trivial baseline, we simply concatenate the morpheme definitions in order, without using the LLM. This provides a point of comparison for evaluating the improvements due to text-to-text generation.

-Dictionary: GPT-3 has the capacity to translate many languages in a few-shot setting, and might have been exposed to definitions of Inuktitut words from the same web resources we are using. We use a prompt modeled on French-to-English few-shot translation (without dictionary definitions of morphemes, but with definitions of our few-shot words) to test whether this setting also works for Inuktitut.

Our next two methods evaluate the usefulness of specific parts of the dictionary entries. In the **definition only** condition, we provide textual definitions of each morpheme; if a morpheme matches multiple dictionary entries, we concatenate them with ";

or, " as the separator. In the **definition+example** condition, we also provide the English translation of an example word in which the morpheme is used (if the dictionary contains one).

We evaluate two more sophisticated methods for dealing with morphemes with multiple possible meanings. First, we ask GPT-3 textually to list all possible meanings for the word, rather than producing only a single one; we call this setting **multianswer**. Second, we enumerate all combinations of morpheme meanings which could make up the word, and create a separate prompt for each one. (This method requires much more computing time than simply prompting for more than one answer.) We call this setting **multiprompt**. In each case, the separate answers are aggregated in two different ways—average and oracle performance—as described in Section 3.

We consider two methods for injecting grammatical information into GPT-3's processing. First, we preface the morpheme decomposition with a short hand-written **grammar description**. Our grammatical description is intended to focus GPT-3 on some common issues we noticed in development. It explains that Inuktitut words begin with a root morpheme which usually determines the syntactic type of the word. Verbs must be translated as English sentences whose subject and object are given by agreement markers at the end of the word, while nouns must be translated as noun phrases or prepositional phrases. We also explain that intermediate morphemes can change the part of speech and contribute other elements to the meaning.

We also experiment with a **chain-of-thought** method in which the system is instructed to explicitly identify the syntactic category of the root, the category of the target translation, the subject and object (if any) from agreement morphology, and the function of any intermediate morphemes before translating.

We evaluate all the prompts, except the chain-of-thought and multiprompt methods, in both zero-shot and few-shot settings. The chain-of-thought method is used only in few-shot mode, since this allows us to model what the intermediate reasoning steps should look like. The multiprompt method is used only in zero-shot mode as, since a prompt is generated for each combination of definitions, it is extremely expensive to run with longer prompts. Our few-shot prompts are always filled in with a pre-selected list of the same five words, with definitions and grammatical decompositions from an Inuktitut pedagogy site, `tusaalanga.ca`. Three of these are translated as sentences, one as a noun phrase and one as a locative prepositional phrase. Two of the sentences have intransitive subject agreement markers and one has transitive subject-object agreement. We fill out the possible answers in the multi-answer condition and the chain of thought reasoning steps manually based on Tusaalanga.

4.1 Results

Table 4 shows the results. Overall, metric scores are low. Confidence intervals[3] are also very wide given the small size of the test set.

Existing NMT systems for Inuktitut can score around 30%, although these use more data and are not tested on exclusively multimorphemic words. BLEU scores in the 30s reflect generally intelligible though sometimes errorful translations; scores in the 20s are considered potentially useful under some circumstances, while not entirely accurate nor fluent. BLEURT scores, meanwhile, range between 0 and 1. Garcia et al. (2023) provides BLEURT scores for a variety of few-shot translation models. Scores for high-resourced German and Chinese are roughly 0.63-0.77; for less-resourced Icelandic they are 0.60-0.76.

Despite these caveats, some trends in the scores are evident. First, the scores of the **-Dictionary** condition compared to the rest show that GPT-3 has no useful prior knowledge of Inuktitut. The trivial **Concatenative** system scores higher, producing output which has some resemblance to the references, but is outperformed by the LLM systems, since it cannot rearrange content from the definitions into fluent translations.

Examining the non-trivial systems, we see that it is helpful to gather examples of morphemes in use, as well as definitions, from dictionary entries; these improve scores in both zero-shot and few-shot settings. Comparing the **multianswer** and **multiprompt** settings, we find that it is not very helpful to create multiple prompts to deal with polysemous morphemes; GPT-3 can handle polysemy naturally if asked to create multiple definitions. Finally, we find that the grammar lesson is unhelpful;

[3]Because BLEU scores represent global precision across the entire test set, we do not compute confidence intervals. We compute BLEURT confidence intervals using the SCIPY bootstrap method applied to the scores of each individual sentence.

Sys	BLEU	BLEURT (95% conf.)
Concat	6.19	0.43 (0.41 - 0.44)
-Dict	0.44	0.13 (0.12 - 0.14)
Def	9.63	0.48 (0.45 - 0.51)
Def+ex	13.29	0.51 (0.48 - 0.54)
Multians-avg	11.31	0.46 (0.44 - 0.48)
Multians-orac	19.83	0.62 (0.59 - 0.64)
Multipr-avg	17.42	0.50 (0.47 - 0.53)
Multipr-orac	23.30	0.59 (0.56 - 0.62)
Grammar	12.46	0.48 (0.45 - 0.51)
Few-shot		
Def	13.48	0.49 (0.46 - 0.52)
Def+ex	16.65	0.52 (0.48 - 0.55)
Multians-avg	18.47	0.51 (0.48 - 0.54)
Multians-orac	20.18	0.54 (0.51 - 0.57)
Grammar	17.30	0.53 (0.49 - 0.56)
Chain	13.91	0.43 (0.40 - 0.47)

Table 4: Metric scores for single-word translation. BLEURT scores are followed by bootstrapped 95% confidence intervals.

it is comparable to definitions and examples only in both zero-shot and few-shot settings. The **chain-of-thought** method, meanwhile, is actively unhelpful.

To gain more insight into the results, we show some translations of selected words in Table 5; the table contains two long verbs, one noun and one locative. The **-Dictionary** translations bear no resemblance to the references; although GPT-3 produces plausible and confident-seeming output, the meanings are completely confabulated. We do not observe wholesale hallucination in the definitions using the dictionary, although some grammatical features can be added incorrectly. For instance, the **definition only** system interprets the first word as a question despite the absence of any interrogative marker.

The **chain-of-thought** system has a tendency to lose information due to incomplete deductions. In example #2 (*tuktuliaqsimajut*), it identifies *tuktu* "caribou" correctly as a noun, but then fails to identify the verbalizing morpheme *liaq* "hunt"; because of this, it then states that there is no subject or object because the translation must be nominal and fails to translate the subject marker *jut* "they (3+)."

The other prompting strategies yield translations which are more similar to one another. In many cases, deviations from the reference reflect legitimate information from the definitions: in Example #1, *savik* can mean both "metal; steel" or "snow-

```
kisarvik is an Inuktitut word which means "a place to anchor a boat". It is made up of the following parts:
kisaq: (currently unknown)
vik: place where the action of the verb takes place, as in "hospital; nursing station"; or, finality: 'for good'; 'forever', as in "He/she is leaving for good."; or, marks something that is immense or impressive in size, as in "ocean"
kisaq means:
```

Figure 2: An example prompt for definition elicitation.

knife". In #3, *sana* is defined as "to work at something; to fabricate, make something". In many cases, the translations obtained seem potentially useful for practical purposes.

On the other hand, morphemes with multiple meanings can lead to mistranslations. Uqausiit defines *unga* as "(root) to long or yearn for a person or a living thing"; "(root) the far side, the beyond of something"; "(locative) to (a place/location)". In the context of #4 *uvunga*, the locative meaning is applicable, since *unga* appears as a suffix, but this is apparently not sufficiently explained by our prompts. In addition, some of the systems appear to conflate information from multiple definitions of the morpheme.

5 Definition creation

We experiment with a single prompt for eliciting definitions. This prompt (Figure 2) provides the definition of all but a single morpheme, and the translation of the phrase as a whole, then asks for the definition of the missing item. GPT-3 is somewhat less likely to restrict itself to the prompted format in this case. We cut off elicited definitions at the first newline. For 20 of the roots, and 3 functional morphemes, GPT-3 repeats the prompt phrase "currently unknown."

Table 6 shows the results, which are much poorer than those for translation. This is partly due to the wide stylistic range of the definitions— reference definitions may contain more or fewer alternative synonyms, so that it is difficult to predict the correct length. However, the results of the task are also genuinely less reliable.

Inspection of the definitions (Table 7) echoes the numerical results, revealing some potential but also problematic tendencies. The system produces a correct definition of *aullaq* "leave" in Example #1, and arguably of *ijaq* "be cold" in #2. Such definitions could provide a starting point for a native speaker to rapidly expand a dictionary with new entries.

Inuktitut	#1 saviggirunnaqtutit	#2 tuktuliaqsimajut	#3 sanaji	#4 uvunga
Reference	You can bring your knife.	They are out caribou hunting.	a worker	to this spot here
-Dict	We are thankful (0.17)	We are learning (0.11)	I understand (0.04)	Peace (0.08)
Def only	are you able to bring a snow-knife? (0.52)	they have gone caribou hunting (0.74)	worker (0.36)	longing for (0.06)
Def+ex	you are able to bring a snow-knife (0.48)	they have gone caribou hunting (0.74)	a worker; a maker (0.61)	longing for (0.06)
Multianswer	You are able to bring metal along (0.39)	They (3+) have gone caribou hunting (0.62) They (3+) are away caribou hunting (0.62)	worker (0.36) maker (0.05) fabricator (0.03)	longing for something near here (0.55) yearning for something far away (0.14)
Grammar	you are able to bring a snow-knife (0.48)	they have gone hunting caribou (0.74)	a worker; someone who works (0.65)	longing/yearning for a place (0.39)
Chain	you can make it (0.23)	hunted caribou (0.31)	worker (0.36)	long for here (0.38)

Table 5: Examples of translations by -Dict and few-shot systems. Parenthesized numbers are BLEURT scores.

Data	BLEU	BLEURT (95% conf.)
Roots	2.88	0.33 (0.30 - 0.36)
Func.	2.97	0.27 (0.24 - 0.29)

Table 6: Metric scores for definition induction. BLEURT scores are followed by bootstrapped 95% confidence intervals.

On the other hand, the definitions of *qingaq* "nose" in #2 and *kisaq* "to anchor" in #3 are motivated by the provided examples, but too specific. *kisarvik* (#3), for instance, is made up of the target morpheme *kisaq* and *vik*, which creates a place nominal from a verb. The system therefore should infer that the target morpheme is a verb and does not contribute the meaning element "place". Instead, it proposes the nominal meaning "an anchorage or place to tie up a boat."

The system also hallucinates some entirely unmotivated definitions, such as "bay, inlet or cove" for *vik*. This definition is likely taken from the system's knowledge of a different language such as Norwegian or Swedish, in which *vik* has this meaning. The extra work of filtering out these misleading definitions detracts from any benefit of using the system for dictionary expansion, since more time may be wasted than gained. These proposed definitions are also not suitable for presentation to a language learner, who may be misled by their seeming plausibility.

6 Conclusion

Our results clearly establish that GPT-3's capacity for monolingual text understanding and generation are sophisticated enough to allow it to translate some complex words with the aid of a dictionary alone. Investigation of various prompt tuning techniques leads to a few tentative conclusions. Usage examples from the dictionary are helpful in combination with definitions. So are few-shot examples (even when only 5 are available). We investigated asking GPT-3 to generate multiple translations, and found some evidence that it might be helpful, particularly when the user already has some idea of how the word might be disambiguated based on the context in which it was encountered. Experiments on better-resourced agglutinative languages, such as Finnish and Hungarian, would be useful in better differentiating the performance of different prompting techniques.

On the other hand, we were not able to show much benefit from adding information on grammar to the prompts. There are two possible reasons: Perhaps we engineered the prompts poorly and could have obtained better results with more careful decisions about what information to include. Or perhaps the GPT-3 system is not yet sophisticated enough to relate relatively abstract grammar information to the concrete task of translation.

We believe both of these explanations are valid to some extent. Evidence that our prompt engineering is at fault comes from examining the failures of the chain-of-thought system in more detail (Appendix B). As stated above, the system sometimes misses nominalizers and verbalizers; although the prompt states that these exist, we could have included more detailed information on how to recognize them.

On the other hand, the system also sometimes creates complex chains of thought in which it loses track of content morphemes. This is why it predicts the meaning "you can make it" for #1 in Table 5 rather than "you can bring your knife", forgetting the initial element *savik*. Similar problems apply to some words expressing emotion— *tautugusunn-*

Example	#1 aullarli "Let him/her depart!"	#2 qingaijaqtunga "I have a cold nose."	#3 kisarvik "a place to anchor a boat"	#4 kanunga "to that spot down there"
		Content (root) morphemes		
Inuktitut	aullaq	qingaq	kisaq	kan
Reference	to leave; to depart; to go away	nose	to anchor something	a place/spot down here/there
System	to go away; to leave; to depart; to move away; to go out. (0.74)	to be cold, shivering, chilly or having a cold nose (0.31)	an anchorage or place to tie up a boat (0.37)	that (0.02)
		Functional morphemes		
Inuktitut	li	ijaq	vik	unga
Reference	let him/her/it...! (command)	(1) to remove; to have something removed (2) to experience coldness of body parts	place where the action of the verb takes place	to (a place/location)
System	him/her (0.28)	to be cold (0.35)	bay, inlet, or cove (0.26)	to go, as in "to go down there" (0.33)

Table 7: Examples of definitions induced by a one-shot system morphemes, with BLEURT scores.

gittara "I don't feel like watching it" is translated as "I love him/her/it" because the system expands *gusuk* "feel an emotion" into "love", replacing the legitimate main verb "watch".

While better prompting could potentially remedy some of these issues, we believe more sophisticated instruction-following models may perform even better given the same resources. Moreover, models with very long context windows might be able to read in large sections of pedagogical material from sites like Tusaalanga directly, reducing the necessity to create abbreviated grammar lessons specifically for use in prompting LLMs. We are also interested to see to what extent more sophisticated LLMs can improve at suggesting dictionary definitions, especially to the extent that hallucinations can be controlled. On the other hand, it would be potentially interesting to see whether these results can be replicated with smaller, more cost and computation-effective LLMs such as T5.

While this work emphasizes how much is possible without an NMT system, we also believe that it can contribute to NMT development in the very low-resource case. Curriculum learning for translation (e.g. Platanios et al., 2019) uses translations of shorter or simpler constructions earlier in pretraining, but suitable "easy" instances may be rare in corpus data, or their distribution may be skewed towards formulaic language. Few-shot dictionary-based translation could be used to bootstrap towards a larger NMT system by providing candidate definitions for single words from the corpus.

Although the scope of the present work is limited to an exploratory demonstration, we are eager to see the many ways in which it can be expanded upon. One particular direction is to explore the extent to which an LLM can exploit linguistic context to disambiguate between various potential translations, hopefully leading to a narrowing of the gap between average and oracle performances. More closely integrating segmentation into the prompting system, either by having the LLM produce its own segmentations or rank multiple segmentations based on the plausibility of their meanings, would reduce dependence on an accurate canonical segmentation system.

We are (to our knowledge) the first to evaluate dictionary-based translation in the absence of a base NMT system, and the first to deploy it on a polysynthetic language. While our results are not yet competitive with fully trained translation, we believe our results represent good news for communities in which limited resources must be distributed among efforts to develop community-facing resources or parallel corpora. A community that focuses its effort on developing dictionaries for human learners can nonetheless enjoy some of the benefits of MT without developing a conventional NMT system, helping to bring language revitalization and language technologies closer together.

Limitations

The results of this work may be limited in reliability and replicability due to some hard-to-avoid aspects of the low-resource setting.

Our numerical results have low statistical power, as illustrated by the wide BLEURT confidence intervals in Tables 4 and 6. Without a large test set, most differences are not statistically significant at the accepted level. They should be treated as trends which can motivate further investigation rather than solid conclusions. The significant findings are that the no dictionary system is worse than the concatenative baseline, which is in turn worse than the LLM systems; multianswer and multiprompt oracles surpass the definition-only system in zero and few-shot settings.

Human evaluations would also improve the reliability of our evaluations, which are currently entirely automated. However, we do not have access to Inuktitut native speakers. Human evaluations could also be used to improve the automated metrics by fine-tuning BLEURT.

Reproducibility of our experiments is limited by potential changes to the OpenAI models we use; OpenAI might withdraw or update them at any time. We estimate that the project incurred total costs under $70 in payments for the GPT-3 API. The multiprompt experiment (which generates a prompt for each combination of morpheme definitions, and did not meaningfully improve over asking GPT-3 to provide multiple answers) was responsible for much of this cost. Few-shot prompts are also more expensive than zero-shot due to their length. We believe that only a few dollars would be necessary to reproduce the most successful system here and run it on hundreds of examples.

Finally, our method assumes access to a canonical segmentation system, which potentially limits its applicability to very low-resourced languages where such a system may be unavailable. By filtering out incorrectly segmented examples, we do not assess the potential impact of segmentation errors on translation.

Ethics Statement

We reached out to the Inuit Uqausinginnik Taiguusiliuqtiit with regard to their stance on extracting datasets from Uqausiit but have not received any reply. We therefore do not plan to make the datasets available to the community for download.

If a system for word translation based on this paper were deployed, it should be in the context of clear labeling. It would be important to indicate the morpheme analysis and morpheme definitions for the word being analyzed, and clearly separate the automatically generated proposed translation, which should be designated as the product of a system which lacks native-speaker expertise. Because most systems in this task did not hallucinate definitions, we believe that a clearly labeled system of this type might do more good than harm in the context of a revitalization effort.

If a system for definition induction based on this paper were deployed, it would be extremely important that only native speakers were allowed to use computer-authored definitions as sources for dictionary entries, and that they be told clearly that the system was provided only as a labor-saving device, rather than as a source of native-like expertise. Scots Wikipedia is one widely cited case where a naive user added a large amount of misleading data to an online resource under the impression that they were being helpful (Brooks and Hern, 2020). Our definition induction system has the potential for this kind of misuse.

Acknowledgements

We thank the Clippers computational discussion group for comments on a preliminary version of this work. We thank four anonymous reviewers for their suggestions, including feedback which helped us to correct a serious problem with our evaluation procedures.

References

Loïc Barrault, Magdalena Biesialska, Ondřej Bojar, Marta R. Costa-jussà, Christian Federmann, Yvette Graham, Roman Grundkiewicz, Barry Haddow, Matthias Huck, Eric Joanis, Tom Kocmi, Philipp Koehn, Chi-kiu Lo, Nikola Ljubešić, Christof Monz, Makoto Morishita, Masaaki Nagata, Toshiaki Nakazawa, Santanu Pal, Matt Post, and Marcos Zampieri. 2020. Findings of the 2020 conference on machine translation (WMT20). In Proceedings of the Fifth Conference on Machine Translation, pages 1–55, Online. Association for Computational Linguistics.

Libby Brooks and Alex Hern. 2020. Shock an aw: Us teenager wrote huge slice of scots wikipedia. nineteen-year-old says he is "devastated" after being accused of cultural vandalism. The Guardian, 26.

Tom Brown, Benjamin Mann, Nick Ryder, Melanie Subbiah, Jared D Kaplan, Prafulla Dhariwal, Arvind Neelakantan, Pranav Shyam, Girish Sastry, Amanda Askell, et al. 2020. Language models are few-shot learners. Advances in neural information processing systems, 33:1877–1901.

Georgiana Dinu, Prashant Mathur, Marcello Federico, and Yaser Al-Onaizan. 2019. Training neural machine translation to apply terminology constraints. In Proceedings of the 57th Annual Meeting of the Association for Computational Linguistics, pages

3063–3068, Florence, Italy. Association for Computational Linguistics.

Zi-Yi Dou and Graham Neubig. 2021. Word alignment by fine-tuning embeddings on parallel corpora. In Proceedings of the 16th Conference of the European Chapter of the Association for Computational Linguistics: Main Volume, pages 2112–2128, Online. Association for Computational Linguistics.

Benoit Farley. 2012. Uqailaut Inuktitut morphological analyzer.

Xavier Garcia, Yamini Bansal, Colin Cherry, George Foster, Maxim Krikun, Fangxiaoyu Feng, Melvin Johnson, and Orhan Firat. 2023. The unreasonable effectiveness of few-shot learning for machine translation.

Nikesh Garera and David Yarowsky. 2008. Translating compounds by learning component gloss translation models via multiple languages. In Proceedings of the Third International Joint Conference on Natural Language Processing: Volume-I.

Marjan Ghazvininejad, Hila Gonen, and Luke Zettlemoyer. 2023. Dictionary-based phrase-level prompting of large language models for machine translation.

Stig-Arne Grönroos, Katri Hiovain, Peter Smit, Ilona Erika Rauhala, Päivi Kristiina Jokinen, Mikko Kurimo, and Sami Petteri Virpioja. 2016. Low-resource active learning of morphological segmentation. Northern European Journal of Language Technology.

Eva Hasler, Felix Stahlberg, Marcus Tomalin, Adrià de Gispert, and Bill Byrne. 2017. A comparison of neural models for word ordering. In Proceedings of the 10th International Conference on Natural Language Generation, pages 208–212, Santiago de Compostela, Spain. Association for Computational Linguistics.

Jennifer Hu and Roger Levy. 2023. Prompt-based methods may underestimate large language models' linguistic generalizations. Lingbuzz preprint.

Eric Joanis, Rebecca Knowles, Roland Kuhn, Samuel Larkin, Patrick Littell, Chi-kiu Lo, Darlene Stewart, and Jeffrey Micher. 2020. The Nunavut Hansard Inuktitut–English parallel corpus 3.0 with preliminary machine translation results. In Proceedings of the Twelfth Language Resources and Evaluation Conference, pages 2562–2572, Marseille, France. European Language Resources Association.

Chen Liang, Haoming Jiang, Xiaodong Liu, Pengcheng He, Weizhu Chen, Jianfeng Gao, and Tuo Zhao. 2021. Token-wise curriculum learning for neural machine translation. In Findings of the Association for Computational Linguistics: EMNLP 2021, pages 3658–3670, Punta Cana, Dominican Republic. Association for Computational Linguistics.

Zoey Liu, Robert Jimerson, and Emily Prud'hommeaux. 2021. Morphological segmentation for Seneca. In Proceedings of the First Workshop on Natural Language Processing for Indigenous Languages of the Americas, pages 90–101, Online. Association for Computational Linguistics.

Thang Luong, Ilya Sutskever, Quoc Le, Oriol Vinyals, and Wojciech Zaremba. 2015. Addressing the rare word problem in neural machine translation. In Proceedings of the 53rd Annual Meeting of the Association for Computational Linguistics and the 7th International Joint Conference on Natural Language Processing (Volume 1: Long Papers), pages 11–19, Beijing, China. Association for Computational Linguistics.

Manuel Mager, Özlem Çetinoğlu, and Katharina Kann. 2020. Tackling the low-resource challenge for canonical segmentation. In Proceedings of the 2020 Conference on Empirical Methods in Natural Language Processing (EMNLP), pages 5237–5250, Online. Association for Computational Linguistics.

Manuel Mager, Ximena Gutierrez-Vasques, Gerardo Sierra, and Ivan Meza-Ruiz. 2018a. Challenges of language technologies for the indigenous languages of the Americas. In Proceedings of the 27th International Conference on Computational Linguistics, pages 55–69, Santa Fe, New Mexico, USA. Association for Computational Linguistics.

Manuel Mager, Elisabeth Mager, Alfonso Medina-Urrea, Ivan Vladimir Meza Ruiz, and Katharina Kann. 2018b. Lost in translation: Analysis of information loss during machine translation between polysynthetic and fusional languages. In Proceedings of the Workshop on Computational Modeling of Polysynthetic Languages, pages 73–83, Santa Fe, New Mexico, USA. Association for Computational Linguistics.

Mick Mallon. 2000. Inuktitut linguistics for technocrats.

Jeffrey Micher. 2017. Improving coverage of an Inuktitut morphological analyzer using a segmental recurrent neural network. In Proceedings of the 2nd Workshop on the Use of Computational Methods in the Study of Endangered Languages, pages 101–106, Honolulu. Association for Computational Linguistics.

Simon Mille, Anya Belz, Bernd Bohnet, Thiago Castro Ferreira, Yvette Graham, and Leo Wanner. 2020. The third multilingual surface realisation shared task (SR'20): Overview and evaluation results. In Proceedings of the Third Workshop on Multilingual Surface Realisation, pages 1–20, Barcelona, Spain (Online). Association for Computational Linguistics.

Sarah Moeller and Mans Hulden. 2021. Integrating automated segmentation and glossing into documentary and descriptive linguistics. In Proceedings of the 4th Workshop on the Use of Computational Methods in the Study of Endangered Languages Volume 1 (Papers), pages 86–95, Online. Association for Computational Linguistics.

Tan Ngoc Le and Fatiha Sadat. 2020. Revitalization of indigenous languages through pre-processing and neural machine translation: The case of Inuktitut. In Proceedings of the 28th International Conference on Computational Linguistics, pages 4661–4666, Barcelona, Spain (Online). International Committee on Computational Linguistics.

Jan Niehues. 2021. Continuous learning in neural machine translation using bilingual dictionaries. In Proceedings of the 16th Conference of the European Chapter of the Association for Computational Linguistics: Main Volume, pages 830–840, Online. Association for Computational Linguistics.

Hyunji Hayley Park, Katherine J. Zhang, Coleman Haley, Kenneth Steimel, Han Liu, and Lane Schwartz. 2021. Morphology matters: A multilingual language modeling analysis. Transactions of the Association for Computational Linguistics, 9:261–276.

Ngoc-Quan Pham, Jan Niehues, and Alexander Waibel. 2018. Towards one-shot learning for rare-word translation with external experts. In Proceedings of the 2nd Workshop on Neural Machine Translation and Generation, pages 100–109, Melbourne, Australia. Association for Computational Linguistics.

Emmanouil Antonios Platanios, Otilia Stretcu, Graham Neubig, Barnabas Poczos, and Tom Mitchell. 2019. Competence-based curriculum learning for neural machine translation. In Proceedings of the 2019 Conference of the North American Chapter of the Association for Computational Linguistics: Human Language Technologies, Volume 1 (Long and Short Papers), pages 1162–1172, Minneapolis, Minnesota. Association for Computational Linguistics.

Matt Post. 2018. A call for clarity in reporting BLEU scores. In Proceedings of the Third Conference on Machine Translation: Research Papers, pages 186–191, Brussels, Belgium. Association for Computational Linguistics.

Christian Roest, Lukas Edman, Gosse Minnema, Kevin Kelly, Jennifer Spenader, and Antonio Toral. 2020. Machine translation for English–Inuktitut with segmentation, data acquisition and pre-training. In Proceedings of the Fifth Conference on Machine Translation, pages 274–281, Online. Association for Computational Linguistics.

Thibault Sellam, Dipanjan Das, and Ankur Parikh. 2020. BLEURT: Learning robust metrics for text generation. In Proceedings of the 58th Annual Meeting of the Association for Computational Linguistics, pages 7881–7892, Online. Association for Computational Linguistics.

Zewei Sun, Qingnan Jiang, Shujian Huang, Jun Cao, Shanbo Cheng, and Mingxuan Wang. 2022. Zero-shot domain adaptation for neural machine translation with retrieved phrase-level prompts.

Adam Wiemerslage, Miikka Silfverberg, Changbing Yang, Arya McCarthy, Garrett Nicolai, Eliana Colunga, and Katharina Kann. 2022. Morphological processing of low-resource languages: Where we are and what's next. In Findings of the Association for Computational Linguistics: ACL 2022, pages 988–1007, Dublin, Ireland. Association for Computational Linguistics.

Tong Zhang, Long Zhang, Wei Ye, Bo Li, Jinan Sun, Xiaoyu Zhu, Wen Zhao, and Shikun Zhang. 2021. Point, disambiguate and copy: Incorporating bilingual dictionaries for neural machine translation. In Proceedings of the 59th Annual Meeting of the Association for Computational Linguistics and the 11th International Joint Conference on Natural Language Processing (Volume 1: Long Papers), pages 3970–3979, Online. Association for Computational Linguistics.

Xuan Zhang and Kevin Duh. 2021. Approaching sign language gloss translation as a low-resource machine translation task. In Proceedings of the 1st International Workshop on Automatic Translation for Signed and Spoken Languages (AT4SSL), pages 60–70, Virtual. Association for Machine Translation in the Americas.

Yuhao Zhang, Ziyang Wang, Runzhe Cao, Binghao Wei, Weiqiao Shan, Shuhan Zhou, Abudurexiti Reheman, Tao Zhou, Xin Zeng, Laohu Wang, Yongyu Mu, Jingnan Zhang, Xiaoqian Liu, Xuanjun Zhou, Yinqiao Li, Bei Li, Tong Xiao, and Jingbo Zhu. 2020. The NiuTrans machine translation systems for WMT20. In Proceedings of the Fifth Conference on Machine Translation, pages 338–345, Online. Association for Computational Linguistics.

A Example prompts

We show the complete zero-shot prompt of each type for Example #1 of Table 5, *saviggirunnaqtutit* "You can bring your knife." The outputs are shown in the table.

No dictionary:

Translate Inuktitut to English:
saviggirunnaqtutit =>

Definition only:

The Inuktitut word saviggirunnaqtutit is made up of the following parts:
savik: (1) metal; steel; iron (2) snow-knife; or, to be fitted with a metal point (harpoon; spear)
ggiq: to bring someone or something along

runnaq: to be able to perform a certain action

tutit: you

In English, saviggirunnaqtutit means roughly:

Definition+example:

The Inuktitut word saviggirunnaqtutit is made up of the following parts:

savik: (1) metal; steel; iron (2) snow-knife; or, to be fitted with a metal point (harpoon; spear)

ggiq: to bring someone or something along, as in "Don't bring your gun along."

runnaq: to be able to perform a certain action, as in "Could you find that out if he/she arrived"

tutit: you, as in "you sleep"

In English, saviggirunnaqtutit means roughly:

Multianswer:

The Inuktitut word saviggirunnaqtutit is made up of the following parts:

savik: (1) metal; steel; iron (2) snow-knife; or, to be fitted with a metal point (harpoon; spear)

ggiq: to bring someone or something along, as in "Don't bring your gun along."

runnaq: to be able to perform a certain action, as in "Could you find that out if he/she arrived"

tutit: you, as in "you sleep"

Give all possible translations of saviggirunnaqtutit:

Grammar lesson:

An Inuktitut word is made up of a root and some optional modifiers; for verbs, this will be followed by a verb ending which acts as an agreement marker.

If the root is a verb, the whole word will usually be translated as a sentence. If the root is a noun, the whole word will be translated as a noun phrase or a prepositional phrase. If the word ends with a locative modifier (like "in" or "on"), translate it as a prepositional phrase.

Some words contain a nominalizer which turns a verb into a noun, like "someone who does the action" or "location where the action takes place". These should be translated as noun phrases even though the root is a verb.

If the translation is a sentence, its subject (and object if there is one) will be given by a verb ending.

Other modifiers within the sentence can introduce auxiliary verbs, adverbs or discourse particles.

The material above is repeated only once in the few-shot setting; the material below is copied for each few-shot word.

The Inuktitut word saviggirunnaqtutit is made up of the following parts:

savik: (1) metal; steel; iron (2) snow-knife; or, to be fitted with a metal point (harpoon; spear)

ggiq: to bring someone or something along, as in "Don't bring your gun along."

runnaq: to be able to perform a certain action, as in "Could you find that out if he/she arrived"

tutit: you, as in "you sleep"

In English, saviggirunnaqtutit means roughly:

Chain-of-thought:

Since we use chain-of-thought prompting only in few-shot mode, we show a few-shot prompt.

An Inuktitut word is made up of a root and some optional modifiers; for verbs, this will be followed by a verb ending which acts as an agreement marker.

To translate an Inuktitut word, first, identify the part of speech of the root.

If the root is a verb, the whole word will usually be translated as a sentence.

If the root is a noun, the whole word will be translated as a noun phrase or a prepositional phrase. If the word ends with a locative modifier (like "in" or "on"), translate it as a prepositional phrase.

Some words contain a nominalizer which turns a verb into a noun, like "someone who does the action" or "location where the action takes place". These should be translated as noun phrases even though the root is a verb.

State the syntactic category of the translation.

If the translation is a sentence, its subject (and object if there is one) will be given by a verb ending. Using this ending, state the subject and object.

Other modifiers within the sentence can introduce auxiliary verbs, adverbs or discourse particles. State the meaning of each modifier.

Finally, translate the word into English.

The Inuktitut word aquttunnaqtuq is made up of the following parts:
aqut: to steer or drive a vehicle or boat, as in "Who is going to drive?"
junnaq: to be able to perform a certain action, as in "He/she can hear."
juq: he/she/it, as in "he/she/it sees"
The root aqut is a verb.
The translation will be a sentence.
The subject is he/she/it and there is no object.
junnaq means 'can', creating the meaning "can drive"
The translation is => he/she/it can drive

The Inuktitut word quviasuppit is made up of the following parts:
quviak: to be happy, joyful, as in "they were happy while they did something"
suk: added to verb roots that normally are transitive (double) to make them intransitive (single), as in "He/she is afraid."
vit: the...of your..., as in "the window of your (1) house"; or, Are you...?; Do you...?, as in "Are you eating?"
The root quviak is a verb.
The translation will be a sentence.
The subject is you and there is no object.
suk makes the verb intransitive, creating the meaning "be happy"
The translation is => are you happy?

The Inuktitut word maligaliurvik is made up of the following parts:
malik: (1) to follow someone or something) (2) to obey someone or something, as in "Kiviuq followed a person into the tent."
gaq: changes a verb to a noun with a passive meaning: 'something that one...', as in "a drink of something; a soft drink"
liq: an action that is underway or starting; also marks a change from one state to another, as in "He/she is going out right now."
uq: marks a continuous, prolonged or repeated action, as in

"He pulled in the long rope."
vik: place where the action of the verb takes place, as in "hospital; nursing station"; or, finality: 'for good'; 'forever', as in "He/she is leaving for good."; or, marks something that is immense or impressive in size, as in "ocean"
The root malik is a verb.
The translation will be a noun phrase because of the nominalizer vik.
There is no subject or object because it is a noun phrase.
gaq makes the verb passive, creating the meaning "be obeyed"
liq and uq together indicate association with a habit or profession, creating the meaning "legislation"
vik indicates the place in which legislation happens, creating the meaning "legislative assembly"
The translation is => Legislative Assembly

The Inuktitut word allavvimmi is made up of the following parts:
allak: used to tell someone to do something quickly or for a particular reason, as in "Sleep a little! (before you do something else)"; or, to write or draw vik: place where the action of the verb takes place, as in "hospital; nursing station"; or, finality: 'for good'; 'forever', as in "He/she is leaving for good."; or, marks something that is immense or impressive in size, as in "ocean" mi: of his/her own...; or, of their (2)...; or, also; too, as in "I saw it, too."; or, of his/her own..., as in "the pole of his/her own tent"; or, in/on/at...(one of something), as in "He sleeps in the tent"
The root allak is a verb
The translation will be a prepositional phrase because of the nominalizer vik and the locative marker mi.
There is no subject or object because it is a noun phrase.
vik indicates the place in which writing happens, creating the meaning "office" The translation is "in/at the office"

The Inuktitut word saviggirunnaqtutit is made up of the following parts:
savik: (1) metal; steel; iron (2) snow-knife; or, to be fitted with a metal point (harpoon; spear)
ggiq: to bring someone or something along, as in "Don't bring your gun along."
runnaq: to be able to perform a certain action, as in "Could you find that out if he/she arrived"
tutit: you, as in "you sleep"
The root

B Chain-of-thought output

We show the full model output for the example words in Table 5; see the previous appendix for the prompt format.

saviggirunnaqtutit "You can bring your knife":
savik is a verb.
The translation will be a sentence.
The subject is you and there is no object.
ggiq and runnaq together indicate the ability to make something, creating the meaning "make"
The translation is => you can make it.

tuktuliaqsimajut "They are out caribou hunting":
tuktu is a noun.
The translation will be a noun phrase.
There is no subject or object because it is a noun phrase.
liaq indicates hunting and sima indicates the result of the hunting, creating the meaning "hunted caribou"
The translation is => hunted caribou.

sanaji "a worker"
sana is a verb.
The translation will be a noun phrase because of the nominalizer ji.
The subject is one who performs the action and there is no object.
ji indicates that the verb is turned into a noun, creating the meaning "worker"
The translation is => worker

uvunga "to this spot here": Is the font size change here significant?
unga is a verb.
The translation will be a prepositional phrase because of the locative marker uv.
There is no subject or object because it is a noun phrase.
unga indicates a sense of longing, creating the meaning "long for"
The translation is => long for here.

Evaluating Cross Lingual Transfer for Morphological Analysis: a Case Study of Indian Languages

Siddhesh Pawar*
Google Research
siddheshmp@google.com

Partha Talukdar
Google Research
partha@google.com

Pushpak Bhattacharyya
IIT Bombay
pb@cse.iitb.ac.in

Abstract

Recent advances in pretrained multilingual models such as Multilingual T5 (mT5) have facilitated cross-lingual transfer by learning shared representations across languages. Leveraging pre-trained multilingual models for scaling morphology analyzers to low-resource languages is a unique opportunity that has been under-explored so far. We investigate this line of research in the context of Indian languages, focusing on two important morphological subtasks: root word extraction and tagging morphosyntactic descriptions (MSD), viz., gender, number, and person (GNP). We experiment with six Indian languages from two language families (Dravidian and Indo-Aryan) to train a multilingual morphology analyzers for the first time for Indian languages. We demonstrate the usability of multilingual models for few-shot cross-lingual transfer through an average 7% increase in GNP tagging in a cross-lingual setting as compared to a monolingual setting through controlled experiments. We provide an overview of the state of the datasets available related to our tasks and point-out a few modeling limitations due to datasets. Lastly, we analyze the cross-lingual transfer of morphological tags for verbs and nouns, which provides a proxy for the quality of representations of word markings learned by the model.

1 Introduction

Morphology analysis is the first step of processing in the classical NLP pipeline. Even in the transformer era, wherein the entire NLP pipeline is replaced with a transformer, the use of morphological segmentation for tokenization instead of statistical subword tokenization has been shown to produce better embeddings, especially for morphologically rich languages (Nzeyimana and Rubungo, 2022). The statistical subword tokenization used in tokenizers such as wordpiece cannot capture morphological alternations (e.g. wordpiece doesn't treat contextual allomorphs as related) and non-concatenative morphology (Klein and Tsarfaty, 2020).

One of the tasks that we analyze in our work is root word extraction, which forms an integral component of morphologically informed segmentation. A morphology analyzer can also help speed up language documentation efforts for endangered languages, Moeller et al. (2020) leveraged interlinear glossed text to generate unseen forms of inflectional paradigm using a morphology analyzer. Availability of morphological information can also benefit various downstream tasks such as parsing (Seeker and Çetinoğlu, 2015), machine translation (Tamchyna et al., 2017), language modeling (Park et al., 2021), etc. Our scope of this work is inflectional and concatenative morphology. We also envision our work to be used in bias-aware machine translation, especially from morphologically poor languages to morphologically richer languages. For example, if we want to translate the sentence "My friend was a doctor" to Hindi, we would ideally prefer to have both masculine and feminine translations "Mera dost doctor tha" (masculine) and "Meri dost doctor thi"(feminine), as English sentence has no mention of gender and for Hindi, the gender markers are present on verbs (tha\thi) and pronouns (mera\meri).

Although high-quality morphology analyzers have been built for some Indian languages, they are either rule-based such as Agarwal et al. (2014), or are neural models trained on annotated data which is available in sufficient quantities only for high resource languages (Jha et al., 2018). Building morphology analyzers for low-resource languages remains a challenging task. For low-resource languages, morphological resources are sparse or virtually nonexistent. Multilingual models have shown promising results for cross-lingual transfer from high-resource to low-resource languages (Wu

*Work done while at IIT Bombay

Proceedings of the 20th SIGMORPHON workshop on Computational Research in Phonetics, Phonology, and Morphology, pages 14–26
July 14, 2023

Percentage of data points with a particular feature marking is present							
Gender	Number	Person	Tense	Aspect	Case	Modality	Others
60.4	94.8	82.1	58.5	35.5	11.0	11.0	27.5

Table 1: Combined statistics of annotated data (across languages) available for various tags. We work with gender, number, and person as they have the highest proportion as compared to other features and are common to noun and verb morphology. We don't use tense as it is not relevant to nouns. More details in section 3

and Dredze, 2019; Lauscher et al., 2020). The main goal of our work is to increase NLP inclusivity. The primary obstacle one encounters while expanding the coverage of NLP models is the lack of usable (annotated) data for most languages; collecting (annotated) data is a painstaking task, especially for endangered languages. When data is sparse, we turn to linguistics to help exploit universalities across languages.

In this work, we study the multilingual capability of mT5 (Xue et al., 2021) to carry out cross-lingual transfer of morphological features and extract the root words given the surface forms. We also test the multilinguality hypothesis that, in the presence of annotated examples of source languages, the required number of annotated examples of the target language to get identical results reduces. We carry out this analysis of cross-lingual transfer within language families and across (language) families and provide pointers to effective usage of multilingual data. The languages we carry out morphological analysis are of the Dravidian family (Tamil, Telugu, and Kannada) and the Indo-Aryan family (Bengali, Hindi, and Marathi). We also give a brief account of the state of datasets available for morphological analysis and their challenges. We finetune mT5 for gender, number, and person tagging for verbs and nouns in six Indian languages: *Marathi, Hindi, Bengali, Tamil, Telugu, and Kannada*. The features: gender, number, and person (GNP) are hereby referred to as morphosyntactic description (MSD) tags. The current state of the datasets and inconsistency of annotation across languages limits our analysis to GNP tags of verbs and nouns.

Our contributions are as follows:

- We test the multilinguality hypothesis that the availability of annotated data of source languages reduces the number of examples of target language required to outperform the monolingual baseline.
- We study inter-family and intra-family transfer in the context of GNP tagging and root word extraction for languages from Dravidian and Indo-Aryan families.
- We analyze how multilingualism helps in the morphological analysis of verbs and nouns, root word extraction, and test the model's ability to generalize to unseen suffixes.

2 Related Work

Morphological analysis: For morphological analysis, SIGMORPHON (Nicolai et al., 2021) has been one of the venues organizing shared tasks and workshops related to computational morphology and multilingual morphological analysis, especially in the low resource scenarios. Shared tasks such as Cotterell et al. (2016, 2017, 2018), etc. looked at morphological reinflection with an increasing number of languages each year. For morphological reinflection, the output is the surface form, and the inputs are: a root word (or any other form of the root word) and desired features in the surface form (the output). Task 2 in Cotterell et al. (2018) as well as McCarthy et al. (2019) explored morphological analysis and reinfection in context. Jin et al. (2020) and Wiemerslage et al. (2021) were aimed at unsupervised clustering of paradigms, wherein given a lemma list, the goal is to output all the possible forms of a lemma. Morphosyntactic lexicon generation is one task closely related to morphological analysis; Faruqui et al. (2016) used graph-based semi-supervised learning for label propagation. Hulden et al. (2014) used a semi-supervised approach for lexicon construction from concrete inflection tables by generalizing the inflection paradigms from the tables provided. For morphology resources, apart from UniMorph (Batsuren et al., 2022; McCarthy et al., 2020), the MorphyNet database (Batsuren et al., 2021) is a large dataset of methodologically annotated surface forms spanning 15 languages and is extracted from Wiktionary. There have also been efforts to create task-specific models for various components of cross-lingual morphological tagging (Cotterell and Heigold, 2017a; Malaviya et al., 2018)

Indian language morphology: Regarding resources for Indian languages, Arora et al. (2022) points out resource scatteredness (rather than scarcity) as the primary obstacle to developing South Asian language technology and proposes the study of language history and contact as one of the potential solutions. Workshops like Dravidian-LangTech (Chakravarthi et al., 2021) and WILDRE (Jha et al., 2020) are dedicated specifically to the development of technologies and resources for Indian languages. The UniMorph database (McCarthy et al., 2020) has been one of the recent efforts to extend the coverage of computational morphological resources. Cotterell and Heigold (2017b) trained bidirectional character-based LSTM-based models to demonstrate the effectiveness of the cross-lingual transfer. They have trained bilingual models for languages from Romance, Slavic Germanic, and Uralic families. Gupta et al. (2020) trained various sequence labelling models for Sanskrit. Nguyen et al. (2021) trained transformer-based models for various NLP tasks such as PoS tagging, Morphological feature tagging, and dependency parsing for over 100 languages. Nair et al. (2021) carried out a comparative study of existing morphological analyzers for Indian languages to conclude that although morphological analyzers exist for Indian languages like Sanskrit and Malayalam, they are not accurate as compared to the high resource baselines. Elsner (2021) probed an analogical memory-based framework for one-shot morphological transfer to study the abstract representational concepts learned by the transfer networks.

3 Dataset Challenges

Creating a multilingual morphology analyzer would require a union of the sets of features across all the languages and all the parts of speech. The morphological features are modeled as categorical variables in fixed output space. The modeling difficulties arise primarily due to the following: (1) absence of feature annotations for Indian languages, (2) lack of data for all the parts of speech (PoS) except verbs and nouns and (3) variance of markings across PoS and languages. The dataset only contains data for verbs and nouns, which restricts our analysis to those PoS. For these PoS, the feature data is primarily available for Gender, number, and person compared to other features, so we carry out transfer analysis for only those features. We provide a summary of annotated data available in Table 1. Gender, number, and person also happen to be morphological features that are common to nouns and verbs. We provide detailed statistics of the UniMorph dataset in appendix A.

We have used various data sources to demonstrate the scalability of the morphology analyzer to 6 Indian languages. For languages Hindi, Telugu, Kannada, and Bengali, we have used the UniMorph 3.0 (McCarthy et al., 2020) dataset. The number of examples varies across languages. For Bengali, the number of examples available is 4443; for Kannada, it is around 6400; for Hindi, there are about 54K examples, while Telugu has about 1500 examples. All the examples in the UniMorph dataset are either verbs or nouns. For Tamil, morphologically annotated data from the Tamil dependency treebank (Ramasamy and Žabokrtský, 2014) was used. The number of annotated words (verbs+nouns) in the tree bank is 9521, all of which were used. For Marathi, we used the dataset from Bapat et al. (2010). The dataset consists of around 21k annotated words, out of which we used 15k words, nouns, or verbs, to have consistency with other datasets. Although there are other sources of data, such as Bhat et al. (2017), we stick to the UniMorph dataset wherever possible to ensure higher annotation accuracy. The scope of our work limits demonstrating the usefulness of cross-lingual transfer for morphological analysis, so dataset selection and optimizing the number of examples for creating the best morphology analyzer remains a challenge for future research.

4 Modelling Details

4.1 Morphological analysis as text to text problem

The Multilingual T5 (Xue et al., 2021) is a massively multilingual pre-trained text-to-text transformer model released by Google in 2020. It is pre-trained on the Common Crawl-based dataset and covers 101 languages. It is an encoder-decoder sequence generation model, unlike mBERT, which is an encoder-only multilingual model. Our task of root word extraction requires the generation of text sequences, so we use an encoder-decoder model to avoid training a decoder separately for the given languages. We use the mT5 base model with 580 million parameters for our experiments.

As mT5 is a text-to-text sequence generation model, the tags are generated as a sequence of text, one after the other. The input to the model is the surface form of the words, and the model generates the gender, number, and person tags as a text sequence. Not all the words in the dataset would be

Modeling Strategy	Accuracies For Marathi			
	Monolingual		Multilingual	
	Root Word	MSD Tagging	Root Word	MSD Tagging
Joint model	42.2	79.7	53.2	84.6
Multitask model	26.2	**86.5**	52.2	88.2
Independent Model	**78.2**	81.2	**86.4**	**95.2**

Table 2: Comparing three modeling strategies for root word extraction and MSD tagging. Training a separate multilingual model for both tasks is the best-performing strategy. We provide details in section 4.2

morphologically marked for GNP; for example, in the case of person marking for nouns, the markings are only present on the pronouns (and the surface form changes according to the person). In contrast, the surface form remains the same for common and proper nouns, irrespective of the person. In such cases, where the marking is either trivial or marking is not present on the word or where the marking cannot be inferred from the surface form itself, the model's expected output is the tag 'unknown'. The datasets we use contain morphological tags without context; we, therefore, predict the tags solely based on the markings present on the words rather than the context and assign the tag 'unknown' to the words for which tags cannot be predicted without context. For all the experiments, unless and otherwise stated: we use the following evaluation strategy: We firstly remove the 20% data (randomly sampled) for each language (which is used for evaluation) and use the remaining 80% data for experiments. We ensure that the randomly sampled data contains unseen paradigms; no surface form of the lemma is present in the training dataset. Across the monolingual and multilingual experiments, the evaluation data remains the same. To avoid the error variation due to bias in sampling (wherein the test set contains all the paradigms available in the training set), we use k-fold cross-validation (with k=5) and report average numbers. The epochs used were 7-15 based on performance on validation data. As far as metrics for measuring model performance are concerned, we report per-tag accuracy for each of the GNP tags, and overall accuracy. The overall accuracy denotes the percentage of instances for which all three tags are predicted correctly by the model. For root word extraction, we consider exact-string match based accuracy.

4.2 Three modelling strategies

We consider three modelling strategies for MSD tagging and root word extraction.

- **Joint model**: We first use the mT5 as a sequence prediction model wherein the input is the surface form, and the outputs are the root words and MSD tags. The root word and MSD tags are generated as a sequence, with the root word being generated first, followed by MSD tags: gender, number, and person (in that order).
- **Multitask model**: In the second setting, we use mT5 as multitask model, with MSD tagging and root word extraction being treated as two separate tasks. We prepend a prefix (string) to the input to specify which task should be performed.
- **Independent model**: In the third setting, we train separate models for root word extraction and MSD tagging, with MSD tags being predicted as a sequence of letters and the input being the surface form.

The input to the model for the second task is the surface form, along with a prefix specifying the task. It should be noted that the choice of prefixes is arbitrary, as long as they are different for each task. While fine-tuning, we add explicit language flags with the respective surface words.

We compare the training strategies in Table 2. The joint sequential prediction leads to the least accuracy in both tasks. Although the multitask framework has higher accuracy than the joint prediction for MSD tagging, it has the lowest accuracy for root word prediction. The multitask framework is expected to have high accuracies because both tasks (MSD tagging and root word extraction) are closely related to each other in the following way: The suffix determines the MSD tags of the surface form, and thus identifying the suffix is an important part of MSD tagging while stripping away the suffix is one of the aspects of root word extraction. The joint multitask training leads to the mixing of outputs (the outputs of both the tasks are in different languages: The MSD tags are in English while

Language	Monolingual accuracies				Multilingual accuracies			
	Gender	Number	Person	Overall	Gender	Number	Person	Overall
Tamil	80.1	87.9	86.3	79.3	86.3	91.7	89.7	**85.4**
Telugu	78.9	97.7	87.4	76.2	78.6	98.3	87.6	**76.5**
Kannada	84.0	88.1	82.6	70.1	87.3	95.7	86.8	**81.7**
Marathi	88.2	87.2	89.3	90.2	96.7	95.9	97.7	**95.6**
Hindi	92.1	85.1	56.9	**53.5**	99.0	89.1	58.3	52.6
Bengali	99.3	94.3	85.0	85.8	99.2	98.3	90.8	**90.4**

Table 3: Demonstrating the benefit of multilingual models over monolingual models for all three tags. The per-tag accuracies and overall accuracies show an increase for all languages except Hindi and Telugu, which show a slight decrease in overall accuracy (but the per-tag accuracy increases for all languages). We provide details of the experiments in section 4.1

the root words are in the same language as the surface form), as observed during the performance on the test set. Training a separate model for both tasks yields the highest performance, and we use the strategy for all our subsequent experiments.

5 Low Resource Morphological Analysis Experiments

5.1 Multilinguality hypothesis

We test the multilinguality hypothesis by comparing monolingual models with multilingual models. As seen in Table 3, which shows per-tag accuracy for each gender, number, person tag, along with overall accuracy, multilingual models outperform the monolingual models for most of the languages except for Hindi and Telugu. One of the reasons for worse performance of multilingual model for Hindi is that the Hindi data containers phrases and post-positions with GNP markings, which are not present in other languages. Thus, adding multilingual data leads to drop in model performance due to confusion between word-based markers and post-position based markers. For Dravidian languages, the overall increase in the accuracy of the multilingual model is negligible in the case of Telugu (as compared to the monolingual baseline), the other two languages, Tamil and Kannada, show around 7.8% increase in overall accuracy. Multilingual models also show better scores in the case of per-tag accuracies for all the Dravidian languages, with gender tag having the highest average increase of 4.03% (averaged over languages).

As also seen in column 2 of Table 2, there is an increase in the accuracy of root word extraction and MSD tagging for Marathi. We show more evidence of the multilinguality hypothesis for MSD tagging through controlled experiments on Bengali and Kannada. We chose these two languages to study the transfer because (1) Kannada shows the highest increase in overall accuracy among the Dravidian languages, and (2) the number of annotated examples of Bengali is the least among the Indo-Aryan languages. Choosing these two languages helps us clearly observe the effect of cross-lingual transfer and the low resource scenario. Tables 4 and 5 show that the multilingual models outperform the monolingual models irrespective of the source languages, with the increase in accuracy being the highest (around 54% for Bengali and 33% for Kannada) in sparse data scenario, where the number of examples of the target language is 1000. Tables 6 and 7 show evidence of the multilinguality hypothesis for root word extraction.

5.2 Inter-family and intra-family transfer

To study cross-family and intra-family transfer, we use Bengali and Kannada. Bengali has the least number of examples in the Indo-Aryan family and shows the highest increase in accuracy with the addition of multilingual data. Kannada shows the highest increase in overall accuracy when going from a monolingual to a multilingual setting. We do this by varying the number of examples of Bengali in the train set to simulate the low-resource scenario. We also add various sets of languages as a source to check inter-family and intra-family transfer. Note that the last row in all the tables named 'All Languages' implies that the data of all six languages were used for training. We study the effectiveness of (family-based) multilingual data by analyzing inter-family and intra-family transfer. In the case of Bengali, we observe that intra-family transfer from languages of the Indo-Aryan family, viz., Marathi and Hindi, lead to, on average, 2.82% more accuracy as compared to transfer from the Dravidian family for MSD tagging (Table 4). For Kannada, the increase in accuracy from monolingual baselines is more from the languages of the Dravidian family as compared to the Indo-Aryan family when the number of examples of Kannada in the training data is 1000 (Table 5). In all other cases, the increase in accuracy with Dravidian languages is either less or similar to that with Indo-Aryan languages as a source. When languages from both families are used as source languages, we observe a sharp increase in accuracy for the root word extraction in Bengali and Kannada. For both the languages, Bengali and Kannada, there is a decrease in accuracy when all the languages are used as source languages, compared to the setting where languages from a particular family are used as source languages.

6 Analysis

In this section, we provide further analysis of the cross-lingual transfer of MSD tags for verbs and nouns and root word extraction.

6.1 GNP tagging for verbs and nouns

In Table 3, we note that the increase in overall accuracy in the case of the multilingual model is the highest for Kannada in the Dravidian family as compared to the monolingual model. Bengali has the least number of annotated examples and shows the highest increase in accuracy from monolingual baseline in the Indo-Aryan family. We dive further into the accuracies of Kannada and Bengali. To investigate the sources of multilingual signals, we conduct experiments separately for nouns and verbs.

Nouns: For nouns, the person feature is trivially third (except for pronouns), and the number feature can be inferred from the suffix, but the gender assignment is arbitrary, and we may require a dictionary to get the gender of the nouns. So, if the nouns (present in the test set) have not been seen during training by the model, one of the potential sources of signal regarding gender is the multilingual data. Another source of signals for gender is also the context that the model has seen during the pretraining (for example, the gender of the nouns is marked on verbs). It is hoped that the gender signals will be captured in the representations learned during the multilingual pretraining. The shared latent space, learned by the multilingual models, is assumed to cluster the words of the same meaning in different languages close to each other.

To test the hypothesis regarding the gender of nouns, we test the accuracy of Kannada and Bengali nouns with various training data from multiple languages. As the gender signal can be dictionary-based, we see that the accuracy increases irrespective of the source languages, as shown in Table 9 and Table 12 in appendix B. For both the languages, Bengali and Kannada, we note that the gender accuracy is higher when the source languages are Marathi and Hindi. The higher accuracy is because the number of training examples of Hindi and Marathi combined is around 70k, while the number of examples of all Dravidian languages combined is about 17K, so more the number of nouns in the training set, more would be the hope of getting dictionary signals. As additional evidence, we also carry out zero-shot transfer for nouns of each language. The training data consists of nouns from all the available languages, and the test data contains nouns from the target language, as shown in Table 13 in the appendix B. The zero-shot gender predic-

Source Languages	Number of Bengali training examples		
	1000	2000	3000
Monolingual	30.8	82.2	85.8
Marathi, Hindi	**85.5**	**89.4**	**90.4**
Tamil, Telugu, Kannada	83.1	87.6	86.1
All languages	73.8	88.9	89.8

Table 4: Bengali MSD tagging accuracies demonstrating effectiveness of intrafamily transfer and multilinguality over monolingual model for low resource setting. More details in section 5.2

Source Languages	Number of Kannada training examples			
	1000	2000	3000	4000
Monolingual	33.2	52.8	65.1	81.7
Marathi, Hindi, Bengali	63.9	77.2	81.4	84.9
Tamil, Telugu,	69.4	74.8	**82.8**	**85.4**
All languages	**69.8**	**76.3**	78.3	82.2

Table 5: Kannada MSD tagging accuracies demonstrating effectiveness of intra-family transfer and multilinguality over monolingual model for low resource setting. More details in section 5.2

Source Languages	Number of Kannada training examples			
	1000	2000	3000	4000
Monolingual	23.2	31.2	40.9	51.2
Marathi, Hindi, Bengali	67.2	70.8	76.7	80.2
Tamil, Telugu,	69.1	71.5	72.9	77.5
All languages	**70.4**	**72.6**	**78.8**	**83.2**

Table 6: Kannada root word extraction accuracies demonstrating multilinguality hypothesis. More details in section 5.1

tion accuracy is non-trivially high for all languages except Tamil (as compared to the case where only verbs are used as source data, wherein we get trivial test accuracies). Tamil has less accuracy for gender as compared to other languages because the number of genders in the Tamil dataset is five, and in a zero-shot setting, the model has no way of knowing the presence of five genders.

Verbs: In the case of verbs, all the features: gender, number, and person can be inferred from the suffix. Our hypothesis here is that increase in the accuracy of verbs in the multilingual setting depends on the source language data available for training. As seen in Table 8, the highest increase in the accuracy of Bengali verbs is seen when the source languages are from the same family. The gender accuracy is almost the same for all the languages as Bengali is a gender-less language, and there are no markings of gender on verbs. In the case of Kannada, as shown in Table 11, the highest increase is observed when the source language is Tamil and Marathi. A Significant increase in accuracy when source data from Marathi is used provides evidence of historical contact between these two languages, as has been discussed in Sengupta and Saha (2015).

Source Languages	Number of Bengali training examples		
	1000	2000	3000
Monolingual	32.2	51.2	74.8
Marathi, Hindi	85.2	92.3	95.2
Tamil, Telugu, Kannada	84.6	91.2	93.3
All languages	**90.1**	**92.8**	**96.9**

Table 7: Bengali root word extraction accuracies demonstrating positive transfer from various subsets of source languages. More details in section 5.1

Source language	Accuracy for Bengali Verbs			
	Gen	Num	Per	Overall
Monolingual	99.3	94.2	84.6	76.2
Marathi	99.2	92.6	89.4	88.9
Hindi	99.2	**93.2**	**90.7**	**90.0**
Tamil	99.6	92.6	86.8	86.8
Telugu	99.1	91.6	84.2	83.9
Kannada	99.2	91.3	88.2	87.3
Hindi, Marathi	99.8	**93.4**	**90.5**	84.1
Tamil, Telugu, Kannada	99.8	91.6	89.8	85.8

Table 8: Analysis of Bengali Verbs demonstrating transfer from various families and languages. More discussions in section 11

Training languages	Accuracy on Kannada Nouns		
	Gender	Number	Overall
Monolingual	96.0	90.4	82.9
Tamil, Telugu	94.0	94.9	89.4
Marathi, Hindi	**96.9**	97.3	94.4
All Languages	96.0	**97.7**	**95.7**

Table 9: Testing cross-lingual transfer for Gender and Number tags in the case of Kannada Nouns

The historical contact also shows the reason behind the highest increase in overall accuracy when the source languages are Marathi and Hindi (Table 9).

Generalization: We also test the model's generalization ability to unseen patterns. For example, the suffix 'raha hei' in Hindi represents masculine, third person, and singular. We remove all instances of the suffix from the train set, add them to the test set, and check the accuracy of the model on it in multilingual and monolingual settings. In the case of monolingual and multilingual settings, the model's overall accuracy is 50% for GNP tagging; the tags gender and number are correctly predicted for all the test instances, while the person tag is correctly predicted for 50% of all the instances. The number and gender can be inferred from the suffix itself; however, the person tag depends on the verb as well as the context, thus leading to confusion for the model (as we are not using the context currently.)

Number of training examples	Bengali		Kannada	
	(1) Input same as outputs	(2) Surface forms and roots	(1) Input same as outputs	(2) Surface forms and roots
zero-shot	12.2	18.2	8.6	12.1
1000	90.3	90.1	72.2	70.4
2000	94.8	92.2	71.2	72.6
3000	**97.9**	96.9	73.9	78.8
4000	-	-	74.4	**83.2**

Table 10: Role of copy bias in root word extraction. Adding inputs same as outputs for source languages has results comparable to the case when inputs are surface form and outputs are root words. (Note: Number of available training examples of Bengali is 3000) More details in section 6.2

Source language	Accuracy for Kannada Verbs			
	Gen	Num	Per	Overall
Monolingual	83.0	95.8	82.7	73.1
Marathi	87.6	**96.3**	83.3	76.0
Hindi	85.6	95.5	90.3	81.9
Tamil	88.0	96.7	92.3	**84.1**
Telugu	80.6	94.6	74.1	66.1
Bengali	84.6	97.4	91.8	81.8
Hindi, Marathi, Bengali	81.4	94.4	83.9	76.0
Tamil, Telugu	**87.7**	97.2	91.6	83.5

Table 11: Analysis of Kannada Verbs demonstrating transfer from related families and languages. More discussions in section

6.2 Root word extraction

To test cross-lingual transfer in the case of root word extraction, we test the copy bias learned by the model. The copy bias is an essential part of the learning process for root word extraction, as the output contains most of the characters present in the input except for a suffix. As can be seen in Tables 7 and 6, the root word extraction accuracy increases to a similar extent, irrespective of the source language. We test the copy bias by adding training examples from source languages such that the input and output are the same. The comparison of the effect of copy bias with our standard setup where the source inputs are surface form and source outputs are root words is shown in Table 10. The table highlights that copy bias plays a role in root word extraction and cross-lingual transfer of morphological knowledge (such as the similarity between morphemes) across the shared embedding space is limited.

7 Conclusions

In this paper, we tested the multilinguality hypothesis for root word extraction and morphosyntactic descriptors (MSD) tagging. We trained multilingual models for MSD tagging and root word extraction using data of six Indian languages spanning two families of the Indian subcontinent. We demonstrated the effectiveness of data from languages of the same and different families and how it can be leveraged to train morphological analysis models for low resource languages. We also analyzed how cross-lingual transfer of morphological knowledge happens for nouns and verbs along with the copy bias, which forms a significant component of the root word extraction. Our framework can be extended to multiple tags as well as more low resources languages as annotated data becomes available. We see our work as an important step in the direction of bias-aware machine translation to morphologically rich languages.

8 Limitations

One of the limitations of our work is the unavailability of context data and unavailability of phrase-based annotations for all languages except Hindi. The unavailability of phrase-based annotations prevents the usage of universal tags because markings that are present on a single word in highly agglutinative languages like Marathi or Tamil get expressed on 2–3 words in isolating or fusional languages like Hindi or Bengali (where markings are present on post-positions). The benefits of using phrase level morphology over token level morphology have been discussed in Goldman and Tsarfaty

(2021). For example, the word 'sochega' in Hindi will have MSD tags: future tense and male gender, while in English, it would take two words, 'he will think' to express the same amount of morphological information. The presence of contextual data can also help to disambiguate MSD tags. The other limitation of our work is the mismatch between the languages for which pretrained models (especially encoder-decoder models) are available and the languages for which we have the annotated data. For example, UniMorph dataset contains annotated examples for Assamese and Sanskrit, but we do not have multilingual pretrained encoder-decoder models for these languages.

9 Ethics Considerations\Broader Impact

Our work is on morphological analysis of low resource languages. We aim to increase the coverage of NLP tools through our work. It is inline with making language technologies accessible for wider range of audiences who do-not have commonly researched high resource languages like English, French as their native language. Our work is also a step towards automating the process of documentation of endangered languages.

Acknowledgements

We thank Simran Khanuja for participating in the early phases of this research. We also thank CFILT Lab, IIT Bombay for providing resources and some of the datasets. We thank Kuzman Ganchev and Srini Narayanan for comments on the draft. We would like to thank CMiNDS department, IIT Bombay along with Google India Research Lab for providing with the opportunity for conducting this research. Finally, we would like to thank Matthias Bauer for providing help with writing and structuring of the final draft.

References

Ankita Agarwal, Pramila, Shashi Singh, Ajai Kumar, and Hemant Darbari. 2014. Morphological analyser for hindi – a rule based implementation. *International Journal of Advanced Computer Research*, 4.

Aryaman Arora, Adam Farris, Samopriya Basu, and Suresh Kolichala. 2022. Computational historical linguistics and language diversity in South Asia. In *Proceedings of the 60th Annual Meeting of the Association for Computational Linguistics (Volume 1: Long Papers)*, pages 1396–1409, Dublin, Ireland. Association for Computational Linguistics.

Mugdha Bapat, Harshada Gune, and Pushpak Bhattacharyya. 2010. A paradigm-based finite state morphological analyzer for Marathi. In *Proceedings of the 1st Workshop on South and Southeast Asian Natural Language Processing*, pages 26–34, Beijing, China. Coling 2010 Organizing Committee.

Khuyagbaatar Batsuren, Gábor Bella, and Fausto Giunchiglia. 2021. Morphynet: a large multilingual database of derivational and inflectional morphology. In *Proceedings of the 18th sigmorphon workshop on computational research in phonetics, phonology, and morphology*, pages 39–48.

Khuyagbaatar Batsuren, Omer Goldman, Salam Khalifa, Nizar Habash, Witold Kieraś, Gábor Bella, Brian Leonard, Garrett Nicolai, Kyle Gorman, Yustinus Ghanggo Ate, Maria Ryskina, Sabrina Mielke, Elena Budianskaya, Charbel El-Khaissi, Tiago Pimentel, Michael Gasser, William Abbott Lane, Mohit Raj, Matt Coler, Jaime Rafael Montoya Samame, Delio Siticonatzi Camaiteri, Esaú Zumaeta Rojas, Didier López Francis, Arturo Oncevay, Juan López Bautista, Gema Celeste Silva Villegas, Lucas Torroba Hennigen, Adam Ek, David Guriel, Peter Dirix, Jean-Philippe Bernardy, Andrey Scherbakov, Aziyana Bayyr-ool, Antonios Anastasopoulos, Roberto Zariquiey, Karina Sheifer, Sofya Ganieva, Hilaria Cruz, Ritván Karahóğa, Stella Markantonatou, George Pavlidis, Matvey Plugaryov, Elena Klyachko, Ali Salehi, Candy Angulo, Jatayu Baxi, Andrew Krizhanovsky, Natalia Krizhanovskaya, Elizabeth Salesky, Clara Vania, Sardana Ivanova, Jennifer White, Rowan Hall Maudslay, Josef Valvoda, Ran Zmigrod, Paula Czarnowska, Irene Nikkarinen, Aelita Salchak, Brijesh Bhatt, Christopher Straughn, Zoey Liu, Jonathan North Washington, Yuval Pinter, Duygu Ataman, Marcin Wolinski, Totok Suhardijanto, Anna Yablonskaya, Niklas Stoehr, Hossep Dolatian, Zahroh Nuriah, Shyam Ratan, Francis M. Tyers, Edoardo M. Ponti, Grant Aiton, Aryaman Arora, Richard J. Hatcher, Ritesh Kumar, Jeremiah Young, Daria Rodionova, Anastasia Yemelina, Taras Andrushko, Igor Marchenko, Polina Mashkovtseva, Alexandra Serova, Emily Prud'hommeaux, Maria Nepomniashchaya, Fausto Giunchiglia, Eleanor Chodroff, Mans Hulden, Miikka Silfverberg, Arya D. McCarthy, David Yarowsky, Ryan Cotterell, Reut Tsarfaty, and Ekaterina Vylomova. 2022. UniMorph 4.0: Universal Morphology. In *Proceedings of the Thirteenth Language Resources and Evaluation Conference*, pages 840–855, Marseille, France. European Language Resources Association.

Riyaz Ahmad Bhat, Rajesh Bhatt, Annahita Farudi, Prescott Klassen, Bhuvana Narasimhan, Martha Palmer, Owen Rambow, Dipti Misra Sharma, Ashwini Vaidya, Sri Ramagurumurthy Vishnu, et al. 2017. The hindi/urdu treebank project. In *Handbook of linguistic annotation*, pages 659–697. Springer.

Bharathi Raja Chakravarthi, Ruba Priyadharshini, Anand Kumar M, Parameswari Krishnamurthy, and

Elizabeth Sherly, editors. 2021. *Proceedings of the First Workshop on Speech and Language Technologies for Dravidian Languages*. Association for Computational Linguistics, Kyiv.

Ryan Cotterell and Georg Heigold. 2017a. Cross-lingual character-level neural morphological tagging. In *Proceedings of the 2017 Conference on Empirical Methods in Natural Language Processing*, pages 748–759.

Ryan Cotterell and Georg Heigold. 2017b. Cross-lingual character-level neural morphological tagging. In *Proceedings of the 2017 Conference on Empirical Methods in Natural Language Processing*, pages 748–759, Copenhagen, Denmark. Association for Computational Linguistics.

Ryan Cotterell, Christo Kirov, John Sylak-Glassman, Géraldine Walther, Ekaterina Vylomova, Arya D. McCarthy, Katharina Kann, Sabrina J. Mielke, Garrett Nicolai, Miikka Silfverberg, David Yarowsky, Jason Eisner, and Mans Hulden. 2018. The CoNLL–SIGMORPHON 2018 shared task: Universal morphological reinflection. In *Proceedings of the CoNLL–SIGMORPHON 2018 Shared Task: Universal Morphological Reinflection*, pages 1–27, Brussels. Association for Computational Linguistics.

Ryan Cotterell, Christo Kirov, John Sylak-Glassman, Géraldine Walther, Ekaterina Vylomova, Patrick Xia, Manaal Faruqui, Sandra Kübler, David Yarowsky, Jason Eisner, and Mans Hulden. 2017. CoNLL-SIGMORPHON 2017 shared task: Universal morphological reinflection in 52 languages. In *Proceedings of the CoNLL SIGMORPHON 2017 Shared Task: Universal Morphological Reinflection*, pages 1–30, Vancouver. Association for Computational Linguistics.

Ryan Cotterell, Christo Kirov, John Sylak-Glassman, David Yarowsky, Jason Eisner, and Mans Hulden. 2016. The SIGMORPHON 2016 shared Task—Morphological reinflection. In *Proceedings of the 14th SIGMORPHON Workshop on Computational Research in Phonetics, Phonology, and Morphology*, pages 10–22, Berlin, Germany. Association for Computational Linguistics.

Micha Elsner. 2021. What transfers in morphological inflection? experiments with analogical models. In *Proceedings of the 18th SIGMORPHON Workshop on Computational Research in Phonetics, Phonology, and Morphology*, pages 154–166, Online. Association for Computational Linguistics.

Manaal Faruqui, Ryan McDonald, and Radu Soricut. 2016. Morpho-syntactic lexicon generation using graph-based semi-supervised learning. *Transactions of the Association for Computational Linguistics*, 4:1–16.

Omer Goldman and Reut Tsarfaty. 2021. Well-defined morphology is sentence-level morphology. In *Proceedings of the 1st Workshop on Multilingual Representation Learning*, pages 248–250, Punta Cana, Dominican Republic. Association for Computational Linguistics.

Ashim Gupta, Amrith Krishna, Pawan Goyal, and Oliver Hellwig. 2020. Evaluating neural morphological taggers for sanskrit. In *Proceedings of the 17th SIGMORPHON Workshop on Computational Research in Phonetics, Phonology, and Morphology*, pages 198–203.

Mans Hulden, Markus Forsberg, and Malin Ahlberg. 2014. Semi-supervised learning of morphological paradigms and lexicons. In *Proceedings of the 14th Conference of the European Chapter of the Association for Computational Linguistics*, pages 569–578, Gothenburg, Sweden. Association for Computational Linguistics.

Girish Nath Jha, Kalika Bali, Sobha L., S. S. Agrawal, and Atul Kr. Ojha, editors. 2020. *Proceedings of the WILDRE5– 5th Workshop on Indian Language Data: Resources and Evaluation*. European Language Resources Association (ELRA), Marseille, France.

Saurav Jha, Akhilesh Sudhakar, and Anil Kumar Singh. 2018. Multi task deep morphological analyzer: Context aware joint morphological tagging and lemma prediction. *ArXiv*, abs/1811.08619.

Huiming Jin, Liwei Cai, Yihui Peng, Chen Xia, Arya McCarthy, and Katharina Kann. 2020. Unsupervised morphological paradigm completion. In *Proceedings of the 58th Annual Meeting of the Association for Computational Linguistics*, pages 6696–6707, Online. Association for Computational Linguistics.

Stav Klein and Reut Tsarfaty. 2020. Getting the ##life out of living: How adequate are word-pieces for modelling complex morphology? In *Proceedings of the 17th SIGMORPHON Workshop on Computational Research in Phonetics, Phonology, and Morphology*, pages 204–209, Online. Association for Computational Linguistics.

Anne Lauscher, Vinit Ravishankar, Ivan Vulić, and Goran Glavaš. 2020. From zero to hero: On the limitations of zero-shot language transfer with multilingual Transformers. In *Proceedings of the 2020 Conference on Empirical Methods in Natural Language Processing (EMNLP)*, pages 4483–4499, Online. Association for Computational Linguistics.

Chaitanya Malaviya, Matthew R. Gormley, and Graham Neubig. 2018. Neural factor graph models for cross-lingual morphological tagging. In *Proceedings of the 56th Annual Meeting of the Association for Computational Linguistics (Volume 1: Long Papers)*, pages 2653–2663, Melbourne, Australia. Association for Computational Linguistics.

Arya D. McCarthy, Christo Kirov, Matteo Grella, Amrit Nidhi, Patrick Xia, Kyle Gorman, Ekaterina Vylomova, Sabrina J. Mielke, Garrett Nicolai, Miikka Silfverberg, Timofey Arkhangelskiy, Nataly Krizhanovsky, Andrew Krizhanovsky, Elena

Klyachko, Alexey Sorokin, John Mansfield, Valts Ernštreits, Yuval Pinter, Cassandra L. Jacobs, Ryan Cotterell, Mans Hulden, and David Yarowsky. 2020. UniMorph 3.0: Universal Morphology. In *Proceedings of the 12th Language Resources and Evaluation Conference*, pages 3922–3931, Marseille, France. European Language Resources Association.

Arya D. McCarthy, Ekaterina Vylomova, Shijie Wu, Chaitanya Malaviya, Lawrence Wolf-Sonkin, Garrett Nicolai, Christo Kirov, Miikka Silfverberg, Sabrina J. Mielke, Jeffrey Heinz, Ryan Cotterell, and Mans Hulden. 2019. The SIGMORPHON 2019 shared task: Morphological analysis in context and cross-lingual transfer for inflection. In *Proceedings of the 16th Workshop on Computational Research in Phonetics, Phonology, and Morphology*, pages 229–244, Florence, Italy. Association for Computational Linguistics.

Sarah Moeller, Ling Liu, Changbing Yang, Katharina Kann, and Mans Hulden. 2020. IGT2P: From interlinear glossed texts to paradigms. In *Proceedings of the 2020 Conference on Empirical Methods in Natural Language Processing (EMNLP)*, pages 5251–5262, Online. Association for Computational Linguistics.

Jayashree Nair, L. S. Aiswarya, and P. R. Sruthy. 2021. A study on morphological analyser for indian languages: A literature perspective. In *Advances in Computing and Data Sciences*, pages 112–123, Cham. Springer International Publishing.

Minh Van Nguyen, Viet Dac Lai, Amir Pouran Ben Veyseh, and Thien Huu Nguyen. 2021. Trankit: A light-weight transformer-based toolkit for multilingual natural language processing. In *Proceedings of the 16th Conference of the European Chapter of the Association for Computational Linguistics: System Demonstrations*, pages 80–90, Online. Association for Computational Linguistics.

Garrett Nicolai, Kyle Gorman, and Ryan Cotterell, editors. 2021. *Proceedings of the 18th SIGMORPHON Workshop on Computational Research in Phonetics, Phonology, and Morphology*. Association for Computational Linguistics, Online.

Antoine Nzeyimana and Andre Niyongabo Rubungo. 2022. Kinyabert: a morphology-aware kinyarwanda language model. In *Proceedings of the 60th Annual Meeting of the Association for Computational Linguistics (Volume 1: Long Papers)*, pages 5347–5363.

Hyunji Hayley Park, Katherine J. Zhang, Coleman Haley, Kenneth Steimel, Han Liu, and Lane Schwartz. 2021. Morphology Matters: A Multilingual Language Modeling Analysis. *Transactions of the Association for Computational Linguistics*, 9:261–276.

Loganathan Ramasamy and Zdeněk Žabokrtský. 2014. Tamil dependency treebank v0.1. LINDAT/CLARIAH-CZ digital library at the Institute of Formal and Applied Linguistics (ÚFAL), Faculty of Mathematics and Physics, Charles University.

Wolfgang Seeker and Özlem Çetinoğlu. 2015. A Graph-based Lattice Dependency Parser for Joint Morphological Segmentation and Syntactic Analysis. *Transactions of the Association for Computational Linguistics*, 3:359–373.

Debapriya Sengupta and Goutam Saha. 2015. Study on similarity among indian languages using language verification framework. *Advances in Artificial Intelligence*, 2015:1–24.

Aleš Tamchyna, Marion Weller-Di Marco, and Alexander Fraser. 2017. Modeling target-side inflection in neural machine translation. In *Proceedings of the Second Conference on Machine Translation*, pages 32–42, Copenhagen, Denmark. Association for Computational Linguistics.

Adam Wiemerslage, Arya D McCarthy, Alexander Erdmann, Garrett Nicolai, Manex Agirrezabal, Miikka Silfverberg, Mans Hulden, and Katharina Kann. 2021. Findings of the sigmorphon 2021 shared task on unsupervised morphological paradigm clustering. In *Proceedings of the 18th SIGMORPHON Workshop on Computational Research in Phonetics, Phonology, and Morphology*, pages 72–81.

Shijie Wu and Mark Dredze. 2019. Beto, bentz, becas: The surprising cross-lingual effectiveness of BERT. In *Proceedings of the 2019 Conference on Empirical Methods in Natural Language Processing and the 9th International Joint Conference on Natural Language Processing (EMNLP-IJCNLP)*, pages 833–844, Hong Kong, China. Association for Computational Linguistics.

Linting Xue, Noah Constant, Adam Roberts, Mihir Kale, Rami Al-Rfou, Aditya Siddhant, Aditya Barua, and Colin Raffel. 2021. mt5: A massively multilingual pre-trained text-to-text transformer. In *Proceedings of the 2021 Conference of the North American Chapter of the Association for Computational Linguistics: Human Language Technologies*, pages 483–498.

A Appendix: Satistics of UniMorph Dataset

The UnimOrph dataset's statistics are shown in table 14. A total of 26 features are available in the meta-data of the UniMorph dataset. They include Aktionsart, Animacy, Argument marking, Aspect, Case, Comparison, Definiteness, Deixis, Evidentiality, Finiteness, Gender, Information Structure, Interrogativity, Language Specific features, Mood, Number, Other, Part of speech, Person, Polarity, Politeness, Possession, Switch reference, Tense, Valency, Voice. For most Indic languages, the annotations are present for not more than eight features per language. The set of features for which annotations are current varies across languages. We give the proportion of words in the dataset for which feature annotations are present. We provide statistics for Gender, Number, Person, Tense, Aspect, and Modality, characteristic features of verbal morphology. We also provide statistics for case, number, number, and person for nouns. The 'others' section represents the features with the highest proportion of tags, from gender, number, person, tense, aspect, modality, and case. Also, one thing that must be noted is that the amount of data available for verbs is almost 5 times the data available for nouns for most of the languages, so the number in the 'total' row is dominated by statistics of verb. For Hindi, the nouns data is completely absent.

B Appendix: Cross-Lingual transfer Nouns—Additional Tables

Training languages	Accuracy on Bengali Nouns		
	Gen	Num	Overall
Monolingual	96.81	79.62	76.85
Tamil, Telugu, Kannada	95.18	91.66	85.18
Marathi, Hindi	98.21	92.23	87.37
All	**98.45**	**92.7**	**90.7**

Table 12: Testing cross-lingual transfer for Gender and Number tags in the case of Bengali Nouns

Target language	Zero Shot Test accuracy for nouns		
	Gender	Number	Overall
Marathi	68.2	76.4	66.4
Telugu	69.6	59.7	48.1
Bengali	55.1	65.5	50.2
Kannada	56.2	61.2	47.3
Tamil	15.1	67.1	13.2

Table 13: Zero-shot accuracies for gender and number tagging of nouns showing the help of multilingual signals for gender. More details in section 6.1

Lang	POS for which data is available	Percentage of data points with a particular feature marking is present							
		Gen	Num	Per	Ten	Aspect	Case	Modality	Others
Hindi	Verbs	94.7	99.0	95.2	34.1	89.1	0	27.0	35.2
	Nouns	-	-	-	-	-	-	-	-
	Total	94.7	99.0	95.2	34.1	89.1	0	27.0	35.2
Bengali	Verbs	-	100	86.9	86.9	60.8	-	2.1	52.1
	Nouns	66.6	-	-	-	-	80.8	-	19.8
	Total	8.0	88.9	75.6	75.6	52.9	10.5	1.8	45.3
Kannada	Verbs	46.6	100	89.2	46.2	-	-	19.6	20.7
	Nouns	-	100	-	-	-	100	-	-
	Total	36.6	91.4	70.5	37.1	0	20.9	15.5	16.8
Telugu	Verbs	50.0	100	100	100	-	-	-	13.7
	Nouns	-	100	-	-	-	100	-	-
	Total	43.7	100	87.2	87.2	0	12.7	0	11.3
Combined	Verbs	47.8	99.7	92.8	77.5	37.4	-	12.1	30.4
	Nouns	16.6	50	-	-	-	70.2	-	4.9

Table 14: Statistics of UniMorph dataset

Joint Learning Model for Low-Resource Agglutinative Language Morphological Tagging

Gulinigeer Abudouwaili[1,2], **Kahaerjiang Abiderexiti**[1,2], **Nian Yi** [1,2,] and **Aishan Wumaier**[1,2,*]
[1]School of Information Science and Engineering, Xinjiang University
[2]Laboratory of Multi-Language Information Technology, Xinjiang University
107556518131@stu.xju.edu.cn, kaharjan@aliyun.com, 15709918429@163.com and Hasan1479@xju.edu.cn

Abstract

Due to the lack of data resources, rule-based or transfer learning is mainly used in the morphological tagging of low-resource languages. However, these methods require expert knowledge, ignore contextual features, and have error propagation. Therefore, we propose a joint morphological tagger for low-resource agglutinative languages to alleviate the above challenges. First, we represent the contextual input with multi-dimensional features of agglutinative words. Second, joint training reduces the direct impact of part-of-speech errors on morphological features and increases the indirect influence between the two types of labels through a fusion mechanism. Finally, our model separately predicts part-of-speech and morphological features. Part-of-speech tagging is regarded as sequence tagging. When predicting morphological features, two-label adjacency graphs are dynamically reconstructed by integrating multilingual global features and monolingual local features. Then, a graph convolution network is used to learn the higher-order intersection of labels. A series of experiments show that the proposed model in this paper is superior to other comparative models.

1 Introduction

Morphological tagging describes the lexical information of a word in a sentence from the part-of-speech (PoS) and morphological features (MFs; case, person, mood, tense, etc.) (Özateş and Çetinoğlu, 2021) and is an essential task in agglutinative language information processing. Morphological tagging can analyze semantics (Klimaszewski and Wróblewska, 2021), so some morphological knowledge will be added to many downstream tasks, such as dependency parsing (Klimaszewski and Wróblewska, 2021), named entity recognition (Kim and Kim, 2020), language models (Park et al., 2021), and machine translation (Jon et al., 2021), to assist the model in learning semantics and improve interpretability. An example is given in Table 1. The first line shows a sentence, the second line shows its lemma, and the third line shows the morphosyntactic description (MSD) labels.

The	cats	are	sleeping	.
the	cat	be	sleep	.
DET	N;PL	V;PRS;3;PL	V;V.PTCP;PRS	PUNT

Table 1: An example of morphological analysis in English

In recent years, there have been many achievements in morphological tagging, among which SIGMORPHON 2019 shared task 2 is a significant milestone (McCarthy et al., 2019), and many cross-lingual morphological tagging models have been proposed. High-resource languages usually use deep learning models and regard morphological tagging as a sequence labeling (Özateş and Çetinoğlu, 2021) or sequence generation task (Oh et al., 2019). The study of English and Chinese morphological tasks began relatively early. Supported by large-scale labeled datasets and large language models, the morphological tagging technology of these languages has reached a mature level. However, the morphological tagging of low-resource languages remains to be further researched. Finite-state transducer (FST) and transfer learning are the primary strategies for constructing morphological tagger in low-resource languages (Wiemerslage et al., 2022; Ibrahim et al., 2018; Rueter et al., 2021; Cotterell and Heigold, 2017). The FST model represents orthographic rules as state transition conditions and can be understood as the transfer of surface relations. Graph convolution networks (GCN) can also explore label relationships (Ma et al., 2021; Zhou et al., 2023). Morphological tagging based on FST focuses on lexical rules of words, which require many linguistic rules. In addition, there are

*:Corresponding author

Proceedings of the 20th SIGMORPHON workshop on Computational Research in Phonetics, Phonology, and Morphology, pages 27–37
July 14, 2023

problems such as poor semantic ability, ambiguity, rule conflicts, and the inability to express deep lexical rules. In transfer learning, high-resource language knowledge is transferred to a low-resource language, and a tagging model is built by deep learning models. If a sequence labeling or generation model based on deep learning is used with low resources languages, error prediction at the previous time cause error propagation.

In agglutinative languages, a word is formed with a lemma and several suffixes. In the Uyghur word, "almidi" (translation: he/she/they did not pick up), "al" is lemma, "mi(a)", "d" and "i" are suffixes, its MSD label: 'V;SG/PL;3;NEG;PST'. The lemma represents the word's meaning, and the suffix represents the grammatical category (Pan et al., 2020). Each suffix represents grammatical information and corresponds to a morphosyntactic description label (Seker and Tsarfaty, 2020). Morphological taggers in low-resource agglutinative language mainly focus on rule-based and statistical models (Ibrahim et al., 2018; WUSIMAN et al., 2019; Tolegen et al.), while relatively few studies are based on transfer learning or deep learning (Toleu et al., 2017; Liu et al., 2021; Toleu et al., 2022). Conventional methods rely on human-designed rules, which are limited to surface rules in the dataset and cannot capture hidden rules and learn or represent deep grammar rules.

In this paper, we investigate (1) which features in agglutinative language are related to MSD labels, (2) how to reduce the direct impact of error propagation, and (3) whether it is possible to accurately predict more complete MSD labels using label relationships and word representation in low-resource languages. Therefore, to overcome these issues, we first represent the input word by contextual and word-formation features. Second, to reduce error propagation caused by PoS, morphological tagging is divided into PoS tagging and MF tagging. Through literature research and experiments, it has been found that PoS can alleviate ambiguity, and PoS affects the prediction of morphological feature labels. Inspired by the work of (Li et al., 2021), a fusion mechanism is adopted for the middle layer of the two tasks. Finally, the output of the fusion mechanism is input into the conditional random field (CRF) layer to predict the PoS of each word. We pretrain labels in the MF tagging model and calculate relevant label co-occurrence statistics for the high-resource agglutinative language to learn the relationship between labels. The co-occurrence of irrelevant labels is calculated for the Uyghur (Ug), Kazakh (Kz), Tatar (Tt), and Yakut (Yk) datasets. A dynamic adjacency graph is reconstructed by using the above relationships and a GCN to learn the label relationship again to find the hidden relationships between labels. Then, the MF labels of each word are predicted by using the word feature and label relationship. We evaluate our model on four low-resource agglutinative languages, Uyghur, Kazakh, Tatar, and Yakut, in universal dependencies (UD), and experiments show that the performance of the model proposed in this paper is superior to that of other comparable models. The model's average accuracy in four languages reaches 85.29%, and the average F1 score reaches 92.61%.

Our contributions are highlighted as follows:

- This paper proposes a joint morphological tagging model that divides morphological tagging into PoS and MF tagging. Furthermore, the middle layer is fused to transform direct influence into indirect influence.

- To further explore the subtle and hidden relationships between MF labels of low-resource agglutinative languages, this paper describes the universal relationship of agglutinative languages and the characteristic relationship of a monolingual language. The final relationship representation of the monolingual MF labels is dynamically constructed through a GCN.

- We conduct experiments on the Uy, Kz, Tt, and Yk datasets, and the experimental results prove the effectiveness of the model proposed in this paper. This paper also fills the gap in the research on fine-grained morphological tagging of low-resource agglutinative language based on deep learning.

2 Related Work

Morphological processing is the primary task of natural language processing. Relevant tasks include but are not limited to the following: morphological tagging (Özateş and Çetinoğlu, 2021), morphological segmentation (Batsuren et al., 2022), lemmatization (Zalmout and Habash, 2020), and morphological analysis (Wiemerslage et al., 2022). There is also a close connection between these subtasks. For example, morphological analysis can be split into lemmatization and morphological tagging. Similar to other tasks, morphological tagging tasks can also be summarized as rule learning (Forbes et al., 2021; Kuznetsova and Tyers, 2021), statistical learning (Çöltekin and Barnes, 2019; Mueller et al., 2013), and deep learning(Seker and Tsarfaty, 2020; Li and Girrbach, 2022), according to different research methods. Recurrent neural networks or pretrained language models have been widely used in morphological tagging for high-resource languages. Nine cross-lingual models were submitted for SIGMORPHON 2019 shared task 2, significantly promoting the development of morphological analysis (McCarthy et al., 2019). The winning model, UDify, was proposed by Kondratyuk (2019) and combines a multilingual pretrained language model and several fine-tuning strategies. They trained multilingually over all treebanks in the first stage and then monolingually used saved multilingual weights in the second stage. Finally, the model predicts each grammatical category. Klimaszewski and Wróblewska (2021) proposed a fully neural natural tagging model, COMBO, for accurate PoS tagging, morphological analysis, lemmatization, and (enhanced) dependency parsing. It is a BERT-based end-to-end multilingual model. Li and Girrbach (2022) studied word segmentation and morphological analysis of Sanskrit and proposed three models: word segmentation, morphological analysis, and combined segmentation and analysis models. The combined segmentation and analysis model is an end-to-end pipeline model. Nicolai et al. (2020) proposed a morphological analysis and generation model for more than one thousand languages. They leveraged a parallel corpus to project from English to other low-resource languages and exploited a morphological annotation tool. Two separate sequence transduction models, one neural and one nonneural network model, were trained, and each model produced an N-best list. The tagging model achieved better performance in high resources. Cotterell and Heigold (2017) trained character-level recurrent neural taggers through language transfer to predict the morphological tagger of high and low resource languages. Learning joint character representations among multiple related languages successfully enables knowledge transfer from the high-resource languages to the low-resource, improving accuracy by up to 30%.

It is difficult to achieve high accuracy using a deep learning or cross-lingual transfer learning model for low-resource languages. Because neither FST nor CRF requires a large dataset, it is common to achieve morphological tagging by using these two models for low-resource languages. In the FST method (Tolegen et al.; Kuznetsova and Tyers, 2021), researchers construct language resources, such as morphological and orthographic rules, and then design a morphological analyzer. WUSIMAN et al. (2019) proposed a character-level morphological collaborative analysis model based on the CRF. Morphological segmentation, annotations, and phonetic changes were combined into a composite label for each character. Toleu et al. (2022) proposed a sequence-to-sequence model of morphological disambiguation. It was hypothesized that the vector representation of the correct analysis should be closer to that of the context vector, and the model predicts the correct MSD label by calculating the similarity. FST and statistical methods require many morphological rules or high-quality annotated data, leading to expensive labor costs. Furthermore, the model cannot be combined with contextual features very well, which can easily cause ambiguity problems. In addition, some problems, such as lexical rule conflicts and long running times, may occur.

Therefore, to avoid ambiguity and improve the model performance of predicting more complete MSD labels, the proposed model uses a pretrained model to represent words via contextual features. By jointly training PoS and MF tags, the direct impact of PoS tags on MF tags is reduced. The related morphological tag relations of the agglutinative language in the treebank are learned and transferred to low-resource languages, and introducing irrelevant tag relations between the low-resource languages and dynamically reconstructing the relations between tags, thus alleviating the problem of data resource scarcity.

3 Joint Learning Model for Morphological Tagging

3.1 Task definition

Morphological tagging is a word-level task, and labels are analyzed in terms of context (Wiemerslage et al., 2022). The definition of the morphological tagging task is as follows: a sentence S consists of n words, $S = \{w_1, w_2, \ldots, w_n\}$. The morphological label of the word w_i is T_i, $T_i = \{t_1, t_2, \ldots, t_m\}$, where t_1 is the PoS label, and the following label is the MF label. Therefore, when the input of the model is sentence S, the output is each word's morphological label, namely, $\{T_1, T_2, \ldots, T_n\}$.

3.2 Model framework

The overall structure of the joint morphological tagging model is shown in Figure 1. We divide the morphological tagging task into two subtasks, PoS tagging and MF tagging. The input sentence is $S = \{\mathbf{E_1}, \mathbf{E_2}, \ldots, \mathbf{E_n}\}$, where $\mathbf{E_i} \in \mathbb{R}^{d_e}$ is the vector of the word w_i, and d_e is the dimension of the vector. First, we input the vector into the BiLSTM layer for each task and encode the sentence through the BiLSTM layer to obtain the hidden state of the context vector, $\mathbf{H} = [\mathbf{h_1}, \mathbf{h_2}, ..., \mathbf{h_n}]$, where $\mathbf{h_i} \in \mathbb{R}^{2d}$. Second, to achieve mutual influence between the two labels, we fuse the output of the BiLSTM layer. Finally, the fused results are input into the inference layer of the model.

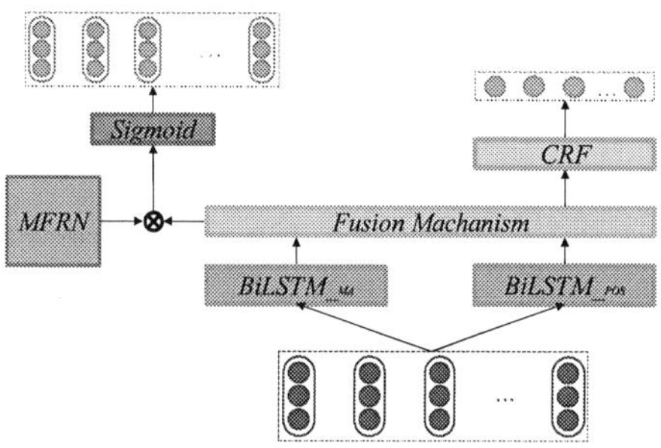

Figure 1: The overall model architecture

The CRF model in the inference layer predicts the PoS label of the word. The morphological feature relation network (MFRN) in the inference layer is dot multiplied by the fused output. We deploy a sigmoid activation function to acquire the probability of each tag, and a tag with a probability value higher than 0.5 is output. The total loss function of the model is:

$$\mathcal{L} = (1 - \lambda)\mathcal{L}_{PoS} + \lambda\mathcal{L}_{MT} \quad (1)$$

where L_{PoS} is the loss function of the CRF layer, L_{MT} is the loss function of the MFRN network, λ is the manually set weight value, and $\lambda \in [0, 1]$. Through experiments, it is found that when $\lambda = 0.6$, the model performance is the best. The loss function of the PoS tagger is a negative log-likelihood function, as shown in Equation 2. Given N training data, x^i represents the ith input sequence, y^i represents the real tag sequence of the ith sequence, and $(y^i \mid x^i)$ is the probability of the real tag sequence. The MF tagging loss function is the binary cross-entropy loss function, as shown in Equation 3. Similarly, given N training data, each input sequence has M words, z represents the real label, and $\bar{z}$ represents the label predicted by the model. z^{ijk} indicates whether the $k-th$ label is in the jth word of the ith input sequence.

$$\mathcal{L}_{PoS} = -\sum_{i=1}^{N} \log p(y^i \mid x^i) \quad (2)$$

$$\mathcal{L}_{MT} = -\sum_{i=1}^{N}\sum_{j=1}^{M}\sum_{k=1}^{|L_{MT}|} z^{ijk} \log \bar{z}^{ijk} + \left(1 - z^{ijk}\right) \log\left(1 - \bar{z}^{ijk}\right) \quad (3)$$

3.2.1 Input embedding layer

The input embedding $\mathbf{E_i}$ consists of three parts: word embedding $\mathbf{W_i}$, morphological embedding $\mathbf{M_i}$ and local context embedding $\mathbf{C_i}$. The dimension of each embedding is d_e. The embeddings of words and local context are generated by the pretrained language model. We use the Chinese minority pretrained language model[1] (CINO) for Uyghur and the pretrained cross-lingual language model[2] (XLM)-RoBERTa for Kazakh, Tatar and Yakut. Since the pretrained models break the morphological rules by splitting words into different subwords, we use a BiLSTM layer to generate Ug and Kz morphological embeddings (Abuduwaili et al., 2022; Makhambetov et al., 2015) (Tt and Yk have no available morphological segmentation tools, and no morphological embeddings are added, only char-based embeddings are used). The final input is generated by concatenating the word, local context and morphological embeddings. The structure of the input layer is shown in Figure 2.

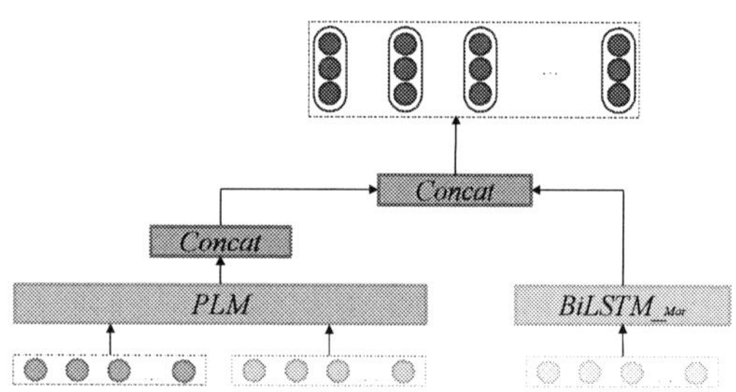

Figure 2: Input layer structure

[1]https://huggingface.co/hfl/cino-base-v2
[2]https://huggingface.co/xlm-roberta-base

3.2.2 Fusion mechanism

We design a fusion mechanism to effectively exchange information between the $\mathrm{BiLSTM_{PoS}}$ and $\mathrm{BiLSTM_{MF}}$ layers. The output results of the $\mathrm{BiLSTM_{PoS}}$ layer, where $\mathbf{H_{PoS}} = [\mathbf{h_1^{PoS}}, \mathbf{h_2^{PoS}}, ..., \mathbf{h_n^{PoS}}]$, and $\mathrm{BiLSTM_{MF}}$ layer, where $\mathbf{H_{MF}} = [\mathbf{h_1^{MF}}, \mathbf{h_2^{MF}}, ..., \mathbf{h_n^{MF}}]$, are nonlinearly transformed to generate $\mathbf{H_{PoS}^{new}}$ and $\mathbf{H_{MF}^{new}}$, and $\sigma(\cdot)$ denotes the softmax activation function, as follows:

$$\mathbf{H}_{MF}^{new} = \sigma\left(\left(\mathbf{W}_{MF}\mathbf{H}_{MF}\right) \times \mathbf{H}_{PoS}^{T}\right) \times \mathbf{H}_{PoS} \tag{4}$$

$$\mathbf{H}_{PoS}^{new} = \sigma\left(\left(\mathbf{W}_{PoS}\mathbf{H}_{PoS}\right) \times \mathbf{H}_{MF}^{T}\right) \times \mathbf{H}_{MF} \tag{5}$$

3.2.3 Morphological feature relation network

The input of this module consists of three parts: the relevant label adjacency (RLA) matrix, irrelevant label adjacency (ILA) matrix, and label embedding (LE). A detailed description of the label relation is provided in the Appendix A. In this paper, we construct an MF label dataset using agglutinative languages for UD datasets. We utilize the label's co-occurrence to obtain the label embedding in this dataset. Given the label set $L = \{l_1, l_2, ..., l_n\}$, the label embedding after training is $\mathbf{E}_l \in \mathbb{R}^{|n| \times d_l}$, where n is the number of label types and d_l is the embedding dimension. Each label embedding is:

$$\mathbf{e}_l^i = \mathbf{E}_l(l_i) \tag{6}$$

The initial label input of the MFRN is the pre-trained label embedding, which is finetuned during the training. The structure of the MFRN is shown in Figure 3.

The two adjacency matrices represent the relationships between relevant and irrelevant labels. Due to the lack of morphological tagging datasets in both languages, we construct a label adjacency matrix to explore the universal relationship between labels more thoroughly using the above labeled datasets. Each language has characteristic features that affect the relationships between related labels. Therefore, four irrelevant label adjacency matrices are constructed for the Ug, Kz, Tt and Yk datasets. The relevant label adjacency matrix is constructed on all languages, which has universal features, while the irrelevant label adjacency matrices have unique features for each language.

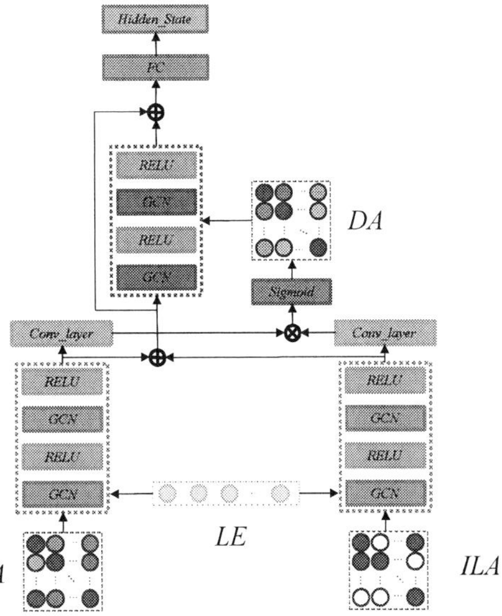

Figure 3: The MFRN structure

Then, we utilize a GCN (Kipf and Welling, 2016) to learn the different relationships between labels guided by the label adjacency matrices. Therefore, labels are treated as nodes and label relationships as edges, and morphological relationships are projected into undirected graphs. An undirected graph $\mathfrak{g}$ with n nodes is represented by an adjacency matrix, $\mathbf{RLA} \in \mathbb{R}^{n \times n}$. Similarly, $\mathbf{ILA} \in \mathbb{R}^{n \times n}$. Each element $\mathbf{A}_{ij}$ in the matrix indicates the relationship between the ith and the jth nodes. Specifically, $\mathbf{ILA}_{ij} = 1$ if the ith node is connected to the jth node, and $\mathbf{ILA}_{ij} = 0$ otherwise. After that, the two matrices are normalized as follows:

$$\widetilde{\mathbf{RLA}} = \mathbf{D}_{RLA}^{-\frac{1}{2}}\overline{\mathbf{RLA}}\mathbf{D}_{RLA}^{-\frac{1}{2}} \tag{7}$$

$$\widetilde{\mathbf{ILA}} = \mathbf{D}_{ILA}^{-\frac{1}{2}}\overline{\mathbf{ILA}}\mathbf{D}_{ILA}^{-\frac{1}{2}} \tag{8}$$

where $\mathbf{D}_{RLA}$ and $\mathbf{D}_{ILA}$ are diagonal degree matrices with entries $\mathbf{D}_{RLA_{ij}} = \sum_j \mathbf{RLA}_{ij}$, and $\mathbf{D}_{ILA_{ij}} = \sum_j \mathbf{ILA}_{ij}$, respectively. We add a self-loop for each node in the GCN. $\overline{\mathbf{ILA}} = \mathbf{ILA} + \mathbf{I}_N$ and $\overline{\mathbf{RLA}} = \mathbf{RLA} + \mathbf{I}_N$, where $\mathbf{I}_N$ is the identity matrix. The multilayer GCN learns the relationship between labels. The output of layer $\mathbf{H}^l$ is:

$$\mathbf{H}^l = \sigma\left(\bar{\mathbf{A}}\mathbf{H}^{l-1}\mathbf{W}^{l-1}\right) \tag{9}$$

where $\sigma(\cdot)$ denotes the leaky rectified linear unit activation function, $\bar{\mathbf{A}}$ represents the normalized adjacency matrix ($\overline{\mathbf{RLA}}$ and $\overline{\mathbf{ILA}}$), $\mathbf{H}^{l-1}$ represents the output of the previous layer, and $\mathbf{W} \in \mathbb{R}^{d_l \times d'}$

represents the parameter to be learned. $\mathbf{H}^0$ is the initial label embedding. The final outputs of the two multilayer GCNs are concatenated to represent the new label embedding, as follows:

$$\mathbf{LE} = \mathbf{H}_{RL}^2 \oplus \mathbf{H}_{IL}^2 \tag{10}$$

where $\mathbf{H}_{RL}^2$ and $\mathbf{H}_{IL}^2$ represent the output of the relevant label and irrelevant label fed into the multilayer GCN, respectively, and the new label embedding $\mathbf{LE} \in \mathbb{R}^{|n| \times 2d'}$. It is difficult to find the hidden relationship between labels only by the statistical rules of labels in the training data, and there will also be noise. Therefore, we utilize the GCN to extract the features from $\mathbf{H}_{RL}^2$ and $\mathbf{H}_{IL}^2$, and multiply the two results to dynamically reconstruct the adjacency graph $\mathbf{DA}$:

$$\mathbf{DA} = \sigma\left(\left(\mathbf{W}_a \mathbf{H}_{RL}^2\right) \times \left(-\mathbf{W}_b \mathbf{H}_{IL}^2\right)^T\right) \tag{11}$$

where $\mathbf{W}_a$ and $\mathbf{W}_b$ are 1×1 convolution layers, and $\sigma(\cdot)$ denotes the sigmoid activation function. We normalize the reconstruction adjacency matrix and obtain a new dynamic reconstruction adjacency matrix $\widetilde{\mathbf{DA}}$. The newly generated label embedding and adjacency matrix are input into another multilayer GCN, and the output result of the dynamic reconstruction network $\mathbf{H}^4$ is obtained. Finally, we combine the output of each GCN layer through a fully connected layer to output the final label representation $\mathbf{HS}$, where $\mathbf{H}^F \in \mathbb{R}^{|n| \times 3d'}$, as follows:

$$\mathbf{H}^F = \mathbf{H}^4 \oplus \mathbf{H}_{RL}^2 \oplus \mathbf{H}_{IL}^2 \tag{12}$$

$$\mathbf{HS} = \mathbf{W}_c \mathbf{H}^F \tag{13}$$

4 Experiments

4.1 Data

We evaluate the proposed model with low-resource agglutinative languages in the UD treebank (version 2.10), such as the Uyghur, Kazakh, Tatar, and Yakut (UKTY) datasets[3]. The UD treebank is a sentence-level dataset that includes many types of PoS labels. Since the annotation type in UD is in the CoNLL-U format, to ensure the integrity of morphological labels and the comparability of experimental results, we use a tool (McCarthy et al., 2018) to convert the data in CoNLL-U format into the UniMorph format and split all datasets into training, testing, and validation sets in an 8:1:1 proportion. The statistics of the dataset are shown in Table 2.

[3]https://universaldependencies.org/#download

4.2 Experimental results and analysis

4.2.1 Overall performance

We seek to compare our model to recurrent cross-lingual models with the best performance in this experiment. The experimental results are shown in Table 3. A detailed description of implementation details is provided in Appendix B.

Neural tagger (McCarthy et al., 2019): This is the baseline model of SIGMORPHON 2019 shared task 2. It generates the morphological tag sequence of each word through a multilayer BiLSTM model. **Multi-Team**: Üstün et al. (2019) proposed a multi-team (multi-attention and multi-decoder) morphological analysis model. The model's performance is improved by introducing pretrained word embeddings to initialize the input. **Morpheus** (Yildiz and Tantuğ, 2019): This model generates word embedding and context-aware word embedding using LSTM and BiLSTM and then inputs the two kinds of word embedding into a decoder to generate morphological labels. **UDify**: Kondratyuk (2019) proposed a morphological tagging model based on multilingual bidirectional encoder representations from transformers (BERT). This model was the winner of SIGMORPHON 2019 shared task 2. **UDPipe**: This model proposed by Straka and Straková (2020) adds pretrained contextualized embeddings (generated by BERT) to the input and uses individual morphological features for regularization. UDPipe placed second in SIGMORPHON 2019 shared task 2. **COMO**: Klimaszewski and Wróblewska (2021) proposed a fully neural NLP tagging system of PoS, morphological analysis, lemmatization, and dependency parsing. It achieved better prediction quality than that of SOTA methods at the time.

Table 3 shows the experimental results of several SOTA models and our model for the UKTY datasets. We measure the performance of models in terms of precision (P), recall (R), F1 score, and accuracy (ACC). The model proposed in this paper achieves a high F1 score and accuracy. Because UDify, UDPipe, and COMBO models are based on BERT, we also conducted comparative experiments on BERT. The experimental results of these models show that except in the Tt, the accuracy and F1 score are not significantly different, and the F1 score is slightly lower. This is because MSD is a set of labels, and the accuracy evaluates the integrity of the predicted MSD label, while the F1 score (P and R) evaluates whether the prediction results for each

Dataset	UD_Uyghur-UDT				UD_Kazakh-KTB				UD_Tatar-NMCTT				UD_Yakut-YKTDT			
	Train	Valid	Test	Label	Train	Valid	Test	Label	Train	Valid	Test	Label	Train	Valid	Test	Label
#Sentences	2764	346	346	45	862	108	108	57	118	15	15	50	231	29	29	36
#Words	32174	3538	4615		8483	1085	1121		1776	222	282		1144	131	128	

Table 2: Dataset statistics.

Lang	Ug				Kz				Tt				Yk				Avg.	
	P	R	F1	ACC.	P	R	F1	ACC.	P	R	F1	ACC.	P	R	F1	ACC.	F1	ACC.
Neural tagger	85.90	87.30	86.60	79.40	87.39	86.86	87.12	78.31	**84.77**	**83.22**	**83.99**	**75.80**	**88.31**	**85.80**	**87.04**	**84.38**	86.19	79.47
Multi-Team	89.56	**89.86**	89.71	82.54	88.91	88.71	88.81	80.38	79.16	79.72	79.44	65.25	84.38	82.09	83.22	77.42	85.30	76.40
Morpheus	**90.38**	89.09	**89.73**	**83.90**	88.39	86.82	87.60	78.50	59.27	54.93	57.02	39.01	70.07	67.19	68.60	62.50	75.74	65.98
UDify	88.42	88.16	88.29	83.73	**92.79**	**92.52**	**92.66**	**86.98**	83.38	82.50	82.94	75.53	85.53	84.94	85.25	78.91	87.29	81.29
UDPipe*	88.15	89.43	88.79	81.13	-	-	-	-	-	-	-	-	-	-	-	-	88.79	81.13
COMBO**	86.48	86.07	86.27	77.14	-	-	-	-	-	-	-	-	-	-	-	-	86.27	77.14
Our model-BERT	90.87	87.05	88.92	81.05	95.24	95.16	95.20	88.40	85.27	83.38	84.31	65.38	87.58	86.95	87.26	77.31	88.86	76.73
Our model-XLM/CINO	**94.87**	**96.18**	**95.52**	**91.60**	**96.92**	**97.32**	**97.12**	**92.82**	**89.18**	**87.20**	**88.18**	**76.40**	**90.03**	**89.23**	**89.63**	80.34	**92.61**	**85.29**

* The UDPipe web service can be accessed directly via API. And only the Uyghur model is available, so only Uyghur is tested in the test set.

** The COMBO model is only available on Uyghur, and the trained model is loaded in the test.

Table 3: Experimental results of morphological tagging.

label in the MSD label are correct. In languages with extremely low resources (Yk and Tt), neural tagger is superior to other baseline models. UDify demonstrated stable performance in four languages. For the Ug dataset, compared with the results of Morpheus, our CINO-based model increases the F1 score and accuracy by 5.79% and 7.70%, respectively. For the Kz dataset, compared with the results of UDify, our XLM-based model increases the F1 score and accuracy by 4.46% and 5.84%, respectively. For the Tt dataset, compared with the results of neural tagger, our XLM-based model increases the F1 score and accuracy by 4.19% and 0.60%, respectively. For the Yk dataset, compared with the results of neural tagger, our XLM-based model increases the F1 score by 2.59% and decreases the accuracy by 4.04%.

4.2.2 Analysis and discussion

To further verify the impact of each module on the model performance, we perform a series of experiments. The experiments mainly explore the influence of the input, fusion mechanism, and different label relationships on the model performance.

Different inputs. Morphology and context will influence the morphological labels of words. Therefore, to explore the impact of different input features on the model performance, a group of ablation experiments is conducted around words, morphology, and local context, and the experimental results are shown in Table 4.

From the experimental results in Table 4, it is found that local context and morphology can affect morphological tagging. Adding local context in low-resource agglutinative language can increase the model's accuracy, but sentence length can affect the growth rate. Because the sentence is shorter, the model learns less critical contextual information and more noise. Based on Table 2, it is found that the average sentence level of the Yk dataset is less than 5 (the average length of sentence is 4.41), so when the window size is 5-7, the model's accuracy starts to drop. Therefore, considering the dataset and practical application, this model uses the local context feature with a window size of 3 in the model. Words are composed of lemma and suffixes (morpheme) in agglutinative languages. The suffixes deeply affect morphological labels. In Table 4, adding morphological features to the Ug and Kz languages can also significantly improve the accuracy of the model.

Lang.	w	w+3g	w+5g	w+7g	w+m	w+m+3g
Ug	86.64	89.32	90.31	90.45	88.95	91.60
Kz	86.79	91.17	90.56	91.08	90.24	92.82
Tt	75.80	76.40	76.80	79.12	-	-
Yk	75.31	80.34	74.53	62.34	-	-

Table 4: The impact of different inputs on model accuracy (%). 'w' represents word, 'g' represents gram, and 'm' represents morphology.

Fusion mechanism. We jointly train the PoS and MF tagging models to reduce the impact of error propagation. However, the impact of the two labels on each other cannot be ignored in morphological tagging. Table 5 shows the experimental results without a fusion mechanism:

Compared to the four datasets, the fusion mechanism performs more significantly on datasets with smaller datasets (Tt and Yk). From the experimental results, it was found that the average F1 score

Lang.	F1	ACC.
Ug	94.05 (↓1.47)	89.64(↓1.96)
Kz	96.11(↓1.01)	91.10(↓1.72)
Tt	80.07(↓8.11)	73.67(↓2.73)
Yk	78.46(↓11.17)	63.91(↓16.43)
Avg.	↓Δ5.44	↓Δ5.71

Table 5: The influence of the fusion mechanism on the model.

and average accuracy of the model with the fusion mechanism increased by 5.44% and 5.71%, respectively. It also proves that the two labels have an interactive relationship, and the fusion mechanism also plays an indirect constraint role.

Different label relationships. We conduct ablation experiments for adding initial label (INL) relationships, irrelevant label (IRL) relationships, pretrained label (PL) relationships and reconstructed label (RL) relationships in the model. The experimental results are shown in Table 6.

Relation	Ug	Kz	Tt	Yk
baseline	86.75	88.01	70.53	72.66
baseline + INL	85.61	70.05	39.33	42.72
baseline+INL+IRL	88.62	88.91	73.97	75.44
baseline+PL+IRL	89.97	91.01	75.67	78.99
baseline+PL+IRL+RL	91.60	92.82	76.40	80.34

Table 6: The influence of different label relationships. We report accuracy (%) of MSD label for all tokens.

In Table 6, the baseline represents the model without any relationship learning. The baseline learns and represents the relationship between the surface and the inside of the label by adding different label relationships and finally outputs the MF label of the word in combination with the input content. In the experiment, when adding the initial label relationship (statistical relationship), the accuracy of the model in Tt and Yk significantly decreases. After adding irrelevant label relationships, the accuracy rate shows an upward trend. Although prior knowledge was added to the model, it was difficult to fully learn the relationships between labels due to the small dataset with various labels. After adding prior knowledge of irrelevant labels, it can constrain the relationships between labels. We believe that there are similarities between languages of the same language family. After adding pretrained label embedding, the model learns the universal relationship of the agglutinative MF labels. Adding the reconstruction relationship enables the model to capture more label relationships in dynamic learning. These methods can learn the hidden relationship between labels, thus improving the robustness of the model.

Error analysis. This paper selects Kazakh, which has the more types of morphological labels (57) and has the longest morphological labels (8) in the dataset, as an example to further analyze the model's performance in predicting long labels compared to other models. The model proposed in this paper can effectively predict short- or long-label problems through label relationships. The experimental results are shown in Table 7.

Label length	1-3	4	5	6	7	8
Overlap	53.82	23.53	20.00	56.00	54.35	57.14
Neural tagger	20.21	29.41	60.00	28.00	32.61	21.43
Multi-Team	17.99	27.45	60.00	26.00	30.43	28.57
Morpheus	18.74	35.29	80.00	30.00	39.13	50.00
UDify	9.84	37.25	60.00	30.00	26.09	21.43
Our model	5.82	13.73	40.00	18.00	13.04	7.14

Table 7: The impact of label length and both (word and lemma) overlaps (%) on model error rate (%). Both overlap means the word and lemma occur in the training and test set.

From Table 7, it is found that in addition to the impact of data size on model performance, the length of labels and the overlap can also affect model performance. The label length is short (1-3), and the overlap is high, so the model's error rate is also relatively low. When the label length is 5, the overlap is the lowest, and the model's error rate is the highest. When the overlap is approximately similar (length=1-3 and length=7, Δ=0.53%), the label length is longer, and the model's error rate is higher. Compared with a label length of 6 and 8, although the overlap is slightly different (Δ=1.14%), the neural tagger, UDify, and our model have lower errors when the label length is 8. This is the result of overlap influencing the model. Compared to other models, our model is less affected by label length and overlap.

5 Conclusion

This paper proposes a joint morphological tagging model based on a neural network for low-resource agglutinative languages. First, to effectively capture the multi-dimensional information of the input words, the model uses the morphological, word and local context features to represent the input words. Second, to reduce the impact of the PoS label on the MF label, the two models are jointly trained, and a fusion mechanism is used to complete the interaction between the two middle layers. Finally, PoS tagging is regarded as sequence labeling, and the CRF model predicts the PoS tag. MF tagging is regarded as a classification task, and a new adjacency graph is dynamically reconstructed by using the two relationships between labels and GCNs. GCNs are used to express the higher-order relationship between labels. This model combines the universal features of agglutinative languages and the characteristic features of UKTY languages, learns the relationship between labels, and effectively alleviates the problems caused by data scarcity. The experiments conducted with UD treebanks show that the proposed morphological tagging model outperforms other models. We explore the morphological tagging model based on a neural network under low resources as an example. In future research, we will continue to optimize the model's relationship representation and threshold selection abilities, and further improving the model's performance.

Limitations

The method proposed in this paper has some limitations:

(1) This model learns not only the features of words, word formation, and context but also the relationships between labels. When there is too much noise, it can disturb the relationship between labels.

(2) The model needs more training time than other models to learn pretrained label relationships.

Acknowledgements

We gratefully thank the anonymous reviewers for their insightful comments. This work is supported by the National Natural Science Foundation of China (grant numbers 62166044, 61762084) and the Natural Science Foundation of Xinjiang Uyghur Autonomous Region under Grant No.2021D01C079.

References

Gulinigeer Abuduwaili, Kahaerjing Abiderexiti, Yunfei Shen, and Aishan Wumaier. 2022. Research on the uyghur morphological segmentation model with an attention mechanism. *Connection Science*, 34:2577–2596.

Khuyagbaatar Batsuren, Gábor Bella, Aryaman Arora, Viktor Martinovic, Kyle Gorman, Zdeněk Žabokrtský, Amarsanaa Ganbold, Šárka Dohnalová, Magda Ševčíková, Kateřina Pelegrinová, Fausto Giunchiglia, Ryan Cotterell, and Ekaterina Vylomova. 2022. The SIGMORPHON 2022 shared task on morpheme segmentation. In *Proceedings of the 19th SIGMORPHON Workshop on Computational Research in Phonetics, Phonology, and Morphology*, pages 103–116, Seattle, Washington. Association for Computational Linguistics.

Çağrı Çöltekin and Jeremy Barnes. 2019. Neural and linear pipeline approaches to cross-lingual morphological analysis. In *Proceedings of the Sixth Workshop on NLP for Similar Languages, Varieties and Dialects*, pages 153–164, Ann Arbor, Michigan. Association for Computational Linguistics.

Ryan Cotterell and Georg Heigold. 2017. Cross-lingual character-level neural morphological tagging. In *Proceedings of the 2017 Conference on Empirical Methods in Natural Language Processing*, pages 748–759, Copenhagen, Denmark. Association for Computational Linguistics.

Clarissa Forbes, Garrett Nicolai, and Miikka Silfverberg. 2021. An FST morphological analyzer for the gitksan language. In *Proceedings of the 18th SIGMORPHON Workshop on Computational Research in Phonetics, Phonology, and Morphology*, pages 188–197, Online. Association for Computational Linguistics.

Tuergun Ibrahim, Kahaerjiang Abiderexiti, Aishan Wumaier, and Maihemuti Maimaiti. 2018. A survey of central asian language processing. *Journal of Chinese Information Processing*, 32(5):14.

Josef Jon, João Paulo Aires, Dusan Varis, and Ondřej Bojar. 2021. End-to-end lexically constrained machine translation for morphologically rich languages. In *Proceedings of the 59th Annual Meeting of the Association for Computational Linguistics and the 11th International Joint Conference on Natural Language Processing (Volume 1: Long Papers)*, pages 4019–4033, Online. Association for Computational Linguistics.

Hongjin Kim and Harksoo Kim. 2020. Integrated model for morphological analysis and named entity recognition based on label attention networks in korean. *Applied Sciences*, 10(11):3740.

Thomas N. Kipf and Max Welling. 2016. Semi-Supervised Classification with Graph Convolutional Networks. *arXiv e-prints*, page arXiv:1609.02907.

Mateusz Klimaszewski and Alina Wróblewska. 2021. COMBO: State-of-the-art morphosyntactic analysis. In *Proceedings of the 2021 Conference on Empirical Methods in Natural Language Processing: System Demonstrations*, pages 50–62, Online and Punta Cana, Dominican Republic. Association for Computational Linguistics.

Dan Kondratyuk. 2019. Cross-lingual lemmatization and morphology tagging with two-stage multilingual BERT fine-tuning. In *Proceedings of the 16th Workshop on Computational Research in Phonetics,*

Phonology, and Morphology, pages 12–18, Florence, Italy. Association for Computational Linguistics.

Anastasia Kuznetsova and Francis Tyers. 2021. A finite-state morphological analyser for Paraguayan Guaraní. In *Proceedings of the First Workshop on Natural Language Processing for Indigenous Languages of the Americas*, pages 81–89, Online. Association for Computational Linguistics.

Jingwen Li and Leander Girrbach. 2022. Word Segmentation and Morphological Parsing for Sanskrit. *arXiv e-prints*, page arXiv:2201.12833.

Ruifan Li, Hao Chen, Fangxiang Feng, Zhanyu Ma, Xiaojie Wang, and Eduard Hovy. 2021. Dual graph convolutional networks for aspect-based sentiment analysis. In *Proceedings of the 59th Annual Meeting of the Association for Computational Linguistics and the 11th International Joint Conference on Natural Language Processing (Volume 1: Long Papers)*, pages 6319–6329, Online. Association for Computational Linguistics.

Chang Liu, Abudoukelilu ABULIZI, Dengfeng YAO, and Halidanmu ABUDUKELIMU. 2021. Survey for uyghur morphological analysis. *Computer Engineering and Applications*, 57(15):42–61.

Qianwen Ma, Chunyuan Yuan, Wei Zhou, and Songlin Hu. 2021. Label-specific dual graph neural network for multi-label text classification. In *Proceedings of the 59th Annual Meeting of the Association for Computational Linguistics and the 11th International Joint Conference on Natural Language Processing (Volume 1: Long Papers)*, pages 3855–3864, Online. Association for Computational Linguistics.

Olzhas Makhambetov, Aibek Makazhanov, Islam Sabyrgaliyev, and Zhandos Yessenbayev. 2015. Data-driven morphological analysis and disambiguation for kazakh. In *Computational Linguistics and Intelligent Text Processing*, pages 151–163, Cham. Springer International Publishing.

Arya D. McCarthy, Miikka Silfverberg, Ryan Cotterell, Mans Hulden, and David Yarowsky. 2018. Marrying Universal Dependencies and Universal Morphology. In *Proceedings of the Second Workshop on Universal Dependencies (UDW 2018)*, pages 91–101, Brussels, Belgium. Association for Computational Linguistics.

Arya D. McCarthy, Ekaterina Vylomova, Shijie Wu, Chaitanya Malaviya, Lawrence Wolf-Sonkin, Garrett Nicolai, Christo Kirov, Miikka Silfverberg, Sabrina J. Mielke, Jeffrey Heinz, Ryan Cotterell, and Mans Hulden. 2019. The SIGMORPHON 2019 shared task: Morphological analysis in context and cross-lingual transfer for inflection. In *Proceedings of the 16th Workshop on Computational Research in Phonetics, Phonology, and Morphology*, pages 229–244, Florence, Italy. Association for Computational Linguistics.

Thomas Mueller, Helmut Schmid, and Hinrich Schütze. 2013. Efficient higher-order CRFs for morphological tagging. In *Proceedings of the 2013 Conference on Empirical Methods in Natural Language Processing*, pages 322–332, Seattle, Washington, USA. Association for Computational Linguistics.

Garrett Nicolai, Dylan Lewis, Arya D. McCarthy, Aaron Mueller, Winston Wu, and David Yarowsky. 2020. Fine-grained morphosyntactic analysis and generation tools for more than one thousand languages. In *Proceedings of the Twelfth Language Resources and Evaluation Conference*, pages 3963–3972, Marseille, France. European Language Resources Association.

Byung-Doh Oh, Pranav Maneriker, and Nanjiang Jiang. 2019. THOMAS: The hegemonic OSU morphological analyzer using seq2seq. In *Proceedings of the 16th Workshop on Computational Research in Phonetics, Phonology, and Morphology*, pages 80–86, Florence, Italy. Association for Computational Linguistics.

Şaziye Betül Özateş and Özlem Çetinoğlu. 2021. A language-aware approach to code-switched morphological tagging. In *Proceedings of the Fifth Workshop on Computational Approaches to Linguistic Code-Switching*, pages 72–83, Online. Association for Computational Linguistics.

Yirong Pan, Xiao Li, Yating Yang, and Rui Dong. 2020. Multi-task neural model for agglutinative language translation. In *Proceedings of the 58th Annual Meeting of the Association for Computational Linguistics: Student Research Workshop*, pages 103–110, Online. Association for Computational Linguistics.

Hyunji Hayley Park, Katherine J. Zhang, Coleman Haley, Kenneth Steimel, Han Liu, and Lane Schwartz. 2021. Morphology matters: A multilingual language modeling analysis. *Transactions of the Association for Computational Linguistics*, 9:261–276.

Jack Rueter, Niko Partanen, Mika Hämäläinen, and Trond Trosterud. 2021. Overview of open-source morphology development for the Komi-Zyrian language: Past and future. In *Proceedings of the Seventh International Workshop on Computational Linguistics of Uralic Languages*, pages 29–39, Syktyvkar, Russia (Online). Association for Computational Linguistics.

Amit Seker and Reut Tsarfaty. 2020. A pointer network architecture for joint morphological segmentation and tagging. In *Findings of the Association for Computational Linguistics: EMNLP 2020*, pages 4368–4378, Online. Association for Computational Linguistics.

Milan Straka and Jana Straková. 2020. UDPipe at EvaLatin 2020: Contextualized embeddings and treebank embeddings. In *Proceedings of LT4HALA 2020 - 1st Workshop on Language Technologies for Historical and Ancient Languages*, pages 124–129, Marseille, France. European Language Resources Association (ELRA).

G. Tolegen, A. Toleu, and R. Mussabayev. A finite state transducer based morphological analyzer for the kazakh language. In *2022 7th International Conference on Computer Science and Engineering (UBMK)*, pages 01–06.

Alymzhan Toleu, Gulmira Tolegen, and Aibek Makazhanov. 2017. Character-aware neural morphological disambiguation. In *Proceedings of the 55th Annual Meeting of the Association for Computational Linguistics (Volume 2: Short Papers)*, pages 666–671, Vancouver, Canada. Association for Computational Linguistics.

Alymzhan Toleu, Gulmira Tolegen, and Rustam Mussabayev. 2022. Language-independent approach for morphological disambiguation. In *Proceedings of the 29th International Conference on Computational Linguistics*, pages 5288–5297, Gyeongju, Republic of Korea. International Committee on Computational Linguistics.

Ahmet Üstün, Rob van der Goot, Gosse Bouma, and Gertjan van Noord. 2019. Multi-team: A multi-attention, multi-decoder approach to morphological analysis. In *Proceedings of the 16th Workshop on Computational Research in Phonetics, Phonology, and Morphology*, pages 35–49, Florence, Italy. Association for Computational Linguistics.

Adam Wiemerslage, Miikka Silfverberg, Changbing Yang, Arya McCarthy, Garrett Nicolai, Eliana Colunga, and Katharina Kann. 2022. Morphological processing of low-resource languages: Where we are and what's next. In *Findings of the Association for Computational Linguistics: ACL 2022*, pages 988–1007, Dublin, Ireland. Association for Computational Linguistics.

Tuergong WUSIMAN, YaTing Yang, Aizizi TUERXUN, and Li CHENG. 2019. Collaborative analysis of uyghur morphology based on character level. *Acta Scientiarum Naturalium Universitatis Pekinensis*, 55(01):47–54.

Eray Yildiz and A. Cüneyd Tantuğ. 2019. Morpheus: A neural network for jointly learning contextual lemmatization and morphological tagging. In *Proceedings of the 16th Workshop on Computational Research in Phonetics, Phonology, and Morphology*, pages 25–34, Florence, Italy. Association for Computational Linguistics.

Nasser Zalmout and Nizar Habash. 2020. Joint diacritization, lemmatization, normalization, and fine-grained morphological tagging. In *Proceedings of the 58th Annual Meeting of the Association for Computational Linguistics*, pages 8297–8307, Online. Association for Computational Linguistics.

Xiaotang Zhou, Tao Zhang, Chao Cheng, and Shinan Song. 2023. Dynamic multichannel fusion mechanism based on a graph attention network and bert for aspect-based sentiment classification. *Applied Intelligence*, 53:6800–6813.

A Label Relationship

We divide label relationships into two categories: relevant and irrelevant relationships. As shown in the label adjacency matrix in Table 8, if there are nonzero data in the relative position of two labels, they are relevant; otherwise, they are irrelevant. For example, labels A and B are relevant, and labels A and D are irrelevant.

	A	B	C	D
A	0	5	10	0
B	5	0	4	0
C	10	4	0	0
D	0	0	0	0

Table 8: Label adjacency matrix

B Implementation Details

The experimental environment is based on Python 3.8 [4] and the PyTorch 1.9.0 deep learning framework [5]. The word vector dimension is 768, the morphological embedding dimension is 300, the number of $\text{BiLSTM}_{\text{mor}}$ hidden units is 768, and the local context vector dimension is 768. $\text{BiLSTM}_{\text{PoS}}$ and $\text{BiLSTM}_{\text{MT}}$ each have 768 hidden units, and the label embedding dimension is 300. The Adam optimizer is used for training, and a dropout rate of 0.5 is enforced during training. We train each configuration using a batch size of 64, a learning rate of 0.01, and the leaky rectified linear unit activation function in the GCN.

[4] https://www.python.org/downloads/

[5] https://pytorch.org/

Revisiting and Amending Central Kurdish Data on UniMorph 4.0

Sina Ahmadi
Department of Computer Science
George Mason University, Fairfax, USA
ahmadi.sina@outlook.com

Aso Mahmudi
Faculty of Engineering and IT
University of Melbourne, Australia
aso.mehmudi@gmail.com

Abstract

UniMorph–the Universal Morphology project is a collaborative initiative to create and maintain morphological data and organize numerous related tasks for various language processing communities. The morphological data is provided by linguists for over 160 languages in the latest version of UniMorph 4.0. This paper sheds light on the Central Kurdish data on UniMorph 4.0 by analyzing the existing data, its fallacies, and systematic morphological errors. It also presents an approach to creating more reliable morphological data by considering various specific phenomena in Central Kurdish that have not been addressed previously, such as Izafe and several enclitics.

1 Introduction

Computational morphology, the study of word formation using computational methods, is one of the important tasks in natural language processing (NLP) and computational linguistics. This field has been one of the prevailing and longstanding tasks with many applications in syntactic parsing, lemmatization and machine translation (Roark and Sproat, 2007). There have been remarkable advances and paradigm shifts in approaches to analyze and generate morphology: starting from ad-hoc approaches in the earlier systems, then rule formalisms and finite-state models since the 1980s (Karttunen and Beesley, 2005) with the notable example of KIMMO two-level morphological analyzer (Karttunen et al., 1983), followed by statistical and classical machine learning since the 1990s as in (Goldsmith, 2001; Schone and Jurafsky, 2001), and more recently, approaches relying on neural network models since 2000s. Lastly, more robust techniques are proposed using monolingual data hallucination (Anastasopoulos and Neubig, 2019), transfer learning (Kann et al., 2017) and pretrained models (Hofmann et al., 2020).

Unlike the progress in approaches, the dependence of systems on clean and reliable data, regardless of the size, for accurate morphological analysis and generation has not changed much. In order to bring together various linguistic communities to create datasets and incentivize further studies in the field, the UniMorph[1] (Batsuren et al., 2022) project has been a leading initiative in this vein. In UniMorph 4.0, the latest version of the project, there are 168 languages from various language families for which morphological data is provided according to the UniMorph schema (Sylak-Glassman, 2016). Additionally, the ACL Special Interest Group on Computational Morphology and Phonology (SIGMORPHON)[2] has played an important role to organize workshops and shared tasks using the UniMorph data. Some of the previous shared tasks focus on cross-linguality and context in morphology (McCarthy et al., 2019), unsupervised morphological paradigm clustering (Wiemerslage et al., 2021) and morphological inflection generation, segmentation, and interlinear glossing in this year's task.

One of the languages that is of interest in this paper and is also included in UniMorph is Central Kurdish, also known as Sorani (`ckb`). Central Kurdish, as a variant of the Indo-European language Kurdish, has a fusional morphology with several distinctive features due to its split-ergativity, erratic patterns in morphotactics and, several endoclitics used in verbal forms. These characteristics seem to be known to the UniMorph community, as described in Pimentel et al. (2021, p. 8). However, the current data available for Central Kurdish contains systematic errors and lacks coverage in morphological forms. The data is also provided in a script that is not used by Kurdish speakers, thus of no utility to downstream tasks in reality. Consequently, these result in poor performance of sys-

[1] https://UniMorph.github.io
[2] https://sigmorphon.github.io

Proceedings of the 20th SIGMORPHON workshop on Computational Research in Phonetics, Phonology, and Morphology, pages 38–48
July 14, 2023

- Bound morphemes:
  - Clitics
    - Enclitics : *=im*, *=î*, *=ît*, *=e*, *=în*, *=in*
    - Endoclitics: *=im*, *=it*, *=î*, *=man*, *=tan*, *=yan*, *=îş*
  - Affixes
    - Inflectional
      - Noun:*-êk*, *-an*, *-gel*, *-ha*, *-at*, *-eke*, *-ekan*, *-e*, *-ane*, *-gele*, *-î* (OBL), *-ê*, *-îne*, {*-î*, *-e*} (IZ)
      - Verb:*-in*, *de-*, *e-*, *bi-*, *we-*, *ne-*, *na-*, *me-*
      - Adjective:*-tir*, *-tirîn*
      - Adverb:*-ane*
    - Derivational:*-a*, *-and*, *-ard*, *-d*, *-îşt*, *-ird*, *-t*, *-û*, *-y*, *-ên*, *-êr*, *-dira*, *-ra*, *-ewe*, *ber-*, *da-*, *der-*, *heł-*, *ser-*, *řa-*, *řo-*, *wer-*

Figure 1: A classification of Central Kurdish bound morphemes in the Latin-based script of Kurdish. Allomorphs and zero morphemes (∅) are not included.

tems that rely on the data in real scenarios.

Contributions This paper summarizes some of the salient features in Central Kurdish morphology. It also aims to discuss the main issues of Central Kurdish data on UniMorph 4.0. Moreover, the paper provides a new dataset of quality with considerable coverage and carries out experiments on the newly annotated data.

2 Central Kurdish Morphology

Kurdish is an Indo-European language spoken by over 25 million speakers in the Kurdish regions in Turkey, Iran, Iraq and Syria, and also by the Kurdish diaspora around the world (McCarus, 2007). Central Kurdish, also known as Sorani is the Kurdish variant that is mostly spoken by the Kurds within the Iranian and Iraqi regions of Kurdistan. Central Kurdish is a null-subject language and has a subject-object-verb (S-O-V) order and can be distinguished from other Indo-Iranian languages by its ergative-absolutive alignment which appears in past tenses of transitive verbs (Ahmadi and Masoud, 2020). In this section, we provide a brief description of Central Kurdish morphology by focusing on morphemes and morphological processes.

2.1 Bound Morphemes

Morphemes are classified into free and bound. While free morphemes are meaningful as they are, bound morphemes only carry meaning when affixed with other words. Bound morphemes are classified into two categories of affixes and clitics. Affixes and clitics are similar in the way that they cannot constitute a word and they lean on a prosodic host, i.e. a word for stress assignment. Clitics can appear with hosts of various syntactic categories while affixes only combine with syntactically-related stems (Haspelmath and Sims, 2013, p. 198). The clitics and affixes in Central Kurdish have been widely studied previously and have been shown to be challenging considering the general theory of clitics (W. Smith, 2014; Gharib and Pye, 2018). This problem is particularly observed with respect to the direct and oblique person markers which can appear in different positions within a word-form depending on the functionality. In this section, the clitics and affixes in Central Kurdish are described. Figure 1 provides the most frequent clitics and affixes in Central Kurdish.

2.1.1 Clitics

Clitics are categorized based on their position with respect to the host. A clitic is called proclitic and enclitic, if it appears before and after the host, respectively. There are two other forms of clitics which are non-peripherical and exist only among a few natural languages. If a clitic appears between the host and another affix, it is called a mesoclitic. A different type of non-peripheral clitic is endoclitic which appears within the host itself and is unique to a few languages around the world, such as Udi (W. Smith, 2014), Degema (Kari, 2002) and also Central Kurdish.

Central Kurdish has two types of endoclitics: pronominal makers, also introduced as mobile person markers by Walther (2012), and the emphasis endoclitic یش *=îş* which can be translated as 'also' or 'too' (Ahmadi et al., 2023). The pronominal endoclitics function as agent markers for transitive

0						girt						past stem of GIRTIN (to take, to get)
1						girt	im					I got.
2						girt	im	in				I got them.
3						girt	im	in	e			I got them to/with.
4						girt	im	in	e	ewe		I got them to/with again.
5						girt	îş	im	in	e	ewe	I got them also to/with again.
6			ne	îş	im	girt	in	e	ewe			I did not get them also to/with again.
7		ne	îş	im	de	girt	in	e	ewe			I was not getting them also to/with again.
8	da	îş	im	ne	de	girt	in	e	ewe			I was not taking down them also to/with again.

Table 1: The placement of the endoclitic *=îş* (in green boxes) and agent marker *=im* (in blue boxes) with respect to the base and each other in a verb form. Note that Central Kurdish is a null-subject language.

verbs in the past tenses or endoclitics as a patient marker for transitive verbs in the present tenses. This is due to the split ergativity feature of Central Kurdish where the agent and patient markers are specified differently. The following examples show the alignment in present and past tenses of کەوتن (KEWTIN, 'to fall') and گرتن (GIRTIN, 'to get'). The agent marker ن *-in* in intransitive present tenses (examples 1 & 3) serves as a patient marker in transitive past tenses (examples 2 & 4) due to ergativity while another morpheme یان *=yan* appears as the agent marker in the transitive verb (example 4).

(1) *dekew**in*** دەکەون
*de-kew-**in***
fall.PRS.PROG.INTR.3PL
'(they) are falling.'

(2) *degir**in*** دەگرن
*de-gir-**in***
get.PRS.PROG.TR.3PL
'(they) are getting.'

(3) *kewt**in*** کەوتن
*kewt-**in***
fall.PST.PROG.INTR.3PL
'(they) fell.'

(4) *girtyan**in*** گرتیانن
*girt=yan-**in***
get.PST.PROG.TR.ERG.3PL.3PL
'(they) got (them).'

Furthermore, the two endoclitic categories of Central Kurdish appear in an erratic pattern within a word form or a phrase. If a prefix appears before the stem of a transitive verb in the past tense, the agent marker postpends to the leftmost morpheme; in other cases, the agent marker appears after the verb stem following a varying morphotactic rule depending on the tense, mood, aspect and transitivity of the verb. Table 1 presents an example where the 1SG marker م (*=im*) and the emphasis endoclitic *=îş* appear after and before the host, i.e. گرت (*girt*), depending on the presence of other bound morphemes such as negation prefix نە (*ne-*) or the verbal particle دا (*da*). It is worth mentioning that this pattern may vary based on the Central Kurdish sub-dialects.

Moreover, the present form of the copula in Central Kurdish are also used as clitics with nouns and adjectives. Table 1 shows these as enclitics.

2.1.2 Affixes

In comparison to clitics, a higher number of bound morphemes in Central Kurdish belong to affixes. Affixes can be categorized into inflectional and derivational based on their ability to create new lexemes. The most frequent affixes in Central Kurdish appear as prefixes and suffixes. Some of the inflectional affixes of Central Kurdish belonging to open-class parts of speech, namely nouns, verbs, adjectives and adverbs, are shown in Table 2. In addition, Izafe particle *-î* and its allomorph *-e* which appear between a head and its dependents in a noun phrase are frequently used to create possessive constructions, as in ناوی من (*naw-î min* 'my name').

In addition to compound words, Central Kurdish relies on derivational morphemes to create new lexemes, particularly new verbal lexemes. To this end, verbal suffix ەوە (*-ewe*) and verbal particles such as دا (*da-*) and هەڵ (*heł-*) are used. It is worth noting that the passive form of verbs is derived from the verb stem by using را/رێ (*-ra/-rê*) or their allomorphs درا/درێ (*-dira/-dirê*) suffixes, unlike Kurmanji Kurdish which relies on periphrastic forms with HATIN (to come) (Ahmadi, 2021b).

In the following, we summarize some of the distinct features of affixes in Central Kurdish.

Nouns	Verbs	Adjectives	Adverbs
number (SG, PL)	**number** (SG, PL)	**number** (SG, PL)	**degree** (COMP, SUPL)
person (1, 2, 3)	**person** (1, 2, 3)	**degree** (COMP, SUPL)	
determiners (DEF, IND, DEM)	**mood** (IND, SBJV, IMP, COND)	**determiners** (DEF, IND, DEM)	
case (OBL, LOC, VOC)	**aspect** (PRF, IMP, PROG)		
gender (M, F)	**tense** (PST, PRS)		

Table 2: Inflectional features and values of Central Kurdish. It should be noted that the function of cases and genders vary among Sorani subdialects.

Discontinuous Morphemes A morpheme that gets interrupted by the insertion of another morphological unit is known as a discontinuous morpheme. Two categories of discontinuous morphemes exist in Central Kurdish: a) demonstratives "*em ...-e*" 'this.DEM' and "*ew ...-e*" 'that.DEM' and, b) circumpositions such as "*be ...-da*", "*le ...-da*" and "*bo ...-ewe*", respectively meaning 'through', 'in' and 'toward' where "..." refers to the position of another morphological unit between the two discontinuous morphemes. While the Latin-based orthography of Kurdish suggests writing such morphemes detached from the preceding word, they are usually concatenated in the Perso-Arabic-based script.

Postverbal Complement *-e* and Pronominal Adverb *-ê* In Central Kurdish, a verb that has the valency of a prepositional phrase with prepositions *be* 'to' or *bo* 'for' can take the postverbal complement *-e* to replace the preposition. In this case, it is compulsory for a noun phrase to come after the verb (Edmonds, 1961, p. 236). Furthermore, the pronominal adverb *-ê* can replace the antecedent prepositional object, and the postverbal complement *-e*, oblique pronoun, accusative nouns or locative adverb. This is particularly used with two verbs of DAN 'to give' and GEYIŞTIN 'to arrive'.

A more detailed description of Central Kurdish morphology, including adpositions and pronouns as free morphemes, is provided in (Ahmadi, 2021a) and (Naserzade et al., 2023).

3 Central Kurdish on UniMorph 4.0

In this section, we analyze the existing morphological data for Central Kurdish on UniMorph 4.0 and describe some of the current fallacies.

The UniMorph project provides a dataset for Central Kurdish that contains 24,316 word-forms.[3] This dataset was initially created within the Alexina Framework (Sagot, 2010) by Walther and Sagot (2010) and focuses on inflectional morphology by providing a set of forms of the paradigms of 252 lemmas with noun or verb part-of-speech tags. Overall, 33 morphological features based on UniMorph are used in the dataset, including LGSPEC1 and LGSPEC2 which are respectively used for Izafe morpheme *-î* and its allomorph *-e*. The number of features combined together is 226 features for all the word forms. In other terms, 0.98% of the word forms are assigned a unique combination of features. Analogous to the notion of 'leakage' in syntactic parsing (Krasner et al., 2022) that reveals the overlap of the train and test sets, such a repetitive usage of the features can cause an erroneously high performance of analysis models. As such, we believe that the dataset has very limited coverage of word forms and lacks diversity.

In the following, we categorize some of the major issues of the Central Kurdish data on UniMorph. Table 3 provides a few examples based on the dataset and categorizes their issues as well.

3.1 Unconventional Writing

Unlike Northern Kurdish which is mostly written in a Latin-based Kurdified script known as *Bedirxan*'s orthography, Central Kurdish is more conventionally written in a Perso-Arabic script. The Kurdish data on UniMorph is written in an unconventional Latin-based orthography that is not used in practice. Furthermore, the character <i> for phoneme /ɪ/ is not represented in the selected script, even though it is frequently used in many morphemes and undergoes various morphophonological alternations. This phoneme, also known as *Bizroke* (Ahmadi, 2019), is represented by <i> in the Latin-based script of Kurdish while is missing in the Perso-Arabic script. We transliterate the original forms in the dataset in the Latin-based script of Kurdish in Table 3.

[3]Available at `https://github.com/UniMorph/ckb`

Lemma	Feature	Form in UniMorph 4.0 (Incorrect)		Correct form	Issue
		Original	Transliterated		
aw 'WATER'	N;FOC	′awš	awş	awîş ئاویش	morphophonology
bûrîn 'FORGIVE'	V;PROG;IND;SG;3;PRS;PASS	debwwrrěět	debûrrêêt	debûrêt دەبووریێت	morphophonology
kirdin 'DO'	V;PROG;IND;SG;3;PRS	dekeě	dekeê	deka دەکا	morphophonology
bezandin 'DEFEAT (TR)'	V;PRF;SBJV;SG;1;NEG;PST	nembezandbwwayě	nembezandbuwayê	nembezandibuwaye نەمبەزاندبووایە	unknown morpheme *-yê*
bestin 'CLOSE (TR)'	V;PFV;SBJV;SG;1;PST	bbestmbayě	bibestimbayê	bimbestibaye بمبەستبایە	morphotactics
kirdin 'DO'	V;PROG;IND;PL;2;NEG;PRS;PASS	nakerěn	nakerên	nakirên ناکرێن	missing alternation
kokîn 'COUGH'	V;IMP;SG;NEG	mekok	mekok	mekoke مەکۆکە	missing morpheme *-e*

Table 3: Some of the categorical issues with the Central Kurdish data on UniMorph 4.0. The forms are transliterated into the conventional Latin-based script of Kurdish. The lemmata and the forms in the Perso-Arabic-based script of Kurdish are removed due to space limitations. The correct forms in both conventional scripts of Kurdish are reconstructed based on the features.

3.2 Morphotactics

As described in § 2, Central Kurdish has a complex morphotactics when it comes to verbs. This is also reflected in the inflection of verbal forms of the UniMorph dataset where some verbal word forms do not conform to the morphology of Central Kurdish and its dialects. This is particularly observed in transitive verbs in which the agent markers should appear before the verb stem and after the leftmost prefix in past tenses (see §2.1.1). However, this morphotactic rule is not systematically present in the verb forms. It is worth mentioning that this phenomenon is not the case in closely-related variants, i.e. Northern Kurdish and Southern Kurdish, or the closely-related language Persian. Therefore, we believe that the annotation was mistakenly and inaccurately carried out under the influence of such variants and languages.

3.3 Morphophonological Alternations

Many morphemes in Central Kurdish alter based on morphophonological rules. This is particularly the case of bound morphemes starting with a vowel, such as *-eke* as the singular definite marker and *-e* as a demonstrative suffix that respectively appear as *-ke*/*-yeke* and *-ye* depending on the preceding phoneme. In the UniMorph data, such alternations are not consistently taken into account. An eye-catching issue of this type is N;FOC which is associated with nouns that appear with the clitic *=îş*. The allomorph *=ş* of this clitic that appears after vowels seems to be universally used in the dataset regardless of the morphophonological rule. Therefore, word forms associated to this tag and other similar tags like N;LGSPEC2 are potentially wrong.

3.4 Incorrect Morphemes

A less severe problem of incorrect inflections is due to incorrect morphemes, particularly allomorphs. We believe that the unconventional script may have aggravated such issues. For instance, the singular imperative form of verbs, i.e. `v;imp;sg` are missing the suffix *-e* as in the incorrect form of *bbexš* (*bibexş*) instead of *bibexşe* (FORGIVE.IMP.2SG) and the morpheme *-yě* (*-yê*) is frequently and incorrectly used instead of the morpheme *-ye* to indicate the conditional mood of the verb. Nevertheless, such issues have been discussed, particularly concerning allomorphs, within the UniMorph community (Gorman et al., 2019).

Taking these issues into account, we estimate that 25% of the forms of Central Kurdish data on UniMorph 4.0 are incorrect.

4 Methodology

Given the fallacies of the Central Kurdish dataset on UniMorph 4.0, we believe that a new dataset is required for a thorough morphological analysis of this language. Although we correct the existing dataset on UniMorph 4.0, we also extend it with new lemmata and more complete paradigms. This measure was taken to ensure the quality of the forms based on a corpus and more importantly, in both conventional scripts of Kurdish, namely the

Perso-Arabic-based and the Latin-based scripts. In this section, we discuss our approach to creating a new dataset for Central Kurdish.

4.1 Modeling Central Kurdish on UniMorph

During the data preparation process, we noticed that the UniMorph schema described by Sylak-Glassman (2016) lacks several features that are commonly used in not only Central Kurdish but also, most Iranic languages, such as Izafe (Windfuhr, 2009). In the schema, the label LGSPEC with a consistent ID is considered for language-specific features. Using this, we also introduce a few features that are currently unsupported and map these new features to LGSPEC with an ID to be consistent with the current schema of UniMorph. Table 4 provides a list of such features.

Type	Function	Ours	UniMorph
Affix	Izafe	[IZAFE]	LGSPEC1
Affix	postverb adpositions	[E] [EE]	LGSPEC2
Affix	postverb adverbial /ewe/	[EWE1]	LGSPEC3
Affix	disc. adpositions	[DA],[RA], [EWE2]	LGSPEC4
Clitic	adverbial clitic	[ISH]	LGSPEC5
Clitic	demonstrative	[DEM]	LGSPEC6
Clitic	copula	[COP]	LGSPEC7
Clitic	pronominal markers (argument/possessive) on transitive past verbs	[PM]	LGSPEC8
Clitic	argument markers on noun/adjectives	[AM]	LGSPEC9

Table 4: Our proposed tags for the new Central Kurdish data in our dataset containing more customized tags and LGSPEC tags for the future versions of UniMorph

It is worth noting that in the current Central Kurdish data on UniMorph 4.0, LGSPEC1 and LGSPEC2 are respectively used for Izafa suffix <î/y> and its allomorph <e>. Similarly, the endoclitic *=îş* is specified as FOC. These are the only language-specific tags that are currently used in this dataset.

4.2 Finite-State Transducers

Relying on Naserzade et al. (2023)'s finite state transducers, we develop a morphological analyzer and generator that can handle all possible well-formed inflected forms of a given word in Central Kurdish. The analyzer takes a word and yields all possible morphological tags. Similarly, the generator takes as input a lemma and its part-of-speech tag, in addition to the past and present stems and transitivity for verbs, and inflects the lemma accordingly. The output words are formed according to Central Kurdish standard orthography and morphophonological rules. The number of forms with unique features is 3,032 for a general noun lemma, 9,096 for a gradable adjective, 3,180 for a transitive verb, and 636 for an intransitive verb. Figure 2 illustrates a transducer to generate noun forms.

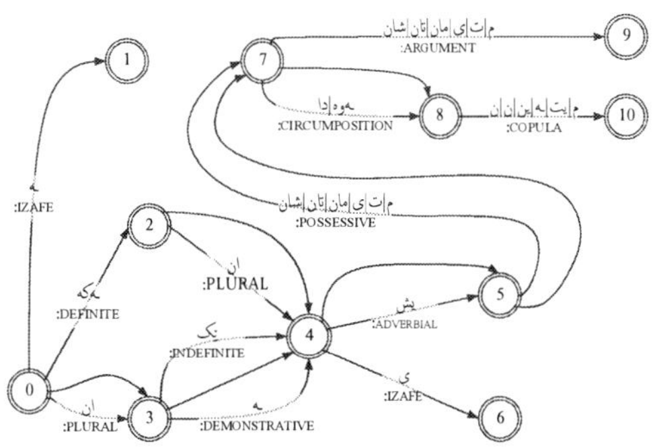

Figure 2: A finite-state transducer for generating nouns in Central Kurdish

4.3 Data Generation

Using the finite-state transducers, we generate two datasets containing a diverse set of word forms and part-of-speech tags as follows:

Gold-standard We first randomly extract 1,000 words from Veisi et al. (2020)'s corpus and then use the finite-state transducers to analyze them. Given that the transducers do not take word context into account, this step was followed by a manual verification to make sure that only the relevant analysis and tags are selected based on the context.

Silver-standard We also create another dataset that contains full paradigms for 10 nouns, 5 adjectives, 17 intransitive verbs (including three passive and two causative verbs) and 12 transitive verbs. As this dataset doesn't rely on context, we refer to it as silver-standard. These words are listed in Table A. To cover all morphophonological changes that occur in the inflectional forms, we select words having stems ending with a consonant, vowels <*a, e, ê, î, o, û*>, approximants <*y*> and <*w/*>, and diphthong <*wê*>. Note that vowels <*i*> and <*u*> do not occur in word-final positions.

During the generation processing, we set a few restrictions in our dataset. In the conjugation of transitive verbs, it is not possible to have both the subject and object pronouns in either the first or second person. This is due to the reflexive con-

Dataset	Noun		Adjective		Verb		Proper Noun		Other		Total	
UniMorph 4.0	1,729	141	0	0	22,291	112	0	0	0	0	24,020	253
Gold-standard	442	375	153	133	181	107	143	139	81	65	1,000	819
Silver-standard	30,320	10	45,447	5	35,116	25	0	0	0	0	110,883	40

Table 5: Number of inflected forms and unique lemmata (second column) by part-of-speech in Central Kurdish in the current dataset of UniMorph 4.0, our proposed datasets aggregated over all splits. The gold-standard presents a more diverse set of forms with part-of-speech tags for fewer lemmata while the silver-standard dataset presents full paradigms of more lemmata.

struction in Central Kurdish that does not commonly appear in the verb form. For example, **de-m=nas=im* '*I know me' and **de-tan-nas-ît* '*you know you' are ill-formed. For this purpose, the adverb *xo* 'self' is commonly used.

Table 5 summarizes the number of forms in our datasets in comparison to the current UniMorph 4.0 data. We present our datasets in both conventional scripts of Kurdish, the Arabic-based and Latin-based ones. The latter is more widely used for Northern Kurdish facilitating cross-dialectal comparisons. Moreover, we provide the corpus-based context of word forms and our customized tags in Table 4 in a separate dataset.

5 Analysis

5.1 Morphological Reinflection

To evaluate our datasets, we carry out an analysis on morphological reinflection introduced as the non-neural baseline for task 1 of SIGMORPHON 2018 that extracts lemma-to-form transformations heuristically (Cotterell et al., 2018). To do so, we first shuffled the datasets and created a 70–10–20 train–dev–test split. During the process, we made sure that identical samples were selected in the two scripts to make the comparison of performances valid. We then run the non-neural baseline using

Dataset (script)	**Accuracy**	**AED**
UniMorph 4.0	48.7%	0.97
Gold-standard (L)	63.5%	0.99
Gold-standard (A)	67.5%	0.88
Silver-standard (L)	61.2%	0.98
Silver-standard (A)	65.0%	0.75

Table 6: Experimental results of test sets on morphological re-inflection for the current UniMorph 4.0 in comparison to our datasets in terms of accuracy (higher is better) and average edit distance (lower is better). AED refers to average edit distance.

the train sets of the three datasets and evaluate the models on the three test sets. Table 6 presents the accuracy and average edit distance in the three datasets. Although it would have been interesting to compare the performance of the baseline system across test sets, e.g., training and testing on different datasets, such comparison could only be valid if the same set of tags has been used which is not the case in the current UniMorph data. Based on the results of the systems that participated in the SIGMORPHON 2021 Shared Task on morphological reflection (Pimentel et al., 2021), an accuracy of over 90% can be achieved.

5.2 Error Analysis

In order to better understand the challenges of reinflection models, we manually checked the wrong outputs of the models trained and tested on our data to determine failure points. Since we have generated all possible inflectional forms of several lemmas and the data is shuffled before building the model, some complex forms do not occur in the train set. Therefore, the model failed to cover those forms. Another difficulty of the baseline model is in tackling the morphophonological changes. As we have covered stems with different final phoneme types, the majority of errors that have lower edit distance are in handling these changes. For example, the failure in alternating the indefinite suffix '*-êk*' to '*-yek*' after a vowel is a primary source of the errors.

In Kurdish, verbs have different past and present stems. For many verbs, the present stem is made by removing the final consonant or vowel of the past stem; for instance, the past and present stems of *girtin* 'to get' are *girt* and *gir*, respectively. However, numerous exceptions enforce computational studies to consider the present verb stems as irregular and look them up from a table, as in the present stems *lê* or *bêj* for *gutin* 'to say' and *xo* for *xwardin* 'to eat'. Analyzing the reinflectional errors showed that detecting such alternations is another major source of error.

Regarding the accuracy based on the scripts, the accuracy of the baseline on data written in the Latin-based (L) script is slightly lower than the Arabic-based script (A). This can be explained by the missing character *Bizroke* (*i*) in the Arabic-based script that plays an important role in Central Kurdish morphology (see §3.1) while the Latin-based character uses it.

5.3 Inflectional Synthesis Degree

As an additional analysis, we calculate the synthesis degree of inflected forms in Central Kurdish by averaging the number of morphemes per form in the gold and silver datasets. According to the degrees reported by Greenberg (1960), Central Kurdish has a relatively high synthetic degree of 2.22 comparable to Old English (2.12), Yakut (2.17), and Swahili (2.55). Among the selected part-of-speech tags, adjectives exhibit the highest level of synthesis as they can function with nominal affixes and clitics and also, a few other distinct ones such as *-tir* and *-tirîn* as comparative and superlative suffixes.

Although prefixing is not used in nouns and adjectives of Central Kurdish, verbs have a higher synthesis in prefixing, mainly due to the verbal prefixes related to negation such as *ne-*, *na-* and *me-* but also subjunctive *bi-* and progressive markers *e-* and *de-*. Moreover, transitive verbs show the highest ratios of synthesis in prefixing in comparison to intransitive verbs. This is due to the erratic patterns of pronominal endoclitics that may appear before or after the stem, while that's not the case in intransitive verbs (see §2.1.1).

It should be noted that these results are expected to be different in derivational morphology.

POS		Morpheme per form		
		pre-stem	post-stem	average
Noun		0	3.63	3.63
Adjective		0	4.30	4.30
Verb	INTR	1.05	2.32	1.68
	TR	1.65	2.46	2
Average		1.35	3.1	**2.22**

Table 7: Degree of synthesis in inflectional morphology of Central Kurdish based on our datasets

6 Conclusion

In this paper, we discuss some of the fallacies of the current data of Central Kurdish on UniMorph 4.0. We argue that the dataset is not only lacking coverage but also misrepresents Kurdish morphology by incorrect morphemes, unconventional writing and inaccurate morphotactics. Additionally, we propose a new dataset with a few additional labels for some of the features of Central Kurdish, such as Izafe and various clitics. Our dataset is generated using finite-state transducers with the human in the loop and are transliterated in the Latin-based script of Kurdish in addition to the Perso-Arabic-based ones. The transliteration of the word-forms facilitates comparative studies, particularly with Northern Kurdish which is mainly written in a Latin-based script. For each word-form, we also look it up in a corpus and provide the context in addition to the morphological features. Moreover, we create a baseline by training models in various setups and evaluating them on our dataset and the current Central Kurdish data on UniMorph 4.0. Finally, we suggest this dataset be added to the future version of UniMorph.

Limitations One of the limitations of our dataset is the lower number of word-forms belonging to a close-class part-of-speech as we chiefly focus on nouns, verbs (transitive and intransitive) and adjectives. On the other hand, we only include inflectional morphology without paradigms of word formation. Furthermore, we only address the morphology of the standard variety of Central Kurdish, i.e. that of Sulaymaniyah. We plan to extend our work to include other varieties of Central Kurdish along with derivational morphology. Given that Central Kurdish lacks a treebank, it will be compelling to bridge Central Kurdish morphology and syntax as well.

Another limitation of the current work is due to the UniMorph schema. Using the LGSPEC tag is not recommended for features that are found across languages but for those that are limited to specific languages (Sylak-Glassman, 2016, p.30). Given that some of the features of Central Kurdish, such as Izafe and pronominal copula, are also found in other closely-related languages, we believe that the current schema should be extended to use specific tags for such features or a better schema, akin to Guriel et al. (2022)'s hierarchical model, is needed for languages with rich morphology like Kurdish.

Acknowledgments

The authors are grateful for the constructive comments of the anonymous reviewers. Sina Ahmadi is generously supported by the National Science Foundation under DLI-DEL award BCS-2109578.

References

Sina Ahmadi. 2019. A rule-based Kurdish text transliteration system. *ACM Transactions on Asian and Low-Resource Language Information Processing (TALLIP)*, 18(2):1–8.

Sina Ahmadi. 2021a. A Formal Description of Sorani Kurdish Morphology. *arXiv preprint arXiv:2109.03942*.

Sina Ahmadi. 2021b. Hunspell for Sorani Kurdish Spell Checking and Morphological Analysis. *arXiv preprint arXiv:2109.06374*.

Sina Ahmadi, Antonios Anastasopoulos, and Géraldine Walther. 2023. A corpus-based study of endoclitic *=îş* in Kurdish. In *Book of abstracts of the the 56th Annual Meeting of the Societas Linguistica Europaea*, Athens, Greece. the 56th Annual Meeting of the Societas Linguistica Europaea.

Sina Ahmadi and Maraim Masoud. 2020. Towards Machine Translation for the Kurdish Language. In *Proceedings of the 3rd Workshop on Technologies for MT of Low Resource Languages*, pages 87–98.

Antonios Anastasopoulos and Graham Neubig. 2019. Pushing the limits of low-resource morphological inflection. In *Proceedings of the 2019 Conference on Empirical Methods in Natural Language Processing and the 9th International Joint Conference on Natural Language Processing (EMNLP-IJCNLP)*, pages 984–996, Hong Kong, China. Association for Computational Linguistics.

Khuyagbaatar Batsuren, Omer Goldman, Salam Khalifa, Nizar Habash, Witold Kieraś, Gábor Bella, Brian Leonard, Garrett Nicolai, Kyle Gorman, Yustinus Ghanggo Ate, et al. 2022. UniMorph 4.0: Universal Morphology. In *Proceedings of the Thirteenth Language Resources and Evaluation Conference*, pages 840–855.

Ryan Cotterell, Christo Kirov, John Sylak-Glassman, Géraldine Walther, Ekaterina Vylomova, Arya D McCarthy, Katharina Kann, Sabrina J Mielke, Garrett Nicolai, Miikka Silfverberg, et al. 2018. The conll–sigmorphon 2018 shared task: Universal morphological reinflection. *arXiv preprint arXiv:1810.07125*.

C. J. Edmonds. 1961. Kurdish Dialect Studies, Vol. Oxford University Press. *Journal of the Royal Asiatic Society*, 94(3-4).

Hiba Gharib and Clifton Pye. 2018. The clitic status of person markers in Sorani Kurdish. *University of Kansas Department of Linguistics*.

John Goldsmith. 2001. Unsupervised learning of the morphology of a natural language. *Computational linguistics*, 27(2):153–198.

Kyle Gorman, Arya D. McCarthy, Ryan Cotterell, Ekaterina Vylomova, Miikka Silfverberg, and Magdalena Markowska. 2019. Weird inflects but OK: making sense of morphological generation errors. In *Proceedings of the 23rd Conference on Computational Natural Language Learning, CoNLL 2019, Hong Kong, China, November 3-4, 2019*, pages 140–151. Association for Computational Linguistics.

Joseph H Greenberg. 1960. A quantitative approach to the morphological typology of language. *International journal of American linguistics*, 26(3):178–194.

David Guriel, Omer Goldman, and Reut Tsarfaty. 2022. Morphological reinflection with multiple arguments: An extended annotation schema and a Georgian case study. In *Proceedings of the 60th Annual Meeting of the Association for Computational Linguistics (Volume 2: Short Papers)*, pages 196–202, Dublin, Ireland. Association for Computational Linguistics.

Martin Haspelmath and Andrea D Sims. 2013. *Understanding morphology*. Routledge.

Valentin Hofmann, Janet Pierrehumbert, and Hinrich Schütze. 2020. DagoBERT: Generating derivational morphology with a pretrained language model. In *Proceedings of the 2020 Conference on Empirical Methods in Natural Language Processing (EMNLP)*, pages 3848–3861, Online. Association for Computational Linguistics.

Katharina Kann, Ryan Cotterell, and Hinrich Schütze. 2017. One-shot neural cross-lingual transfer for paradigm completion. In *Proceedings of the 55th Annual Meeting of the Association for Computational Linguistics (Volume 1: Long Papers)*, pages 1993–2003, Vancouver, Canada. Association for Computational Linguistics.

Ethelbert E Kari. 2002. On endoclitics: Some facts from Degema. *Journal of Asian and African Studies*, 63:37–53.

Lauri Karttunen and Kenneth R Beesley. 2005. Twenty-five years of finite-state morphology. *Inquiries Into Words, a Festschrift for Kimmo Koskenniemi on his 60th Birthday*, pages 71–83.

Lauri Karttunen et al. 1983. KIMMO: a general morphological processor. In *Texas Linguistic Forum*, volume 22, pages 163–186. Texas, USA.

Nathaniel Krasner, Miriam Wanner, and Antonios Anastasopoulos. 2022. Revisiting the effects of leakage on dependency parsing. In *Findings of the Association for Computational Linguistics: ACL 2022*, pages 2925–2934, Dublin, Ireland. Association for Computational Linguistics.

Arya D. McCarthy, Ekaterina Vylomova, Shijie Wu, Chaitanya Malaviya, Lawrence Wolf-Sonkin, Garrett Nicolai, Christo Kirov, Miikka Silfverberg, S. J. Mielke, Jeffrey Heinz, Ryan Cotterell, and Mans Hulden. 2019. The SIGMORPHON 2019 shared task: Morphological analysis in context and cross-lingual transfer for inflection. *CoRR*, abs/1910.11493.

Ernst M McCarus. 2007. Kurdish morphology. *Morphologies of Asia and Africa*, 2:1021–1049.

Morteza Naserzade, Aso Mahmudi, Hadi Veisi, Hawre Hosseini, and Mohammad Mohammadamini. 2023. CKMorph: a comprehensive morphological analyzer for Central Kurdish. *International Journal of Digital Humanities*.

Tiago Pimentel, Maria Ryskina, Sabrina J. Mielke, Shijie Wu, Eleanor Chodroff, Brian Leonard, Garrett Nicolai, Yustinus Ghanggo Ate, Salam Khalifa, Nizar Habash, Charbel El-Khaissi, Omer Goldman, Michael Gasser, William Lane, Matt Coler, Arturo Oncevay, Jaime Rafael Montoya Samame, Gema Celeste Silva Villegas, Adam Ek, Jean-Philippe Bernardy, Andrey Shcherbakov, Aziyana Bayyr-ool, Karina Sheifer, Sofya Ganieva, Matvey Plugaryov, Elena Klyachko, Ali Salehi, Andrew Krizhanovsky, Natalia Krizhanovsky, Clara Vania, Sardana Ivanova, Aelita Salchak, Christopher Straughn, Zoey Liu, Jonathan North Washington, Duygu Ataman, Witold Kieraś, Marcin Woliński, Totok Suhardijanto, Niklas Stoehr, Zahroh Nuriah, Shyam Ratan, Francis M. Tyers, Edoardo M. Ponti, Grant Aiton, Richard J. Hatcher, Emily Prud'hommeaux, Ritesh Kumar, Mans Hulden, Botond Barta, Dorina Lakatos, Gábor Szolnok, Judit Ács, Mohit Raj, David Yarowsky, Ryan Cotterell, Ben Ambridge, and Ekaterina Vylomova. 2021. SIGMORPHON 2021 shared task on morphological reinflection: Generalization across languages. In *Proceedings of the 18th SIGMORPHON Workshop on Computational Research in Phonetics, Phonology, and Morphology*, pages 229–259, Online. Association for Computational Linguistics.

Brian Roark and Richard Sproat. 2007. *Computational approaches to morphology and syntax*, volume 4. OUP Oxford.

Benoît Sagot. 2010. The Lefff, a freely available and large-coverage morphological and syntactic lexicon for French. In *7th international conference on Language Resources and Evaluation (LREC 2010)*, Valletta, Malta.

Patrick Schone and Dan Jurafsky. 2001. Knowledge-free induction of inflectional morphologies. In *Second meeting of the North American chapter of the association for computational linguistics*.

John Sylak-Glassman. 2016. The composition and use of the universal morphological feature schema (UniMorph Schema). *Johns Hopkins University*.

Hadi Veisi, Mohammad MohammadAmini, and Hawre Hosseini. 2020. Toward Kurdish language processing: Experiments in collecting and processing the AsoSoft text corpus. *Digital Scholarship in the Humanities*, 35(1):176–193.

Peter W. Smith. 2014. Non-peripheral cliticization and second position in Udi and Sorani Kurdish. In *Paper under revision at Natural Language and Linguistic Theory*, `https://user.uni-frankfurt.de/~psmith/docs/smith_non_peripheral_cliticization.pdf` edition. (Date accessed: 12.05.2020).

Géraldine Walther. 2012. Fitting into morphological structure: accounting for Sorani Kurdish endoclitics. In *Mediterranean Morphology Meetings*, volume 8, pages 299–321. [Online; accessed 19-Mar-2019].

Géraldine Walther and Benoît Sagot. 2010. Developing a large-scale lexicon for a less-resourced language: General methodology and preliminary experiments on Sorani Kurdish. In *Proceedings of the 7th SaLTMiL Workshop on Creation and use of basic lexical resources for less-resourced languages (LREC 2010 Workshop)*.

Adam Wiemerslage, Arya D. McCarthy, Alexander Erdmann, Garrett Nicolai, Manex Agirrezabal, Miikka Silfverberg, Mans Hulden, and Katharina Kann. 2021. Findings of the SIGMORPHON 2021 shared task on unsupervised morphological paradigm clustering. In *Proceedings of the 18th SIGMORPHON Workshop on Computational Research in Phonetics, Phonology, and Morphology*, pages 72–81, Online. Association for Computational Linguistics.

Gernot Windfuhr. 2009. *The Iranian Languages*. Routledge London.

A Appendix

Noun	Adjective	Verb (present stem)	
		Intransitive	Transitive
dar / دار 'tree'	*lar* / لار 'crooked'	*kewtin* (*kew-*) / کەوتن 'fall'	*girtin* (*gir-*) / گرتن 'get'
pyaw / پیاو 'man'	*zana* / زانا 'shrewd'	*mirdin* (*mir-*) / مردن 'die'	*birdin* (*bir-*) / بردن 'take'
mey / مەی 'wine'	*taze* / تازە 'fresh'	*çûn* (*ç-*) / چوون 'go'	*xwardin* (*xo-*) / خواردن 'eat'
xesû / خەسوو 'step-mother'	*namo* / نامۆ 'weird'	*řoyştin* (řo-) / ڕۆیشتن 'leave'	*biřîn* (*biř-*) / بڕین 'cut'
masî / ماسی 'fish'	*nwê* / نوێ 'new'	*nûstin* (*nû-*) / نووستن 'sleep'	*pêwan* (*pêw-*) / پێوان 'measure'
ajawe / ئاژاوە 'chaos'		*westan* (*west-*) / وەستان 'stop'	*kirdin* (*ke-*) / کردن 'do'
bira / برا 'brother'		*pijmîn* (*pijm-*) / پژمین 'sneeze'	*dan* (*de-*) / دان 'give'
diro / درۆ 'lie'		*tirsan* (*tirs-*) / ترسان 'fear.CAUS'	*firoştin* (*firoş-*) / فرۆشتن 'sell'
girê / گرێ 'knot'		*birjan* (birjê-) / برژان 'grill'	*gwastin* (*gwaz-*) / گواستن 'carry'
gwê / گوێ 'ear'		*biřan* (*biřê-*) / بڕان 'cut'	*pařan* (*pařê-*) / پاڕان 'beg'
		kizan (*kizê-*) / کزان 'singe'	
		leran (*lerê-*) / لەران 'wobble'	
		geşan (*geşê-*) / گەشان 'blow'	
		biran (*bir-*) / بران 'carry.PASS'	
		pirsiran (*pirsir-*) / پرسران 'ask.PASS'	
		niran (*nir-*) / نران 'put.PASS'	
		bezîn (*bez-*) / بەزین 'defeat.CAUS'	

Table A.1: Selected words for which full paradigms are generated and included in our dataset

Investigating Phoneme Similarity with Artificially Accented Speech

Margot Masson, Julie Carson-Berndsen
SFI Centre for Research Training in Digitally-Enhanced Reality (d-real)
School of Computer Science, University College Dublin, Ireland
margot.masson@ucdconnect.ie, julie.berndsen@ucd.ie

Abstract

While the deep learning revolution has led to significant performance improvements in speech recognition, accented speech remains a challenge. Current approaches to this challenge typically do not seek to understand and provide explanations for the variations of accented speech, whether they stem from native regional variation or non-native error patterns. This paper seeks to address non-native speaker variations from both a knowledge-based and a data-driven perspective. We propose to approximate non-native accented-speech pronunciation patterns by the means of two approaches: based on phonetic and phonological knowledge on the one hand and inferred from a text-to-speech system on the other. Artificial speech is then generated with a range of variants which have been captured in confusion matrices representing phoneme similarities. We then show that non-native accent confusions actually propagate to the transcription from the ASR, thus suggesting that the inference of accent specific phoneme confusions is achievable from artificial speech.

1 Introduction

Automatic speech recognition (ASR) systems, while achieving high levels of performance on US-accented English, still struggle to handle accents for which they have not been trained (Hinsvark et al., 2021). Thus, accent robustness is an important challenge for the field of speech recognition, especially since such systems have become widespread and are used worldwide.

Various approaches have been tried to build accent-robust ASR systems. The most straightforward one, building accent-specific models, is limited because of the low availability of data for most accents which are mostly not well sourced. The lack of sourced data for training and testing makes the task of recognising accented speech extremely difficult. This lack of data is mainly due to the wide diversity of accents (native and non-native) leading to the complexity of recording enough examples for each, and the difficulty of accurately labelling and transcribing speech data.

Some attempts to overcome both lack of data and accent robustness have been proposed. These include multi-task training (Ghorbani and Hansen, 2018; Yang et al., 2018; Viglino et al., 2019), features adaptation (Gong et al., 2021) or adversarial training (Sun et al., 2018). However, these methods do not completely solve the problem of the lack of data, as data would still be needed for testing. Instead, generating artificial speech data seems promising, as data augmentation has been proven to be efficient for improving the recognition of accented speech (Fukuda et al., 2018), and the use of artificial data has been around for some time (Goronzy et al., 2004; Ueno et al., 2021).

This paper investigates the extent to which artificial speech data can be used to infer accent-related phoneme confusions. We do this by using an off-the-shelf speech synthesis system, in this case Microsoft Azure TTS[1], to synthesise artificially accented speech data and then using the Wav2Vec 2.0 ASR (Baevski et al., 2020), to produce a confusion matrix for this data. This matrix is then been examined and compared to other confusion matrices, in order to evaluate its relevance in representing a particular accent. In this paper, we focus on non-native accents, although the same study could have been applied to native accents.

The remainder of the paper is structured as follows. Section 2 discusses related work. Section 3 describes the process of generating accent related phoneme confusions for artificial accented speech. In sections 4 and 5, we compare the confusions obtained with alternative methods and discuss the extent to which text-to-speech systems can capture accent related phoneme confusions.

[1] https://microsoft/azure/text-to-speech

Proceedings of the 20th SIGMORPHON workshop on Computational Research in Phonetics, Phonology, and Morphology, pages 49–57
July 14, 2023

2 Related Work

Recent approaches for automatic speech recognition use end-to-end deep neural networks,(e.g. CTC-based, transformer-based and attention-based models) and have been really successful for this task. Commercial options exhibit extremely high performance; however, none of them achieve the same performance on accented speech. Attempts to improve end-to-end ASR performance on accented speech have had mixed results, and rely mainly on the training process. Indeed, the complexity of these architectures makes the understanding of the actual learning process difficult, if not impossible, and leads to an increasing need for explainability. This challenge has been the focus of a number of studies. Scharenborg et al. (2019) highlight the link between linguistic representations of speech and deep learning representation clusters. English et al. (2022) look to investigate in more detail the utility of attention layers, which is used in recent ASR systems. In the test community, Asyrofi et al. (2021) have proposed a testing framework for ASR systems. The work presented in this paper aligns with the goals of these approaches.

Accents are defined as variation in phoneme realisation due to several factors such as geographical location. In the case of non-native accents, which is the focus of this paper, the differences in pronunciation compared to the native language (L1) come mainly from the differences that exist between the phonetic rules of the native language and those of the target language (L2) (Flege, 1995). Thus, many pronunciation difficulties are due to phonological transfer - which involves applying L1 rules to L2 pronunciation - are linked to the non-existence of certain L2 characteristics in the L1, and result from discrepancies between the phonetic systems of the two languages. These challenges may include difficulties in producing and perceiving specific segmentals (Olsen, 2012) - like phonemes, consonant clusters, vowels - or suprasegmentals (Trofimovich and Baker, 2006) - like stress patterns, rhythm and intonation patterns - that are present in the L2 but absent or different in the L1.

Thus, non-native speakers commonly tend to approximate the pronunciation of phonemes which do not exist in their native language, by known ones they perceive as similar, as showed by Stefanich and Cabrelli (2021). For instance, pronouncing the English phoneme [ð] - corresponding to the grapheme sequence "th" as in "those" - as the French phonemes [z] or [d] is common amongst French people when speaking English (Capliez, 2011), since [ð] is not a phoneme of French (International Phonetic Association, 1999). While this is a very simplified version of the concept of accent, which does not include phenomena such as prosodic or phonotactic constraints, we focus in this paper on that definition of an accent, i.e. as the replacement of L2-but-not-L1 phonemes by L1 phonemes. This *paradigmatic* definition is intended to evolve into a more complete definition to include the *syntagmatic* and *suprasegmental* aspects in future work.

In order to understand the way in which non-native speakers switch from a phoneme of the target language (L2) to another phoneme of their native language (L1), we need to characterise phonemes and define what similarity between phonemes means. Several phonetic-based feature systems have been proposed to describe the specific phonemes of a language. Chomsky and Halle (1968) proposed a system to analyse the phonological structure of a language from a generative perspective. They described phonemes through binary features, organised along major features (that distinguish vowels from consonants), place of articulation, manner of articulation and source features (like voicing). Since then, multiple phonological feature sets have been proposed and have been used to capture similarities between phoneme classes.

This description of phonemes with features allow us to calculate their similarity using distance metrics such as Jaccard index (as defined in Equation 1, the Jaccard index between two sets U and V), that can easily be used as a similarity measure between phonemes, assuming that they are represented by their binary features. However, while it is a simple similarity to implement as baseline for the work presented in this paper, this measure is not satisfactory in the sense that all features have the same weight and, therefore, it does not take into account the difference in distance between the phonetic realisation of two features. Furthermore, it is only an a priori knowledge-based similarity, that does not necessarily follow the real-world realisations of phonemes.

$$Jaccard(U, V) = \frac{|U \cap V|}{|U \cup V|} \tag{1}$$

While Bailey and Hahn (2005) argued that knowledge-based feature based measures are better at predicting similarity, data driven techniques offer new opportunities to identify confusions and similarities. As an example of a data-driven approach, Kane and Carson-Berndsen (2016) built a confusion matrix over the TIMIT (Garofolo et al., 1992) dataset, which contains recordings of 8 major US-English dialects. They created what they call an enhanced confusion matrix, by excluding an acoustic model iteratively, in order to restrict the recognition process and identify what phonemes are recognised in place of those that are missing from the model. This process ends up with a lot more confusions for each phoneme, thus retrieving more similarities. They found that this confusion matrix corresponds better to theoretical expectations. Furthermore, phoneme embeddings have been used as the basis of data-driven similarity, in the context of sound analogies (Silfverberg et al., 2018), for determining allophonic relationships (Kolachina and Magyar, 2019) and for capturing distributional properties (O'Neill and Carson-Berndsen, 2019).

3 Introduction of Non-Native Variations

The overall method presented in this paper for synthesising accented speech consists, broadly, of 1) transforming texts into phoneme sequences, 2) applying variations to the phoneme sequence according the target accent, and 3) synthesising speech from the phoneme sequence using a text-to-speech (TTS) engine. This workflow is illustrated in Figure 1 and is referred in the remainder of the paper as "variation method". The core of this accented speech synthesis lies in the way we choose and apply variations to the phoneme sequence. This is done by 1) selecting the phonemes to vary using a mapping between the phonemes of the different languages - this mapping is called the *phonetic compatibility matrix*, and 2) varying the selected phonemes by replacing them with their nearest neighbour phonemes in terms of similarity. This mimics the way non-native speakers adjust to the target language pronunciation. These replacements could be regarded as *mispronunciations*.

The construction of the *phonetic compatibility matrix* is very straightforward. It is built as a boolean matrix, associating the different languages with their phonemes, the values being 1 if the phoneme exists in the target language, and 0 otherwise. Table 1 shows a sample of a compatibility matrix. For example, it shows that French and Spanish speakers are likely to approximate the [ð] phoneme, while English speakers will probably approximate the [ʁ] phoneme when speaking French. This matrix is based on the IPA handbook (International Phonetic Association, 1999) charts for the different languages.

Phone	English	French	Spanish
d	1	1	1
ð	1	0	0
θ	1	0	1
z	1	1	0
s	1	1	1
t	1	1	1
ʁ	0	1	0

Table 1: Section of the compatibility matrix

When applied, the variation method replaces the incompatible phonemes (i.e. the English phonemes identified in the *phonetic compatibility matrix* as not existing in the target language) with their nearest neighbour (that is with the higher similarity, or smallest distance to the original phoneme) in the *similarity matrix*, amongst the phonemes that exist both in English and in the target language. As we saw in the related work, the similarity between phonemes can be defined in several ways. In this paper, we will briefly introduce three different methods we used for building the *similarity matrix*, with a focus on similarity identification using artificial accented speech data. Thus, the next two subsections explore these methods for defining a *similarity matrix*, which can be separated into two paradigms: knowledge-based and data-driven.

3.1 Knowledge-Based Similarity

As outlined in Section 2, features have been used for describing phonemes and for calculating similarity between them. Thus, a similarity matrix can be constructed based on the Jaccard distance between the phonemes. This method for building a similarity matrix and using it for generating artificially accented speech is referred to as method **KB1** in the remainder of the paper.

However, Jaccard-based similarity does not take into account the difficulty of switching from one articulatory position and manner to another. For instance, switching from [p] to [q] is more counter intuitive than switching from [p] to [m] while they are equally similar along the Jaccard distance (equal to 0.5). Thus, for weighting the features along their physical distance in the mouth, we have positioned

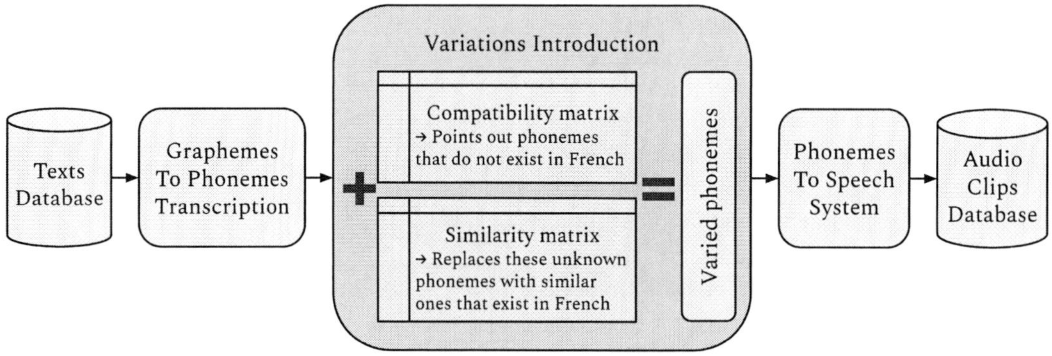

Figure 1: Overview of the generation of speech with non-native variations.

the phonemes in a three dimensional space (Figure 2), representing the features positioned along three axes corresponding to the *place of articulation*, the *manner of articulation* and the *voicing*; this is used as a measure of phonetic neighbourhood.

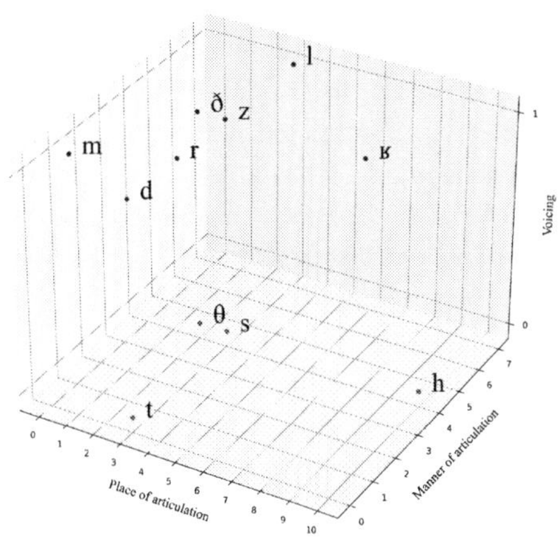

Figure 2: 3D representation of some phonemes

The coordinates of the phonemes in this space (depicted in Table 2) are used to calculate the Euclidean distance between the phonemes, as a similarity measure. For instance, in this space, the coordinates of [ð] are (3,5,1) and the coordinates of [z] are (4,2,1), which results in a Euclidean distance of 3.16 in a space where greatest distance is 13, resulting in a normalised distance of 0.24 (0.76 in similarity). This construction highlights the positional similarity of phonemes. For instance, in this space the distance between [p] and [q] (0.69) is now bigger than that between [p] and [m] (0.11). These distances are stored in the similarity matrix corresponding to that method. This 3-dimensional representation, in addition to its use for building the corresponding similarity and generating artificial accented speech, will now be referred as **KB2**.

The two similarity matrices presented in this subsection, KB1 and KB2, are entirely knowledge-based and do not necessarily highlight other constraints such as phonotactics, pitch or tone. In this sense, the data-driven paradigm presented in the next subsection can be seen as more representative of what may happen in natural accented speech.

3.2 Data-Driven Similarity

One method that has been used previously for synthesizing artificial accented speech is to rely exclusively on deep learning architectures of TTS systems to generate accented speech. This method consists of processing text inputs with a TTS engine, configured with the pronunciation patterns of the target accent. For instance, for generating a French accent in English, we input English text, to be read by the TTS engine as if it was French. We implemented this using an off-the-shelf text-to-speech system (Microsoft Azure TTS) for generating French-accented speech. This method is referred as **DD1** in the remainder of the paper and is explained in more detail in the next section.

However, the above method implies the use of a model that has been trained specifically to synthesize the target language, which brings us back to the problem of lack of data. Besides, the work conducted by Kane and Carson-Berndsen (2016) and presented in Section 2 suggests that phone confusions can be derived directly from speech data. This work motivated the development of our second data-driven method for generating accented speech. This method, denoted **DD2**, consists in running an

	Bilabial	...	Glottal
Plosive	(0,0,0) | (0,0,1)	...	(10,0,0) | (10,0,1)
...	(.., ..,0) | (.., ..,1)	...	(.., ..,0) | (.., ..,1)
Lateral Approximant	(0,7,0) | (0,7,1)	...	(10,7,0) | (10,7,1)

Table 2: Illustration of the construction of the 3D representation of phonemes

ASR system on accented speech data for retrieving the non-native confusions. These confusions can then be used for generating speech with variations as per the method described at the beginning of this section. Given the lack of natural French-accented English data, we decided to look at the recovery of phonetic confusions from artificial data. Section 4 delves into this method in more detail.

4 Artificial Speech Confusions

As introduced in the previous section, DD2 method has three stages: 1) generating artificial French-accented speech by using an off-the-shelf TTS system, 2) generating the recognition confusion matrix using an ASR system, and 3) introducing variations in speech, as per the variation method (see Figure 1), by using the previously obtained confusion matrix as the so-called *similarity matrix* for choosing the phonemes to vary.

The generation of artificial French accented speech is done by providing text inputs (i.e. textual sentences from TIMIT dataset) to the Microsoft Azure TTS, with its two parameters *language* set to English and *voice* set to one of the Azure French voices: *fr-FR-DeniseNeural* or *fr-FR-HenriNeural*. This configuration allows the TTS to synthesize the English sentences with a French pronunciation, that is reading the sentences as if they were written in French. At the end of this process, we end up with a set of artificially accented speech audios.

Then, the second step is the generation of the French confusions. For obtaining that matrix, we use Wav2Vec 2.0 ASR with a subsequent grapheme to phoneme mapping and we align the phoneme sequences with the original ones obtained from TIMIT. The confusion matrix created from these alignments is expected to capture the confusions specifically due to the target French accent.

Lastly, the confusion matrix we just created can be used as the *similarity matrix* described in Section 3 for getting the replacement phonemes for the phonemes that do not exist in French. As for KB1 and KB2, the variation method first selects the English phonemes that do not exist in French, then selects their replacements in the *similarity matrix* and finally a Phoneme-To-Text engine creates the varied speech. This aims to mimic the way French speakers approximate the pronunciation of English.

In the next sections, we evaluate the relevance of the similarity matrix described in this section - i.e. based on artificial non-native confusions - in the context of accented speech generation. This evaluation is done by comparing the results obtained by the ASR on speech generated using the variation method with the above matrix, referred to as **method DD2** in the remainder of the paper, against the other ones described in the paper.

5 Experiments

The experiments aim to evaluate the extent to which it is possible to infer accent-related phonemes confusions from artificially accented speech. For that purpose, we compare the performance of the ASR on the data generated as in Section 4, that is the speech synthesised from artificial confusions, with respect to the other methods described in Section 3, and with respect to speech without variations (artificial and natural native US English speech) as baseline. As a summary, we have the following methods:

- **NV1** is a baseline corresponding to natural US-English speech data from TIMIT.
- **NV2** is a baseline corresponding to artificial US-English speech obtained using Azure TTS.
- **KB1** corresponds to the representation of phonemes as sets of features, and their similarity as Jaccard distance.

- **KB2** corresponds to the representation of phonemes into a 3-dimensional space, and their similarity as Euclidean distance.
- **DD1** corresponds to the use of Azure TTS as a generator of accented speech, with the so-called *voice* parameter set to a French voice.
- **DD2** corresponds to the confusion matrix obtained after running an ASR on the audio files obtained by applying method DD1. This is the main focus of the paper, and has been described in Section 4.

For comparing the different methods, we use three criteria: word error rate (WER), phoneme error rate (PER) and visual inspection of hierarchical similarity clustering in dendogram representations. Global metrics, i.e. WER and PER, are used to consider the impact that variations have on recognition. The hierarchical view of similarity values of some selected phonemes provides an insight into the impact of specific variations on the recognition. That is, it is possible to see if the variation patterns propagate to the output via the confusions.

For the purpose of this paper, we built four similarity matrices, following the methodology described in sections 3 and 4. That is, we built the matrices corresponding to knowledge-based methods KB1 and KB2, as well as the similarity matrices for data driven methods DD1 and DD2. For creating these matrices, we selected 1000 sentences out of the 2366 sentences of TIMIT corpus as a text corpus. The ASR system used for conducting these experiments is Wav2Vec 2.0. The target accent is French, and the reference language is US English.

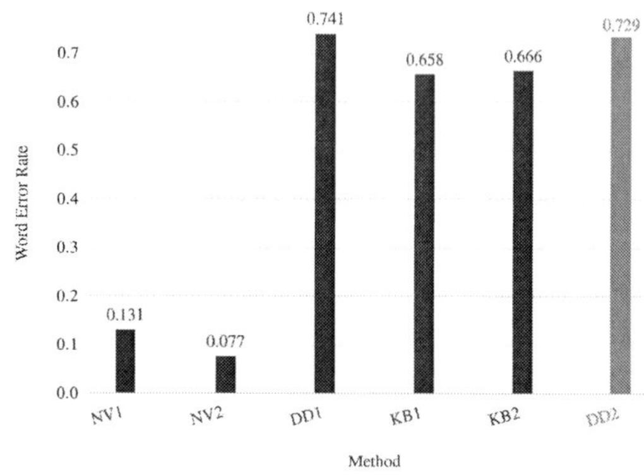

Figure 3: WER scores for DD2 vs other methods.

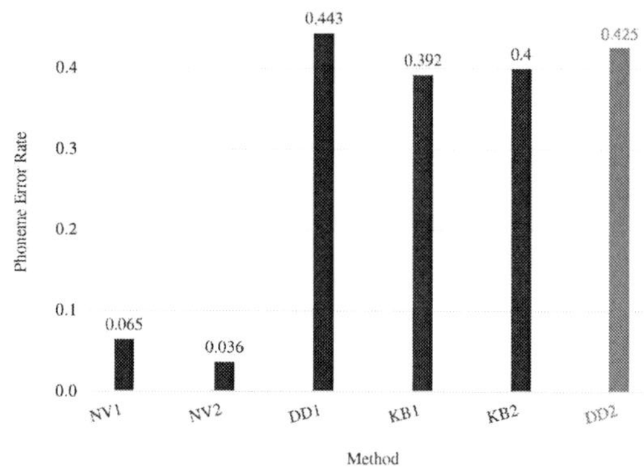

Figure 4: PER scores for DD2 vs other methods.

6 Results and Discussion

6.1 WER and PER

Figures 3 and 4 depict WER and PER values respectively with ASR on the six different methods. As expected, artificial speech with variations obtained higher WER scores $\approx$+0.57 than speech without variation, thus confirming that Wav2Vec 2.0 performs better on speech without variation. We thus obtained a drop of more than 50% between accented and non-accented speech recognition accuracy, which corresponds to the drop reported in the literature. Unsurprisingly, the PER follows the same tendencies as the WER. This indicates to an extent that the confusions we obtained are due to the difficulties for Wav2Vec2.0 in handling the *mispronunciations* we introduced in our varied speech at the phonemic level.

These results confirm the interest of our variation method for challenging ASR systems, and they are also encouraging for the identification of non-native speech learning patterns. Indeed, we can expect that the drop in accuracy between knowledge-based variation methods and data-driven variation methods is caused by the addition of new variations patterns. While the knowledge-based approaches only apply phoneme substitutions, many more other phenomena are represented by the data-driven approaches, such as phonotactics, coarticulation or prosodic transfer. The low value of the drop, however, could indicate that phoneme substitutions are the main source of errors for ASR systems, but this needs to be investigated further.

6.2 Phoneme Similarities

In order to look at the similarities which emerge from the ASR, we used hierarchical clustering of the output confusions matrices. Dendrograms visu-

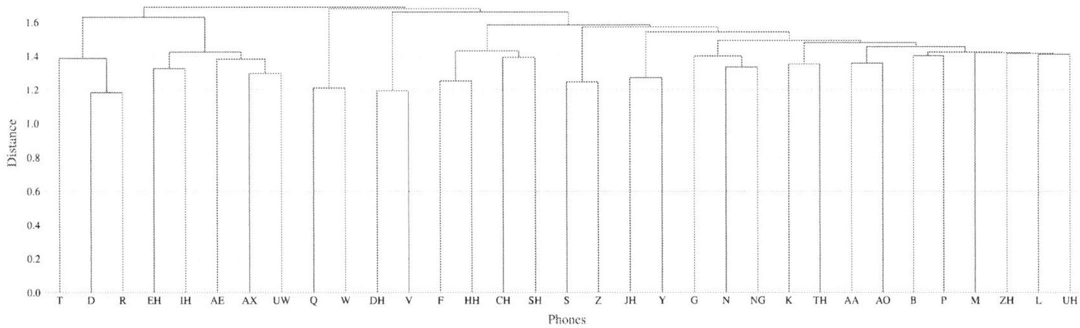

Figure 5: Hierarchical view of the confusions obtained with KB1 method.

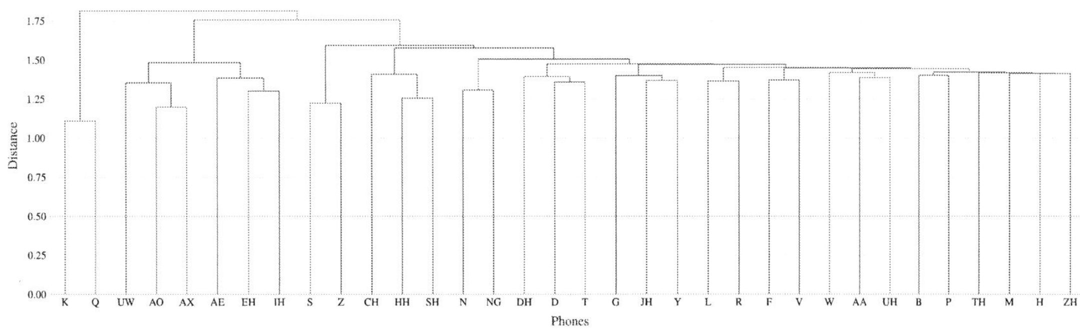

Figure 6: Hierarchical view of the confusions obtained with DD1 method.

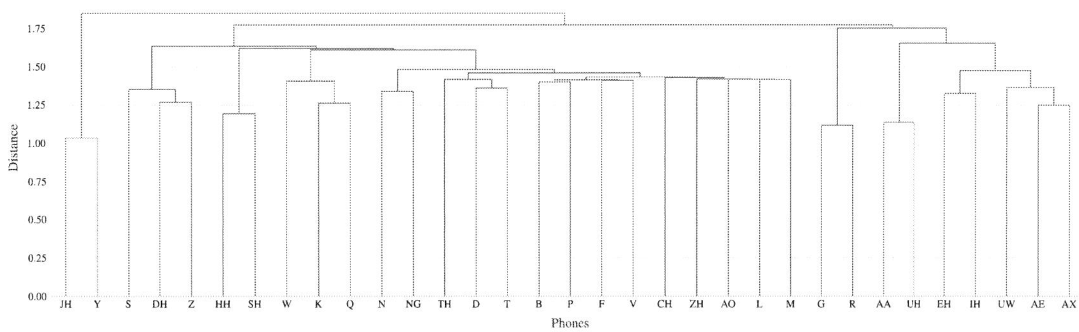

Figure 7: Hierarchical view of the confusions obtained with DD2 method.

alising this clustering can be found in Figures 5, 6 and 7 for KB1, DD1 and DD2 methods respectively [2]. The dendograms highlight some overall interesting patterns in the confusions. KB1 exhibits place-of-articulation clusters (e.g [t], [d], [r] alveolars for instance), which was expected knowing that its similarity matrix was constructed around phonetic features. However, we are looking to investigate whether the variants propagate through the ASR and provide insights into how variants cluster and emerge in a deep learning model. While the differences between the dendograms require further detailed analysis examining the contexts in which the errors occur, it can be seen, for instance, that the [ð] has moved closer to the [s] and [z] in DD2 in Figure 7, and to [d] and [t] in DD1 in Figure 6. These two confusions correspond to typical L1-French pronunciation of the *th* English grapheme. Furthermore, *r* in French is pronounced differently and it can also be seen in DD2 that [r] and [g] now cluster together; this is an indication that these sounds are both articulated further back.

This analysis of phoneme confusions highlighted that Wav2Vec2.0 was not able to correct the vari-

[2] Note that ARPABET rather than the IPA is used in these figures

ations we introduced in the input, and that these variations propagated through the ASR to the transcriptions. Indeed, confusions for KB1 and KB2 relate precisely to the variations we applied. This opens up perspectives for further analysis of the notion of similarity for ASR systems, including for artificial speech.

7 Conclusions

In this paper, we used artificially accented speech for retrieving non-native similarity patterns. We generated accented speech TTS with French voices and were able to use that output for calculating the corresponding confusion matrix. By using this matrix as a representation of similarity for introducing variations in speech, we found that these correspond to actual non-native variations. In the near future, we plan to enhance our knowledge-based methods with other types of variation, in particular phonotactic constraints. In the longer term, there are two motivations for the approach presented in this paper. The first is to investigate and model non-native speech variants as they are captured in deep learning models and the second is to provide a methodology for challenging ASR systems to determine how far a variant can be from the expected phoneme and still be recognised correctly.

Limitations

The speech recognition used was the Wav2Vec 2.0 model. Some of the errors may have been influenced by the fine tuning of the final layers; this could lead to errors being corrected by the language model. Furthermore, Wav2Vec 2.0 produces character output which we transformed to phonemes using a grapheme-to-phoneme tool; this will lead to some loss in the variation. These limitations can be overcome to some extent by using a Wav2Vec 2.0 phoneme model which we plan for our next experiments. We have only worked on French to date, even though we believe that the method is applicable to other languages. Finally, the experiments were done only on TIMIT. While this is a balanced dataset, use of other datasets will likely lead to better insights.

Ethics Statement

We have used existing speech datasets and off-the-shelf tools for speech recognition and synthesis. The use of the existing voices of the native speaker of one language, in this case French, to synthesise artificial non-native English speech is taken as representative of an L2 learner speaking English for the first time. There is much to be learned about speech variation from such artificially generated speech but is should not be regarded as mocking non-native speaker endeavours to learn a language. Indeed the variants learned from such data can provide useful insights for speaker accommodation.

Acknowledgements

This work was conducted with the financial support of the Science Foundation Ireland Centre for Research Training in Digitally-Enhanced Reality (d-real) under Grant No. 18/CRT/6224. For the purpose of Open Access, the author has applied a CC BY public copyright licence to any Author Accepted Manuscript version arising from this submission.

References

Muhammad Hilmi Asyrofi, Zhou Yang, and David Lo. 2021. Crossasr++: a modular differential testing framework for automatic speech recognition. In *Proceedings of the 29th ACM Joint Meeting on European Software Engineering Conference and Symposium on the Foundations of Software Engineering*. ACM.

Alexei Baevski, Henry Zhou, Abdelrahman Mohamed, and Michael Auli. 2020. wav2vec 2.0: A framework for self-supervised learning of speech representations. *CoRR*, abs/2006.11477.

Todd M. Bailey and Ulrike Hahn. 2005. Phoneme similarity and confusability. *Journal of Memory and Language*, 52(3):339–362.

Marc Capliez. 2011. Typologie des erreurs de production d'anglais des francophones.

Noam. Chomsky and Morris Halle. 1968. *The Sound Pattern of English*. Harper and Row New York.

Patrick Cormac English, John D. Kelleher, and Julie Carson-Berndsen. 2022. Domain-informed probing of wav2vec 2.0 embeddings for phonetic features. In *Proceedings of the 19th SIGMORPHON Workshop on Computational Research in Phonetics, Phonology, and Morphology*, pages 83–91, Seattle, Washington. Association for Computational Linguistics.

James E Flege. 1995. Second language speech learning: Theory, findings, and problems. *Speech perception and linguistic experience: Issues in cross-language research*, 92:233–277.

Takashi Fukuda, Raul Fernandez, Andrew Rosenberg, Samuel Thomas, Bhuvana Ramabhadran, Alexander Sorin, and Gakuto Kurata. 2018. Data Augmentation Improves Recognition of Foreign Accented Speech. In *Proc. Interspeech 2018*, pages 2409–2413.

J. Garofolo, Lori Lamel, W. Fisher, Jonathan Fiscus, D. Pallett, N. Dahlgren, and V. Zue. 1992. Timit acoustic-phonetic continuous speech corpus. *Linguistic Data Consortium.*

Shahram Ghorbani and John H.L. Hansen. 2018. Leveraging Native Language Information for Improved Accented Speech Recognition. In *Proc. Interspeech 2018*, pages 2449–2453.

Xun Gong, Yizhou Lu, Zhikai Zhou, and Yanmin Qian. 2021. Layer-Wise Fast Adaptation for End-to-End Multi-Accent Speech Recognition. In *Proc. Interspeech 2021*, pages 1274–1278.

Silke Goronzy, Stefan Rapp, and Ralf Kompe. 2004. Generating non-native pronunciation variants for lexicon adaptation. *Speech Communication*, 42:109–123.

Arthur Hinsvark, Natalie Delworth, Miguel Del Rio, Quinten McNamara, Joshua Dong, Ryan Westerman, Michelle Huang, Joseph Palakapilly, Jennifer Drexler, Ilya Pirkin, Nishchal Bhandari, and Miguel Jette. 2021. Accented speech recognition: A survey. *CoRR*, abs/2104.10747.

The International Phonetic Association. 1999. *Handbook of the International Phonetic Association: A Guide to the Use of the International Phonetic Alphabet.* Cambridge University Press.

Mark Kane and Julie Carson-Berndsen. 2016. Enhancing Data-Driven Phone Confusions Using Restricted Recognition. In *Proc. Interspeech 2016*, pages 3693–3697.

Sudheer Kolachina and Lilla Magyar. 2019. What do phone embeddings learn about phonology? *Proceedings of the 16th Workshop on Computational Research in Phonetics, Phonology, and Morphology.*

Michael K. Olsen. 2012. The l2 acquisition of spanish rhotics by l1 english speakers: The effect of l1 articulatory routines and phonetic context for allophonic variation. *Hispania*, 95(1):65–82.

Emma O'Neill and Julie Carson-Berndsen. 2019. The Effect of Phoneme Distribution on Perceptual Similarity in English. In *Proc. Interspeech 2019*, pages 1941–1945.

Odette Scharenborg, Nikki van der Gouw, Martha Larson, and Elena Marchiori. 2019. The representation of speech in deep neural networks. In *MultiMedia Modeling: 25th International Conference, MMM 2019, Thessaloniki, Greece, January 8–11, 2019, Proceedings, Part II 25*, pages 194–205. Springer.

Miikka P Silfverberg, Lingshuang Mao, and Mans Hulden. 2018. Sound analogies with phoneme embeddings. *Proceedings of the Society for Computation in Linguistics (SCiL) 2018*, pages 136–144.

Sara Stefanich and Jennifer Cabrelli. 2021. The effects of l1 english constraints on the acquisition of the l2 spanish alveopalatal nasal. *Frontiers in Psychology*, 12:640354.

Sining Sun, Ching-Feng Yeh, Mei-Yuh Hwang, Mari Ostendorf, and Lei Xie. 2018. Domain adversarial training for accented speech recognition. *CoRR*, abs/1806.02786.

Pavel Trofimovich and Wendy Baker. 2006. Learning second language suprasegmentals: Effect of l2 experience on prosody and fluency characteristics of l2 speech. *Studies in Second Language Acquisition*, 28(1):1–30.

Sei Ueno, Masato Mimura, Shinsuke Sakai, and Tatsuya Kawahara. 2021. Data augmentation for asr using tts via a discrete representation. In *2021 IEEE Automatic Speech Recognition and Understanding Workshop (ASRU)*, pages 68–75.

Thibault Viglino, Petr Motlicek, and Milos Cernak. 2019. End-to-End Accented Speech Recognition. In *Proc. Interspeech 2019*, pages 2140–2144.

Xuesong Yang, Kartik Audhkhasi, Andrew Rosenberg, Samuel Thomas, Bhuvana Ramabhadran, and Mark Hasegawa-Johnson. 2018. Joint modeling of accents and acoustics for multi-accent speech recognition.

Generalized Glossing Guidelines: An Explicit, Human- and Machine-Readable, Item-and-Process Convention for Morphological Annotation

David R. Mortensen[*†] **Ela Gulsen**[*†] **Taiqi He**[†]
Nathaniel Robinson[†] **Jonathan D. Amith**[‡] **Lindia Tjuatja**[†]
Lori Levin[†]
[†]Carnegie Mellon University [‡]Gettysburg College
[†]{dmortens, egulsen, taiqih, nrrobins, lindiat, levin}@andrew.cmu.edu
[‡]jonamith@gmail.com

Abstract

We introduce a YAML notation for multi-line interlinear glossed text (IGT) that represents non-concatentative processes such as infixation, reduplication, mutation, truncation, and tonal overwriting in a consistent, formally rigorous way, on par with affixation, using an Item-and-Process (IP) framework. Our new notation—Generalized Glossing Guidelines (GGG)—is human- and machine-readable and easy to edit with general purpose tools. A GGG representation has four fields: (1) A Surface Representation (`sr`) with curly brackets to show where non-concatenative morphological processes have applied. (2) A Lexical Representation (`lx`) that explicitly shows non-concatenative processes as insertions, deletions, and substitutions as they apply to the basic form of morphemes. (3) A gloss field (`gl`) that associates glosses with morphemes and morphological processes in the `sr` and `lx` lines. (4) A metalanguage translation. We demonstrate the linguistic adequacy of GGG and compare it to two other IGT annotation schemes.

1 Introduction

As part of the ongoing wav2gloss project, we are generating Interlinear Glossed Text (IGT) from speech using an end-to-end system. In producing IGT for various languages of the Americas, we encountered a challenge: traditional interlinear glossing schemes are well-suited for the representation of concatenative morphology (Comrie et al., 2008) where morphological properties are realized by spans of phonological material (Goodman et al., 2015; Maeda and Bird, 2000; Bird and Liberman, 1999; Bird et al., 2000; Ide and Suderman, 2007). However, the languages that we are working with—Mixtec, Nahuatl, and Totonac—are permeated by morphological operations such as truncation, tonal overwriting, reduplication, apophony, and segmental overwriting, that cannot be adequately expressed as the concatenation (or even interleaving) of strings. The shortcoming of most IGT notations is that they represent the alignment of affixes with glosses, but they do not explicitly show how non-concatenative processes align to glosses.

The contrast between concatenative and non-concatenative "models of grammatical description" goes back at least to a seminal article by Charles Hockett (1954) in which he observed that morphology can be viewed as the concatenation of morphemes (item-and-arrangement or IA) or as the application of processes to morphemes (item-and-process or IP). Whatever their ontological nature may be, some morphological operations—for example, apophony and truncation—are more easily expressed as processes than morphemes. In order to gloss these operations (and give them the same status as affixation), we needed to develop an annotation scheme more general than those currently available. Therefore, we propose Generalized Glossing Guidelines (or GGG), that build upon existing conventions such as the Leipzig Glossing Rules (Comrie et al., 2008) but make the framework formally explicit and add consistent and comprehensive support for non-concatenative morphological alternations such as infixation, reduplication, transfixation, apophony, tonal overwriting, and truncation.

Figure 1 gives an example of GGG from Yoloxóchitl Mixtec. It shows metadata as well as the four fields, `sr` (Surface Representation), `lx` (Lexical Representation), `gl` (gloss), and `tr` (translation). It shows tonal overwriting in curly brackets, with citicization shown by `=`.

[*]Denotes equal contribution.

Proceedings of the 20th SIGMORPHON workshop on Computational Research in Phonetics, Phonology, and Morphology, pages 58–67
July 14, 2023 ©2023 Association for Computational Linguistics

2 Background

A large number of glossing conventions, from the very formal (e.g., Xigt; Goodman et al. 2015) to the relatively informal (e.g., the Leipzig Glossing Rules or LGR; Comrie et al. 2008) have been proposed and employed in computational applications. For example, a recent SIGMORPHON shared task on glossing used representations based on LGR.[1]

These conventions play two roles: (1) They allow linguists and language workers to communicate with one another with clarity and minimal ambiguity; (2) They allow humans and computers to communicate with one another with respect to the morphosyntax of human languages. In our use-case, they allow neural models to communicate the details of their morphosyntactic analyses to language workers. As such, these annotation conventions need to be both human readable (whether directly or through some kind of user interface) and expressive, without sacrificing explicitness.

Although LGR largely satisfies these critera when only concatenative morphology occurs, non-concatenative operations are only supported in a limited and sometimes inexplicit way in this convention. The following example shows the LGR notation for apophony (umlaut) in German:

(1) Ich habe vier Brüder
1.SG have.1.SG four brother\PL
'I have four brothers.'

The sequence "\PL" indicates that plural is marked by a non-concatenative process (in this case, apophony), but it does not index the morphological property to a specific formal change. In the Generalized Glossing Guidelines described here, the same example would be the following:[2]

(2) Ich habe vier Br{u>ü}der
1.SG have.1.SG four brother{PL}
'I have four brothers.'

LGR also has conventions for annotating reduplication and infixation, but each of these notations is different. Compare these examples from Motu:

(3) a. ma~mahuta
PL sleep
'to sleep'

b. {>ma}mahuta
sleep{PL}
'to sleep'

In LGR (3a), reduplicants are delimited with a tilde. In the GGG version (3b), again showing only `lx`, reduplication is notated with the same arrow notation as all other non-concatenative processes.

Compare the following well-known example of infixation in Tagalog:

(4) a. s<um>ulat
<COMPL>write
'write'

b. s{>um}ulat
write{COMPL}
'write'

In LGR (4a), infixes are surrounded by angle brackets. In the GGG version (4b), infixes are indicated with the same notation as reduplication and all other processes. Maximal empirical coverage is achieved with minimal formal equipment.

Another important framework for representing IGT (and morphosyntactic annotations, generally) is Xigt (Goodman et al., 2015), an XML-based format that associates annotations with spans. It, too, is highly general, machine-readable, and formally rigorous, but its opaque structure makes it difficult to read and write without special software tools.

We propose GGG to take the best of the both frameworks. It has the following properties:

- General and adaptable
- Human readable
- Machine readable and unambiguous
- Editable with general-purpose tools
- Consistent and formally-rigorous in its representation of non-concatenative processes

2.1 Lexical Representations

The core of the GGG format is the lexical or `lx` representation. To understand `lx`, one must distinguish morphological processes from phonological processes and imagine a pipeline in which morphological processes precede phonological processes.

Morphological processes are associated with meaning or grammatical features. For example, the Mixtec tone changes shown in Figure 1 mark the habitual aspect. Phonological processes, in contrast, are not associated with meanings. They are processes that apply when phonological conditions are met. For example, tone sandhi in many languages is purely phonological (does not realize any morphosyntactic properties).

[1] `https://github.com/sigmorphon/2023GlossingST`

[2] We show only `lx` here, structuring fields as in a conventional glossed example, and omit `sr` for the sake of comparison to LGR.

In Item-and-Process Morphology, there are two kinds of constructs associated with meaning: morphemes (items) and processes. The pipeline assumed by GGG is one in which morphemes are first assembled via concatenation (a MORPHEMIC REPRESENTATION). At this level, each instance of the same morpheme has the same form (except in cases of suppletion). Then, processes apply to these strings. Together, the items and processes form the lexical representation (`lx`) in GGG. This representation is the output of the morphology and the input to the phonology.[3]

Phonological rules may apply to the `lx` representation, yielding phonologically conditioned allomorphy. Some cases of nasalization shown in the `sr` field in Figure 1 are phonological. Since nasalization is not associated with any meaning, it does not correspond to labels in the gloss (`gl`).

In GGG, the `lx` represents the application of processes to morphemes—mapping between a MORPHEMIC REPRESENTATION and an UNDERLYING REPRESENTATION. The bracket-and-arrow notation shown in (3b) and (4b) above describes rewrites between the morphemic form and the underlying form. That is to say, the morphemic representation is everything outside of the brackets interspersed with everything to the left of the arrows (>) and the underlying representation is everything outside of the brackets interspersed with everything to the right of the arrows. The surface representation, in contrast, is the output of the phonology.

2.2 GGG is purely descriptive

The goal of GGG is **not** to provide a deep theoretical account of morphology but rather to be purely descriptive. Thus—for example—even when we believe that a morphological process is best explained by autosegmental tones being "bumped" from one mora to the following mora, GGG represents this process as the deletion of a tone from one mora of the morphemic representation and the simultaneous insertion of an identical tone on the following mora in the underlying representation (with some loss of generality). This is done to explicitly state the formal relationship between a morphemic form and underlying form while making a minimum of theory-internal assumptions. For example, in Yoloxóchitl Mixtec, the habitual is formed by overwriting a /4/ (high) tone to the first mora. Two examples are given in (5):

(5) a. chio'{1>4}o{>1}4
cook_boiling{HAB;1,2}
habitually cook by boiling'

b. sa{3>4}ta{>3}4
sa{3>4}ta{>2}4
buy{HAB;1,2}
'habitually buy'

Note that these changes are morphologically (not phonologically) conditioned. In (5a), GGG represents the tonal morphology as /1/ being replaced by /4/ and (the second) /4/ being preceded by an inserted /1/, focusing on the superficial (insertion of /1/ in the second mora) rather than the deep relationship (reassingment of the same /1/ to the second mora) between the morphemic representation and the underlying representation (the input to the phonological rules).

3 The Guidelines

GGG attempts to represent IGT examples like those in the preceding section in a YAML format, [4] preserving to the degree possible the conventions that are present when linguists typeset linguistic data for the consumption of other linguists. This allies it with the SIL Shoebox format and differentiates it from Xigt (Goodman et al., 2015) and other highly explicit IGT formats. This also makes it relatively easy to edit GGG text using off-the-shelf tools (e.g., text editors and transcription tools).

3.1 General Data Structure

An illustration of a YAML file for GGG is presented in Figure 1. The top level object is a map, consisting of metadata fields (`obj_lang` for "object language" and `meta_lang` for "meta language" are required), and `segs`, which is an array of "discourse segments" (roughly, sentences). The field `obj_lang` consists of a single ISO 639-3 code (as a string). The field `meta_lang` is an array of ISO 639-3 codes. Each discourse segment is a map with the following fields:

src The audio or video document from which the segment derives.

start The start time of the interval in the source file from which the segment derives (in seconds since the beginning of the recording).

[3]Note that this approach assumes a non-trivial and controversial assumption about the phonology-morphology interface. It excludes interleaving between morphological and phonological alternations. This is done to make the glossing format tractable and is characteristic of glossing formats generally. However, when cyclic phonology results in a two-step change, GGG allows this to be represented.

[4]`https://yaml.org`

```
obj_lang: xty
meta_lang: eng
segs:
-
src: xty0002.wav
start: 256
end: 265
speaker: 3
lx: "ja'{3>4}nda2 =nã1 =e1 ka4 nda{3>4}sa3 ba'1a3 =na2 yu'3u4 =run4"
sr: "ja'{4}nda2 =nã1 =e1 kã4 nda{4}sa3 ba'1a3 =nã2 yu'3u4 =run4"
gl: "cut{HAB} =3.PL =3.INAM there convert{HAB} good =3.PL mouth =wood"
tr: "...they cut it and convert it into a bifurcated stick."
```

Figure 1: Sample of GGG from Yoloxóchit Mixtec showing the use of bracket-and-arrow notation to indicate tonal overwriting and differences between lexical and surface forms produced by phonological rules. The numerals after vowels represent tones (/4/ is high; /1/ is low) associated with the preceding mora (for our purposes, vowel).

end The end time of the interval in the source file from which the segment derives (in seconds since the beginning of the recording).

speaker ID for speaker in this discourse segment.

lx The lexical representation of the discourse segment—the mapping between a MORPHEMIC representation in which all morphemes are represented in their canonical form (to which all processes have applied) and the underlying form that is the input to the phonology; consists of tokens (corresponding to morphemes) delimited by spaces.

sr The surface representation of the discourse segment—the output of the phonology, consisting of tokens delimited by spaces.

gl The glosses of each of the tokens in the lx and `sr` strings, delimited by spaces.

tr An idiomatic translation of the discourse segment (as a string).

Crucially, when split on white space, the `lx`, `sr`, and `gl` fields must consist of exactly the same number of strings. An alternative and equivalent representation would be to have these fields be arrays of objects, each corresponding to a word. This would enforce the alignment between words and glosses directly. However, it is much less readable than the proposed format and would be harder to edit with off-the-shelf tools.

Each of the tokens in the `lx` and `sr` strings consists of either a root, affix, or clitic and one or more processes that have been applied to it, as described in §3.2. Each of the tokens in the `gloss` string also consist of roots, affixes, clitics, and processes. Each word must have the same number of each of these categories of items. Except for processes, these must occur in the same order in forms and glosses. The roots, affixes, and clitics that make up the words are "morpheme-like units" (or tokens) and are delimited by spaces. Each process is associated with a single morpheme-like unit.[5]

3.2 Space-Delimited Form Tokens

Form tokens are sequences with components of the types shown in Table 1.

TYPE	CONN.	PREC. BASE?	EXAMPLE	GLOSS
root	n/a	n/a	Kind	child
prefix	-	Y	un- likely	NEG- likely
suffix	-	N	Kind -er	child -PL
procliti	=	Y	j'= aime	1.SG= like
enclitic	=	N	child ='s	child =POSS

Table 1: Types of tokens.

When lexical glosses consist of multiple words, they are joined with the underscore, as in Hmong `lug` '`come_back`'. In this case, an optional rule from LGR is made mandatory. The use of a period to compose complex glosses is not to be used for this purpose. Instead, it is used strictly in cases of cumulative exponence (that is, where a single morpheme realizes and is glossed with more than one property) as in English `-s` '-3.SG.PRS'.

[5]In a few cases, this has proven problematic and has resulted in redundancy, but in the general case, it has worked well.

Form tokens may contain annotations for MORPHOLOGICAL PROCESSES such as the following:

- Reduplication
- Infixation
- Transfixation
- Apophony
- Tonal overwriting
- Segmental overwriting

These are indicated with bracketed expressions. In lexical forms (`lx`), these consist of `{A>B}` where `A` and `B` can be any string including the empty string. These indicate a process in which `A` has been replaced by `B`. Examples include English `t{u>i}θ` 'tooth{PL}.' In `srs`, these consist of `{A}`, where `A` can be any string (including the empty string). These indicate substrings that are the result of the application of a process. Take, for example, English `t{i}θ` 'tooth{PL}'. For a complete example, see Figure 1. In some cases, there may be a hierarchical relationship between processes, where one process "feeds" another. This is indicated by providing additional steps using the bracket-and-arrow notation, e.g., `{3>1>4}` as in the following examples from Yoloxóchitl Mixtec. In (6a) and (6b) the irrealis transitive *ta'3bi4* and instransitive *ta'1bi4* are changed to the habitual, with tone /4/ on the first mora. We analyze the shift of /3/>/1/ as a detransitivising process and thus in example (6b) both DTR and HAB are represented by {3>1>4}. The low tone /1/ is then reassigned to the second mora (shown in GGG as the "insertion" of /1/ on /i/). In many cases this "push" of first mora's original tone (/1/ or /3/) onto the second mora occurs, forming a contour tones (e.g., /14/ and underlying /34/ (surface /24/ by phonological rule after the mora-initial tone 4 of the habitual).

(6) a. ta'{3>4}bi4
break{HAB}
'habitually break (transitive)'

b. ta'{3>1>4}bi{>1}4
break{DTR.HAB;1,2}
'habitually break (intransitive)'

3.3 Covert elements

When the absence of an affix is significant, it can be represented as 0- or -0 (standing in for $\varnothing$ or ϵ).

3.4 Distinguishing Morphology from Phonology

The process notations are not meant to represent purely phonological alternations. If an alternation can be accounted for by a rule that is wholly conditioned by the surrounding phonological segments or syllable structure and prosodic context, it should be treated as phonological and not directly represented in the `lx` field. The `lx` field should contain only information that is derivable from the lexical, derivational, and inflectional properties of a token and is not predictable on another basis.

3.5 Space-Delimited Gloss Tokens

Type	Example	Glosss
Infixation	s{>um}ulat	write{PFV}
Reduplication	{>su}sulat	write{PROSP}
Transfixation	k{i>u}t{a>u}b	book{PL;1,2}
Apophony	t{u>i}θ	tooth{PL}
Segmental overwriting	{xi>ku}3xi3	eat{IRR}
Tonal overwriting	ku{3>14}ni2	want{NEG}

Table 2: Example forms and glosses for a range of morphological processes.

Conventions for associating gloss tokens with morpheme tokens (see Table 2) are based on the Leipzig glossing conventions with significant extensions. When possible, labels for categories are derived from the Unimorph schema (Sylak-Glassman, 2016).

Each gloss token consists of a lexical or morpheme gloss followed by a sequence of process glosses (each enclosed in curly brackets) and zero or one delimiters {`=`, `-`} which may be either preposed or postposed. Process glosses consist of lexical glosses or morpheme glosses and an optional semicolon followed by a list of numbers separated by commas. The numbers indicate the index of spans (starting from 1) in the corresponding form the gloss applies to. For example, in Arabic `k{i>u}t{a:>u}b` 'book{PL;1,2}', the PL property is realized by two changes ({>u} and {>u}) and this is indicated by the span indices (1,2) after the semicolon. For ease of annotation, if there is only one process in a word, the index can be omitted.

Some form tokens have more than one associated process. The corresponding glosses are provided in successive bracketed expressions after that lexical or morpheme gloss. For example, in Arabic `k{>a}t{>:}{>a}b{>a}` 'write{PST;1,3}{CAUS;2}{3.SG.M;4}', there are three processes, indicated by the three properties in brackets with their respective indices. The use of indices means the alignment between bracketed expressions in forms and glosses is deterministic. The orders of the processes (bracketed expressions) in the gloss can be arbitrary, but—as a group—they should appear only at the end of the gloss.

Morpheme glosses are drawn from the Unimorph Schema (Sylak-Glassman, 2016) when possible.[6] When glosses for derivational morphology are present in the Leipzig Rules but not in Unimorph, the Leipzig gloss should be used. When a needed category is not represented in either resource, it will be added to the standard.

Super-categories of features are representated as `CATEGORY::`. Thus, first-person plural subject is represented as `SUBJ::1.PL`.

3.6 Disjunctions

Disjunctions between properties can indicated with the pipe (`|`) operator and grouping can be indicated with square brackets. The `|` operator binds more closely than the `.` operator. Thus, English *you* may be glossed (out of context) as `2.SG|PL.NOM|ACC` (second person, singular or plural and nominative or accusative. Square brackets can be used for grouping. German *sie* can be glossed (out of context) as `3.[SG.FEM]|[PL.NOM|ACC]` (third person, either feminine singular or unspecified for gender and plural and either nominative or accusative). Disjunctions are to be used when the exact analysis of a wordform, in context, is not clear to an annotator. In general, their use should be minimized as the quality of the annotations improves.

3.7 Translations

Each discourse segment should be accompanied by an idiomatic translation into the metalanguage.

3.8 Parsing GGG

Parsing GGG is more complicated than parsing Xigt because GGG is, effectively, an $A^n B^n C^n$ language. To validate or parse GGG, one must ensure that three sequences, `lx`, `sr`, and `gl`, are the same length (when split into tokens on white space). This means that context-free parsing for GGG is not possible. This adds some overhead to writing tools for GGG. However, we have written parsing, generation, and validation tools for GGG without excessive investments.[7]

4 Linguistic Adequacy

The adequacy of GGG for annotating concatenative morphology is identical to that of LGR, since the mechanism is borrowed from LGR directly. The only modification is that morphemes within a word are divided by spaces in addition to hyphens and equal signs. This means that the headedness of compounds must be stated explicitly (with dependents treated like affixes).

The GGG approach, however, has a distinct advantage in the treatment of non-concatenative morphology, as it is able to achieve complete adequacy (though not theoretical correctness or depth of generalization) through the use of a single annotation mechanism: {A?>B?(;C)?}. We show that the convention works well for infixation, reduplication, truncation, apophony, tonal overwriting, segmental overwriting, transfixation, and other similar processes.

4.1 Infixation

Infixation involves the inserting of a morpheme into a morpheme. Take the following examples from Ulwa, a Misumalpan language of Nicaragua. Possessives are denoted by affixes such as "ka" (3.SG) and "ki" (1.SG), which may occur as either suffixes or infixes depending on the syllable structure of the word. Therefore, in all of these cases, we are treating the affixes as morphological processes. McCarthy and Prince (1993)

```
-
  lx: "wahai{>ki}"
  sr: "wahai{ki}"
  gl: "brother{POSS::1.SG}"
  tr: "my brother"
-
  lx: "sû{>ki}lu"
  sr: "sû{ki}lu"
  gl: "dog{POSS::1.SG}"
  tr: "my dog"
```

Using LGR, the first two URs would be annotated as `wahai<ki>` and `sû<ki>lu`. Consider a similar example from Latin:

[6] See, also `https://unimorph.github.io/schema/`

[7] See `https://github.com/cmu-llab/generalized-glossing-guidelines`.

Operation	GGG	LGR	Xigt
prefix	un- likely NEG- likely	un-likely NEG-likely	✓
suffix	Kind -er child -PL	Kind-er child-PL	✓
infix	sû{>ki}lu dog{1.SG}	sû<ki>lu dog<1.SG>	✓
prefixing reduplication	{>su}sulat write{PROSP}	su~sulat PROSP~write	✓
infixing reduplication	ma{>m}vit̪ lion{PL}	?	✓
suffixing reduplication	kuk{>uk} bark{PROG}	kuk~uk bark~PROG	✓
subtractive morphology	nyoo{n>} lamb{PL}	✗	✗
apophony	c{ea>i}nn head{PL}	cinn head\PL	✗
tonal overwriting	xi{3>4}xi3 eat{HAB}	✗	✗
segmental overwriting	{ki>ka}3{xa>sa}3 do{IRR; 1,2}	✗	✗
transfixation	k{i>u}t{a:>u}b book{PL;1,2}	✗	✓
score	11	6.5	7

Table 3: Comparison of the representation of different morphological processes by glossing convention.

```
-
  lx: "ta{>n}g{>o}"
  sr: "ta{n}g{o}"
  gl: "touch{1.SG.PRS.IND}"
  tr: "I touch."
```

Both of these systems are equally adequate for representing infixation (at least of this kind). Infixing reduplication, however, is possibly a different matter, as shown in §4.2 below.

4.2 Reduplication

Reduplication refers to the realization of a morphological property by repeating material from a base. In this example from Mangap-Mbula, a VC-sequence is reduplicated after the base, to mark progressive aspect: (Bugenhagen, 1995)

```
-
  lx: "kuk{>uk}"
  sr: "kuk{uk}"
  gl: "bark{PROG}"
  tr: "be barking"
```

GGG can deal with relatively complex types of redupulication such as occur in Balsas Nahuatl[8], in which the repeated material can ultimately be realized as a high tone and/or a lengthened vowel (which are not necessarily contiguous):

```
-
  lx: "ti- ne:{>ó}ch- {>te}te:mowa -0"
  sr: "ti- ne:{ó}x- {te}te:mowa -0"
  gl: "SUBJ::2SG- OBJ::1SG- \
       {RED_H;1,2}look\_for -PRS.IND.SG"
  tr: "You look for me."
-
  lx: "ni- mi{>:ó}ts- te:mowa -0"
  sr: "ni- mi{:ó}s- te:mowa -0"
  gl: "SUBJ::1SG- OBJ::2SG- \
```

[8]The acute accent indicates a high tone. Unlike other varieties of Nahuatl, Balsas Nahuatl is tonal (Guion and Amith, 2005; Guion et al., 2010).

```
    {RED_H;1}look\_for -PRS.IND.SG"
  tr: "I look for you."
```

GGG is uniquely able to formalize Balsas Nahuatl reduplication with a fixed coda laryngeal (RDP_H), a reduplicant that can be realized on the the stem in various ways (first, third, and fourth examples) or on a prefix (second example). The commonality of all four cases is established by the common gloss: (RDP_H). Reduplication may be prefixing, suffixing, or infixing. The case of infixing reduplication is particularly problematic for LGR, since it is not clear which convention—the tilde convention for reduplication or the angle-bracket notation for infixation—should take precedence. In GGG, the notation is the same and this decision is not necessary. Take the following example from Pima (Riggle, 2006):

```
-
  lx: "ma{>m}vit̪"
  sr: "ma{m}vit̪"
  gl: "lion{PL}"
  tr: "lions"
-
  lx: "tʃɨ{>tʃ}mait̪"
  sr: "tʃɨ{tʃ}mait̪"
  gl: "drum{PL}"
  tr: "drums"
```

A similar pattern of infixing reduplication can be found in Latin:

```
-
  ur: "s{>po}pond{>ī}"
  sr: "s{po}pond{ī}"
  gl: "perform{1.SG.PRF.IND;1,2}
```

4.3 Subtractive morphology

Subtractive morphology involves the deletion of a segmental material from a base. The Murle language in the Surmic family subtracts the last consonant of a noun to change it from singular to plural: (Arensen, 1982)

```
  lx: "nyoo{n>0}"
  sr: "nyoo{}"
  gl: "lamb{PL}"
  tr: "lambs"
-
  lx: "wawo{c>0}"
  sr: "wawo{}"
  gl: "white_heron{PL}"
  tr: "white herons"
```

There appears to be no standard way of notating this in LGR. In Xigt, we believe that subtractive morphology could be notated by aligning a gloss with an empty string, but this would make it indistinguishable from realizing a morphological property via no change to the form.

4.4 Apophony

Apophony refers to a process in which a morphological property is realized through an alternation in phonemes. Take the following examples from Irish, in which vowel alternation is used to turn singular nouns into plural (Fife and King, 2017).

```
-
  lx: "c{ea>i}nn"
  sr: "c{i}nn"
  gl: "head{PL}"
  tr: "heads"
-
  lx: "m{ui>a}r{>a}"
  sr: "m{a}r{a}"
  gl: "sea{PL;1,2}"
  tr: "seas"
```

Apophony in Totonac often involves consonants changes, like changing /ʃ/ to /s/:

```
-
  lx: "{ʃ>s}kú'ta'"
  sr: "{s}kú'ta'"
  gl: "sour{DIM}"
  tr: "a little sour"
-
  lx: "{ʃ>s}uːni'"
  sr: "{s}uːni'"
  gl: "bitter{DIM}"
  tr: "a little bitter"
```

LGR allows one to indicate that apophonony affects a morpheme, but does not apply a notation for specifying its locus. Apparently Xigt has no way to distinguish apophony from infixation.

4.5 Tonal overwriting

Tonal overwriting refers to the class of morphological processes in which a tonal "affix" overwrites the existing tonal melody on a base. Examples from Yoloxóchitl Mixtec—which uses tonal overwriting to indicate different verbal inflections, such as habitual and negative—follow:

```
-
  lx: "ta'{3>1>4}bi{>1}4"
```

```
sr: "ta'{4}bi{14}"
gl: "get-broken{HAB;1,2}"
tr: "habitually get broken"
```

In Xigt, there is not a clear way of distinguishing these changes from infixation. In LGR, these can be represented with the backslash notation used for apophony, with the same drawbacks.

4.6 Segmental overwriting

Tonal overwriting is fairly common. The analogous segmental process—in which a string of segments is overwritten by other segments—is relatively rare, but does exist. The following example from Yoloxóchitl Mixtec employs segmental overwriting to inflect a class of verbs as irrealis:

```
-
  lx: "{xi>ku}3xi3"
  sr: "{ku}3xi3"
  gl: "eat{IRR}"
  tr: "eat"
```

4.7 Transfixation

Transfixation involves interspersing affixal spans into a root morpheme. In Semitic languages such as Arabic and Hebrew, words are mostly associated with 3-consonant roots. In Arabic, *k-t-b* is a root meaning "write" and *d-r-s* is a root meaning "study". These roots are combined with patterns of vowels to form words.

Transfixation is particularly tricky to represent using LGR, and it is unclear which convention should be used to do so (the angle-bracket infix notation or the backslash non-concatenative notation). In GGG, all of the patterns inserted into the root are treated as morphological processes, using the bracket notation.

Take the following examples from Arabic, which show how different vowel patterns can distinguish between singular and plural nouns, as well as different forms of verbs.

```
  lx: "q{a>u}l{>uu}b"
  sr: "q{u}l{uu}b"
  gl: "heart{PL;1,2}"
  tr: "hearts"
-
  lx: "d{>a}r{>a}s{>a}"
  sr: "d{a}r{a}s{a}"
  gl: "study{PST;1,2}{3.SG.M;3}"
  tr: "he studied"
```

Transfixation can be combined with other processes as well. For example, gemination on the 2nd consonant of the root is used to turn a Form I verb into a causative Form II verb (Haspelmath and Sims, 2010).

```
-
  lx: "d{>a}r{>:}{>a}s{>a}"
  sr: "d{a}r{:}{a}s{a}"
  gl: "study{PST;1,3}{CAUS;2}{3.SG.M;4}"
  tr: "he taught"
```

A scorecard comparing the adequacy of GGG, LGR, and Xigt is shown in Table 3.

5 Conclusions

As should be clear from Table 1, most of the attested types of morphological processes can be represented in all three annotation formats. However, GGG has clear advantages in some areas. For example, if a linguist wants to know how nouns with a particular singular form are realized in the plural, without knowing in advance what processes are involved, they could discover this through relatively simple processing of GGG—because it is completely explicit. It would be immediately evident whether the process was a particular kind of apophony, reduplication, tonal overwriting, etc. For the other two annotation formats, this kind of research—if non-concatenative processes are involved—is considerably more complicated.

One cost, because of its explicitness, is that GGG annotation cannot be completed until a linguist has a thorough (though fundamental) analysis of a language's morphology. Our goal is to develop tools to facilitate this analysis: to go from basic recordings to interlinear annotations with reduced human intervention. We hope that GGG will be an important part of this ongoing work. But the benefits are great. We are currently using GGG with great success in our ongoing research and hope that other investigators will find it similarly useful.

Acknowledgments

We gratefully acknowledge the support of US National Science Foundation, grant number 2211951, numerous examples Mixtec examples from Rey Castillo Garcia, and generous contributions from three anonymous reviewers.

References

Jonathan E. Arensen. 1982. *Murle grammar*, volume 2 of *Occasional Papers in the Study of Sudanese Languages*. Summer Institute of Linguistics and University of Juba, Juba, Sudan.

Steven Bird, David S. Day, John S. Garofolo, John Henderson, Christophe Laprun, and Mark Y. Liberman. 2000. Atlas: A flexible and extensible architecture for linguistic annotation. *ArXiv*, cs.CL/0007022.

Steven Bird and Mark Y. Liberman. 1999. A formal framework for linguistic annotation. *ArXiv*, cs.CL/9903003.

R.D. Bugenhagen. 1995. *A Grammar of Mangap-Mbula: An Austronesian Language of Papua New Guinea*. Books Series. Department of Linguistics, Research School of Pacific and Asian Studies, Australian National University.

Bernard Comrie, Martin Haspelmath, and Balthasar Bickel. 2008. The leipzig glossing rules: Conventions for interlinear morpheme-by-morpheme glosses. *Department of Linguistics of the Max Planck Institute for Evolutionary Anthropology & the Department of Linguistics of the University of Leipzig. Retrieved January*, 28:2010.

James Fife and Gareth King. 2017. *Celtic (Indo-European)*, chapter 24. John Wiley & Sons, Ltd.

Michael Wayne Goodman, Joshua Crowgey, Fei Xia, and Emily M. Bender. 2015. Xigt: extensible interlinear glossed text for natural language processing. *Language Resources and Evaluation*, 49(2):455–485.

Susan G Guion and Jonathan D Amith. 2005. The effect of [h] on tonal development in nahuatl. *The Journal of the Acoustical Society of America*, 117(4):2490–2490.

Susan G Guion, Jonathan D Amith, Christopher S Doty, and Irina A Shport. 2010. Word-level prosody in balsas nahuatl: The origin, development, and acoustic correlates of tone in a stress accent language. *Journal of Phonetics*, 38(2):137–166.

M. Haspelmath and A.D. Sims. 2010. *Understanding Morphology*. Understanding language series. Hodder Education.

Charles Francis Hockett. 1954. Two models of grammatical description. *WORD*, 10:210–234.

Nancy Ide and Keith Suderman. 2007. Graf: A graph-based format for linguistic annotations. In *LAW@ACL*.

Kazuaki Maeda and Steven Bird. 2000. A formal framework for interlinear text. Paper presented at the workshop on Web-Based Language Documentation and Description.

John J McCarthy and Alan Prince. 1993. *Prosodic Morphology: Constraint Interaction and Satisfaction*. Linguistics Department Faculty Publication Series. 14. University of Massachusettes Amherst.

Jason Riggle. 2006. Infixing reduplication in pima and its theoretical consequences. *Natural Language & Linguistic Theory*, pages 857–891.

John Sylak-Glassman. 2016. The composition and use of the universal morphological feature schema (unimorph schema). Ms., Center for Language and Speech Processing, Johns Hopkins University.

JAMBU: A historical linguistic database for South Asian languages

Aryaman Arora
Georgetown University
aa2190@georgetown.edu

Adam Farris
Stanford University
adfarris@stanford.edu

Samopriya Basu
Simon Fraser University
samopriya_basu@sfu.ca

Suresh Kolichala
Microsoft
suresh.kolichala@gmail.com

Abstract

We introduce JAMBU, a cognate database of South Asian languages which unifies dozens of previous sources in a structured and accessible format. The database includes 287k lemmata from 602 lects, grouped together in 23k sets of cognates. We outline the data wrangling necessary to compile the dataset and train neural models for reflex prediction on the Indo-Aryan subset of the data. We hope that JAMBU is an invaluable resource for all historical linguists and Indologists, and look towards further improvement and expansion of the database.[1]

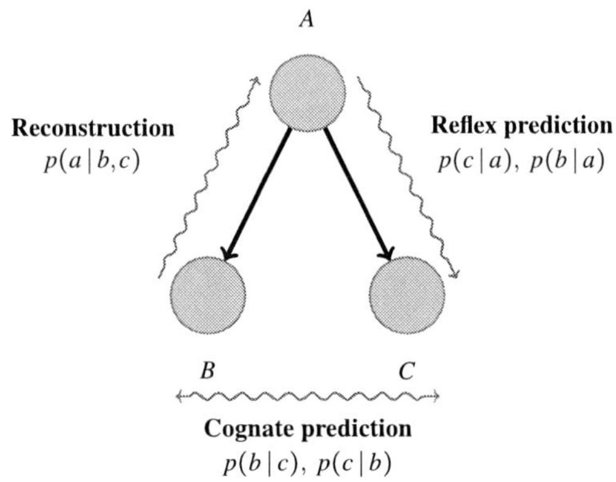

Figure 1: Three tasks of interest in computational historical linguistics. In this diagram, *A* is the ancestor language of *B* and *C*.

1 Introduction

A particular concern of historical linguists is studying relatedness and contact between languages. Two languages are related if they share words the arose from a common source, having undergone (potentially different) regular sound changes.[2] For example, the German words *schlafen* and *Schiff* are cognate to the English words *sleep* and *ship* respectively, with the German words having undergone the sound change /p/ → /f/. Using evidence like this from all of the Germanic languages, historical linguists have reconstructed the historical words that gave rise to these terms: **slāpan* and **skipą* (Kroonen, 2013).

Computational historical linguistics is a growing field that seeks to apply modern computational methods to studying this kind of change (Jäger, 2019; List, 2023). Massive datasets of multilingual cognates are necessary for much of the current research in this area, e.g. on multilingual cognate detection and phoneme-level alignment (List et al., 2018) and automatic comparative reconstruction of historical ancestors of languages (Ciobanu and Dinu, 2018).

South Asia[3] as a region is home to a complex historical mesh of language contact and change, especially between the Indo-Aryan and Dravidian language families (Masica, 1976). Yet, South Asia is relatively understudied by linguists compared to the linguistic diversity of the region (Arora et al., 2022). There is no cross-family lexical dataset to facilitate computational study on South Asian historical and contact linguistics. In order to improve this unfortunate state of affairs, we introduce the **JAMBU** cognate database for South Asian languages. JAMBU includes all cognacy information from the major printed etymological dictionaries for the Indo-Aryan (Turner, 1962–1966) and Dravidian (Burrow and Emeneau, 1984) languages, as well as data from several more recent sources. In this paper, we introduce and analyse our database and train neural models on the reflex prediction task. We hope that this resource brings us closer to the ultimate goal of understanding how the lan-

[1]The entire dataset is available at `https://github.com/moli-mandala/data`, and a web interface for browsing it is at `https://neojambu.herokuapp.com/`.

[2]Per the Neogrammarian hypothesis, sound changes are regular and *exceptionless* (Osthoff and Brugmann, 1878; Paul, 1880). The reality of sound change is sometimes less ideal.

[3]When using the term *South Asia* we refer to the Indian Subcontinent.

Proceedings of the 20th SIGMORPHON workshop on Computational Research in Phonetics, Phonology, and Morphology, pages 68–77
July 14, 2023

guages of South Asia have evolved and interacted over time.

2 Related work

CLDF format. CLDF was proposed by Forkel et al. (2018) as a standard, yet highly flexible, format for linguistic data (including cognate databases, etymological dictionaries with reconstructions, and even dictionaries). We use this format for the JAMBU database. Many etymological databases use CLDF to effectively encode complex relations (e.g. loaning) and metadata (e.g. references, phonetic forms, alignments). Some which informed our database design were Rankin et al. (2015); Greenhill et al. (2008).

Cognates. Batsuren et al. (2019) compiled a *cognate database* covering 338 languages from Wiktionary. They noted that the meaning of *cognate* varies between research communities—for our purposes as historical linguists, we prefer grouping terms with shared direct etymological sources, while much computational work (e.g. Kondrak et al., 2003) takes a broader definition which includes loanwords or even all semantic equivalents as cognates.

As shown in figure 1, computational historical linguistics has taken on tasks involving cognates such as automatic *cognate identification* from wordlists (Rama et al., 2018; List et al., 2018; Rama, 2016), *cognate/reflex prediction*, i.e. predicting the form of a cognate in another language based on concurrent or historical data (List et al., 2022; Bodt and List, 2022; Fourrier et al., 2021; Marr and Mortensen, 2020), and *reconstruction* of the ancestor form of a cognate set (Durham and Rogers, 1969; Bouchard et al., 2007; Ciobanu and Dinu, 2018; Meloni et al., 2021; He et al., 2022, *inter alia*).

Other South Asian cognate databases. Cathcart (2019a,b, 2020) and Cathcart and Rama (2020) also previously made use of data from Turner (1962–1966) by scraping the version hosted online by *Digitial Dictionaries of South Asia*.

There was an effort to create a new digital South Asian etymological dictionary in the early 2000s, termed the **SARVA** (South Asian Residual Vocabulary Assemblage) project (Southworth, 2005a). This was unsuccessful however, and only a small portion of the possible cross-family entries were complete. Our database does not incorporate it.

	Languages	Cognate sets	Lemmata
Indo-Aryan	433	16,464	194,834
Dravidian	78	5,649	78,502
Nuristani	22	3,645	12,088
Other	52	163	311
Munda	15	129	1,352
Burushaski	2	41	48
Total	602	23,024	287,135

Table 1: Statistics about the JAMBU database, factored by language family. **Cognate sets** counts the number of such sets that include at least one cognate from that family (and so does not sum to the total).

3 Database

The JAMBU database incorporates data from three major language families of South Asia: Indo-European (the Indo-Aryan and Nuristani subbranches), Dravidian, and Austroasiatic (the Munda subbranch). This comes out to 287k lemmata from 602 lects across 23k cognate sets (table 1).

The data is stored in the CLDF structured data format. The overall database structure is described in the file `Wordlist-metadata.json`, which includes information about the type of data recorded in each column of each file. The file `forms.csv` includes all lemmata (word form) and associated etymological and linguistic information. The files `parameters.csv` and `cognates.csv` include all cognateset headwords and etymological notes for each. The file `languages.csv` lists all languages in the database and their geographical location. Finally, `sources.bib` lists all data references in BibTeX format.

For each lemma in `forms.csv`, we store the following information: a unique *form ID*; the *language ID*; the *cognate set ID*, linking it to other cognate lemmata; a *normalised* representation of the lemma itself, using our transcription scheme; a *gloss* in English; the spelling of the lemma in the *native script*; the phonemic *IPA* representation of the lemma; the *unnormalised* form of the lemma taken from the original source; a finer-grained *cognate set ID*; *notes*; and *references*.

For each cognate set, we store a **headword**, which is usually a common ancestor of the words in that cognateset or a reconstruction of that ancestor if possible. We also store desiderata such as definitions and etymological notes.

Finally, we take an expansive view of what constitutes a "language" in our database. If a word is

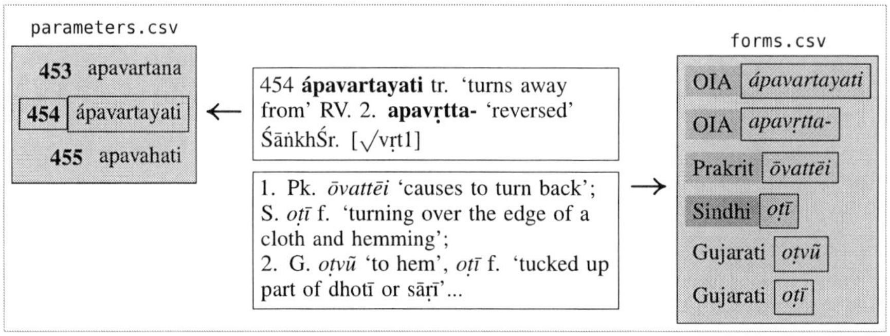

Figure 2: Diagram of some of the data in JAMBU parsed from CDIAL entry 454 (*ápavartayati*, 'turns away from').

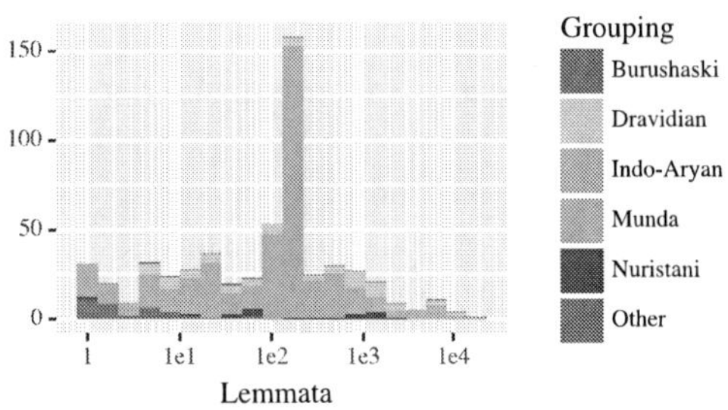

Figure 3: Distribution of languages by number of lemmata entered in JAMBU.

known to only be attested in a particular dialect, we list that dialect separately. For example, for the Shina language (northwestern Indo-Aryan), we list 32 geographical dialects. The distribution of languages by number of lemmata is depicted in figure 3.

3.1 Data sources and scraping

The two major data sources are CDIAL (Turner, 1962–1966) and DEDR (Burrow and Emeneau, 1984), which have been scraped in their entirety from web versions hosted by the University of Chicago's Digital Dictionaries of South Asia project.[4] Since the raw data is in HTML with limited structured markup, extracting CLDF-suitable data is a significant hurdle, including matching lemmata to the appropriate language and grouping associated metadata like grammatical gender and etymological notes under the correct form (figure 2). Further cleanup of data from these two sources will have to be done manually.

Since CDIAL and DEDR have not been updated in decades, we are also incorporating more recent sources that refer to them into our database, as well as etymologising newer fieldwork data manually. The additional sources we added (some partially) are listed in appendix B.

3.2 Transcriptions

One serious issue has been reconciling differing transcription systems from different sources; transcription schemes vary across sources even for the same language, since there is no standard transcription for South Asian linguistics. An illustrative example of this issue is the variable transcription of the labiodental fricative as *v* or *w*.

Turner (1962–1966) normalises entries from various sources into a relatively mundane Indological transcription, i.e., IAST[5] with many extensions for the varying phonologies of South Asian languages, but not always consistently. For example, the phoneme /eː/ is notated ⟨ē⟩ for Sanskrit entries, but ⟨e⟩ for Hindi (and in Burrow and Emeneau (1984), as ⟨é⟩ for Malto entries). Elsewhere, e.g., in Bengali and Punjabi, transcriptions adhere to the written form, which do not always adhere to any phonemic analysis of the languages in question. In the case of Kashmiri, Shina, and many other languages, there are now better analyses to base romanisation on than existed at the time of compilation of the sources of Turner (1962–1966). Meanwhile, (Burrow and Emeneau, 1984) does not attempt to conventionalise transcription at all, instead strictly copying the transcription from the original source; e.g. all Bengali entries strictly reflect spelling and do not indicate the differing surface realisations of the orthographic schwa (Johny and Jansche, 2018).

We created a new, more rigidly standardised transcription system based on Indological conventions to unify all our data. We did not want to use pure IPA because it obscures useful cross-lingual pat-

[4] https://dsal.uchicago.edu/dictionaries/

[5] https://en.wikipedia.org/wiki/International_Alphabet_of_Sanskrit_Transliteration

Language	Original	Normalised
Old Indo-Aryan	*anugr̥bhāyati	*anugr̥b^{h}āyati
European Romani	učhar	uc^{h}ar
Shumashti	ắšin	ǽśin
Palula	beedhríi	bēd^{h}rî
Pashai: Degano	dew'âz	devắz

Table 2: Examples showing how our orthographic normalisation process affected forms from various sources.

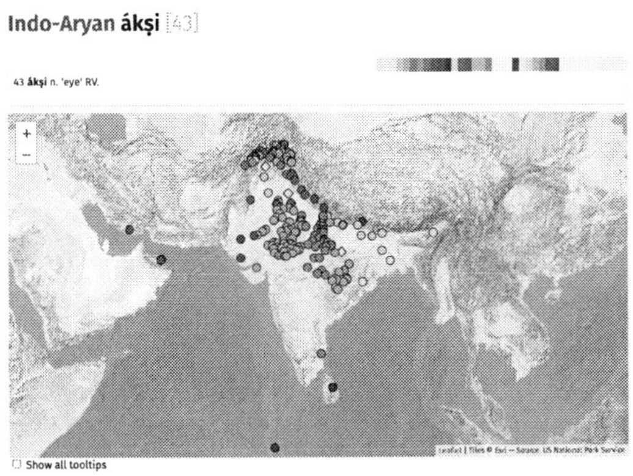

Figure 4: Web interface for Jambu, displaying reflexes of CDIAL entry 43 (*ákṣi*, 'eye'). See `https://neojambu.herokuapp.com/entries/43`.

terns[6] and is not conventional in the Indological research community (especially considering that the database may be of use to non-linguist Indologists as well). For that reason, we use a modified IAST (for instance, using a superscript ⟨^{h}⟩ to notate aspiration and breathy voice distinguishing these from genuine h-clusters) to suit cross-linguistic needs. Some contrasts are made more explicit while notational consistency is maintained across the board.

We used the `segments` Python library to create orthography normalisation profiles for each source's transcription scheme (Moran and Cysouw, 2018); some examples of the changes are shown in table 2. So far, forms from all source have not yet been orthographically standardised to our system. However, we developed standardisation scripts covering 204k lemmata, of which 99.7% were automatically converted without errors.

3.3 Web interface

Finally, we developed a web interface for the JAMBU database; see figure 4. Originally, we used the pre-existing `clld` webapp toolkit for the publication of Cross-Linguistic Linked Data,[7] but we later switched to a custom Flask web app designed from scratch in order to have finer control over the database structure and to execute searches on the backend more efficiently. This web interface supports search, filtering, and geographical visualisation. We hope this supersedes the unstructured search interfaces currently available for browsing older etymological dictionaries for these languages (Turner, 1962–1966; Burrow and Emeneau, 1984).

Model	Perplexity	BLEU	TER
GRU	2.57	55.91	**34.40**
Transformer	**2.53**	**56.03**	35.15

Table 3: Performance of the two models on reflex prediction on the Indo-Aryan segment of JAMBU.

4 Experiment

As a demonstration of the usability of the dataset for computational historical linguistics, we replicate the reflex prediction task of Cathcart and Rama (2020). We train neural models on the task of reflex prediction in Indo-Aryan languages, i.e. predicting the descendant of an Old Indo-Aryan word in a given Indo-Aryan language. Rather than being restricted to data from Turner (1962–1966), we can draw on all the sources present in JAMBU.

We train on 80% of the data and test on the remaining 20%. We compare two models: a bidirectional GRU encoder-decoder with Bahdanau attention and a transformer encoder-decoder with learned positional embeddings. The optimised hyperparameters for the GRU are a learning rate of $2 \cdot 10^{-3}$, 4 layers, and embedding and hidden size of 64. The transformer had a learning rate of 1 (using the parameter-based adjustment and warmup/decay schedule from Huang et al., 2022), 3 layers, 4 attention heads per layer, embedding size of 64, and FFN size of 128. Both models were trained for 50 epochs without early stopping with a batch size of 1024 on a single Quadro RTX 6000, with a run completing in about 15 minutes.

We evaluate BLEU and TER on the held-out set using the SacreBLEU implementation (Post, 2018), treating a single phoneme as a 'word'. Even after comprehensive hyperparameter tuning we find that both models achieve similar performances, per the results in table 3. We leave analysis of these models for future work.

[6] E.g. the Indological *a* (called a schwa) varies in pronunciation across South Asia, from [a̱] (Telugu) to [ɜ] (Hindi) to [ɔ~o] (Bengali) to [ʌ] (Nepali).

[7] `https://github.com/clld/clld`

5 Conclusion

In this paper, we introduced JAMBU, the largest and most up-to-date cognate database for South Asian languages. We are continuing to expand the database, incorporating all lexical data that has so far been unused in comparative linguistic work on the region. We believe that the open questions of South Asian historical linguistics cannot be resolved without examining all the information (both synchronic and diachronic) that linguists have collected about language of the region. The old etymological dictionaries are in desparate need of an update. However, much work remains. We briefly discuss some avenues of future work.

Many sources are yet to be incorporated, especially those recording loanwords from external languages (especially Persian, Arabic, English, and Portuguese) and from local literary languages (particularly Sanskrit). We have yet to distentangle cross-lectal interactions and mark lexical isoglosses, which seem necessary to understand the history of language interactions in the region; Kalyan et al. (2018)'s wave model of linguistic change has been thought by many scholars to be suited for South Asian languages, but it has not been operationalised yet due to a lack of comprehensive data (Toulmin, 2006; Kogan, 2017).

Another significant task ahead is extending our database structure to support indicating and analysing more complex cross-lingual interactions. For example, the database as it stands does not distinguish between inheritance from the parent language and loaning mediated by a sibling language.

We have also been working on a consistent orthography for tonemes in the languages where tones are contrastive, such as the northwestern Indo-Aryan languages (Baart, 2014). Older data from these languages either does not notate tone at all (for tonality was not yet recognized, as in Gawri and Torwali), or represents it indirectly through diachronically correct, but synchronically confusing, spelling systems (as in Punjabi and Kishtwari). So, our work will also involve analyzing and incorporating new data from tonal languages, both from existing sources and our own fieldwork.

Finally, we hope to manually improve data quality once the parsing of old sources is stable. This includes fixing known mistakes, reorganising entries to better indicate indirect derivations and cross-lectal loans, and etymological notes that summarise the extant literature.

References

Binny Abraham, Binoy Koshy, and Vimal Raj R. 2012. Sociolinguistic survey of selected Rajasthani speech varieties of Rajasthan, India, volume 2: Mewari. *Journal of Language Survey Reports*.

Said Al Jahdhami. 2017. Zadjali: The dying language. *International Journal of Language and Linguistics*, 4.

Said Humaid Al Jahdhami. 2022. Maimani language and Lawati language: Two sides of the same coin? *Journal of Modern Languages*, 32(1):37–57.

Aryaman Arora and Ahmed Etebari. 2020–2021. Kholosi dictionary.

Aryaman Arora, Adam Farris, Samopriya Basu, and Suresh Kolichala. 2022. Computational historical linguistics and language diversity in South Asia. In *Proceedings of the 60th Annual Meeting of the Association for Computational Linguistics (Volume 1: Long Papers)*, pages 1396–1409, Dublin, Ireland. Association for Computational Linguistics.

Joan Baart. 2014. Tone and stress in north-west Indo-Aryan. *Above and beyond the segments: Experimental linguistics and Phonetics, Amsterdam: John Benjamins*, pages 1–13.

Joan L. G. Baart. 1997. *The sounds and tones of Kalam Kohistani: with wordlist and texts*. National Institute of Pakistan Studies, Quaid-i-Azam University and Summer Institute of Linguistics, Islamabad.

Peter C. Backstrom and Carla F. Radloff. 1992. *Sociolinguistic Survey of Northern Pakistan, Volume 2. Languages of Northern Areas*. National Institute of Pakistan Studies, Islamabad.

Khuyagbaatar Batsuren, Gábor Bella, and Fausto Giunchiglia. 2019. CogNet: A large-scale cognate database. In *Proceedings of the 57th Annual Meeting of the Association for Computational Linguistics*, pages 3136–3145, Florence, Italy. Association for Computational Linguistics.

Theodor Gipson Benjamin and Liahey Ngwazah. 2012. Sociolinguistic survey of selected Rajasthani speech varieties of Rajasthan, India, volume 5: Dhundari and Shekhawati. *Journal of Language Survey Reports*.

Hermann Berger. 1998. *Die Burushaski-Sprache von Hunza und Nager*. Harrassowitz.

Murli D. Bhawnani. 1979. *Descriptive analysis of Thari: A dialect of Sindhi language*. Ph.D. thesis, Deccan College Post Graduate and Research Institute Pune, Pune.

Timotheus A. Bodt and Johann-Mattis List. 2022. Reflex prediction: A case study of Western Kho-Bwa. *Diachronica*, 39(1):1–38.

Ed Boehm. 2017. *A Sociolinguistic Profile of Bundeli*. Journal of Language Survey Reports. SIL International, Dallas, Texas.

Edward Daniel Boehm. 1998. A phonological reconstruction of Proto-Tharu. Master's thesis, The University of Texas at Arlington.

Kelly Kilgo Boehm. 2002. *A Preliminary Sociolinguistic Survey of the Chhattisgarhi-Speaking Peoples of India*. SIL International, Dallas, Texas.

Alexandre Bouchard, Percy Liang, Thomas Griffiths, and Dan Klein. 2007. A probabilistic approach to diachronic phonology. In *Proceedings of the 2007 Joint Conference on Empirical Methods in Natural Language Processing and Computational Natural Language Learning (EMNLP-CoNLL)*, pages 887–896, Prague, Czech Republic. Association for Computational Linguistics.

Thomas Burrow and Murray Barnson Emeneau. 1984. *A Dravidian Etymological Dictionary*, 2 edition. Clarendon Press, Oxford.

Chundra Cathcart. 2019a. Gaussian process models of sound change in Indo-Aryan dialectology. In *Proceedings of the 1st International Workshop on Computational Approaches to Historical Language Change*, pages 254–264, Florence, Italy. Association for Computational Linguistics.

Chundra Cathcart. 2019b. Toward a deep dialectological representation of Indo-Aryan. In *Proceedings of the Sixth Workshop on NLP for Similar Languages, Varieties and Dialects*, pages 110–119, Ann Arbor, Michigan. Association for Computational Linguistics.

Chundra Cathcart. 2020. A probabilistic assessment of the Indo-Aryan Inner–Outer Hypothesis. *Journal of Historical Linguistics*, 10(1):42–86.

Chundra Cathcart and Taraka Rama. 2020. Disentangling dialects: a neural approach to Indo-Aryan historical phonology and subgrouping. In *Proceedings of the 24th Conference on Computational Natural Language Learning*, pages 620–630, Online. Association for Computational Linguistics.

Sajayan Chacko and Liahey Ngwazah. 2012. Sociolinguistic survey of selected Rajasthani speech varieties of Rajasthan, India, volume 6: Marwari, Merwari, and Godwari. *Journal of Language Survey Reports*.

Alina Maria Ciobanu and Liviu P. Dinu. 2018. Ab initio: Automatic Latin proto-word reconstruction. In *Proceedings of the 27th International Conference on Computational Linguistics*, pages 1604–1614, Santa Fe, New Mexico, USA. Association for Computational Linguistics.

Stanton P. Durham and David Ellis Rogers. 1969. An application of computer programming to the reconstruction of a proto-language. In *International Conference on Computational Linguistics COLING 1969: Preprint No. 5*, Sånga Säby, Sweden.

Josef Elfenbein. 1994. Notes on Khetrāni phonology. *Studien zur Indologie und Iranistik*, 19:71–82.

M. B. Emeneau and T. Burrow. 1962. *Dravidian Borrowings from Indo-Aryan*. Number 26 in University of California Publications in Linguistics. University of California Press, Berkeley.

Robert Forkel, Johann-Mattis List, Simon J Greenhill, Christoph Rzymski, Sebastian Bank, Michael Cysouw, Harald Hammarström, Martin Haspelmath, Gereon A Kaiping, and Russell D Gray. 2018. Cross-Linguistic Data Formats, advancing data sharing and re-use in comparative linguistics. *Scientific data*, 5(1):1–10.

Clémentine Fourrier, Rachel Bawden, and Benoît Sagot. 2021. Can cognate prediction be modelled as a low-resource machine translation task? In *Findings of the Association for Computational Linguistics: ACL-IJCNLP 2021*, pages 847–861, Online. Association for Computational Linguistics.

Sonja Fritz. 2002. *The Dhivehi language: a descriptive and historical grammar of Maldivian and its dialects*. Ergon-Verlag.

Harjeet Singh Gill. 1973. *Linguistic atlas of the Punjab*. Munshiram Manoharlal Publishers, Delhi.

Simon J. Greenhill, Robert Blust, and Russell D. Gray. 2008. The Austronesian Basic Vocabulary Database: From bioinformatics to lexomics. *Evolutionary Bioinformatics*, 4:EBO.S893. PMID: 19204825.

Andre He, Nicholas Tomlin, and Dan Klein. 2022. Neural unsupervised reconstruction of protolanguage word forms. *arXiv*, abs/2211.08684.

Austin Huang, Suraj Subramanian, Jonathan Sum, Khalid Almubarak, and Stella Biderman. 2022. The annotated transformer.

Mathews John and Bezily P. Varghese. 2021. The Kannauji-speaking people of Uttar Pradesh: A sociolinguistic profile. *Journal of Language Survey Reports*.

Cibu C Johny and Martin Jansche. 2018. Brahmic schwa-deletion with neural classifiers: Experiments with bengali. In *Proc. The 6th Intl. Workshop on Spoken Language Technologies for Under-Resourced Languages*, pages 259–263.

Thomas Jouanne. 2014. *A Preliminary Analysis of the Phonological System of the Western Pahāṛī Language of Kvār*. Ph.D. thesis, University of Oslo, Oslo.

Gerhard Jäger. 2019. Computational historical linguistics. *Theoretical Linguistics*, 45(3–4):151–182.

Siva Kalyan, Alexandre François, et al. 2018. Freeing the comparative method from the tree model: A framework for historical glottometry. *Senri Ethnological Studies*, 98:59–89.

Masato Kobayashi. 2022. Proto-Dravidian origins of the Kuṛux-Malto past stems. *Bhasha. Journal of South Asian Linguistics, Philology and Grammatical Traditions*, 1(2):263–282.

Anton I Kogan. 2017. Genealogical classification of New Indo-Aryan languages and lexicostatistics. *Journal of Language Relationship*, 14(3–4):227–258.

Grzegorz Kondrak, Daniel Marcu, and Kevin Knight. 2003. Cognates can improve statistical translation models. In *Companion Volume of the Proceedings of HLT-NAACL 2003 - Short Papers*, pages 46–48.

Binoy Koshy. 2012. Sociolinguistic survey of selected Rajasthani speech varieties of Rajasthan, India, volume 3: Hadothi. *Journal of Language Survey Reports*.

Guus Kroonen. 2013. *Etymological Dictionary of Proto-Germanic*. Leiden Indo-European Etymological Dictionary Series; 11. Brill, Leiden, Boston.

Henrik Liljegren. 2013. Notes on Kalkoti: A Shina language with strong Kohistani influences. *Linguistic Discovery*, 11(1):129–160.

Henrik Liljegren. 2019. Palula dictionary. *Dictionaria*, (3):1–2700.

Johann-Mattis List. 2023. Computational historical linguistics.

Johann-Mattis List, Ekaterina Vylomova, Robert Forkel, Nathan Hill, and Ryan Cotterell. 2022. The SIGTYP 2022 shared task on the prediction of cognate reflexes. In *Proceedings of the 4th Workshop on Research in Computational Linguistic Typology and Multilingual NLP*, pages 52–62, Seattle, Washington. Association for Computational Linguistics.

Johann-Mattis List, Mary Walworth, Simon J Greenhill, Tiago Tresoldi, and Robert Forkel. 2018. Sequence comparison in computational historical linguistics. *Journal of Language Evolution*, 3(2):130–144.

Clayton Marr and David R. Mortensen. 2020. Computerized forward reconstruction for analysis in diachronic phonology, and Latin to French reflex prediction. In *Proceedings of LT4HALA 2020 - 1st Workshop on Language Technologies for Historical and Ancient Languages*, pages 28–36, Marseille, France. European Language Resources Association (ELRA).

Colin P. Masica. 1976. *Defining a Linguistic Area: South Asia*. University of Chicago Press.

Eldose K. Mathai. 2011. Bagri of Rajasthan, Punjab, and Haryana: A sociolinguistic survey. *Journal of Language Survey Reports*.

Eldose K. Mathai. 2012. Sociolinguistic survey of selected Rajasthani speech varieties of Rajasthan, India, volume 4: Mewati. *Journal of Language Survey Reports*.

Carlo Meloni, Shauli Ravfogel, and Yoav Goldberg. 2021. Ab antiquo: Neural proto-language reconstruction. In *Proceedings of the 2021 Conference of the North American Chapter of the Association for Computational Linguistics: Human Language Technologies*, pages 4460–4473, Online. Association for Computational Linguistics.

Steven Moran and Michael Cysouw. 2018. *The Unicode Cookbook for Linguists: Managing writing systems using orthography profiles*. Language Science Press.

Ram Dayal Munda. 1968. Proto-Kherwarian phonology. Master's thesis, University of Chicago.

Hermann Osthoff and Karl Brugmann. 1878. *Morphologische Untersuchungen auf dem Gebiete der indogermanischen Sprachen*. Hirzel, Leipzig, Germany.

Hukam Chand Patyal. 1982. Etymological notes on some Maṇḍyāḷī words (Indo-Aryan Studies II). *Indo-Iranian Journal*, 24:289–294.

Hukam Chand Patyal. 1983. Etymological notes on some Maṇḍyāḷī words (Indo-Aryan Studies IV). *Indo-Iranian Journal*, 25:41–49.

Hukam Chand Patyal. 1984. Etymological notes on some Maṇḍyāḷī words (Indo-Aryan Studies V). *Indo-Iranian Journal*, 27:121–132.

Hukam Chand Patyal. 1991. Etymological notes on some Ḍogri words (Indo-Aryan Studies III). *Indo-Iranian Journal*, 34:123–124.

Hermann Paul. 1880. *Prinzipien der Sprachgeschichte*. Max Niemeyer, Halle, Germany.

Martin Pfeiffer. 2018. *Kurux Historical Phonology Reconsidered: With a Reconstruction of Pre-Kurux-Malto Phonology*. PubliQation.

Matt Post. 2018. A call for clarity in reporting BLEU scores. In *Proceedings of the Third Conference on Machine Translation: Research Papers*, pages 186–191, Belgium, Brussels. Association for Computational Linguistics.

Taraka Rama. 2016. Siamese convolutional networks for cognate identification. In *Proceedings of COLING 2016, the 26th International Conference on Computational Linguistics: Technical Papers*, pages 1018–1027, Osaka, Japan. The COLING 2016 Organizing Committee.

Taraka Rama, Johann-Mattis List, Johannes Wahle, and Gerhard Jäger. 2018. Are automatic methods for cognate detection good enough for phylogenetic reconstruction in historical linguistics? In *Proceedings of the 2018 Conference of the North American Chapter of the Association for Computational Linguistics: Human Language Technologies, Volume 2 (Short Papers)*, pages 393–400, New Orleans, Louisiana. Association for Computational Linguistics.

Robert L. Rankin, Richard T. Carter, A. Wesley Jones, John E. Koontz, David S. Rood, and Iren Hartmann, editors. 2015. *Comparative Siouan Dictionary*. Max Planck Institute for Evolutionary Anthropology, Leipzig.

Felix Rau. 2019. Munda cognate set with proto-munda reconstructions.

Khawaja A. Rehman and Joan L. G. Baart. 2005. A first look at the language of Kundal Shahi in Azad Kashmir. *SIL Electronic Working Papers*.

Ruth Laila Schmidt and Vijay Kumar Kaul. 2008. A comparative analysis of Shina and Kashmiri vocabularies. *Acta Orientalia*, 69:231–302.

Christopher Shackle. 1995. *A Guru Nanak Glossary*. Routledge.

F. C. Southworth. 2005a. The SARVA (South Asia Residual Vocabulary Assemblage) project.

Franklin C. Southworth. 2005b. Prehistoric implications of the Dravidian element in the NIA lexicon with special reference to Marathi. *International Journal of Dravidian Linguistics*, 34(1):17–28.

Franklin C Southworth. 2006. Proto-Dravidian agriculture. In *Proceedings of the Pre-symposium of Rihn and 7th ESCA Harvard-Kyoto Roundtable. Research Institute for Humanity and Nature, Kyoto*, pages 121–150.

Richard F. Strand. 1997–2021. Nuristân: Hidden land of the Hindu-Kush.

Matthew William Stirling Toulmin. 2006. *Reconstructing linguistic history in a dialect continuum: The Kamta, Rajbanshi, and Northern Deshi Bangla subgroup of Indo-Aryan*. Ph.D. thesis, The Australian National University.

Ralph Lilley Turner. 1962–1966. *A comparative dictionary of the Indo-Aryan languages*. Oxford University Press, London.

Govindaswamy Srinivasa Varma. 1970. *Vaagri boli, an Indo-Aryan language*. Ph.D. thesis, Annamalai University.

Stephen Watters. 2013. A sociolinguistic profile of the Bhils of northern Dhule district. *Journal of Language Survey Reports*.

Claus Peter Zoller. 2005. *A grammar and dictionary of Indus Kohistani: Dictionary*, volume 1. Walter de Gruyter.

Saeed Zubair. 2016. A phonological description of Wadiyari, a language spoken in Pakistan. Master's thesis, Payap University, Chiang Mai, Thailand.

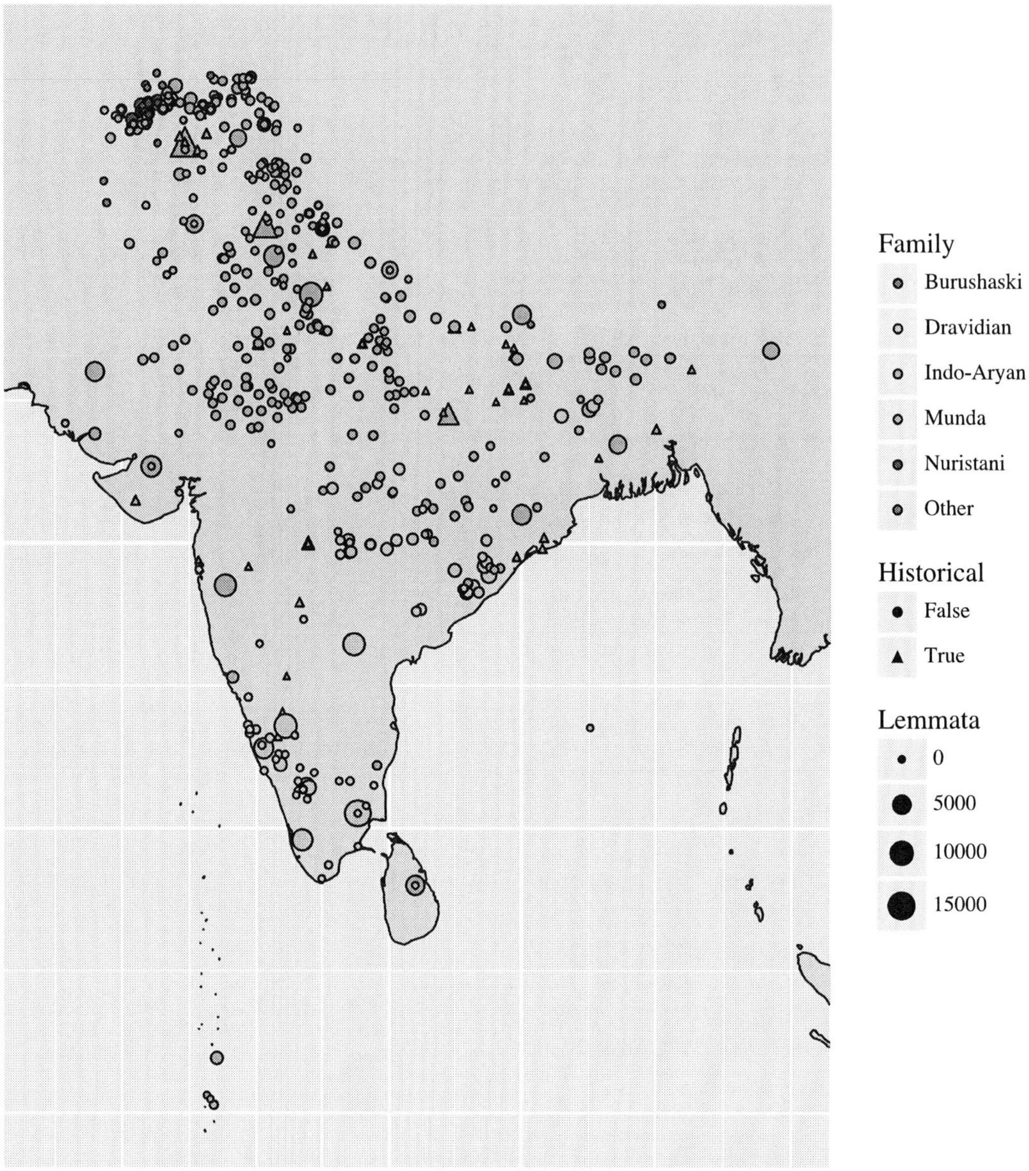

Figure 5: Map of South Asian languages present in JAMBU, coloured by phylogenetic grouping and sized by number of lemmata included in the database. 74 lects (mostly varieties of Romani, an Indo-Aryan language, spoken in Europe and the Middle East) are not visible within the bounds of this map.

A Licensing

Data from Burrow and Emeneau (1984) and Turner (1962–1966) has been scraped using the approval of the SARVA project (of which one of the authors was previously involved in) for strictly academic purposes. Additional data added to the dataset has either been manually etymologised (and therefore is an original academic contribution) or obtained with permission of the respective authors.

B Other data sources

Language(s)	Reference	Etymologised?	In JAMBU?
Burushaski	Berger (1998)	✓	†
Dravidian	Burrow and Emeneau (DEDR; 1984)	✓	✓
	Emeneau and Burrow (DBIA; 1962)	✓	
	Southworth (2006)	✓	✓
	Southworth (2005b)	✓	✓
Kurux, Malto	Kobayashi (2022)	✓	†
	Pfeiffer (2018)	✓	†
Indo-Aryan	Turner (CDIAL; 1962–1966)	✓	✓
Bagri	Mathai (2011)		✓
Bhil	Watters (2013)		
Bundeli	Boehm (2017)		✓
Chhattisgarhi	Boehm (2002)		✓
Dhivehi	Fritz (2002)	✓	✓
Dogri	Patyal (1991)	✓	✓
Gawri	Baart (1997)		✓
Indus Kohistani	Zoller (2005)	✓	
Kalkoti	Liljegren (2013)		✓
Kamtapuri, etc.	Toulmin (2006)	✓	✓
Kannauji	John and Varghese (2021)		†
Khetrani	Elfenbein (1994)		✓
Kholosi	Arora and Etebari (2020–2021)	✓	✓
Kundal Shahi	Rehman and Baart (2005)		✓
Kvari	Jouanne (2014)		✓
Maimani, Luwati	Al Jahdhami (2022)		†
Mandeali	Patyal (1982, 1983, 1984)	✓	✓
Palula	Liljegren (2019)	✓	✓
Punjabi, etc.	Gill (1973)		†
	Shackle (1995)	✓	†
Rajasthani	Abraham et al. (2012)		✓
	Benjamin and Ngwazah (2012)		✓
	Chacko and Ngwazah (2012)		✓
	Koshy (2012)		✓
	Mathai (2012)		✓
Shina, Domaaki	Backstrom and Radloff (1992)		✓
Shina, Kashmiri	Schmidt and Kaul (2008)		†
Thari	Bhawnani (1979)		†
Tharu	Boehm (1998)		✓
Vaagri Boli	Varma (1970)	✓	†
Wadiyara Koli	Zubair (2016)		†
Zadjali	Al Jahdhami (2017)		✓
Munda	Rau (2019)	✓	✓
	Munda (1968)	✓	
Nuristani	Strand (1997–2021)	✓	✓

Table 4: All sources included in JAMBU, grouped together by language and family. **Etymologised?** indicates whether the original sources provided etymologies for the terms it listed; if not, we manually proposed etymologies. **In JAMBU?** indicates what portion of the work has been incorporated into the current version of the database; ✓ means entirely while † means partially.

Lightweight morpheme labeling in context: Using structured linguistic representations to support linguistic analysis for the language documentation context

Bhargav Shandilya and Alexis Palmer
University of Colorado Boulder
{bhargav.shandilya,alexis.palmer}@colorado.edu

Abstract

Linguistic analysis is a core task in the process of documenting, analyzing, and describing endangered and less-studied languages. In addition to providing insight into the properties of the language being studied, having tools to automatically label words in a language for grammatical category and morphological features can support a range of applications useful for language pedagogy and revitalization. At the same time, most modern NLP methods for these tasks require both large amounts of data in the language and compute costs well beyond the capacity of most research groups and language communities.

In this paper, we present a **gloss-to-gloss (g2g)** model for linguistic analysis (specifically, morphological analysis and part-of-speech tagging) that is lightweight in terms of both data requirements and computational expense.

The model is designed for the interlinear glossed text (IGT) format, in which we expect the source text of a sentence in a low-resource language, a translation of that sentence into a language of wider communication, and a detailed glossing of the morphological properties of each word in the sentence. We first produce silver standard parallel glossed data by automatically labeling the high-resource translation. The model then learns to transform source language morphological labels into output labels for the target language, mediated by a structured linguistic representation layer. We test the model on both low-resource and high-resource languages, and find that our simple CNN-based model achieves comparable performance to a state-of-the-art transformer-based model, at a fraction of the computational cost.

1 Introduction

Linguistic analysis is a core task in the documentation, analysis, and description of endangered and less-studied languages. One frequent goal of language documentation projects is to produce a corpus of **interlinear glossed texts**, or IGT (Figure 1 shows an example from the Mayan language Uspanteko). IGT can take many different forms, but canonically consists of the target language sentence, morphological segmentation of each word, glossing of each word with its stem translation and any relevant morphosyntactic features, and a translation into a language of wider communication.

xk'amch			ritz'iq+	
x-	k'am	-ch	r-	itz'yeq
COM	recibir	MOV	E3	ropa
trajeron ropa				

Figure 1: Example of IGT: Uspanteko (usp) sentence.

In addition to providing insight into the properties of the language being studied, the linguistic information in IGT can support a range of applications useful for language teaching and revitalization. Modern NLP methods typically require both large amounts of annotated data in the target language and compute resources beyond the capacity of most research groups and language communities. In this paper we address the task of **lightweight** morpheme labeling in context (McCarthy et al., 2019), developing a model which achieves reasonable accuracy with minimal requirements for *both* labeled data and computational expense.

Following previous work (Moeller and Hulden, 2021; Moeller et al., 2021; McMillan-Major, 2020; Zhao et al., 2020; Baldridge and Palmer, 2009, among others), **we aim to predict the parts of speech (POS) and morphosyntactic features for each word in the target sentence**, producing the third line of Figure 1, with stem translations replaced by POS labels. This model can produce a first-pass labeling for correction by human experts working on the documentation project, saving large amounts of time (as shown by Baldridge and Palmer, 2009) and freeing experts to work on more complex aspects of linguistic analysis.

To match the language documentation context,

Proceedings of the 20th SIGMORPHON workshop on Computational Research in Phonetics, Phonology, and Morphology, pages 78–92
July 14, 2023 ©2023 Association for Computational Linguistics

where we often have a transcription and translation of the text before any other labeled data, we model morpheme labeling as a translation task. Specifically, the model should learn to transform labels for the high-resource translation into labels for the target language; hence the name **gloss-to-gloss (g2g)**.

For initial model development, we use data labeled in the UniMorph[1] format, so that we can test the model's performance on a range of languages. Next, we test the same model on Uspanteko data from a language documentation project (Pixabaj et al., 2007), which involves the steps of:

a) Converting the morpheme labels from the Uspanteko IGT into the UniMorph format, which includes mapping Uspanteko-specific labels into the UniMorph tag set;

b) Replacing stem translations (e.g. *ropa* (clothes)) with part-of-speech labels;

c) Translating the Spanish translations of the Uspanteko sentences into English, then automatically labeling the English text with UniMorph labels;

d) Using our g2g model to predict labels for the Uspanteko sentences.

For step (a), the expected UniMorph representation for the Uspanteko sentence above might be:

```
xk'amch      ritz'iq
V;PFV;ALL    N;ERG;3;PL
```

For example, the tag COM (completive aspect) from the Uspanteko IGT is mapped to the UniMorph label PFV (perfective aspect), and the tag E3 (ergative 3rd person plural) is converted to the UniMorph trio of ERG, 3, and PL.

Step (c) creates pseudo-parallel English data for the texts. For Figure 1, this step yields the following (noisy) morphological analysis:

```
[they]PRO;3;PL  [brought]V;PST
[clothes]N;PL
```

Even in this simple example, we see that the morphological information expressed in the two languages is similar but not identical, and the morphological features are distributed differently across the words. Our model additionally incorporates a layer that maps morpheme labels to their linguistic dimensions, following the dimensions defined by the UniMorph schema (Sylak-Glassman, 2016). Mapping to linguistic dimension is a first step toward incorporating linguistic knowledge for the task of morpheme glossing in context.

In step (d), we concatenate a vector of the English morpheme labels with static word embeddings for the English lexical items; this combined representation serves as input to the final classification layers, whose task is to produce the appropriate labels for the target language.

To keep computational demands low, we use a rather simple CNN-based architecture, and compare to a fine-tuned BERT (Devlin et al., 2019) model. On standard evaluations, the CNN model achieves performance comparable to the BERT model, at a fraction of the computational expense.

The contributions of this work are:

1. A lightweight (low computational expense, reasonable data requirements) model for morpheme labeling in context, with an architecture designed for a modified IGT (interlinear glossed text) format;

2. A simple structured linguistic representation in the form of linguistic dimensions, used to guide predictions;

3. Evaluation of the model on language documentation data (IGT) for the Mayan language Uspanteko, and additional evaluations on a range of high-resource languages.

We described related work in Section 2, our approach to data representation in Section 3, and the model architecture in Section 4. Section 5 describes results for the high-resource language development experiments, and Section 6 presents our core results on IGT for Uspanteko. We wrap up with discussion and conclusions.

2 Background and related work

One goal of this work is to develop time-saving tools for use in the language documentation context. Specifically, we aim to support the production of interlinear glossed text (IGT) with a lightweight model that can be run on a standard laptop, using whatever previously-produced IGT might be available for the target language.

2.1 Computational support for IGT

IGT is a standard format for representing rich linguistic information associated with text. It is a

[1]https://unimorph.github.io/

common representation in linguistic literature and a frequent product of language documentation and description projects.

At the same time, creating IGT is a time-consuming and expertise-demanding process, bringing together a collection of skilled tasks. Depending on the original data source, IGT production may require transcription and translation of recorded audio or video, as well as morphological segmentation and morphological analysis. An increasing amount of research effort has recently been devoted to finding low-resource solutions for each stage of the process, with work in transcription (for example, Adams et al., 2017; Wisniewski et al., 2020), translation (see Haddow et al. (2022) for a survey), and segmentation (Ruokolainen et al., 2013; Eskander et al., 2019; Mager et al., 2020, among others) tasks. Work on automatic morphological inflection for low-resource languages is also related, though it approaches the task from a different direction (Anastasopoulos and Neubig, 2019; Liu and Hulden, 2021; Muradoglu and Hulden, 2022; Wiemerslage et al., 2022, among others).

Representing IGT. Early computational efforts in this area focused on defining data formats for representing the complex relationships between the various tiers of IGT (Hughes et al., 2003, 2004; Palmer and Erk, 2007). The Xigt project (Goodman et al., 2015) improves upon and modernizes previous formats, offering an easily-serializable representation for IGT. In this study we take a different approach, extracting the morpheme labels from the IGT and clustering the labels for morphemes associated with a particular word into a UniMorph-style format (Batsuren et al., 2022). By using UniMorph, we depart from an important property of IGT: the direct and ordered association of labels with the morphemes they describe.

Morpheme glossing. The task of automatically producing IGT is the focus of a current (2023) shared task competition at SIGMORPHON.[2] Given a paired source text and translation, participants in the competition are asked to output, for each word, the appropriate stem translation and morpheme labels. Data are provided for seven different low-resource languages.

The earliest work on this task we are aware of (Baldridge and Palmer, 2009; Palmer et al., 2009, 2010) takes segmented data as input and outputs part-of-speech labels and morpheme labels, ignoring the stem translation part of the task. Samardžić et al. (2015) break the task down into two steps, starting with part-of-speech and morpheme labels and then filling in stem translations using dictionary resources, with predicted labels helping to disambiguate. Sequence labeling approaches, including Conditional Random Fields (CRFs), Hidden Markov Models, and Recurrent Neural Networks are explored by Barriga Martínez et al. (2021) for the Otomi language, and Moeller and Hulden (2018) consider both neural and non-neural sequence labeling approaches for several endangered languages. McMillan-Major (2020), who merge the outputs of two CRF models, one training on the source text, the other on the translation. Zhao et al. (2020) also leverage the translation signal for glossing.

In this work, we draw inspiration from earlier work in our focus on the morpheme labels (leaving aside the stem translation) and in our use of the translation to guide learning. We use a CNN to capture relationships between the source and target morpheme labels, combined with static word embeddings for the translated task to boost the semantic signal. The combination of these elements gives us a low-compute solution.

2.2 CNNs, and treating language as images

Convolutional Neural Networks (CNNs) have been used to some degree in NLP for static classification tasks and to capture latent structures in text. Before attention-based models became the standard approach to sequential prediction, CNNs were shown to achieve results that were comparable to other traditional language models such as RNNs and LSTMs. Pham et al. (2016) show that CNNs can be effective for dynamic sequence prediction tasks where both local and long-range dependency information needs to be captured. Their CNN model for statistical language modeling has a perplexity score comparable to popular RNN-based approaches.

A radically different approach to image-driven NLP is taken by Rust et al. (2023) to overcome vocabulary bottlenecks in languages. Their encoder approach (PIXEL) renders text as images and models orthographic similarity between languages. Although their approach does match BERT's performance on syntactic and semantic language tasks, PIXEL proves to be a more robust option for noisy

[2] https://github.com/sigmorphon/2023GlossingST

In 1923 she became a member of the Lägerdorf ADGB action committee. [adp, num, 3;fem;nom;pro;sg, pst;ind;fin;v, det;indf, n;sg, adp, det;def, n;sg, sg;propn, n;sg, n;sg, _]
1923 wurde sie Mitglied des Lägerdorfer ADGB - Aktionsausschusses. [num, ind;3;v;sg;pst;fin;pass, 3;fem;sg;pro;nom, n;neut;sg;nom, gen;sg;def;det;masc, propn, sg;gen;masc;propn, _, n;sg;gen;masc, _]

Table 1: Example of fully-prepared pseudo-parallel data. The source text is automatically-translated and glossed English; the target text is German.

text inputs. Kim et al. (2015) use a CNN coupled with an LSTM at the character level to perform language modeling. Although their model has 60% fewer parameters than popular LSTM architectures of the time, it outperforms word-level and morpheme-level LSTM baselines. Our work differs from this approach in that we encode both word order and morpheme-level information in two dimensions instead of using character-level representations.

3 Data and its representation

For model development, we start with data from the 2019 SIGMORPHON shared task on morphological analysis in context.[3] Once the model has been developed and tested, we apply it to a true low-resource language (Section 6.)

The shared task data is a collection of datasets of varying sizes, from 68 different languages and/or varieties, with sentence level morphological analysis in the UniMorph (Batsuren et al., 2022; McCarthy et al., 2020) style. Here we report results for 9 languages, selected for diversity of morphological systems. For each language, we select the first 10,000 sentences from the corpus and use a train/dev/test split of 60/20/20.

3.1 UniMorph data

The UniMorph (Universal Morphological Feature) schema is a set of morphological feature labels. This set of labels is intended to serve as an interlingua for annotation of (mostly) inflectional morphology, providing a universal schema into which any tag set can be mapped. The data consists of sentences, with lemmas and morphological labels assigned to each word within the sentence.

Pseudo-parallel data. Recall that our model treats morphological analysis as a translation task, "translating" the source-side labels into labels for the target-side sentence, assuming semantic equivalence. The UniMorph-labeled texts described above are not parallel, and we are not aware of any parallel texts with UniMorph-style labels. Therefore, we produce pseudo-parallel data by automatically translating each dataset into English and then labeling the English sentences with a morphological labeler trained on English UniMorph data. An instance of the fully prepared source data appears in Table 1.[4] We use the Google Translate API[5] to back-translate target text to English, our choice of high-resource anchor (source) language. We train a 64-unit BiLSTM model (Figure 8) with categorical cross-entropy loss to generate morphological labels for each word in the source language. We also trained a GRU model for the same purpose, but found that the BiLSTM is superior in terms of F1, as shown in Table 2.

3.2 Linguistic dimensions (LDs)

UniMorph's more than 200 individual labels are grouped into 23 linguistic dimensions, ranging from Aktionsart to voice, and including domains such as information structure and politeness (see Sylak-Glassman for details). For example, the marker PFV on the Uspanteko verb indicates completive aspect and can be mapped to the dimension of ASPECT. The marker PST on the Spanish verb indicates past tense, mapped to the linguistic dimension TENSE. We use the UniMorph linguistic dimensions in our model.

[3] https://sigmorphon.github.io/sharedtasks/2019/task2/

[4] Further preprocessing involves removal of punctuation and conversion to all-lowercase letters.

[5] https://cloud.google.com/translate/docs

Model	Loss	Accuracy	F1
Bidirectional LSTM	0.111	0.969	0.922
GRU	0.126	0.963	0.876

Table 2: Performance of English glossing models.

	SG	ADP	NUM	...	NOM
Word 1	0	1	0	...	0
Word 2	0	0	1	...	0
...					
Word n					

Figure 2: Multi-hot encoding for morpheme labels.

3.3 Structured representation for morphological features

Prior to encoding, the dataset consists of tokenized sentence and gloss pairs for the source and target languages. Each word in a sentence is naturally associated with one or more morphological features. This presents a multi-class encoding problem that is solved by using a categorical heat-map representation (Section 4), in which each column represents a single label (morphological feature or part-of-speech), and each row represents one word in the sentence. Considering the first three words in the sentence shown in Table 1, the encoding would be: *[In]->[adp], [1923]->[num], [she]->[3,fem,nom,pro,sg]*. The input to the model is a full 2-D binary representation where the column headers are the set of all possible individual morpheme labels and the rows consist of all words, with additional padding to standardize the input format. An example of the binary multi-hot encoding is shown in Figure 2. The gloss labels are then mapped to their linguistic dimensions (LDs).

4 Gloss-to-gloss (g2g) model

Figure 3 shows the architecture of the g2g system, and Figure 4 schematizes the model's workflow for one sample input sentence. Gloss labels for both source and target text are mapped to their linguistic dimensions (LDs) and encoded as heat maps, transforming the problem of glossing to an image-to-image prediction problem. The CNN generates heat maps with expectations over output gloss labels. These heat maps can be seen be seen as binary images, or alternately as sparse tensors. The heat maps, concatenated with pre-trained word2vec embeddings for the source language text, serve as inputs to shallow three-layer network for final labeling. The model's output prediction is a 2-D tensor of the same dimensions containing values that represent the probability of each morpheme label for each word in the sentence. We do not perform extensive parameter search, instead adopting standard settings (Appendix B).

4.1 Motivation

We assume parallel meaning between the source and target language texts. We also expect variability in how that meaning is expressed. **Translational divergence** can include challenges like differences in the structures employed by the two languages, differences in the morphological systems and their inventories, and variation with respect to what types of grammatical resources the languages use to convey the intended meaning. From a linguistic perspective, it is optimistic to expect a g2g approach to yield accurate target language glosses.

At the same time, we know that there are regularities to these divergences, and we expect our model to learn some of these mappings. To boost performance, we use word embeddings to capture meaning; these embeddings may also encode some information about morphology (Schwartz et al., 2022; Avraham and Goldberg, 2017; Soricut and Och, 2015). We use LDs to abstract away from particular labels into linguistic categories, and we use an extra probabilistic component (Section 4.3) to decide when to stop predicting labels.

4.2 Morphological representation and training

Before the morphological data is fed into the primary CNN model, we prime the representation with established classes/dimensions. For instance, we classify labels such as `ACC`, `NOM`, and `DAT` into the `CASE` category. This mapping reduces the count of label types by 60% on average for all source-target language pairs, consequently improving model accuracy and preventing mistakes that pertain to multiple category labels being predicted for the same word.

The heat map representation allows us to transform the sequence learning problem into a 2D image-based learning problem. The input is a binary image and the model output is a heat map that represents the probability values for the possible morpheme labels for each word in the sentence. Using this encoding format, we can create lightweight CNN models that can take inputs of any arbitrary padding (rows) and morphological feature (column) size. Due to the relatively small number of parameters, we can train a unique model for each language pair.

The input heat map images are fed to a standard convolutional neural network (CNN).[6] We obtain

[6]Further model details in Appendix B.

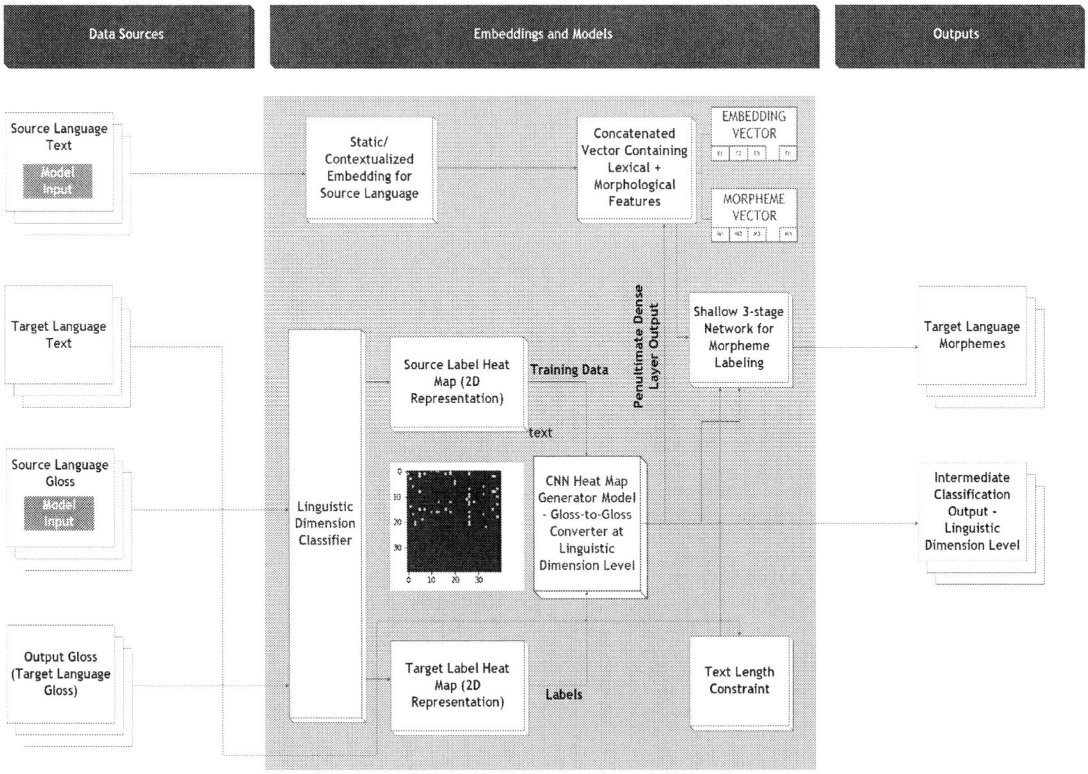

Figure 3: Architecture of g2g system.

a discretized output of linguistic dimension predictions by setting a threshold and assigning hard categories to each cell (0 or 1). The threshold is considered a pipeline parameter for each language pair and is set by performing an optimal parameter search that maximizes the F1 score post-facto. The threshold for German, for instance, is set at 0.35.

4.3 Adding lexical information and probabilistic length modeling

To capture lexical semantics, we concatenate w2v embeddings (Mikolov et al., 2013) for the source side words with the penultimate dense layer of the CNN. We then train a shallow network with 3 dense layers on the concatenated vectors, outputting a flattened version of the heat map of target glosses. This one-dimensional representation is then transformed back into a 2D representation and decoded to obtain the target language gloss.

One challenge of the heat map approach is uncertainty about when to stop predicting labels. Sentence lengths vary, but the model always predicts a standard 40-word heat map. To address this issue, we use the sentence length of the target text (without lexical information; Zhao et al., 2020 use a similar approach) and a probabilistic model that determines the likelihood of a combination of morpheme labels occurring together and drops low-probability combinations (such as PRPN;PL (plural proper noun) for English) from the output heat map until the number of rows matches the number of words in the target language sentence. The selection is based on the joint probabilities of co-occurring morphological labels drawn from a likelihood lookup table constructed using the frequency of various possible morphological combinations in our training sets.

4.4 Training an LLM for morphological labeling - BERT

Since there is no easily available baseline for parallel text glossing, we train a BERT model to act as a comparable computationally-expensive baseline. Pre-trained cased weights are used since our common source language for all target languages is English. The possible gloss combinations in the target language form their own separate vocabulary and are together treated as a language of their own. The problem is reduced to a standard translation problem where English is the source and the gloss

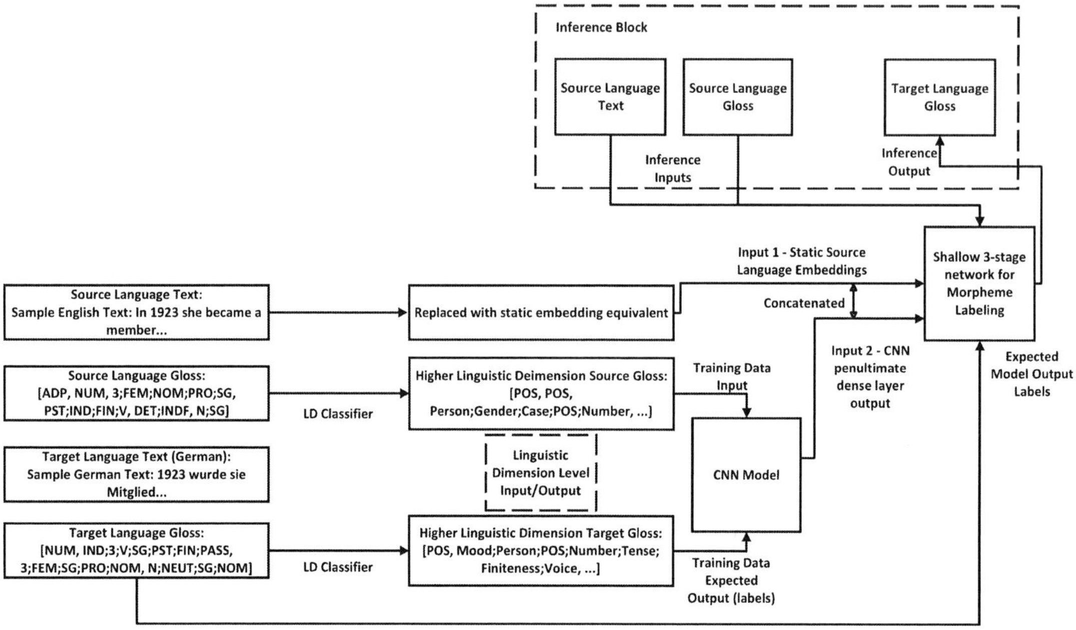

Figure 4: Workflow of g2g system for the sample input from Table 1.

	morpheme F1		LD F1		POS acc.	
	BERT	CNN	BERT	CNN	BERT	CNN
Basque	0.75	0.69	0.87	0.86	0.91	0.86
Finnish	0.81	0.77	0.86	0.84	0.92	0.84
French	0.81	0.83	0.85	0.89	0.95	0.91
German	0.78	0.75	0.91	0.79	0.88	0.83
Italian	0.79	0.75	0.84	0.82	0.94	0.91
Russian	0.82	0.73	0.89	0.78	0.88	0.84
Spanish	0.73	0.65	0.88	0.87	0.96	0.92
Turkish	0.78	0.66	0.79	0.78	0.87	0.80
English	0.84	0.82	0.95	0.89	0.95	0.89

Table 3: Performance of CNN and BERT models across languages. Morpheme-level=F1 over all labels, LD-level=F1 over linguistic dimension categories, POS=accuracy. F1 is computed following SIGMORPHON 2019 shared task metric.

vocabulary is the target. Concatenating the source language morphology vector with the BERT embedding did not significantly affect the output, so we use only contextual and positional embeddings to fine-tune the model, with a separate fine-tuned model for each source-target language pair.

5 Experiments, results, and discussion

To evaluate performance of the model, we test it on nine different language pairs (see Table 3). For all non-English languages, we back-translate to English. For English, our source language is German.

As a baseline, we fine-tune a pre-trained BERT model for the morpheme labeling task, using the same data and splits, but in a standard supervised learning set-up (i.e. no parallel data and no LDs).

The CNN model experiments were run on a 2.6 GHz Intel(R) Core(TM) CPU, taking an average of **8.5 minutes** to train. The BERT baseline experiments were run on a multi-GPU cluster, taking an average of **3.5 hours** to train.

Evaluation. Table 3 shows results for both models across all languages, with accuracy for POS labels and, for morpheme labels and linguistic dimensions, F1 as defined for the SIGMORPHON 2019 shared task: true positives are the set intersection of the gold and predicted labels for a word, and false positives are labels in the predicted set but not the gold.[7] All measures are computed at the heatmap level for each row (sentence) and averaged over the full dataset.

Results. Some patterns hold across most language pairs. For the most part, the CNN does not quite match the performance of the transformer. Crucially, though, the CNN trains on a single laptop in under 10 minutes, where the transformer needs a compute cluster and multiple hours to train. The CNN performance is generally within 5 percentage points of the BERT model, and this may be

[7]NOTE: although we use the same data and evaluation as the shared task, our CNN results are not directly comparable, because, unlike almost all participating teams, we do not use target language lexemes or labels as training input.

an acceptable performance in most documentation contexts - an empirical question for future work.

The POS score represents the proportion of the part of speech predictions that were correct. Because there are latent associations between POS category and morpheme labels (for example, it would be highly unusual to see aspectual features marked on nouns), the POS score should be directly proportional to the final F1 scores that we obtain for each language. This is reflected across our results. While both models struggle with Turkish and Russian, the CNN also performs poorly on Basque.

At the LD level, the model's performance is somewhat similar across the three Romance languages we considered (Spanish, French and Italian). While the CNN fails to perform better than the transformer in most scenarios, it is interesting to note that the CNN performs marginally better than the transformer on French. However, both models show a significant performance dip when it comes to Spanish.

The CNN's F1 dips to 0.66 for Turkish and 0.73 for Russian. This may be due to their high morphological complexity.

6 Applying the model to language documentation data

Finally, we apply our model to data from the Mayan language Uspanteko (Pixabaj et al., 2007), using the train/dev/test splits defined for the SIGMORPHON 2023 shared task: training on 21 texts (9774 sentences), and using one text each for dev and test (around 200 sentences each). The model's performance on language documentation data parallels the results for high-resource languages.

Experimental setup and data preparation Translations of the Uspanteko sentences are available in Spanish. To remain consistent, we translate the Spanish sentences to English using the Google Translate API.

It is important to note that this translation step adds compounding errors to the model's final gloss output.

IGT to UniMorph Mapping The labels used in the Uspanteko IGT belong to the glossing conventions selected by the language documentation project. The label set is particular to the linguistic properties of the language, and as such they make some different distinctions than those encoded by UniMorph. Some of the mappings between UniMorph and IGT are shown in Table 9. The custom mapping table that we built to convert IGT to UniMorph are available in our repository.[8]

Model	F1
BERT Linguistic Dimension Level	0.80
CNN Linguistic Dimension Level	0.76
BERT Morpheme Level	0.71
CNN Morpheme Level	0.63

Table 4: Performance of models on Uspanteko data.

Results and Discussion As seen in Table 4, the model performance on Uspanteko is comparable to its performance on morphologically complex high-resource languages like Turkish. This leads us to believe that our computationally efficient approach can indeed be used in the low-resource language documentation context to produce a first pass labeling, thus reducing the time an expert needs to spend on labeling. To better understand the system's errors, we show the label distribution for false positives output by the CNN model (Figure 5) at the level of linguistic dimension. 33% of these are the `unk` (unknown) label, which occurs when the model fails to make a confident prediction on the linguistic dimension. These are precisely the cases where the human expert should intervene.

We note that the model is not over-predicting the LD of part-of-speech, despite the fact that 42% of gold labels in the test set are part-of-speech labels. Instead, the model makes more errors for the categories of case, person, and number. We expect that the prevalence of case errors comes from the fact that Uspanteko uses an ergative-absolutive case system, with patterning entirely different from the rather impoverished nominative-accusative case system of English. Uspanteko also uses a number of grammatical categories not present in English, such as directionals and relational nouns (Tyers and Henderson, 2021). Looking at particular parts of speech, the model does well on conjunctions (84% accuracy), and struggles with adverbs and adjectives. 24% of adverb predictions are confused with adjective tags and about 13% of adverbs and adjectives are labeled 'unknown'.

[8] `https://github.com/bhargav-ns/G2G_Conversion`

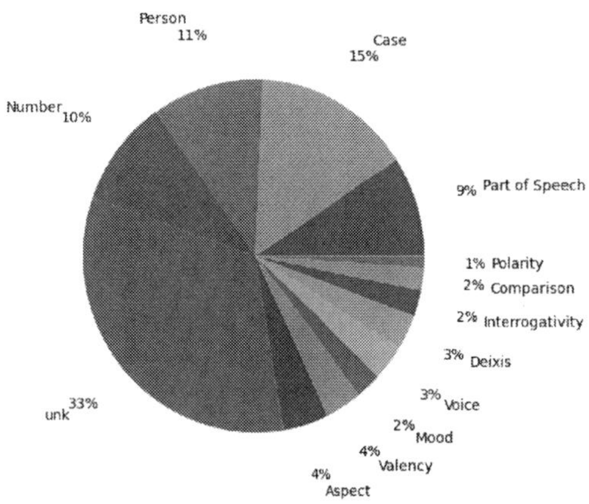

Figure 5: CNN: distribution of false positive predictions at the linguistic dimension level for Uspanteko.

7 Conclusion

We have presented the g2g model, a new architecture for morphological analysis that dramatically reduces compute time by modeling the task as, essentially, an image-to-image translation task. The model incorporates knowledge of linguistic categories by mapping labels to their linguistic dimensions, with the effect of narrowing the space of possible outputs. These strategies result in an enormous reduction of compute time and a system more suitable for use in low-resource scenarios than the large language models currently achieving top performance for this and similar tasks.

Model variants and future work. Working with language documentation data adds several layers of complexity. In this work, our model's output lacks the ordered association with individual morphemes typical of most IGT. We use an unordered set of labels to describe the morphological features of a word, as shown in Table 1.

In addition, there is wide variability in both the label sets and the glossing scheme across language documentation projects. One widely-used scheme is encoded in the Leipzig Glossing Rules (Bernard Comrie, 2008); Table 5 shows an example of a German phrase glossed according to Leipzig conventions. In future work we aim to produce outputs that mimic the glossing conventions used in the original data, including the order of the labels, the nature of the labels, and the glossing syntax.

The Sigmorphon 2023 shared task on interlinear glossing[9] hews closer to this goal. In this shared

unser-	n	Väter-	n
our-	DAT.PL	father	DAT.PL
"To	our	fathers."	

Table 5: German phrase labeled using Leipzig Glossing Rules.

task, the source language text and target language text are used as inputs to obtain the target language glosses in Leipzig format. This is fundamentally different from our input format, as we attempt to obtain the target language glosses without the target language text. Instead, we use all the information available from the high-resource source language (text and glosses) as inputs to the model.

Our next step is to work directly with documentary linguists to evaluate whether and how such tools can be usefully deployed by field linguists and/or language community members. Another planned direction is to work on more sophisticated approaches to incorporating linguistic knowledge.

Limitations and ethical considerations. First, the system's performance is constrained by the use of automated systems to produce pseudo-parallel data. Errors in translation and morpheme labeling on the high-resource side propagate to the output and cause mistakes in target side labeling. We have not yet performed the extensive error analyses needed to understand how much error propagation might be affecting the system.

Second, we have not yet tested the system in an actual documentation project. When working on NLP with endangered and/or indigenous languages in mind, there is a clear risk of perpetuating existing oppression (Bird, 2020; Schwartz, 2022). We hope to avoid some of these harms by using data from a wide range of non-threatened languages first, waiting to involve language community members and documentary linguists until we have a system with good enough results that we expect it could actually be helpful in real world contexts. We have already developed collaborations with several speakers of endangered languages and linguists working on documentation projects, and we look forward to continuing this work with their guidance and involvement.

Acknowledgements

We thank the anonymous reviewers for very useful suggestions and feedback. Thanks also to the CLASIC cohort, FOLTA lab members, and CompSem

[9] https://github.com/sigmorphon/2023glossingST

lab members at CU Boulder for helpful discussions and feedback. This material is based upon work supported by the National Science Foundation under Grant No. 2149404,"CAREER: From One Language to Another". Any opinions, findings, and conclusions or recommendations expressed in this material are those of the authors and do not necessarily reflect the views of the National Science Foundation.

References

Oliver Adams, Trevor Cohn, Graham Neubig, and Alexis Michaud. 2017. Phonemic transcription of low-resource tonal languages. In *Proceedings of the Australasian Language Technology Association Workshop 2017*, pages 53–60, Brisbane, Australia.

Antonios Anastasopoulos and Graham Neubig. 2019. Pushing the limits of low-resource morphological inflection. In *Proceedings of the 2019 Conference on Empirical Methods in Natural Language Processing and the 9th International Joint Conference on Natural Language Processing (EMNLP-IJCNLP)*, pages 984–996, Hong Kong, China. Association for Computational Linguistics.

Oded Avraham and Yoav Goldberg. 2017. The interplay of semantics and morphology in word embeddings. In *Proceedings of the 15th Conference of the European Chapter of the Association for Computational Linguistics: Volume 2, Short Papers*, pages 422–426, Valencia, Spain. Association for Computational Linguistics.

Jason Baldridge and Alexis Palmer. 2009. How well does active learning *actually* work? Time-based evaluation of cost-reduction strategies for language documentation. In *Proceedings of the 2009 Conference on Empirical Methods in Natural Language Processing*, pages 296–305, Singapore. Association for Computational Linguistics.

Diego Barriga Martínez, Victor Mijangos, and Ximena Gutierrez-Vasques. 2021. Automatic interlinear glossing for Otomi language. In *Proceedings of the First Workshop on Natural Language Processing for Indigenous Languages of the Americas*, pages 34–43, Online. Association for Computational Linguistics.

Khuyagbaatar Batsuren, Omer Goldman, Salam Khalifa, Nizar Habash, Witold Kieraś, Gábor Bella, Brian Leonard, Garrett Nicolai, Kyle Gorman, Yustinus Ghanggo Ate, Maria Ryskina, Sabrina Mielke, Elena Budianskaya, Charbel El-Khaissi, Tiago Pimentel, Michael Gasser, William Abbott Lane, Mohit Raj, Matt Coler, Jaime Rafael Montoya Samame, Delio Siticonatzi Camaiteri, Esaú Zumaeta Rojas, Didier López Francis, Arturo Oncevay, Juan López Bautista, Gema Celeste Silva Villegas, Lucas Torroba Hennigen, Adam Ek, David Guriel, Peter Dirix, Jean-Philippe Bernardy, Andrey Scherbakov, Aziyana Bayyr-ool, Antonios Anastasopoulos, Roberto Zariquiey, Karina Sheifer, Sofya Ganieva, Hilaria Cruz, Ritván Karahóǧa, Stella Markantonatou, George Pavlidis, Matvey Plugaryov, Elena Klyachko, Ali Salehi, Candy Angulo, Jatayu Baxi, Andrew Krizhanovsky, Natalia Krizhanovskaya, Elizabeth Salesky, Clara Vania, Sardana Ivanova, Jennifer White, Rowan Hall Maudslay, Josef Valvoda, Ran Zmigrod, Paula Czarnowska, Irene Nikkarinen, Aelita Salchak, Brijesh Bhatt, Christopher Straughn, Zoey Liu, Jonathan North Washington, Yuval Pinter, Duygu Ataman, Marcin Wolinski, Totok Suhardijanto, Anna Yablonskaya, Niklas Stoehr, Hossep Dolatian, Zahroh Nuriah, Shyam Ratan, Francis M. Tyers, Edoardo M. Ponti, Grant Aiton, Aryaman Arora, Richard J. Hatcher, Ritesh Kumar, Jeremiah Young, Daria Rodionova, Anastasia Yemelina, Taras Andrushko, Igor Marchenko, Polina Mashkovtseva, Alexandra Serova, Emily Prud'hommeaux, Maria Nepomniashchaya, Fausto Giunchiglia, Eleanor Chodroff, Mans Hulden, Miikka Silfverberg, Arya D. McCarthy, David Yarowsky, Ryan Cotterell, Reut Tsarfaty, and Ekaterina Vylomova. 2022. UniMorph 4.0: Universal Morphology. In *Proceedings of the Thirteenth Language Resources and Evaluation Conference*, pages 840–855, Marseille, France. European Language Resources Association.

B. Bickel Max Planck Institute for Evolutional Anthropology Bernard Comrie, M. Haspelmath. 2008. *The Leipzig Glossing Rules: Conventions for Interlinear Morpheme-by-morphene Glosses.*

Steven Bird. 2020. Decolonising speech and language technology. In *Proceedings of the 28th International Conference on Computational Linguistics*, pages 3504–3519, Barcelona, Spain (Online). International Committee on Computational Linguistics.

Jacob Devlin, Ming-Wei Chang, Kenton Lee, and Kristina Toutanova. 2019. BERT: Pre-training of deep bidirectional transformers for language understanding. In *Proceedings of the 2019 Conference of the North American Chapter of the Association for Computational Linguistics: Human Language Technologies, Volume 1 (Long and Short Papers)*, pages 4171–4186, Minneapolis, Minnesota. Association for Computational Linguistics.

Ramy Eskander, Judith Klavans, and Smaranda Muresan. 2019. Unsupervised morphological segmentation for low-resource polysynthetic languages. In *Proceedings of the 16th Workshop on Computational Research in Phonetics, Phonology, and Morphology*, pages 189–195, Florence, Italy. Association for Computational Linguistics.

Michael Wayne Goodman, Joshua Crowgey, Fei Xia, and Emily M. Bender. 2015. Xigt: extensible interlinear glossed text for natural language processing. *Language Resources and Evaluation*, 49(2):455–485.

Barry Haddow, Rachel Bawden, Antonio Valerio Miceli Barone, Jindřich Helcl, and Alexandra Birch. 2022. Survey of low-resource machine translation. *Computational Linguistics*, 48(3):673–732.

Baden Hughes, Steven Bird, and Catherine Bow. 2003. Encoding and presenting interlinear text using XML technologies. In *Proceedings of the Australasian Language Technology Workshop 2003*, pages 61–69, Melbourne, Australia.

Baden Hughes, Catherine Bow, and Steven Bird. 2004. Functional requirements for an interlinear text editor. In *Proceedings of the Fourth International Conference on Language Resources and Evaluation (LREC'04)*, Lisbon, Portugal. European Language Resources Association (ELRA).

Yoon Kim, Yacine Jernite, David Sontag, and Alexander M. Rush. 2015. Character-aware neural language models.

Ling Liu and Mans Hulden. 2021. Backtranslation in neural morphological inflection. In *Proceedings of the Second Workshop on Insights from Negative Results in NLP*, pages 81–88, Online and Punta Cana, Dominican Republic. Association for Computational Linguistics.

Manuel Mager, Özlem Çetinoğlu, and Katharina Kann. 2020. Tackling the low-resource challenge for canonical segmentation. In *Proceedings of the 2020 Conference on Empirical Methods in Natural Language Processing (EMNLP)*, pages 5237–5250, Online. Association for Computational Linguistics.

Arya D. McCarthy, Christo Kirov, Matteo Grella, Amrit Nidhi, Patrick Xia, Kyle Gorman, Ekaterina Vylomova, Sabrina J. Mielke, Garrett Nicolai, Miikka Silfverberg, Timofey Arkhangelskiy, Nataly Krizhanovsky, Andrew Krizhanovsky, Elena Klyachko, Alexey Sorokin, John Mansfield, Valts Ernštreits, Yuval Pinter, Cassandra L. Jacobs, Ryan Cotterell, Mans Hulden, and David Yarowsky. 2020. UniMorph 3.0: Universal Morphology. In *Proceedings of the Twelfth Language Resources and Evaluation Conference*, pages 3922–3931, Marseille, France. European Language Resources Association.

Arya D. McCarthy, Ekaterina Vylomova, Shijie Wu, Chaitanya Malaviya, Lawrence Wolf-Sonkin, Garrett Nicolai, Christo Kirov, Miikka Silfverberg, Sabrina J. Mielke, Jeffrey Heinz, Ryan Cotterell, and Mans Hulden. 2019. The SIGMORPHON 2019 shared task: Morphological analysis in context and cross-lingual transfer for inflection. In *Proceedings of the 16th Workshop on Computational Research in Phonetics, Phonology, and Morphology*, pages 229–244, Florence, Italy. Association for Computational Linguistics.

Angelina McMillan-Major. 2020. Automating gloss generation in interlinear glossed text. In *Proceedings of the Society for Computation in Linguistics 2020*, pages 355–366, New York, New York. Association for Computational Linguistics.

Tomas Mikolov, Wen-tau Yih, and Geoffrey Zweig. 2013. Linguistic regularities in continuous space word representations. In *Proceedings of the 2013 Conference of the North American Chapter of the Association for Computational Linguistics: Human Language Technologies*, pages 746–751, Atlanta, Georgia. Association for Computational Linguistics.

Sarah Moeller and Mans Hulden. 2018. Automatic glossing in a low-resource setting for language documentation. In *Proceedings of the Workshop on Computational Modeling of Polysynthetic Languages*, pages 84–93, Santa Fe, New Mexico, USA. Association for Computational Linguistics.

Sarah Moeller and Mans Hulden. 2021. Integrating automated segmentation and glossing into documentary and descriptive linguistics. In *Proceedings of the 4th Workshop on the Use of Computational Methods in the Study of Endangered Languages Volume 1 (Papers)*, pages 86–95, Online. Association for Computational Linguistics.

Sarah Moeller, Ling Liu, and Mans Hulden. 2021. To POS tag or not to POS tag: The impact of POS tags on morphological learning in low-resource settings. In *Proceedings of the 59th Annual Meeting of the Association for Computational Linguistics and the 11th International Joint Conference on Natural Language Processing (Volume 1: Long Papers)*, pages 966–978, Online. Association for Computational Linguistics.

Saliha Muradoglu and Mans Hulden. 2022. Eeny, meeny, miny, moe. how to choose data for morphological inflection. In *Proceedings of the 2022 Conference on Empirical Methods in Natural Language Processing*, pages 7294–7303, Abu Dhabi, United Arab Emirates. Association for Computational Linguistics.

Alexis Palmer and Katrin Erk. 2007. IGT-XML: An XML format for interlinearized glossed text. In *Proceedings of the Linguistic Annotation Workshop*, pages 176–183, Prague, Czech Republic. Association for Computational Linguistics.

Alexis Palmer, Taesun Moon, and Jason Baldridge. 2009. Evaluating automation strategies in language documentation. In *Proceedings of the NAACL HLT 2009 Workshop on Active Learning for Natural Language Processing*, pages 36–44, Boulder, Colorado. Association for Computational Linguistics.

Alexis Palmer, Taesun Moon, Jason Baldridge, Katrin Erk, Eric Campbell, and Telma Can. 2010. Computational strategies for reducing annotation effort in language documentation: A case study in creating interlinear texts for Uspanteko. *Linguistic Issues in Language Technology*, 3.

Ngoc-Quan Pham, German Kruszewski, and Gemma Boleda. 2016. Convolutional neural network language models. In *Proceedings of the 2016 Conference on Empirical Methods in Natural Language Processing*, pages 1153–1162, Austin, Texas. Association for Computational Linguistics.

Telma Can Pixabaj, Miguel Angel Vicente Méndez, María Vicente Méndez, and Oswaldo Ajcot Damián. 2007. Text Collections in Four Mayan Languages, Archived in the Archive of the Indigenous Languages of Latin America.

Teemu Ruokolainen, Oskar Kohonen, Sami Virpioja, and Mikko Kurimo. 2013. Supervised morphological segmentation in a low-resource learning setting using conditional random fields. In *Proceedings of the Seventeenth Conference on Computational Natural Language Learning*, pages 29–37, Sofia, Bulgaria. Association for Computational Linguistics.

Phillip Rust, Jonas F. Lotz, Emanuele Bugliarello, Elizabeth Salesky, Miryam de Lhoneux, and Desmond Elliott. 2023. Language modelling with pixels.

Tanja Samardžić, Robert Schikowski, and Sabine Stoll. 2015. Automatic interlinear glossing as two-level sequence classification. In *Proceedings of the 9th SIGHUM Workshop on Language Technology for Cultural Heritage, Social Sciences, and Humanities (LaTeCH)*, pages 68–72, Beijing, China. Association for Computational Linguistics.

Lane Schwartz. 2022. Primum Non Nocere: Before working with Indigenous data, the ACL must confront ongoing colonialism. In *Proceedings of the 60th Annual Meeting of the Association for Computational Linguistics (Volume 2: Short Papers)*, pages 724–731, Dublin, Ireland. Association for Computational Linguistics.

Lane Schwartz, Coleman Haley, and Francis Tyers. 2022. How to encode arbitrarily complex morphology in word embeddings, no corpus needed. In *Proceedings of the first workshop on NLP applications to field linguistics*, pages 64–76, Gyeongju, Republic of Korea. International Conference on Computational Linguistics.

Radu Soricut and Franz Och. 2015. Unsupervised morphology induction using word embeddings. In *Proceedings of the 2015 Conference of the North American Chapter of the Association for Computational Linguistics: Human Language Technologies*, pages 1627–1637, Denver, Colorado. Association for Computational Linguistics.

John Sylak-Glassman. 2016. The composition and use of the universal morphological feature schema (unimorph schema). *Johns Hopkins University*.

Francis Tyers and Robert Henderson. 2021. A corpus of k'iche' annotated for morphosyntactic structure. In *Proceedings of the First Workshop on Natural Language Processing for Indigenous Languages of the Americas*, pages 10–20, Online. Association for Computational Linguistics.

Adam Wiemerslage, Miikka Silfverberg, Changbing Yang, Arya McCarthy, Garrett Nicolai, Eliana Colunga, and Katharina Kann. 2022. Morphological processing of low-resource languages: Where we are and what's next. In *Findings of the Association for Computational Linguistics: ACL 2022*, pages 988–1007, Dublin, Ireland. Association for Computational Linguistics.

Guillaume Wisniewski, Séverine Guillaume, and Alexis Michaud. 2020. Phonemic transcription of low-resource languages: To what extent can preprocessing be automated? In *Proceedings of the 1st Joint Workshop on Spoken Language Technologies for Under-resourced languages (SLTU) and Collaboration and Computing for Under-Resourced Languages (CCURL)*, pages 306–315, Marseille, France. European Language Resources association.

Xingyuan Zhao, Satoru Ozaki, Antonios Anastasopoulos, Graham Neubig, and Lori Levin. 2020. Automatic interlinear glossing for under-resourced languages leveraging translations. In *Proceedings of the 28th International Conference on Computational Linguistics*, pages 5397–5408, Barcelona, Spain (Online). International Committee on Computational Linguistics.

A Dataset Preparation Details

Truncation and padding. Since 95% of the sample sentences in the dataset had fewer than 40 words per sentence, we set the padding/truncation limit to 40, thus making each feature map to be a 40x40 pixel heat-map that encodes the labels for all the words in a sentence.

Heat maps. The entire source and target morphological data is represented as a 3-dimensional cuboidal heat map. Each sentence (entry) in the dataset is a single 2-D slice of the cuboid, the dimensions of which are [Padding Length] x [Number of Morpheme Categories]. The English-German pair, for example, has a sentence map dimension of [40 x 20]. Padding length is manually set based on the 95th percentile of sentence lengths across the dataset. Each row in the heat map would represent the morphological labels for a single word within the larger sentence. An example heat map excerpt is shown in figure 6.

B Details of the CNN model

A sequential convolutional network with 3 blocks of standard Convolution - Max Pool - Dropout - Batch Norm layers are used in the network. Relu activation and 'same' padding are used for all of the convolutional layers and a pool size of (2,2) is used for each MaxPooling2D layer. A fixed dropout of 0.2 is applied after each pooling layer in the three blocks. The output of the third block is up-sampled and flattened into a single-dimensional

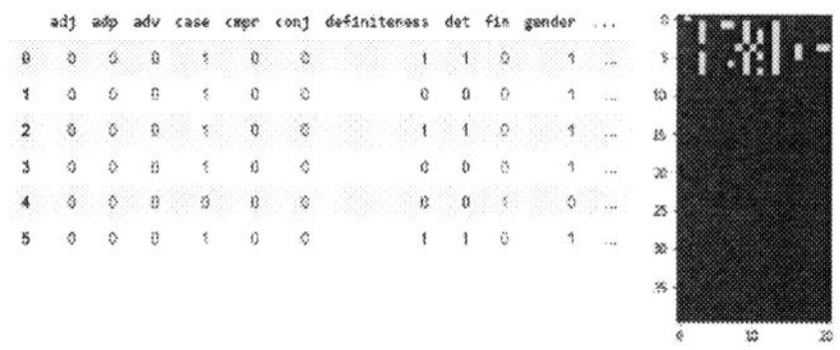

Figure 6: Heat map representation

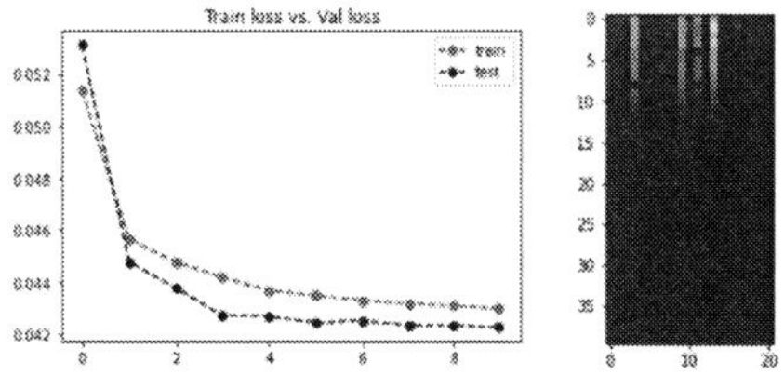

Figure 7: Sample output prediction

vector of length [categories x padding size]. A sigmoid activation is used in the final dense layer to facilitate the prediction of a probability score for every possible linguistic dimension of a word. The model is compiled with MSE as the loss function. A sample output prediction is shown in figure 7

C Fine-grained evaluations

Evaluation metrics of different granularities were explored to evaluate the model's performance. All the measures are computed at the heatmap level for each row (sentence) and averaged out over the entire dataset. We take standard accuracy, precision, and F1 scores for the flattened feature map vectors of the gold and predicted labels. Each feature map is originally of size `padding cut-off` times `number of linguistic dimensions` . Each unit of the predicted vector is independently compared with its corresponding gold label vector unit to evaluate the model output for different languages.

To get a more fine-grained sense of the model's performance, we explore two additional evaluation measures:

1. Proportion of missing labels
2. Proportion of extra labels

Tables 6 and 7 show fine-grained evaluations for both models. The missing label score represents the ratio of labels that are present in the gold gloss set but are absent in the model predictions. Similarly, the excess label score is the fraction of labels that have been wrongly predicted by the model.

D Variable training data experiments

Table 8 show results from experiments varying the amount of training data used.

Certain language families seem to demonstrate a significantly higher threshold for variance explainability based on dataset size. Spanish, French, and Italian (all romance languages) show massive jumps in accuracy from 20% to 40% training data but improve less drastically beyond the 60% training data mark. On the other hand, German and English show a rise in accuracy from 60% to 100% training data. Russian and Finnish demonstrate large jumps from 40% to 60% training data. Since the datasets' size was normalized before training, we might be able to conclude that these patterns are endemic to language families. For instance, it might be possible to conclude that the model requires significantly lesser training data to reach peak performance for romance languages as compared to Germanic languages. This generalization cannot be drawn from our small subset of languages and morphological tests, and therefore requires further investigation.

E Bi-directional LSTM for English Glossing

Figure 8 shows the model architecture for the Bi-directional LSTM that was used to gloss our source data and generate our source dataset for training purposes. The data was encoded with static w2v embeddings and the model was trained for 20 epochs (until convergence) on an English dataset containing UniMorph tags from the 2019 SIGMORPHON shared task referenced earlier. Model performance is detailed in table 2.

	CNN - Proportion of Missing Labels	CNN - Proportion of Extra Labels	CNN - POS Accuracy
Spanish	0.234	0.243	0.92
French	0.23	0.17	0.91
Basque	0.38	0.33	0.86
Italian	0.27	0.26	0.91
German	0.236	0.238	0.83
English	0.23	0.24	0.89
Turkish	0.39	0.32	0.8
Russian	0.36	0.33	0.84
Finnish	0.24	0.13	0.92

Table 6: CNN - Morpheme Tagging Scores, fine-grained evaluation

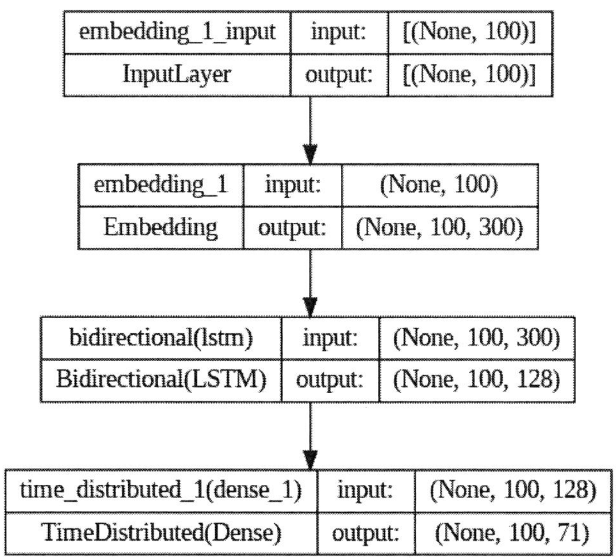

Figure 8: LSTM Model for English Text Glossing - Pseudo-parallel data generation

	BERT - Missing Labels	BERT - Extra Labels	BERT - POS Accuracy
Spanish	0.17	0.19	0.96
French	0.21	0.22	0.95
Basque	0.27	0.13	0.91
Italian	0.2	0.16	0.94
German	0.18	0.2	0.88
English	0.17	0.09	0.95
Turkish	0.25	0.13	0.87
Russian	0.24	0.28	0.88
Finnish	0.18	0.09	0.92

Table 7: BERT Morpheme Tagging Scores, fine-grained evaluation

Limited Train Data - F1 Score	20%	40%	60%	80%
Spanish	0.38	0.48	0.55	0.63
French	0.46	0.52	0.62	0.76
Basque	0.36	0.37	0.49	0.52
Italian	0.41	0.45	0.59	0.68
German	0.49	0.56	0.64	0.72
English	0.49	0.59	0.68	0.73
Turkish	0.33	0.38	0.52	0.58
Russian	0.39	0.4	0.64	0.71
Finnish	0.47	0.53	0.71	0.73

Table 8: Variable Training Data - Results

IGT Abbreviation	UniMorph Abbreviation
???	Unk
A1P	['ABS', '1', 'PL']
A1S	['ABS', '1', 'SG']
A2P	['ABS', '2', 'PL']
A2S	['ABS', '2', 'SG']
ADJ	ADJ
ADV	ADV
AFE	V
AFI	POS
AGT	AGFOC
AP	ANTIP
APLI	APPL
ART	ART, INDF
CAU	CAUS
CLAS	CLF
COM	PRF
COND	COND
CONJ	CONJ

Table 9: IGT to UniMorph Mappings

Improving Automated Prediction of English Lexical Blends Through the Use of Observable Linguistic Features

Jarem Saunders
M.A. Student, Department of Linguistics
University of North Carolina at Chapel Hill
jsaunders1@unc.edu jarem.saunders@gmail.com

Abstract

The process of lexical blending is difficult to reliably predict. This difficulty has been shown by machine learning approaches in blend modeling, including attempts using then state-of-the-art LSTM deep neural networks trained on character embeddings, which were able to predict lexical blends given the ordered constituent words in less than half of cases, at maximum. This project introduces a novel model architecture which dramatically increases the correct prediction rates for lexical blends, using only Polynomial regression and Random Forest models. This is achieved by generating multiple possible blend candidates for each input word pairing and evaluating them based on observable linguistic features. The success of this model architecture illustrates the potential usefulness of observable linguistic features for problems that elude more advanced models which utilize only features discovered in the latent space.

1 Introduction

1.1 Descriptive Research on Lexical Blends

Lexical blends have long been noted as a linguistic phenomenon with little consistent predictability. Researchers have described many different factors which affect how much of two given input words will be preserved in the resulting blend. This is often described in terms of the "switchpoint," or point at which each input word is truncated.

Factors described in the literature include a tendency for words to split at syllable constituent boundaries (Gries 2012, Kelly 2009), an observation that blends tend to match the length of the 2nd input word (Bat-El 2006), and a finding that the prosodic structure (Arndt-Lappe & Plag 2013). None of these noted tendencies or a combination thereof has thus far been used to create a predictive model of blending.

1.2 Predictive Models of Lexical Blends

Researchers who have used data-driven methods to model blending have instead opted for the use phoneme-by-phoneme insertion and deletion counts or the use of character embeddings. The former of these approaches was used by Deri & Knight (2015) as part of a multi-tape FST model that used grapheme-phoneme alignments to train the model on transformations to the phoneme sequence and produce the correct orthographic output, achieving a maximum of 45.75% correct blend predictions.

Gangal et. al. (2017) used the latter approach, training a then state-of-the-art LSTM deep neural network on character embeddings to attempt to generate English-like blends. This was shown to improve the rate of correct predictions to 48.75%, and found that the best performing models entertained multiple blend candidates and selected the most probable form, described as "exhaustive generation", rather than using greedy decoding from the vector space. Both of these models often produced sequences which were phototactically invalid, though sometimes these were orthographically plausible.

Because of the overall limited success of the models, including only a small increase in performance between the models despite a large increase in model complexity, we have developed an alternative model architecture which utilizes the same grapheme/phoneme alignment system as Deri & Knight and the exhaustive generation strategy laid out by Gangal et. al., but uses

Proceedings of the 20th SIGMORPHON workshop on Computational Research in Phonetics, Phonology, and Morphology, pages 93–97
July 14, 2023

linguistically-motivated features which were directly observable from the input forms. The use of linguistically-informed feature spaces was shown to improve performance in blend prediction using a modified form of the Gangal et. al. LSTM architecture, though improvements were once again quite modest (Kulkarni & Wang 2018). This paper proposes a more dramatic change in architecture which uses a novel feature set based primarily on the descriptive blend characteristics of Arndt-Lappe & Plag (2013).

For the purpose of this analysis, we constraint the blend structures entertained to only be those that follow typical English blend formation patterns by keeping some initial portion of the first word and some final portion of the second word. This model architecture was applied to 3 different corpora of lexical blends and was compared to previous model performance on each corpus, when applicable.

2 Methods

The model architecture laid out in this paper included the following elements:

- A component to generate all plausible blend candidates from the two input words and extract linguistically-based feature values using grapheme/phoneme alignments and syllable structure information.
- A component which uses the extracted features to calculate the probability of being a valid blend for each blend candidate.
- A feature to select the most probable candidate from each input word pairing.

The generation process was performed by iteratively creating prefixes from the first input word and suffixes from the second input word using grapheme-phoneme alignments, such that the substring consisted of a contiguous sequence of phonemes and their corresponding graphemes. Each prefix was then concatenated with each suffix to produce the full candidate set for each input word pair.

Feature values were calculated for each candidate using a set of phonemically-defined features, modified from Arndt-Lappe & Plag (2013). Labels were assigned to each candidate based on whether the graphemes of the candidate matched the desired blend output. Candidates with feature values which were identical to a candidate already in the feature set were removed.

Feature names	**Description**
W1/W2 length	number of syllables
Candidate length	number syllables
Medial overlap	whether candidate has contiguous phonemes shared by prefix/suffix
W1/W2 left/right edge to primary stress	number of syllables from input word edges to primary stress
W1 left edge to switchpoint	number of syllables from W1 left edge to switchpoint
W2 left edge to switchpoint	number of syllables from W2 right edge to switchpoint
Switchpoint syllable bound	whether switchpoint occurs at onset, nucleus, or coda boundary, or not at boundary
W1/W2 primary stress preserved	whether candidate preserves primary stress of input(s)
W1/W2 segments preserved	proportion of segments from each input preserved in candidate
W1/W2 syllables preserved	proportion of syllable nuclei from each input preserved in candidate
Switchpoint at W2 primary stress syllable	whether switchpoint in W2 falls within primary syllable bearing primary stress

Table 1: Complete set of linguistically-based model features utilized in trials

Given the feature values for all candidates, we used Random Forest classifiers and Polynomial regression models to learn probabilities for each candidate based on the extracted feature values. Rather than assign each data instance to a class, probabilities are retained for each candidate so that the candidate with the maximum probability can be selected. Random Forest and Polynomial regression were chosen for this experiment because they are easier to train and interpret than deep neural approaches.

Finally, a selection component was used to find the candidate from each input word pairing with the greatest probability of being a valid blend of English. This candidate was then chosen as the model's predicted output for that input word pairing.

2.1 Feature Set

The model used features which were modeled after the most relevant cues for blends discussed in previous linguistic literature on blend formation and structure. Among these are features that track whether the switchpoint aligns with syllable structure boundaries, the proportion of the input word that is preserved, and which word (if any) has it's stress patterns preserved.

In addition to these phonological features derived directly from the phoneme representations of input words, the model uses the phonotactic markedness score calculated by the BLICK phonotactic learner, which returns a score to indicate how well a sequence of phonemes follows English phonotactics (Hayes 2012). This is expressed as a sum of weighted violations of MaxEnt grammar constraints learned from a large sample of words from the CMU pronouncing dictionary (Hayes 2008). This feature was included to improve the phonotactic plausibility of output candidates. Specific names and descriptions for all model features are given in Table 1.

3 Experiments

The specific trials the model was used for are given here, along with the datasets utilized in training/testing for those trials.

3.1 Datasets

Three separate corpora were used in training and testing the model. The first two corpora were those used in the previous machine learning models of blending, Deri & Knight (2015) and Gangal et. al. (2017), respectively. These were both acquired through online resources such as Wikipedia, Wiktionary, and Urban Dictionary. The final corpus used comes from Shaw (2014) and is a curation of an earlier dictionary assembled by Thurner (1993). After filtering to meet the project design, 322 blends were used in trials of the Deri & Knight corpus, 1092 were used from Gangal et. al., and 1096 were used from Shaw.

3.2 Trials Performed

For each corpus, the model architecture was tested and evaluated using three different learners: LASSO regression, 2nd order Polynomial regression (with interaction terms), and Random Forest classifiers. Due to high collinearity among the feature set, we selected subset of the model features was selected to minimize correlations and maximize coefficient values by removing measures of syllable proportion, word length, and syllable distances to the switchpoint from the feature set. Each learner was trained once using the full feature set and once using the manually selected subset of features. Each trial was validated using 10-fold cross validation.

Learner	Features	Correct	Edit dist.
LASSO	Full	56.13%	1.05
Polynomial	Full	64.42%	0.72
RF	Full	60.39%	0.81
LASSO	Subset	55.21%	1.09
Polynomial	Subset	63.83%	0.79
RF	Subset	60.39%	0.83
Previous benchmark		45.39%	1.59

Table 2: Model Performance on D.&K. Corpus

Learner	Features	Correct	Edit dist.
LASSO	Full	47.72%	1.36
Polynomial	Full	59.51%	0.89
RF	Full	57.32%	0.89
LASSO	Subset	46.17%	1.43
Polynomial	Subset	54.21%	1.06
RF	Subset	57.32%	0.95
Previous benchmark		48.75%	1.12

Table 3: Model Performance on G. et. al. Corpus

Learner	Features	Correct	Edit dist.
LASSO	Full	66.09	0.93
Polynomial	Full	74.13%	0.58
RF	Full	73.96%	0.58
LASSO	Subset	64.17%	0.98
Polynomial	Subset	71.67%	0.66
RF	Subset	72.58%	0.65

Table 4: Model Performance on Shaw Corpus

4 Results

Model predictions were evaluated on the average percentage of blends correctly predicted and the average Levenshtein edit distance between the predicted output form and the correct blend form.

4.1 Quantitative Results

Models trained and tested on the Deri & Knight corpus outperformed the benchmark set by the multi-tape FST on both measures of model performance for every variation of the model. For the Gangal et. al. corpus, only the variation of the model using the LASSO regression learner failed to outperform the benchmark set by the LSTM model using character embeddings. The Shaw corpus demonstrated the highest performance of any model, with an average of 74.13% of blends correctly predicted with the best performing model trained on this corpus.

For all corpora, the model variations that used Polynomial regression learners outperformed all others, and models using full data set outperformed those with the manually curated subset, in spite of the high collinearity of the dataset.

A comparison of the highest performing models to date for all corpora is given in Figure 1.

4.2 Qualitative Results

Qualitative error analysis shows that the best performing model across all corpora, the Polynomial regression with full features trained on the Shaw corpus, tends to over-preserve phonemic material from both input words, rather than over-delete. In a random sample of 100 instances in which this model selected an incorrect candidate, 40 of them preserved too many contiguous segments from the first word, compared to 15 instances in which the output candidate had a sequence from the first word which was too short. Similarly, the sample demonstrated that 33 candidates had over-preserved segmental material from the second input word, compared to 18 instances in which too many segments of the word were deleted. In general, this resulted in a greater number of candidates that were longer than the desired output than candidates that were too short.

5 Discussion

5.1 Usefulness of Observable Features

Results from the trials we have conducted so far provide a compelling argument for the potential usefulness of observable linguistic features in the generation of lexical blends. This, in turn, may provide a framework for dealing with similar linguistic processes which exhibit some degree of unpredictability or are infrequently attested in natural language text data and accordingly are difficult for models which rely on features obtained in the latent space.

Little work has been done to date to tune hyperparameters or optimize the feature set used by the models. Future research into these areas could lead further improvements in the prediction rates that has already gained by using this model architecture, including research into measures to reduce the apparent model bias toward longer candidates.

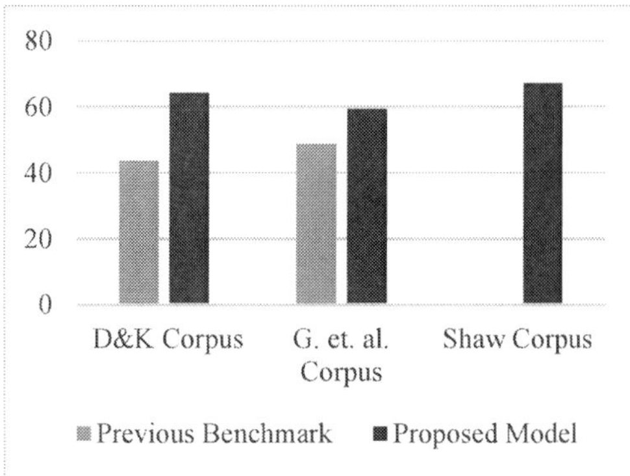

Figure 1: Maximum Model Correct Prediction Rates by Corpus

5.2 Potential Linguistic Applications

The architecture may also be useful for testing hypotheses about blend generation. Because the learners used in this model architecture are more interpretable than neural networks, the actual feature weights and decision tree splits used by the model can be directly examined and can be used as a datapoint in evaluating the relative importance of different factors that affect blend formation. Given the fact that there are often many possible blends that speakers can produce from an input word pair before it enters the lexicon (Gries 2012), testing the model's performance on novel blend forms and comparing it to blends produced by human speakers would be the most informative way to test how well this model truly does at replicating human-like blend generation behavior.

Such a trial would also be informative in comparing this methodology against modern large language models, as it provides a chance to use genuinely held-out data to evaluate them. One drawback of this architecture is its lack of generalizability to low resource languages.

5.3 Limitations of the Model Architecture

While this methodology does not require the large amount of text data utilized by more advanced models, it does depend on access to grapheme/phoneme alignment information for all input words. This does limit the usefulness of the model for languages with little linguistically-tagged data available, though the success of the small Deri & Knight corpus does indicate that the model architecture can be made to function effectively with a limited amount of annotated data.

References

Arndt-Lappe, S., & Plag, I. (2013). The role of prosodic structure in the formation of English blends. English Language & Linguistics, 17(3), 537-563.

Deri, A., & Knight, K. (2015). How to make a frenemy: Multitape FSTs for portmanteau generation. In Proceedings of the 2015 Conference of the North American Chapter of the Association for Computational Linguistics: Human Language Technologies (pp. 206-210).

Gangal, V., Jhamtani, H., Neubig, G., Hovy, E., & Nyberg, E. 2017. Charmanteau: Character embedding models for portmanteau creation. arXiv preprint arXiv:1707.01176.

Gries, S. T. 2004. Shouldnt it be breakfunch? A quantitative analysis of blend structure in English.

Gries, S. T. 2006. Cognitive determinants of subtractive word formation: A corpus-based perspective.

Gries, S. T. 2012. Quantitative corpus data on blend formation: Psycho-and cognitive-linguistic perspectives. Cross-disciplinary perspectives on lexical blending, 252, 145.

Hayes, B. 2012. BLICK: a phonotactic probability calculator (manual).

Hayes, B., & Wilson, C. 2008. A maximum entropy model of phonotactics and phonotactic learning. Linguistic inquiry, 39(3), 379-440.

Kelly, M. H. 1998. To "brunch" or to "brench": Some aspects of blend structure.

Kubozono, H. 1990. Phonological constraints on blending in English as a case for phonology-morphology interface. Yearbook of morphology, 3, 1-20.

Kulkarni, V., & Wang, W. Y. (2018, June). Simple models for word formation in slang. In Proceedings of the 2018 Conference of the North American Chapter of the Association for Computational Linguistics: Human Language Technologies, Volume 1 (Long Papers) (pp. 1424-1434).

Shaw, K. E., White, A. M., Moreton, E., & Monrose, F. 2014. Emergent faithfulness to morphological and semantic heads in lexical blends. In Proceedings of the annual meetings on phonology (Vol. 1, No. 1).

Thurner, Dick. 1993. Portmanteau dictionary: Blend words in the English language, including trademarks and brand names. Jefferson, NC: McFarland & Co.

Colexifications for Bootstrapping Cross-lingual Datasets: The Case of Phonology, Concreteness, and Affectiveness

Yiyi Chen
Department of Computer Science
Aalborg University, Copenhagen
Denmark
yiyic@cs.aau.dk

Johannes Bjerva
Department of Computer Science
Aalborg University, Copenhagen
Denmark
jbjerva@cs.aau.dk

Abstract

Colexification refers to the linguistic phenomenon where a single lexical form is used to convey multiple meanings. By studying cross-lingual colexifications, researchers have gained valuable insights into fields such as psycholinguistics and cognitive sciences (Jackson et al., 2019; Xu et al., 2020; Karjus et al., 2021; Schapper and Koptjevskaja-Tamm, 2022; François, 2022). While several multilingual colexification datasets exist, there is untapped potential in using this information to bootstrap datasets across such semantic features. In this paper, we aim to demonstrate how colexifications can be leveraged to create such cross-lingual datasets. We showcase curation procedures which result in a dataset covering 142 languages across 21 language families across the world. The dataset includes ratings of concreteness and affectiveness, mapped with phonemes and phonological features. We further analyze the dataset along different dimensions to demonstrate potential of the proposed procedures in facilitating further interdisciplinary research in psychology, cognitive science, and multilingual natural language processing (NLP). Based on initial investigations, we observe that i) colexifications that are closer in concreteness/affectiveness are more likely to colexify; ii) certain initial/last phonemes are significantly correlated with concreteness/affectiveness intra language families, such as /k/ as the initial phoneme in both Turkic and Tai-Kadai correlated with concreteness, and /p/ in Dravidian and Sino-Tibetan correlated with Valence; iii) the type-to-token ratio (TTR) of phonemes are positively correlated with concreteness across several language families, while the length of phoneme segments are negatively correlated with concreteness; iv) certain phonological features are negatively correlated with concreteness across languages. The dataset is made public online for further research[1].

[1]https://github.com/siebeniris/ColexPhon

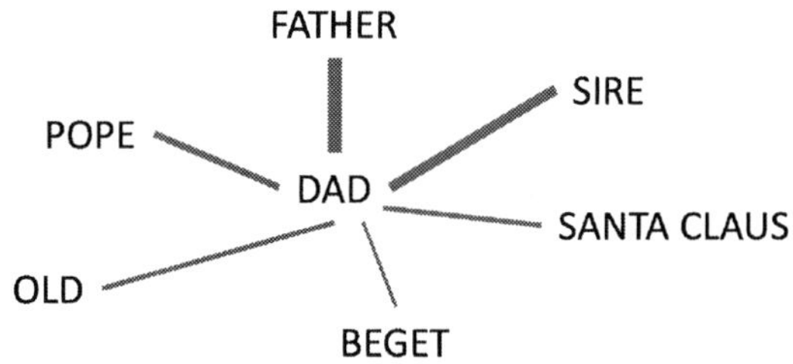

Figure 1: Colexification subgraph for DAD. The weight of the edges are proportional to the frequency of the colexification pattern in the dataset.

1 Introduction

Semantic typology studies cross-lingual semantic categorization (Evans et al., 2010). Within this area, the term "colexification" was first introduced and used by François (2008) and Haspelmath (2003) to create semantic maps. The study of colexifications focuses on cross-lingual colexification patterns, where the same lexical form is used in distinct languages to express multiple concepts. For instance, *mapu* in Mapudungun and *apakee* in Ignaciano both express the concepts EARTH and WORLD (Rzymski et al., 2020). Colexifications have been found to be pervasive across languages and cultures. The investigation of colexifications have led to interesting findings across different fields, such as linguistic typology (Schapper and Koptjevskaja-Tamm, 2022), psycholinguistics (Jackson et al., 2019), cognitive science (Gibson et al., 2019), but remain relatively unexplored in NLP (Harvill et al., 2022; Chen et al., 2023).

In recent years, with the increasing popularity of automatic methods and big data in linguistics, datasets such as Concepticon (List et al., 2022) and BabelNet (Navigli and Ponzetto, 2012) have been developed, affording large-scale cross-lingual semantic comparisons. The Database of Cross-lingual Colexifications (CLICS^3) (Rzymski et al., 2020) was created based on the Concepticon con-

Proceedings of the 20th SIGMORPHON workshop on Computational Research in Phonetics, Phonology, and Morphology, pages 98–109
July 14, 2023

cepts, including 4,228 colexification patterns across 3,156 languages, to facilitate research in colexifications. Studies have also been shown to curate large-scale colexification networks from BabelNet, consisting of over 6 million synsets across 520 languages (Harvill et al., 2022; Chen et al., 2023).

While syntactic typology is relatively well-established in NLP (Malaviya et al., 2017; Bjerva and Augenstein, 2018a,b, 2021; Cotterell et al., 2019; Bjerva et al., 2019a,b,c, 2020; Stanczak et al., 2022; Östling and Kurfalı, 2023; Fekete and Bjerva, 2023), semantic typology has so far only been subject to limited research (Chen et al., 2023; Chen and Bjerva, 2023; Liu et al., 2023). As a relatively new topic in both semantic typology and NLP, colexifications covers a wide-range of languages and language families. In contrast, although the concepts of concreteness/abstractness and affectiveness (e.g., valence, dominance and arousal) have long been in the center stage of interdisciplinary research fields such as cognitive science, psychology, linguistics and neurophysiology (Warriner et al., 2013; Solovyev, 2021; Brysbaert et al., 2014), language coverage of such resources is severely limited, and curation prohibitively expensive.

The study of phonemes and phonological features have furthermore been essential to, e.g., address the problems of non-arbitrariness in languages and investigating universals of spoken languages (de Varda and Strapparava, 2022). Studies such as Gast and Koptjevskaja-Tamm (2022) demonstrate the genealogical stability (persistence) and susceptibility to change (diffusibility) via studying the patterns the phonemes/phonological forms and the colexifications across European languages. However, this study is limited to a small range of languages, and the investigated concepts are also restricted to 100-item Swadesh list (Swadesh, 1950). With the proposed procedures, a wider range of concepts and the phonological forms across language families are curated.

In this paper, we create a synset graph based on multilingual WordNet (Miller, 1995) data from BabelNet 5.0. We then develop a cross-lingual dataset that includes ratings of concreteness and affectiveness, as this approach yields more comprehensive data than using CLICS^3. In addition, we meticulously select and organize phonemes and phonological features for the lexicons that represent the concepts. Our methodology for data creation is not limited to the constructed dataset, as it has potential for broader applications. We showcase the versatility of our approach through analysis across various dimensions, and make our dataset freely available.

2 Related Work

Colexifications The creation of semantic maps using cross-linguistic colexifications was initially formalized by François (2008). Semantic maps are graphical representations of the relationship between recurring expressions of meaning in a language (Haspelmath, 2003). This method is based on the idea that language-specific colexification patterns indicate the semantic proximity or relatedness between the meanings that are colexified (Hartmann et al., 2014). When analyzed cross-linguistically, colexification patterns can provide insights into various fields, such as cognitive principles recognition (Berlin and Kay, 1991; Schapper et al., 2016; Jackson et al., 2019; Gibson et al., 2019; Xu et al., 2020; Brochhagen and Boleda, 2022), diachronic semantic shifts in individual languages (Witkowski and Brown, 1985; Urban, 2011; Karjus et al., 2021; François, 2022), and language contact evolution (Heine and Kuteva, 2003; Koptjevskaja-Tamm and Liljegren, 2017; Schapper and Koptjevskaja-Tamm, 2022).

Jackson et al. (2019) conducted a study on cross-lingual colexifications related to emotions and found that different languages associate emotional concepts differently. For example, Persian speakers associate GRIEF closely with REGRET, while Dargwa speakers associate it with ANXIETY. The variations in cultural background and universal structure in emotion semantics provide interesting insights into the field of NLP. Bao et al. (2021) analyzed colexifications from various sources, including BabelNet, Open Multilingual WordNet, and CLICS^3, and demonstrated that there is no universal colexification pattern.

In the field of NLP, Harvill et al. (2022) constructed a synset graph from BabelNet to boost performance on lexical semantic similarity task. More recently, Chen et al. (2023) use colexifications to construct language embeddings and further model language similarities. Our goal is to utilize colexifications to construct cross-lingual datasets, including diverse ratings and phonological forms and features, to support further research, particularly in low-resource languages where norms and ratings are notably scarce.

Norms and Ratings A large number of words in high-resource languages have been assigned norms and ratings by researchers in psychology (Brysbaert et al., 2014; Warriner et al., 2013). Norms and ratings of words are essential components in psychology, linguistics, and recently being widely used in NLP. Norms refer to the typical frequency and context in which words are used in a particular language, while ratings represent subjective judgements of individuals on various dimensions such as concreteness, valence, arousal, and imageability. These norms and ratings can improve the performance on downstream tasks, such as sentiment analysis, emotion recognition, word sense disambiguation, and affective computing (Kwong, 2008; Tjuka et al., 2022; Strapparava and Mihalcea, 2007; Mohammad and Turney, 2010).

The study of concreteness and abstractness of concepts is interdisciplinary and spans across various fields, including linguistics, psychology, psycholinguistics, and neurophysiology (Solovyev, 2021). Concrete concepts are those that can be perceived by the senses, such as CAT and MOUNTAIN, while abstract concepts, like RELATIONSHIP and UNDERSTANDING, cannot be perceived by the senses. Brysbaert et al. (2014) conducted a study on concreteness ratings for 37,058 English words and 2,896 two-word expressions, involving over 4,000 participants, which has provided insights across various linguistic disciplines. The concreteness ratings are based on a scale of 1 (abstract) to 5 (concrete). These ratings have been used in conjunction with various tasks such as classification of metaphoricity (Haagsma and Bjerva, 2016) and animacy (Bjerva, 2014), as well as cultural studies (Berger and Packard, 2022).

Apart from concreteness, affective ratings are also essential for interdisciplinary research in psychology, linguistics and NLP. The affective norms for English words (ANEW) dataset, providing ratings of valence, arousal and dominance for English words, has been widely used in both psychology and NLP research (Bradley and Lang, 1999). Subsequently, the affective norms for French Words (FAN) and the affective norms for German words (ANGST) datasets, proving similar affective ratings for French and German words, respectively, have also been developed (Monnier and Syssau, 2014; Schmidtke et al., 2014). The Spanish version of ANEW is developed by Redondo et al. (2007). Extending the English ANEW, Warriner et al. (2013) covers nearly 14,000 English lemmas, providing ratings for valence (the pleasantness of a stimulus), arousal (the intensity of emotion provoked by a stimulus), and dominance (the degree of control exerted by a stimulus). For creating our dataset, we use the ratings from Warriner et al. (2013), see details in Section 3.

The data for linguistic norms and ratings is usually collected only for one language. For low-resource languages, such data is obviously lacking. Using our procedures, the norms and ratings can be bootstrapped for low-resource languages by sharing cross-lingual concepts through colexifications.

Phonemes and Phonological Features While direct phonetic comparison across languages is difficult, a common practice in comparing phonological characteristics across languages is to combine similar sounds into one multilingual phone set (Salesky et al., 2020). While more advanced methods for phonological typology do exist, e.g. Cotterell and Eisner (2017, 2018), a basic approach to phonology is found via the International Phonetic Alphabet (IPA), which classifies sounds based on general phonological properties. In this vein, WikiPron is created to serve as an open-source tool for mining phonemic pronunciation data from Wikitionary and still under continuous maintenance (Lee et al., 2020). To this date, it contains more than 1,8 million word/pronunciations across 543 languages.[2] The pronunciations are given in IPA, and segmented in a way that IPA diacritics can be properly recognized (Lee et al., 2020).

Demonstrating that phonological features outperform character-based models, PanPhon is created and used for various NER-related tasks (Mortensen et al., 2016). To date, PanPhon is a database relating over 5,000 IPA segments to 24 subsegmental articulatory features.[3] It has been used for various purposes, such as cross-modal and cross-lingual study of iconicity in languages (Zhu et al., 2021), and cross-linguistic phonosemantic correspondence using a deep-learning framework (de Varda and Strapparava, 2021).

In this paper, we build upon this work by diving into the relationship between phonological features, and the concreteness and affectiveness of sense lemmas across a wide set of languages. The paper is inspired by findings such that the sounds of words can influence their meaning and emotional

[2] https://github.com/CUNY-CL/wikipron

[3] https://github.com/dmort27/panphon

impact. For example, words with round vowel sounds are often associated with positive emotions, while harsher, more angular sounds can convey negative emotions (Ćwiek et al., 2022). This study aims to initiate the study on the intricate interplay between sound and affective/abstract meanings.

3 Dataset Curation

A *colexification pattern* refers to a case where two concepts are colexified, such as DAD-POPE shown in Figure 1. Specifically, a *colexification* is an instance of a *colexification pattern*, such as *far* in Danish, as shown in Table 1.

In order to leverage colexifications to create a cross-lingual dataset incorporating norms and ratings in psychology and other fields, we propose the following procedures for data curation and creation, as illustrated in Fig. 2.

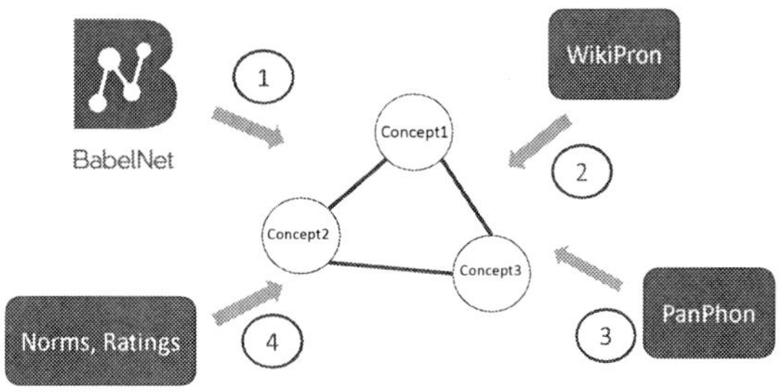

Figure 2: The Workflow of the Procedures for Creating the cross-lingual Dataset using Colexifications.

Building the Synset/Concept Graph In WordNet, a sense is a discrete representation of one aspect of the meaning of a word. For example, the lemma *bank* can either mean the sense FINANCIAL INSTITUTION or the sense SLOPING MOUND. The set of near-synonyms for a sense is called a **synset**, which is a primitive in WordNet (Jurafsky and Martin, 2023). Synsets are groups of words sharing the same concept. In order to construct of colexification networks, i) the WordDNet synsets are extracted from BabelNet; ii) for each synset, all the included word senses with their lemmas in the regarding language are elicitated; iii) finally, the sets of synsets sharing the same lemmas are extracted to represent a sysnet graph, with nodes being the synsets and the edges being the lemmas and their languages. The construction of a synset graph from BabelNet is first formalized in (Harvill et al., 2022), and adapted by (Chen et al., 2023) incorporating information of the languages and lemmas, see the Algorithm 1.

We adopt the algorithm presented in Chen et al. (2023) to construct a large-scale synset graph from WordNet synsets for our study. The difference in Chen et al. (2023) and Harvill et al. (2022) lies in the addition of G_s at line 3 and line 9, as shown in Algorithm 1. G_s affords the construction of colexification patterns and modeling language relations.

Algorithm 1 Construction of Colexification Graph: Given a set of languages L and corresponding vocabularies V, create graph edges between all colexified synset pairs (nodes), consisting of the set of tuples of lemmas and their language.

1: **function** CONSTRUCTGRAPH(L,V)
2: $CSP \leftarrow \{\}$ ▷ Colexified Synset Pairs
3: $G_s \leftarrow$ **graph**
4: **for** $l \in L$ **do**
5: **for** $x \in V_l$ **do**
6: **if** $|S_x| \geq 2$ **then**
7: **for** $\{s_1, s_2\} \in \binom{S_x}{2}$ **do**
8: $CSP \leftarrow CSP \cup \{s_i, s_j\}$
9: $G_s(s_1, s_2) \leftarrow \{x, l\}$
10: **end for**
11: **end if**
12: **end for**
13: **end for**
14: $G \leftarrow$ **graph**
15: **for** $s_1, s_2 \in CSP$ **do**
16: $G(s_1, s_2) \leftarrow 1$
17: **end for**
18: **return** G
19: **return** G_s
20: **end function**

A WordNet synset comprises a sense word, a Part-of-speech (POS) tag, and a sense number, e.g., dad#n#1. The sense numbers indicate the prevalence of the use of senses, with the most frequently used sense labeled 1. The frequency of use is determined by how often a sense is tagged in semantic concordance texts.[4] Our assumption is that the mean score of lexicon ratings, annotated by multiple humans across domains and languages, represents the ratings for the most prevalent sense. However, when it comes to cross-lingual synset-to-concept mapping, there may be variations in the sense annotations between languages. Suppose that in French the main sense KNOT is knot#n#4, which

[4]https://wordnet.princeton.edu/documentation/wndb5wn

refers to *a unit of speed*, while in English, the annotation for KNOT likely refers to *an actual knot that you tie*, which is the 1st sense for the synset. As a result, we cannot expect the same ratings of concreteness or affectiveness for these two different senses. Therefore, to map synsets to concepts, we always select the initial sense of the synsets..

Once filtered by the 1st sense of the synsets, as illustrated in Table 1, we derive concepts by extracting the sense word from each synset. The resulting concept graph comprises nodes representing the 1st senses of synsets and edges indicating the corresponding languages and sense lemmas.

Phonemes Extraction To facilitate analysis of phonetic characteristics cross-lingually in the context of colexifications and against ratings of concreteness and affectiveness, we extract phonemes from WikiPron, which to this date includes 1,882,240 word/pronunciation pairs in 543 languages.[5] To map the pronunciations to our data, we mapped their word/language code pairs to the pairs of sense lemma/language code extracted from BabelNet. As a result, there are 139,698 sense lemma/ phonemes pairs across 142 languages, presented as in Table 1. In our dataset, the median size of the phonemes per language is 32.

Phonological Features Extraction Phonological features have been proposed as the foundation of spoken language universals. Despite variations in phones across languages, the set of phonological features remains constant. Phones can be constructed from a set of phonological features. In our study, we extract phonemes for sense lemmas and then further extract phonological (articulatory) features based on the subsegments using PanPhon. PanPhon generates 24 phonological features for each segment, such as syllabic, sonorant, consonantal, continuant, delayed release, lateral, nasal, strident, voice, spread glottis, constricted glottis, anterior, coronal, distributed, labial, high (vowel/consonant, not tone), low (vowel/consonant, not tone), back, round, elaric airstream mechanism (click), tense, long, hitone, hireg [6]. Each feature is assigned a value of '1', '-1', or '0', where '1' indicates a positive value of the feature, '-1' indicates a negative value of the feature, and '0' indicates that the feature is absent for that sound. For instance, a vowel cannot possess consonant features, so it is marked as '0'. We use PanPhon to convert each phone into a vector with length 24 in our dataset.

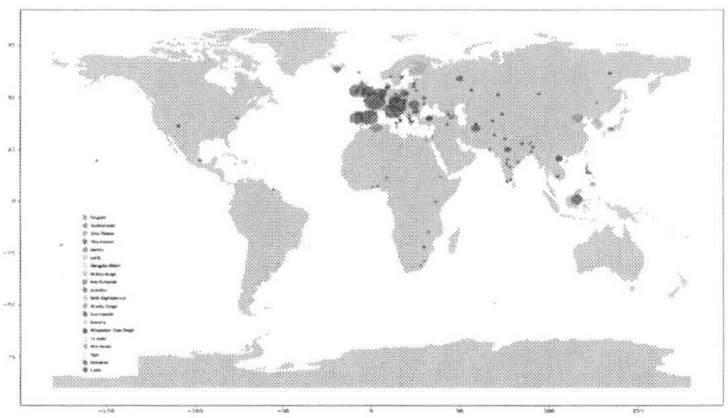

Figure 3: The map of language families of our data. The size of the points are proportional to the number of concepts in each language. Colors represent language families.

Incorporating Norms and Ratings Having built the concept graph from the synset graph by selecting the 1st senses of the synsets across languages, we map the concepts from databases containing norms and ratings to the concept graph. As shown in Table 1, the concept 1 DAD is mapped from concreteness/affectiveness rating lists to the synset 1 dad#n#1, while the concept 2 POPE is mapped to the synset 2 pope#n#1 by intersecting the datasets by the sense words. When each concept in the colexification pair has a rating, the distance of the concreteness/affectiveness can be calculated by computing the absolute distance of the two. When concept 1 has a (mean) concreteness of $conc_1$ and concept 2 has a (mean) concreteness of $conc_2$, then the $Conc.Dist$ is calculated as $|conc_1 - conc_2|$. Similar procedures are used for computing distance of valence ($V.Dist$), arousal ($A.Dist$) and dominance ($D.Dist$).

To conduct analysis of the correlations between phonemes/phonological features against the concreteness/affectiveness, the ratings for each phonemes are calculated as the average of the ratings of the included concepts, grouped by the phonemes and its language, respectively.

Undergoing these procedures, we create a dataset in 142 languages across 21 language families, including ratings in concreteness/affectivness, and phonemes for lemmas. The overall statistics of the data is shown in Table 2. The map for the data color coded by language families is presented in Fig. 3. As shown, the data is highly skewed towards Indo-European languages, and the data is quite scarce in Americas.

[5] https://github.com/CUNY-CL/wikipron

[6] https://github.com/dmort27/panphon

Sense Lemma	Language	Phonemes	Synset 1	Synset 2	Concept 1	Concept 2	Conc.Dist	V.Dist	A.Dist	D.Dist
پاپ	Persian	p ɑː p	dad#n#1	pope#n#1	DAD	POPE	0.42	1.96	0.16	1.88
بابا	Arabic	b ɑː b ɑː	dad#n#1	pope#n#1	DAD	POPE	0.42	1.96	0.16	1.88
папа	Russian	p a p ə	dad#n#1	pope#n#1	DAD	POPE	0.42	1.96	0.16	1.88
far	Danish	-	dad#n#1	sire#n#1	DAD	SIRE	-	0.74	0.05	0.57
pare	Castilian	p a ɾ e	Santa_Claus#n#1	dad#n#1	SANTA CLAUS	DAD	0.17	-	-	-

Table 1: An example of the dataset. {CONC,V,D,A}.Dist represent the distance of the concreteness, valence, dominance and arousal of the pair of concepts for each lexicon. The value is unknown(-) if either of the concepts does not have a rating.

#Entries	Colex. Patterns	#Synset	#Lexicalization	#Phone/Lemma pairs	#Concept	#Concept w/ Aff.	#Concept w/ Conc.
186,6558	676,594	72,604	68,249	613,906	84,084	10,353	19,179

Table 2: Statistics of the Dataset.

4 Analysis and Results

4.1 Colexifications vs. Closeness in Concreteness/Affectivness

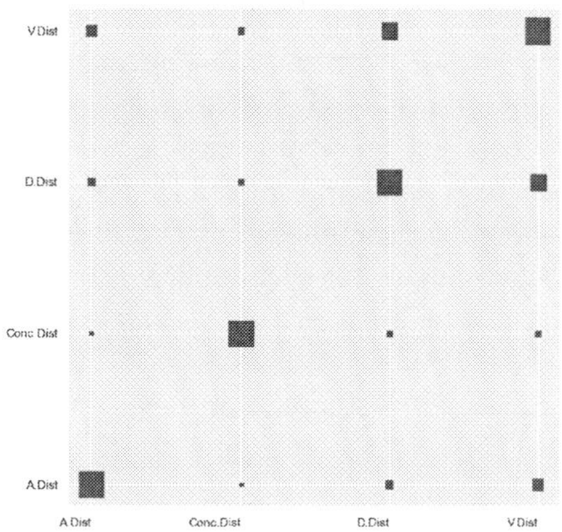

Figure 4: Correlation between Affectiveness- and Concreteness-Distances between the Colexified Concepts. The size of the squares represent correlation coefficients.

	Conc.Dist	V.Dist	A.Dist	D.Dist
#Colex.	-0.4716*	-0.4192*	-0.5798*	-0.5083*
Colex. Patterns	-0.4634*	-0.4115*	-0.581033*	-0.5065*
#Languages	-0.4727*	-0.4178*	-0.5798*	-0.5090*

Table 3: Correlation between #Colexifications and the Concreteness/Affectivness Distances between the Colexified Concepts, p-values are in the brackets. The sign * indicates the statistical significance of the correlation at 95% ($p < 0.0001$).

Previous studies show that abstract concepts are often understood by reference to more concrete concepts (Lakoff and Johnson, 2008), and words that first arise with concrete meanings often later gain an abstract one (Xu et al., 2017). Xu et al. (2020) leans on these findings to show that concepts more dissimilar in concreteness and affective valence are more likely to colexify. To test this, we calculate the correlation coefficients[7] between the number of colexifications and concreteness/affectiveness distances of the colexified concepts across languages. However, the results show the exact contrary to the previous theories and findings. As shown in Table 3, there is a statistically significant and relatively strong negative correlation between colexifications and the distance of concreteness, valence, arousal and dominance. This verifies that it is more likely for a pair of concepts to colexify when they are closer in concreteness and affectiveness. Our results about affectivness in colexifications is also corroborated by Di Natale et al. (2021).

Since both distances of conreteness and affectiveness are correlated with colexifications, it is intuitive to assume they might be correlated to each other. To test this, we calcuate the correlation coefficients between each dimension of concreteness and affectiveness. As shown in Fig. 4, the distances of valence and dominance are correlated with each other stronger than other pairs. And, concreteness distance is not significantly correlated with any dimension of affectiveness.

4.2 Phonemes vs. Concreteness/Affectiveness

Previous studies suggest that characteristics of the initial and the last phoneme have the most significant impact on the phonetic characteristics of the whole phone set (Pimentel et al., 2020). To test whether there are universals between the initial/last phoneme and the concreteness/affectiveness, we calculate the correlations between them per language family.

Since the whole results are too large to present,

[7]All the correlation analyses done in this study are using the SciPy implementation of Pearson correlation algorithm.

Lang. Family	#Lang.	# Sample	# Phonemes	Initial Phoneme	Last Phoneme
Turkic	7	2453	53	k (0.1148), t (0.1020)	-
Tai-Kadai	3	2701	20	k (-0.1122), n (0.1066)	-
Austroasiatic	2	3400	26	ʔ (0.1028)	-
Austronesian	7	21365	33	-	ŋ (0.1053)
Uralic	5	23352	37	ʋ (-0.1082)	i (0.1423), n (-0.1983), ɒ (0.1005)
Dravidian	3	339	22	p (0.2072)	ɭ (-0.2738)
Sino-Tibetan	5	7567	39	y (-0.1189)	^{1} (-0.1428), ^{4} (0.1092), ^{5} (0.1066)
Afro-Asiatic	5	862	44	e (-0.1450)	o (-0.1107), r (-0.1582), β (-0.1074), χ (-0.1432)

Table 4: Correlation between the Initial/Last Phoneme and the Concreteness of Sense Lemma across Languages per Language Family. All the presented coefficients (in the brackets) are statistically significant and at least bigger than 0.1 or smaller than -0.1, corrected with Bonferroni correction ($p < 0.05/\#Lang.$*).

Features	Tai-Kadai (2822/3)	Austroasiatic (3555/2)	Indo-European (229661/75)	Uralic (26795/6)
syl	-0.1570*	-0.1870*	-0.1851*	-0.2716*
son	-0.1533*	-0.1698*	-0.1453*	-0.2783*
cons	-0.1734*	-0.2252*	-0.1284*	-0.2092*
cont	-0.1567*	-0.1768*	-0.1520*	-0.2692*
nas	-	-0.1038*	-0.1120*	-0.1718*
voi	-0.1524*	-0.1546*	-0.1726*	-0.2486*
sg	-	-0.1185*	-	-
ant	-0.1217*	-0.1407*	-0.1553*	-0.2670*
cor	-0.1574*	-0.1956*	-0.1215*	-0.2195*
distr	-	-	-	-0.1719*
lab	-	-	-	-0.1706*
lo	-	-	-	-0.1244*
hi	-0.1194*	-0.1678*	-0.1015*	-
lo	-0.1424*	-	-	-
back	-0.1009*	-0.1513*	-	-
tense	-0.1631*	-0.1175*	-0.1350*	-0.2675*

Table 5: Correlation between Phonological Features and the Concreteness of Sense Lemma per Language Family. All the presented coefficients are statistically significant and at least bigger than 0.1 or smaller than -0.1, corrected with Bonferroni correction ($p < 0.05/\#Lang.$*).

we report here only the results where the correlations are statistically significant, and the absolute value of which are bigger than 0.1. To prevent data from incorrectly appearing to be statistically significant, we correct the p-value with Bonferroni correction by dividing it with the number of the languages within the language family that is tested on. Only the results, that are statistically significant at 95% after applying Bonferroni correction, are reported.

We can observe that, as in Table 4, by correlating against the concreteness distance, the p as the initial phoneme and the last ɭ is significantly and stronger correlated within Dravidian languages, and a in Artificial languages as the first phoneme, compared to others. While across language families, k is correlated with concreteness.

Similarly, we test the correlations against the affectivness distance. Only the results with valence is reported, since the correlations of the phonemes against other affective ratings are not significant. As shown in Table 6, p as initials present correlations with affectiveness cross language families, i.e., Sino-Tibetan and Dravidian.

To represent the complexity of phonemes intra language families, we calculate the TTR as the ratio of unique phonemes and the length of all the phonemes for each lemma. Furthermore, the correlation between the TTR and the concreteness/arousal is computed, as shown in Table 4. And also the length of the phoneme segments are calculated for similar correlation test. Across all 8 language families, the segment length is statistically negatively correlated with the concreteness, but positively correlated with arousal. While, the correlations between TTR and the concreteness shows that the more concrete concept, the more diverse (complex) the phonemes are.

4.3 Phonological Features vs. Concreteness/Affectiveness

To test whether phonological features of the phonemes correlate with concreteness or affectiveness, for each phoneme/lemma pair, the phonological feature vectors are calculated and the values are aggregated by frequency of the present features. As indicated in Table 5, in the reported data, all the phonological features are negatively correlated with the concreteness. While the correlation coefficients in general are quite small, this hints at the possible existence of effects of these phonological features on concreteness. For instance, the *coronal obstruent (cor)* feature in all four language families is highly negatively correlated with concreteness, indicating that there is a general preference for such

Lang. Family	#Lang.	# Sample	# Phonemes	Initial Phoneme	Last Phoneme
Turkic	7	2453	53	c (-0.1178), a (-0.1284)	p (-0.1412), y (-0.1158)
Austroasiatic	2	3400	26	-	h (-0.1169)
Artificial Language	2	448	24	m (-0.2464)	-
Dravidian	3	339	22	p (0.1667), r (-0.2044)	ɭ (-0.2693)
Sino-Tibetan	5	7567	39	p (-0.1337), u (-0.1272), y (0.1010)	-
Afro-Asiatic	5	862	44	i (-0.1070), j (0.1065), z (-0.1058), ɡ (-0.1268), ʔ (0.1091)	ɾ (0.1353), ʔ (-0.1588)

Table 6: Correlation between the Initial/Last Phoneme and the Valence of Sense Lemma across Languages per Language Family. All the presented coefficients (in the brackets) are statistically significant and at least bigger than 0.1 or smaller than -0.1, corrected with Bonferroni correction ($p < 0.05/\#Lang.$).

words to be abstract in meaning.

Lang. Family	#Lang.	# Sample	TTR	LEN
vs. Concreteness				
Turkic	8	2557	-	-0.1373*
Tai-Kadai	3	2701	0.1511*	-0.1834*
Austroasiatic	2	3398	0.1794*	-0.2715*
Uralic	6	23508	0.1876*	-0.2402*
Dravidian	3	339	-	-0.2585*
Indo-European	75	211371	-	-0.1697*
Sino-Tibetan	5	7567	0.1257*	-0.1184*
vs. Arousal				
Austroasiatic	2	3398	-	0.1157*
Mongolic-Khitan	3	66	-	0.3294*

Table 7: Correlation between TTR (Type-to-Token Ratio)/ Segment Length and the Concreteness of Sense Lemma per Language Family. All the presented coefficients (in the brackets) are statistically significant and at least bigger than 0.1 or smaller than -0.1, corrected with Bonferroni correction ($p < 0.05/\#Lang.$).

5 Conclusion and Future Work

In this study, we proposed a set of procedures to leverage colexifications to bootstrap cross-lingual datasets, incorporating human ratings of concreteness and affective meanings. The created dataset presents data in 142 languages across 21 language families and 5 language macro areas. However, the procedures can be applied beyond the datasets used in this paper.

Inspired by previous works, we test the correlations between i) the distance of concreteness/affectiveness and the number of colexifications; ii) the phonemes and concreteness/ affectiveness; and iii) the phonological features and the ratings. It is shown that i) colexifications closer in concreteness/effectiveness are more likely to colexify; ii) certian initial/last phonemes do present statistically significant correlations with the ratings across languages; and iii) there is a positive correlation between the phoneme diversity and concreteness; finally iv) certain phonological features are negatively correlated with the ratings. While it is difficult to draw any meaningful conclusions from this finding without a prior hypothesis, we hope that future work can use this dataset to make well-founded findings on the interactions between phonology, concreteness, and affectiveness.

We have showcased the soundness and validity of our approach to curate data from different domains and create a cross-lingual dataset mapping the information. The initial analyses and findings could inspire further applications in NLP and also other fields, such as psychology and psycholingusitics, which we will explore extensively for future work.

Nevertheless, the analyses conducted in this study are confined to individual correlation tests, which are inadequate for reaching definitive conlusions. For future work, we will employ multivariate modeling techniques utilizing affective/concrete ratings and the phonetic features to delve deeper into understanding the connections between human conceptualization and sounds across diverse languages and cultures.

Limitations

A limitation of this study is the fact that the concreteness ratings of Brysbaert et al. (2014) are curated solely from self-identified U.S. residents. And the affectiveness ratings of Warriner et al. (2013) are solely curated in English. As such, there is a risk of an anglocentric bias in the created dataset. Nonetheless, the goal of this study is to explore the potential of leveraging colexifications to bootstrap cross-lingual datasets in as many languages as possible, including a lot of low-resource languages.

Ethics Statement

Related to the limitations of this work, while this work increases research potential for low-resource languages, this comes with the main ethical risk of potential of propagating the anglocentric bias of some of the source datasets further.

Acknowledgements

This work is supported by the Carlsberg Foundation under a *Semper Ardens: Accelerate* career grant held by JB, entitled 'Multilingual Modelling for Resource-Poor Languages', grant code CF21-0454. We are furthermore grateful to the anonymous SIGMORPHON reviewers for pointing out issues that needed clarification in this work.

References

Hongchang Bao, Bradley Hauer, and Grzegorz Kondrak. 2021. On universal colexifications. In *Proceedings of the 11th Global Wordnet Conference*, pages 1–7, University of South Africa (UNISA). Global Wordnet Association.

Jonah Berger and Grant Packard. 2022. Using natural language processing to understand people and culture. *American Psychologist*, 77(4):525.

Brent Berlin and Paul Kay. 1991. *Basic color terms: Their universality and evolution*. Univ of California Press.

Johannes Bjerva. 2014. Multi-class animacy classification with semantic features. In *Proceedings of the Student Research Workshop at the 14th Conference of the European Chapter of the Association for Computational Linguistics*, pages 65–75.

Johannes Bjerva and Isabelle Augenstein. 2018a. From phonology to syntax: Unsupervised linguistic typology at different levels with language embeddings. In *Proceedings of the 2018 Conference of the North American Chapter of the Association for Computational Linguistics: Human Language Technologies, Volume 1 (Long Papers)*, pages 907–916.

Johannes Bjerva and Isabelle Augenstein. 2018b. Tracking typological traits of uralic languages in distributed language representations. In *Proceedings of the Fourth International Workshop on Computational Linguistics of Uralic Languages*, pages 76–86.

Johannes Bjerva and Isabelle Augenstein. 2021. Does typological blinding impede cross-lingual sharing? In *Proceedings of the 16th Conference of the European Chapter of the Association for Computational Linguistics: Main Volume*, pages 480–486, Online. Association for Computational Linguistics.

Johannes Bjerva, Yova Kementchedjhieva, Ryan Cotterell, and Isabelle Augenstein. 2019a. A probabilistic generative model of linguistic typology. In *Proceedings of the 2019 Conference of the North American Chapter of the Association for Computational Linguistics: Human Language Technologies, Volume 1 (Long and Short Papers)*, pages 1529–1540, Minneapolis, Minnesota. Association for Computational Linguistics.

Johannes Bjerva, Yova Kementchedjhieva, Ryan Cotterell, and Isabelle Augenstein. 2019b. Uncovering probabilistic implications in typological knowledge bases. In *Proceedings of the 57th Annual Meeting of the Association for Computational Linguistics*, pages 3924–3930, Florence, Italy. Association for Computational Linguistics.

Johannes Bjerva, Robert Östling, Maria Han Veiga, Jörg Tiedemann, and Isabelle Augenstein. 2019c. What do language representations really represent? *Computational Linguistics*, 45(2):381–389.

Johannes Bjerva, Elizabeth Salesky, Sabrina J Mielke, Aditi Chaudhary, Celano Giuseppe, Edoardo Maria Ponti, Ekaterina Vylomova, Ryan Cotterell, and Isabelle Augenstein. 2020. Sigtyp 2020 shared task: Prediction of typological features. In *The Second Workshop on Computational Research in Linguistic Typology*, pages 1–11. Association for Computational Linguistics.

Margaret M. Bradley and Peter J. Lang. 1999. Affective norms for english words (anew): Instruction manual and affective ratings.

Thomas Brochhagen and Gemma Boleda. 2022. When do languages use the same word for different meanings? the goldilocks principle in colexification. *Cognition*, 226:105179.

Marc Brysbaert, Amy Beth Warriner, and Victor Kuperman. 2014. Concreteness ratings for 40 thousand generally known english word lemmas. *Behavior research methods*, 46:904–911.

Yiyi Chen, Russa Biswas, and Johannes Bjerva. 2023. Colex2Lang: Language embeddings from semantic typology. In *Proceedings of the 24th Nordic Conference on Computational Linguistics (NoDaLiDa)*, pages 673–684, Tórshavn, Faroe Islands. University of Tartu Library.

Yiyi Chen and Johannes Bjerva. 2023. Patterns of closeness and abstractness in colexifications: The case of indigineous languages in the americas. In *Third Workshop on NLP for Indigenous Languages of the Americas*. Association for Computational Linguistics.

Ryan Cotterell and Jason Eisner. 2017. Probabilistic typology: Deep generative models of vowel inventories. In *Proceedings of the 55th Annual Meeting of the Association for Computational Linguistics (Volume 1: Long Papers)*, pages 1182–1192, Vancouver, Canada. Association for Computational Linguistics.

Ryan Cotterell and Jason Eisner. 2018. A deep generative model of vowel formant typology. In *Proceedings of the 2018 Conference of the North American Chapter of the Association for Computational Linguistics: Human Language Technologies, Volume 1 (Long Papers)*, pages 37–46, New Orleans, Louisiana. Association for Computational Linguistics.

Ryan Cotterell, Christo Kirov, Mans Hulden, and Jason Eisner. 2019. On the complexity and typology of inflectional morphological systems. *Transactions of the Association for Computational Linguistics*, 7:327–342.

Aleksandra Ćwiek, Susanne Fuchs, Christoph Draxler, Eva Liina Asu, Dan Dediu, Katri Hiovain, Shigeto Kawahara, Sofia Koutalidis, Manfred Krifka, Pärtel Lippus, et al. 2022. The bouba/kiki effect is robust across cultures and writing systems. *Philosophical Transactions of the Royal Society B*, 377(1841):20200390.

Andrea Gregor de Varda and Carlo Strapparava. 2021. A layered bridge from sound to meaning: Investigating cross-linguistic phonosemantic correspondences. In *Proceedings of the annual meeting of the cognitive science society*, volume 43.

Andrea Gregor de Varda and Carlo Strapparava. 2022. A cross-modal and cross-lingual study of iconicity in language: Insights from deep learning. *Cognitive Science*, 46(6):e13147.

Anna Di Natale, Max Pellert, and David Garcia. 2021. Colexification networks encode affective meaning. *Affective Science*, 2(2):99–111.

Nicholas Evans et al. 2010. Semantic typology. In *The Oxford handbook of linguistic typology*. Oxford University Press.

Marcell Richard Fekete and Johannes Bjerva. 2023. Gradual language model adaptation using fine-grained typology. In *Proceedings of the 5th Workshop on Research in Computational Linguistic Typology and Multilingual NLP*, pages 153–158, Dubrovnik, Croatia. Association for Computational Linguistics.

Alexandre François. 2008. Semantic maps and the typology of colexification. *From polysemy to semantic change: Towards a typology of lexical semantic associations*, (106):163.

Alexandre François. 2022. Lexical tectonics: Mapping structural change in patterns of lexification. *Zeitschrift für Sprachwissenschaft*, 41(1):89–123.

Volker Gast and Maria Koptjevskaja-Tamm. 2022. Patterns of persistence and diffusibility in the european lexicon. *Linguistic Typology*, 26(2):403–438.

Edward Gibson, Richard Futrell, Steven P. Piantadosi, Isabelle Dautriche, Kyle Mahowald, Leon Bergen, and Roger Levy. 2019. How efficiency shapes human language. *Trends in Cognitive Sciences*, 23(5):389–407.

Hessel Haagsma and Johannes Bjerva. 2016. Detecting novel metaphor using selectional preference information. In *Proceedings of the Fourth Workshop on Metaphor in NLP*, pages 10–17.

Iren Hartmann, Martin Haspelmath, and Michael Cysouw. 2014. Identifying semantic role clusters and alignment types via microrole coexpression tendencies. *Studies in Language. International Journal sponsored by the Foundation "Foundations of Language"*, 38(3):463–484.

John Harvill, Roxana Girju, and Mark Hasegawa-Johnson. 2022. Syn2Vec: Synset colexification graphs for lexical semantic similarity. In *Proceedings of the 2022 Conference of the North American Chapter of the Association for Computational Linguistics: Human Language Technologies*, pages 5259–5270, Seattle, United States. Association for Computational Linguistics.

Martin Haspelmath. 2003. The geometry of grammatical meaning: Semantic maps and cross-linguistic comparison. In *The new psychology of language*, pages 217–248. Psychology Press.

Bernd Heine and Tania Kuteva. 2003. On contact-induced grammaticalization. *Studies in Language. International Journal sponsored by the Foundation "Foundations of Language"*, 27(3):529–572.

Joshua Conrad Jackson, Joseph Watts, Teague R. Henry, Johann-Mattis List, Robert Forkel, Peter J. Mucha, Simon J. Greenhill, Russell D. Gray, and Kristen A. Lindquist. 2019. Emotion semantics show both cultural variation and universal structure. *Science*, 366(6472):1517–1522.

Dan Jurafsky and James H Martin. 2023. Speech and language processing (3rd (draft) ed.).

Andres Karjus, Richard A Blythe, Simon Kirby, Tianyu Wang, and Kenny Smith. 2021. Conceptual similarity and communicative need shape colexification: An experimental study. *Cognitive Science*, 45(9):e13035.

Maria Koptjevskaja-Tamm and Henrik Liljegren. 2017. *Semantic Patterns from an Areal Perspective*, Cambridge Handbooks in Language and Linguistics, page 204–236. Cambridge University Press.

Oi Yee Kwong. 2008. A preliminary study on the impact of lexical concreteness on word sense disambiguation. In *Proceedings of the 22nd Pacific Asia Conference on Language, Information and Computation*, pages 235–244, The University of the Philippines Visayas Cebu College, Cebu City, Philippines. De La Salle University, Manila, Philippines.

George Lakoff and Mark Johnson. 2008. *Metaphors we live by*. University of Chicago press.

Jackson L. Lee, Lucas F.E. Ashby, M. Elizabeth Garza, Yeonju Lee-Sikka, Sean Miller, Alan Wong, Arya D. McCarthy, and Kyle Gorman. 2020. Massively multilingual pronunciation modeling with WikiPron. In *Proceedings of the Twelfth Language Resources and Evaluation Conference*, pages 4223–4228, Marseille, France. European Language Resources Association.

Johann Mattis List, Annika Tjuka, Christoph Rzymski, Simon Greenhill, and Robert Forkel. 2022. Clld concepticon 3.0.0 as cldf dataset.

Yihong Liu, Haotian Ye, Leonie Weissweiler, and Hinrich Schütze. 2023. Crosslingual transfer learning for low-resource languages based on multilingual colexification graphs. *arXiv preprint arXiv:2305.12818*.

Chaitanya Malaviya, Graham Neubig, and Patrick Littell. 2017. Learning language representations for typology prediction. In *Proceedings of the 2017 Conference on Empirical Methods in Natural Language Processing*, pages 2529–2535, Copenhagen, Denmark. Association for Computational Linguistics.

George A Miller. 1995. Wordnet: a lexical database for english. *Communications of the ACM*, 38(11):39–41.

Saif Mohammad and Peter Turney. 2010. Emotions evoked by common words and phrases: Using Mechanical Turk to create an emotion lexicon. In *Proceedings of the NAACL HLT 2010 Workshop on Computational Approaches to Analysis and Generation of Emotion in Text*, pages 26–34, Los Angeles, CA. Association for Computational Linguistics.

Catherine Monnier and Arielle Syssau. 2014. Affective norms for french words (fan). *Behavior research methods*, 46(4):1128–1137.

David R. Mortensen, Patrick Littell, Akash Bharadwaj, Kartik Goyal, Chris Dyer, and Lori S. Levin. 2016. Panphon: A resource for mapping IPA segments to articulatory feature vectors. In *Proceedings of COLING 2016, the 26th International Conference on Computational Linguistics: Technical Papers*, pages 3475–3484. ACL.

Roberto Navigli and Simone Paolo Ponzetto. 2012. Babelnet: The automatic construction, evaluation and application of a wide-coverage multilingual semantic network. *Artificial Intelligence*, 193:217–250.

Tiago Pimentel, Brian Roark, and Ryan Cotterell. 2020. Phonotactic complexity and its trade-offs. *Transactions of the Association for Computational Linguistics*, 8:1–18.

Jaime Redondo, Isabel Fraga, Isabel Padrón, and Montserrat Comesaña. 2007. The spanish adaptation of anew (affective norms for english words). *Behavior research methods*, 39(3):600–605.

Christoph Rzymski, Tiago Tresoldi, Simon J Greenhill, Mei-Shin Wu, Nathanael E Schweikhard, Maria Koptjevskaja-Tamm, Volker Gast, Timotheus A Bodt, Abbie Hantgan, Gereon A Kaiping, et al. 2020. The database of cross-linguistic colexifications, reproducible analysis of cross-linguistic polysemies. *Scientific data*, 7(1):1–12.

Elizabeth Salesky, Eleanor Chodroff, Tiago Pimentel, Matthew Wiesner, Ryan Cotterell, Alan W Black, and Jason Eisner. 2020. A corpus for large-scale phonetic typology. In *Proceedings of the 58th Annual Meeting of the Association for Computational Linguistics*, pages 4526–4546, Online. Association for Computational Linguistics.

Antoinette Schapper and Maria Koptjevskaja-Tamm. 2022. Introduction to special issue on areal typology of lexico-semantics. *Linguistic Typology*, 26(2):199–209.

Antoinette Schapper, Lila San Roque, and Rachel Hendery. 2016. *12. Tree, firewood and fire in the languages of Sahul*, pages 355–422. De Gruyter Mouton, Berlin, Boston.

David S Schmidtke, Tobias Schröder, Arthur M Jacobs, and Markus Conrad. 2014. Angst: Affective norms for german sentiment terms, derived from the affective norms for english words. *Behavior research methods*, 46:1108–1118.

Valery Solovyev. 2021. Concreteness/abstractness concept: State of the art. In *Advances in Cognitive Research, Artificial Intelligence and Neuroinformatics: Proceedings of the 9th International Conference on Cognitive Sciences, Intercognsci-2020, October 10-16, 2020, Moscow, Russia 9*, pages 275–283. Springer.

Karolina Stanczak, Edoardo Ponti, Lucas Torroba Hennigen, Ryan Cotterell, and Isabelle Augenstein. 2022. Same neurons, different languages: Probing morphosyntax in multilingual pre-trained models. In *Proceedings of the 2022 Conference of the North American Chapter of the Association for Computational Linguistics: Human Language Technologies*, pages 1589–1598, Seattle, United States. Association for Computational Linguistics.

Carlo Strapparava and Rada Mihalcea. 2007. SemEval-2007 task 14: Affective text. In *Proceedings of the Fourth International Workshop on Semantic Evaluations (SemEval-2007)*, pages 70–74, Prague, Czech Republic. Association for Computational Linguistics.

Morris Swadesh. 1950. Salish internal relationships. *International Journal of American Linguistics*, 16(4):157–167.

Annika Tjuka, Robert Forkel, and Johann-Mattis List. 2022. Linking norms, ratings, and relations of words and concepts across multiple language varieties. *Behavior Research Methods*, 54(2):864–884.

Matthias Urban. 2011. Asymmetries in overt marking and directionality in semantic change. *Journal of Historical Linguistics*, 1(1):3–47.

Amy Beth Warriner, Victor Kuperman, and Marc Brysbaert. 2013. Norms of valence, arousal, and dominance for 13,915 english lemmas. *Behavior research methods*, 45:1191–1207.

Stanley R. Witkowski and Cecil H. Brown. 1985. Climate, clothing, and body-part nomenclature. *Ethnology*, 24(3):197–214.

Yang Xu, Khang Duong, Barbara C. Malt, Serena Jiang, and Mahesh Srinivasan. 2020. Conceptual relations predict colexification across languages. *Cognition*, 201:104280.

Yang Xu, Barbara C Malt, and Mahesh Srinivasan. 2017. Evolution of word meanings through metaphorical mapping: Systematicity over the past millennium. *Cognitive psychology*, 96:41–53.

Chengrui Zhu, Keyu An, Huahuan Zheng, and Zhijian Ou. 2021. Multilingual and crosslingual speech recognition using phonological-vector based phone embeddings. In *2021 IEEE Automatic Speech Recognition and Understanding Workshop (ASRU)*, pages 1034–1041. IEEE.

Robert Östling and Murathan Kurfalı. 2023. Language embeddings sometimes contain typological generalizations.

Character Alignment Methods for Dialect-to-Standard Normalization

Yves Scherrer
Department of Digital Humanities
University of Helsinki
Helsinki, Finland
yves.scherrer@helsinki.fi

Abstract

This paper evaluates various character alignment methods on the task of sentence-level standardization of dialect transcriptions. We compare alignment methods from different scientific traditions (dialectometry, speech processing, machine translation) and apply them to Finnish, Norwegian and Swiss German dialect datasets. In the absence of gold alignments, we evaluate the methods on a set of characteristics that are deemed undesirable for the task. We find that trained alignment methods only show marginal benefits to simple Levenshtein distance. On this particular task, *eflomal* outperforms related methods such as GIZA++ or *fast_align* by a large margin.

1 Introduction

In recent research, a wide range of character transduction tasks (Wu and Cotterell, 2019) have been studied, such as modernization of historical spellings, correction of non-standard spellings in user-generated content, lemmatization, or grapheme-to-phoneme conversion (G2P). While most work aims at creating and improving generative models that produce the target representation given its source representation, we focus in this paper on the task of aligning characters when both representations are given. Character alignment is a key step in the training pipeline of certain character transduction models such as those based on the statistical machine translation (SMT) paradigm.

Other lines of research have been concerned with finding distances between strings, e.g., to compare different dialectal pronunciations (dialectometry) or to identify cognate pairs in corpora of related languages. While most research in these areas focuses on finding the optimal distance metric for a given task, we rather look at the alignments produced by these distance metrics here. Indeed, character alignments are a by-product of distance computations and readily available.

In most cases, both character transduction and distance computation are performed at word level, i.e., one word at a time. However, we argue that it is beneficial to carry them out at sentence level (if appropriate corpora are available) to enable contextual disambiguation, to avoid relying on preexistent tokenization and to capture assimilation effects at word boundaries.

In this work, we focus on sentence-level standardization of dialect transcriptions. We compare character alignment methods from different scientific traditions and apply them to corpora of transcribed dialectal speech from three languages, namely Finnish, Norwegian and Swiss German. In the absence of gold alignments, we evaluate the alignment methods on a set of characteristics (e.g., the amount of vowel-to-consonant alignments) that are deemed undesirable for dialect-to-standard character alignment.

2 Alignment Methods

Character alignment methods have been proposed for different purposes in different fields, but all of them can be meaningfully applied to sentence-level dialect-to-standard alignment.

Dialectometry The core idea of dialectometry is to obtain abstract representations of dialect landscapes from large numbers of individual features (see e.g. Nerbonne and Kretzschmar, 2003; Wieling and Nerbonne, 2015). One way to achieve this is to compute distances between phonetic transcriptions of a given word in different dialects, followed by aggregating the distances over all words of the dataset. Levenshtein distance (Levenshtein, 1966) is generally used as a starting point for such undertakings, but over the years, several extensions have been proposed, such as vowel-sensitive Levenshtein distance, or the possibility to learn the edit weights from a corpus (Heeringa et al., 2006). While most work focuses on the obtained distance

Proceedings of the 20th SIGMORPHON workshop on Computational Research in Phonetics, Phonology, and Morphology, pages 110–116
July 14, 2023

	docs	sents	words	sents/doc	words/doc	words/sent	chars/word	$\|C_\cup\|$	$\|C_\cap\|$
SKN	99	51,254	841,859	518	8504	16.4	5.7	243	70
NDC	648	145,961	1,937,905	225	2991	13.3	4.4	93	84
ArchiMob	6	11,959	93,450	1993	15575	7.8	5.3	49	33

Table 1: Key figures of the three datasets. The table shows the absolute number of documents, sentences and words, as well as the average number of sentences per document, words per document, words per sentence, and characters per word. $|C_\cup|$ refers to the size of the union of dialectal and standardized character sets, $|C_\cap|$ to their intersection.

values and their correlation to existing dialectological findings, Wieling et al. (2009) specifically evaluate the alignments obtained by such distance metrics.

Cognate identification Similar distance metrics have been employed for identifying cognates in large corpora of related languages (e.g. Mann and Yarowsky, 2001; Kondrak and Sherif, 2006).

Grapheme-to-phoneme conversion Many text-to-speech systems contain a G2P component that turns words spelled in conventional orthography into sequences of phoneme symbols that correspond to the actual pronunciation of the word. Before neural sequence-to-sequence models were used, the standard approaches for G2P relied on stochastic transducers or HMMs with weights learned from training data using expectation-maximization (EM). For example, Ristad and Yianilos (1998) introduced a stochastic memoryless transducer. Jiampojamarn et al. (2007) proposed an extension to this model that also covers multi-character graphemes and phonemes.

Statistical machine translation Word alignment is a crucial ingredient of the SMT paradigm introduced at the beginning of the 1990s (Brown et al., 1993). GIZA++, an open-source aligner that has become standard over the years, uses a pipeline of increasingly complex word alignment models (Och and Ney, 2000). Follow-up work such as *fast_align* (Dyer et al., 2013) and *eflomal* (Östling and Tiedemann, 2016) introduced simpler, faster and less memory-hungry alignment approaches with only minor sacrifices in accuracy.

Although designed to align words in sentence pairs, the word alignment models can also operate on single characters. This approach has become popular as character-level SMT and has been used e.g. to translate between closely-related languages (Tiedemann, 2009) or for historical text modernization (Scherrer and Erjavec, 2013).

3 Data

We use existing dialect corpora from Finnish, Norwegian and Swiss German for our experiments:

SKN – Finnish The Samples of Spoken Finnish corpus (*Suomen kielen näytteitä*, hereafter SKN) (Institute for the Languages of Finland, 2021) consists of 99 interviews conducted mostly in the 1960s. It includes data from 50 Finnish-speaking locations, with two speakers per location (with one exception). The interviews have been transcribed phonetically on two levels of granularity (detailed and simplified) and normalized manually by linguists. We use the detailed transcriptions here.[1]

NDC – Norwegian The Norwegian Dialect Corpus (Johannessen et al., 2009, hereafter NDC) was compiled between 2006 and 2010 in the context of a larger initiative to collect dialect data of the North Germanic languages. Typically, four speakers per location were recorded, and each speaker appears both in an interview with a researcher and in an informal conversation with another speaker. The recordings were transcribed phonetically and thereafter semi-automatically normalized to the Bokmål standard.[2]

ArchiMob – Swiss German The ArchiMob corpus (Scherrer et al., 2019) consists of oral history interviews conducted between 1999 and 2001. It contains 43 phonetically transcribed interviews, but only six of them were normalized manually. We only use these six documents for our experiments.

Some quantitative information about the datasets is given in Table 1. One may note that ArchiMob has the longest documents and NDC the shortest. On the other hand, ArchiMob has the shortest sentences. SKN has the most detailed transcriptions

[1]Details about the availability of the corpora are given in Table 6 in the appendix.

[2]The publicly available phonetic and orthographic transcriptions are not well aligned. We use (and provide) an automatically re-aligned version of the corpus, cf. Table 6.

SKN:
mä oon syänys "seittemäŋ "silakkaa , 'aiva niin , 'häntä erellä .
minä olen syönyt seitsemän silakkaa , aivan niin , häntä edellä .
'I have eaten seven herrings, that's right, tail first'

NDC:
å får eg sje sjøra vår bil før te påske
og får jeg ikke kjøre vår bil før til påske
'and I don't get to drive our car until Easter'

ArchiMob:
aber meer hènd den furchpaari finanzijelli schwirigkaite gchaa
aber wir haben dann furchtbare finanzielle schwierigkeiten gehabt
'but then we had terrible financial difficulties'

Table 2: Example sentence pairs from the three datasets. The top row presents the phonetic dialectal transcription, the middle row the standardized version, and the bottom row provides an English gloss. Although the number of transcribed and standardized tokens is the same in the three shown examples, we do not presuppose this for our experiments. Likewise, we do not presuppose that the data is aligned at token level.

and therefore the largest character vocabulary. Table 2 provides some example sentences.

4 Experimental Setup

4.1 Data Preparation

We reformat the three datasets in such a way that the utterances are split into sequences of characters and that the word boundaries are marked with a special symbol (_), as exemplified in Figure 1.

```
_ å _ f å r _ e g _ s j e _ s j ø r a _
_ o g _ f å r _ j e g _ i k k e _ k j ø r e _
```

Figure 1: Tokenized example sentence, dialectal transcription above and orthographic normalization below.

Since all alignment methods are unsupervised and there are no gold alignments for evaluation, we do not split the data into training and test sets. We train one alignment model per document, using the dialectal transcriptions as the source and the orthographic normalizations as the target.

4.2 Alignment Methods

We apply the following alignment methods:

- Levenshtein distance with default edit operation weights (`leven`).
- Weighted Levenshtein distance using PMI scores as edit operation weights (Wieling et al., 2009). We extract the PMI scores from the concatenation of all Levenshtein-aligned documents of a corpus (`leven-pmi`).
- Stochastic memoryless unigram transducer with weights trained iteratively on single documents (Ristad and Yianilos, 1998) (`unigram`).[3]
- Stochastic memoryless bigram transducer (Jiampojamarn et al., 2007); we override the default settings and allow deletions and insertions, as well as mappings of two bigrams (`bigram`).
- `GIZA++` with default parameters.
- `fast_align` with default parameters.
- `eflomal` with default parameters.
- *eflomal* can extract prior alignment probabilities from a previously aligned dataset to initialize a new alignment model. We concatenate all documents of a corpus to extract the probabilities (`eflomal-priors`).

To summarize, our experiments cover one untrained model (`leven`), five models trained on document-level data (`unigram`, `bigram`, `GIZA++`, `fast_align`, `eflomal`) and two models trained on corpus-level data (`leven-pmi`, `eflomal-priors`).

4.3 Symmetrization

Word alignment algorithms can only produce one-to-many alignments, but no many-to-one alignments. Therefore, it is standard practice to run the models twice, once in the "forward" direction and once in the "reverse" direction. The produced alignments are then symmetrized, e.g., by taking the intersection if precision is favored, or the union if recall is favored. Heuristics such as the popular *grow-diag-final-and* method produce a more balanced result (Och and Ney, 2003). For consistency, we apply symmetrization to all methods.

4.4 Adding Adjacent Identicals

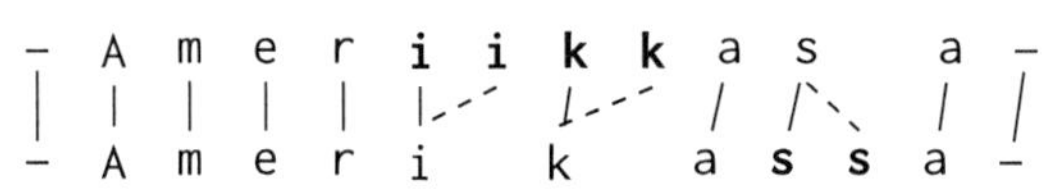

Figure 2: Additional alignments (dashed lines) are added to the initial alignments (solid lines) on the basis of consecutive identical characters (in bold).

Levenshtein-based models only produce one-to-one alignments, but leave inserted and deleted characters unaligned. To reduce the amount of

[3]We use the implementation by (Jiampojamarn et al., 2007) available at `https://github.com/letter-to-phoneme/m2m-aligner`.

unaligned characters, we add a simple heuristic that identifies two consecutive identical characters on one side and, if one of them is unaligned, introduces a new many-to-one alignment link (see Figure 2 for an example).

4.5 Evaluation Criteria

In a similar study, Wieling et al. (2009) compare various alignment methods with a set of manually verified gold alignments. Unfortunately, such annotations are not available for the three datasets used in this work. Instead, we gather four statistics about various phenomena that we consider undesirable for the given task, and rank the alignment methods according to these phenomena. They include:

U-src proportion of unaligned source characters,
U-tgt proportion of unaligned target characters,
V-C proportion of vowel-to-consonant and consonant-to-vowel alignments (disregarding semi-vowels, nasals, laterals and suprasegmentals),
X proportion of crossing alignment pairs (swaps).

We aggregate these proportions over all documents of a given dataset.

Note that we do not expect the optimal values of these proportions to be 0. The expected values depend on the languages and dialects, and reliable estimates would require access to a gold-aligned development set. However, based on our knowledge of the languages and dialects, we estimate **V-C** to lie below 1% and **X** below 0.2%. **U-tgt** is expected to be higher than **U-src**,[4] but both proportions are unlikely to exceed 15%.

Besides these quality indicators, we also report run times (on 1 CPU) and memory usage of the alignment methods.[5]

5 Results

5.1 Symmetrization Strategies

Table 3 exemplifies the effect of different symmetrization strategies on the basis of *eflomal* and the SKN dataset, but similar results are obtained for the other methods and datasets. It can be seen that recall-focused strategies (union) provide the lowest number of unaligned characters, whereas precision-focused strategies (intersection) show the lowest amounts of vowel-consonant alignments and crossing alignments. The *grow-diag-final-and* (`gdfa`) strategy is largely similar to union, but greatly reduces the number of crossing alignments. We find that `gdfa` provides the best compromise overall and select this symmetrization method for all subsequent experiments.

	forward	reverse	intersect	union	gdfa
U-src	9.39	9.51	13.77	**7.53**	7.63
U-tgt	6.00	7.18	11.11	**4.64**	4.76
V-C	0.17	0.15	**0.11**	0.21	0.20
X	0.50	0.49	**0.02**	1.00	0.12

Table 3: Impact of alignment symmetrization strategies. All values are percentages and refer to *eflomal* alignments on the SKN dataset.

5.2 Adding Adjacent Identicals

Table 4 shows that the adjacent-identicals heuristic effectively reduces the number of unaligned characters on both source and target sides, but leaves the other measures largely unaffected. In the following, we add this heuristic to all Levenshtein- and unigram-based methods and apply it after symmetrization with `gdfa`.

	SKN		NDC		ArchiMob	
	−aai	+aai	−aai	+aai	−aai	+aai
U-src	9.27	**8.85**	5.09	**1.25**	4.57	**2.65**
U-tgt	6.18	**5.22**	8.10	**7.92**	13.76	**12.78**
V-C	0.31	0.31	0.36	0.38	1.37	1.34
X	0.00	0.00	0.00	0.00	0.02	0.02

Table 4: Impact of adding adjacent identicals (`+aai`) on Levenshtein alignment. All values are percentages.

5.3 Method Comparison

The comparison between the eight alignment methods enumerated in Section 4.2 is shown in Table 5.

Two methods, `GIZA++` and `fast_align`, yield unrealistically high proportions of unaligned characters, leaving half of all characters unaligned in the worst case. The same methods also show higher-than-expected amounts of swaps. On the other hand, the `bigram` transducer produces unexpectedly large amounts of vowel-consonant alignments. These three methods can therefore not be recommended for character alignment with the used parameters.

[4]In SKN, **U-src** may be higher than **U-tgt** because of the suprasegmentals occurring in the source.

[5]The code for all experiments is available at `https://github.com/Helsinki-NLP/dialect-align-sigmorphon23`.

		Leven	Leven+PMI	unigram	bigram	GIZA++	fast_align	eflomal	eflomal+priors
SKN	U-src	8.85	8.11	9.83	9.60	*39.99*	*50.13*	7.63	7.67
	U-tgt	5.22	4.67	6.47	7.35	*38.56*	*48.66*	4.76	4.65
	V-C	0.31	0.46	0.07	*8.51*	0.20	0.24	0.20	0.25
	X	0.00	0.00	0.00	0.05	*0.75*	*0.26*	0.12	*0.40*
NDC	U-src	1.25	1.11	1.95	5.17	*15.34*	*26.64*	2.49	3.22
	U-tgt	7.92	7.54	8.85	8.13	*21.03*	*31.59*	7.51	7.45
	V-C	0.38	0.46	0.15	*6.36*	0.39	*1.26*	0.43	0.38
	X	0.00	0.00	0.00	0.07	*0.39*	*0.32*	0.02	0.13
ArchiMob	U-src	2.65	2.66	13.54	3.74	7.45	13.91	2.33	3.67
	U-tgt	12.78	12.85	*23.59*	10.51	*17.52*	*23.95*	9.14	12.61
	V-C	*1.34*	*1.39*	0.63	*7.81*	0.71	*1.48*	*2.00*	*1.22*
	X	0.02	0.00	0.00	0.07	*0.50*	*0.63*	0.12	0.14
CPU time (hh:mm)		0:30	11:17	20:20	105:27	30:36	0:45	12:32	16:18
Memory (MB)		69	76	1290	2350	58	34	263	268

Table 5: Evaluation of character alignment methods. All values are percentages, lower values are assumed to be better. Values violating our expectations are shown in italics.

The Levenshtein-based and `unigram` models do not permit swaps, leaving the corresponding measure at 0.[6] Since this is a technical limitation of the models, it should not be considered as an argument in their favor.

Learning the weights over the entire corpus (`leven-pmi`, `eflomal-priors`) does not consistently improve (nor worsen) results. We would have expected this approach to be useful especially for SKN and NDC with their short texts. This also contrasts with the findings of Wieling et al. (2009), who obtained significant error rate reductions with PMI-based Levenshtein distance. More thorough inspection of the results will be required to explain this divergence.

Three models (`leven`, `unigram`, `eflomal`) show similar performance over our criteria. They can be recommended in different situations. If crossing alignments (swaps) are expected to occur in the data, `eflomal` is the only recommended solution. If phonological consistency is highly rated, the `unigram` transducer is the method of choice because it produces the lowest rate of vowel-consonant alignments, at the expense of slightly higher amounts of unaligned tokens. Finally, plain Levenshtein distance remains remarkably competitive compared to the trained models. It is also one of the fastest and least memory-hungry approaches.

[6]It is nevertheless possible to obtain swaps through symmetrization. It has also been proposed to add a swap transition to Levenshtein distance, but preliminary experiments have shown that this addition negatively affects the other measures.

6 Discussion

Our evaluation of character alignment methods is based on a set of "undesirable characteristics" of the task. In this section, we would like to discuss some issues arising from this experimental setup.

In Swiss German and Finnish, a common pattern is the lack of final *n* in the dialectal pronunciation. For Swiss German *müesse / müssen*, two solutions are available: (a) a one-to-many alignment containing both *e–e* and *e–n*, and (b) leaving *n* unaligned. Although both options can be considered linguistically equivalent, our evaluation favors solution (a). In the opposite direction, the same argument holds for the suprasegmental symbols in the SKN corpus.

The transcription systems of Norwegian and Swiss German are based on conventional orthography and render some phonemes by multiple characters (e.g. Norwegian ***sje / ikke***). It is unclear how alignment errors inside such multi-character graphemes should be evaluated.

Alignment can be performed left-to-right or right-to-left. For Norwegian *æin / en*, the former yields *æ–e* and the latter *i–e*. Although symmetrization minimizes the effects of alignment direction, its impact on the evaluation scores is not entirely clear.

Despite these yet unsolved questions, we believe that our evaluation provides interesting insights into the performance of character alignment methods for sentence-level dialect-to-standard normalization.

Limitations

A major limitation of the current work is the absence of gold alignments for evaluating the different methods. Gold alignments would also enable us to provide more reliable estimates of the prevalence of the evaluated phenomena in the three datasets. We are not aware of any other similar corpora that come with gold character alignments. The work of Wieling et al. (2009) uses word lists, not entire sentences.

Furthermore, our work currently only covers European languages in Latin script. Some of the presented techniques also assume identical writing systems in the transcribed and normalized layers. Our setup may therefore not generalize well to the dialectal variation and writing systems present in other parts of the world. For example, the **V-C** proportion cannot be easily determined in scripts that do not specify all vowels. Although there is an extensive amount of research in particular on Arabic and Japanese dialects and their normalization (e.g., Abe et al., 2018; Eryani et al., 2020), we currently limit our experiments to data written in Latin script.

Ethics Statement

All experiments are based on publicly available corpora. Even though some of the corpora contain personal information, they have been cleared for publication. The reported experiments do not introduce any new artifacts that would be problematic from an ethical point of view.

References

Kaori Abe, Yuichiroh Matsubayashi, Naoaki Okazaki, and Kentaro Inui. 2018. Multi-dialect neural machine translation and dialectometry. In *Proceedings of the 32nd Pacific Asia Conference on Language, Information and Computation*, Hong Kong. Association for Computational Linguistics.

Peter F. Brown, Stephen A. Della Pietra, Vincent J. Della Pietra, and Robert L. Mercer. 1993. The mathematics of statistical machine translation: Parameter estimation. *Computational Linguistics*, 19(2):263–311.

Chris Dyer, Victor Chahuneau, and Noah A. Smith. 2013. A simple, fast, and effective reparameterization of IBM model 2. In *Proceedings of the 2013 Conference of the North American Chapter of the Association for Computational Linguistics: Human Language Technologies*, pages 644–648, Atlanta, Georgia. Association for Computational Linguistics.

Fadhl Eryani, Nizar Habash, Houda Bouamor, and Salam Khalifa. 2020. A spelling correction corpus for multiple Arabic dialects. In *Proceedings of the Twelfth Language Resources and Evaluation Conference*, pages 4130–4138, Marseille, France. European Language Resources Association.

Wilbert Heeringa, Peter Kleiweg, Charlotte Gooskens, and John Nerbonne. 2006. Evaluation of string distance algorithms for dialectology. In *Proceedings of the Workshop on Linguistic Distances*, pages 51–62, Sydney, Australia. Association for Computational Linguistics.

Institute for the Languages of Finland. 2021. Samples of Spoken Finnish, VRT Version.

Sittichai Jiampojamarn, Grzegorz Kondrak, and Tarek Sherif. 2007. Applying many-to-many alignments and hidden Markov models to letter-to-phoneme conversion. In *Human Language Technologies 2007: The Conference of the North American Chapter of the Association for Computational Linguistics; Proceedings of the Main Conference*, pages 372–379, Rochester, New York. Association for Computational Linguistics.

Janne Bondi Johannessen, Joel James Priestley, Kristin Hagen, Tor Anders Åfarli, and Øystein Alexander Vangsnes. 2009. The Nordic Dialect Corpus – an advanced research tool. In *Proceedings of the 17th Nordic Conference of Computational Linguistics (NODALIDA 2009)*, pages 73–80, Odense, Denmark. Northern European Association for Language Technology (NEALT).

Grzegorz Kondrak and Tarek Sherif. 2006. Evaluation of several phonetic similarity algorithms on the task of cognate identification. In *Proceedings of the Workshop on Linguistic Distances*, pages 43–50, Sydney, Australia. Association for Computational Linguistics.

Vladimir I. Levenshtein. 1966. Binary Codes Capable of Correcting Deletions, Insertions and Reversals. *Soviet Physics Doklady*, 8(10):707–710.

Gideon S. Mann and David Yarowsky. 2001. Multipath translation lexicon induction via bridge languages. In *Second Meeting of the North American Chapter of the Association for Computational Linguistics*.

John Nerbonne and William Kretzschmar. 2003. Introducing computational techniques in dialectometry. *Computers and the Humanities*, 37(3):245–255.

Franz Josef Och and Hermann Ney. 2000. Improved statistical alignment models. In *Proceedings of the 38th Annual Meeting of the Association for Computational Linguistics*, pages 440–447, Hong Kong. Association for Computational Linguistics.

Franz Josef Och and Hermann Ney. 2003. A systematic comparison of various statistical alignment models. *Computational Linguistics*, 29(1):19–51.

Robert Östling and Jörg Tiedemann. 2016. Efficient word alignment with Markov Chain Monte Carlo. *Prague Bulletin of Mathematical Linguistics*, 106:125–146.

Eric Ristad and Peter Yianilos. 1998. Learning string edit distance. *Pattern Analysis and Machine Intelligence, IEEE Transactions on*, 20:522 – 532.

Yves Scherrer and Tomaž Erjavec. 2013. Modernizing historical Slovene words with character-based SMT. In *Proceedings of the 4th Biennial International Workshop on Balto-Slavic Natural Language Processing*, pages 58–62, Sofia, Bulgaria. Association for Computational Linguistics.

Yves Scherrer, Tanja Samardžić, and Elvira Glaser. 2019. Digitising Swiss German: how to process and study a polycentric spoken language. *Language Resources and Evaluation*, 53(4):735–769.

Jörg Tiedemann. 2009. Character-based PSMT for closely related languages. In *Proceedings of the 13th Annual conference of the European Association for Machine Translation*, Barcelona, Spain. European Association for Machine Translation.

Martijn Wieling and John Nerbonne. 2015. Advances in dialectometry. *Annual Review of Linguistics*, 1(1):243–264.

Martijn Wieling, Jelena Prokić, and John Nerbonne. 2009. Evaluating the pairwise string alignment of pronunciations. In *Proceedings of the EACL 2009 Workshop on Language Technology and Resources for Cultural Heritage, Social Sciences, Humanities, and Education (LaTeCH – SHELT&R 2009)*, pages 26–34, Athens, Greece. Association for Computational Linguistics.

Shijie Wu and Ryan Cotterell. 2019. Exact hard monotonic attention for character-level transduction. In *Proceedings of the 57th Annual Meeting of the Association for Computational Linguistics*, pages 1530–1537, Florence, Italy. Association for Computational Linguistics.

A Appendix

The appendix provides further information about the used datasets (Table 6).

Dataset	Licence	URL
SKN	CC-BY	`http://urn.fi/urn:nbn:fi:lb-2021112221`
NDC	CC BY-NC-SA 4.0	`http://www.tekstlab.uio.no/scandiasyn/download.html`
(realigned)	CC BY-NC-SA 4.0	`https://github.com/Helsinki-NLP/ndc-aligned`
ArchiMob	CC BY-NC-SA 4.0	`https://www.spur.uzh.ch/en/departments/research/textgroup/ArchiMob.html`

Table 6: Datasets used in the experiments.

SIGMORPHON–UniMorph 2023 Shared Task 0: Typologically Diverse Morphological Inflection

Omer Goldman[1] **Khuyagbaatar Batsuren**[2] **Salam Khalifa**[3] **Aryaman Arora**[4]
Garrett Nicolai[5] **Reut Tsarfaty**[1] **Ekaterina Vylomova**[6]
[1]Bar-Ilan University [2]National University of Mongolia [3]Stony Brook University
[4]Georgetown University [5]University of British Columbia [6]University of Melbourne
omer.goldman@gmail.com vylomovae@unimelb.edu.au

Abstract

The 2023 SIGMORPHON–UniMorph shared task on typologically diverse morphological inflection included a wide range of languages: 26 languages from 9 primary language families. The data this year was all lemma-split, to allow testing models' generalization ability, and structured along the new hierarchical schema presented in (Batsuren et al., 2022). The systems submitted this year, 9 in number, showed ingenuity and innovativeness, including hard attention for explainability and bidirectional decoding. Special treatment was also given by many participants to the newly-introduced data in Japanese, due to the high abundance of unseen Kanji characters in its test set.[1]

1 Introduction

As a long-running shared task, the SIGMORPHON-UniMorph task on morphological inflection is a major engine behind the surging interest in computational morphology, as it facilitated both the building of UniMorph as a large multilingual morphological dataset, and the development and testing of morphological inflection models. In its first few installments (Cotterell et al., 2016, 2017, 2018; Vylomova et al., 2020) the focus of the task was first and foremost on generalization across languages, with the their number raising steadily from 10 languages in the task of 2016 to 90 languages in 2020.

Later studies, both in the 2021 shared task (Pimentel et al., 2021) and otherwise (Goldman et al., 2022a), discovered that the impressive results achieved by systems submitted to these tasks were in large part due the presence of test lemmas in the train set. As a result, the 2022 shared task (Kodner et al., 2022) focused on generalization to both unseen lemmas and unseen feature combinations.

In this task we continue to test systems on the challenging lemma-split setting while circling back to the inclusivity objective that guided the task from its inception. To this end, we employ the hierarchical annotation schema of UniMorph 4.0 (Batsuren et al., 2022) that allows more natural annotation of languages with complex morphological structures such as case stacking and polypersonal agreement. This year we include 26 languages from 9 primary language families: Albanian, Amharic, Ancient Greek, Arabic (Egyptian and Gulf), Armenian, Belarusian, Danish, English, Finnish, French, Georgian, German, Hebrew, Hungarian, Italian, Japanese, Khaling, Macedonian, Navajo, Russian, Sámi, Sanskrit, Spanish, Swahili and Turkish. The inclusion of Japanese, written in Kanji characters that are rarely shared across lemmas, compelled all systems this year to find ways to deal with unseen characters in the test set.

In total, 9 systems were submitted by 3 teams, both neural and non-neural models, and they were compared against 2 baselines, neural and non-neural as well. The submitted systems experimented with innovative ideas for morphological inflection as well as for sequence-to-sequence modeling in general. Girrbach (2022) introduced an elaborate attention mechanism between static representations for explainability, and Canby and Hockenmaier (2023) experimented with a new type of decoder for transformer models that is able to decode from both left to right and vise versa simultaneously. Lastly, Kwak et al. (2023) improved the non-neural affixing system used as a baseline.

The results show that although on average systems achieve impressive results in inflecting unseen lemmas, some languages still present a substantial challenge, mostly extinct languages like Ancient Greek and Sanskrit or low resourced languages like Navajo and Sámi. In addition, the results point to a dependency on the writing system that could be further explored in future shared tasks.

[1]Data, evaluation scripts, and predictions are available at: https://github.com/sigmorphon/2023InflectionST

Proceedings of the 20th SIGMORPHON workshop on Computational Research in Phonetics, Phonology, and Morphology, pages 117–125
July 14, 2023 ©2023 Association for Computational Linguistics

Family	Subfamily	ISO 639-2	Language	Source of Data	Annotators
Afro-Asiatic	Semitic	afb	Arabic, Gulf	Obeid et al. (2020)	Salam Khalifa
		arz	Arabic, Egyptian		Nizar Habash
		amh	Amharic	Gasser (2011)	Michael Gasser
		heb	Hebrew	Wiktionary	Omer Goldman
Indo-European	Albanian	sqi	Albanian	Wiktionary	Kirov et al. (2016)
	Armenian	hye	Eastern Armenian	Wiktionary	Hossep Dolatian
	Balto-Slavic	bel	Belarusian	Wiktionary	Ekaterina Vylomova
		mkd	Macedonian	Wiktionary	Ekaterina Vylomova
		rus	Russian	Wiktionary	Ekaterina Vylomova
	Germanic	dan	Danish	Wiktionary	Mans Hulden Khuyagbaatar Batsuren
		eng	English	Wiktionary	Mans Hulden Khuyagbaatar Batsuren
		deu	German	Wiktionary	Ryan Cotterell
	Helenic	grc	Ancient Greek	Wiktionary	Kirov et al. (2016)
	Indo-Aryan	san	Sanskrit	Huet's inflector	Aryaman Arora
	Romance	fra	French	Wiktionary	Géraldine Walther
		ita	Italian	Wiktionary	Géraldine Walther
		fra	Spanish	Wiktionary	Géraldine Walther
Japonic		jap	Japanese	Wiktionary	Khuyagbaatar Batsuren Omer Goldman
Kartvelian		kat	Georgian	Guriel et al. (2022)	David Guriel Simon Guriel Silvia Guriel-Agiashvili Nona Atanelov
Na-Dené	Southern Athabascan	nav	Navajo	Wiktionary	Mans Hulden Rob Malouf
Niger–Congo	Bantu	swa	Swahili	Goldman et al. (2022b)	Lydia Nishimwe Shadrak Kirimi Omer Goldman
Sino-Tibetan	Kiranti	klr	Khaling	Walther et al. (2013)	Géraldine Walther
Turkic	Oghuz	tur	Turkish	Wiktionary	Omer Goldman Duygu Ataman
Uralic	Finnic	fin	Finnish	Wiktionary	Mans Hulden
		sme	Sámi	Wiktionary	Mans Hulden
	Ugric	hun	Hungarian	Wiktionary	Judit Ács Khuyagbaatar Batsuren Gábor Bella, Ryan Cotterell Christo Kirov

Table 1: Languages presented in this year's shared task

2 Task Description

This year's task was organized in a very similar fashion to previous iterations. Participants were asked to design supervised learning systems which could predict an inflected form given a lemma and a morphological feature set corresponding to an inflectional category, or a cell in a morphological paradigm. They were provided with a training set of several thousands of examples, as well as a development set and test set for each language. The training data consisted of (`lemma`, `feature set`, `inflected form`) triples, while the inflected forms were held out from the test set. The development set was provided in both train- and test-like formats.

Data was made available to participants in two phases. In the first phase, the training and development sets were provided for most languages. In the second phase, training and development sets were released for some extra ("surprise") languages and the test sets were provided for all languages.[2]

Schema Differences The data this year followed the hierarchical annotation schema that was suggested by Guriel et al. (2022) and adopted in UniMorph 4.0 (Batsuren et al., 2022). The difference that was most pronounced in the data was the replacement of opaque tags that grouped several features such as AC3SM(a 3rd person singular masculine accusative argument) with the hierarchically combined features ACC(3,SG,MASC), i.e. without introducing a new tag for each feature combination in the cases of polypersonal agreement.

[2]The surprise languages were: Albanian, Belarusian, German, Gulf Arabic, Khaling, Navajo, Sámi and Sanskrit.

3 The Languages

The selection of languages used in this year's task is varied at almost any dimension. In terms of language genealogy we have representatives of 9 language families, some are widely used, like English and Spanish, and others are endangered or extinct, like Khaling and Sanskrit. The languages employ a wide variety of orthographic systems with varying degrees of transparency (Sproat and Gutkin, 2021): alphabets (e.g., German), abugidas (e.g., Sanskrit), abjads (e.g., Hebrew), and even one logographs using language (Japanese).

In light of the new annotation schema, many languages in this year's selection employ forms that refer to multiple arguments. Possessors are marked on nouns in 6 of the languages: Hebrew, Hungarian, Amharic, Turkish, Armenian and Finnish. In addition, polypersonal agreement appears in verbs of 5 of the languages: Georgian, Spanish, Hungarian, Khaling and Swahili.[3] Other notable morphological characteristics include, among others, the ablaut-extensive Semitic languages and prefix-inclined Navajo.

All in all, Table 1 enumerates the languages included in the shared task.

Languages new to UniMorph A couple of languages, namely Swahili and Sanskrit, have seen their respective UniMorph data increased substantially in size for this task. The Swahili data, that previously had partial inflection tables, was expanded using the clause morphology data of Goldman et al. (2022b), so a Swahili verbal inflection table includes more that 14,000 forms rather than mere 180. The Sanskrit data was massively expanded, mostly in terms of the number of lemmas, by incorporating data from Gérard Huet's Sanskrit inflector.[4]

In addition, one previously unrepresented language was introduced to UniMorph — Japanese. The data was crawled from Wiktionary and canonicalized to match the UniMorph 4.0 format. The usage of Kanji characters, logograms of Chinese origin that are completely unrepresentative of the pronunciation and almost uniquely used per lemma, can pose an interesting challenge to inflection systems that will have to deal with many unseen characters.

[3]Nouns in Arabic also mark their possessor and Verbs in Navajo also agree with multiple arguments, but the UniMorph data includes partial inflection tables for these languages.

[4]https://sanskrit.inria.fr/index.fr.html

# Inflection Tables	Languages
500	fin, fra, grc, heb, hun, hye, ita kat, klr, nav, san, sme, spa, sqi swa, tur
1000	amh, bel, deu, jap, mkd, rus
2000	dan
3000	afb, arz, eng

Table 2: Results of all the systems, submitted and baselines over the test sets in all languages. the best system(s) per language in marked in **bold**. The systems are ordered by the averaged success.

4 Data Preparation

All data for this task is provided in standard UniMorph format, with training items consisting of (`lemma, morphosyntactic features, inflected form`) triples. Since the goal of the task is to predict inflected forms, the test set was presented as (`lemma, features`) pairs. The data for all languages was lemma-split (Goldman et al., 2022a).

For each language, a number of inflection tables (i.e., lemmas) were sampled from the entire UniMorph dataset. 80% of the tables were used for the train set, and the rest were split between the validation and the test sets, then 10,000 forms were sampled from the inflection tables of the train set, and 1,000 forms were sampled for the validation and test sets from the respective tables. The number of inflection tables used was capped at 500, in cases where the tables were too small to generate enough data more tables were added until it was sufficient. Table 2 details the amount of tables used for each language.

5 The systems

5.1 Baseline Systems

The baseline systems provided this year are a recurrent appearance of the baselines of yesteryears: a **neural** character-level transformer (Wu et al., 2021, details in Appendix A), and a **non-neural** statistical application of affixing rules firstly used by Cotterell et al. (2017).

5.2 Submitted Systems

University of Arizona Kwak et al. (2023) submitted several non-neural models. Their first system (**AZ1**) is a re-implementation of the non-neural baseline, while another system of theirs (**AZ2**) uses the same framework but improves the rules used for both processing of the training data and making the predictions over the test set. In addition, they experimented with a weighted finite-state transducers (WFST; **AZ3**), and they provided an ensemble of the WFST with AZ2 (**AZ4**).

University of Tübingen Girrbach (2023) focused on explainability of the predictions of a neural inflection model. They did not get into debate on whether soft attention between model's hidden states is a good explanation (Jain and Wallace, 2019; Wiegreffe and Pinter, 2019), but rather applied a hard attention mechanism directly over static character representations. The models complexity comes solely from the attention module itself, that includes a LSTMs that run over the example's source and target.

University of Illinois Canby and Hockenmaier (2023) provided the most extensive set of experiments with transformer-based neural models. The ultimate focus of their work was the directionality of the decoder. Rather than decoding left-to-right, their first system (**IL1**) used two unidirectional models and chose a prediction that got the higher probability assessed by its respective model. In addition, they experimented with a model capable of deciding whether to decode from left or right at each step separately and used it either to select between unidirectional predictions (**IL2**) or as a standalone model (**IL3**). Lastly, they equipped IL3 with a beam re-ranker (**IL4**).

Common system characteristics The Japanese data, with its high abundance of unseen characters, posed a major problem to the neural submitted systems. Thus, they all gave the Japanese data special treatment and replaced the unseen characters with special place holders that were filled in with the lemma characters as a post-processing step.[5]

None of the systems submitted made explicit use of the hierarchy of the features. The teams opted for flattening the structure and letting the models understand the relations between the features from the order. Thus, for example, the feature bundle V;PRS;NOM(1,SG);ACC(2,PL) was treated as V;PRS;NOM;1;SG;ACC;2;PL, with multiple person and number features on the same level.

6 Results and analysis

Table 3 summarizes the accuracy results of all systems over all languages based on the exact match between the prediction and gold outputs. In addition, we also provide macro-averaged score over languages.

System performance In terms of averaged performance, all neural systems outperformed the non-neural systems, with IL4 having the best performance. When examining the results per language, the neural baseline and three of the Illinois-submitted systems take the lead in about 6 languages each. The exceptions to this are English, Danish and French, in which the non-neural baseline is the best performing system. Partial explanation may be the small size of the inflection tables in Danish and English that necessitated inclusion of many lemmas in the training set and may facilitated better generalization ability of the non-neural baseline. Admittedly, this explanation is not valid for French, but this language was proven difficult in previous shared tasks (Cotterell et al., 2017, 2018) and in other works (Silfverberg and Hulden, 2018; Goldman and Tsarfaty, 2021).

The neural baseline system was significantly hampered by the lack of a special mechanism for the unseen characters in Japanese. When discarding the Japanese performance for all systems, the neural baseline is second in averaged performance. That is to say that devising a strategy to deal with unseen characters is highly necessary when inflecting lemma-split data in general, and logographic languages in particular.

Being the neural system with the lowest averaged accuracy, TÜB seem to trade some predictive power in favor of having more explainable outputs, as exemplified in Figure 1.

Although the WFST system that is AZ3 is the system with the lowest scores, including it as part of an ensemble resulted in some advantages and helped producing the best non-neural system — AZ4.

Language performance The performance of the per-language best system over most languages is quite impressive, and in some cases like Swahili and Khaling even exceptionally impressive. How-

[5]Another possible solution to this bind could have been to introduce a copy mechanism in the model itself, such as the one used by Makarov and Clematide (2018). However, no team chose this path.

Language	AZ3	AZ1	Baseline Non-neural	AZ2	AZ4	TÜB	Baseline Neural	IL1	IL2	IL3	IL4
macro average	56.1	67.2	69.6	71.7	72.4	76.9	81.6	82.6	84.0	84.1	**84.3**
afb	34.5	30.8	30.8	52.7	52.7	75.8	80.1	80.7	82.2	84.1	**84.6**
amh	59.9	65.4	65.4	74.0	74.0	83.8	82.2	88.9	**90.6**	88.9	88.6
arz	75.7	77.2	77.9	80.8	80.8	87.6	**89.6**	89.2	88.7	89.1	88.7
bel	46.2	68.1	68.1	64.5	64.5	56.3	74.5	73.5	**74.7**	72.9	72.9
dan	64.8	**89.5**	**89.5**	87.4	87.4	85.7	88.8	88.8	**89.5**	86.5	87.5
deu	59.9	79.8	79.8	77.9	77.9	74.5	**83.7**	79.7	79.7	80.2	79.7
eng	67.0	**96.6**	**96.6**	96.2	96.2	96.0	95.1	95.6	95.9	94.6	95.0
fin	48.2	80.8	80.8	80.6	80.6	67.6	85.4	79.2	80.6	85.7	**86.1**
fra	76.7	**77.7**	**77.7**	76.3	76.3	67.9	73.3	69.3	74.7	71.7	72.9
grc	40.4	52.6	52.6	54.8	54.8	36.7	54.0	48.9	53.7	**56.0**	**56.0**
heb	51.6	64.5	64.5	76.7	76.7	81.3	83.2	77.3	79.3	**83.7**	83.6
heb$_{voc}$	34.7	30.9	30.9	65.3	65.3	82.7	92.0	**92.9**	92.6	90.9	91.0
hun	45.9	74.7	74.7	74.7	74.7	75.9	80.5	76.3	79.8	84.3	**85.0**
hye	88.9	86.3	86.3	86.2	88.9	85.9	91.0	88.4	91.5	**94.4**	94.3
ita	78.0	75.0	75.0	63.6	78.0	84.7	94.1	95.8	**97.2**	92.1	92.2
jap	67.0	64.1	64.1	64.1	67.0	**95.3**	26.3	92.8	94.2	94.9	94.9
kat	71.7	82.0	82.0	82.1	82.1	70.5	84.5	84.1	**84.7**	81.3	82.9
klr	27.8	54.5	54.5	53.1	53.1	96.4	**99.5**	99.4	99.4	99.4	99.4
mkd	64.9	91.6	91.6	90.8	90.8	86.7	**93.8**	91.9	92.4	92.1	92.4
nav	23.7	35.8	35.8	41.8	41.8	53.6	52.1	54.0	55.1	55.1	**55.6**
rus	66.8	86.0	86.0	85.6	85.6	82.1	**90.5**	87.4	87.3	84.2	85.5
san	47.0	62.2	62.2	62.1	62.1	54.5	66.3	63.3	**69.1**	67.7	65.9
sme	30.1	56.0	56.0	49.7	49.7	58.5	**74.8**	69.9	71.8	67.4	67.3
spa	86.3	87.8	87.8	87.4	87.4	88.7	93.6	90.9	91.4	**93.8**	93.1
sqi	73.8	19.3	83.4	78.1	78.1	71.5	85.9	87.6	88.9	**92.0**	91.6
swa	56.2	60.5	60.5	65.0	65.0	94.7	93.7	93.1	93.1	**96.6**	**96.6**
tur	28.1	64.6	64.6	64.6	64.6	81.8	**95.0**	90.9	90.8	90.3	92.0

Table 3: Results of all the systems, submitted and baselines over the test sets in all languages. the best system(s) per language in marked in **bold**. The systems are ordered by the averaged success.

ever, there are still some languages over which no system achieves over 80% accuracy. These are: Navajo, Ancient Greek, Sanskrit, Belarusian, Sami and French. While there is no one characteristic shared between all of these languages, it is worth noting that this list includes the only two extinct languages tested in this task, and the only mostly prefixing language. Perhaps further development of tailored models could close this gap.

Language	AZ4	IL4
afb	52.7	84.6
afb no diacr.	80.8	89.2
arz	80.8	88.7

Table 4: Results of all the best neural and non-neural systems over Gulf Arabic, with and without omission of diacritics. Results over Egyptian Arabic are provided for reference. Further evaluations and results for all systems appear in Appendix B.

The orthography's influence As in previous years, the Hebrew data was provided in two formats: the standard unvocalized abjad where vowels are largely omitted from the text, and the rarely used fully vocalized form that is computationally equivalent to an alphabet.

For most systems, the difference in performance between the two variants is stark. In general, the non-neural systems succeeded better over the unvocalized variant, presumably because omitting the vowels masks the non-concatenative ablauts. However, the neural systems fared better over the vocalized data, potentially due to the far lower level of ambiguity it exhibits.

However, the Arabic data complicates this picture. Although Egyptian and Gulf Arabic are closely related dialects with marginal differences in the inflectional system, most systems' success rates differ significantly between these two Arabic varieties. Error analysis revealed that inconsistent diacritization in the Gulf data is the main driving factor in this discrepancy in performance. Unlike the Egyptian Arabic data, not all forms in the Gulf data are diacritized. While all lemmas are diacritized in Gulf, only a subset of the verbal inflected forms are diacritized and the rest are not. In total, around 46% of the training data is diacritized.

The result is that the non-neural systems failed to generate vowel diacritics in the same somewhat arbitrary pattern unlike the neural systems, which

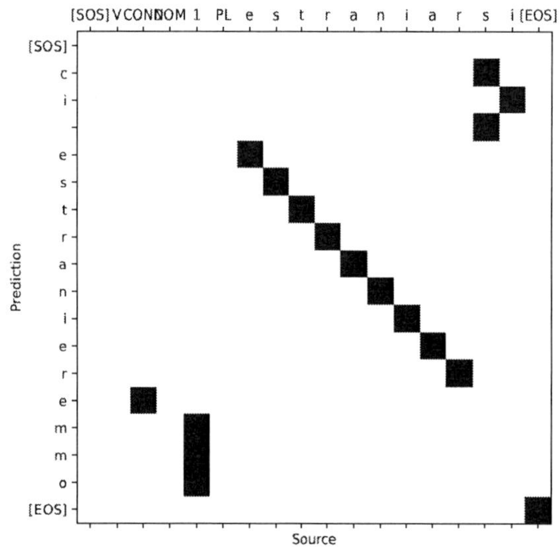

Figure 1: An example of explained inflection by TÜB. Each predicted character is anchored in one input symbol, other conditioning symbols omitted and can be found in Girrbach (2023).

managed to deal well with the inconsistency in the data. The exact match accuracy for Gulf Arabic for the best neural and non-neural systems, which was calculated after omission of all diacritics, is presented in Table 4 and detailed for all systems in Appendix B. It shows that without this source of inconsistency, the performance of Gulf Arabic is in line with the performance of Egyptian.

All in all, it seems like a consistent indication of vowels does not have the same effects in Hebrew and Arabic, despite their typological and orthographic similarity. The results over Arabic dialects are similar regardless of whether diacritics were omitted, while in Hebrew the vocalization played a greater role. This conundrum may point to a need to investigate further the role of the orthographic system in the success rate of inflection models, both neural and non-neural.

7 Conclusions

This year's shared task further promoted the goals of the recurring UniMorph inflection task: we tested innovative inflection systems on a challenging lemma-split data, and did so in an inclusive fashion both in terms of typological diversity of the languages included and the annotation schema that allows treatment of more complex morphological phenomena.

We received 9 submitted systems and tested them on 16 typologically diverse languages. The most interesting pattern arising from our results is the greatly varied performance between languages, with the best performing system ranging from 55.6 to 99.4 accuracy percentage. We thus conclude that further research is needed to close this gap.

Moreover, this year's task gave a prominent role to the orthographic systems of the languages selected, both by including for the first time a logographically written language and by analysing the role of abjad-vocalization in Semitic languages. We believe that this direction is a promising lead for promoting the understanding of the factors influencing the performance of inflection models.

Acknowledgements

The research of Omer Goldman and Reut Tsarfaty was funded by a grant from the European Research Council, ERC-StG grant number 677352, and a grant from the Israeli Ministry of Science and Technology (MOST), grant number 3-17992, for which they are grateful. All of Salam Khalifa's contributions were supported by the department of Linguistics and the Institute of Advanced Computational Science (IACS) at Stony Brook University.

References

Khuyagbaatar Batsuren, Omer Goldman, Salam Khalifa, Nizar Habash, Witold Kieraś, Gábor Bella, Brian Leonard, Garrett Nicolai, Kyle Gorman, Yustinus Ghanggo Ate, Maria Ryskina, Sabrina Mielke, Elena Budianskaya, Charbel El-Khaissi, Tiago Pimentel, Michael Gasser, William Abbott Lane, Mohit Raj, Matt Coler, Jaime Rafael Montoya Samame, Delio Siticonatzi Camaiteri, Esaú Zumaeta Rojas, Didier López Francis, Arturo Oncevay, Juan López Bautista, Gema Celeste Silva Villegas, Lucas Torroba Hennigen, Adam Ek, David Guriel, Peter Dirix, Jean-Philippe Bernardy, Andrey Scherbakov, Aziyana Bayyr-ool, Antonios Anastasopoulos, Roberto Zariquiey, Karina Sheifer, Sofya Ganieva, Hilaria Cruz, Ritván Karahóǧa, Stella Markantonatou, George Pavlidis, Matvey Plugaryov, Elena Klyachko, Ali Salehi, Candy Angulo, Jatayu Baxi, Andrew Krizhanovsky, Natalia Krizhanovskaya, Elizabeth Salesky, Clara Vania, Sardana Ivanova, Jennifer White, Rowan Hall Maudslay, Josef Valvoda, Ran Zmigrod, Paula Czarnowska, Irene Nikkarinen, Aelita Salchak, Brijesh Bhatt, Christopher Straughn, Zoey Liu, Jonathan North Washington, Yuval Pinter, Duygu Ataman, Marcin Wolinski, Totok Suhardijanto, Anna Yablonskaya, Niklas Stoehr, Hossep Dolatian, Zahroh Nuriah, Shyam Ratan, Francis M. Tyers, Edoardo M. Ponti, Grant Aiton, Aryaman Arora, Richard J. Hatcher, Ritesh Kumar, Jeremiah Young, Daria Rodionova, Anastasia Yemelina, Taras Andrushko,

Igor Marchenko, Polina Mashkovtseva, Alexandra Serova, Emily Prud'hommeaux, Maria Nepomniashchaya, Fausto Giunchiglia, Eleanor Chodroff, Mans Hulden, Miikka Silfverberg, Arya D. McCarthy, David Yarowsky, Ryan Cotterell, Reut Tsarfaty, and Ekaterina Vylomova. 2022. UniMorph 4.0: Universal Morphology. In *Proceedings of the Thirteenth Language Resources and Evaluation Conference*, pages 840–855, Marseille, France. European Language Resources Association.

Marc E. Canby and Julia Hockenmaier. 2023. A framework for bidirectional decoding: Case study in morphological inflection.

Ryan Cotterell, Christo Kirov, John Sylak-Glassman, Géraldine Walther, Ekaterina Vylomova, Arya D. McCarthy, Katharina Kann, Sabrina J. Mielke, Garrett Nicolai, Miikka Silfverberg, David Yarowsky, Jason Eisner, and Mans Hulden. 2018. The CoNLL–SIGMORPHON 2018 shared task: Universal morphological reinflection. In *Proceedings of the CoNLL–SIGMORPHON 2018 Shared Task: Universal Morphological Reinflection*, pages 1–27, Brussels. Association for Computational Linguistics.

Ryan Cotterell, Christo Kirov, John Sylak-Glassman, Géraldine Walther, Ekaterina Vylomova, Patrick Xia, Manaal Faruqui, Sandra Kübler, David Yarowsky, Jason Eisner, and Mans Hulden. 2017. CoNLL-SIGMORPHON 2017 shared task: Universal morphological reinflection in 52 languages. In *Proceedings of the CoNLL SIGMORPHON 2017 Shared Task: Universal Morphological Reinflection*, pages 1–30, Vancouver. Association for Computational Linguistics.

Ryan Cotterell, Christo Kirov, John Sylak-Glassman, David Yarowsky, Jason Eisner, and Mans Hulden. 2016. The SIGMORPHON 2016 shared Task—Morphological reinflection. In *Proceedings of the 14th SIGMORPHON Workshop on Computational Research in Phonetics, Phonology, and Morphology*, pages 10–22, Berlin, Germany. Association for Computational Linguistics.

Michael Gasser. 2011. Hornmorpho: a system for morphological processing of amharic, oromo, and tigrinya. In *Conference on Human Language Technology for Development, Alexandria, Egypt*, pages 94–99.

Leander Girrbach. 2022. SIGMORPHON 2022 shared task on morpheme segmentation submission description: Sequence labelling for word-level morpheme segmentation. In *Proceedings of the 19th SIGMORPHON Workshop on Computational Research in Phonetics, Phonology, and Morphology*, pages 124–130, Seattle, Washington. Association for Computational Linguistics.

Leander Girrbach. 2023. Tü-CL at SIGMORPHON 2023: Straight-through gradient estimation for hard attention. In *Proceedings of the 20th SIGMORPHON Workshop on Computational Research in Phonetics, Phonology, and Morphology*, Toronto, Canada. Association for Computational Linguistics.

Omer Goldman, David Guriel, and Reut Tsarfaty. 2022a. (un)solving morphological inflection: Lemma overlap artificially inflates models' performance. In *Proceedings of the 60th Annual Meeting of the Association for Computational Linguistics (Volume 2: Short Papers)*, pages 864–870, Dublin, Ireland. Association for Computational Linguistics.

Omer Goldman, Francesco Tinner, Hila Gonen, Benjamin Muller, Victoria Basmov, Shadrack Kirimi, Lydia Nishimwe, Benoît Sagot, Djamé Seddah, Reut Tsarfaty, and Duygu Ataman. 2022b. The MRL 2022 shared task on multilingual clause-level morphology. In *Proceedings of the The 2nd Workshop on Multi-lingual Representation Learning (MRL)*, pages 134–146, Abu Dhabi, United Arab Emirates (Hybrid). Association for Computational Linguistics.

Omer Goldman and Reut Tsarfaty. 2021. Minimal supervision for morphological inflection. In *Proceedings of the 2021 Conference on Empirical Methods in Natural Language Processing*, pages 2078–2088, Online and Punta Cana, Dominican Republic. Association for Computational Linguistics.

David Guriel, Omer Goldman, and Reut Tsarfaty. 2022. Morphological reinflection with multiple arguments: An extended annotation schema and a Georgian case study. In *Proceedings of the 60th Annual Meeting of the Association for Computational Linguistics (Volume 2: Short Papers)*, pages 196–202, Dublin, Ireland. Association for Computational Linguistics.

Sarthak Jain and Byron C. Wallace. 2019. Attention is not Explanation. In *Proceedings of the 2019 Conference of the North American Chapter of the Association for Computational Linguistics: Human Language Technologies, Volume 1 (Long and Short Papers)*, pages 3543–3556, Minneapolis, Minnesota. Association for Computational Linguistics.

Christo Kirov, John Sylak-Glassman, Roger Que, and David Yarowsky. 2016. Very-large scale parsing and normalization of Wiktionary morphological paradigms. In *Proceedings of the Tenth International Conference on Language Resources and Evaluation (LREC'16)*, pages 3121–3126, Portorož, Slovenia. European Language Resources Association (ELRA).

Jordan Kodner, Salam Khalifa, Khuyagbaatar Batsuren, Hossep Dolatian, Ryan Cotterell, Faruk Akkus, Antonios Anastasopoulos, Taras Andrushko, Aryaman Arora, Nona Atanalov, Gábor Bella, Elena Budianskaya, Yustinus Ghanggo Ate, Omer Goldman, David Guriel, Simon Guriel, Silvia Guriel-Agiashvili, Witold Kieraś, Andrew Krizhanovsky, Natalia Krizhanovsky, Igor Marchenko, Magdalena Markowska, Polina Mashkovtseva, Maria Nepomniashchaya, Daria Rodionova, Karina Scheifer, Alexandra Sorova, Anastasia Yemelina, Jeremiah Young, and Ekaterina Vylomova. 2022. SIGMORPHON–UniMorph 2022 shared task 0: Generalization and typologically diverse morphological inflection. In *Proceedings of the 19th SIGMORPHON Workshop on Computational Research in Phonetics, Phonology, and Morphology*, pages 176–203, Seattle, Washington. Association for Computational Linguistics.

Alice Kwak, Michael Hammond, and Cheyenne Wing. 2023. Morphological reinflection with weighted finite-state transducers. In *Proceedings of the 20th SIGMORPHON Workshop on Computational Research in Phonetics, Phonology, and Morphology*, Toronto, Canada. Association for Computational Linguistics.

Peter Makarov and Simon Clematide. 2018. Neural transition-based string transduction for limited-resource setting in morphology. In *Proceedings of the 27th International Conference on Computational Linguistics*, pages 83–93, Santa Fe, New Mexico, USA. Association for Computational Linguistics.

Ossama Obeid, Nasser Zalmout, Salam Khalifa, Dima Taji, Mai Oudah, Bashar Alhafni, Go Inoue, Fadhl Eryani, Alexander Erdmann, and Nizar Habash. 2020. CAMeL tools: An open source python toolkit for Arabic natural language processing. In *Proceedings of the Twelfth Language Resources and Evaluation Conference*, pages 7022–7032, Marseille, France. European Language Resources Association.

Tiago Pimentel, Maria Ryskina, Sabrina J. Mielke, Shijie Wu, Eleanor Chodroff, Brian Leonard, Garrett Nicolai, Yustinus Ghanggo Ate, Salam Khalifa, Nizar Habash, Charbel El-Khaissi, Omer Goldman, Michael Gasser, William Lane, Matt Coler, Arturo Oncevay, Jaime Rafael Montoya Samame, Gema Celeste Silva Villegas, Adam Ek, Jean-Philippe Bernardy, Andrey Shcherbakov, Aziyana Bayyr-ool, Karina Sheifer, Sofya Ganieva, Matvey Plugaryov, Elena Klyachko, Ali Salehi, Andrew Krizhanovsky, Natalia Krizhanovsky, Clara Vania, Sardana Ivanova, Aelita Salchak, Christopher Straughn, Zoey Liu, Jonathan North Washington, Duygu Ataman, Witold Kieraś, Marcin Woliński, Totok Suhardijanto, Niklas Stoehr, Zahroh Nuriah, Shyam Ratan, Francis M. Tyers, Edoardo M. Ponti, Grant Aiton, Richard J. Hatcher, Emily Prud'hommeaux, Ritesh Kumar, Mans Hulden, Botond Barta, Dorina Lakatos, Gábor Szolnok, Judit Ács, Mohit Raj, David Yarowsky, Ryan Cotterell, Ben Ambridge, and Ekaterina Vylomova. 2021. SIGMORPHON 2021 shared task on morphological reinflection: Generalization across languages. In *Proceedings of the 18th SIGMORPHON Workshop on Computational Research in Phonetics, Phonology, and Morphology*, pages 229–259, Online. Association for Computational Linguistics.

Miikka Silfverberg and Mans Hulden. 2018. An encoder-decoder approach to the paradigm cell filling problem. In *Proceedings of the 2018 Conference on Empirical Methods in Natural Language Processing*, pages 2883–2889, Brussels, Belgium. Association for Computational Linguistics.

Richard Sproat and Alexander Gutkin. 2021. The taxonomy of writing systems: How to measure how logographic a system is. *Computational Linguistics*, 47(3):477–528.

Ekaterina Vylomova, Jennifer White, Elizabeth Salesky, Sabrina J. Mielke, Shijie Wu, Edoardo Maria Ponti, Rowan Hall Maudslay, Ran Zmigrod, Josef Valvoda, Svetlana Toldova, Francis Tyers, Elena Klyachko, Ilya Yegorov, Natalia Krizhanovsky, Paula Czarnowska, Irene Nikkarinen, Andrew Krizhanovsky, Tiago Pimentel, Lucas Torroba Hennigen, Christo Kirov, Garrett Nicolai, Adina Williams, Antonios Anastasopoulos, Hilaria Cruz, Eleanor Chodroff, Ryan Cotterell, Miikka Silfverberg, and Mans Hulden. 2020. SIGMORPHON 2020 shared task 0: Typologically diverse morphological inflection. In *Proceedings of the 17th SIGMORPHON Workshop on Computational Research in Phonetics, Phonology, and Morphology*, pages 1–39, Online. Association for Computational Linguistics.

Géraldine Walther, Guillaume Jacques, and Benoît Sagot. 2013. Uncovering the inner architecture of khaling verbal morphology. In *3rd workshop on Sino-Tibetan languages of Sichuan*.

Sarah Wiegreffe and Yuval Pinter. 2019. Attention is not not explanation. In *Proceedings of the 2019 Conference on Empirical Methods in Natural Language Processing and the 9th International Joint Conference on Natural Language Processing (EMNLP-IJCNLP)*, pages 11–20, Hong Kong, China. Association for Computational Linguistics.

Shijie Wu, Ryan Cotterell, and Mans Hulden. 2021. Applying the transformer to character-level transduction. In *Proceedings of the 16th Conference of the European Chapter of the Association for Computational Linguistics: Main Volume*, pages 1901–1907, Online. Association for Computational Linguistics.

A Hyper Parameters of the Neural Baseline

For the neural baseline models we used the standard hyper parameters of Wu et al. (2021). These are:

- 4 transformer layers
- 4 attention heads
- 256 dimensions in the embeddings
- 1024 dimensions in the hidden feed forward layers
- 0.3 dropout chance
- 400 examples per batch
- 20,000 training steps at max
- Inverse square root scheduler with 4,000 worm up steps
- Adam optimizer with β of 0.98
- learning rate of 0.001
- label smoothing with α of 0.1

Language	AZ3	AZ1	Baseline Non-neural	AZ2	AZ4	TÜB	Baseline Neural	IL1	IL2	IL3	IL4
afb original	34.5	30.8	30.8	52.7	52.7	75.8	80.1	80.7	82.2	84.1	84.6
afb mixed	66.9	70.7	70.7	70.3	70.3	77.4	82.2	83.1	84.5	86.0	86.5
afb no diacr.	74.4	77.4	77.4	80.8	80.8	81.9	87.9	87.8	89.2	89.0	89.2
arz	75.7	77.2	77.9	80.8	80.8	87.6	89.6	89.2	88.7	89.1	88.7

Table 5: Results of all the systems over Gulf Arabic with different considerations for inconsistent diacritization of the original data. Results over Egyptian Arabic are provided for reference.

B Detailed evaluations for Gulf Arabic

Table 5 details several evaluations done over Gulf Arabic, with the results of Egyptian Arabic provided for reference. Specifically:

- *original* is the evaluation done over the inconsistently diacritized data, as it appears in Table 3.
- *mixed* is the evaluation done after removing diacritics only the predictions whose respective gold contains no diacritics
- *no diacr.* is the evaluation done after removing all diacritics from both predictions and gold outputs.

SIGMORPHON–UniMorph 2023 Shared Task 0, Part 2: Cognitively Plausible Morphophonological Generalization in Korean

Canaan Breiss[1] **Jinyoung Jo**[2]
[1]Massachusetts Institute of Technology [2]University of California, Los Angeles
canaan@mit.edu jinyoungjo@ucla.edu

Abstract

This paper summarises data collection and curation for Part 2 of the 2023 SIGMORPHON-UniMorph Shared Task 0, which focused on modeling speaker knowledge and generalization of a pair of interacting phonological processes in Korean. We briefly describe how modeling the generalization task could be of interest to researchers in both Natural Language Processing and linguistics, and then summarise the traditional description of the phonological processes that are at the center of the modeling challenge. We then describe the criteria we used to select and code cases of process application in two Korean speech corpora, which served as the primary learning data. We also report the technical details of the experiment we carried out that served as the primary test data. [1]

1 Introduction

This paper summarises data collection and curation for Part 2 of the 2023 SIGMORPHON-UniMorph Shared Task 0, which focused on modeling speaker knowledge and generalization of a pair of interacting phonological processes in Korean. We briefly describe how modeling the generalization task could be of interest to researchers in both Natural Language Processing and linguistics, and then summarise the traditional description of the phonological processes that are at the center of the modeling challenge. We then describe the criteria we used to select and code cases of process application in two Korean speech corpora, which served as the primary learning data. We also report the technical details of the experiment we carried out that served as the primary test data.

1.1 Motivation

In this subtask, we sought to build on the success of the human-generalization subtasks (*wug*-tests) in the 2021 and 2022 SIGMORPHON Shared Tasks by creating a dataset that would be of interest to both researchers in NLP and those working in linguistic theory, with the goal of sparking further mutually beneficial collaboration and exchange of ideas between the two fields. The dataset that we gathered documented two phonological processes in Korean that sometimes overlap in their scope of application. Thus, the data bear on questions of linguistic interest about whether human language users generate language in a derivation-based (serial) or output-oriented (parallel) manner. This question of cognitive architecture has clear parallels in computational models of language, where there is a range of statistical, mathematical, and neural methods that embody both the extreme ends, and wide middle, of this architectural range.

Of relevance to both NLP researchers and linguistics is our finding that the disambiguating learning data is also quite sparse: in a child-directed speech corpus of 53,000 words, we found that the environment crucial to learn what happens when rule conditioning contexts overlap appears only 12 times (The Ko Corpus, Ko et al. (2020)). In a corpus of adult speech, the forms occur a total of about 1,000 times in 900,000 phrases (The NIKL Korean Dialogue Corpus; National Institute of Korean Language (2022)). This poses a challenge for models that need large amounts of data to reliably learn linguistic patterns. By pairing the generalization task with the curation of corpus data, we hope to shed light on what kind of generalizations human learners form in the face of such sparse data. These data can be then used to inform the further the development of cognitively plausible linguistic theories, and can also be used to benchmark the development of machine learning models that learn to generalize from sparse data to novel out-of-domain items in a human-like way.

[1]All data discussed here are available at: https://github.com/sigmorphon/2023InflectionST

Proceedings of the 20th SIGMORPHON workshop on Computational Research in Phonetics, Phonology, and Morphology, pages 126–131
July 14, 2023 ©2023 Association for Computational Linguistics

2 Description of the phonological processes

We bring to bear data from the interaction of two phonological processes in Korean, Post-Obstruent Tensification (POT) and Cluster Simplification (CS). When their conditioning environments overlap, we can observe crucial evidence about how (or whether) the processes are ordered (Kim-Renaud, 1974; Sohn, 1999; Kim, 2003). Note that throughout we use the International Phonetic Alphabet for linguistic data, augmented with the symbol "*" to indicate the tense stop series in Korean; we use the symbol "C" to represent an obstruent consonant, and the symbol "V" to represent a vowel. We follow convention in the linguistic literature by using /slashes/ to represent underlying representations (URs) presumed to be represented in the speaker's mental lexicon, and [brackets] to represent surface representations (SRs) which are taken to be the intended phonetic targets of phonological computation.

2.1 Post-obstruent tensification (POT)

POT causes a lenis consonant to tensify after an obstruent; using SPE-style rewrite rules (Chomsky and Halle, 1968), the process can be expressed as: lax C → tense C / [p, t, k] _. For example, 잡다 /cap-ta/ is realized as [cap-t*a] 'to hold-DECL' ; 받고 /pat-ko/ → [pat-k*o] 'to receive-and' . POT is described as nearly categorical within the accentual phrase (Jun, 1998), a finding which we also observe in the data we report here, and applies in nearly all possible morphological and phrasal environments.

2.2 Cluster simplification (CS)

CS targets underlying consonant clusters in coda position, yielding simplification when followed by a C-initial suffix or a word boundary. The process can be expressed using SPE rules as: CC → C / _{#, C}. For example, in 앉는 /anc-nɨn/, the final /c/ is deleted in the surface form [an-nɨn] 'to sit-COMP' ; a similar outcome is seen in 굶나 /kulm-na/ → [kum-na] 'to starve-INTERROG' . The process also applies at word boundaries, such that underlying 닭 /talk/ surfaces as [tak] 'chicken'. CS is variable depending on verb identity and final consonant place (Kwon et al., 2023), and the conditioning context exists in verbs and nouns.

2.3 Overlapping contexts

When verbs that end in an /-lC/ consonant cluster are suffixed with a lax obstruent-initial affix (denoted /C-/), the conditioning contexts for both processes are met. In verbs, the majority outcome is that the /lC/ cluster is simplified to singleton [l], and the following stop is tensed. For example, 맑고 /malk-ko/ is realized as [mal-k*o] 'to be clear-and', with a tense [k*] in spite of the triggering context having been deleted; a similar example is 낡고 /nalk-ko/ → [nal-k*o] 'to be old-and'. These types of form suggest that the two processes apply "in sequence", with POT ordered before CS, as shown in table 1.

UR	/pat-ko/ to receive-and	/anc-nɨn/ to sit.COMP	/malk-ko/ to be clear-and
POT	pat-k*o	—	malk-k*o
CS	—	an-nɨn	mal-k*o
SR	[pat-k*o]	[an-nɨn]	[mal-k*o]

Table 1: Example of apparent ordering between POT and CS in Korean /-lC/-final verbs.

This type of process interaction is known in the phonological literature as *counter-bleeding opacity* (Kiparsky, 1968): CS would destroy the conditioning environment for POT (removing the obstruent in the cluster), but applies too late to do so, resulting in an apparent "overapplication" of CS – it seems to have applied outside its conditioning environment. Note that in general, post-liquid tensification is absent from the language (e.g. 줄다 /cul-ta/ →[cul-ta], not *[cul-t*a] 'to decrease-DECL'), so the observed outcome 맑고 / malk-ko/ → [mal-k*o] cannot be attributed to other phonological processes at work.

Although the opaque outcome, as in 맑고 /malk-ko/ → [mal-k*o], is the canonical and majority type, the literature contains reports of variability in how CS and POT apply when overlapping. For example, (Kim, 2003) reports that the target of CS may vary between coda /l/ and coda /C/; for example 밟고 /palp-ko/ → [pal-k*o]~[pap-k*o] 'to step on-and'; 낡지 /nalk-ci/ → [nal-c*i]~[nak-c*i] 'to be old-CONN'. Further, while in /-lC/-final verbs the opaque outcome obtains when an obstruent-initial suffix is attached, in nouns of the same shape the outcome is not opaque; CS always targets the /l/ rather than the /C/, yielding outcomes like 닭도 /talk-to/ → [tak-t*o] 'chicken-also' and 흙과 /hɨlk-kwa/ → [hɨk-k*wa] 'soil-and' (Tak, 2008). Thus, we suspect that further examination of more naturalistic data in corpora and in the generalization task may surface a more complex pattern of variation.

3 Task description

The task was to predict human responses to a generalization task (a *wug*-test, cf. Berko (1958)), involving existing high-frequency verb stems, existing low-frequency verb stems, and novel verb stems. The stems were paired with affixes that created environments that were designed to condition POT alone (as in 막다 /mak-ta/ 'to block-DECL'), CS alone (as in 밟는 /palp-nɨn/ 'to step on-COMP'), the critical overlapping context (as in 밟고 /palp-ko/ 'to step on-and'), or designed to trigger neither process, so that the underlying consonant cluster is resyllabified across the syllable boundary and survives deletion (as in 넓어 /nʌlp-ʌ/ 'to be wide-DECL').

Training data came in two types: a list of the 53 /-lC/-final verbs in the frequency list of Korean from Kang and Kim (2004), and counts and hand-coding of the outcome of environments that could condition POT and/or CS in verbs from an adult-directed speech corpus and an infant-directed speech corpus.

The list and corpus counts were designed to be used as the primary training data, and results of the generalization task were divided up into *train*, *dev*, and *test* splits. The *train* and *dev* splits were intended to be used during model development, and model performance calculated on the *test* set.

4 Corpus data collection

To approximate the data that a learner of Korean might be exposed to while acquiring their phonology, we culled relevant data from two corpora of spoken Korean.

4.1 Adult-directed speech corpus

For adult-directed speech, we used the NIKL dialogue corpus (National Institute of Korean Language, 2022), which consists of approx. 900,000 phrases of semi-spontaneous speech, together with orthographic and phonemic transcription. We extracted each suffixed /-lC/ verb from the corpus (7,570 tokens, 1,395 types), and manually annotated them for pronunciation. We excluded words with /-lh/-final stems because they participate in additional processes, such as coalescence with the following stop that yields aspiration instead of tensification 잃다 /ilh-ta/ → [il-t^{h}a], not *[il-t*a] 'to lose-DECL') (Kim-Renaud, 1974; Sohn, 1999). We did not extract POT-only contexts (simple /-C/-final verbs with following /C-/-initial suffixes) because they were extremely frequent, and impressionistic judgements of the second author align with the literature (Jun, 1998) that POT applies nearly obligatorily within phrases. In the smaller infant corpus and the results of the generalization task, such environments were extracted and coded.

4.2 Infant-directed speech corpus

For infant-directed speech, we used the Ko corpus (Ko et al., 2020), collected from interactions of mother-child pairs in a free-play session. The corpus consists of approx. 53,000 words of spontaneous infant-directed speech, paired with orthographic and phonemic transcription. We extracted and hand-checked all affixed /-lC/ verbs in the corpus (289 tokens, 38 types), as well as all simple /-C/ verbs with a following /C-/-initial affix (1,083 tokens, 171 types). Exclusions were the same as for the adult-directed speech corpus.

5 Experimental data collection

To probe how adult speakers represent CS, POT, and their interaction in existing words, and how they generalize this knowledge to entirely novel contexts, we carried out a production task where speakers were asked to produce inflected forms of verbs, and record their productions.

5.1 Stimuli

Stimuli had two stem types (/-lC/ and /-C/), and three frequency levels (high-frequency, low-frequency, and nonce). Frequency levels were calculated using information from Kang and Kim (2004). We selected 10 stimuli in each of the six resulting categories, and paired each with three affix types (/-a, ʌ/ -아, 어 'DECLARATIVE, INTERROGATIVE, IMPERATIVE',[2] /-na/ -나 'INTERROGATIVE', and /-ta/ -다 'DECLATIVE'). This yielded 180 stimuli, selected to elicit the four types of contexts exemplified in section 3: contexts where POT and CS could apply non-overlappingly, contexts where we

[2]The distribution of these allomorphs is governed by vowel harmony which is unrelated to the consonantal phenomena under investigation here; see Ahn (1985) for a traditional description, and Jo (forthcoming) for a recent overview of the empirical landscape.

could observe the form of the stem with no phonological effects at all, and contexts where POT and CS overlap.

5.2 Participants

Our goal was to recruit 30 speakers of Korean who were born in Korea and grew up with Korean as their dominant language. We used a combination of recruitment on Prolific, word-of-mouth, and posting on online forums to recruit participants, and ended up with 23 by the deadline for data release. We released data from 12 speakers to teams at that time as *train* data and 4 for as *dev*, held back data from 7 speakers as *test* and released their demographic info and trial information without the right answers, and continued collecting data. By the time the due date for releasing test data came, we had collected data from 6 more speakers, and so the correct answers were released for the original 7 *test* subjects, plus 6 "surprise" speakers. 1 more participant's data was collected after test data were released, to reach the total target of 30. Participants recruited through Prolific were paid for their time.

5.3 Design and procedure

The design leveraged the fact that, although Korean has a number of phonological processes that cross both morpheme-boundaries within words and word-boundaries within prosodic phrases (Sohn, 1999), the standard practice in writing Korean using the Hangul orthography is to write each morpheme as though no phonological processes had applied to it (approximating phonological URs). In spite of this norm, however, the orthography is still capable of expressing and uniquely identifying the full range of phonetic realizations that these alternations give rise to (approximating the SRs). For example, the underlying form of 'to block-DECL' is /mak-ta/, and is written in Hangul as 막다 and when POT applies, it is produced as [mak-t*a]; this can be represented in the spelling as 막따, though the normal written form is 막다. These facts about Korean orthographic norms allowed us to rely on the "self-transcription" method of Moore-Cantwell (2020), where participants spoke their response out loud in response to the standard written form of the stimulus (indicating the UR), and then were asked to choose an orthographic form that most closely matched the form they produced where the different possible surface realizations (SRs) were disambiguated.

The experiment was carried out over the internet using the Labvanced experimental platform (Finger et al., 2017). Participants were instructed to find a quiet room to complete the experiment, and that it would take approximately an hour. They were told that they would be asked to read a series of inflected words out loud while being recorded, and then select one of several multiple-choice options that matched what they had said the most closely. After, they would be asked to indicate whether they knew the word or not.

The experiment began with four practice trials, after which each participant completed the 180 inflection trials in a random order. On each inflection trial, the target word would be shown to participants with a V-initial suffix not included in the experimental design (/-ajo, ʌjo/ -아요, -어요 'DECLARATIVE, INTERROGATIVE, IMPERATIVE-polite'), and they would be asked to say the word out loud with one of the three affixes (/-a, ʌ/, /-na/, /-ta/), depending on the trial. Then, after producing the form and the recording was complete, they were asked to choose which of a number of multiple-choice options they had said. The number of multiple-choice items differed from trial to trial based on the type of stem (/-lC/- or /-C/-final) and suffix (vowel-, sonorant-, or obstruent-initial). The options always included transcriptions where each expected phonological process (POT and/or CS, depending on the stem and affix) either applied or not independently, and also overlapped; in cases with sonorant-initial affixes, candidates also included outcomes for possible application of lateralization and nasalization (Sohn, 1999) – the latter two are not the focus of study here, but were included for the sake of completeness. On each trial, the prompt was shown while participants were being recorded, then when they stopped the recording, the display was changed to show only a button to allow a replay of their own production, and the range of possible outcomes. There was always an "other" case listed, where participants were allowed to write their pronunciation if none of the options provided matched their pronunciation. In practice this was extremely rare; see section 5.4 for details.

After the production task, the second phase of the experiment was a vocabulary test. On each screen, participants saw a stem with the same non-target vowel-initial affix as in the prompt on the production task, and then indicated using a 5-point

Likert scale how familiar they were with the word, ranging from 1 ("I don't know this word at all") to 5 ("I am extremely familiar with the word").

Finally, participants were asked to provide some background information about themselves, including whether they had begun speaking Korean in some context before the age of seven, and what other languages they spoke. No recruited participants were excluded on grounds of having a language background that did not meet our criteria for inclusion described in section 5.2.

5.4 Data coding

Spot-checks were carried out to make sure that the forms produced by the speakers were consistent with the forms that they indicated that they produced; in general, subjects were extremely accurate in reporting what they said; "other" responses were excluded, which comprised only an extremely small percentage of the data.

After data checking, existing stems that were rated as 1 (="I don't know this word at all") by a given subject were re-classified as novel for that subject. This was done to allow for accurate estimation of the knowledge of each subject, and to avoid making the assumption that all participants know all words in the study.

6 Discussion

As stated in section 1, the goal of this subtask was to spur collaboration and cross-talk between two communities; thus, we set aside here a discussion of the contents of the dataset, referring the reader to the paper by Jeong et al. (2023) to summarise the findings in of the one team that worked on this subtask. The model and discussion found in their paper notwithstanding, we hope the data we gathered in this subtask may also have broader utility in testing linguistic theories of learning and representation, and in benchmarking models that attempt to reach human-like levels generalization while maintaining human-like requirements in terms of data efficiency. It is our hope that it may continue to be of use outside the context of this subtask going forward.

Acknowledgements

Thanks to Ryan Cotterell, Omer Goldman, Roger Levy, Garrett Nicolai, Ekaterina Vylomova, and the audience at the 97th LSA Annual Meeting for helpful comments, feedback, and guidance. We are grateful to the MIT Computational Psycholinguistics Lab for funding the data collection; CB also acknowledges the MIT-IBM Watson AI Lab for individual funding.

References

Sang-Cheol Ahn. 1985. *The interplay of phonology and morphology in Korean*. Ph.D. thesis, University of Illinois at Urbana-Champaign.

Jean Berko. 1958. The child's learning of english morphology. *Word*, 14(2-3):150–177.

Noam Chomsky and Morris Halle. 1968. The sound pattern of English.

Holger Finger, Caspar Goeke, Dorena Diekamp, Kai Standvoß, and Peter König. 2017. Labvanced: a unified javascript framework for online studies. In *International Conference on Computational Social Science (Cologne)*.

Chongnam Jeong, Dominic Schmitz, Akhilesh Kakolu Ramarao, Anna Stein, and Kevin Tang. 2023. Linear discriminative learning: a competitive non-neural baseline for morphological inflection. In *Proceedings of the 20th SIGMORPHON Workshop on Computational Research in Phonetics, Phonology, and Morphology*.

Jinyoung Jo. forthcoming. Korean vowel harmony has weak phonotactic support and has limited productivity. *Phonology*.

Sun-Ah Jun. 1998. The accentual phrase in the korean prosodic hierarchy. *Phonology*, 15(2):189–226.

Beom-Mo Kang and Hung-Gyu Kim. 2004. *Hankwuke hyengtayso mich ehwi sayong pintouy pwunsek2 [Frequency analysis of Korean morpheme and word usage2]*. Institute of Korean Culture, Korea University, Seoul.

Seoncheol Kim. 2003. *Phyocwun Palum Silthay Cosa II [A Survey of Standard Pronunciation II]*. National Institute of Korean Language, Seoul.

Young-Key Kim-Renaud. 1974. *Korean Consonantal Phonology*. Ph.D. thesis, University of Hawaii.

Paul Kiparsky. 1968. *Linguistic universals and linguistic change*.

Eon-Suk Ko, Jinyoung Jo, Kyung-Woon On, and Byoung-Tak Zhang. 2020. Introducing the ko corpus of korean mother–child interaction. *Frontiers in Psychology*, 11:3698.

Soohyun Kwon, Taejin Yoon, Sujin Oh, and Jeon-Im Han. 2023. Variable realization of consonant clusters in seoul and gyeongsang korean. Poster at HISPHONCOG 2023.

Claire Moore-Cantwell. 2020. Weight and final vowels in the English stress system. *Phonology*, 37(4):657–695.

National Institute of Korean Language. 2022. NIKL Korean Dialogue Corpus (audio) 2020(v.1.3).

Ho-Min Sohn. 1999. *The Korean Language*. Cambridge University Press, Cambridge, UK.

Jin-young Tak. 2008. A uniform analysis of tensification in korean: An optimality approach. *Korean Journal of Linguistics*, 33:545–564.

Morphological reinflection with weighted finite-state transducers

Alice Kwak and **Michael Hammond** and **Cheyenne Wing**
Dept. of Linguistics
U. of Arizona
Tucson, AZ 85721, USA
{alicekwak,hammond,cheyennewing}@arizona.edu

Abstract

This paper describes the submission by the University of Arizona to the SIGMORPHON 2023 Shared Task on typologically diverse morphological (re-)infection. In our submission, we investigate the role of frequency, length, and weighted transducers in addressing the challenge of morphological reinflection. We start with the non-neural baseline provided for the task and show how some improvement can be gained by integrating length and frequency in prefix selection. We also investigate using weighted finite-state transducers, jump-started from edit distance and directly augmented with frequency. Our specific technique is promising and quite simple, but we see only modest improvements for some languages here.

1 Introduction

This paper describes the submission by the University of Arizona to the SIGMORPHON 2023 Shared Task on typologically diverse morphological (re-)infection. The goal of the Shared Task is to model inflectional morphology. The specific task is to learn how to inflect for a language generally from a limited number of examples.

In this task, we are given $10,000$ examples of inflected forms in 27 languages along with the morphological category and the generally accepted lemma form. For example, in English, we have data as in Table 1.

...		
argue	V;NFIN	argue
argue	V;PRS;NOM(3,SG)	argues
argue	V;PST	argued
argue	V;V.PTCP;PRS	arguing
argue	V;V.PTCP;PST	argued
ascertain	V;NFIN	ascertain
ascertain	V;PRS;NOM(3,SG)	ascertains
ascertain	V;PST	ascertained
ascertain	V;V.PTCP;PRS	ascertaining
...		

Table 1: Some English training data

Morphosyntactic information is in Unimorph format (Guriel et al., 2022). The logic is that we are given complete paradigms for n lemmas for each language where the number of lemmas we see in the training data is a function of the size of the paradigms. Specifically, if paradigms are small, we see more lemmas than if paradigms are big.

The goal is to build a system that learns the relationship between lemmas L, morphosyntactic descriptions M, and inflected words W. The system effectively computes a function from $L \times M$ to W. More details on the task are given in Goldman et al. (2023).

The organizers provided two baseline systems, a neural and a non-neural one. We decided to focus our efforts on a non-neural solution and so we began our work by attempting to understand the non-neural baseline more clearly.

For comparison purposes, we ultimately submitted four sets of results: i) our implementation of the non-neural baseline; ii) a version of the non-neural baseline with adjustments for prefix frequency and length; iii) an approach using weighted finite-state transducers; and iv) an ensemble approach using both prefix frequency/length and weighted transducers.

In the following sections, we first review the structure of the baseline non-neural system. We then outline our approaches and present our results. We conclude with a discussion of shortcomings and next steps.[1]

2 Non-neural baseline

The non-neural baseline system (Cotterell et al., 2017) was inspired by (Liu and Mao, 2016). It

[1]All of our code is available at https://github.com/hammondm/sigmorphon23/.

Proceedings of the 20th SIGMORPHON workshop on Computational Research in Phonetics, Phonology, and Morphology, pages 132–137

Prefix	Stem	Suffix
∅	happ	y
un	happ	iness

Table 2: Alignment of *happy* and *unhappiness*

Prefixes	Suffixes
(<ha, <unha)	(py>, piness>)
(<, <un)	(>, ess>)
(<hap, <unhap)	(happy>, happiness>)
(<happ, <unhapp)	(>, s>)
(<h, <unh)	(>, ness>)
	(appy>, appiness>)
	(y>, iness>)
	(ppy>, ppiness>)
	(>, ss>)
	(>, >)

Table 3: Hypothesized rules for *happy* and *unhappiness* (angled brackets are word boundaries)

aligns lemmas and surface forms utilizing Hamming distance and Levenshtein distance and uses this alignment to hypothesize potential prefixes and suffixes.

For example, if the system were presented *happy* and *unhappiness*, it would hypothesize the morphological analysis in Table 2.[2]

This alignment would be used to extract potential prefix rules and suffix rules as in Table 3. During inference, the best prefix rule and suffix rule are chosen based on length and frequency. Specifically, the longest rule that produces the most identical forms is chosen.

Our first submission is essentially as described above.

3 Non-neural Baseline improvements

For our second submission, we made two revisions to the non-neural baseline system.

First, we replaced the input for extracting prefix rules, which was originally specified as the concatenation of lemma's prefix and surface form's root, with the concatenation of lemma's prefix and lemma's root. Given the alignment algorithm described above, this shouldn't have an effect in most cases, but it actually produced a small improvement. Presumably, this is because of cases where the lemma and word form do not share an obvious root.

Second, we changed the criteria for choosing the best prefix rule. The criteria for choosing the best rule had been set up asymmetrically for prefix rules and suffix rules. For suffix rules, the longest-matching rule(s) given an input and the morphosyntactic description was chosen as the best rule. If there are ties, the most frequent rule was chosen. For prefix rules, frequency had been the only criterion and the length of the match had not been considered. We revised the system so that the same criteria apply to both prefix rules and the suffix rules.

We were able to get a modest improvement in performance as a result of these revisions (non-neural baseline: 69.60%, revised system: 71.71%).[3]

4 Weighted finite-state transducers

We also built a system, inspired by the non-neural baseline described above, but which uses weighted finite-state transducers instead. Similar techniques have been tried before, for example, Durrett and DeNero (2013) and Forsberg and Hulden (2016). In fact, a number of them showed up in the 2016 version of this task, e.g. Alegria and Etxeberria (2016), Nicolai et al. (2016), Liu and Mao (2016), and King (2016).[4]

Durrett and DeNero (2013) learns a set of transformations: separate ones for prefixes, stems, and suffixes. They use a conditional random field (CRF) to combine and apply them.

Forsberg and Hulden (2016) generate probabilistic and non-probabilistic morphological analyzers in an automatic way by converting morphological inflection tables into unweighted and weighted FSTs.

Alegria and Etxeberria (2016) uses *Phonetisaurus*, a WFST-based system (Novak et al., 2012). This system directly learns a single WFST to model the lemma-to-word relation. The model thus includes a role for frequency, but not length. Morphosyntactic information is directly encoded in the WFST.

Nicolai et al. (2016) uses DirecTL+ (Jiampojamarn et al., 2008), a discriminative transducer that

[2]The example in the text is an instance of derivational morphology. Unfortunately, English does not have inflectional prefixes, so we use this.

[3]Our implementation of the non-neural baseline gets a slightly different macro average, so we cite the organizers' macro average here.

[4]Merzhevich et al. (2022) use transducers as well, but they are constructed by hand, not learned from data.

searches for a sequence of character transformation rules. It uses a version of the MIRA algorithm (McDonald et al., 2005) to assign weights to each feature. Transformations are N-gram-based and combined to produce surface forms.

Liu and Mao (2016) use a linear-chain conditional random field model with contextual features, e.g. what is a consonant or vowel.

King (2016) uses conditional random fields as well. Separate edit rules are induced from edit distance comparisons and combined at inference. Other features like position in the string were also incorporated.

In our model, we use edit distance to calculate the precise overlap between a lemma and a surface form and then build a weighted finite-state transducer (WFST) from that that specifies changes with interleaving variables. The weights penalize degrees of mismatch with the variables.

For example, take a lemma-word pair like *break* and *broken*. First, we use edit distance to calculate an optimal alignment. We then replace all identical spans with variables that penalize mismatches. In this example, *br* would be a variable and *k* would be a variable. Our transducers are implemented in *pyfoma*[5]. Using the formalism of that system, the resulting transducer would be specified as below:

$$(.*<\mathrm{n}>|\mathrm{br})(\mathrm{ea}:\mathrm{o})(.*<\mathrm{n}>|\mathrm{k})('':\mathrm{en})<\mathrm{m}>$$

Here there is a penalty associated with not matching the spans where the two forms align. In the formalism above, we've specified these as n to indicate that we experimented with different weighting options. There is a penalty associated with the rule as a whole, indicated above as m. This was used to incorporate different possible costs for the length of the rule. Again, we tried different options here, but the general strategy was to penalize shorter less frequent rules.

In training, we built transducers in this way for all training items, separated by morphosyntactic descriptions. For inference, we generated all possible outputs for a lemma with the WFSTs for that morphosyntactic description and chose the one that had the lowest cost.

We expected such a system would be better able to capture *nonconcatenative* morphological systems, systems where morphological categories might be marked by stem-internal changes as opposed to prefixes or suffixes. In fact, as we discuss below, this was not the case.

Based on development split performance, we saw that the frequency of forms played a role: as with the baseline system, more frequent output forms were preferred. To handle this, we adjusted our weighting scheme so that if multiple WFSTs produced the same output, those got lowered scores.

Our approach differs from previous WFST-based approaches in three main respects. First, our alignment and overall system is extremely simple, as described above. Second, our weights are naive, not trained, and assigned on the basis of a general theory of what should matter, as described above. Finally, our system employs only transducers.

One strength of our system is that it's very straightforward and easy to manipulate the weights. It can be used to test the effect each factor (e.g., form frequency, length of rules, etc.) has over the system's performance.

5 Ensemble system

We found that our system generally did not perform as well as the non-neural baseline or our revision of it, but we saw improved performance for some languages with development data, specifically Japanese, Armenian, and Italian. Therefore we also submitted a ensemble system. where we generated test outputs using our improved baseline and our WFST system and selected the test results based on development data performance.

6 Results

Results for our four submissions are given in Table 4.

Submission 1 is our execution of the non-neural baseline. It is here simply for comparison purposes.[6]

Submission 2 is our simple adaptation of the non-neural baseline to make prefixation and suffixation sensitive to the same variables of length and frequency of surface forms. The adapted system performed better than the non-neural baseline (67.1% vs. 71.7%).

[5] `https://github.com/mhulden/pyfoma`

[6] Just for completeness, our version of the non-neural baseline differs from the organizer's in one key line where lists of strings are zipped together. In the organizer's version that object is then converted directly to a list; in our version, it is not.

Submission 3 is the WFST-based system. It does not perform very well in general (56.1%), but, as noted above, it does better than the systems 1 and 2 in a couple of cases: Armenian, Italian, and Japanese.

Finally, submission 4 is the ensemble system, where we draw on systems 2 and 3 depending on which performed better with development data.

7 Discussion

We focused our efforts on a non-neural approach and thus did not expect competitive results. That said, we did manage to improve over the non-neural baseline. Our intention was to understand more deeply how morphological systems could be modeled in the simplest finite-state terms. To this end, we conducted several experiments with our WFST system.

One of the experiments we did is to create the WFST with individual characters, instead of spans, as variables. In our submitted system, spans that are identical in a lemma-word pair are replaced with variables. We revised the system to replace individual matching characters with variables. For example, take the lemma-word pair *break* and *broken* once again. In our submitted system, identical spans *br* and *k* are replaced with variables that penalize mismatches. In the revised system, individual characters *b*, *r*, and *k* are replaced with variables. Thus the first variable in the formula below is replaced as shown.

$$(.*<n>|\mathrm{br})(\mathrm{ea}:\mathrm{o})(.*<n>|\mathrm{k})('':\mathrm{en})<m>$$

not split:	$(.*<n>\|\mathrm{br})$
split:	$(.*<n>\|\mathrm{b})(.*<n>\|\mathrm{r})$

The motivation for this experiment was to see if penalizing each unmatched character, rather than the whole span, would enhance the system's performance. Our hypothesis was that penalizing individual characters would improve the system, as it would give a more specific penalty to an unmatched span.

This was not the case. At least for the various weightings we tried, the individual character variable versions did not perform as well as system 3 above.

In addition, the individual variable versions entailed much larger transducers and much longer run times. For the systems we submitted, running the languages in parallel meant a complete run always took less than an hour. For the individual variable versions, running the languages in parallel took over 15 hours on our campus supercomputer.

Our expectation is that with a compiled transducer system like Foma or OpenFST and with more aggressive parallelization, we could reduce this runtime significantly.

Another experiment we did is to adjust weights based on the frequency of the form produced by the candidate WFSTs. During error analysis, we found out that there are many WFST candidates producing the same form. In many cases these frequent forms were the correct ones, but they were not selected as the optimal forms due to high weights. In order to mitigate this issue, we tried adjusting the weights of the WFSTs based on the frequency of the form the transducer produced. As a result of this adjustment, we were able to obtain a boost of approximately 5% in system performance on development data (from 51% to 56%).

8 Conclusion

In conclusion, we developed three non-neural models. The first combined frequency and length in the selection of prefixes. The second used WFSTs built from edit distance alignments. The third model combined the results of the first two models.

The direct baseline changes resulted in overall improvements, but the WFST system did not. However, there were specific language improvements from the WFST solution and we were able to incorporate these in our ensemble system.

9 Limitations

While the WFST model didn't perform very well overall, our sense is that it is worth pursuing further. Specifically, there are several moves worth exploring.

First, we should move to a compiled system so that we can test the "individual variable" models more thoroughly.

Second, we should try models where we set the variable weights by training, rather than naively in advance.

Third, in an individual variable setting, it would be promising to weight the variables by locality. Specifically, do mismatched variables have more effect when they are closer to where the changes happen? Similarly, we might adjust the granularity of the variables as a function of position, with

Language	1	2	3	4
Arabic, Gulf	0.308	0.527	0.345	0.527
Amharic	0.654	0.74	0.599	0.74
Arabic, Egyptian	0.772	0.808	0.757	0.808
Belarusian	0.681	0.645	0.462	0.645
Danish	0.895	0.874	0.648	0.874
German	0.798	0.779	0.599	0.779
English	0.966	0.962	0.67	0.962
Finnish	0.808	0.806	0.482	0.806
French	0.777	0.763	0.767	0.763
Ancient Greek	0.526	0.548	0.404	0.548
Hebrew	0.309	0.653	0.347	0.653
Hebrew (Unvoc)	0.645	0.767	0.516	0.767
Hungarian	0.747	0.747	0.459	0.747
Armenian	0.863	0.862	0.889	0.889
Italian	0.75	0.636	0.78	0.78
Japanese	0.641	0.641	0.67	0.67
Georgian	0.82	0.821	0.717	0.821
Khaling	0.545	0.531	0.278	0.531
Macedonian	0.916	0.908	0.649	0.908
Navajo	0.358	0.418	0.237	0.418
Russian	0.86	0.856	0.668	0.856
Sanskrit	0.622	0.621	0.47	0.621
Sami	0.56	0.497	0.301	0.497
Spanish	0.878	0.874	0.863	0.874
Albanian	0.193	0.781	0.738	0.781
Swahili	0.605	0.65	0.562	0.65
Turkish	0.646	0.646	0.281	0.646
macro	0.671	0.717	0.561	0.724

Table 4: Language-by-language results for our four submissions

single-character variables sometimes and variable spans in other cases.

Fourth, We had individual WFSTs for each lemma, but with a compiled system it makes sense to put them all together into a single WFST.

References

Iñaki Alegria and Izaskun Etxeberria. 2016. EHU at the SIGMORPHON 2016 shared task. a simple proposal: Grap heme-to-phoneme for inflection. In *Proceedings of the 14th SIGMORPHON Workshop on Computational Research in Phonetics, Phonology, and Morphology*, pages 27–30, Berlin, Germany. Association for Computational Linguistics.

Ryan Cotterell, Christo Kirov, John Sylak-Glassman, Géraldine Walther, Ekaterina Vylomova, Patrick Xia, Manaal Faruqui, Sandra Kübler, David Yarowsky, Jason Eisner, and Mans Hulden. 2017. CoNLL-SIGMORPHON 2017 shared task: Universal morphological reinflection in 52 languages. In *Proceedings of the CoNLL SIGMORPHON 2017 Shared Task: Universal Morphological Reinflection*, pages 1–30, Vancouver. Association for Computational Linguistics.

Greg Durrett and John DeNero. 2013. Supervised learning of complete morphological paradigms. In *Proceedings of the 2013 Conference of the North American Chapter of the Association for Computational Linguistics: Human Language Technologies*, pages 1185–1195, Atlanta, Georgia. Association for Computational Linguistics.

Markus Forsberg and Mans Hulden. 2016. Learning transducer models for morphological analysis from example inflections. In *Proceedings of the SIGFSM Workshop on Statistical NLP and Weighted Automata*, pages 42–50, Berlin, Germany. Association for Computational Linguistics.

Omer Goldman, Khuyagbaatar Batsuren, Khalifa Salam, Aryaman Arora, Garrett Nicolai, Reyt Tsarfaty, and Ekaterina Vylomova. 2023. SIGMORPHON–UniMorph 2023 shared task 0: Typologically diverse morphological inflection. In *Proceedings of the 20th SIGMORPHON Workshop on Computational Research in Phonetics, Phonology, and Morphology*, Toronto, Canada. Association for Computational Linguistics.

David Guriel, Omer Goldman, and Reut Tsarfaty. 2022. Morphological reinflection with multiple arguments: An extended ann otation schema and a Georgian case study. In *Proceedings of the 60th Annual Meeting of the Association for Computational Linguistics (Volume 2: Short Papers)*, pages 196–202, Dublin, Ireland. Association for Computational Linguistics.

Sittichai Jiampojamarn, Colin Cherry, and Grzegorz Kondrak. 2008. Joint processing and discriminative training for letter-to-phoneme conversion. In *Proceedings of ACL-08: HLT*, pages 905–913, Columbus, Ohio. Association for Computational Linguistics.

David King. 2016. Evaluating sequence alignment for learning inflectional morphology. In *Proceedings of the 14th SIGMORPHON Workshop on Computational Research in Phonetics, Phonology, and Morphology*, pages 49–53, Berlin, Germany. Association for Computational Linguistics.

Ling Liu and Lingshuang Jack Mao. 2016. Morphological reinflection with conditional random fields and unsup ervised features. In *Proceedings of the 14th SIGMORPHON Workshop on Computational Research in Phonetics, Phonology, and Morphology*, pages 36–40, Berlin, Germany. Association for Computational Linguistics.

Ryan McDonald, Koby Crammer, and Fernando Pereira. 2005. Online large-margin training of dependency parsers. In *Proceedings of the 43rd Annual Meeting of the Association for Computational Linguistics (ACL'05)*, pages 91–98, Ann Arbor, Michigan. Association for Computational Linguistics.

Tatiana Merzhevich, Nkonye Gbadegoye, Leander Girrbach, Jingwen Li, and Ryan Soh-Eun Shim. 2022. SIGMORPHON 2022 task 0 submission description: Modelling morpholo gical inflection with data-driven and rule-based approaches. In *Proceedings of the 19th SIGMORPHON Workshop on Computational Research in Phonetics, Phonology, and Morphology*, pages 204–211, Seattle, Washington. Association for Computational Linguistics.

Garrett Nicolai, Bradley Hauer, Adam St Arnaud, and Grzegorz Kondrak. 2016. Morphological reinflection via discriminative string transduction. In *Proceedings of the 14th SIGMORPHON Workshop on Computational Research in Phonetics, Phonology, and Morphology*, pages 31–35, Berlin, Germany. Association for Computational Linguistics.

Josef R. Novak, Nobuaki Minematsu, and Keikichi Hirose. 2012. WFST-based grapheme-to-phoneme conversion: Open source tools for alignment, model-building and decoding. In *Proceedings of the 10th International Workshop on Finite State Methods and Natural Language Processing*, pages 45–49, Donostia–San Sebastián. Association for Computational Linguistics.

Linear Discriminative Learning: a competitive non-neural baseline for morphological inflection

Cheonkam Jeong[†]
Department of Linguistics
University of Arizona
Tucson, AZ, 85721, United States

Dominic Schmitz[†] and **Akhilesh Kakolu Ramarao**[†]
Department of English Language and Linguistics
Institute of English and American Studies
Heinrich-Heine-University
Düsseldorf, 40225, Germany

Anna Sophia Stein
Institute of Linguistics
Heinrich-Heine-University
Düsseldorf, 40225, Germany

Kevin Tang
Department of English Language and Linguistics
Institute of English and American Studies
Heinrich-Heine-University
Düsseldorf, 40225, Germany

Abstract

This paper presents our submission to the SIGMORPHON 2023 task 2 of Cognitively Plausible Morphophonological Generalization in Korean. We implemented both Linear Discriminative Learning and Transformer models and found that the Linear Discriminative Learning model trained on a combination of corpus and experimental data showed the best performance with the overall accuracy of around 83%. We found that the best model must be trained on both corpus data and the experimental data of one particular participant. Our examination of speaker-variability and speaker-specific information did not explain why a particular participant combined well with the corpus data. We recommend Linear Discriminative Learning models as a future non-neural baseline system, owning to its training speed, accuracy, model interpretability and cognitive plausibility. In order to improve the model performance, we suggest using bigger data and/or performing data augmentation and incorporating speaker- and item-specifics considerably.

1 Introduction

There has been a heated debate on whether human language users generate language in a generative manner (e.g., Chomsky and Halle (1968)) or an output-oriented manner (e.g., Prince and Smolensky (2004)). In accordance with the theoretical stance, computational models have been proposed. The generative approach is essentially rule-based at an abstract level. The Minimal Generalisation Learner (MGL) by Albright and Hayes (2003) is a traditional, symbolic rule learner. More recent rule-based computational approaches include Allen and Becker (2015) and Belth et al. (2021).

With the availability of large corpus data, output-oriented models have become widely popular. Output-oriented models can be rule-based or end-to-end. The former includes Prince and Smolensky (2004) and Lignos et al. (2009); in the former, a search procedure is implemented on a set of candidates, or outputs, in order to find the surface form that is most compatible with the underlying representation. On the other hand, output-oriented models can be rule-free. For instance, Malouf (2017) showcased a recurrent deep learning model to predict paradigm forms. Similarly, Kirov and Cotterell (2018) proposed a encoder-decoder network architecture to model linguistic phenomena.

Both approaches have their own advantages and disadvantages. However, in terms of model performance, output-oriented models surpass generative ones presumably due to difficulty of incorporating many other variations in conversation. Nevertheless, output-oriented models are not panacea. They are not as cognitively motivated, thus making them less appealing for cognitive research. Deep learning-based models, in particular, show great performance, but they lack interpretability. These shortcomings necessitate a hybrid model, which is i) cognitively motivated, ii) more agnostic than generative models, and iii) more transparent than deep learning-based models.

Recently, Baayen et al. (2019) proposed Linear Discriminative Learning (LDL), part of the discriminative lexicon (Chuang and Baayen, 2021). As the model follows the Rescorla-Wagner Rule and Widrow-Hoff Rules, some insight into human cognition can be obtained through model imple-

[†] These authors contributed equally to this work.

Senior and corresponding author: Kevin Tang (kevin.tang@hhu.de)

Proceedings of the 20th SIGMORPHON workshop on Computational Research in Phonetics, Phonology, and Morphology, pages 138–150
July 14, 2023

mentation. Moreover, as it implements a linear mapping between form and meaning in simple two layers without any hidden layer, LDL features higher interpretability and embraces linguistic engineering. Considering these advantages, an LDL model was chosen as the main model for the SIGMORPHON 2023 shared task 2, which aims to generalize morphological inflections in Korean. A transformer model, which has been state-of-the-art models for various NLP tasks, was also implemented for comparison. The code and data are available here: `https://github.com/hhuslamlab/sigmorphon2023`

2 Related Work

While neural-based systems typically dominate SIGMORPHON challenges, perhaps because they generally perform well in morphological inflection tasks, their limitations can be better examined using wug testing. For instance, McCurdy et al. (2020) examined the ability of modern Encoder-Decoder (ED) architectures to inflect German plurals and concluded that ED does not show human-like variability as shown in wug data. In fact, recent SIGMORPHON challenges involve learning from corpora that better represent the actual linguistic input of children (such as child-directed speech) and evaluating on phonetically-transcribed spoken production by children or adults in corpora or in experiments. For instance, the SIGMORPHON 2021 shared Task 0 Part 2 was to predict the judgement ratings of wug words (Calderone et al., 2021) as opposed to using real words held-out from the training data as test data. Similarly, the SIGMORPHON 2022 challenge involved computational modeling of the data drawn from corpora of child-directed speech and evaluation on children's learning trajectories and erroneous productions (Kodner and Khalifa, 2022; Kakolu Ramarao et al., 2022).

Turning to studies from the field of laboratory phonology, there is a long history of training models on corpora to learn specific aspects of morpho-phonological grammar and evaluating their productivity with experimental data (wug-test and acceptability judgement). For instance, Jun (2010)'s study on stem-final obstruent variation in Korean trained a model with multiple stocastic rules (Albright and Hayes (2002)'s Paradigm Learning Model) in which the acquisition of morphology is based on the distributional pattern of the learning data, using the Sejong corpus, and evaluated on acceptability judgement data. Related to the linguistic phenomenon in this study, Albright and Kang (2009) conducted a computational modeling of inflected forms of Korean verbs using the Minimal Generalization Learner algorithm (Albright and Hayes, 2002) and evaluated the model's performance with attested child errors and historical changes.

Finally, there is a growing number of morphological inflection studies that use the Linear Discriminative Learning model (which will be introduced later) to train on corpus data and evaluate on experimental data (Nieder et al., 2021; Heitmeier et al., 2021; Chuang et al., 2020; Heitmeier and Baayen, 2020; Baayen et al., 2018) and they typical yielded relatively high performance (compared to traditional, symbolic rule learner) while being easy to interpret and cognitively motivated.

3 Task and Evaluation Details

We challenge the shared task 2 Cognitively Plausible Morphophonological Generalization in Korean. The aim of this task is to predict human responses to a generalization task (wug-test), considering high-frequency, low-frequency, and pseudoword items. This implies that human responses may vary depending on the word frequency and familiarity.

The phonological phenomenon to be tested through this task is Korean Post-Obstruent Tensification (henceforth, POT). In Korean, when a lenis consonant in the coda is followed by another obstruent, it can be tensified. However, when a consonant cluster occurs in the coda position, it undergoes Consonant Simplification (henceforth, CS) before POT if the following segment is either an obstruent or a sonorant. On the other hand, neither CS nor POT does occur when the following segment is a vowel.

Depending on the type of the deleted consonant, variation can occur, which can be affected by such speaker- and item-specific features as language familiarity and frequency. In this regard, the main task can be rephrased as predicting features as completely as possible in accordance with those in the answers. For this task, both corpus and experimental data are provided, which include variation patterns. Models are to be evaluated on the accuracy of the prediction of the feature vectors given the corresponding features in the answers from unseen participants.

4 Data

Both corpus and experimental data are provided for this task. The National institute of Korean Language (NIKL) Korean Dialogue corpus (NIKL, 2021) is provided as the main corpus data. All the word tokens affixed with `-lC verbs`, except for `-lh` final stems, are provided after manual annotation by the organizers. They further are categorized as `lC+Obstruent`, `lC+Sonorant`, and `lC+Vowel`, depending on the type of the consequent segment. `lC+Obstruent` and `lC+Sonorant` data each include target words with morphological boundaries and produced words with syllable breaks both in a Romanized form and Korean orthography. Whether target words undergo POT is also provided, as well as such features as obstruent deletion and lateral deletion pertinent to CS and POT.

On the other hand, `lC+Vowel` data only provide target words with morphological boundaries both in a Romanized form and Korean orthography. They do not include produced word information as this condition is not subject to POT and CS; thus, all the feature values of obstruent deletion and lateral deletion are labeled as 0 with the POT value being labeled as 0. Whether the target is lateralizated or nasalized is marked only in the `lC+Sonorant` data while labeled as `NA` in the others. The number of tokens in `lC+Obstruent` data is 876, that of tokens in `lC+Sonorant` data is 95, and that of tokens in `lC+Vowel` data is 2,525 with 514 types–1,485 if frequency information in `lC+Vowel` data is ignored. Thus, the total number of tokens in the NIKL data is 3,496.

In addition to the adult corpus, some part of a child spontaneous speech corpus, the Ko corpus (Ko et al., 2020), is provided. As with the NIKL data, the Ko corpus provides target words and their production but solely in a Romanized form. The POT value with the lateralization and nasalization feature values are labeled. As it does not include any lC verbs followed by a sonorant, both nasalization and lateralization are not applicable. A total of 336 tokens are provided.

In the case of experimental data, the experimental responses of 12 participants, in addition to 4 participants for the development data, are provided. They include what are included in the corpus data with the experimental specifics: the trial number, the trial ID, the subject ID, option, language familiarity, and word frequency. A total of 2,843 tokens are provided.

5 System Description

The main task is to accommodate as many variation patterns as possible. We navigated through all the corpus and experimental data, in which process we found inconsistencies in transcription in the data. In particular, the Ko corpus includes items transcribed in a very detailed manner, including phonological processes, such as deletion and insertion, other than those pertinent to the task. We also found that the target item does not always feature one-to-one mapping, but more-than-one mapping.

Based on the observations above, data preprocessing was of primary importance and was the most time-consuming component. We manually corrected the Ko corpus and automatically unified the transcription style. We then selected models adequate to this task. Considering the nature of the shared task that investigates morphological variations with both corpus and experimental data and the time constraint, LDL was chosen as the main model, along with a Transformer model that has demonstrated great performance in NLP. For each of the two modelling approaches we conducted two studies: Study 1 experimented with systems that train only on the corpus data and/or only on the experimental data; Study 2 used the insights from Study 1, and experimented with systems that train on both the corpus and the experimental data.

5.1 Linear Discriminative Model

LDL generates a system of form-meaning relations by discriminating between different forms and meanings, with forms and meanings being represented by numerical vectors. Form vectors are based either on segmental representations of various lengths, or on representations of acoustic transitions gleaned directly from the speech signal (Arnold et al., 2017; Shafaei-Bajestan et al., 2021). Meaning itself is taken to be a dynamic concept, being emergent from the context in which words are being used, and is represented by semantic vectors, similar to approaches in distributional semantics (Boleda, 2020). The idea is that if both forms and meanings can be expressed numerically, we can mathematically connect form and meaning, i.e. map meaning onto form and vice versa. In this system of mappings, the two sets of vectors are combined into matrices – a form matrix and a semantic matrix. The form vectors are mapped onto semantic vectors to model comprehension, and semantic vectors are mapped onto form vectors to model production. The mapping between them at the theoretical end-state of learning is predicted using multivariate multiple linear regression (hence the term 'Linear Discriminative Learning'). The network is simple and interpretable, because, in contrast to deep learning networks, it features just two layers (i.e. the form and meaning matrices), both of which are linguistically transparent.

5.1.1 Data Preprocessing

Due to the time limitation, we decided to winnow out the data that are only pertinent to POT and CS from the Ko corpus. To be specific, the Ko corpus includes tokens involving other phonological processes, like insertion, as well. For instance, there are 6 instances of `ipko` and the produced forms are `ikgo`, `lipgo`, `tipgo`, `ikgu`, `linkgo`, and `nipgo`. Considering POS and CS rules, the ideal outputs are `ipgo` and `ikgo`. Moreover, based on the tendency of negative vowelization of the mid rounded vowel in conversation, `ikgu` is another candidate. The others are also producible, especially considering that the Ko corpus consists of children speech, but they are definitely not canonical outputs from the pertinent rules. Thus, if the input and the output are hugely different from each other because of other phonological processes, the tokens were discarded. All the duplicated tokens were also removed. Thus, 286 tokens were left from 336 tokens. Lastly, morphological boundary and feature representation were manually incorporated following the style of the other data.

We also observed that there are inconsistencies in transcription style between the two corpus data and the experimental data. The following data transformations were performed on the corpus data. In the Production_R, the tense forms of the plosives `p*,t*,k*` are replaced with `b,d,g`, and those of the alveolar fricative and the alveolo-palatal affricate `S,c*` are replaced with `s*, J`, respectively. Moreover, there are several inconsistencies in transcription style between the input (Morphology_R) and the output (Production_R). First, the middle yin diphthong `yv` or `jv` in Morphology_R is replaced with `jv` or `yv` in Production_R. Second, the alveolar fricative `S` in Morphology_R is replaced with `s*`, but the reverse transformation is conducted in Production_R. Lastly, the tense stops in Korean orthography `P, T, K` in Morphology_R are replaced with `p, t, k`, except when they occur in the word-initial position.

As a result, the pre-processed data contained `s*` as phone representation. That is, a single phone is represented by two symbols. For triphones, this would lead to unwanted consequences: Triphones which contain information only on two phones, i.e. `s*` and any other phone, and triphones which contain only one of the two parts of `s*`. Therefore, `s*` was replaced with `S` for the implementations of LDL presented in the subsequent sections.

5.1.2 General Model Architecture

The form matrices C used for the present implementations of LDL consisted of triphones, i.e. sequences of three phones within a word form. Triphones overlap and can be understood as proxies for phonological transitions. In each word's individual form vector c, the presence of a triphone is marked with 1, while the absence is marked with 0. The form vectors of all words of a set of words constitute its C matrix and each row in such a C matrix represents a word form, while the columns of the C matrix represent all triphones of its underlying word set. Triphones were used as previous studies found overall good performance for triphones (e.g. Chuang et al. 2021; Schmitz et al. 2021).

The semantic matrices S used for the present implementations of LDL deviate from those usually found in studies using LDL. Commonly, semantics are introduced via semantic vectors obtained by methods of distributional semantics, e.g. via fastText (Bojanowski et al., 2016) or naive discriminative learning (Baayen et al., 2011). However, with the small amount of language data provided, the computation of such semantic vectors is barely feasible. While creating semantic vectors based on a larger corpus of Korean may be one option to solve this issue, we decided against this solution as it would mean using data that is not part of the current challenge. Instead, semantic vectors were created based on morphemes and in a binary fashion. That is, similar to the form vectors, in each word's individual semantic vector s, the presence of a morpheme is marked with 1, while the absence is marked with 0. The semantic vectors of all words of a set of words constitute its S matrix.

With C and S, one can straightforwardly map forms onto meanings and meanings onto forms:

$$CF = S$$

$$SG = C$$

If one wants to predict the forms or semantics for words that are not yet part of the implementation, additional steps are required. Predicting semantics for newly introduced forms, one computes
with C' denoting the Moore-Penrose generalised inverse. Using the transformation matrix F and a combined form matrix for previously and newly introduced forms $C_{combined}$, then

$$S = C_{combined}F$$

Using this method, previous studies have analysed the semantics of pseudowords (Cassani et al., 2020; Chuang et al., 2021; Schmitz et al., 2021). Adapting this method for the prediction of forms, as for the present study, one computes

$$G = S'C$$

Then, using the transformation matrix G and a combined semantic matrix for previously and newly introduced words, the following is solved:

$$C = S_{combined}G$$

Note that this method comes with an important caveat: Newly introduced words must not contain any triphones that are not part of the original C matrix when predicting their meaning, and, in the present case, they must not contain any morphemes that are not part of the original S matrix.

5.1.3 Study 1

For a first implementation of LDL, the following rationale was adopted. First, the combined data of the NIKL and Ko corpora were taken to represent the mental lexicon of a speaker of Korean. That is, we assumed that this knowledge is shared by all participants. Second, based on this shared prior knowledge, participants individually produced word forms during the experiment. Predicting these forms, and in turn the phonological processes underlying them, via prior knowledge was the aim of this implementation.

The combined NIKL and Ko corpus data were used as initial word set ($n = 632$ after duplicate removal). Based on the corpus data, C and S matrices were created following the specifications in Section 5.1.2. After obtaining the required transformation matrix G via $G = S'C$, G was based on the triphone to morpheme relations found in the corpus data it was trained on. In a next step, one would then use G to compute $C = S_{combined}G$. However, the experimental data contained 111 triphones (out of 247) that were not part of the corpus data. As G was not trained to predict these triphones, any further computations were rendered meaningless.

5.1.4 Study 2

Instead, a second LDL network was implemented. The rationale of this implementation was to first create individual networks for all sixteen train and dev participants. Each participant's network was trained on the combined corpus data and on their experimental data. In a second step, each of the sixteen participants and their networks were then used to predict all other participants' produced word forms. This provided insight in how far pertinent participants were able to predict other participant's productions, allowing the selection of a 'best' participant to then predict the test participants' produced word forms.

First, for each of the sixteen train and dev participants a data set containing the combined NIKL and Ko corpus data ($n = 632$ after duplicate removal) as well as their experimental data was created ($n = 175$ to $n = 180$). Based on this data set, C and S matrices were created and comprehension as well as production were modeled following the specifications outlined in Section 5.1.2.

Second, each of the sixteen participants' G matrices was used to predict the forms produced by all other train and dev participants in the experiment. In contrast to Section 5.1.3, this computation did not pose a problem as experiment items and their triphones were already introduced during the first step. As a result, we obtained prediction accuracies for all sixteen participants by all sixteen participants. Accuracy here refers to whether a word form was predicted correctly. The overall and individual accuracies for low-, high-frequency, and pseudoword items are available on GitHub.

Across all sixteen train and dev participants, it was found that participant 597515 clearly outperformed the other fifteen participants in terms of prediction accuracy across all experimental items. Their mean prediction accuracy across all experimental items was 73%, with 76% for low frequency, 71% for high frequency, and 73% for pseudoword items. Their overall Precision, Recall, and F1 scores for the training data are given in Table 1.

In an attempt to understand why this particular participant showed the best prediction results for the other fifteen train and dev participants and to find out whether we could determine differ-

	Precision	Recall	F1
simplify_delete_obstruent	0.48	0.57	0.43
simplify_delete_lateral	0.60	0.69	0.60
nasalization	0.60	0.69	0.60
lateralization	0.72	0.58	0.46
tensification	0.64	0.77	0.67

Table 1: Precision, Recall, and F1 of participant 597515 for the five phonological processes in the training data

ent 'best' participants for different participants to be predicted, we implemented three multiple regression models for each of the sixteen train and dev participants, i.e. one for high frequency, one for low frequency, and one for pseudoword items. For a given participant's multiple regression models, the dependent variable was the set of prediction accuracies reached by the other participants for that participant. As predictors, the biographical background information, LANGUAGEPREFERENCE and AGESTARTEDSPEAKING, were introduced. Across the sixteen low frequency item models, we found that one participant with a LANGUAGEPREFERENCE of 3 showed an effect for LANGUAGEPREFERENCE ($p = 0.02$). This presumably indicated that the other participant with a LANGUAGEPREFERENCE of 3 was the 'best' prediction candidate for this participant. Across the sixteen high frequency item models, we found that both participants with a LANGUAGEPREFERENCE of 3 showed an effect for LANGUAGEPREFERENCE ($p = 0.02$; $p = 0.0002$), indicating that they were each other's best prediction candidates. Another participant showed a barely significant effect of LANGUAGEPREFERENCE ($p = 0.046$), and yet another participant showed a significant effect of AGESTARTEDSPEAKING ($p = 0.03$) . Across the pseudoword item models, no effects were found. As these results were inconclusive, we decided to drop this attempt and to use participant 597515's G matrix to predict the forms, and hence the underlying phonological processes, for the seven test participants.

The predicted forms and their underlying representations were used to derive information on which of the five phonological processes of interest were predicted for a pertinent word form.

5.2 Neural Network

5.2.1 Data Preprocessing

See the data preprocessing steps in Section 5.1.1.

5.2.2 Model Architecture

Our model closely follows the formulation of the encoder-decoder Transformer for character-level transduction model proposed by Wu et al. (2021). We use multi-headed Transformers with self-attention and implement them with Fairseq (Ott et al., 2019) tool, a PyTorch-based sequence modeling toolkit. Both Encoder and Decoder have four layers with four attention heads, an embedding size of 256 and hidden layer size of 1,024. We use Adam Optimizer (Kingma and Ba, 2015), with an initial learning rate of 0.001, a batch size of 400, 0.1 label smoothing and 1.0 gradient clip threshold. Models are trained for a maximum of 3,000 optimizer updates. Checkpoints are saved every 10 epochs. Beam search is used at the decoding time with a beam width of 5.

The checkpoint with the smallest loss on the development data is chosen as the best model.

For the evaluation, we consider the models' *sequence accuracy* (henceforth, *accuracy*), where only instances for which the entire output sequence equals the target are considered correct.

5.2.3 Study 1

The inputs to each model are the individual characters of the romanized. For example, for the model trained against the raw NIKL dataset, the input is `J a l p - k o` and the output is `J a l . g o`

Model Training Three models were trained on i) the raw NIKL dataset (with a total of 1485 tokens), ii) the raw Ko corpus (with a total of, and iii) the combined datasets (NIKL and Ko). The data in each model were split into train (70%), dev (10%), test (20%) sets. The sequence accuracies of the three models are 71.7% (raw NIKL)[1], 35.3% (raw Ko) and 65.5% (the combined dataset). Furthermore, we trained a model on all experimental items following the same train-test split as stated above and the accuracy was found to be 69.4%.

While these models were evaluated on a different set of test data, their accuracies can nonetheless suggest how the different datasets should be used in Study 2 (Section 5.2.4). Training on the Ko corpus alone is unlikely to be sufficient as it yielded the lowest accuracy. While combining NIKL with Ko yielded a poorer model compared to just using

[1]We experimented with a model using the NIKL dataset but without syllable boundaries, and it yielded an accuracy of 71.6% – a negligible difference compared to the model with syllable boundaries 71.7%

NIKL alone, the Ko corpus should not be excluded given that it is arguably more ecologically valid than NIKL and the amount of training data is already small in this challenge. Finally, training only on experimental items resulted in a comparable performance as the combined dataset. This model was not used as it was explicitly discouraged by the challenge.

To determine how well a model trained only on corpus data would perform on the experimental data, we evaluated the best model (trained on raw NIKL) against the experimental data (and removed the syllable boundaries in the predictions to match the transcription style of the experimental data) and it yielded a much lower accuracy of 29.9%, suggesting that we should incorporate the experimental data as part of training.

5.2.4 Study 2

In this study, we primarily used the pre-processed dataset (using methods described in section 5.2.1) that consists of both NIKL and child spontaneous speech dataset. We then incorporate parts of experimental data along with the combined dataset during both training and development phase. The test data provided by the organizers is used during the testing phase.

Model Training We first incorporated models with training the combined dataset using i) productions from best participant and ii) productions from worst participant, as development data , that yielded accuracy scores of 43.8% and 39.4%.

Next, we trained a model on the combined dataset (NIKL, and the Ko corpus) with the productions from 4 best participants and using responses from a random participant as development data which produced an accuracy score of 68.1%.

Finally, a model was trained on all participants' except the best participant's responses with the combined dataset (NIKL, and the Ko corpus) and using the productions from best participant as development data that yielded an accuracy of 69.2%. The accuracies of this model for: i) low-frequency ii) high-frequency and iii) pseudoword items are 64.4%, 77.7% and 65.38% respectively. The overall Precision, Recall and F1 scores for the five phonological processes in the test data are given in Appendix A.

	Precision	Recall	F1
simplify_delete_obstruent	0.69	0.70	0.67
simplify_delete_lateral	0.79	0.75	0.75
nasalization	0.79	0.75	0.75
lateralization	0.44	0.53	0.41
tensification	0.98	0.98	0.98

Table 2: Precision, Recall, and F1 of participant 597515 for the five phonological processes in the test data

5.3 Results

Predicting the seven test participants' productions using the 'best' participant's LDL network as detailed in Section 5.1.4, an overall accuracy of 83.32% was reached. The accuracies of this model for: i) low-frequency ii) high-frequency and iii) pseudoword items are 83.56%, 83.58% and 82.84%. The overall Precision, Recall, and F1 scores for the test data are given in Table 2. The model performed best on tensification (F1: 0.98), and worst on lateralisation (F1: 0.41). The mean perplexity scores for the train and dev as well as for the test data are 2.11 and 1.97 respectively. The performance of the model on the test data is similar to that on the training data (Table 1) with the exception of simplify delete obstruent being better predicted than lateralization in the test data. Comparing to the best Transformer model, LDL performed better in terms of the overall accuracies of the model; however, the relative performances of the five phonological processes (Precision, Recall and F1 scores) are largely the same (Appendix A).

6 Variability: Items and Participants

To examine the variability of the phenomenon, Shannon entropy (base 2) (Shannon, 1948) was used to quantify how variable are the items in the experimental data and how variable are the participants. In this study, we considered sixteen possible combinations of the five phonological processes (therefore sixteen events in entropy's term) (See Appendix C). With sixteen combinations, the highest possible entropy value is 4 which means each combination has a probability of 1/16 indicating a high level of variability, and the lowest possible entropy is 0 which means there is only one attested combination indicating no variability. For detailed analyses, see Appendix B.

First, we computed the by-item entropy values by computing the proportion of the sixteen response combinations using the sixteen participants (training and development). The 180 experimental items have a mean entropy of 0.584. Pseudoword items have the highest mean entropy (0.612), followed by high-frequency items (0.596) and low-frequency items (0.544). These entropy values suggest that the experimental items in general have low variability and unsurprisingly the pseudoword items were particularly variable compared to the real words. However, these differences in entropy values were not statistically significant ($ps > 0.3842$).

Second, we computed by-participant entropy values by computing the proportion of the sixteen response combinations. Across all the experimental items, the sixteen participants have a mean entropy of 2.143. Participants show the lowest mean entropy with the high-frequency items (2.049) , followed by low-frequency items (2.111) and pseudoword items (2.112). However, these differences in entropy values were not statistically significant ($ps > 0.2542$). Our 'best' participant 597515 has an entropy of 2.192 across all items, 2.176 for high-frequency, 2.154 for low-frequency and 2.140 for pseudoword items, with all values similar to their means. Therefore, the participant's superiority is not purely due to their responses being more variable.

7 Discussion and Conclusion

We demonstrated that LDL is capable of modelling morphological inflection trained on limited corpus and experimental data. Its performance is competitive to that of the Transformer model that we experimented with. Past SIGMORPHON shared tasks (2017–2022) with a focus on morphological inflection have generally received more neural-based systems than non-neural ones and found that neural-based ones tend to be superior (Kodner and Khalifa, 2022; Kodner et al., 2022; Pimentel et al., 2021; Vylomova et al., 2020; McCarthy et al., 2019; Cotterell et al., 2018, 2017, 2016). Amongst the submitted non-neural systems, LDL has never been utilized. Our study cannot conclude that LDL is superior to the transformer architecture as the latter was not fully optimized. However, it has great potential to serve as a non-neural baseline system for future shared tasks as well as allowing researchers to conduct rapid experiments, because of its architecture simplicity, performance (with accuracies from 59% to 99% in a range of languages, e.g. Heitmeier et al. 2021; Schmitz et al. 2021; Stein and Plag 2021; Chuang et al. 2020; Baayen et al. 2019) and speed (in our study one model required on average 35 seconds of CPU processing on an i7-9750H 2.60 GHz system with 32 GB memory).

Our study found that training on the corpus data alone was insufficient and that our models require at least one participant's experimental data in order to inflect the experimental items well. However, from an ecological perspective, a model should only be trained on the corpus data (NIKL and Ko), excluding the experimental data, as the corpus data serve to represent the participants' actual linguistic input. The corpus data we have are likely unrepresentative of the actual linguistic input of our participants. Firstly, the verbs were not embedded in an utterance, and even if the full utterances were used the overall amount of data would still be small with only 53,000 words from the Ko corpus, and 900,000 phrases from the NIKL corpus. Based on spoken speech input alone, Brysbaert et al. (2016) estimated that for American English, the total input from social interactions (in a dialogue) would be equal to 11.688 million word tokens per year and a 20-year-old would have been exposed to about 234 million word tokens. Using a much larger speech-like or transcribed corpus such as SUBTLEX-KR (Tang and de Chene, 2014) (90 million eojeols) is a promising approach for examining morphological inflection patterns (see de Chene (2014) on regularisation in Korean noun inflection).

Our item variability analyses suggest that the three item types (high-, low-frequency and pseudowords) are not particularly different in their variability. This might be reflecting how the LDL model reported in Section 5.3 performed similarly with them (high: 83.58%, low: 83.56%, and pseudowords: 82.84%). However, the best Transfomer model was sensitive to item types yielding a higher accuracy for the high-frequency items (77.7%), than the low-frequency (64.4%) and pseudoword (65.38%) items.

Our attempts in understanding why the 'best' participant was the best in predicting individual participants' productions were not successful. Response variability was unable to explain why our 'best' participant was the best, as it has neither high nor low in variability compared to the other 15 participants. Our regression analyses predicting individual participant accuracies using the participants' demographics was inconclusive. While one may assume that the LDL prediction results should improve when one predicts speakers of similar backgrounds, the nonetheless satisfying LDL prediction results suggest that demographics-matching was not needed. Overall, our results suggest that LDL is suitable for tasks such as the one at hand.

Limitations

The small amount of training data provided in this shared task poses a challenge for models that need large amounts of data to reliably learn linguistic patterns. While we did not employ any data augmentation techniques, we suggest future work to train the models on all the possible feature combinations (weighted with the probabilities as the experimental data) for the stems in the two corpora.

Owning to the lack of time and computing resources, we did not fully optimize our transformer models and we did not fully utilize and explore i) speaker-specific information, especially for the transformer models, ii) token frequency information in the corpora, as we assumed extension of morphological patterns is based on type, not token, frequency (Bybee, 2001; Pierrehumbert, 2001). Furthermore, we did not experiment with training models with either high-frequency, low-frequency and pseudoword items. It is possible that some speakers' high/low/pseudoword items would be better served as part of the training set.

The LDL model in Section 5.1.3 was not able to evaluate the experimental items due to the unattested triphones. This shortcoming can be mitigated by using phonological features (Tang and Baer-Henney, 2023).

Ethics Statement

In the beginning of the challenge, we discovered the answers of the experimental test data were accidentally released early by the organisers. We immediately informed the organisers and as requested, we deleted the test data and committed to not use it until it was officially released. Our work was trained on speech corpora of adults which were recorded with ethics approval. The broader impact of the work includes i) improving how morphological inflection models can be trained with low-resource languages or phenomena, ii) developing speaker-specific morphological inflection models, iii) establishing a new baseline model architecture (LDL) that has a low carbon footprint.

CRediT authorship contribution statement

CJ, DS, and AKR contributed equally to this work. KT served as the senior and corresponding author on this paper.

We follow the CRediT taxonomy[2]. Conceptualization: KT; Data curation: CJ, AKR; Formal Analysis: AS, DS; Investigation: KT, DS, CJ, AKR; Methodology: KT; Supervision: KT; Visualization: AS; and Writing – original draft: KT and Writing – review & editing: KT, AS, CJ, DS, AKR.

Acknowledgements

We gratefully acknowledge the support of the central HPC system "HILBERT" at Heinrich-Heine-University, Düsseldorf.

References

Adam Albright and Bruce Hayes. 2002. Modeling English past tense intuitions with minimal generalization. In *Proceedings of the ACL-02 Workshop on Morphological and Phonological Learning - Volume 6*, MPL '02, page 58–69, USA. Association for Computational Linguistics.

Adam Albright and Bruce Hayes. 2003. Rules vs. analogy in English past tenses: A computational/experimental study. *Cognition*, 90(2):119–161.

Adam Albright and Yoonjung Kang. 2009. Predicting innovative alternations in Korean verb paradigms. *Current issues in unity and diversity of languages: Collection of the papers selected from the CIL 18, held at Korea University in Seoul*, pages 1–20.

Blake Allen and Michael Becker. 2015. Learning alternations from surface forms with sublexical phonology. *Unpublished manuscript. Available as lingbuzz/002503*.

Denis Arnold, Fabian Tomaschek, Konstantin Sering, Florence Lopez, and R. Harald Baayen. 2017. Words from spontaneous conversational speech can be recognized with human-like accuracy by an error-driven learning algorithm that discriminates between meanings straight from smart acoustic features, bypassing the phoneme as recognition unit. *PLOS ONE*, 12:e0174623.

R. Harald Baayen, Yu-Ying Chuang, and James P. Blevins. 2018. Inflectional morphology with linear mappings. *The Mental Lexicon*, 13(2):230–268.

R. Harald Baayen, Yu-Ying Chuang, Elnaz Shafaei-Bajestan, and James P. Blevins. 2019. The discriminative lexicon: A unified computational model for

[2]`https://www.ucl.ac.uk/library/research-support/open-access/credit-taxonomy`

the lexicon and lexical processing in comprehension and production grounded not in (de) composition but in linear discriminative learning. *Complexity*, 2019:1–39.

R. Harald Baayen, Petar Milin, Dusica Filipović Đurđević, Peter Hendrix, and Marco Marelli. 2011. An amorphous model for morphological processing in visual comprehension based on naive discriminative learning. *Psychological Review*, 118:438–481.

Caleb Belth, Sarah Payne, Deniz Beser, Jordan Kodner, and Charles Yang. 2021. The greedy and recursive search for morphological productivity.

Piotr Bojanowski, Edouard Grave, Armand Joulin, and Tomas Mikolov. 2016. Enriching word vectors with subword information. *Transactions of the Association for Computational Linguistics*, 5:135–146.

Gemma Boleda. 2020. Distributional semantics and linguistic theory. *Annual Review of Linguistics*, 6:213–234.

Marc Brysbaert, Michaël Stevens, Paweł Mandera, and Emmanuel Keuleers. 2016. How many words do we know? practical estimates of vocabulary size dependent on word definition, the degree of language input and the participant's age. *Frontiers in psychology*, 7:1116.

Joan Bybee. 2001. *Phonology and language use*. Cambridge University Press, Cambridge.

Basilio Calderone, Nabil Hathout, and Olivier Bonami. 2021. Not quite there yet: Combining analogical patterns and encoder-decoder networks for cognitively plausible inflection. In *Proceedings of the 18th SIGMORPHON Workshop on Computational Research in Phonetics, Phonology, and Morphology*, pages 274–282, Online. ACL.

Giovanni Cassani, Yu-Ying Chuang, and R Harald Baayen. 2020. On the semantics of nonwords and their lexical category. *Journal of Experimental Psychology: Learning, Memory, and Cognition*, 46(4):621.

Noam Chomsky and Morris Halle. 1968. *The sound pattern of English*. New York: Harper & Row.

Yu-Ying Chuang and R. Harald Baayen. 2021. Discriminative learning and the lexicon: NDL and LDL. *Oxford Research Encyclopedia of Linguistics*.

Yu-Ying Chuang, Kaidi Lõo, James P. Blevins, and R. Harald Baayen. 2020. Estonian case inflection made simple: A case study in word and paradigm morphology with linear discriminative learning. In Lívia Körtvélyessy and Pavol Štekauer, editors, *Complex Words: Advances in Morphology*, page 119–141. Cambridge University Press.

Yu-Ying Chuang, Marie Lenka Vollmer, Elnaz Shafaei-Bajestan, Susanne Gahl, Peter Hendrix, and R Harald Baayen. 2021. The processing of pseudoword form and meaning in production and comprehension: A computational modeling approach using linear discriminative learning. *Behavior research methods*, 53:945–976.

Ryan Cotterell, Christo Kirov, John Sylak-Glassman, Géraldine Walther, Ekaterina Vylomova, Arya D McCarthy, Katharina Kann, Sabrina J Mielke, Garrett Nicolai, Miikka Silfverberg, David Yarowsky, Jason Eisner, and Mans Hulden. 2018. The CoNLL–SIGMORPHON 2018 shared task: Universal morphological reinflection. In *Proceedings of the CoNLL–SIGMORPHON 2018 Shared Task: Universal Morphological Reinflection*, pages 1–27, Brussels, Belgium. Association for Computational Linguistics.

Ryan Cotterell, Christo Kirov, John Sylak-Glassman, Géraldine Walther, Ekaterina Vylomova, Patrick Xia, Manaal Faruqui, Sandra Kübler, David Yarowsky, Jason Eisner, and Mans Hulden. 2017. CoNLL-SIGMORPHON 2017 shared task: Universal morphological reinflection in 52 languages. In *Proceedings of the CoNLL-SIGMORPHON 2017 Shared Task: Universal Morphological Reinflection*, Vancouver, Canada. Association for Computational Linguistics.

Ryan Cotterell, Christo Kirov, John Sylak-Glassman, David Yarowsky, Jason Eisner, and Mans Hulden. 2016. The SIGMORPHON 2016 shared task—morphological reinflection. In *Proceedings of the 14th SIGMORPHON Workshop on Computational Research in Phonetics, Phonology, and Morphology*, Berlin, Germany. Association for Computational Linguistics.

Brent de Chene. 2014. Probability matching versus probability maximization in morphophonology: The case of Korean noun inflection. *Theoretical and applied linguistics at Kobe Shoin*, 17:1–13.

Maria Heitmeier and R. Harald Baayen. 2020. Simulating phonological and semantic impairment of english tense inflection with linear discriminative learning. *The Mental Lexicon*, 15(3):385–421.

Maria Heitmeier, Yu-Ying Chuang, and R. Harald Baayen. 2021. Modeling morphology with linear discriminative learning: Considerations and design choices. *Frontiers in Psychology*, 12.

Jongho Jun. 2010. Stem-final obstruent variation in Korean. *Journal of East Asian Linguistics*, 19:137–179.

Akhilesh Kakolu Ramarao, Yulia Zinova, Kevin Tang, and Ruben van de Vijver. 2022. HeiMorph at SIGMORPHON 2022 shared task on morphological acquisition trajectories. In *Proceedings of the 19th SIGMORPHON Workshop on Computational Research in Phonetics, Phonology, and Morphology*, pages 236–239, Seattle, Washington. Association for Computational Linguistics.

Diederik P. Kingma and Jimmy Ba. 2015. Adam: A method for stochastic optimization. In *3rd International Conference on Learning Representations, ICLR 2015, San Diego, CA, USA, May 7-9, 2015, Conference Track Proceedings*.

Christo Kirov and Ryan Cotterell. 2018. Recurrent neural networks in linguistic theory: Revisiting Pinker and Prince (1988) and the past tense debate. *Transactions of the Association for Computational Linguistics*, 6:651–665.

Eon-Suk Ko, Jinyoung Jo, Kyung-Woon On, and Byoung-Tak Zhang. 2020. Introducing the Ko corpus of Korean mother–child interaction. *Frontiers in Psychology*, 11:602623.

Jordan Kodner and Salam Khalifa. 2022. SIGMORPHON–UniMorph 2022 shared task 0: Modeling inflection in language acquisition. In *Proceedings of the 19th SIGMORPHON Workshop on Computational Research in Phonetics, Phonology, and Morphology*, pages 157–175, Seattle, Washington. Association for Computational Linguistics.

Jordan Kodner, Salam Khalifa, Khuyagbaatar Batsuren, Hossep Dolatian, Ryan Cotterell, Faruk Akkus, Antonios Anastasopoulos, Taras Andrushko, Aryaman Arora, Nona Atanalov, Gábor Bella, Elena Budianskaya, Yustinus Ghanggo Ate, Omer Goldman, David Guriel, Simon Guriel, Silvia Guriel-Agiashvili, Witold Kieraś, Andrew Krizhanovsky, Natalia Krizhanovsky, Igor Marchenko, Magdalena Markowska, Polina Mashkovtseva, Maria Nepomniashchaya, Daria Rodionova, Karina Scheifer, Alexandra Sorova, Anastasia Yemelina, Jeremiah Young, and Ekaterina Vylomova. 2022. SIGMORPHON–UniMorph 2022 shared task 0: Generalization and typologically diverse morphological inflection. In *Proceedings of the 19th SIGMORPHON Workshop on Computational Research in Phonetics, Phonology, and Morphology*, pages 176–203, Seattle, Washington. Association for Computational Linguistics.

Constantine Lignos, Erwin Chan, Mitchell P. Marcus, and Charles Yang. 2009. A rule-based unsupervised morphology learning framework. In *Working Notes for CLEF 2009 Workshop co-located with the 13th European Conference on Digital Libraries (ECDL 2009) , Corfù, Greece, September 30 - October 2, 2009*, volume 1175 of *CEUR Workshop Proceedings*. CEUR-WS.org.

Robert Malouf. 2017. Abstractive morphological learning with a recurrent neural network. *Morphology*, 27:431–458.

Arya D. McCarthy, Ekaterina Vylomova, Shijie Wu, Chaitanya Malaviya, Lawrence Wolf-Sonkin, Garrett Nicolai, Christo Kirov, Miikka Silfverberg, Sabrina J. Mielke, Jeffrey Heinz, Ryan Cotterell, and Mans Hulden. 2019. The SIGMORPHON 2019 shared task: Morphological analysis in context and cross-lingual transfer for inflection. In *Proceedings of the 16th Workshop on Computational Research in Phonetics, Phonology, and Morphology*, pages 229–244, Florence, Italy. Association for Computational Linguistics.

Kate McCurdy, Adam Lopez, and Sharon Goldwater. 2020. Conditioning, but on which distribution? grammatical gender in German plural inflection. In *Proceedings of the Workshop on Cognitive Modeling and Computational Linguistics*, pages 59–65, Online. Association for Computational Linguistics.

Jessica Nieder, Yu-Ying Chuang, Ruben van de Vijver, and R. H Baayen. 2021. A discriminative lexicon approach to word comprehension, production and processing: Maltese plurals.

NIKL. 2021. NIKL Korean dialogue corpus (audio) 2020(v.1.3).

Myle Ott, Sergey Edunov, Alexei Baevski, Angela Fan, Sam Gross, Nathan Ng, David Grangier, and Michael Auli. 2019. fairseq: A fast, extensible toolkit for sequence modeling. In *Proceedings of the 2019 Conference of the North American Chapter of the Association for Computational Linguistics: Human Language Technologies, NAACL-HLT 2019, Minneapolis, MN, USA, June 2-7, 2019, Demonstrations*, pages 48–53. Association for Computational Linguistics.

Janet Pierrehumbert. 2001. Exemplar dynamics: Word frequency, lenition and contrast. In Joan Bybee and Paul Hopper, editors, *Frequency and the emergence of linguistic structure*, pages 137–157. John Benjamins, Amsterdam.

Tiago Pimentel, Maria Ryskina, Sabrina J. Mielke, Shijie Wu, Eleanor Chodroff, Brian Leonard, Garrett Nicolai, Yustinus Ghanggo Ate, Salam Khalifa, Nizar Habash, Charbel El-Khaissi, Omer Goldman, Michael Gasser, William Lane, Matt Coler, Arturo Oncevay, Jaime Rafael Montoya Samame, Gema Celeste Silva Villegas, Adam Ek, Jean-Philippe Bernardy, Andrey Shcherbakov, Aziyana Bayyr-ool, Karina Sheifer, Sofya Ganieva, Matvey Plugaryov, Elena Klyachko, Ali Salehi, Andrew Krizhanovsky, Natalia Krizhanovsky, Clara Vania, Sardana Ivanova, Aelita Salchak, Christopher Straughn, Zoey Liu, Jonathan North Washington, Duygu Ataman, Witold Kieraś, Marcin Woliński, Totok Suhardijanto, Niklas Stoehr, Zahroh Nuriah, Shyam Ratan, Francis M. Tyers, Edoardo M. Ponti, Grant Aiton, Richard J. Hatcher, Emily Prud'hommeaux, Ritesh Kumar, Mans Hulden, Botond Barta, Dorina Lakatos, Gábor Szolnok, Judit Ács, Mohit Raj, David Yarowsky, Ryan Cotterell, Ben Ambridge, and Ekaterina Vylomova. 2021. SIGMORPHON 2021 shared task on morphological reinflection: Generalization across languages. In *Proceedings of the 18th SIGMORPHON Workshop on Computational Research in Phonetics, Phonology, and Morphology*, pages 229–259, Online. Association for Computational Linguistics.

Alan Prince and Paul Smolensky. 2004. *Optimality Theory: Constraint interaction in generative grammar*. John Wiley & Sons.

Dominic Schmitz, Ingo Plag, Dinah Baer-Henney, and Simon David Stein. 2021. Durational differences of word-final /s/ emerge from the lexicon: Modelling morpho-phonetic effects in pseudowords with linear discriminative learning. *Frontiers in Psychology*, 12.

Elnaz Shafaei-Bajestan, Masoumeh Moradipour-Tari, Peter Uhrig, and R. Harald Baayen. 2021. Ldl-auris: a computational model, grounded in error-driven learning, for the comprehension of single spoken words. *Language, Cognition and Neuroscience*, pages 1–28.

Claude Elwood Shannon. 1948. A mathematical theory of communication. *The Bell System Technical Journal*, 27(3):379–423.

Simon David Stein and Ingo Plag. 2021. Morpho-phonetic effects in speech production: Modeling the acoustic duration of english derived words with linear discriminative learning. *Frontiers in Psychology*, 12.

Kevin Tang and Dinah Baer-Henney. 2023. Modelling L1 and the artificial language during artificial language learning. *Laboratory Phonology: Journal of the Association for Laboratory Phonology*, 14(1):1–54.

Kevin Tang and Brent de Chene. 2014. A new corpus of colloquial Korean and its applications. Presented at The 14th Laboratory Phonology Conference (LabPhon 14), Tachikawa, Tokyo, Japan.

Ekaterina Vylomova, Jennifer White, Elizabeth Salesky, Sabrina J. Mielke, Shijie Wu, Edoardo Maria Ponti, Rowan Hall Maudslay, Ran Zmigrod, Josef Valvoda, Svetlana Toldova, Francis Tyers, Elena Klyachko, Ilya Yegorov, Natalia Krizhanovsky, Paula Czarnowska, Irene Nikkarinen, Andrew Krizhanovsky, Tiago Pimentel, Lucas Torroba Hennigen, Christo Kirov, Garrett Nicolai, Adina Williams, Antonios Anastasopoulos, Hilaria Cruz, Eleanor Chodroff, Ryan Cotterell, Miikka Silfverberg, and Mans Hulden. 2020. SIGMORPHON 2020 shared task 0: Typologically diverse morphological inflection. In *Proceedings of the 17th SIGMORPHON Workshop on Computational Research in Phonetics, Phonology, and Morphology*, pages 1–39, Online. Association for Computational Linguistics.

Shijie Wu, Ryan Cotterell, and Mans Hulden. 2021. Applying the transformer to character-level transduction. In *Proceedings of the 16th Conference of the European Chapter of the Association for Computational Linguistics: Main Volume, EACL 2021, Online, April 19 - 23, 2021*, pages 1901–1907. Association for Computational Linguistics.

A Appendix: Evaluation metrics for the Neural Network model

	Precision	Recall	F1
simplify_delete_obstruent	0.70	0.71	0.68
simplify_delete_lateral	0.79	0.72	0.72
nasalization	0.79	0.72	0.72
lateralization	0.44	0.53	0.41
tensification	0.98	0.98	0.98

Table 3: Precision, Recall, and F1 for the five phonological processes in the test data for the best performing neural network model

B Appendix: Variability analyses

	mean	sd	min.	max.
All	0.58	0.52	0.00	1.68
High-frequency	0.60	0.54	0.00	1.68
Low-frequency	0.54	0.52	0.00	1.47
Pseudoword	0.61	0.50	0.00	1.65

Table 4: Summary statistics of by-item entropy: Mean, standard deviation (sd), minimum (min.) and maximum (max.) entropy values of all items computed over all items, as well as subsets of items (high-frequency, low-frequency and pseudoword items)

	mean	sd	min.	max.
All	2.14	0.14	1.83	2.33
High-frequency	2.05	0.16	1.67	2.25
Low-frequency	2.11	0.10	1.88	2.25
Pseudoword	2.11	0.15	1.85	2.33

Table 5: Summary statistics of by-participant entropy: Mean, standard deviation (sd), minimum (min.) and maximum (max.) entropy values of all participants computed over all items, as well as subsets of items (high-frequency, low-frequency and pseudoword items)

participant	all	pseudoword	low	high
597515	2.19	2.14	2.15	2.18
592117	2.20	2.11	2.14	2.18
563118	2.19	2.13	2.15	2.10
556014	2.26	2.25	2.19	2.21
578085	2.16	2.04	2.23	2.03
559838	2.14	2.14	2.05	2.00
589028	2.03	2.01	2.04	1.99
594939	2.05	1.97	2.07	2.02
581952	2.22	2.25	2.19	2.02
565631	1.89	1.85	1.95	1.79
578698	2.24	2.25	2.19	2.18
556505	2.23	2.25	2.08	2.13
592166	2.26	2.22	2.25	2.18
556033	2.33	2.33	2.15	2.21
585660	1.84	1.87	1.88	1.67
575760	2.04	2.00	2.07	1.91

Table 6: Breakdown of by-participant entropy values: Entropy values for all participants in the experimental dataset (excluding the test set) computed over all items, as well as subsets of items (pseudoword, low-frequency (low) and high-frequency (high) items)

C Appendix: Feature combinations

Tens.	Nasal.	L del.	C del.	Lateral.
0	N/A	0	0	N/A
N/A	0	0	0	0
1	N/A	0	1	N/A
N/A	1	N/A	N/A	N/A
1	N/A	N/A	N/A	N/A
0	N/A	N/A	N/A	N/A
N/A	0	1	0	0
1	N/A	0	0	N/A
N/A	1	1	0	0
N/A	0	0	1	0
N/A	0	N/A	N/A	N/A
1	N/A	1	0	N/A
N/A	1	0	0	0
0	N/A	1	0	N/A
1	N/A	1	1	N/A
0	N/A	0	1	N/A
N/A	0	0	1	1

Table 7: Feature combinations used in the entropy calculation. The features are tensification (Tens.), nasalization (Nasal.), laterial deletion (L del.), obstruent deletion (C del.) and lateralization (Lateral.). The combination '1, N/A, 1, 1, N/A' was excluded as it had only one attestation across the dev and train set.

Tü-CL at SIGMORPHON 2023: Straight-Through Gradient Estimation for Hard Attention

Leander Girrbach
University of Tübingen
leander.girrbach@uni-tuebingen.de

Abstract

This paper describes our systems participating in the 2023 SIGMORPHON Shared Task on Morphological Inflection (Goldman et al., 2023) and in the 2023 SIGMORPHON Shared Task on Interlinear Glossing. We propose methods to enrich predictions from neural models with discrete, i.e. interpretable, information. For morphological inflection, our models learn deterministic mappings from subsets of source lemma characters and morphological tags to individual target characters, which introduces interpretability. For interlinear glossing, our models learn a shallow morpheme segmentation in an unsupervised way jointly with predicting glossing lines. Estimated segmentation may be useful when no ground-truth segmentation is available. As both methods introduce discreteness into neural models, our technical contribution is to show that straight-through gradient estimators are effective to train hard attention models.

1 Introduction

This paper describes our systems participating in the SIGMORPHON–UniMorph Shared Task on Typologically Diverse and Acquisition-Inspired Morphological Inflection Generation (Goldman et al., 2023) and the SIGMORPHON 2023 Shared Task on Interlinear Glossing. For morphological inflection, we participate in part 1, and for interlinear glossing we mainly target the closed track.

Morphological Inflection is the task of predicting the correct inflected form given a lemma and set of morphological tags. An example from the Italian dataset in the shared task is

$$\text{votare (“to vote”)} \xrightarrow{\text{V;IND;FUT;NOM(1,PL)}} \text{voteremo.}$$

The organisers of the shared task provide train, validation and test splits for 26 languages. In the case of Hebrew, 2 datasets are provided. Train splits contain 10K (lemma, tags, form) triples, validation and test splits contain 1K triples.

Interlinear glossing is the task of predicting glossing lines, which is a sequence of morphological tags, including lexical translations for each token, on the sentence level given the surface text and optionally a translation. An example of interlinear glossing taken from the train portion of the Gitksan dataset in the shared task is:

(1) *Iin* *dip* *gidax̱* *guhl* *wilt.*
CCNJ-1.I 1PL.I ask what-CN LVB-3.II

“And we asked what he did.”

The organisers of the shared task provide train, validation and test splits for 7 typologically diverse languages. Dataset sizes differ for each language. Furthermore, the shared task features a closed track, where only surface text and a translation is available for each sentence, and an open track, where canonical morpheme segmentation and POS tags are provided as additional information.

Especially when the main focus of training machine learning models is scientific discovery, even the notoriously good performance of deep neural models (Jiang et al., 2020) may not be satisfactory. Instead, models should also yield insights into what they learn about the data. However, clear and interpretable explanations are often hard to derive from models by post-hoc analysis, although many methods exist (Holzinger et al., 2020; Burkart and Huber, 2021; Rao et al., 2022). On the other hand, self-interpretable models, i.e. models whose calculations directly reveal discrete information, are generally hard to train with gradient methods and do not reach the same effectiveness as fully continuous models (Niepert et al., 2021).

Therefore, in this work we aim at narrowing the gap between inherently interpretable models and fully continuous deep sequence-to-sequence models by demonstrating the effectiveness of straight-through gradient estimators in optimising discrete intermediate representations by gradient methods.

Proceedings of the 20th SIGMORPHON workshop on Computational Research in Phonetics, Phonology, and Morphology, pages 151–165
July 14, 2023

As applications, we construct a model type for morphological inflection that shows, without ambiguity, which subset of lemma characters and tags causes the prediction of a form character. Our proposed model for interlinear glossing enriches the given surface text with shallow morpheme segmentation.

Our main contributions are: (1) We show the effectiveness of straight-through gradient estimators for learning hard attention; (2) We present a model for morphological inflection that unambiguously shows which subset of lemma characters and tags lead to the prediction of a form character; (3) We present a model that learns shallow morpheme segmentation jointly with interlinear glossing in an unsupervised fashion.

2 ST Optimization of Hard Attention

We discuss hard attention as mappings of the following form: Let $k \in \mathbb{N}$ be the number of target positions (e.g. the number of decoder positions in a encoder-decoder sequence-to-sequence model), and $\mathbf{X} \in \mathbb{R}^{n \times d}$ the matrix containing d-dimensional feature vectors of n source elements (e.g. learned embedding vectors). Each target element $\mathbf{y}_i$, $i \in \{1, \ldots, K\}$ is calculated as a sum of source element encodings, formally $\mathbf{y}_i = \sum_{j \in \rightarrow_i} \mathbf{x}_j$ where $\mathbf{x}_j$ is the jth row vector in $\mathbf{X}$ and $\rightarrow_i \subseteq \{1, \ldots, n\}$ is the set of source elements aligned to target position i. Note that a source element may be aligned to multiple target elements, i.e. appear in $\rightarrow_i$ for different i.

This mapping can be calculated by a matrix multiplication $\xi \cdot \mathbf{X} = \mathbf{Y} \in \mathbb{R}^{k \times d}$, where columns of $\xi \in \{0,1\}^{k \times n}$ are the multi-hot encodings of index sets $(\rightarrow_i)_{i \in \{1,\ldots,K\}}$. Formally, this means

$$\xi_{i,j} = \begin{cases} 1 & \text{if } j \in \rightarrow_i \\ 0 & \text{if } j \notin \rightarrow_i \end{cases}$$

We assume ξ is a sample from a underlying categorical distribution where we can compute the marginals $\hat{\xi}_{i,j}$ that specify the probability

$$\hat{\xi}_{i,j} = \Pr[j \in \rightarrow_i]$$

of j being included in $\rightarrow_i$. For example, in the case of dot-product attention, we have $\mathbf{z} \in \mathbb{R}^{k \times n}$ the matrix product of decoder states and encoder states. Then, we obtain $\hat{\xi}$ by $\mathrm{softmax}$ over rows, and ξ by sampling from the categorical distributions defined by rows of $\hat{\xi}$. At test time, argmax is used instead of sampling.

The main problem is how to side-step sampling during gradient-based optimization, because sampling is not differentiable. One solution is the so-called straight-through estimator (Bengio et al., 2013; Jang et al., 2017; Cathcart and Wandl, 2020) which means using ξ for the forward pass, i.e. when computing model outputs, but using $\hat{\xi}$ for backpropagation, i.e. when computing gradients of model parameters w.r.t. the loss.

However, gradients of $\mathbf{X}$ are affected by the discreteness of ξ as well, because $\xi_{i,j} = 0$ also means $\mathbf{x}_j$ does not receive gradients from $\mathbf{y}_i$. Therefore, when using straight-through gradient estimation, we should use $\hat{\xi}$ when computing gradients of $\mathbf{X}$. Formally, for some differentiable function f that is applied to $\mathbf{Y}$, we set

$$\frac{\partial f(\xi \cdot \mathbf{X})}{\partial \hat{\xi}} = \mathbf{X}^T \frac{\partial f(\mathbf{Y})}{\partial \mathbf{Y}}$$

$$\frac{\partial f(\xi \cdot \mathbf{X})}{\partial \mathbf{X}} = \left(\frac{\partial f(\mathbf{Y})}{\partial \mathbf{Y}}\right)^T \cdot \hat{\xi},$$

which can be implemented as

$$\mathbf{Y} = \hat{\xi} \cdot \mathbf{X} - \mathrm{sg}\left((\hat{\xi} - \xi) \cdot \mathbf{X}\right), \qquad (1)$$

where sg is the stop-gradient function (van den Oord et al., 2017) which behaves like the identity during forward pass, but has 0 partial derivatives everywhere.

3 Applications

In this section, we describe how to apply the method from Section 2 to sequence transduction (Section 3.1) and sequence segmentation (Section 3.2). We keep formulations more general than necessary for the shared tasks, because we want to highlight that the methods apply to similar problems as well.

3.1 Sequence Transduction

Sequence Transduction means transforming an input or source sequence $s_{1:n} = s_1, \ldots, s_n$ into an output or target sequence $t_{1:m} = t_1, \ldots, t_m$. Successful model types for this tasks are neural encoder-decoder networks with attention (Bahdanau et al., 2015). These models use an encoder which computes contextual source symbol representations $\mathbf{s}_1, \ldots, \mathbf{s}_n$ and a decoder which computes autoregressive target symbol representations $\mathbf{t}_1, \ldots, \mathbf{t}_m$. Entries of the attention matrix $\hat{\xi}$ are dot products[1] of source representations and target representations, normalised to a categorical distribution over source symbols for every target symbol. Output symbols are predicted from the concatenation of the respective previous autoregressive target representation with the weighted sum of source symbol representations, where weights correspond to probabilities of the respective attention distribution. In terms of interpretability, this type of model has two problems:

Soft Attention The role of soft attention (i.e. using $\hat{\xi}$ directly) with regard to explaining model predictions is not entirely understood (Jain and Wallace, 2019; Wiegreffe and Pinter, 2019). Therefore, we want to replace soft attention with hard attention, whose interpretability is undisputed. We replace soft attention with hard attention by sampling source elements from rows of $\hat{\xi}$ during training. The sampled index sets are used to discretise $\hat{\xi}$ into ξ. We enable end-to-end training through Equation (1).

Contextual Representations Contextual symbol encodings represent information about the whole sequence, not just the encoded symbol. In deep models, it is therefore not clear what information actually is encoded (Meister et al., 2021). For this reason, we want to use non-contextual symbol embeddings for prediction and use contextual symbol encodings only for computing $\hat{\xi}$.

However, only selecting one single source symbol by hard attention and then not using any contextual information is not sufficient for successful transduction. For example, in the case of morphological inflection discussed here, predictions have to take morphological tags and surrounding characters into account when transducing a source character. Therefore, we use two attention heads computing different kinds of attention:

1. Softmax-normalised attention $\hat{\xi}_{\text{symbol}}$ to select a single symbol to transduce.

2. Sigmoid-normalised attention $\hat{\xi}_{\text{cond}}$ to select multiple symbols as conditions. In this case, the sigmoid function σ is applied to every dot-product of encoder states and decoder states individually, yielding a Bernoulli distribution for every combination. ξ_{cond} is the result of sampling from each Bernoulli distribution. At test time, we round to 0 or 1 instead of sampling to ensure deterministic predictions.

Predictions are computed from the combined context vectors, formally

$$\begin{aligned} \mathbf{Y}^{\text{symbol}} &= \xi_{\text{symbol}} \cdot \mathbf{X}_{\text{embed}} \\ \mathbf{Y}^{\text{cond}} &= \xi_{\text{cond}} \cdot \mathbf{X}_{\text{embed}} \\ p_j(\bullet \mid s_{1:n}) &= \text{MLP}([\mathbf{Y}_j^{\text{symbol}}, \mathbf{Y}_j^{\text{cond}}]) \end{aligned} \tag{2}$$

where $\bullet$ is a placeholder to indicate distributions over the target alphabet, p_j is the distribution for the jth target symbol, and $\mathbf{X}_{\text{embed}}$ is the matrix containing non-contextual source symbol embeddings.

In this formulation, the decoder is still autoregressive, but is only involved in computing attention scores, not predictions any more. Therefore, it is entirely transparent which source symbols are responsible for which predictions. Also, the condition vector is a sum of equally weighted non-contextual symbol embeddings. The only non-transparent computation are the attention scores. Formally, the model learns a mapping $\mathcal{S} \times 2^{\mathcal{S} \times \mathbb{N}} \rightarrow \mathcal{T}$ where $\mathcal{S}$ is the source alphabet, $\mathbb{N}$ are the natural numbers (to account for multiplicities of symbols), and $2^{\mathcal{S} \times \mathbb{N}}$ indicates the power set. $\mathcal{T}$ is the target alphabet. The attention mechanism selects the contextually appropriate arguments for this mapping. A more detailed description of the concrete model architecture is in Appendix B.

Of course, the increased transparency limits the expressivity of the model. One problem is that gradient signals for encoder and decoder are insufficient, because their only remaining role is to compute attention matrices. Therefore, we train sequence transduction models in a multi-task setting, using the interpretable mechanism described above together with the typical mechanism, i.e. predicting the next target symbol from decoder state and combined contextual source symbol encodings. However, we use the same attention matrices in both cases. Predictions of type one-to-many (e.g. converting a single morphological tag to a suffix consisting of multiple characters) are also problematic: For each single target symbol, a different source symbol or condition is required. Possible solutions are augmenting the target alphabet with symbol ngrams (Liu et al., 2017) or allowing for local non-autoregressive predictions (Libovický and Helcl, 2018). However, we leave exploration of such methods to future work. Finally, condition

[1]There are different ways to calculate unnormalised attention scores (Luong et al., 2015; Brauwers and Frasincar, 2023), but without loss of generality we restrict the discussion to dot-product attention.

vectors $\mathbf{Y}^{\text{cond}}$ are insensitive to order due to summing being a commutative operation. This problem can be mitigated by positional encodings, but we do not observe improvements in preliminary experiments and do not explore this option here.

3.2 Sequence Segmentation

We combine hard attention with Structured Attention proposed by Kim et al. (2017). In particular, we consider the case of sequence segmentation and propose an end-to-end trainable interlinear glossing model (for the closed tack, where this information is not given) that first performs shallow morphological segmentation[2] on input words and then predicts the gloss label for each morpheme. Note that the method is also applicable to other tasks that require sequence segmentation and further processing of resulting segments, such as joint Sandhi segmentation and morphological parsing in Sanskrit (Li and Girrbach, 2022). In contrast to Kim et al., our segment encodings respect a particular sampled segmentation due to hard attention, and do not represent expected feature values.

Encoder Model Given a sentence as input to the glossing model, we first apply a character level encoder such as BiLSTM (Hochreiter and Schmidhuber, 1997; Graves and Schmidhuber, 2005), to compute contextual character representations on the sentence level. Then, we continue processing on the word level and denote a word w by its characters $w = s_1, \ldots, s_n$. Each word consists of a sequence of characters that are represented by contextual features computed in the previous step. For each character at position i, we predict a Bernoulli distribution parametrised by probability $p_i^{\text{seg}} \in (0; 1)$ that indicates whether the corresponding character is the last character of a (shallow) morpheme segment in our case. We also adopt the method by Raffel et al. (2017) to add Gaussian noise to unnormalised scores during training to encourage discreteness of segmentation probabilities.

Furthermore, each word is paired with the number of morphemes in the word. According to Leipzig Glossing Conventions (Comrie et al., 2008, Rule 2), the number of morphemes in a word is given by the number of hyphen-separated labels assigned to a word. During inference, the number of labels and therefore morphemes is not given. In this case, a straightforward solution is to start a new morpheme whenever the segmentation probability exceeds a certain threshold τ. However, we found trivial solutions for τ like $\frac{1}{2}$ not to work well, while learning to predict the number of morphemes in a word from the max-pooled character representations by a MLP works well in our case. Therefore, we adopt the latter option and leave exploration of the former method to future work. In cases where we have no information about the number of segments during training, marginalising the number of segments still remains as option.

Computing Marginals Character-level segmentation scores p_i^{seg} have to be converted to the attention matrix $\hat{\xi}$ by marginalising all segmentations. For each source element s_i, marginalisation computes the marginal probability of having a morpheme boundary at s_i. Adopting the terminology of Section 2, morphemes correspond to target elements and characters to source elements. Each source element is aligned to exactly one target element and the alignment is monotonic. This means each source element can only be aligned to the same target element as the immediately preceding source element or alternatively it can be aligned to the next target element. Accordingly, we compute marginals, i.e. distributions over targets for each source element, by the forward-backward algorithm, same as Kim et al. (2017). The forward recursion is given by $\alpha_{1,1} = 1$ and

$$\alpha_{i,j} = \alpha_{i-1,j} \cdot (1 - p_{i-1}^{\text{seg}}) + \alpha_{i-1,j-1} \cdot p_{i-1}^{\text{seg}}$$

for $i > 1, j \geq 1$ where $p_i^{\text{seg}} \in (0; 1)$ is the predicted segmentation probability of the ith source element. Note that the first source element is always part of the first segment. Backward scores are computed as $\beta_{n,k} = 1$ and

$$\beta_{i,j} = \beta_{i+1,j} \cdot (1 - p_{i,j}^{\text{seg}}) + \beta_{i+1,j+1} \cdot p_{i,j}^{\text{seg}}$$

for $i < n$ and $j \leq k$. Finally, marginals are given by $\hat{\xi}_{i,j} = \frac{\alpha_{i,j} \cdot \beta_{i,j}}{\alpha_{n,k}}$. In practise, computations are performed in log-space.

Training For discretising segmentations, it is most convenient to simply choose the maximum likelihood segmentation, which corresponds to starting new segments at the $k-1$ indices with maximum segmentation probabilities. The corresponding target segment representations are computed by $\mathbf{Y} = \xi \cdot \mathbf{X}$, where $\mathbf{X}$ is the matrix of

[2]Shallow morphological segmentation means only segmenting the surface string. Contrast this to canonical segmentation, which also restores a latent canonical form of present morphemes (Kann et al., 2016).

source element representations. Note that we use the discrete assignments ξ for computing segment representations and Equation (1) for training.

In the case of interlinear glossing, distributions over labels for each morpheme are computed by a MLP taking morpheme representations, i.e. rows in $\mathbf{Y}$, as input. Loss, then, is the cross-entropy between predicted distributions over labels and ground-truth labels. Note that in this case, and in contrast to Section 3.1, we compute morpheme representations from contextualised character representations, and not from non-contextual embeddings, because we think that only sets of characters of shallow morpheme segments are not sufficient to compute the semantic information necessary for glossing, especially the correct translations.

This has two consequences, first of all the model is not transparent (i.e. interpretable), and character encodings may be "fuzzy" in the sense that information is locally spread across multiple characters which may obscure precise morpheme boundaries. A similar effect has been shown for sparse attention by Meister et al. (2021). We leave exploring more interpretable models similar to the model described in Section 3.1 and biasing models towards more precise morpheme segmentation to future work. In this work, our main focus is to provide shallow morpheme segmentation as additional predictions, not to build an entirely interpretable glossing model.

4 Evaluation

Here, we evaluate the methods presented in Section 3 by participating in the shared task on morphological inflection and in the shared task on interlinear glossing. Technical details of the experimental setup and hyperparameters are in Appendix A.

4.1 Baselines

For the morphological inflection shared task, the organisers provide a neural and a non-neural baseline. For the interlinear glossing shared task, the organisers provide a transformer-based neural baseline. Furthermore, we add a CTC-based sequence labelling model (Graves et al., 2006) as baseline. The CTC model encodes the source sentence on the character level by a BiLSTM encoder and predicts a label or blank from each character. Here, we exploit that the number of labels is the same as the number of morphemes, and each word has at least as many characters as morphemes.

4.2 Data Representation

For a detailed description of the shared task data, refer to the respective shared task overview papers. In the case of morphological inflection, we convert (lemma, tags, form) triples to (source, target) pairs by removing all punctuation from the tags and prepending the remaining sequence of tags to the lemma characters. Special pre- and postprocessing is applied to Japanese in order to eliminate Kanji, see Appendix C.

In the case of interlinear glossing, no modification is necessary for the closed track. However, for the open track, we replace the source text by hyphen-separated morphemes. We assume they contain more information than the original unsegmented text, and the unsegmented text does not add any information when the segmented morphemes are available. In this case, we also do not learn shallow segmentation, but predict a single label from each morpheme. The CTC baseline flexibly learns alignments of labels to characters in both cases. In both cases, we approach interlinear glossing as a sequence labelling problem.

4.3 Results

Morphological Inflection In Table 1, we report macro-averaged test set accuracy and edit distance. Full results for all languages achieved by our model and the baselines are in Appendix D. For clarity, we only report results of the best system for every participating team. Results show that our interpretable model loses on performance compared to more flexible neural models, such as the Transformer baseline. On 22 of 27 languages, the neural baseline beats our model. However, results also show that introducing interpretability does not have catastrophic consequences regarding performance. With some advantages in macro-averaged scores, our model performs roughly on par with the non-neural baseline, beating it on 14 of 27 languages. In summary, these results suggest that introducing interpretability to neural models causes some decrease in performance, but having neural interpretable models still gives better results than having interpretable non-neural models.

To illustrate patterns learned by our models, we show examples of the selected source symbols and condition symbols. The first example in Figure 1 is taken from the French (validation) dataset, namely the target inflection is

$$\textit{juger} \text{ “to judge”} \xrightarrow{\text{V;COND;NOM(1,PL)}} \text{“jugerions”}.$$

	Accuracy ↑	ED ↓
Illinois	84.27	0.35
Baseline (Neural)	81.61	0.40
Ours	**76.91**	**0.58**
Arizona	72.45	0.75
Baseline (¬ Neural)	69.60	0.81

Table 1: Morphological Inflection: Best macro-averaged test set results for accuracy and edit distance (ED) of each team. Results of our model are highlighted in bold.

In this case, the prediction is correct. We can see how the model first selects characters of the stem to copy. Here, few if any other source symbols are selected as conditions. Then, for predicting the inflection suffix "-ions", the model selects tag symbols both to transduce and as conditions.

Next, we consider an example from the Italian dataset, namely

$$\textit{estraniarsi}\ \text{“to alienate onself”} \xrightarrow{\text{V;IND;PRS;NOM(1,PL)}} \text{“ci estranieremmo”}.$$

The corresponding selected symbols and conditions are shown in Figure 2. This example shows an interesting non-monotonic pattern, namely moving the reflexive pronoun "si" to the front and changing it to the correct number and person, in this case 1st plural. The model correctly captures this, as we can see from the selected transduction symbols (left side). Also, the model learned which conditions to select for changing the "s" in "si" to "c". After this transform, the model copies the stem by selecting stem characters as transduction symbols and conditions. Finally, the model generates the inflectional suffix by selecting mainly tags as transduction characters and conditions.

Interlinear Glossing In Table 2, we report macro-averaged word level and morpheme level test set accuracies. Both our additional CTC baseline and our morpheme-segmentation model, henceforth referred to as "morph", compare favourably to the transformer baseline. Furthermore, our morph model achieves better performance than competing models on track 1, where the unsupervised learning of morpheme segmentation is relevant, which shows that learning additional linguistically relevant structures can improve performance by injecting useful inductive biases in the model. Furthermore, we again conclude that using discrete structure as intermediate representations does not necessarily decrease performance catastrophically. Instead, it seems helpful in this case. Finally, we note that translations are not necessary for current glossing models to achieve strong performance, since we do not use them.

We also show examples of shallow segmentation learned by the morph model. We focus only on the segmentation, because this is the main contribution of our model. Note that all segmentations were learned in an unsupervised way for track 1 alongside the main objective, i.e. predicting the glossing line. For track 1, morphological segmentation is not given, unlike for track 2.

Because our model learns shallow segmentations, while ground-truth segmentations provided for track 2 are canonical segmentations, we can not conduct a quantitative analysis. Therefore, we restrict the analysis to anecdotal qualitative analysis of 2 example segmentions predicted by our models.

First, we consider a prediction for the following Natugu example:

(2) *Nedr rlilrdr doa nzpwxng* .
Ne-dr r-li-lr-dr doa nz-pwx-ng .
ne-dr r-li-r-dr doa nz-pwx-ngq .

"The two of them had four children."

Morphemes are separated by hyphens "-". The predicted segmentation is in the second line, and the ground-truth segmentation is in the third line. The predicted segmentation differs from the ground-truth, because it copies characters and therefore can not change capitalisation, and two morphemes ("lr" → "r" and "ng" → "ngq") are normalised in the ground-truth segmentation, so that they differ from their surface form.

Next, we consider a Uspanteko example:

(3) *i tiyuq sol ji' tren tib'ek*
i t-iyuq sol ji' t-r-en t-ib'e-k
i ti-yu' sol ji' t-r-en ti-b'e-k

"Y llega solo asi hace se va."

Again, the predicted segmentation is in the second line. In two cases the vowel "i" is assigned to the wrong morpheme, but the predicted glossing line (not shown) is still correct. In this case, incorrect segmentation is apparently not a problem for the subsequent classification of morphemes, but in other cases this may cause problems. Here, we

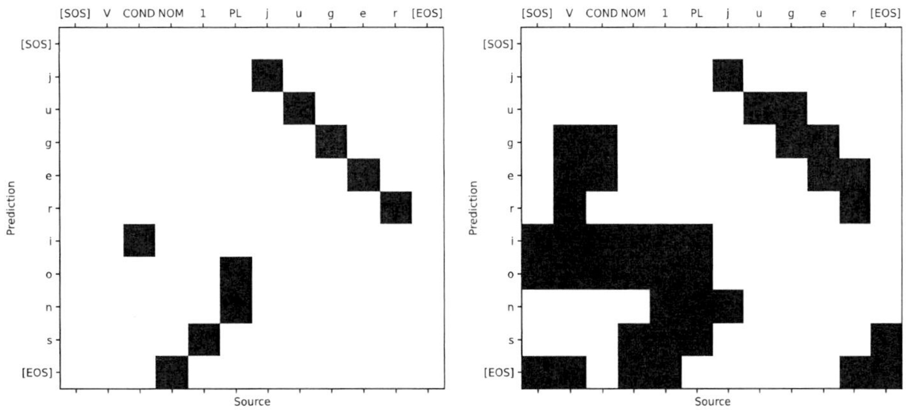

Figure 1: Example for French *juger* "to judge". The target prediction is "juger" $\xrightarrow{\text{V;COND;NOM(1,PL)}}$ "jugerions". The prediction is correct in this case. On the left side, we show the single selected symbols for transduction, on the right side we show the additionally selected condition symbols. Because we use hard attention, attention scores can only be 0 or 1, and we can present them in a black-and-white style.

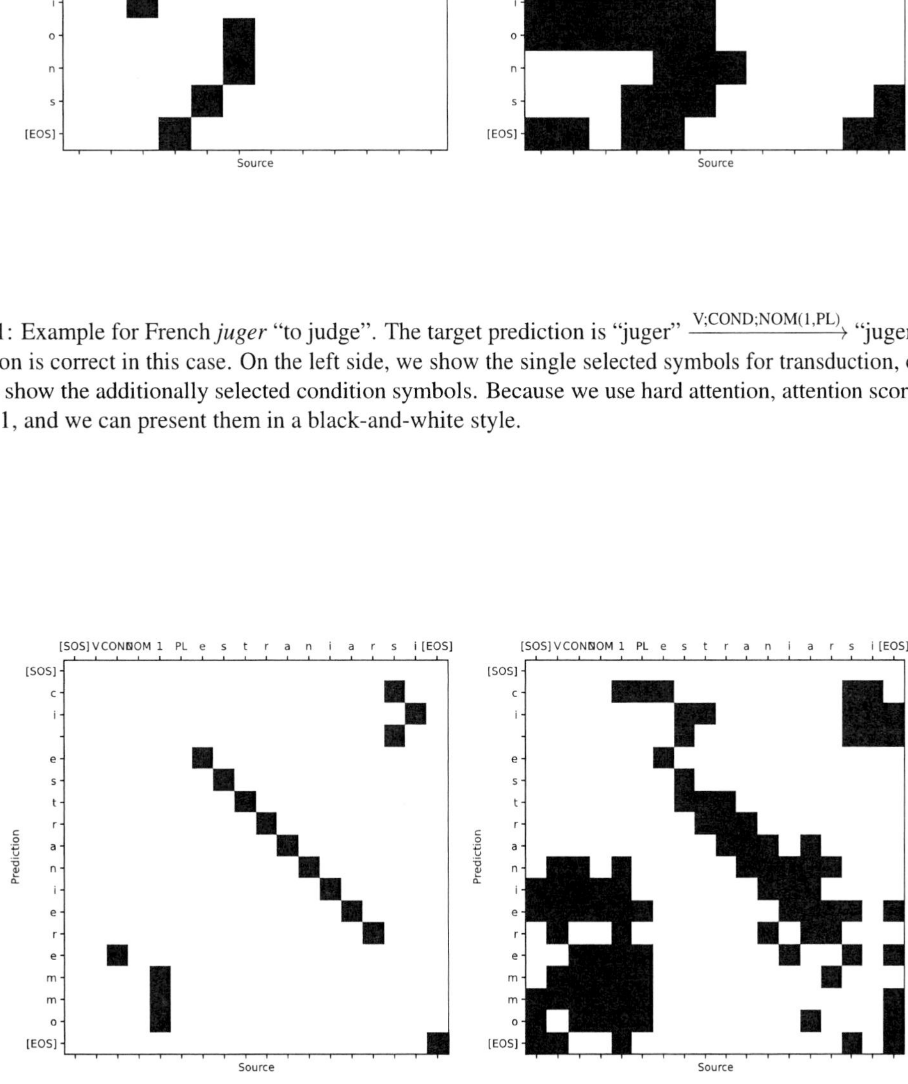

Figure 2: Example for Italian *estraniarsi* "to alienate onself". The target prediction is "estraniarsi" $\xrightarrow{\text{V;COND;NOM(1,PL)}}$ "ci estranieremmo". The prediction is correct in this case. On the left side, we show the single selected symbols for transduction, on the right side we show the additionally selected condition symbols.

	Track 1		Track 2	
	Word Level	Morph. Level	Word Level	Morph. Level
Ours (Morph)	71.30	62.55	76.56	84.21
Ours (CTC)	68.01	60.24	74.43	78.03
Baseline	47.31	33.60	59.14	67.69

Table 2: Interlinear Glossing: Macro-averaged test set accuracy for our models and the baseline. Higher is better.

can see that contextualised character encodings can bypass the discrete morpheme segmentation step.

5 Related Work

Much recent work in character-level transduction aims at making models both more interpretable and stronger by using sparse (Peters and Martins, 2019, 2020) or hard attention (Aharoni and Goldberg, 2017; Wu et al., 2018; Wu and Cotterell, 2019; Makarov and Clematide, 2018b,a). Modifying the attention mechanism is necessary, because for soft attention, which does not realise hard alignment decisions, the relation of model outputs and attention weights is not fully understood (Jain and Wallace, 2019; Wiegreffe and Pinter, 2019). Hard attention does not suffer from this problem, because it realises hard alignment decisions, so that we exactly know which information influences the output of attention. Especially if the main purpose of models is to gain insights into the data and not mainly to achieve better performance on modelling it, interpretability of models is crucial.

However, working with hard attention is notoriously difficult, because it introduces non-differentiability into models. This means that the sophisticated machinery developed for gradient-based optimisation of deep neural models fails in this case. The most popular but also most expensive approach to train hard attention mechanisms is marginalising all alignments (Yu et al., 2016; Raffel et al., 2017; Wu et al., 2018; Wu and Cotterell, 2019) or approximating the marginalisation (Shankar et al., 2018). Different approaches to approximate gradients instead of having exact gradients by marginalisation are using reinforcement learning (Xu et al., 2015; Makarov and Clematide, 2018a), reparametrising discrete distributions or working with continuous relaxations (Jang et al., 2017; Maddison et al., 2017), and perturbation based gradient approximators (Niepert et al., 2021). While all methods to use hard attention with gradient-based optimisation come with problems, we find straight-through gradient estimators (Bengio et al., 2013) very effective to compute informative discrete intermediate representations even for complicated attention scenarios. Similar results have been reported for other fields as well, both practically (Sahoo et al., 2022) and in theoretical analysis (Yin et al., 2019). Therefore, we propose two models, one for interpretable sequence transduction and one for joint segmentation and segment classification, based on straight-through gradient estimators.

6 Conclusion

In this work, we propose to optimise hard attention as building block in deep neural networks, which in principle is non-differentiable, by straight-through gradient estimation. In particular, we describe applications to interpretable sequence-to-sequence models and sequence segmentation models. We evaluate our approaches on two important tasks in computational morphology, namely morphological inflection and interlinear glossing which are shared tasks of the ACL SIGMORPHON 2023 workshop. Our approaches achieve good results in morphological inflection despite of constrained expressivity compared to fully differentiable models, and strong results in interlinear glossing. These results provide encouraging evidence that learning interpretable intermediate representations by deep neural network does not necessarily lead to intolerable sacrifices in performance. We hope that future work can benefit from these insights by combining interpretable representations and the generalisation abilities of neural models for scientific discovery.

Acknowledgements

We thank the organisers of both shared tasks for their efforts and for their help during training and evaluation phases. Also, we thank Çağrı Çöltekin for his feedback on a draft version of this paper and Leonard Salewski for a helpful discussion in the early phase of this project.

References

Roee Aharoni and Yoav Goldberg. 2017. Morphological inflection generation with hard monotonic attention. In *Proceedings of the 55th Annual Meeting of the Association for Computational Linguistics (Volume 1: Long Papers)*, pages 2004–2015, Vancouver, Canada. Association for Computational Linguistics.

Takuya Akiba, Shotaro Sano, Toshihiko Yanase, Takeru Ohta, and Masanori Koyama. 2019. Optuna: A next-generation hyperparameter optimization framework. In *Proceedings of the 25th ACM SIGKDD International Conference on Knowledge Discovery and Data Mining*.

Dzmitry Bahdanau, Kyunghyun Cho, and Yoshua Bengio. 2015. Neural machine translation by jointly learning to align and translate. In *3rd International Conference on Learning Representations, ICLR 2015, San Diego, CA, USA, May 7-9, 2015, Conference Track Proceedings*.

Yoshua Bengio, Nicholas Léonard, and Aaron C. Courville. 2013. Estimating or propagating gradients through stochastic neurons for conditional computation. *CoRR*, abs/1308.3432.

Gianni Brauwers and Flavius Frasincar. 2023. A general survey on attention mechanisms in deep learning. *IEEE Trans. Knowl. Data Eng.*, 35(4):3279–3298.

Nadia Burkart and Marco F. Huber. 2021. A survey on the explainability of supervised machine learning. *J. Artif. Intell. Res.*, 70:245–317.

Chundra Cathcart and Florian Wandl. 2020. In search of isoglosses: continuous and discrete language embeddings in Slavic historical phonology. In *Proceedings of the 17th SIGMORPHON Workshop on Computational Research in Phonetics, Phonology, and Morphology*, pages 233–244, Online. Association for Computational Linguistics.

Bernard Comrie, Martin Haspelmath, and Balthasar Bickel. 2008. The leipzig glossing rules: Conventions for interlinear morpheme-by-morpheme glosses. *Department of Linguistics of the Max Planck Institute for Evolutionary Anthropology & the Department of Linguistics of the University of Leipzig*.

Omer Goldman, Khuyagbaatar Batsuren, Khalifa Salam, Aryaman Arora, Garrett Nicolai, Reyt Tsarfaty, and Ekaterina Vylomova. 2023. SIGMORPHON–UniMorph 2023 shared task 0: Typologically diverse morphological inflection. In *Proceedings of the 20th SIGMORPHON Workshop on Computational Research in Phonetics, Phonology, and Morphology*, Toronto, Canada. Association for Computational Linguistics.

Alex Graves, Santiago Fernández, Faustino J. Gomez, and Jürgen Schmidhuber. 2006. Connectionist temporal classification: labelling unsegmented sequence data with recurrent neural networks. In *Machine Learning, Proceedings of the Twenty-Third International Conference (ICML 2006), Pittsburgh, Pennsylvania, USA, June 25-29, 2006*, volume 148 of *ACM International Conference Proceeding Series*, pages 369–376. ACM.

Alex Graves and Jürgen Schmidhuber. 2005. Framewise phoneme classification with bidirectional LSTM and other neural network architectures. *Neural Networks*, 18(5-6):602–610.

Sepp Hochreiter and Jürgen Schmidhuber. 1997. Long short-term memory. *Neural Comput.*, 9(8):1735–1780.

Andreas Holzinger, Anna Saranti, Christoph Molnar, Przemyslaw Biecek, and Wojciech Samek. 2020. Explainable AI methods - A brief overview. In *xxAI - Beyond Explainable AI - International Workshop, Held in Conjunction with ICML 2020, July 18, 2020, Vienna, Austria, Revised and Extended Papers*, volume 13200 of *Lecture Notes in Computer Science*, pages 13–38. Springer.

Sarthak Jain and Byron C. Wallace. 2019. Attention is not Explanation. In *Proceedings of the 2019 Conference of the North American Chapter of the Association for Computational Linguistics: Human Language Technologies, Volume 1 (Long and Short Papers)*, pages 3543–3556, Minneapolis, Minnesota. Association for Computational Linguistics.

Eric Jang, Shixiang Gu, and Ben Poole. 2017. Categorical reparameterization with gumbel-softmax. In *5th International Conference on Learning Representations, ICLR 2017, Toulon, France, April 24-26, 2017, Conference Track Proceedings*. OpenReview.net.

Yiding Jiang, Behnam Neyshabur, Hossein Mobahi, Dilip Krishnan, and Samy Bengio. 2020. Fantastic generalization measures and where to find them. In *8th International Conference on Learning Representations, ICLR 2020, Addis Ababa, Ethiopia, April 26-30, 2020*. OpenReview.net.

Katharina Kann, Ryan Cotterell, and Hinrich Schütze. 2016. Neural morphological analysis: Encoding-decoding canonical segments. In *Proceedings of the 2016 Conference on Empirical Methods in Natural Language Processing*, pages 961–967, Austin, Texas. Association for Computational Linguistics.

Yoon Kim, Carl Denton, Luong Hoang, and Alexander M. Rush. 2017. Structured attention networks. In *5th International Conference on Learning Representations, ICLR 2017, Toulon, France, April 24-26, 2017, Conference Track Proceedings*. OpenReview.net.

Jingwen Li and Leander Girrbach. 2022. Word segmentation and morphological parsing for sanskrit. *arXiv preprint arXiv:2201.12833*.

Jindřich Libovický and Jindřich Helcl. 2018. End-to-end non-autoregressive neural machine translation with connectionist temporal classification. In *Proceedings of the 2018 Conference on Empirical Methods in Natural Language Processing*, pages 3016–3021, Brussels, Belgium. Association for Computational Linguistics.

Hairong Liu, Zhenyao Zhu, Xiangang Li, and Sanjeev Satheesh. 2017. Gram-ctc: Automatic unit selection and target decomposition for sequence labelling. In *Proceedings of the 34th International Conference on Machine Learning, ICML 2017, Sydney, NSW, Australia, 6-11 August 2017*, volume 70 of *Proceedings of Machine Learning Research*, pages 2188–2197. PMLR.

Ilya Loshchilov and Frank Hutter. 2019. Decoupled weight decay regularization. In *7th International Conference on Learning Representations, ICLR 2019, New Orleans, LA, USA, May 6-9, 2019*. OpenReview.net.

Thang Luong, Hieu Pham, and Christopher D. Manning. 2015. Effective approaches to attention-based neural machine translation. In *Proceedings of the 2015 Conference on Empirical Methods in Natural Language Processing*, pages 1412–1421, Lisbon, Portugal. Association for Computational Linguistics.

Chris J. Maddison, Andriy Mnih, and Yee Whye Teh. 2017. The concrete distribution: A continuous relaxation of discrete random variables. In *5th International Conference on Learning Representations, ICLR 2017, Toulon, France, April 24-26, 2017, Conference Track Proceedings*. OpenReview.net.

Peter Makarov and Simon Clematide. 2018a. Imitation learning for neural morphological string transduction. In *Proceedings of the 2018 Conference on Empirical Methods in Natural Language Processing*, pages 2877–2882, Brussels, Belgium. Association for Computational Linguistics.

Peter Makarov and Simon Clematide. 2018b. Neural transition-based string transduction for limited-resource setting in morphology. In *Proceedings of the 27th International Conference on Computational Linguistics*, pages 83–93, Santa Fe, New Mexico, USA. Association for Computational Linguistics.

Clara Meister, Stefan Lazov, Isabelle Augenstein, and Ryan Cotterell. 2021. Is sparse attention more interpretable? In *Proceedings of the 59th Annual Meeting of the Association for Computational Linguistics and the 11th International Joint Conference on Natural Language Processing (Volume 2: Short Papers)*, pages 122–129, Online. Association for Computational Linguistics.

Mathias Niepert, Pasquale Minervini, and Luca Franceschi. 2021. Implicit MLE: backpropagating through discrete exponential family distributions. In *Advances in Neural Information Processing Systems 34: Annual Conference on Neural Information Processing Systems 2021, NeurIPS 2021, December 6-14, 2021, virtual*, pages 14567–14579.

Adam Paszke, Sam Gross, Francisco Massa, Adam Lerer, James Bradbury, Gregory Chanan, Trevor Killeen, Zeming Lin, Natalia Gimelshein, Luca Antiga, Alban Desmaison, Andreas Kopf, Edward Yang, Zachary DeVito, Martin Raison, Alykhan Tejani, Sasank Chilamkurthy, Benoit Steiner, Lu Fang, Junjie Bai, and Soumith Chintala. 2019. Pytorch: An imperative style, high-performance deep learning library. In H. Wallach, H. Larochelle, A. Beygelzimer, F. d'Alché-Buc, E. Fox, and R. Garnett, editors, *Advances in Neural Information Processing Systems 32*, pages 8024–8035. Curran Associates, Inc.

Ben Peters and André F. T. Martins. 2019. IT–IST at the SIGMORPHON 2019 shared task: Sparse two-headed models for inflection. In *Proceedings of the 16th Workshop on Computational Research in Phonetics, Phonology, and Morphology*, pages 50–56, Florence, Italy. Association for Computational Linguistics.

Ben Peters and André F. T. Martins. 2020. One-size-fits-all multilingual models. In *Proceedings of the 17th SIGMORPHON Workshop on Computational Research in Phonetics, Phonology, and Morphology*, pages 63–69, Online. Association for Computational Linguistics.

Colin Raffel, Minh-Thang Luong, Peter J. Liu, Ron J. Weiss, and Douglas Eck. 2017. Online and linear-time attention by enforcing monotonic alignments. In *Proceedings of the 34th International Conference on Machine Learning, ICML 2017, Sydney, NSW, Australia, 6-11 August 2017*, volume 70 of *Proceedings of Machine Learning Research*, pages 2837–2846. PMLR.

Sukrut Rao, Moritz Böhle, and Bernt Schiele. 2022. Towards better understanding attribution methods. In *IEEE/CVF Conference on Computer Vision and Pattern Recognition, CVPR 2022, New Orleans, LA, USA, June 18-24, 2022*, pages 10213–10222. IEEE.

Subham Sekhar Sahoo, Anselm Paulus, Marin Vlastelica, Vít Musil, Volodymyr Kuleshov, and Georg Martius. 2022. Backpropagation through combinatorial algorithms: Identity with projection works. *arXiv preprint arXiv:2205.15213*.

Shiv Shankar, Siddhant Garg, and Sunita Sarawagi. 2018. Surprisingly easy hard-attention for sequence to sequence learning. In *Proceedings of the 2018 Conference on Empirical Methods in Natural Language Processing*, pages 640–645, Brussels, Belgium. Association for Computational Linguistics.

Aäron van den Oord, Oriol Vinyals, and Koray Kavukcuoglu. 2017. Neural discrete representation learning. In *Advances in Neural Information Processing Systems 30: Annual Conference on Neural Information Processing Systems 2017, December 4-9, 2017, Long Beach, CA, USA*, pages 6306–6315.

Sarah Wiegreffe and Yuval Pinter. 2019. Attention is not not explanation. In *Proceedings of the 2019 Confer-*

ence on Empirical Methods in Natural Language Processing and the 9th International Joint Conference on Natural Language Processing (EMNLP-IJCNLP), pages 11–20, Hong Kong, China. Association for Computational Linguistics.

Shijie Wu and Ryan Cotterell. 2019. Exact hard monotonic attention for character-level transduction. In *Proceedings of the 57th Annual Meeting of the Association for Computational Linguistics*, pages 1530–1537, Florence, Italy. Association for Computational Linguistics.

Shijie Wu, Pamela Shapiro, and Ryan Cotterell. 2018. Hard non-monotonic attention for character-level transduction. In *Proceedings of the 2018 Conference on Empirical Methods in Natural Language Processing*, pages 4425–4438, Brussels, Belgium. Association for Computational Linguistics.

Kelvin Xu, Jimmy Ba, Ryan Kiros, Kyunghyun Cho, Aaron C. Courville, Ruslan Salakhutdinov, Richard S. Zemel, and Yoshua Bengio. 2015. Show, attend and tell: Neural image caption generation with visual attention. In *Proceedings of the 32nd International Conference on Machine Learning, ICML 2015, Lille, France, 6-11 July 2015*, volume 37 of *JMLR Workshop and Conference Proceedings*, pages 2048–2057. JMLR.org.

Penghang Yin, Jiancheng Lyu, Shuai Zhang, Stanley J. Osher, Yingyong Qi, and Jack Xin. 2019. Understanding straight-through estimator in training activation quantized neural nets. In *7th International Conference on Learning Representations, ICLR 2019, New Orleans, LA, USA, May 6-9, 2019*. OpenReview.net.

Lei Yu, Jan Buys, and Phil Blunsom. 2016. Online segment to segment neural transduction. In *Proceedings of the 2016 Conference on Empirical Methods in Natural Language Processing*, pages 1307–1316, Austin, Texas. Association for Computational Linguistics.

A Experimental Setup

Here, we describe our experimental setup, including hyperparameters, in detail. Also note that our code is available on GitHub. Code for morphological inflection is here: `https://github.com/LGirrbach/sigmorphon-2023-glossing`. Code for interlinear glossing is here: `https://github.com/LGirrbach/sigmorphon-2023-inflection`. All models are implemented in `PyTorch` (Paszke et al., 2019) and `pytorch_lightning`.[3]

In all cases, models are optimised using the AdamW optimizer (Loshchilov and Hutter, 2019) without weight decay, learning rate is 0.001, and all other parameters are the PyTorch defaults. We use an exponential decay learning rate scheduler which multiplies the learning rate by factor γ after each epoch. We tune γ for each combination of model and language. Furthermore, we clip gradients with absolute value greater than 1.

Models are trained exclusively on the training splits provided by the shared task organisers. After each training epoch, generalisation performance is estimated by performance on the validation split. In the case of Morphological Inflection, our main metric is normalised edit distance (lower is better). In the case of Interlinear Glossing, our main metric is accuracy of correctly predicted glossing lines (higher is better). If performance does not improve for 3 epochs, training is stopped. Only the best model checkpoint, i.e. the checkpoint 3 epochs before ending training, is retained.

A.1 Hyperparameter Tuning

For each combination of language and model, we optimise hyperparameters independently. The tuned hyperparameters and their corresponding value ranges are in Table 3. Note that other than stated there, the minimum batch size for Morphological Inflection models is always 4. Also, minimum batch size for Arapaho and Uspanteko languages (Interlinear Glossing) is 16. The maximum batch size for Arapaho and Uspanteko is 128. The maximum batch size for Gitksan (Interlinear Glossing) is 16.

In each case, we sample 50 sets of hyperparameters using the `optuna` library (Akiba et al., 2019). For each sampled set, a model is trained and the performance on the validation set is recorded. After sampling 50 sets, the set that resulted in the best performance on the validation set is saved. For training models for submission of results to the shared tasks and all other analyses, we exclusively use hyperparameter that were found best in this hyperparameter study. Since we tune parameters for many models, we do not report the results here. However, they are available in our GitHub repositories.

A.2 Main Evaluation

For submitting results to the shared tasks and further analyses, we retrain 5 models for each combination of model type and language. The models use the hyperparameters from the tuning study described in Appendix A.1. However, they have different initialisations and may therefore perform differently. For submitting results, we select the

[3] `https://github.com/Lightning-AI/lightning/`

Parameter Name	Range
# LSTM Layers	$\{1,2\}$
Hidden Size	$[64; 512]$
Dropout	$[0.0; 0.5]$
Scheduler γ	$[0.9; 1.0]$
Batch Size	$[2; 64]$

Table 3: Ranges for values of tuned hyperparameters. Note that batch size ranges differ in some cases.

model the model with best performance on the validation set. Having multiple copies of the same model type trained with the same hyperparameters is useful, because especially in low-resource scenarios different initialisations can have a relevant impact on the generalisation performance. On the one hand, it is necessary to estimate this variance to see how robust models are, on the other hand this helps mitigating spurious effects in the analyses.

B Sequence Transduction Model: Detailed Description

Here, we provide a more detailed description of the sequence transduction model (see Section 3.1).

For training, we have two paired sequences $s = s_1, \dots, s_n$ and $t = t_1, \dots, t_m$, representing the source and target sequence, respectively. The goal is to maximise the likelihood of transducing the source sequence s to the target sequence t.

The first step is to represent all symbols in both sequences by high-dimensional non-contextual vectors, i.e. embeddings. Thus, we arrive at embedded sequences $\mathbf{s} = \mathbf{s}_1, \dots, \mathbf{s}_n$ and $\mathbf{t} = \mathbf{t}_1, \dots, \mathbf{t}_m$, with $\mathbf{s}_i, \mathbf{t} \in \mathbb{R}^d$. Here, boldfaced lowercase variables represent vectors. Furthermore, we denote the $n \times d$ matrix with source symbol embeddings as rows as $\mathbf{S} \in \mathbb{R}^{n \times d}$ and we denote the $m \times d$ matrix with all target symbol embeddings as $\mathbf{T} \in \mathbb{R}^{m \times d}$. Note, that embeddings of source symbols and target symbols are optimised independently of each other, i.e. they are not paired.

In the next step, we encode the source sequence by a *bidirectional* LSTM and arrive at a contextual representation $\mathbf{h}_i^s$ for each source symbol with index i, $1 \leq i \leq n$. Likewise, we encode the target sequence using a *unidirectional* LSTM and denote the autoregressive encoding of the symbol with index $j, 1 \leq j, \leq m$ as $\mathbf{h}_j^t$. Formally, we can write

$$\mathbf{h}_i^s = \mathrm{BiLSTM}(\mathbf{s}_i \mid \mathbf{s}_1, \dots, \mathbf{s}_n) \tag{3}$$

$$\mathbf{h}_j^t = \mathrm{LSTM}(\mathbf{t}_j \mid \mathbf{t}_1, \dots, \mathbf{t}_{j-1}) \tag{4}$$

and representing all contextualised representations as matrices:

$$\mathbf{H}^s = \mathrm{BiLSTM}(\mathbf{S}) \tag{5}$$

$$\mathbf{H}^t = \mathrm{LSTM}(\mathbf{T}) \tag{6}$$

So far, this formulation is the same as conventional LSTM-based encoder-decoder models. However, the attention mechanism is different. According to the descriptions in Section 2 and Section 3.1, we define attention matrices as follows:

$$\mathbf{Z} = \mathbf{H}^s \cdot (\mathbf{H}^t)^T \tag{7}$$

$$\hat{\xi}_{\text{symbol}} = \mathrm{softmax}(\mathbf{Z}) \tag{8}$$

$$\hat{\xi}_{\text{cond}} = \sigma(\mathbf{Z}) \tag{9}$$

where $\mathbf{Z} \in \mathbb{R}^{n \times m}$ represents the unnormalised dot-product attention scores, softmax is applied to columns of $\mathbf{Z}$ and the sigmoid function σ is applied elementwise. In fact, it seems counterintuitive to use the same unnormalised scores in both attention heads, but this works well in practise. From these attention matrices, we obtain the discretised alignment matrices ξ_{symbol} and ξ_{cond} by sampling columnwise one-hot vectors in the case of ξ_{symbol} and elementwise values $\in \{0, 1\}$ for ξ_{cond}. Then, we calculate context vectors as

$$\mathbf{Y}_{\text{symbol}} = \xi_{\text{symbol}}^T \cdot \mathbf{S} \tag{10}$$

$$\mathbf{Y}_{\text{cond}} = \xi_{\text{cond}}^T \cdot \mathbf{S} \tag{11}$$

Note, that here we use the discretised alignment matrices ξ_{symbol} and ξ_{cond} in place of the real-valued matrices $\hat{\xi}_{\text{symbol}}$ and $\hat{\xi}_{\text{symbol}}$. Because discretisation is non-differentiable, we instead use a way of calculation that enables straight-through gradient estimation, namely Equation (1):

$$\mathbf{Y}_{\text{symbol}} = \hat{\xi}_{\text{symbol}}^T \cdot \mathbf{S} - \mathrm{sg}\left((\hat{\xi}_{\text{symbol}} - \xi_{\text{symbol}})^T \cdot \mathbf{S} \right) \tag{12}$$

$$\mathbf{Y}_{\text{cond}} = \hat{\xi}_{\text{cond}}^T \cdot \mathbf{S} - \mathrm{sg}\left((\hat{\xi}_{\text{cond}} - \xi_{\text{cond}})^T \cdot \mathbf{S} \right) \tag{13}$$

Finally, we predict a distribution over target symbols by a MLP from the concatenation of $\mathbf{Y}_{\text{symbol}}$ and $\mathbf{Y}_{\text{cond}}$ according to Equation (2):

$$p_j(\bullet \mid s_1, \ldots, s_n) = \text{MLP}([\mathbf{Y}_j^{\text{symbol}}, \mathbf{Y}_j^{\text{cond}}]) \quad (14)$$

where $p_j(\bullet \mid s_1, \ldots, s_n)$ indicates the distribution over target symbols at prediction position with index j. Here, the concrete ground truth target symbol is t_j.

To train the model, we use the typical supervised objective, namely minimising the cross-entropy between predicted categorical distributions over target symbols and the one-hot encoded ground truth target symbol at each prediction position. This also means we use teacher forcing for sequential predictions. During inference, t is predicted in a step-wise fashion by greedy decoding.

However, note that in addition to the setup described above, we also use the typical attention mechanism in a multi-tasking fashion, but only during training. We do not use contextualised source symbol representations for inference. The reason why we still use the typical loss as auxiliary loss is that the gradient signal on $\mathbf{H}^s$ and $\mathbf{H}^t$ is weak when their only role is to calculate $\mathbf{Z}$. In this case, we calculate

$$\mathbf{C} = \left(\text{softmax}\left(\mathbf{H}^s \cdot (\mathbf{H}^t)^T\right)\right)^T \cdot \mathbf{H}^s \quad (15)$$

where softmax is applied to columns, and then predict distributions over target symbols as

$$p_j^{\text{aux}}(\bullet \mid s_1, \ldots, s_n) = \text{MLP}(\mathbf{C}) \quad (16)$$

so that we can also calculate the cross-entropy loss on $p_j^{\text{aux}}(\bullet \mid s_1, \ldots, s_n)$ and differentiate model parameter w.r.t. the sum of both losses during training. Note, again, that this is only to stabilise training by optimising the contextual representations, and does not affect the model architecture for inference.

C Preprocessing of Japanese

The Japanese writing system includes 4 alphabets, namely Latin characters (Romaji), Chinese characters (Kanji), and two syllabic scripts (Katakana and Hiragana) that were derived from Chinese characters by simplification and standardisation. The Japanese dataset provided with the shared task contains Kanji, Hiragana, and Katakana. Kanji constitute a problem for character-level models, because they are effectively an open set. The number of Kanji taught in Japanese schools is already ≈ 2000, to which variants, obsolete Kanji, and special Kanji only used in names may be added. Therefore, a model for Japanese language data should have the possibility to process previously unseen Kanji.

In the case of morphological inflection, however, this problem may be ignored, because Kanji are never altered in inflection. Instead, inflectional suffixes are expressed in Hiragana. Kanji may still appear in stems, and have therefore be dealt with.

We apply the following preprocessing: We replace all Kanji by a special placeholder symbol K that is the same for every Kanji. This applies to both source lemmas and target forms. In the case of successful prediction of target lemmas, the number of Kanji in the target form is the same as the number of Kanji in the source lemma. Therefore, we copy Kanji from the source by replacing the predicted placeholders. The order of Kanji in source and target does not change. In case of predicting fewer placeholders in the predicted form than there are Kanji in the source lemma, which is an error, we copy as many Kanji as there are placeholders in the predicted form from left to right. In case of predicting more placeholders in the predicted form than there are Kanji in the source lemma, which also is an error, we leave additional placeholders unchanged, i.e. we do not change the predicted placeholder symbol, but still copy as many Kanji as possible from left to right.

D Full Results

Morphological Inflection In Table 5, we report the official test set accuracies achieved by our model for all languages. For comparison, we also show results of the neural and the non-neural baseline. Likewise, we report official test set edit distances in Table 6.

These results show some interesting patterns. For example, the neural baseline performs worst on Japanese, which we assume is an effect of the alphabet (see Appendix C). Therefore, our proposed pre- and postprocessing for Japanese is important. Alternatively, a copy mechanism could be used.

Another trend is that our model performs strongly on semitic languages (e.g. afb, amh, arz, heb, heb_unvoc), especially compared to the non-neural baseline. Here, non-concatenative morphology gives our model an advantage, because usually individual transforms do not involve multiple characters, such as suffix ngrams. Remember that our model can only predict exactly one form character

	Track 1				Track 2			
	Word Level		Morph. Level		Word Level		Morph. Level	
	CTC	Morph	CTC	Morph	CTC	Morph	CTC	Morph
Arapaho	77.90	78.79	76.56	78.57	85.12	85.80	90.93	91.37
Tsez	80.96	80.94	70.29	73.95	85.68	85.79	91.16	92.01
Gitksan	04.69	21.09	09.26	11.72	13.80	26.56	17.08	50.22
Lezgi	78.10	78.78	62.03	62.10	85.44	83.41	83.45	87.61
Natugu	80.20	81.04	56.38	56.32	87.83	87.92	90.17	92.32
Nyangbo	85.34	85.05	86.74	85.24	85.90	87.98	89.96	91.40
Uspanteko	68.86	71.01	60.42	62.55	77.21	78.46	83.45	84.51

Table 4: Interlinear glossing: Official test set accuracies for all languages. Higher is better. CTC refers to our CTC-based baseline model, "Morph" refers to our model that learns morphological segmentation in a unsupervised way for track 1. In track 2, we simply use the provided representation.

from each combination of transduction lemma character and condition set. This shows that our model is able to capture complex patterns, but may not be optimal to generate extensive surface transforms.

Interlinear Glossing In Table 4, we report official test set accuracies achieved by our models for all languages. In most cases, our Morph model is superior to the CTC model, which confirms the benefit of morpheme segmentations for the task of interlinear glossing. The same conclusion is supported by the stark differences between track 1 and track 2. In track 2, performance is generally much better, especially when looking at morpheme level accuracies. Remember that we only use the ground-truth morpheme segmentation as additional information in track 2. We conclude that research in morpheme segmentation will be useful for computational models for interlinear glossing as well.

	Ours	Neural	¬ Neural
afb	75.8	80.1	30.8
amh	83.8	82.2	65.4
arz	87.6	89.6	77.9
bel	56.3	74.5	68.1
dan	85.7	88.8	89.5
deu	74.5	83.7	79.8
eng	96.0	95.1	96.6
fin	67.6	85.4	80.8
fra	67.9	73.3	77.7
grc	36.7	54.0	52.6
heb	82.7	92.0	30.9
heb(2)	81.3	83.2	64.5
hun	75.9	80.5	74.7
hye	85.9	91.0	86.3
ita	84.7	94.1	75.0
jap	95.3	26.3	64.1
kat	70.5	84.5	82.0
klr	96.4	99.5	54.5
mkd	86.7	93.8	91.6
nav	53.6	52.1	35.8
rus	82.1	90.5	86.0
san	54.5	66.3	62.2
sme	58.5	74.8	56.0
spa	88.7	93.6	87.8
sqi	71.5	85.9	83.4
swa	94.7	93.7	60.5
tur	81.8	95.0	64.6

Table 5: Official test set accuracies for all languages. Higher is better. "Neural" and "¬ Neural" refer to the neural and non-neural baseline, respectively. "heb(2)" refers to the `heb_unvoc` dataset.

	Ours	Neural	¬ Neural
afb	0.49	0.38	1.47
amh	0.22	0.24	0.59
arz	0.24	0.22	0.46
bel	1.31	0.64	0.90
dan	0.34	0.25	0.17
deu	1.00	0.48	0.80
eng	0.07	0.09	0.06
fin	0.63	0.21	0.26
fra	0.86	0.45	0.37
grc	1.43	1.00	1.04
heb	0.44	0.21	1.82
heb(2)	0.30	0.28	0.48
hun	0.57	0.44	0.47
hye	0.43	0.20	0.30
ita	0.43	0.12	0.75
jap	0.09	1.20	0.80
kat	0.79	0.35	0.51
klr	0.05	0.00	0.84
mkd	0.38	0.09	0.15
nav	1.37	1.55	1.88
rus	0.56	0.38	0.46
san	1.01	0.71	0.90
sme	0.88	0.65	0.89
spa	0.31	0.10	0.17
sqi	0.74	0.27	0.38
swa	0.06	0.06	4.10
tur	0.58	0.17	0.87

Table 6: Official test set edit distances for all languages. Lower is better. "Neural" and "¬ Neural" refer to the neural and non-neural baseline, respectively. "heb(2)" refers to the `heb_unvoc` dataset.

The BGU-MeLeL System for the SIGMORPHON 2023 Shared Task on Morphological Inflection

Gal Astrach
Department of Computer Science
Ben Gurion Univeristy
Beer Sheva, Israel
galastra@post.bgu.ac.il

Yuval Pinter
Department of Computer Science
Ben Gurion Univeristy
Beer Sheva, Israel
uvp@cs.bgu.ac.il

Abstract

This paper presents the submission by the MeLeL team to the SIGMORPHON–UniMorph Shared Task on Typologically Diverse and Acquisition-Inspired Morphological Inflection Generation Part 3: Models of Acquisition of Inflectional Noun Morphology in Polish, Estonian, and Finnish. This task requires us to produce the word form given a lemma and a grammatical case, while trying to produce the same error-rate as in children. We approach this task with a reduced-size character-based transformer model, multilingual training and an upsampling method to introduce bias.

1 Background

The SIGMORPHON Shared Task proposed a cross-linguistics modelling of child language acquisition to mediate between the theories of the acquisition of inflectional morphology. Here, unlike previous shared tasks of morphology inflection, the goal is to build a model that shows childlike item-by-item error rates, instead of generating the well-formed inflection.

1.1 Morphological Acquisition

The way that a child or an adult acquires a language is different. Therefore, the way they make mistakes is different. In the past decades there were many studies about the way children acquire a language, but most of the research focus only one language. Granlund et al. (2019) performed a large-scale cross-linguistics study of three languages—Finnish, Estonian and Polish. The research's goal was to find the aspects that indicate what makes children inflect words correctly.

The research found two such aspects: the first is *surface-form frequency*, where the greater the input frequency of the targeted inflectional form (i.e., the exact surface form that the child is attempting to produce in a given context; e.g., Polish książki, 'book-genitive') is, the greater the speed and accuracy of production or recognition. The second is *phonological neighborhood density* (PND), where the greater the number of "neighbours" or "friends"—nouns that are similar in both the base (nominative) form and the relevant target form (e.g., książka → książki; doniczka → doniczki; gruszka → gruszki)—the greater the speed and accuracy of production or recognition.

They also describe how these aspects work together: the effect of phonological neighbourhood density is greater for items with low surface-form frequency. Since low-frequency items are less likely to be successfully retrieved from memory, they must be generated by phonological analogy.

1.2 Modeling Acquisition of Inflectional Noun Morphology

The task of morphological inflection (Cotterell et al., 2017; Kodner et al., 2022) is defined as finding an inflected form for a given lemma and list of morphosyntactic attributes. Most state-of-the-art systems for the tasks to date center on character-level transduction and representation, and naturally attempt to predict the correct inflection with maximum performance. The current task, by contrast, requires imperfect generation by design, and thus solicits different approaches than state-of-the-art.

The data format in this task also differs from previous iteration in that it is more faithful to language children are exposed to. Instances are limited to single-feature inflection of lemmas into various grammatical cases (e.g., accusative, nominative, or genitive), and the lemma and the correct inflection are given in both orthographic and phonetic form (using IPA). In addition, the surface-form frequency of the lemma is provided, and the test set also contains children's error-rate of the inflection. The dataset is split such that lemmas in the training set do not appear in the test set (Goldman et al., 2022). The task expects as system output a list of

Proceedings of the 20th SIGMORPHON workshop on Computational Research in Phonetics, Phonology, and Morphology, pages 166–170
July 14, 2023

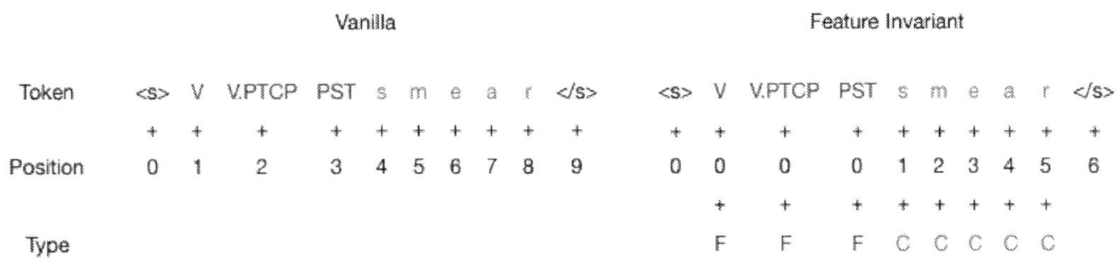

Figure 1: Wu et al. feature invariance (taken from the original paper)

top-10 inflections in IPA, alongside their probabilities. As an example, the following is a training data instance for the Polish lemma zdrowie "health":

`zdrowie GEN zdrowia zdrɔvjɛ zdrɔvja 6,`

where the columns represent (in order): the lemma in standard orthography, grammatical case, the inflection in standard orthography, the lemma in IPA, the inflection in IPA and the surface-form frequency.

1.3 Evaluation

In addition to exact-match accuracy and edit distance, correlation-based evaluation was also used for this task. In our development stage, we extracted the top 10 predictions for each instance with their respective probabilities, using beam search. We then calculated the correlation (both Spearman's and Pearson's) of the correct inflection's error rate and the model's outputs' probabilities. Due to the data format, this evaluation could only be done on the test set. When the correct form is not in top 10 predictions, we assign it zero probability.

2 Model

The base model that we used is the current state-of-the-art character-based transformer model (Wu et al., 2021). We then modified it to fit the task. The code from the model is forked from the public repository[1] with changes relevant to this task, meaning that the learning rate scheduler, early stopping and various training strategies are the same. Our model accepts the lemma in its IPA form.

The purpose of the original base model was to inflect a lemma form to the correct inflection morphological properties given as input. Our settings differ in that the model should inflect according to the children's behavior, and not to the correct inflection. We can do that by modifying the model to work with both of the features introduced above, namely **PND** and **surface-form frequency**. We select our model based on the best epoch according to the overall best evaluation (see §1.3) on the test sets.

2.1 Base Model

The transformer (Vaswani et al., 2017) is a sequence-to-sequence model, used for tasks such as machine translation. The transformer-based model we use as a basis for our task (Wu et al., 2021) is tailored for character-level transduction in order to be applied to tasks such as morphological inflection and grapheme-to-phoneme prediction, illustrated in Figure 1 (taken from the original paper). Crucially, the input provided to the model is the concatenation of the characters of the lemma with the morphosyntactic attributes, assigning embeddings to each character and attribute. Their variant, dubbed **feature-invariant transformer**, differs from the original transformer in two aspects: a smaller model and a feature-invariant architecture.

Feature invariance In morphological inflection tasks, the lemma is a sequence of characters mapped to the inflection which is a different sequence of characters, to be predicted according to the list of morphological attributes. The transformer model deals with sequences as they are ordered. However, the portion of the input consisting of a list of morphological attributes is unordered; moreover, the distance between attributes and the characters within the input is irrelevant. These properties may lead to inconsistencies in data representation and generalization when training a sequence model so sensitive to input order. The feature-invariant transformer therefore receives the positional encoding of features as zeroes, and only begins incrementing position count for the lemma's

[1] https://github.com/shijie-wu/neural-transducer

System	Accuracy	Edit Distance	Pearson's	Spearman's
Baseline (Wu et al.)	1.0000	0	−0.029	−0.061
Base + Smaller Model	.8812	0.229	0.078	−0.047
Base + Upsample	.9890	0.015	−0.015	−0.087
Base + Multilingual	.9978	0.002	−0.106	−0.259
Base + Smaller Model + Upsample	.8099	0.359	0.286	0.237
Base + Smaller Model + Multilingual	.6864	0.548	0.379	0.334
Base + Multilingual + Upsample	.9890	0.013	−0.023	−0.318
Base + Small + Upsample + Multiling	.5526	0.814	**0.467**	**0.438**

Table 1: Model variants' results on the test set. Results for models not specified as multilingual are reported are the macro-average for the three languages. Multilinugal models' correlations are calculated on the concatenated test sets of all three languages. The correlations are the metrics of interest. The system in bold was submitted to the shared task.

characters. Additionally, a special token is used to indicate whether a symbol is a word character or a morphosyntactic attribute.

2.2 Surface Form Frequency

According to Granlund et al. (2019), one of the attributes that correlate with accuracy in children is the frequency of the form in the heard corpus they are exposed to. Therefore, we chose to incorporate this information in our model, by a combination of methods, namely **upsampling** and **surface form frequency embeddings**.

Upsampling We manipulate the training dataset synthetically by upsampling each form in direct proportion to the form-frequency as annotated in the dataset. The way we upsample is that when reading the raw dataset, we add the same sample according to the value in the surface-form-frequency column, meaning that if a sample (a lemma, morphological feature and an inflection) has the value n in the surface-form-frequency column, then it will appear n times in the training set.

Surface-form frequency embedding Since in the test set we cannot upsample, we need to also utilize the form-frequency value by itself. We do that by feeding the value of the surface-form frequency into a linear layer, with the layer's output size the same as the other inputs' embedding dimension, and then concatenating it to the embedding's layer's output. The linear layer has no activation function, in order to act like the embedding layer in the transformer. After concatenation, we apply dropout to the new embedding tensor.

2.3 Multilingual

In order to generalize the modeling of language acquisition, we trained the model multilingually. We did that by adding a tag to the morphosyntactic attributes, together with the grammatical case, which indicates the language. The language tag therefore acts like the rest of the morphosyntactic attributes and provided as input to the embedding layer.

2.4 An Even Smaller Model

As mentioned above, the transformer introduced in Wu et al. (2021) is a smaller transformer than the original. Early experiments led us to suspect that further reducing the model size could better approximate children's performance. We use 4 encoder-decoder layers, 2 self-attention heads, a feed-forward layer with hidden size $d_{\text{FF}} = 128$, embedding size $d_{\text{model}} = 256$, dropout rate 0.5, and a batch size of 100.

3 Results and Discussion

We present the results for our models in Table 1. They show that our methods provide substantial improvement over the baseline, which generates perfect inflections, but correlates poorly with the children's error rates. The best improvement in correlation given by a single method was from decreasing model size; the best overall performance was obtained by using all three methods, indicating that their improvement profiles are complementary. We note that multilingual training was mostly beneficial to model performance, suggesting that the language acquisition process is generalizable across languages.

As noted in the background section, there are two aspects relevant to this task of modeling acquisition which are different than normal, well-formed inflection, namely surface-form frequency and phonological neighborhood density (PND). The model we designed captures the former by the upsampling method and frequency embeddings, whereas PND could theoretically be imbued through the transformer's encoder, which embeds the lemma into a hidden state vector given its IPA representation. As such, it is capable of modeling similarity on the phonetic level, so if two words are pronounced similarly, their hidden states can be similar and thus provide means for PND realization.

4 Conclusion

This paper presents the approach taken by the MeLeL team to solving the SIGMORPHON 2023 Shared Task on Typologically Diverse and Acquisition-Inspired Morphological Inflection Generation. To this end, we designed a model for morphological inflection, based on current state of the art. We adapted the model to the task objectives, modifying hyper-parameters to add "forgetfulness", incorporated surface-form frequency information by adding upsampling and embedding the frequency counts, and trained multilingually to generalize cross-lingual features. Our final system, which correlates with child-produced inflection substantially better than the base system, is informed by two aspects previously shown to be relevant to children's inflectional competence, namely surface-form frequency and neighborhood phonetic distance.

References

Ryan Cotterell, Christo Kirov, John Sylak-Glassman, Géraldine Walther, Ekaterina Vylomova, Patrick Xia, Manaal Faruqui, Sandra Kübler, David Yarowsky, Jason Eisner, and Mans Hulden. 2017. CoNLL-SIGMORPHON 2017 shared task: Universal morphological reinflection in 52 languages. In *Proceedings of the CoNLL SIGMORPHON 2017 Shared Task: Universal Morphological Reinflection*, pages 1–30, Vancouver. Association for Computational Linguistics.

Omer Goldman, David Guriel, and Reut Tsarfaty. 2022. (un)solving morphological inflection: Lemma overlap artificially inflates models' performance. In *Proceedings of the 60th Annual Meeting of the Association for Computational Linguistics (Volume 2: Short Papers)*, pages 864–870, Dublin, Ireland. Association for Computational Linguistics.

Sonia Granlund, Joanna Kolak, Virve Vihman, Felix Engelmann, Elena V.M. Lieven, Julian M. Pine, Anna L. Theakston, and Ben Ambridge. 2019. Language-general and language-specific phenomena in the acquisition of inflectional noun morphology: A cross-linguistic elicited-production study of polish, finnish and estonian. *Journal of Memory and Language*, 107:169–194.

Jordan Kodner, Salam Khalifa, Khuyagbaatar Batsuren, Hossep Dolatian, Ryan Cotterell, Faruk Akkus, Antonios Anastasopoulos, Taras Andrushko, Aryaman Arora, Nona Atanalov, Gábor Bella, Elena Budianskaya, Yustinus Ghanggo Ate, Omer Goldman, David Guriel, Simon Guriel, Silvia Guriel-Agiashvili, Witold Kieraś, Andrew Krizhanovsky, Natalia Krizhanovsky, Igor Marchenko, Magdalena Markowska, Polina Mashkovtseva, Maria Nepomniashchaya, Daria Rodionova, Karina Scheifer, Alexandra Sorova, Anastasia Yemelina, Jeremiah Young, and Ekaterina Vylomova. 2022. SIGMORPHON–UniMorph 2022 shared task 0: Generalization and typologically diverse morphological inflection. In *Proceedings of the 19th SIGMORPHON Workshop on Computational Research in Phonetics, Phonology, and Morphology*, pages 176–203, Seattle, Washington. Association for Computational Linguistics.

Ashish Vaswani, Noam Shazeer, Niki Parmar, Jakob Uszkoreit, Llion Jones, Aidan N. Gomez, Lukasz Kaiser, and Illia Polosukhin. 2017. Attention is all you need. *CoRR*, abs/1706.03762.

Shijie Wu, Ryan Cotterell, and Mans Hulden. 2021. Applying the transformer to character-level transduction. In *Proceedings of the 16th Conference of the European Chapter of the Association for Computational Linguistics: Main Volume*, pages 1901–1907, Online. Association for Computational Linguistics.

Language	In top-10	Acc.	Pear.	Pear-0	Cosine	Cosine-0
Polish	134/150	.73	−0.020	0.231	0.99	0.94
Estonian	121/144	.55	0.547	0.578	0.99	0.94
Finnish	134/162	.44	0.462	0.462	0.98	0.92

Table 2: Submitted model results for each language. "In top-10" means the number of predictions from the test set that were found in the model's top-10 list. "Pear" and "Cosine" are the Pearson's correlation and Cosine Similarity for the predicted probabilities, where the "-0" denotes that when the correct form is not in top-10, the probability assigned is 0.

A Results Per Language

In Table 2 we present the results for each language on the submitted model, as reported in the official task website as of May 18, 2023.

Tü-CL at SIGMORPHON 2023: Straight-Through Gradient Estimation for Hard Attention

Leander Girrbach
University of Tübingen
leander.girrbach@uni-tuebingen.de

Abstract

This paper describes our systems participating in the 2023 SIGMORPHON Shared Task on Morphological Inflection (Goldman et al., 2023) and in the 2023 SIGMORPHON Shared Task on Interlinear Glossing. We propose methods to enrich predictions from neural models with discrete, i.e. interpretable, information. For morphological inflection, our models learn deterministic mappings from subsets of source lemma characters and morphological tags to individual target characters, which introduces interpretability. For interlinear glossing, our models learn a shallow morpheme segmentation in an unsupervised way jointly with predicting glossing lines. Estimated segmentation may be useful when no ground-truth segmentation is available. As both methods introduce discreteness into neural models, our technical contribution is to show that straight-through gradient estimators are effective to train hard attention models.

1 Introduction

This paper describes our systems participating in the SIGMORPHON–UniMorph Shared Task on Typologically Diverse and Acquisition-Inspired Morphological Inflection Generation (Goldman et al., 2023) and the SIGMORPHON 2023 Shared Task on Interlinear Glossing. For morphological inflection, we participate in part 1, and for interlinear glossing we mainly target the closed track.

Morphological Inflection is the task of predicting the correct inflected form given a lemma and set of morphological tags. An example from the Italian dataset in the shared task is

$$\text{votare ("to vote")} \xrightarrow{\text{V;IND;FUT;NOM(1,PL)}} \text{voteremo.}$$

The organisers of the shared task provide train, validation and test splits for 26 languages. In the case of Hebrew, 2 datasets are provided. Train splits contain 10K (lemma, tags, form) triples, validation and test splits contain 1K triples.

Interlinear glossing is the task of predicting glossing lines, which is a sequence of morphological tags, including lexical translations for each token, on the sentence level given the surface text and optionally a translation. An example of interlinear glossing taken from the train portion of the Gitksan dataset in the shared task is:

(1)

Iin	*dip*	*gidax̱*	*guhl*	*wilt.*
CCNJ-1.I	1PL.I	ask	what-CN	LVB-3.II

"And we asked what he did."

The organisers of the shared task provide train, validation and test splits for 7 typologically diverse languages. Dataset sizes differ for each language. Furthermore, the shared task features a closed track, where only surface text and a translation is available for each sentence, and an open track, where canonical morpheme segmentation and POS tags are provided as additional information.

Especially when the main focus of training machine learning models is scientific discovery, even the notoriously good performance of deep neural models (Jiang et al., 2020) may not be satisfactory. Instead, models should also yield insights into what they learn about the data. However, clear and interpretable explanations are often hard to derive from models by post-hoc analysis, although many methods exist (Holzinger et al., 2020; Burkart and Huber, 2021; Rao et al., 2022). On the other hand, self-interpretable models, i.e. models whose calculations directly reveal discrete information, are generally hard to train with gradient methods and do not reach the same effectiveness as fully continuous models (Niepert et al., 2021).

Therefore, in this work we aim at narrowing the gap between inherently interpretable models and fully continuous deep sequence-to-sequence models by demonstrating the effectiveness of straight-through gradient estimators in optimising discrete intermediate representations by gradient methods.

Proceedings of the 20th SIGMORPHON workshop on Computational Research in Phonetics, Phonology, and Morphology, pages 171–185
July 14, 2023

As applications, we construct a model type for morphological inflection that shows, without ambiguity, which subset of lemma characters and tags causes the prediction of a form character. Our proposed model for interlinear glossing enriches the given surface text with shallow morpheme segmentation.

Our main contributions are: (1) We show the effectiveness of straight-through gradient estimators for learning hard attention; (2) We present a model for morphological inflection that unambiguously shows which subset of lemma characters and tags lead to the prediction of a form character; (3) We present a model that learns shallow morpheme segmentation jointly with interlinear glossing in an unsupervised fashion.

2 ST Optimization of Hard Attention

We discuss hard attention as mappings of the following form: Let $k \in \mathbb{N}$ be the number of target positions (e.g. the number of decoder positions in a encoder-decoder sequence-to-sequence model), and $\mathbf{X} \in \mathbb{R}^{n \times d}$ the matrix containing d-dimensional feature vectors of n source elements (e.g. learned embedding vectors). Each target element $\mathbf{y}_i$, $i \in \{1, \ldots, K\}$ is calculated as a sum of source element encodings, formally $\mathbf{y}_i = \sum_{j \in \rightarrow_i} \mathbf{x}_j$ where $\mathbf{x}_j$ is the jth row vector in $\mathbf{X}$ and $\rightarrow_i \subseteq \{1, \ldots, n\}$ is the set of source elements aligned to target position i. Note that a source element may be aligned to multiple target elements, i.e. appear in $\rightarrow_i$ for different i.

This mapping can be calculated by a matrix multiplication $\xi \cdot \mathbf{X} = \mathbf{Y} \in \mathbb{R}^{k \times d}$, where columns of $\xi \in \{0, 1\}^{k \times n}$ are the multi-hot encodings of index sets $(\rightarrow_i)_{i \in \{1, \ldots, K\}}$. Formally, this means

$$\xi_{i,j} = \begin{cases} 1 & \text{if } j \in \rightarrow_i \\ 0 & \text{if } j \notin \rightarrow_i \end{cases}$$

We assume ξ is a sample from a underlying categorical distribution where we can compute the marginals $\hat{\xi}_{i,j}$ that specify the probability

$$\hat{\xi}_{i,j} = \Pr[j \in \rightarrow_i]$$

of j being included in $\rightarrow_i$. For example, in the case of dot-product attention, we have $\mathbf{z} \in \mathbb{R}^{k \times n}$ the matrix product of decoder states and encoder states. Then, we obtain $\hat{\xi}$ by $\mathrm{softmax}$ over rows, and ξ by sampling from the categorical distributions defined by rows of $\hat{\xi}$. At test time, argmax is used instead of sampling.

The main problem is how to side-step sampling during gradient-based optimization, because sampling is not differentiable. One solution is the so-called straight-through estimator (Bengio et al., 2013; Jang et al., 2017; Cathcart and Wandl, 2020) which means using ξ for the forward pass, i.e. when computing model outputs, but using $\hat{\xi}$ for backpropagation, i.e. when computing gradients of model parameters w.r.t. the loss.

However, gradients of $\mathbf{X}$ are affected by the discreteness of ξ as well, because $\xi_{i,j} = 0$ also means $\mathbf{x}_j$ does not receive gradients from $\mathbf{y}_i$. Therefore, when using straight-through gradient estimation, we should use $\hat{\xi}$ when computing gradients of $\mathbf{X}$. Formally, for some differentiable function f that is applied to $\mathbf{Y}$, we set

$$\frac{\partial f(\xi \cdot \mathbf{X})}{\partial \hat{\xi}} = \mathbf{X}^T \frac{\partial f(\mathbf{Y})}{\partial \mathbf{Y}}$$
$$\frac{\partial f(\xi \cdot \mathbf{X})}{\partial \mathbf{X}} = \left(\frac{\partial f(\mathbf{Y})}{\partial \mathbf{Y}} \right)^T \cdot \hat{\xi},$$

which can be implemented as

$$\mathbf{Y} = \hat{\xi} \cdot \mathbf{X} - \mathrm{sg}\left((\hat{\xi} - \xi) \cdot \mathbf{X} \right), \qquad (1)$$

where sg is the stop-gradient function (van den Oord et al., 2017) which behaves like the identity during forward pass, but has 0 partial derivatives everywhere.

3 Applications

In this section, we describe how to apply the method from Section 2 to sequence transduction (Section 3.1) and sequence segmentation (Section 3.2). We keep formulations more general than necessary for the shared tasks, because we want to highlight that the methods apply to similar problems as well.

3.1 Sequence Transduction

Sequence Transduction means transforming an input or source sequence $s_{1:n} = s_1, \ldots, s_n$ into an output or target sequence $t_{1:m} = t_1, \ldots, t_m$. Successful model types for this tasks are neural encoder-decoder networks with attention (Bahdanau et al., 2015). These models use an encoder which computes contextual source symbol representations $\mathbf{s}_1, \ldots, \mathbf{s}_n$ and a decoder which computes autoregressive target symbol representations $\mathbf{t}_1, \ldots, \mathbf{t}_m$. Entries of the attention matrix $\hat{\xi}$ are dot products[1] of source representations and target representations, normalised to a categorical distribution over source symbols for every target symbol. Output symbols are predicted from the concatenation of the respective previous autoregressive target representation with the weighted sum of source symbol representations, where weights correspond to probabilities of the respective attention distribution. In terms of interpretability, this type of model has two problems:

Soft Attention The role of soft attention (i.e. using $\hat{\xi}$ directly) with regard to explaining model predictions is not entirely understood (Jain and Wallace, 2019; Wiegreffe and Pinter, 2019). Therefore, we want to replace soft attention with hard attention, whose interpretability is undisputed. We replace soft attention with hard attention by sampling source elements from rows of $\hat{\xi}$ during training. The sampled index sets are used to discretise $\hat{\xi}$ into ξ. We enable end-to-end training through Equation (1).

Contextual Representations Contextual symbol encodings represent information about the whole sequence, not just the encoded symbol. In deep models, it is therefore not clear what information actually is encoded (Meister et al., 2021). For this reason, we want to use non-contextual symbol embeddings for prediction and use contextual symbol encodings only for computing $\hat{\xi}$.

However, only selecting one single source symbol by hard attention and then not using any contextual information is not sufficient for successful transduction. For example, in the case of morphological inflection discussed here, predictions have to take morphological tags and surrounding characters into account when transducing a source character. Therefore, we use two attention heads computing different kinds of attention:

1. Softmax-normalised attention $\hat{\xi}_{\text{symbol}}$ to select a single symbol to transduce.

2. Sigmoid-normalised attention $\hat{\xi}_{\text{cond}}$ to select multiple symbols as conditions. In this case, the sigmoid function σ is applied to every dot-product of encoder states and decoder states individually, yielding a Bernoulli distribution for every combination. ξ_{cond} is the result of sampling from each Bernoulli distribution. At test time, we round to 0 or 1 instead of sampling to ensure deterministic predictions.

Predictions are computed from the combined context vectors, formally

$$\begin{aligned} \mathbf{Y}^{\text{symbol}} &= \xi_{\text{symbol}} \cdot \mathbf{X}_{\text{embed}} \\ \mathbf{Y}^{\text{cond}} &= \xi_{\text{cond}} \cdot \mathbf{X}_{\text{embed}} \\ p_j(\bullet \mid s_{1:n}) &= \text{MLP}([\mathbf{Y}_j^{\text{symbol}}, \mathbf{Y}_j^{\text{cond}}]) \end{aligned} \tag{2}$$

where $\bullet$ is a placeholder to indicate distributions over the target alphabet, p_j is the distribution for the jth target symbol, and $\mathbf{X}_{\text{embed}}$ is the matrix containing non-contextual source symbol embeddings.

In this formulation, the decoder is still autoregressive, but is only involved in computing attention scores, not predictions any more. Therefore, it is entirely transparent which source symbols are responsible for which predictions. Also, the condition vector is a sum of equally weighted non-contextual symbol embeddings. The only non-transparent computation are the attention scores. Formally, the model learns a mapping $\mathcal{S} \times 2^{\mathcal{S} \times \mathbb{N}} \rightarrow \mathcal{T}$ where $\mathcal{S}$ is the source alphabet, $\mathbb{N}$ are the natural numbers (to account for multiplicities of symbols), and $2^{\mathcal{S} \times \mathbb{N}}$ indicates the power set. $\mathcal{T}$ is the target alphabet. The attention mechanism selects the contextually appropriate arguments for this mapping. A more detailed description of the concrete model architecture is in Appendix B.

Of course, the increased transparency limits the expressivity of the model. One problem is that gradient signals for encoder and decoder are insufficient, because their only remaining role is to compute attention matrices. Therefore, we train sequence transduction models in a multi-task setting, using the interpretable mechanism described above together with the typical mechanism, i.e. predicting the next target symbol from decoder state and combined contextual source symbol encodings. However, we use the same attention matrices in both cases. Predictions of type one-to-many (e.g. converting a single morphological tag to a suffix consisting of multiple characters) are also problematic: For each single target symbol, a different source symbol or condition is required. Possible solutions are augmenting the target alphabet with symbol ngrams (Liu et al., 2017) or allowing for local non-autoregressive predictions (Libovický and Helcl, 2018). However, we leave exploration of such methods to future work. Finally, condition

[1] There are different ways to calculate unnormalised attention scores (Luong et al., 2015; Brauwers and Frasincar, 2023), but without loss of generality we restrict the discussion to dot-product attention.

vectors $\mathbf{Y}^{\text{cond}}$ are insensitive to order due to summing being a commutative operation. This problem can be mitigated by positional encodings, but we do not observe improvements in preliminary experiments and do not explore this option here.

3.2 Sequence Segmentation

We combine hard attention with Structured Attention proposed by Kim et al. (2017). In particular, we consider the case of sequence segmentation and propose an end-to-end trainable interlinear glossing model (for the closed tack, where this information is not given) that first performs shallow morphological segmentation[2] on input words and then predicts the gloss label for each morpheme. Note that the method is also applicable to other tasks that require sequence segmentation and further processing of resulting segments, such as joint Sandhi segmentation and morphological parsing in Sanskrit (Li and Girrbach, 2022). In contrast to Kim et al., our segment encodings respect a particular sampled segmentation due to hard attention, and do not represent expected feature values.

Encoder Model Given a sentence as input to the glossing model, we first apply a character level encoder such as BiLSTM (Hochreiter and Schmidhuber, 1997; Graves and Schmidhuber, 2005), to compute contextual character representations on the sentence level. Then, we continue processing on the word level and denote a word w by its characters $w = s_1, \ldots, s_n$. Each word consists of a sequence of characters that are represented by contextual features computed in the previous step. For each character at position i, we predict a Bernoulli distribution parametrised by probability $p_i^{\text{seg}} \in (0; 1)$ that indicates whether the corresponding character is the last character of a (shallow) morpheme segment in our case. We also adopt the method by Raffel et al. (2017) to add Gaussian noise to unnormalised scores during training to encourage discreteness of segmentation probabilities.

Furthermore, each word is paired with the number of morphemes in the word. According to Leipzig Glossing Conventions (Comrie et al., 2008, Rule 2), the number of morphemes in a word is given by the number of hyphen-separated labels assigned to a word. During inference, the number of labels and therefore morphemes is not given. In this case, a straightforward solution is to start a new morpheme whenever the segmentation probability exceeds a certain threshold τ. However, we found trivial solutions for τ like $\frac{1}{2}$ not to work well, while learning to predict the number of morphemes in a word from the max-pooled character representations by a MLP works well in our case. Therefore, we adopt the latter option and leave exploration of the former method to future work. In cases where we have no information about the number of segments during training, marginalising the number of segments still remains as option.

Computing Marginals Character-level segmentation scores p_i^{seg} have to be converted to the attention matrix $\hat{\xi}$ by marginalising all segmentations. For each source element s_i, marginalisation computes the marginal probability of having a morpheme boundary at s_i. Adopting the terminology of Section 2, morphemes correspond to target elements and characters to source elements. Each source element is aligned to exactly one target element and the alignment is monotonic. This means each source element can only be aligned to the same target element as the immediately preceding source element or alternatively it can be aligned to the next target element. Accordingly, we compute marginals, i.e. distributions over targets for each source element, by the forward-backward algorithm, same as Kim et al. (2017). The forward recursion is given by $\alpha_{1,1} = 1$ and

$$\alpha_{i,j} = \alpha_{i-1,j} \cdot (1 - p_{i-1}^{\text{seg}}) + \alpha_{i-1,j-1} \cdot p_{i-1}^{\text{seg}}$$

for $i > 1, j \geq 1$ where $p_i^{\text{seg}} \in (0; 1)$ is the predicted segmentation probability of the ith source element. Note that the first source element is always part of the first segment. Backward scores are computed as $\beta_{n,k} = 1$ and

$$\beta_{i,j} = \beta_{i+1,j} \cdot (1 - p_{i,j}^{\text{seg}}) + \beta_{i+1,j+1} \cdot p_{i,j}^{\text{seg}}$$

for $i < n$ and $j \leq k$. Finally, marginals are given by $\hat{\xi}_{i,j} = \frac{\alpha_{i,j} \cdot \beta_{i,j}}{\alpha_{n,k}}$. In practise, computations are performed in log-space.

Training For discretising segmentations, it is most convenient to simply choose the maximum likelihood segmentation, which corresponds to starting new segments at the $k-1$ indices with maximum segmentation probabilities. The corresponding target segment representations are computed by $\mathbf{Y} = \xi \cdot \mathbf{X}$, where $\mathbf{X}$ is the matrix of

[2]Shallow morphological segmentation means only segmenting the surface string. Contrast this to canonical segmentation, which also restores a latent canonical form of present morphemes (Kann et al., 2016).

source element representations. Note that we use the discrete assignments ξ for computing segment representations and Equation (1) for training.

In the case of interlinear glossing, distributions over labels for each morpheme are computed by a MLP taking morpheme representations, i.e. rows in $\mathbf{Y}$, as input. Loss, then, is the cross-entropy between predicted distributions over labels and ground-truth labels. Note that in this case, and in contrast to Section 3.1, we compute morpheme representations from contextualised character representations, and not from non-contextual embeddings, because we think that only sets of characters of shallow morpheme segments are not sufficient to compute the semantic information necessary for glossing, especially the correct translations.

This has two consequences, first of all the model is not transparent (i.e. interpretable), and character encodings may be "fuzzy" in the sense that information is locally spread across multiple characters which may obscure precise morpheme boundaries. A similar effect has been shown for sparse attention by Meister et al. (2021). We leave exploring more interpretable models similar to the model described in Section 3.1 and biasing models towards more precise morpheme segmentation to future work. In this work, our main focus is to provide shallow morpheme segmentation as additional predictions, not to build an entirely interpretable glossing model.

4 Evaluation

Here, we evaluate the methods presented in Section 3 by participating in the shared task on morphological inflection and in the shared task on interlinear glossing. Technical details of the experimental setup and hyperparameters are in Appendix A.

4.1 Baselines

For the morphological inflection shared task, the organisers provide a neural and a non-neural baseline. For the interlinear glossing shared task, the organisers provide a transformer-based neural baseline. Furthermore, we add a CTC-based sequence labelling model (Graves et al., 2006) as baseline. The CTC model encodes the source sentence on the character level by a BiLSTM encoder and predicts a label or blank from each character. Here, we exploit that the number of labels is the same as the number of morphemes, and each word has at least as many characters as morphemes.

4.2 Data Representation

For a detailed description of the shared task data, refer to the respective shared task overview papers. In the case of morphological inflection, we convert (lemma, tags, form) triples to (source, target) pairs by removing all punctuation from the tags and prepending the remaining sequence of tags to the lemma characters. Special pre- and postprocessing is applied to Japanese in order to eliminate Kanji, see Appendix C.

In the case of interlinear glossing, no modification is necessary for the closed track. However, for the open track, we replace the source text by hyphen-separated morphemes. We assume they contain more information than the original unsegmented text, and the unsegmented text does not add any information when the segmented morphemes are available. In this case, we also do not learn shallow segmentation, but predict a single label from each morpheme. The CTC baseline flexibly learns alignments of labels to characters in both cases. In both cases, we approach interlinear glossing as a sequence labelling problem.

4.3 Results

Morphological Inflection In Table 1, we report macro-averaged test set accuracy and edit distance. Full results for all languages achieved by our model and the baselines are in Appendix D. For clarity, we only report results of the best system for every participating team. Results show that our interpretable model loses on performance compared to more flexible neural models, such as the Transformer baseline. On 22 of 27 languages, the neural baseline beats our model. However, results also show that introducing interpretability does not have catastrophic consequences regarding performance. With some advantages in macro-averaged scores, our model performs roughly on par with the non-neural baseline, beating it on 14 of 27 languages. In summary, these results suggest that introducing interpretability to neural models causes some decrease in performance, but having neural interpretable models still gives better results than having interpretable non-neural models.

To illustrate patterns learned by our models, we show examples of the selected source symbols and condition symbols. The first example in Figure 1 is taken from the French (validation) dataset, namely the target inflection is

$$\textit{juger}\text{ “to judge”} \xrightarrow{\text{V;COND;NOM(1,PL)}} \text{“jugerions”}.$$

	Accuracy ↑	ED ↓
Illinois	84.27	0.35
Baseline (Neural)	81.61	0.40
Ours	**76.91**	**0.58**
Arizona	72.45	0.75
Baseline (¬ Neural)	69.60	0.81

Table 1: Morphological Inflection: Best macro-averaged test set results for accuracy and edit distance (ED) of each team. Results of our model are highlighted in bold.

In this case, the prediction is correct. We can see how the model first selects characters of the stem to copy. Here, few if any other source symbols are selected as conditions. Then, for predicting the inflection suffix "-ions", the model selects tag symbols both to transduce and as conditions.

Next, we consider an example from the Italian dataset, namely

$$\textit{estraniarsi} \text{ “to alienate onself”} \xrightarrow{\text{V;IND;PRS;NOM(1,PL)}} \text{“ci estranieremmo”}.$$

The corresponding selected symbols and conditions are shown in Figure 2. This example shows an interesting non-monotonic pattern, namely moving the reflexive pronoun "si" to the front and changing it to the correct number and person, in this case 1st plural. The model correctly captures this, as we can see from the selected transduction symbols (left side). Also, the model learned which conditions to select for changing the "s" in "si" to "c". After this transform, the model copies the stem by selecting stem characters as transduction symbols and conditions. Finally, the model generates the inflectional suffix by selecting mainly tags as transduction characters and conditions.

Interlinear Glossing In Table 2, we report macro-averaged word level and morpheme level test set accuracies. Both our additional CTC baseline and our morpheme-segmentation model, henceforth referred to as "morph", compare favourably to the transformer baseline. Furthermore, our morph model achieves better performance than competing models on track 1, where the unsupervised learning of morpheme segmentation is relevant, which shows that learning additional linguistically relevant structures can improve performance by injecting useful inductive biases in the model. Furthermore, we again conclude that using discrete structure as intermediate representations does not necessarily decrease performance catastrophically. Instead, it seems helpful in this case. Finally, we note that translations are not necessary for current glossing models to achieve strong performance, since we do not use them.

We also show examples of shallow segmentation learned by the morph model. We focus only on the segmentation, because this is the main contribution of our model. Note that all segmentations were learned in an unsupervised way for track 1 alongside the main objective, i.e. predicting the glossing line. For track 1, morphological segmentation is not given, unlike for track 2.

Because our model learns shallow segmentations, while ground-truth segmentations provided for track 2 are canonical segmentations, we can not conduct a quantitative analysis. Therefore, we restrict the analysis to anecdotal qualitative analysis of 2 example segmentions predicted by our models.

First, we consider a prediction for the following Natugu example:

(2) *Nedr rlilrdr doa nzpwxng* .
Ne-dr r-li-lr-dr doa nz-pwx-ng .
ne-dr r-li-r-dr doa nz-pwx-ngq .

"The two of them had four children."

Morphemes are separated by hyphens "-". The predicted segmentation is in the second line, and the ground-truth segmentation is in the third line. The predicted segmentation differs from the ground-truth, because it copies characters and therefore can not change capitalisation, and two morphemes ("lr" → "r" and "ng" → "ngq") are normalised in the ground-truth segmentation, so that they differ from their surface form.

Next, we consider a Uspanteko example:

(3) *i tiyuq sol ji' tren tib'ek*
i t-iyuq sol ji' t-r-en t-ib'e-k
i ti-yu' sol ji' t-r-en ti-b'e-k

"Y llega solo asi hace se va."

Again, the predicted segmentation is in the second line. In two cases the vowel "i" is assigned to the wrong morpheme, but the predicted glossing line (not shown) is still correct. In this case, incorrect segmentation is apparently not a problem for the subsequent classification of morphemes, but in other cases this may cause problems. Here, we

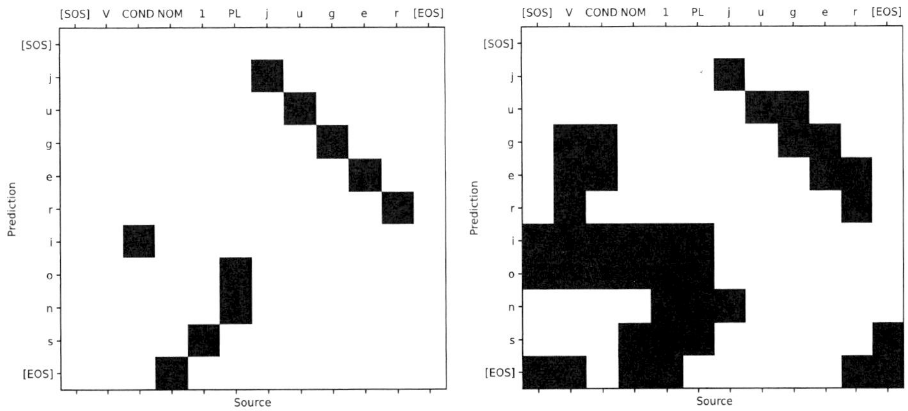

Figure 1: Example for French *juger* "to judge". The target prediction is "juger" $\xrightarrow{\text{V;COND;NOM(1,PL)}}$ "jugerions". The prediction is correct in this case. On the left side, we show the single selected symbols for transduction, on the right side we show the additionally selected condition symbols. Because we use hard attention, attention scores can only be 0 or 1, and we can present them in a black-and-white style.

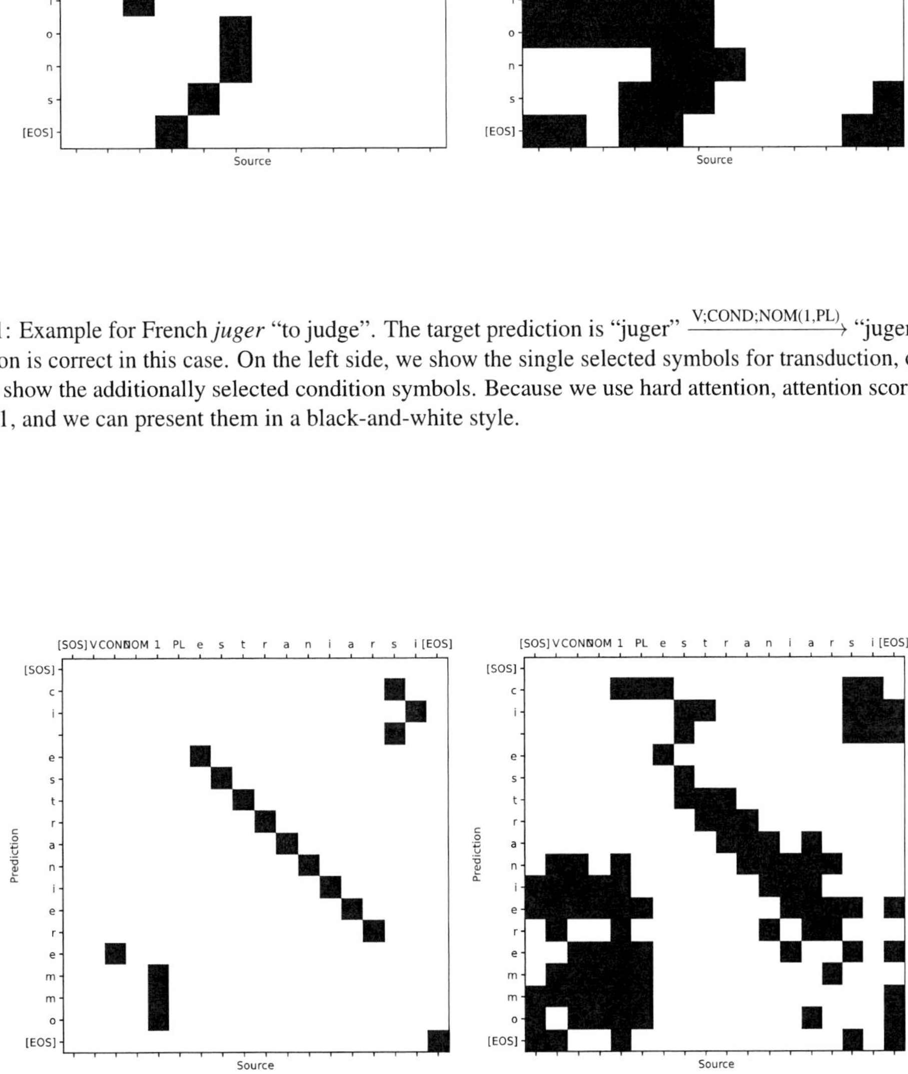

Figure 2: Example for Italian *estraniarsi* "to alienate onself". The target prediction is "estraniarsi" $\xrightarrow{\text{V;COND;NOM(1,PL)}}$ "ci estranieremmo". The prediction is correct in this case. On the left side, we show the single selected symbols for transduction, on the right side we show the additionally selected condition symbols.

	Track 1		Track 2	
	Word Level	Morph. Level	Word Level	Morph. Level
Ours (Morph)	71.30	62.55	76.56	84.21
Ours (CTC)	68.01	60.24	74.43	78.03
Baseline	47.31	33.60	59.14	67.69

Table 2: Interlinear Glossing: Macro-averaged test set accuracy for our models and the baseline. Higher is better.

can see that contextualised character encodings can bypass the discrete morpheme segmentation step.

5 Related Work

Much recent work in character-level transduction aims at making models both more interpretable and stronger by using sparse (Peters and Martins, 2019, 2020) or hard attention (Aharoni and Goldberg, 2017; Wu et al., 2018; Wu and Cotterell, 2019; Makarov and Clematide, 2018b,a). Modifying the attention mechanism is necessary, because for soft attention, which does not realise hard alignment decisions, the relation of model outputs and attention weights is not fully understood (Jain and Wallace, 2019; Wiegreffe and Pinter, 2019). Hard attention does not suffer from this problem, because it realises hard alignment decisions, so that we exactly know which information influences the output of attention. Especially if the main purpose of models is to gain insights into the data and not mainly to achieve better performance on modelling it, interpretability of models is crucial.

However, working with hard attention is notoriously difficult, because it introduces non-differentiability into models. This means that the sophisticated machinery developed for gradient-based optimisation of deep neural models fails in this case. The most popular but also most expensive approach to train hard attention mechanisms is marginalising all alignments (Yu et al., 2016; Raffel et al., 2017; Wu et al., 2018; Wu and Cotterell, 2019) or approximating the marginalisation (Shankar et al., 2018). Different approaches to approximate gradients instead of having exact gradients by marginalisation are using reinforcement learning (Xu et al., 2015; Makarov and Clematide, 2018a), reparametrising discrete distributions or working with continuous relaxations (Jang et al., 2017; Maddison et al., 2017), and perturbation based gradient approximators (Niepert et al., 2021). While all methods to use hard attention with gradient-based optimisation come with problems, we find straight-through gradient estimators (Bengio et al., 2013) very effective to compute informative discrete intermediate representations even for complicated attention scenarios. Similar results have been reported for other fields as well, both practically (Sahoo et al., 2022) and in theoretical analysis (Yin et al., 2019). Therefore, we propose two models, one for interpretable sequence transduction and one for joint segmentation and segment classification, based on straight-through gradient estimators.

6 Conclusion

In this work, we propose to optimise hard attention as building block in deep neural networks, which in principle is non-differentiable, by straight-through gradient estimation. In particular, we describe applications to interpretable sequence-to-sequence models and sequence segmentation models. We evaluate our approaches on two important tasks in computational morphology, namely morphological inflection and interlinear glossing which are shared tasks of the ACL SIGMORPHON 2023 workshop. Our approaches achieve good results in morphological inflection despite of constrained expressivity compared to fully differentiable models, and strong results in interlinear glossing. These results provide encouraging evidence that learning interpretable intermediate representations by deep neural network does not necessarily lead to intolerable sacrifices in performance. We hope that future work can benefit from these insights by combining interpretable representations and the generalisation abilities of neural models for scientific discovery.

Acknowledgements

We thank the organisers of both shared tasks for their efforts and for their help during training and evaluation phases. Also, we thank Çağrı Çöltekin for his feedback on a draft version of this paper and Leonard Salewski for a helpful discussion in the early phase of this project.

References

Roee Aharoni and Yoav Goldberg. 2017. Morphological inflection generation with hard monotonic attention. In *Proceedings of the 55th Annual Meeting of the Association for Computational Linguistics (Volume 1: Long Papers)*, pages 2004–2015, Vancouver, Canada. Association for Computational Linguistics.

Takuya Akiba, Shotaro Sano, Toshihiko Yanase, Takeru Ohta, and Masanori Koyama. 2019. Optuna: A next-generation hyperparameter optimization framework. In *Proceedings of the 25th ACM SIGKDD International Conference on Knowledge Discovery and Data Mining*.

Dzmitry Bahdanau, Kyunghyun Cho, and Yoshua Bengio. 2015. Neural machine translation by jointly learning to align and translate. In *3rd International Conference on Learning Representations, ICLR 2015, San Diego, CA, USA, May 7-9, 2015, Conference Track Proceedings*.

Yoshua Bengio, Nicholas Léonard, and Aaron C. Courville. 2013. Estimating or propagating gradients through stochastic neurons for conditional computation. *CoRR*, abs/1308.3432.

Gianni Brauwers and Flavius Frasincar. 2023. A general survey on attention mechanisms in deep learning. *IEEE Trans. Knowl. Data Eng.*, 35(4):3279–3298.

Nadia Burkart and Marco F. Huber. 2021. A survey on the explainability of supervised machine learning. *J. Artif. Intell. Res.*, 70:245–317.

Chundra Cathcart and Florian Wandl. 2020. In search of isoglosses: continuous and discrete language embeddings in Slavic historical phonology. In *Proceedings of the 17th SIGMORPHON Workshop on Computational Research in Phonetics, Phonology, and Morphology*, pages 233–244, Online. Association for Computational Linguistics.

Bernard Comrie, Martin Haspelmath, and Balthasar Bickel. 2008. The leipzig glossing rules: Conventions for interlinear morpheme-by-morpheme glosses. *Department of Linguistics of the Max Planck Institute for Evolutionary Anthropology & the Department of Linguistics of the University of Leipzig*.

Omer Goldman, Khuyagbaatar Batsuren, Khalifa Salam, Aryaman Arora, Garrett Nicolai, Reyt Tsarfaty, and Ekaterina Vylomova. 2023. SIGMORPHON–UniMorph 2023 shared task 0: Typologically diverse morphological inflection. In *Proceedings of the 20th SIGMORPHON Workshop on Computational Research in Phonetics, Phonology, and Morphology*, Toronto, Canada. Association for Computational Linguistics.

Alex Graves, Santiago Fernández, Faustino J. Gomez, and Jürgen Schmidhuber. 2006. Connectionist temporal classification: labelling unsegmented sequence data with recurrent neural networks. In *Machine Learning, Proceedings of the Twenty-Third International Conference (ICML 2006), Pittsburgh, Pennsylvania, USA, June 25-29, 2006*, volume 148 of *ACM International Conference Proceeding Series*, pages 369–376. ACM.

Alex Graves and Jürgen Schmidhuber. 2005. Framewise phoneme classification with bidirectional LSTM and other neural network architectures. *Neural Networks*, 18(5-6):602–610.

Sepp Hochreiter and Jürgen Schmidhuber. 1997. Long short-term memory. *Neural Comput.*, 9(8):1735–1780.

Andreas Holzinger, Anna Saranti, Christoph Molnar, Przemyslaw Biecek, and Wojciech Samek. 2020. Explainable AI methods - A brief overview. In *xxAI - Beyond Explainable AI - International Workshop, Held in Conjunction with ICML 2020, July 18, 2020, Vienna, Austria, Revised and Extended Papers*, volume 13200 of *Lecture Notes in Computer Science*, pages 13–38. Springer.

Sarthak Jain and Byron C. Wallace. 2019. Attention is not Explanation. In *Proceedings of the 2019 Conference of the North American Chapter of the Association for Computational Linguistics: Human Language Technologies, Volume 1 (Long and Short Papers)*, pages 3543–3556, Minneapolis, Minnesota. Association for Computational Linguistics.

Eric Jang, Shixiang Gu, and Ben Poole. 2017. Categorical reparameterization with gumbel-softmax. In *5th International Conference on Learning Representations, ICLR 2017, Toulon, France, April 24-26, 2017, Conference Track Proceedings*. OpenReview.net.

Yiding Jiang, Behnam Neyshabur, Hossein Mobahi, Dilip Krishnan, and Samy Bengio. 2020. Fantastic generalization measures and where to find them. In *8th International Conference on Learning Representations, ICLR 2020, Addis Ababa, Ethiopia, April 26-30, 2020*. OpenReview.net.

Katharina Kann, Ryan Cotterell, and Hinrich Schütze. 2016. Neural morphological analysis: Encoding-decoding canonical segments. In *Proceedings of the 2016 Conference on Empirical Methods in Natural Language Processing*, pages 961–967, Austin, Texas. Association for Computational Linguistics.

Yoon Kim, Carl Denton, Luong Hoang, and Alexander M. Rush. 2017. Structured attention networks. In *5th International Conference on Learning Representations, ICLR 2017, Toulon, France, April 24-26, 2017, Conference Track Proceedings*. OpenReview.net.

Jingwen Li and Leander Girrbach. 2022. Word segmentation and morphological parsing for sanskrit. *arXiv preprint arXiv:2201.12833*.

Jindřich Libovický and Jindřich Helcl. 2018. End-to-end non-autoregressive neural machine translation with connectionist temporal classification. In *Proceedings of the 2018 Conference on Empirical Methods in Natural Language Processing*, pages 3016–3021, Brussels, Belgium. Association for Computational Linguistics.

Hairong Liu, Zhenyao Zhu, Xiangang Li, and Sanjeev Satheesh. 2017. Gram-ctc: Automatic unit selection and target decomposition for sequence labelling. In *Proceedings of the 34th International Conference on Machine Learning, ICML 2017, Sydney, NSW, Australia, 6-11 August 2017*, volume 70 of *Proceedings of Machine Learning Research*, pages 2188–2197. PMLR.

Ilya Loshchilov and Frank Hutter. 2019. Decoupled weight decay regularization. In *7th International Conference on Learning Representations, ICLR 2019, New Orleans, LA, USA, May 6-9, 2019*. OpenReview.net.

Thang Luong, Hieu Pham, and Christopher D. Manning. 2015. Effective approaches to attention-based neural machine translation. In *Proceedings of the 2015 Conference on Empirical Methods in Natural Language Processing*, pages 1412–1421, Lisbon, Portugal. Association for Computational Linguistics.

Chris J. Maddison, Andriy Mnih, and Yee Whye Teh. 2017. The concrete distribution: A continuous relaxation of discrete random variables. In *5th International Conference on Learning Representations, ICLR 2017, Toulon, France, April 24-26, 2017, Conference Track Proceedings*. OpenReview.net.

Peter Makarov and Simon Clematide. 2018a. Imitation learning for neural morphological string transduction. In *Proceedings of the 2018 Conference on Empirical Methods in Natural Language Processing*, pages 2877–2882, Brussels, Belgium. Association for Computational Linguistics.

Peter Makarov and Simon Clematide. 2018b. Neural transition-based string transduction for limited-resource setting in morphology. In *Proceedings of the 27th International Conference on Computational Linguistics*, pages 83–93, Santa Fe, New Mexico, USA. Association for Computational Linguistics.

Clara Meister, Stefan Lazov, Isabelle Augenstein, and Ryan Cotterell. 2021. Is sparse attention more interpretable? In *Proceedings of the 59th Annual Meeting of the Association for Computational Linguistics and the 11th International Joint Conference on Natural Language Processing (Volume 2: Short Papers)*, pages 122–129, Online. Association for Computational Linguistics.

Mathias Niepert, Pasquale Minervini, and Luca Franceschi. 2021. Implicit MLE: backpropagating through discrete exponential family distributions. In *Advances in Neural Information Processing Systems 34: Annual Conference on Neural Information Processing Systems 2021, NeurIPS 2021, December 6-14, 2021, virtual*, pages 14567–14579.

Adam Paszke, Sam Gross, Francisco Massa, Adam Lerer, James Bradbury, Gregory Chanan, Trevor Killeen, Zeming Lin, Natalia Gimelshein, Luca Antiga, Alban Desmaison, Andreas Kopf, Edward Yang, Zachary DeVito, Martin Raison, Alykhan Tejani, Sasank Chilamkurthy, Benoit Steiner, Lu Fang, Junjie Bai, and Soumith Chintala. 2019. Pytorch: An imperative style, high-performance deep learning library. In H. Wallach, H. Larochelle, A. Beygelzimer, F. d'Alché-Buc, E. Fox, and R. Garnett, editors, *Advances in Neural Information Processing Systems 32*, pages 8024–8035. Curran Associates, Inc.

Ben Peters and André F. T. Martins. 2019. IT–IST at the SIGMORPHON 2019 shared task: Sparse two-headed models for inflection. In *Proceedings of the 16th Workshop on Computational Research in Phonetics, Phonology, and Morphology*, pages 50–56, Florence, Italy. Association for Computational Linguistics.

Ben Peters and André F. T. Martins. 2020. One-size-fits-all multilingual models. In *Proceedings of the 17th SIGMORPHON Workshop on Computational Research in Phonetics, Phonology, and Morphology*, pages 63–69, Online. Association for Computational Linguistics.

Colin Raffel, Minh-Thang Luong, Peter J. Liu, Ron J. Weiss, and Douglas Eck. 2017. Online and linear-time attention by enforcing monotonic alignments. In *Proceedings of the 34th International Conference on Machine Learning, ICML 2017, Sydney, NSW, Australia, 6-11 August 2017*, volume 70 of *Proceedings of Machine Learning Research*, pages 2837–2846. PMLR.

Sukrut Rao, Moritz Böhle, and Bernt Schiele. 2022. Towards better understanding attribution methods. In *IEEE/CVF Conference on Computer Vision and Pattern Recognition, CVPR 2022, New Orleans, LA, USA, June 18-24, 2022*, pages 10213–10222. IEEE.

Subham Sekhar Sahoo, Anselm Paulus, Marin Vlastelica, Vít Musil, Volodymyr Kuleshov, and Georg Martius. 2022. Backpropagation through combinatorial algorithms: Identity with projection works. *arXiv preprint arXiv:2205.15213*.

Shiv Shankar, Siddhant Garg, and Sunita Sarawagi. 2018. Surprisingly easy hard-attention for sequence to sequence learning. In *Proceedings of the 2018 Conference on Empirical Methods in Natural Language Processing*, pages 640–645, Brussels, Belgium. Association for Computational Linguistics.

Aäron van den Oord, Oriol Vinyals, and Koray Kavukcuoglu. 2017. Neural discrete representation learning. In *Advances in Neural Information Processing Systems 30: Annual Conference on Neural Information Processing Systems 2017, December 4-9, 2017, Long Beach, CA, USA*, pages 6306–6315.

Sarah Wiegreffe and Yuval Pinter. 2019. Attention is not not explanation. In *Proceedings of the 2019 Confer-*

ence on Empirical Methods in Natural Language Processing and the 9th International Joint Conference on Natural Language Processing (EMNLP-IJCNLP), pages 11–20, Hong Kong, China. Association for Computational Linguistics.

Shijie Wu and Ryan Cotterell. 2019. Exact hard monotonic attention for character-level transduction. In *Proceedings of the 57th Annual Meeting of the Association for Computational Linguistics*, pages 1530–1537, Florence, Italy. Association for Computational Linguistics.

Shijie Wu, Pamela Shapiro, and Ryan Cotterell. 2018. Hard non-monotonic attention for character-level transduction. In *Proceedings of the 2018 Conference on Empirical Methods in Natural Language Processing*, pages 4425–4438, Brussels, Belgium. Association for Computational Linguistics.

Kelvin Xu, Jimmy Ba, Ryan Kiros, Kyunghyun Cho, Aaron C. Courville, Ruslan Salakhutdinov, Richard S. Zemel, and Yoshua Bengio. 2015. Show, attend and tell: Neural image caption generation with visual attention. In *Proceedings of the 32nd International Conference on Machine Learning, ICML 2015, Lille, France, 6-11 July 2015*, volume 37 of *JMLR Workshop and Conference Proceedings*, pages 2048–2057. JMLR.org.

Penghang Yin, Jiancheng Lyu, Shuai Zhang, Stanley J. Osher, Yingyong Qi, and Jack Xin. 2019. Understanding straight-through estimator in training activation quantized neural nets. In *7th International Conference on Learning Representations, ICLR 2019, New Orleans, LA, USA, May 6-9, 2019*. OpenReview.net.

Lei Yu, Jan Buys, and Phil Blunsom. 2016. Online segment to segment neural transduction. In *Proceedings of the 2016 Conference on Empirical Methods in Natural Language Processing*, pages 1307–1316, Austin, Texas. Association for Computational Linguistics.

A Experimental Setup

Here, we describe our experimental setup, including hyperparameters, in detail. Also note that our code is available on GitHub. Code for morphological inflection is here: `https://github.com/LGirrbach/sigmorphon-2023-glossing`. Code for interlinear glossing is here: `https://github.com/LGirrbach/sigmorphon-2023-inflection`. All models are implemented in `PyTorch` (Paszke et al., 2019) and `pytorch_lightning`.[3]

In all cases, models are optimised using the AdamW optimizer (Loshchilov and Hutter, 2019) without weight decay, learning rate is 0.001, and all other parameters are the PyTorch defaults. We use an exponential decay learning rate scheduler which multiplies the learning rate by factor γ after each epoch. We tune γ for each combination of model and language. Furthermore, we clip gradients with absolute value greater than 1.

Models are trained exclusively on the training splits provided by the shared task organisers. After each training epoch, generalisation performance is estimated by performance on the validation split. In the case of Morphological Inflection, our main metric is normalised edit distance (lower is better). In the case of Interlinear Glossing, our main metric is accuracy of correctly predicted glossing lines (higher is better). If performance does not improve for 3 epochs, training is stopped. Only the best model checkpoint, i.e. the checkpoint 3 epochs before ending training, is retained.

A.1 Hyperparameter Tuning

For each combination of language and model, we optimise hyperparameters independently. The tuned hyperparameters and their corresponding value ranges are in Table 3. Note that other than stated there, the minimum batch size for Morphological Inflection models is always 4. Also, minimum batch size for Arapaho and Uspanteko languages (Interlinear Glossing) is 16. The maximum batch size for Arapaho and Uspanteko is 128. The maximum batch size for Gitksan (Interlinear Glossing) is 16.

In each case, we sample 50 sets of hyperparameters using the `optuna` library (Akiba et al., 2019). For each sampled set, a model is trained and the performance on the validation set is recorded. After sampling 50 sets, the set that resulted in the best performance on the validation set is saved. For training models for submission of results to the shared tasks and all other analyses, we exclusively use hyperparameter that were found best in this hyperparameter study. Since we tune parameters for many models, we do not report the results here. However, they are available in our GitHub repositories.

A.2 Main Evaluation

For submitting results to the shared tasks and further analyses, we retrain 5 models for each combination of model type and language. The models use the hyperparameters from the tuning study described in Appendix A.1. However, they have different initialisations and may therefore perform differently. For submitting results, we select the

[3] `https://github.com/Lightning-AI/lightning/`

Parameter Name	Range
# LSTM Layers	$\{1, 2\}$
Hidden Size	$[64; 512]$
Dropout	$[0.0; 0.5]$
Scheduler γ	$[0.9; 1.0]$
Batch Size	$[2; 64]$

Table 3: Ranges for values of tuned hyperparameters. Note that batch size ranges differ in some cases.

model the model with best performance on the validation set. Having multiple copies of the same model type trained with the same hyperparameters is useful, because especially in low-resource scenarios different initialisations can have a relevant impact on the generalisation performance. On the one hand, it is necessary to estimate this variance to see how robust models are, on the other hand this helps mitigating spurious effects in the analyses.

B Sequence Transduction Model: Detailed Description

Here, we provide a more detailed description of the sequence transduction model (see Section 3.1).

For training, we have two paired sequences $s = s_1, \ldots, s_n$ and $t = t_1, \ldots, t_m$, representing the source and target sequence, respectively. The goal is to maximise the likelihood of transducing the source sequence s to the target sequence t.

The first step is to represent all symbols in both sequences by high-dimensional non-contextual vectors, i.e. embeddings. Thus, we arrive at embedded sequences $\mathbf{s} = \mathbf{s}_1, \ldots, \mathbf{s}_n$ and $\mathbf{t} = \mathbf{t}_1, \ldots, \mathbf{t}_m$, with $\mathbf{s}_i, \mathbf{t} \in \mathbb{R}^d$. Here, boldfaced lowercase variables represent vectors. Furthermore, we denote the $n \times d$ matrix with source symbol embeddings as rows as $\mathbf{S} \in \mathbb{R}^{n \times d}$ and we denote the $m \times d$ matrix with all target symbol embeddings as $\mathbf{T} \in \mathbb{R}^{m \times d}$. Note, that embeddings of source symbols and target symbols are optimised independently of each other, i.e. they are not paired.

In the next step, we encode the source sequence by a *bidirectional* LSTM and arrive at a contextual representation $\mathbf{h}_i^s$ for each source symbol with index i, $1 \leq i \leq n$. Likewise, we encode the target sequence using a *unidirectional* LSTM and denote the autoregressive encoding of the symbol with index $j, 1 \leq j, \leq m$ as $\mathbf{h}_j^t$. Formally, we can write

$$\mathbf{h}_i^s = \mathrm{BiLSTM}(\mathbf{s}_i \mid \mathbf{s}_1, \ldots, \mathbf{s}_n) \tag{3}$$
$$\mathbf{h}_j^t = \mathrm{LSTM}(\mathbf{t}_j \mid \mathbf{t}_1, \ldots, \mathbf{t}_{j-1}) \tag{4}$$

and representing all contextualised representations as matrices:

$$\mathbf{H}^s = \mathrm{BiLSTM}(\mathbf{S}) \tag{5}$$
$$\mathbf{H}^t = \mathrm{LSTM}(\mathbf{T}) \tag{6}$$

So far, this formulation is the same as conventional LSTM-based encoder-decoder models. However, the attention mechanism is different. According to the descriptions in Section 2 and Section 3.1, we define attention matrices as follows:

$$\mathbf{Z} = \mathbf{H}^s \cdot (\mathbf{H}^t)^T \tag{7}$$
$$\hat{\xi}_{\text{symbol}} = \mathrm{softmax}(\mathbf{Z}) \tag{8}$$
$$\hat{\xi}_{\text{cond}} = \sigma(\mathbf{Z}) \tag{9}$$

where $\mathbf{Z} \in \mathbb{R}^{n \times m}$ represents the unnormalised dot-product attention scores, $\mathrm{softmax}$ is applied to columns of $\mathbf{Z}$ and the sigmoid function σ is applied elementwise. In fact, it seems counterintuitive to use the same unnormalised scores in both attention heads, but this works well in practise. From these attention matrices, we obtain the discretised alignment matrices ξ_{symbol} and ξ_{cond} by sampling columnwise one-hot vectors in the case of ξ_{symbol} and elementwise values $\in \{0, 1\}$ for ξ_{cond}. Then, we calculate context vectors as

$$\mathbf{Y}_{\text{symbol}} = \xi_{\text{symbol}}^T \cdot \mathbf{S} \tag{10}$$
$$\mathbf{Y}_{\text{cond}} = \xi_{\text{cond}}^T \cdot \mathbf{S} \tag{11}$$

Note, that here we use the discretised alignment matrices ξ_{symbol} and ξ_{cond} in place of the real-valued matrices $\hat{\xi}_{\text{symbol}}$ and $\hat{\xi}_{\text{symbol}}$. Because discretisation is non-differentiable, we instead use a way of calculation that enables straight-through gradient estimation, namely Equation (1):

$$\mathbf{Y}_{\text{symbol}} = \hat{\xi}_{\text{symbol}}^T \cdot \mathbf{S} - \mathrm{sg}\left((\hat{\xi}_{\text{symbol}} - \xi_{\text{symbol}})^T \cdot \mathbf{S} \right) \tag{12}$$

$$\mathbf{Y}_{\text{cond}} = \hat{\xi}_{\text{cond}}^T \cdot \mathbf{S} - \mathrm{sg}\left((\hat{\xi}_{\text{cond}} - \xi_{\text{cond}})^T \cdot \mathbf{S} \right) \tag{13}$$

Finally, we predict a distribution over target symbols by a MLP from the concatenation of $\mathbf{Y}_{\text{symbol}}$ and $\mathbf{Y}_{\text{cond}}$ according to Equation (2):

$$p_j(\bullet \mid s_1, \ldots, s_n) = \text{MLP}([\mathbf{Y}_j^{\text{symbol}}, \mathbf{Y}_j^{\text{cond}}]) \tag{14}$$

where $p_j(\bullet \mid s_1, \ldots, s_n)$ indicates the distribution over target symbols at prediction position with index j. Here, the concrete ground truth target symbol is t_j.

To train the model, we use the typical supervised objective, namely minimising the cross-entropy between predicted categorical distributions over target symbols and the one-hot encoded ground truth target symbol at each prediction position. This also means we use teacher forcing for sequential predictions. During inference, t is predicted in a step-wise fashion by greedy decoding.

However, note that in addition to the setup described above, we also use the typical attention mechanism in a multi-tasking fashion, but only during training. We do not use contextualised source symbol representations for inference. The reason why we still use the typical loss as auxiliary loss is that the gradient signal on $\mathbf{H}^s$ and $\mathbf{H}^t$ is weak when their only role is to calculate $\mathbf{Z}$. In this case, we calculate

$$\mathbf{C} = \left(\text{softmax}\left(\mathbf{H}^s \cdot (\mathbf{H}^t)^T\right)\right)^T \cdot \mathbf{H}^s \tag{15}$$

where softmax is applied to columns, and then predict distributions over target symbols as

$$p_j^{\text{aux}}(\bullet \mid s_1, \ldots, s_n) = \text{MLP}(\mathbf{C}) \tag{16}$$

so that we can also calculate the cross-entropy loss on $p_j^{\text{aux}}(\bullet \mid s_1, \ldots, s_n)$ and differentiate model parameter w.r.t. the sum of both losses during training. Note, again, that this is only to stabilise training by optimising the contextual representations, and does not affect the model architecture for inference.

C Preprocessing of Japanese

The Japanese writing system includes 4 alphabets, namely Latin characters (Romaji), Chinese characters (Kanji), and two syllabic scripts (Katakana and Hiragana) that were derived from Chinese characters by simplification and standardisation. The Japanese dataset provided with the shared task contains Kanji, Hiragana, and Katakana. Kanji constitute a problem for character-level models, because they are effectively an open set. The number of Kanji taught in Japanese schools is already ≈ 2000, to which variants, obsolete Kanji, and special Kanji only used in names may be added. Therefore, a model for Japanese language data should have the possibility to process previously unseen Kanji.

In the case of morphological inflection, however, this problem may be ignored, because Kanji are never altered in inflection. Instead, inflectional suffixes are expressed in Hiragana. Kanji may still appear in stems, and have therefore be dealt with.

We apply the following preprocessing: We replace all Kanji by a special placeholder symbol K that is the same for every Kanji. This applies to both source lemmas and target forms. In the case of successful prediction of target lemmas, the number of Kanji in the target form is the same as the number of Kanji in the source lemma. Therefore, we copy Kanji from the source by replacing the predicted placeholders. The order of Kanji in source and target does not change. In case of predicting fewer placeholders in the predicted form than there are Kanji in the source lemma, which is an error, we copy as many Kanji as there are placeholders in the predicted form from left to right. In case of predicting more placeholders in the predicted form than there are Kanji in the source lemma, which also is an error, we leave additional placeholders unchanged, i.e. we do not change the predicted placeholder symbol, but still copy as many Kanji as possible from left to right.

D Full Results

Morphological Inflection In Table 5, we report the official test set accuracies achieved by our model for all languages. For comparison, we also show results of the neural and the non-neural baseline. Likewise, we report official test set edit distances in Table 6.

These results show some interesting patterns. For example, the neural baseline performs worst on Japanese, which we assume is an effect of the alphabet (see Appendix C). Therefore, our proposed pre- and postprocessing for Japanese is important. Alternatively, a copy mechanism could be used.

Another trend is that our model performs strongly on semitic languages (e.g. afb, amh, arz, heb, heb_unvoc), especially compared to the non-neural baseline. Here, non-concatenative morphology gives our model an advantage, because usually individual transforms do not involve multiple characters, such as suffix ngrams. Remember that our model can only predict exactly one form character

	Track 1				Track 2			
	Word Level		Morph. Level		Word Level		Morph. Level	
	CTC	Morph	CTC	Morph	CTC	Morph	CTC	Morph
Arapaho	77.90	78.79	76.56	78.57	85.12	85.80	90.93	91.37
Tsez	80.96	80.94	70.29	73.95	85.68	85.79	91.16	92.01
Gitksan	04.69	21.09	09.26	11.72	13.80	26.56	17.08	50.22
Lezgi	78.10	78.78	62.03	62.10	85.44	83.41	83.45	87.61
Natugu	80.20	81.04	56.38	56.32	87.83	87.92	90.17	92.32
Nyangbo	85.34	85.05	86.74	85.24	85.90	87.98	89.96	91.40
Uspanteko	68.86	71.01	60.42	62.55	77.21	78.46	83.45	84.51

Table 4: Interlinear glossing: Official test set accuracies for all languages. Higher is better. CTC refers to our CTC-based baseline model, "Morph" refers to our model that learns morphological segmentation in a unsupervised way for track 1. In track 2, we simply use the provided representation.

from each combination of transduction lemma character and condition set. This shows that our model is able to capture complex patterns, but may not be optimal to generate extensive surface transforms.

Interlinear Glossing In Table 4, we report official test set accuracies achieved by our models for all languages. In most cases, our Morph model is superior to the CTC model, which confirms the benefit of morpheme segmentations for the task of interlinear glossing. The same conclusion is supported by the stark differences between track 1 and track 2. In track 2, performance is generally much better, especially when looking at morpheme level accuracies. Remember that we only use the ground-truth morpheme segmentation as additional information in track 2. We conclude that research in morpheme segmentation will be useful for computational models for interlinear glossing as well.

	Ours	Neural	¬ Neural
afb	75.8	80.1	30.8
amh	83.8	82.2	65.4
arz	87.6	89.6	77.9
bel	56.3	74.5	68.1
dan	85.7	88.8	89.5
deu	74.5	83.7	79.8
eng	96.0	95.1	96.6
fin	67.6	85.4	80.8
fra	67.9	73.3	77.7
grc	36.7	54.0	52.6
heb	82.7	92.0	30.9
heb(2)	81.3	83.2	64.5
hun	75.9	80.5	74.7
hye	85.9	91.0	86.3
ita	84.7	94.1	75.0
jap	95.3	26.3	64.1
kat	70.5	84.5	82.0
klr	96.4	99.5	54.5
mkd	86.7	93.8	91.6
nav	53.6	52.1	35.8
rus	82.1	90.5	86.0
san	54.5	66.3	62.2
sme	58.5	74.8	56.0
spa	88.7	93.6	87.8
sqi	71.5	85.9	83.4
swa	94.7	93.7	60.5
tur	81.8	95.0	64.6

Table 5: Official test set accuracies for all languages. Higher is better. "Neural" and "¬ Neural" refer to the neural and non-neural baseline, respectively. "heb(2)" refers to the `heb_unvoc` dataset.

	Ours	Neural	¬ Neural
afb	0.49	0.38	1.47
amh	0.22	0.24	0.59
arz	0.24	0.22	0.46
bel	1.31	0.64	0.90
dan	0.34	0.25	0.17
deu	1.00	0.48	0.80
eng	0.07	0.09	0.06
fin	0.63	0.21	0.26
fra	0.86	0.45	0.37
grc	1.43	1.00	1.04
heb	0.44	0.21	1.82
heb(2)	0.30	0.28	0.48
hun	0.57	0.44	0.47
hye	0.43	0.20	0.30
ita	0.43	0.12	0.75
jap	0.09	1.20	0.80
kat	0.79	0.35	0.51
klr	0.05	0.00	0.84
mkd	0.38	0.09	0.15
nav	1.37	1.55	1.88
rus	0.56	0.38	0.46
san	1.01	0.71	0.90
sme	0.88	0.65	0.89
spa	0.31	0.10	0.17
sqi	0.74	0.27	0.38
swa	0.06	0.06	4.10
tur	0.58	0.17	0.87

Table 6: Official test set edit distances for all languages. Lower is better. "Neural" and "¬ Neural" refer to the neural and non-neural baseline, respectively. "heb(2)" refers to the `heb_unvoc` dataset.

Findings of the SIGMORPHON 2023 Shared Task on Interlinear Glossing

Michael Ginn[◇] **Sarah Moeller**[♣] **Alexis Palmer**[◇] **Anna Stacey**[♠]
Garrett Nicolai[♠] **Mans Hulden**[◇] **Miikka Silfverberg**[♠]
[◇]University of Colorado Boulder [♣]University of Florida
[♠]University of British Columbia
michael.ginn@colorado.edu miikka.silfverberg@ubc.ca

Abstract

This paper presents the findings of the SIGMORPHON 2023 Shared Task on Interlinear Glossing. This first iteration of the shared task explores glossing of a set of six typologically diverse languages: Arapaho, Gitksan, Lezgi, Natügu, Tsez and Uspanteko. The shared task encompasses two tracks: a resource-scarce closed track and an open track, where participants are allowed to utilize external data resources. Five teams participated in the shared task. The winning team Tü-CL achieved a 23.99%-point improvement over a baseline RoBERTa system in the closed track and a 17.42%-point improvement in the open track.

1 Introduction

Roughly half of the world's languages are currently endangered (Seifart et al., 2018). As a result, language preservation and revitalization have become significant areas of focus in linguistic research. Both of these endeavors require thorough documentation of the language, which is crucial for creating grammatical descriptions, dictionaries, and educational materials that aid in language revitalization. However, traditional manual language documentation is a time-consuming and resource-intensive process due to the costs associated with collecting, transcribing, and annotating linguistic data. Therefore, there is a need to expedite the documentation process through the use of automated methods. While these methods can never fully replace the expertise of a dedicated documentary linguist, they have the potential to greatly facilitate and accelerate the annotation of linguistic data (Palmer et al., 2009).

Linguistic annotation involves several interconnected subtasks, including: (1) transcription of speech recordings, (2) morphological segmentation of transcribed speech, (3) glossing of segmented morphemes, and (4) translation of the transcriptions into a matrix language, such as English. These processes result in a semi-structured output known as an interlinear gloss, as demonstrated in the Natügu example below:

(1) ma yrkr-tx-o-kz-Ø .
house finish-INTS-GDIR.DOWN-also-3MINIS .
Houses were gone too.

This paper presents the findings of the SIGMORPHON 2023 Shared Task on Interlinear Glossing[1], which focuses on automating step (3) of the language documentation pipeline. Notably, this shared task represents the first initiative specifically dedicated to interlinear glossing. Despite the prevalence of interlinear glossed text as a data format in language documentation, the automatic generation of glossed text remains relatively underexplored in the field of natural language processing (NLP). We hope that this shared task can help stimulate further work in automated glossing.

2 Background

Existing work in data driven automated glossing has utilized both traditional feature-based approaches like maximum entropy classifiers (MEMM) (Ratnaparkhi, 1996) and conditional random fields (CRF) (Lafferty et al., 2001) as well as more recent neural models like LSTM encoder-decoders (Sutskever et al., 2014) and transformers (Vaswani et al., 2017). Palmer et al. (2009) investigate active learning for interlinear glossing using the MEMM architecture. McMillan-Major (2020) incorporated translations as auxiliary supervision in a CRF glossing model. Moeller and Hulden (2018) and Barriga Martínez et al. (2021) compare traditional feature-based models and LSTM encoder-decoder models. Zhao et al. (2020) present a modified multi-source transformer model which incorporates translations as auxiliary supervision.

The current literature on automatic glossing exhibits notable gaps, as several techniques that have

[1] https://github.com/sigmorphon/2023glossingST

Proceedings of the 20th SIGMORPHON workshop on Computational Research in Phonetics, Phonology, and Morphology, pages 186–201
July 14, 2023

proven valuable for other morphology tasks have yet to be explored for glossing. There are several intriguing directions for future research, including:

1. Crosslingual training (Çöltekin, 2019; Anastasopoulos and Neubig, 2019) has shown promise for morphological inflection and could be investigated for its potential in glossing.

2. Incorporating additional noisy training data (Wiemerslage et al., 2023) can improve accuracy for low-resource inflection and could help improve the performance of glossing models as well. In the context of interlinear glossing, this data could come from large multilingual databases like ODIN (Lewis and Xia, 2010) which is automatically created with the aid of web crawling and is known to be noisy.

3. Data augmentation techniques (Liu and Hulden, 2021; Anastasopoulos and Neubig, 2019; Silfverberg et al., 2017) are now a well-established technique in morphological inflection and could enhance the training process for glossing models.

4. Hard attention models (Aharoni and Goldberg, 2017; Makarov et al., 2017) have delivered strong performance for several morphology tasks in low-resource settings and could also be applied to interlinear glossing.

5. Multitask training (Rama and Çöltekin, 2018) and meta-learning (Kann et al., 2020) techniques could be leveraged to enhance glossing performance.

6. Finally, pretrained language models like ByT5 (Xue et al., 2022) have demonstrated strong performance in various morphology tasks, yet their potential for interlinear glossing remains unexplored.

The submissions in this shared task explore several of these techniques, including the use of pretrained language models, data augmentation, utilization of external data, and the application of hard attention models.

3 Tasks and Evaluation

3.1 Interlinear Glossed Text

Interlinear Glossed Text (IGT) serves as a means to capture the syntactic and morphological characteristics of words within a corpus. It is a semi-structured format which lacks strict annotation standards, leading to variations in annotation practices among different annotators. These variations can be influenced by documentation requirements, adopted theoretical frameworks, and other factors (Palmer et al., 2009).

For this shared task, the data adheres to the Leipzig glossing conventions (Lehmann, 1982). The Leipzig format follows a three-line documentation style, including morphological segmentation of the input tokens, glosses of individual morphemes, and translations. Below is an example from Arapaho, one of the languages used in the shared task:

(2) nih-bii3ihi-noo nohkuseic
2S.PAST-eat-1S morning
I ate this morning.

In this example, the first line represents the morphological segmentation, the second line provides glosses for each morpheme, and the third line presents the corresponding translation.

The transcription line (*nih-bii3ihi-noo nohkuseic* in Example 2) gives the orthographic transcription of a sentence, phrase or utterance in the source language. The transcription may be segmented with dashes to indicate morpheme boundaries.

The gloss line ("2S.PAST-eat-1S morning" in Example 2) provides a linguistic gloss for each morpheme in the transcription line. For glossing, morphemes are grouped into two distinct categories:

1. *Functional morphemes* or *grams* include affixes and functional words which do not carry their own lexical meaning. Functional morphemes are glossed using uppercase labels like 1S (first-person singular affix) which indicate grammatical category and/or syntactic function. Portmanteau morphs, which denote multiple functions, can be glossed using compound labels like 2S.PAST. Gloss labels typically come from a fixed inventory like UniMorph (Sylak-Glassman, 2016; Kirov et al., 2018; Batsuren et al., 2022b), although conventions are not standardized and are often varied to fit the needs of the language.

2. In contrast to functional morphemes, *lexical morphemes* or *stems* are open-class words and stems which carry semantic meaning. These are glossed in lowercase using their translation

in a matrix language like English or Spanish; thus, for example, *bii3ihi* is glossed as *eat*.

The translation line ('I ate this morning.' in Example 2) of an IGT entry provides a translation in a high-resource language such as English. The tokens in the translation are not necessarily aligned with specific words in the source language, as languages often express equivalent concepts in differing numbers of words.

3.2 The Interlinear Glossing Task

The objective of the shared task is to develop automated systems capable of predicting the gloss of a given input utterance, using its orthographic transcription and translation as input. The glossing task presents several key challenges, such as disambiguation of ambiguous morphemes and accurate translation of word stems. The shared task explores two distinct resource settings, referred to as tracks, which differ in terms of the supervision provided during model training and at test-time.

The Closed Track (Track 1) In the closed track, the input consists of the orthographic transcription of the target utterance, for example, *nihbii3ihinoo nohkuseic* (Arapaho), and its translation to a matrix language like English: 'I ate this morning' (note the lack of morpheme boundaries in the transcription). The aim is to generate a gloss `2S.PAST-eat-1S morning`. This setting poses a significant challenge since the glossing model does not have access to a morphological segmentation of the input utterance. Therefore, it must infer the number of morphemes and the identity of the component morphemes for each input word without any supervision. The closed setting draws inspiration from the work of Zhao et al. (2020), which utilizes a similar setup.

The Open Track (Track 2) In a practical language documentation setting, various types of resources can be available as auxiliary supervision when training glossing systems. These resources may include manually glossed text, morphological segmentations, dictionaries, raw text in the target language, and more. The open track aims to explore the extent of glossing performance achievable when participants are allowed to utilize auxiliary resources. In addition to the data provided in the closed track, morphological segmentations are provided in the open track. For instance, for the Arapaho example mentioned earlier, a morphological segmentation *nih-bii3ihi-noo nohkuseic* would be included. Gold standard segmentations are provided both for model training and at test-time. Moreover, participants are encouraged to make use of external data resources except for additional glossed text in the target language.

3.3 Evaluation of Glossing Performance

We evaluate glossing performance with regard to two metrics: word-level and morpheme-level glossing accuracy. Word-level glossing accuracy is defined as the fraction of words in the test data which received a fully correct gloss like `2S.PAST-eat-1S`:

$$\mathrm{w}_{acc} = \frac{\text{Count(correctly glossed tokens)}}{\text{Count(all tokens)}} \quad (1)$$

Note that all the individual morphemes in the word have to be correctly glossed. In contrast, morpheme-level glossing accuracy is defined as the fraction of morphemes in the test data which received the correct gloss:

$$\mathrm{m}_{acc} = \frac{\text{Count(correctly glossed morphemes)}}{\text{Count(all morphemes)}} \quad (2)$$

In the closed track, where gold standard morphological segmentations are not provided, it may happen that the system predicts too few or too many glosses for an input word. This complicates computation of morpheme-level glossing accuracy. When too few morphemes are predicted, we pad the predictions with `NULL` morphemes until the number of morphemes corresponds to the gold standard gloss (e.g. `2S.PAST-eat` $\rightarrow$ `2S.PAST-eat-NULL`). When too many morphemes are predicted, we discard extra morphemes at the end of the output (e.g. `2S.PAST-eat-1S-PL` $\rightarrow$ `2S.PAST-eat-1S`).

For the official shared task results, we compute accuracy over multiple languages. We then report micro average glossing accuracy across the different languages. Micro average word-level glossing accuracy is used for the official ranking of the participating submissions.

3.4 Comparison to Other NLP Tasks

While interlinear glossing forms a distinct and interesting NLP task in its own right, it has connections to many commonly explored NLP tasks, particularly part-of-speech (POS) tagging, lemmatization, morphological tagging[2], and morphological segmentation (McCarthy et al., 2019; Cotterell and

[2]Also known as morphological analysis in context.

Heigold, 2017; Müller et al., 2015; Batsuren et al., 2022a). All of these tasks involve varying degrees of grammatical analysis.

Interlinear glossing is particularly strongly connected to morphological tagging as both involve morphological annotation in context. However, there are two major differences between the tasks:

1. In interlinear glossing, a morpheme-level annotation of the input sentence is generated. The output of a glossing model provides the order of various morphological elements in the input tokens, indicating the position of different affixal elements. In contrast, morphological tagging provides a more abstracted representation where the order of morphemes is lost.

2. Another difference between morphological tagging and interlinear glossing is related to the treatment of lexical elements. In morphological tagging, it is common to return the lemma of input words along with the associated grammatical information of the inflected input word. In glossing, on the other hand, it is common to annotate word forms with a translation of the input lexeme in a matrix language like English. This substantial difference between the tasks introduces elements of machine translation into the morphology task.

Following the approaches of McMillan-Major (2020) and Zhao et al. (2020), the shared task datasets provide gold standard translations of the input sentences as additional supervision during both training and test time. Thus, the task of lexeme translation involves retrieving the lemma of the correct lexemes from the provided translation.

4 Data

4.1 Languages and Glossed Data

Arapaho [arp] is an Algonquian language with a few hundred speakers in Wyoming, USA. It is highly agglutinating and polysynthetic, with the verb carrying the heaviest morphological load (Cowell and Moss, 2008). Polysynthesis in Arapaho includes noun incorporation, where special forms of certain nouns become part of the verb. The corpus used in this shared task contains narratives and conversation that have been documented starting in the 1880s until the present day, including a few religious texts that are translations from English. It is written in the popular Arapaho orthography. Much of the data is available through the Endangered Languages Archive[3] or the Center for the Study of Indigenous Languages of the West[4].

Gitksan [git] The Gitksan are one of the Indigenous peoples of the northern interior region of British Columbia, Canada. Today, Gitksan is the most vital Tsimshianic language, but is still critically endangered with an estimated 300-850 speakers (Dunlop et al., 2018). The language has an "analytic to synthetic" morphology (Rigsby, 1986, 1989) and, unlike many Canadian Indigenous languages, it is not polysynthetic. It has a rich assortment of derivational morphemes and substantial capacity for compounding; consequently, its degree of word-complexity has been described as similar to German (Tarpent, 1987). The data used for the shared task were extracted from a paper containing three stories by the Gitksan elders Barbara Sennot, Hector Hill and Vincent Gogag (Forbes et al., 2017).

Lezgi [lez] (aka Lezgian) is a Nakh-Daghestanian (Northeast Caucasian) language spoken by over 500,000 speakers in Russia and Azerbaijan (Eberhard et al., 2023). The corpus used is from the Qusar dialect in Azerbaijan (Donet, 2014). It is a highly agglutinative language with overwhelmingly suffixing morphology (Haspelmath, 1993). Noun cases are formed by case-stacking which is a unique characteristic of Nakh-Daghestanian languages. Instead of a unique morpheme for each case, case-stacking composes case inflections by "stacking" sequences of case suffixes as illustrated in Table 1.

Natügu [ntu] belongs to the Reefs-Santa Cruz group in the Austronesian family. It is spoken by about 4,000 people in the Temotu Province of the Solomon Islands. It has primarily agglutinative morphology with complex verb structures (Åshild Næss and Boerger, 2008). The corpus used for the shared task contains transcribed narratives and a large written text.[5]

Tsez [ddo] (aka Dido) belongs to the Tsez-Hinukh branch of the Nakh-Daghestanian family.

[3] https://elar.soas.ac.uk/Collection/MPI189644

[4] https://www.colorado.edu/center/csilw/arapaho-language-archives

[5] Natqgu grammar and large text available at https://www.langlxmelanesia.com/tilp

```
\t heetne'ii'P woowooyoo'ohk heet-ne'ii'cencei'soo'
\m heet-ne'ii'-P woo-wooyoo'-ohk heet-ne'ii'-cen-cei'soo-'
\g FUT-that's.when-pause REDUP-new-SUBJ FUT-that's.when-very-different-0S
\l It will be , pretty soon it will all be different  [ from how it is now ].
```

Figure 1: A glossed Arapaho sentence in the official shared task format for the open track (i.e. track 2).

WORD FORM	GLOSS
itim	SG.ABS 'man'
itim-ar	PL.ABS 'men'
itim-ar-di	PL-ERG 'men'
itim-di-k	OBL-AD.ESS 'near a man'
itim-di-k-di	OBL-AD-DIR 'toward a man'
itim-ar-di-k-ay	PL-OBL-AD-EL 'from men'

Table 1: A simplified example of Lezgi case-stacking on the noun root *itim* 'man'. Absolutive (ABS) and essive (ESS) cases and singular number (SG) are marked by null morphemes. The plural suffix (PL) attaches directly to the noun stem. The ergative (ERG) and the oblique (OBL) suffixes attach after the number. The adessive case (AD.ESS) attaches to the oblique suffix. The elative (EL) and directive (DIR) cases are added in the fourth slot after the root.

It has about 14,000 speakers in Daghestan, Russia. It has a rich agglutinative, suffixing morphology. The corpus is part of the Tsez Annotated Corpus Project (Comrie et al., 2022; Abdulaev and Abdullaev, 2010).[6]

Tutrugbu [nyb] (aka Nyagbo, Nyangbo) is a Niger-Congo language with a few thousand estimated speakers in Ghana (Eberhard et al., 2023). It is a highly agglutinative language that features some reduplication (Essegbey, 2019). The corpus from which the shared task data was extracted contains a variety of spontaneous data supplemented with elicited data collected with a range of documentary techniques.[7]

Uspanteko [usp] (aka Uspantek) belongs to the K'ichean branch of the Mayan language family spoken by as many as 6000 speakers in the Guatemalan highlands and in diaspora communities (Bennett et al., 2016). Uspanteko is a lightly agglutinative language with complex verbal morphology and ergative-absolutive alignment (Coon, 2016). Uspanteko is unusual among Mayan languages for its use of contrastive lexical tone (Bennett et al., 2022).[8] The texts were collected, transcribed, translated and annotated as part of an OKMA Mayan language documentation project (Pixabaj et al., 2007) and are currently accessible via the Archive of Indigenous Languages of Latin America.[9] The corpus includes oral histories, personal experience texts, and stories; preprocessing of the corpus is described in Palmer et al. (2010).

4.2 Shared Task Data

Shared task datasets were generated from original glossed source data in various formats (LaTeX, CLDF[10] and Flex[11]) using dedicated conversion scripts. We aimed to make minimal changes to the original glossed data while ensuring consistent annotation practices across languages. All morpheme boundaries were converted to a unified format using hyphens ("-"), all glossed word stems were lowercased (or titlecased in the case of proper nouns) and all affix glosses were uppercased. Apart from potential changes to casing, gloss symbols were not modified. Portmanteau morphs, where morpheme-boundaries cannot be identified, were glossed using a period syntax (".") as in the examples here.it.is and 2S.PAST.

An example of a glossed Arapaho sentence in the official shared task format is given in Figure 1. This entry comes from the open track (track 2), where morphological segmentations are provided. The following lines are included in the gloss:

`\t` the orthographic representation,

`\m` the morphological segmentation of the orthographic representation,

`\g` the gloss of the orthographic representation and

`\t` the English or Spanish translation.

[6] `https://tsezacp.clld.org/`

[7] 'Unpublished Nyangbo (Tutrugbu) texts' compiled by Dr. James Essegby

[8] Tone is not, however, marked in the shared task dataset.

[9] `https://ailla.utexas.edu`

[10] `https://cldf.clld.org/`

[11] `https://software.sil.org/fieldworks/`

The token counts in the transcription, segmentation and gloss of a given example have to match. However, the token count in the translation line is allowed to differ. Examples in the source data which did not follow this restriction were filtered out.

We split the datsets into non-overlapping training, development and test data. For languages where there was a clear division into separate texts, we aimed to use one complete text for development and testing, respectively, and the rest of the data for training. This was the case for Gitksan and Arapaho.[12] For the rest of the languages, we used 80% of the sentences for training, and 10% for development and testing, respectively. Statistics on data sizes are provided in Table 2. Note that the table gives token counts, not sentence counts, and the counts do not, therefore, exactly correspond to an 80-10-10 split.

Data characteristics The shared task datasets encompass a range of diverse data conditions. The training data size, as shown in Table 2, varies from approximately 140k tokens for Arapaho to a mere 261 tokens for Gitksan, with most languages having between 2k and 15k tokens of training data. With the potential exception of Arapaho and Uspanteko, all the languages qualify as low-resourced datasets. Additional characteristics of the datasets are presented in Table 3:

1. Type-token-ratio (TTR) for most languages falls within the 20-30% range with the notable exception of Gitksan where TTR is 61.3% which is likely to be related to the very small size of the training set.

2. We compute out-of-vocabulary (OOV) rates on the test set. For most languages, OOV rates are below 30% with Gitksan once again being a notable exception with OOV rate of 79.9%. In general, these rates are high compared to typical OOV rates for English text.

3. As a further analysis, we also report morpheme-level OOV rates on the test set, which can be more illuminating for morphologically complex languages. These fall below 10% for most languages with the exception of Gitksan, where morpheme-level OOV is 41.2%, again due to the very small training set.

[12]For Arapaho, text 56 is used for development and text 63 for testing. For Gitksan, we used Hector Hill's story for development and Vincent Gogag's story for testing.

	TRAIN	DEV	TEST
ARAPAHO	139714	17573	17597
GITKSAN	261	388	384
LEZGI	7029	992	886
NATÜGU	10140	1280	1076
NYANGBO	8669	1093	1057
TSEZ	37458	4761	4701
USPANTEKO	41923	928	2405

Table 2: Token counts for shared task train, development and test data. The counts are the same for both the open and closed track.

In Table 3, we also report statistics related to the morphological characteristics of the languages:

1. The average number of morphemes per word can be computed based on the morphological segmentations provided for track 2. For training data, this ranges from 1.4, for Uspanteko, to 2.0 for Tsez, meaning that many multimorphemic words can be found in all of the datasets.

2. Finally, we also compute the gloss ambiguity, that is, the average number of distinct glosses that a morpheme receives in the training data. For example, the English suffix *-s* is ambiguous between two readings because it can be both a number and tense marker. Glossing ambiguity can be seen as one indicator of the difficulty of a glossing task. For most of the shared task languages, it is very close to 1. The only exceptions are Gitksan (1.3) and Uspanteko (1.2), both of which contain frequent and ambiguous affixes.

The shared task datasets also provide English or Spanish translations, which can be valuable when glossing word stems. Table 4 presents statistics on how often the correct stem translation can be found in the utterance translation.[13]. We present separate statistics for in-vocabulary tokens, which have been observed in the training set, and for out-of-vocabulary (OOV) tokens, which are absent from the training set. The coverage ranges from 37% for Uspanteko (40% for OOV tokens) to 71% for

[13]To compute these statistics, the translations in the test set were first lemmatized using the Stanza toolkit (Qi et al., 2020).

Tsez (72% for OOV tokens). This demonstrates that translations are likely to contain valuable information for the glossing task, particularly for OOV tokens, which can be challenging to gloss without access to stem translations.

5 Glossing Systems

5.1 The Baseline System

The baseline system utilizes the RoBERTa architecture with default hyperparameters (Liu et al., 2019). The glossing task is treated as a token classification task, where words or morphemes form the input, and the IGT gloss (or gloss compound) forms the output label. In the closed track, we train word-level models; in the open track, where morphological segmentations are provided, morphemes form the input units to the glossing model. The baseline model is trained on the shared task training data without pretraining. We train one model for each language. For a detailed presentation of the baseline system, please see Ginn (2023).[14]

A transformer-based architecture is an effective choice for this task, as interlinear glossing often involves disambiguating homonymous morphemes based on context. For example, the English plural morpheme *-s* is spelled the same as the present-tense third-person singular verb morpheme, and the correct label must be determined from the lexical and sentence context. We decided to use a masked architecture rather than a sequence-to-sequence setup. During initial development, we also experimented with a sequence-to-sequence architecture, but this required more data to converge, and delievered inferior performance. Error analysis revealed this to be due to isolated insertions and deletions of morphemes. This is difficult to fix because there exists no a priori restriction on the morpheme count generated by the model.

The baseline system includes a number of known limitations which leave room for improvement; particularly, it can not effectively handle out-of-vocabulary words or morphemes, does not perform any segmentation in the closed track, and does not make use of part-of-speech tags or other resources in the open track. The system also does not utilize translations.

[14]Code for the baeline system can be found in the shared task repository `https://github.com/sigmorphon/2023glossingST/tree/main`

5.2 Participant Systems

Here we describe the participating systems. Table 5 provides an overview of the strategies employed by the different teams.

COATES (Coates, 2023) This system is based on the LSTM encoder-decoder architecture (Sutskever et al., 2014) and participated in the closed track of the shared task. The input to the glossing system consists of short context windows centered at the target word. Windows of width 1 and 2 are used to generate candidate predictions and the final output prediction of the model is generated using weighted voting among the output candidates.

LISNTEAM (Okabe and Yvon, 2023) This submission is a hybrid CRF-neural system and participated in the open track of the shared task. The system is a combination of two components: (1) An unsupervised neural alignment system SimAlign (Sabet et al., 2020) originally intended for machine translation, and (2) A CRF sequence labeling system Lost (Lavergne et al., 2011). The alignment system is used during training to associate word stems with lexemes in the translations. It uses cosine similarity of BERT representations (Devlin et al., 2019) to score the association between lexemes in the translation and the word stems in the gloss. Alignment allows the system to learn to pick lexemes from the translation line for stems which do not occur in the training data and thus to gloss unseen word forms. The CRF model is used to gloss the morphemes in the input sentence. The team submitted two systems LISNTEAM_1 and LISNTEAM_2 which differ with regard to the featurization of the CRF model.

SIGMOREFUN (He et al., 2023) This team submitted transformer-based systems and participated in the open track of the shared task. The authors experiment with the pretrained byte-level transformer model ByT5 (Xue et al., 2022) and the multilingual pretrained transformer XLM-RoBERTa (Conneau et al., 2020) fine-tuned for glossing. Interestingly, the ByT5 model falls behind the XLM-RoBERTa model in terms of glossing accuracy. To boost performance, the team incorporate additional glossed data from the ODIN database and, for Gitksan, lexemes from a Gitksan morphological analyzer (Forbes et al., 2021). The team also experiment augmenting the gold standard training sets with artificially generated glossing data. This team incorporated both translations and segmentations into

	ARAPAHO	GITKSAN	LEZGI	NATÜGU	NYANGBO	TSEZ	USPANTEKO
(1) TTR	31.9%	61.3%	27.0%	27.5%	22.3%	29.4%	21.9%
(2) OOV	25.8%	79.9%	15.2%	21.4%	8.4%	18.1%	20.5%
(3) MORPH OOV	3.6%	41.2%	4.9%	2.8%	1.1%	0.5%	5.3%
(4) MORPHS PER WORD	1.8	1.6	1.5	1.6	1.6	2.0	1.4
(5) GLOSSES PER MORPH	1.0	1.3	1.0	1.0	1.0	1.0	1.2

Table 3: Statistics concerning the shared task datasets: (1) TTR type-token-ratio in training data, (2) Amount of OOV, or out-of-vocabulary, tokens in the test set, (3) Amount of OOV morphemes in the test set, (4) average number of morphemes per word in the training data, and (5) Average number of possible glosses per morpheme in the training data.

	TOK. RECALL	OOV TOK. RECALL
ARAPAHO	51.32	49.87
GITKSAN	44.29	44.13
LEZGI	42.98	44.89
NATÜGU	58.72	58.21
TSEZ	71.17	71.66
USPANTEKO	36.49	40.14

Table 4: Amount of stem glosses which are found in the translation of the sentence. We present figures separately for all tokens and OOV tokens which are not found in the training data. Nyangbo is missing from this table because translations are not provided.

the model input using specialized prompts. The team made four submissions to the shared task SIGMOREFUN$_1$ – SIGMORFUN$_4$ displaying different combinations of model and data augmentation strategy.

TEAMSIGGYMORPH (Cross et al., 2023) This team participate both in the open and closed track. They investigate the performance of different input and output representations: character-based, byte-based and subword-based. For the closed track, the team used a vanilla transformer model. For the open track, they applied a BiLSTM encoder-decoder model and the ByT5 byte-level transformer model. The team accomplished stem-translation using a heuristic approach which combines translation statistics computed from the training set and copying of unseen stems, which often represent proper names. Like team SIGMOREFUN, this team also found that ByT5 underperformed compared to other model architectures.

TÜ-CL (Girrbach, 2023) This team participated both in the open and closed track of the shared task (in fact, the team also participated in this year's SIGMORPHON inflection shared task using the same model). The system uses straight-through gradient estimation (Bengio et al., 2013) to train a hard-attentional neural glossing model. For the closed track submission, the system induces a shallow morphological segmentation of the input text. This happens without any segmented training data which is not available in the closed track. Morpheme boundaries are assigned using the hard attention weights learned by the model. For the open track, gold standard segmentations are used. For both tracks, gloss tags and stems are then predicted for each morpheme using an MLP. This model delivers very strong performance while, surprisingly, not utilizing translations in any way.

6 Results and Discussion

6.1 Closed track (track 1)

The official shared task results for the closed track are presented in Table 6. Three teams participated in the closed track and two of these teams presented a complete submission for all shared task languages and beat the baseline system. Only teams with a complete submission (TÜ-CL and COATES) were eligible to participate in the official shared task evaluation. Of these two teams, TÜ-CL achieved the best micro average word-level glossing accuracy 71.30% with their second submission TÜ-CL$_2$. Team TÜ-CL also delivering the best performance for all individual languages in track 1.

It is noteworthy that both teams TÜ-CL and COATES beat the shared task baseline by wide margins: 23.99%-points for TÜ-CL and 12.24%-points for COATES. This demonstrates that even in the resource-scarce closed track setting, large improvements in glossing accuracy are possible over a baseline transformer system. All track 1 submissions strongly outperform the baseline for Nyangbo. Likewise, we see great improvements over the baseline for Lezgi and Natügu.

Results for morpheme-level glossing accuracy

	HA	TRANSFORMER	BYT5	LSTM	CRF-HYBRID	USE TRANSL.	EXT. DATA	DATA AUG.
COATES				X				
LISNTEAM$_1$					X	X		
LISNTEAM$_2$					X	X		
SIGMOREFUN$_1$		X	X			X	X	X
SIGMOREFUN$_2$		X	X			X	X	X
SIGMOREFUN$_3$		X	X			X	X	X
TEAMSIGGYMORPH$_1$		X						
TEAMSIGGYMORPH$_2$		X	X	X				X
TÜ-CL$_1$	X							
TÜ-CL$_2$	X							

Table 5: Summary of design features in the shared task systems: Hard attention (HA), use of transformer architecture TRANSFORMER, use of the BYT5 pretrained model, use of LSTM encoder-decoder architecture, use of a hybrid CRF and neural model (CRF-HYBRID), use of the provided translations (USE TRANSL.), use of external data (EXT. DATA), and use of data augmentation techniques (DATA AUG.).

WORD-LEVEL ACCURACY

Submission	Arp	Ddo	Git	Lez	Ntu	Nyb	Usp	AVG	Complete?
TÜ-CL$_2$	**78.79**	80.94	**21.09**	**78.78**	**81.04**	85.05	**73.39**	71.30	YES
TÜ-CL$_1$	77.90	**80.96**	4.69	78.10	80.20	**85.34**	68.86	68.01	YES
COATES$_1$	55.56	74.45	6.51	65.69	70.63	77.01	66.99	59.55	YES
BASELINE	71.14	73.41	16.93	49.66	42.01	5.96	72.06	47.31	YES
TEAMSIGGYMORPH$_1$	-	52.46	-	22.91	41.82	59.22	57.26	46.73	

MORPHEME-LEVEL ACCURACY

Submission	Arp	Ddo	Git	Lez	Ntu	Nyb	Usp	AVG	Complete?
TÜ-CL$_2$	**78.47**	**73.95**	**11.72**	**62.10**	56.32	85.24	**70.05**	62.55	YES
TÜ-CL$_1$	76.56	70.29	9.26	62.03	**56.38**	**86.74**	60.42	60.24	YES
TEAMSIGGYMORPH$_1$	-	53.19	-	28.13	31.86	66.25	59.73	47.83	
COATES$_1$	45.42	64.43	9.84	40.74	37.55	72.82	56.02	46.69	YES
BASELINE	44.19	51.23	8.54	41.62	18.17	14.22	57.24	33.60	YES

Table 6: Word-level accuracy (above) and morpheme-level accuracy (below) for track 1. The AVG column gives the micro average accuracy across languages. Averages are not comparable for partial submissions, where results for some languages are missing.

largely mirror those of word-level accuracy. Again TÜ-CL delivers the best performance for all languages. A general observation is that morpheme-level accuracies in track 1 are lower than word-level accuracies. This can be attributed to the fact that multi-morphemic words are often difficult to gloss correctly when the morphological segmentation is not give. A single incorrectly identified morpheme boundary will often result in several incorrectly glossed morphemes. To see why this is the case, consider the English past tense verb form *walked*. If the word is incorrectly analyzed as a monolithic adjective, both the stem *walk* and past tense marker *-ed* will be incorrectly glossed. This effect weighs down morpheme-level accuracy for the closed track.

6.2 Open track (track 2)

The official shared task results for the open track are presented in Table 7. In the open track, we got submissions from four teams, two of which presented complete submissions for all shared task languages. Both of these teams beat the baseline with regard to micro averaged word-level glossing accuracy. Similarly as in the closed track, TÜ-CL achieved the best overall performance and the best performance for most languages. For Arapaho, the SIGMORFUN team achieved the best performance and, for Natügu and Gitksan, LISNTEAM achieved the best performance. TÜ-CL beat the baseline system with regard to micro average word-level glossing accuracy by a wide margin of 17.42%-points.

Overall performance in the open track is, un-

WORD-LEVEL ACCURACY

Submission	Arp	Ddo	Git	Lez	Ntu	Nyb	Usp	AVG	Complete?
TÜ-CL$_2$	85.80	**85.79**	26.56	83.41	87.92	**87.98**	**78.46**	76.56	YES
TÜ-CL$_1$	85.12	85.68	13.80	**85.44**	87.83	85.90	77.21	74.43	YES
SIGMOREFUN$_2$	82.92	80.07	31.25	77.77	78.72	85.53	77.51	73.39	YES
LISNTEAM$_1$	-	84.85	28.39	83.41	88.85	-	76.30	72.36	
SIGMOREFUN$_1$	**85.87**	73.77	27.86	74.15	82.99	80.61	73.47	71.25	YES
TEAMSIGGYMORPH$_2$	-	79.28	26.56	81.72	87.73	76.25	75.84	71.23	
SIGMOREFUN$_4$	80.56	82.79	20.57	63.77	77.97	82.59	75.72	69.14	YES
LISNTEAM$_2$	-	-	**31.51**	82.73	**89.31**	-	-	67.85	
BASELINE	85.44	75.71	16.41	34.54	41.08	84.30	76.55	59.14	YES
SIGMOREFUN$_3$	73.27	62.37	4.17	38.60	55.11	69.25	70.85	53.38	YES

MORPHEME-LEVEL ACCURACY

Submission	Arp	Ddo	Git	Lez	Ntu	Nyb	Usp	AVG	Complete?
TÜ-CL$_2$	**91.37**	**92.01**	50.22	**87.61**	92.32	**91.40**	**84.51**	84.21	YES
SIGMOREFUN$_2$	89.34	88.15	**52.39**	82.36	85.53	89.49	83.08	81.48	YES
LISNTEAM$_1$	-	91.39	50.80	87.17	92.60	-	82.42	80.88	
TEAMSIGGYMORPH$_2$	-	88.36	47.76	86.59	92.10	82.74	82.22	79.96	
SIGMOREFUN$_1$	91.36	84.35	47.47	80.17	88.35	85.84	80.08	79.66	YES
TÜ-CL$_1$	90.93	91.16	17.08	83.45	90.17	89.96	83.45	78.03	YES
LISNTEAM$_2$	-	-	51.09	86.52	**92.77**	-	-	76.79	
BASELINE	91.11	85.34	25.33	51.82	49.03	88.71	82.48	67.69	YES
SIGMOREFUN$_4$	80.81	78.24	12.74	50.00	63.39	85.30	73.25	63.39	YES
SIGMOREFUN$_3$	72.10	57.93	2.60	26.24	35.62	70.01	67.73	47.46	YES

Table 7: Word-level accuracy (above) and morpheme-level accuracy (below) for track 2. The AVG column gives the micro average accuracy across languages. Averages are not comparable for partial submissions, where results for some languages are missing.

derstandably, higher than in the closed track due to the fact that gold standard morphological segmentations were provided during training and test time, and additional resources were allowed, which some of the participants utilized. However, absolute improvement over the baseline is lower in the open track than the closed track. This may be a consequence of the fact that the learning problem in the open track is easier. It is also noteworthy that morpheme-level performance is higher than word-level performance for the open track, whereas the opposite is true for the closed track. This is understandable because gold standard morphological segmentations are provided and a single isolated glossing error is less likely to ruin the gloss for the complete word form in the open track.

6.3 Analysis of performance

We now present a more detailed analysis of the shared task results. This analysis is related to Figure 2 which presents average performance of shared task systems on the different languages and their relationship with training data size, out-of-vocabulary (OOV) rate and type-token-ratio (TTR).

Impact of training data size The size of the training set is one of the most influential factors determining the performance of natural language processing systems. This observation also holds true for the shared task results. The training data sizes vary from 261 tokens for Gitksan (git) to 139,714 tokens for Arapaho (arp). It is evident that the highest micro average word-level glossing performance in the open track is achieved for Arapaho, which benefits from the largest training set. In the closed track, Arapaho stands among the top three languages in terms of glossing accuracy, but the best performance is observed for Tsez (ddo), which has approximately 37,000 training tokens. This places it among the higher-resourced languages in the shared task. Conversely, Gitksan, with the smallest training set, consistently exhibits the lowest glossing performance. Overall, a clear trend emerges, demonstrating an improvement in glossing performance as the training data size increases.

Impact of OOV rate While out-of-vocabulary (OOV) rate computed on the test set is an important predictor of performance in tasks like morphological tagging (Müller et al., 2015), it does not seem to have a clear impact on system performance in this shared task. While the highest OOV rate and lowest performance are attained for Gitksan, this is largely an artefact of its very small training data size. If we disregard Gitksan, the impact of OOV rate both for the open and closed track is unclear. In fact, in the open track, the best average glossing performance is attained for Arapaho which has the second-highest OOV rate. Nevertheless, Arapaho also has the largest training set. This might seem like a surprising coincidence but we must remember that Arapaho is highly morphologically complex which tends to lead to higher OOV rates.

Impact of TTR Similarly to OOV, Type-token-ratio in the training set can be seen a measure of the diversity of the training data. We would expect a higher TTR to improve glossing performance. However, according to the statistics presented in Figure 2, the trend is not very clear. While the best performance in the closed track is attained for Tsez, which has moderately high TTR, the second-best performance is attained for Uspanteko with the lowest TTR.

7 Future Directions

The submissions in this shared task have explored several novel techniques that have not been previously applied to automatic interlinear glossing. Surprisingly, pretrained language models like ByT5 did not perform as well as one might expect based on their strong performance on other morphology tasks. This unexpected outcome raises the need for further investigation.

One interesting observation is that the winning submission, TÜ-CL, completely disregards the provided translations. While this could suggest that translations may not be as useful for the glossing task, we believe there is still room for improvement in this area. Incorporating large pretrained English models as a reliable source of translated text could potentially lead to additional enhancements.

Considering the availability of extensive morphological resources for many languages, such as those provided by UniMorph and similar projects, multi-task learning holds promise for interlinear glossing. Additionally, we encourage further exploration of crosslingual approaches, leveraging the ODIN database of interlinear glossed text, which despite being noisy, offers a highly multilingual resource for research purposes.

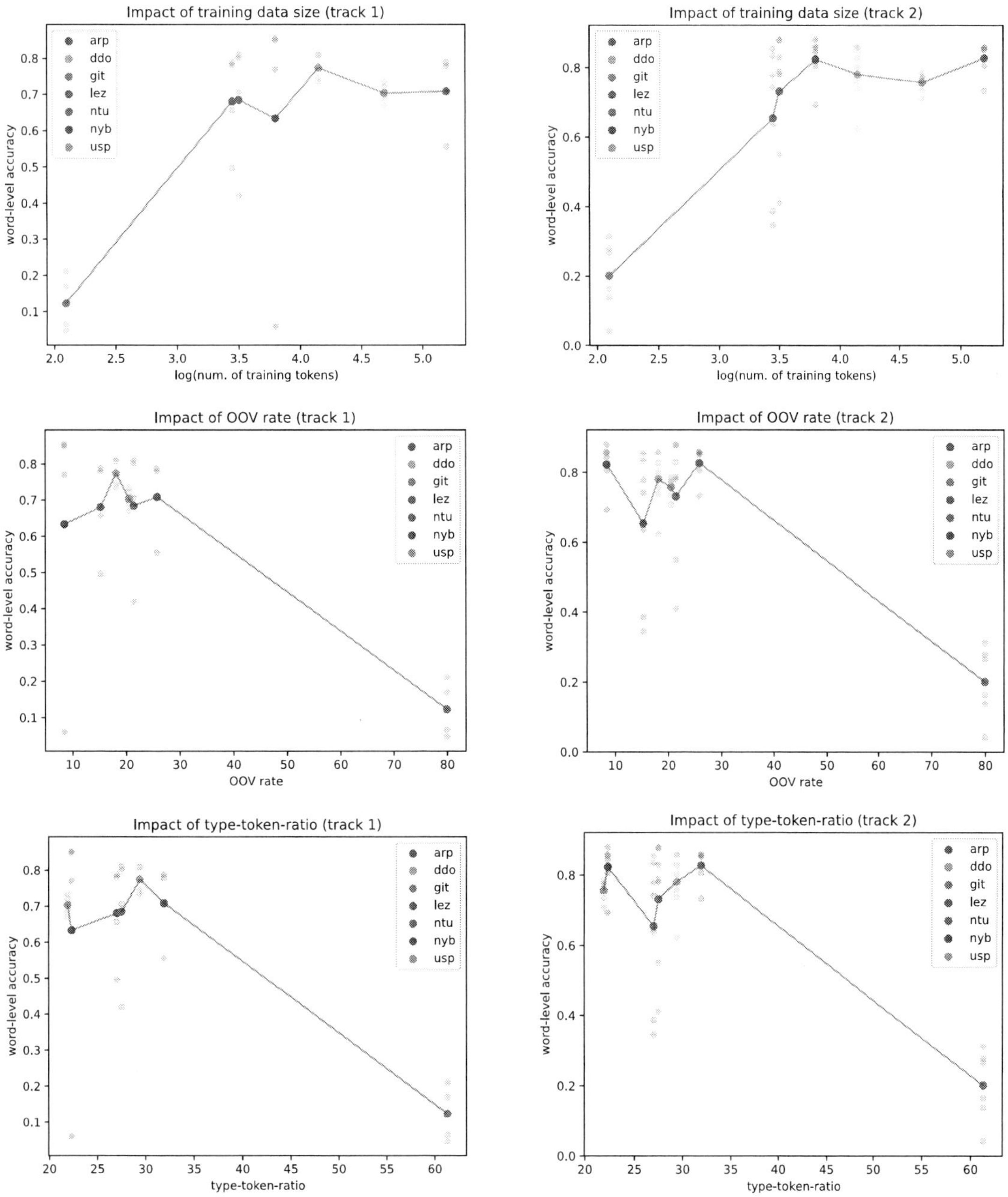

Figure 2: Impact of different data characteristics (training data size, out-of-vocabulary rate and type-token-ratio) on average word-level glossing accuracy. In addition to the average performance, we also plot the performance of each individual system. Only complete complete submissions, for all shared task languages, are included in these plots. Abbreviations refer to languages: Arapaho (arp), Tsez (ddo), Gitksan (git), Lezgi (lez), Natügu (ntu), Nyangbo (nyb) and Uspanteko (usp).

8 Conclusion

The 2023 SIGMORPHON Shared Task on Interlinear Glossing received submissions from five teams which presented a wealth of interesting techniques greatly expanding the field of automated interlinear glossing. The submissions achieved substantial improvements over a baseline RoBERTa system. The winning team TÜ-CL achieved a 23.99%-point improvement over the baseline in the closed track and a 17.42%-point improvement in the open track using a hard attention model.

Acknowledgements

We would like to express our gratitude to the organizers of the SIGMORPHON workshop and all the participants of the shared task for their valuable contributions. We would also like to extend our sincerest thanks to the speakers and linguists who have dedicated their efforts to the development of the corpora used in this shared task. Lastly, Miikka Silfverberg wants to acknowledge the assistance provided by ChatGPT during the editing process of this manuscript.

References

A. K. Abdulaev and I. K. Abdullaev, editors. 2010. *Cezyas folklor/Dido (Tsez) folklore/Didojskij (cezskij) fol'klor.* "Lotos", Leipzig–Makhachkala.

Roee Aharoni and Yoav Goldberg. 2017. Morphological inflection generation with hard monotonic attention. In *Proceedings of the 55th Annual Meeting of the Association for Computational Linguistics (Volume 1: Long Papers)*, pages 2004–2015.

Antonios Anastasopoulos and Graham Neubig. 2019. Pushing the limits of low-resource morphological inflection. In *Proceedings of the 2019 Conference on Empirical Methods in Natural Language Processing and the 9th International Joint Conference on Natural Language Processing (EMNLP-IJCNLP)*, pages 984–996.

Diego Barriga Martínez, Victor Mijangos, and Ximena Gutierrez-Vasques. 2021. Automatic interlinear glossing for Otomi language. In *Proceedings of the First Workshop on Natural Language Processing for Indigenous Languages of the Americas*, pages 34–43, Online. Association for Computational Linguistics.

Khuyagbaatar Batsuren, Gábor Bella, Aryaman Arora, Viktor Martinovic, Kyle Gorman, Zdeněk Žabokrtský, Amarsanaa Ganbold, Šárka Dohnalová, Magda Ševčíková, Kateřina Pelegrinová, et al. 2022a. The sigmorphon 2022 shared task on morpheme segmentation. In *Proceedings of the 19th SIGMORPHON Workshop on Computational Research in Phonetics, Phonology, and Morphology*, pages 103–116.

Khuyagbaatar Batsuren, Omer Goldman, Salam Khalifa, Nizar Habash, Witold Kieraś, Gábor Bella, Brian Leonard, Garrett Nicolai, Kyle Gorman, Yustinus Ghanggo Ate, Maria Ryskina, Sabrina Mielke, Elena Budianskaya, Charbel El-Khaissi, Tiago Pimentel, Michael Gasser, William Abbott Lane, Mohit Raj, Matt Coler, Jaime Rafael Montoya Samame, Delio Siticonatzi Camaiteri, Esaú Zumaeta Rojas, Didier López Francis, Arturo Oncevay, Juan López Bautista, Gema Celeste Silva Villegas, Lucas Torroba Hennigen, Adam Ek, David Guriel, Peter Dirix, Jean-Philippe Bernardy, Andrey Scherbakov, Aziyana Bayyr-ool, Antonios Anastasopoulos, Roberto Zariquiey, Karina Sheifer, Sofya Ganieva, Hilaria Cruz, Ritván Karahóğa, Stella Markantonatou, George Pavlidis, Matvey Plugaryov, Elena Klyachko, Ali Salehi, Candy Angulo, Jatayu Baxi, Andrew Krizhanovsky, Natalia Krizhanovskaya, Elizabeth Salesky, Clara Vania, Sardana Ivanova, Jennifer White, Rowan Hall Maudslay, Josef Valvoda, Ran Zmigrod, Paula Czarnowska, Irene Nikkarinen, Aelita Salchak, Brijesh Bhatt, Christopher Straughn, Zoey Liu, Jonathan North Washington, Yuval Pinter, Duygu Ataman, Marcin Wolinski, Totok Suhardijanto, Anna Yablonskaya, Niklas Stoehr, Hossep Dolatian, Zahroh Nuriah, Shyam Ratan, Francis M. Tyers, Edoardo M. Ponti, Grant Aiton, Aryaman Arora, Richard J. Hatcher, Ritesh Kumar, Jeremiah Young, Daria Rodionova, Anastasia Yemelina, Taras Andrushko, Igor Marchenko, Polina Mashkovtseva, Alexandra Serova, Emily Prud'hommeaux, Maria Nepomniashchaya, Fausto Giunchiglia, Eleanor Chodroff, Mans Hulden, Miikka Silfverberg, Arya D. McCarthy, David Yarowsky, Ryan Cotterell, Reut Tsarfaty, and Ekaterina Vylomova. 2022b. UniMorph 4.0: Universal Morphology. In *Proceedings of the Thirteenth Language Resources and Evaluation Conference*, pages 840–855, Marseille, France. European Language Resources Association.

Yoshua Bengio, Nicholas Léonard, and Aaron Courville. 2013. Estimating or propagating gradients through stochastic neurons for conditional computation. *arXiv preprint arXiv:1308.3432*.

Ryan Bennett, Jessica Coon, and Robert Henderson. 2016. Introduction to Mayan Linguistics. *Lang. Linguistics Compass*, 10:455–468.

Ryan Bennett, Meg Harvey, Robert Henderson, and Tomás Alberto Méndez López. 2022. The phonetics and phonology of uspanteko (mayan). *Language and Linguistics Compass*.

Edith Coates. 2023. An ensembled encoder-decoder system for interlinear glossed text. In *Proceedings of the 20th SIGMORPHON Workshop on Computational Research in Phonetics, Phonology, and Morphology*. Association for Computational Linguistics.

Çağrı Çöltekin. 2019. Cross-lingual morphological inflection with explicit alignment. In *Proceedings of the 16th workshop on computational research in phonetics, phonology, and morphology*, pages 71–79.

Bernard Comrie, A. K. Abdulaev, and I. K. Abdullaev, editors. 2022. *The Tsez Annotated Corpus Project (v1.0)*. Zenodo, Leipzig.

Alexis Conneau, Kartikay Khandelwal, Naman Goyal, Vishrav Chaudhary, Guillaume Wenzek, Francisco Guzmán, Édouard Grave, Myle Ott, Luke Zettlemoyer, and Veselin Stoyanov. 2020. Unsupervised cross-lingual representation learning at scale. In *Proceedings of the 58th Annual Meeting of the Association for Computational Linguistics*, pages 8440–8451.

Jessica Coon. 2016. Mayan morphosyntax. *Lang. Linguistics Compass*, 10:515–550.

Ryan Cotterell and Georg Heigold. 2017. Cross-lingual character-level neural morphological tagging. In *Proceedings of the 2017 Conference on Empirical Methods in Natural Language Processing*, pages 748–759.

Andrew Cowell and Alonzo Moss. 2008. *The Arapaho Language*. University Press of Colorado.

Ziggy Cross, Michelle Yun, Ananya Apparaju, Jata MacCabe, Garrett Nicolai, and Miikka Silfverberg. 2023. Glossy bytes: Neural glossing using subword encoding. In *Proceedings of the 20th SIGMORPHON Workshop on Computational Research in Phonetics, Phonology, and Morphology*. Association for Computational Linguistics.

Jacob Devlin, Ming-Wei Chang, Kenton Lee, and Kristina Toutanova. 2019. Bert: Pre-training of deep bidirectional transformers for language understanding. In *Proceedings of the 2019 Conference of the North American Chapter of the Association for Computational Linguistics: Human Language Technologies, Volume 1 (Long and Short Papers)*, pages 4171–4186.

Charles Donet. 2014. The Importance of Verb Salience in the Followability of Lezgi Oral Narratives. Master's thesis, Graduate Institute of Applied Linguistics, Dallas, TX.

Britt Dunlop, Suzanne Gessner, Tracey Herbert, and Aliana Parker. 2018. Report on the status of BC First Nations languages. Report of the First People's Cultural Council. Retrieved March 24, 2019.

David M. Eberhard, Gary F. Simons, and Charles D. Fennig, editors. 2023. *Ethnologue: Languages of the World*, twenty-sixth edition. SIL International, Dallas, Texas.

James Essegbey. 2019. *Tutrugbu (Nyangbo) Language and Culture*. Brill, Leiden/Boston.

Clarissa Forbes, Henry Davis, Michael Schwan, and the UBC Gitksan Research Laboratory. 2017. Three Gitksan texts. In *Papers for the 52nd International Conference on Salish and Neighbouring Languages*, pages 47–89. UBC Working Papers in Linguistics.

Clarissa Forbes, Garrett Nicolai, and Miikka Silfverberg. 2021. An fst morphological analyzer for the gitksan language. In *Proceedings of the 18th SIGMORPHON Workshop on Computational Research in Phonetics, Phonology, and Morphology*, pages 188–197.

Michael Ginn. 2023. Sigmorphon 2023 shared task of interlinear glossing: Baseline model. *arXiv preprint arXiv:2303.14234*.

Leander Girrbach. 2023. Tü-CL at SIGMORPHON 2023: Straight-Through gradient estimation for hard attention. In *Proceedings of the 20th SIGMORPHON Workshop on Computational Research in Phonetics, Phonology, and Morphology*. Association for Computational Linguistics.

Martin Haspelmath. 1993. *A grammar of Lezgian*. Mouton de Gruyter, Berlin; New York.

Taiqi He, Lindia Tjuatja, Nathaniel Robinson, Shinji Watanabe, David R. Mortensen, Graham Neubig, and Lori Levin. 2023. SigMoreFun submission to the SIGMORPHON shared task on interlinear glossing. In *Proceedings of the 20th SIGMORPHON Workshop on Computational Research in Phonetics, Phonology, and Morphology*. Association for Computational Linguistics.

Katharina Kann, Samuel R Bowman, and Kyunghyun Cho. 2020. Learning to learn morphological inflection for resource-poor languages. In *Proceedings of the AAAI Conference on Artificial Intelligence*, volume 05 (34), pages 8058–8065.

Christo Kirov, Ryan Cotterell, John Sylak-Glassman, Géraldine Walther, Ekaterina Vylomova, Patrick Xia, Manaal Faruqui, Sabrina J. Mielke, Arya D. McCarthy, Sandra Kübler, David Yarowsky, Jason Eisner, and Mans Hulden. 2018. Unimorph 3.0: Universal morphology. *ArXiv*, abs/1810.11101.

John D Lafferty, Andrew McCallum, and Fernando CN Pereira. 2001. Conditional random fields: Probabilistic models for segmenting and labeling sequence data. In *Proceedings of the Eighteenth International Conference on Machine Learning*, pages 282–289.

Thomas Lavergne, Alexandre Allauzen, Josep Maria Crego, and François Yvon. 2011. From n-gram-based to CRF-based translation models. In *Proceedings of the Sixth Workshop on Statistical Machine Translation*, pages 542–553, Edinburgh, Scotland. Association for Computational Linguistics.

Christian Lehmann. 1982. Directions for interlinear morphemic translations. *Folia Linguistica - FOLIA LINGUIST*, 16:199–224.

William D Lewis and Fei Xia. 2010. Developing odin: A multilingual repository of annotated language data for hundreds of the world's languages. *Literary and Linguistic Computing*, 25(3):303–319.

Ling Liu and Mans Hulden. 2021. Backtranslation in neural morphological inflection. In *Proceedings of the Second Workshop on Insights from Negative Results in NLP*, pages 81–88.

Yinhan Liu, Myle Ott, Naman Goyal, Jingfei Du, Mandar Joshi, Danqi Chen, Omer Levy, Mike Lewis, Luke Zettlemoyer, and Veselin Stoyanov. 2019. RoBERTa: A Robustly Optimized BERT Pretraining Approach. ArXiv:1907.11692 [cs].

Peter Makarov, Tatyana Ruzsics, and Simon Clematide. 2017. Align and copy: Uzh at sigmorphon 2017 shared task for morphological reinflection. In *Proceedings of the CoNLL SIGMORPHON 2017 Shared Task: Universal Morphological Reinflection*, pages 49–57.

Arya D McCarthy, Ekaterina Vylomova, Shijie Wu, Chaitanya Malaviya, Lawrence Wolf-Sonkin, Garrett Nicolai, Christo Kirov, Miikka Silfverberg, Sabrina J Mielke, Jeffrey Heinz, et al. 2019. The sigmorphon 2019 shared task: Morphological analysis in context and cross-lingual transfer for inflection. In *Proceedings of the 16th Workshop on Computational Research in Phonetics, Phonology, and Morphology*, pages 229–244.

Angelina McMillan-Major. 2020. Automating gloss generation in interlinear glossed text. In *Proceedings of the Society for Computation in Linguistics 2020*, pages 355–366, New York, New York. Association for Computational Linguistics.

Sarah Moeller and Mans Hulden. 2018. Automatic glossing in a low-resource setting for language documentation. In *Proceedings of the Workshop on Computational Modeling of Polysynthetic Languages*, pages 84–93, Santa Fe, New Mexico, USA. Association for Computational Linguistics.

Thomas Müller, Ryan Cotterell, Alexander Fraser, and Hinrich Schütze. 2015. Joint lemmatization and morphological tagging with lemming. In *Proceedings of the 2015 conference on empirical methods in natural language processing*, pages 2268–2274.

Shu Okabe and François Yvon. 2023. LISN @ SIGMORPHON 2023 shared task on interlinear glossing. In *Proceedings of the 20th SIGMORPHON Workshop on Computational Research in Phonetics, Phonology, and Morphology*. Association for Computational Linguistics.

Alexis Palmer, Taesun Moon, and Jason Baldridge. 2009. Evaluating automation strategies in language documentation. In *Proceedings of the NAACL HLT 2009 Workshop on Active Learning for Natural Language Processing*, pages 36–44.

Alexis Palmer, Taesun Moon, Jason Baldridge, Katrin Erk, Eric Campbell, and Telma Can. 2010. Computational strategies for reducing annotation effort in language documentation. *Linguistic Issues in Language Technology*, 3.

Telma Can Pixabaj, Miguel Angel Vicente Méndez, Mar ía Vicente Méndez, and Oswaldo Ajcot Damián. 2007. *Text Collections in Four Mayan Languages*. Archived in The Archive of the Indigenous Languages of Latin America (AILLA).

Peng Qi, Yuhao Zhang, Yuhui Zhang, Jason Bolton, and Christopher D. Manning. 2020. Stanza: A Python natural language processing toolkit for many human languages. In *Proceedings of the 58th Annual Meeting of the Association for Computational Linguistics: System Demonstrations*.

Taraka Rama and Çağrı Çöltekin. 2018. Tübingen-oslo system at sigmorphon shared task on morphological inflection. a multi-tasking multilingual sequence to sequence model. In *Proceedings of the CoNLL–SIGMORPHON 2018 Shared Task: Universal Morphological Reinflection*, pages 112–115.

Adwait Ratnaparkhi. 1996. A maximum entropy model for part-of-speech tagging. In *Conference on empirical methods in natural language processing*.

Bruce Rigsby. 1986. Gitxsan grammar. Ms., University of Queensland, Australia.

Bruce Rigsby. 1989. A later view of Gitksan syntax. In M. Key and H. Hoenigswald, editors, *General and Amerindian Ethnolinguistics: In remembrance of Stanley Newman*. Mouton de Gruyter, Berlin.

Masoud Jalili Sabet, Philipp Dufter, François Yvon, and Hinrich Schütze. 2020. Simalign: High quality word alignments without parallel training data using static and contextualized embeddings. *arXiv preprint arXiv:2004.08728*.

Frank Seifart, Nicholas Evans, Harald Hammarström, and Stephen C. Levinson. 2018. Language documentation twenty-five years on. *Language*, 94(4):e324–e345.

Miikka Silfverberg, Adam Wiemerslage, Ling Liu, and Lingshuang Jack Mao. 2017. Data augmentation for morphological reinflection. In *Proceedings of the CoNLL SIGMORPHON 2017 Shared Task: Universal Morphological Reinflection*, pages 90–99.

Ilya Sutskever, Oriol Vinyals, and Quoc V Le. 2014. Sequence to sequence learning with neural networks. *Advances in neural information processing systems*, 27.

John Sylak-Glassman. 2016. The composition and use of the universal morphological feature schema (UniMorph Schema).

Marie-Lucie Tarpent. 1987. *A Grammar of the Nisgha Language*. Ph.D. thesis, University of Victoria.

Ashish Vaswani, Noam Shazeer, Niki Parmar, Jakob Uszkoreit, Llion Jones, Aidan N Gomez, Łukasz Kaiser, and Illia Polosukhin. 2017. Attention is all you need. *Advances in neural information processing systems*, 30.

Adam Wiemerslage, Changbing Yang, Garrett Nicolai, Miikka Silfverberg, and Katharina Kann. 2023. An investigation of noise in morphological inflection. *arXiv preprint arXiv:2305.16581*.

Linting Xue, Aditya Barua, Noah Constant, Rami Al-Rfou, Sharan Narang, Mihir Kale, Adam Roberts, and Colin Raffel. 2022. Byt5: Towards a token-free future with pre-trained byte-to-byte models. *Transactions of the Association for Computational Linguistics*, 10:291–306.

Xingyuan Zhao, Satoru Ozaki, Antonios Anastasopoulos, Graham Neubig, and Lori Levin. 2020. Automatic interlinear glossing for under-resourced languages leveraging translations. In *Proceedings of the 28th International Conference on Computational Linguistics*, pages 5397–5408, Barcelona, Spain (Online). International Committee on Computational Linguistics.

Åshild Næss and Brenda H. Boerger. 2008. Reefs–santa Cruz as Oceanic: Evidence from the verb complex. *Oceanic Linguistics*, 47:185–212.

LISN @ SIGMORPHON 2023 Shared Task on Interlinear Glossing

Shu Okabe and **François Yvon**
Université Paris-Saclay & CNRS
LISN, rue du Belvédère
91405 Orsay, France
{shu.okabe,francois.yvon}@limsi.fr

Abstract

This paper describes LISN's submission to the second track (open track) of the shared task on Interlinear Glossing for SIGMORPHON 2023. Our systems are based on Lost, a variation of linear Conditional Random Fields initially developed as a probabilistic translation model and then adapted to the glossing task. This model allows us to handle one of the main challenges posed by glossing, i.e. the fact that the list of potential labels for lexical morphemes is not fixed in advance and needs to be extended dynamically when labelling units are not seen in training. In such situations, we show how to make use of candidate lexical glosses found in the translation and discuss how such extension affects the training and inference procedures. The resulting automatic glossing systems prove to yield very competitive results, especially in low-resource settings.

1 Introduction

LISN participated in the 'open track' of the shared task on interlinear glossing of SIGMORPHON 2023 (Ginn et al., 2023) with two submissions. Figure 1 presents the format of the sentences for this shared task. In this track, the source sentence **T** is overtly segmented into morphemes (**M**), which yields an explicit one-to-one correspondence between each source morpheme and the corresponding gloss (**G**), thanks to the Leipzig Glossing Rules convention (Bickel et al., 2008). A translation **L** in a more-resourced language (English or Spanish) is also provided, except for Nyangbo. An obvious formalisation of the task that we mostly adopt, is thus to view glossing as a sequence labelling task performed at the morpheme level.

As can be seen in Figure 1, there are roughly two categories of glosses: *grammatical glosses* indicating the grammatical function of the morpheme (e.g., GEN1) and *lexical glosses* expressing a meaning (e.g., son).[1] While the grammatical glosses of a language constitute a finite set of labels, the variety of lexical glosses is unknown, which is one of the main challenges of the task, especially in small training data conditions.

T	Nesis	ɬˤono	uži	zown.
M	nesi–s	ɬˤono	uži	zow–n
G	he.OBL–GEN1	three	son	be.NPRS–PST.UNW
L	He had three sons.			

Figure 1: A sample entry in Tsez: source sentence (**T**), and its morpheme-segmented version (**M**), glossed line (**G**), and target translation (**L**)

To accommodate such cases, we assume that lexical glosses can be directly inferred from the translation tier. Recent works on automatic gloss generation, such as (McMillan-Major, 2020; Zhao et al., 2020), also rely on a similar assumption and leverage the available translations. In our model, we will thus consider that the set of possible labels for the morphemes in any given sentence consists of the union of (a) all the grammatical glosses, (b) lemmas occurring in the target translation, (c) frequently-associated labels from the training data. By using a variant of Conditional Random Fields (CRFs) (Lafferty et al., 2001), which enables such local restriction of the set of possible labels, our glossing model can be viewed as an extension of previous sequence labelling systems based on CRFs such as (Moeller and Hulden, 2018; McMillan-Major, 2020; Barriga Martínez et al., 2021). In our approach, using translations as labels during training raises the issue of aligning the translation and the source sentence, which we handle with the neural word alignment model of Jalili Sabet et al. (2020). As alignments are computed at the morpheme level, this technique does not apply for the 'closed track', where the source segmentation is not part of the training annotations.

Our participation is motivated by two factors:

[1]We consider 'compound' glosses such as 'he.OBL' as lexical glosses in our submission.

Proceedings of the 20th SIGMORPHON workshop on Computational Research in Phonetics, Phonology, and Morphology, pages 202–208
July 14, 2023 ©2023 Association for Computational Linguistics

to evaluate the model performance across varying training data sizes (from a few dozen to thousands of sentences) and to challenge its ability to handle a variety of high-resource languages in the target translation. Section 2 describes our system, while Section 3 presents our experimental settings. Section 4 reports the complete set of results obtained with our models.

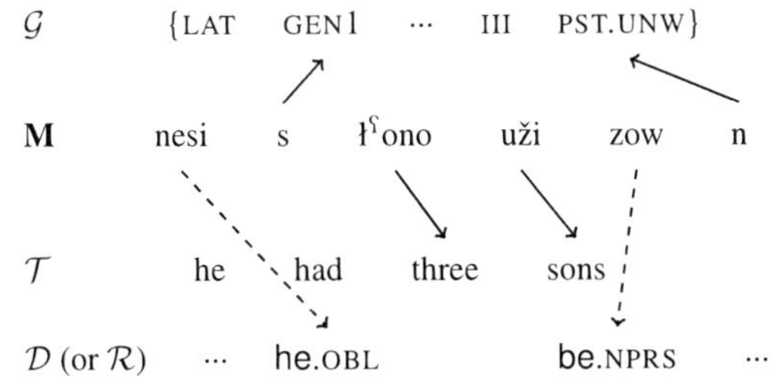

Figure 2: Illustration of our approach to label the example source sentence **M** of Figure 1. $\mathcal{G}$ represents the set of all grammatical glosses in the training data, $\mathcal{T}$ the set of words occuring in the translation **L**, $\mathcal{D}$ the set of lexical labels from the training dictionary, and $\mathcal{R}$ the reference lexical labels seen in training. During training, automatic alignments between **M** and $\mathcal{T}$ are used.

2 System description

Our glossing system uses two main technological components: we (a) rely on an automatic alignment model between the lexical glosses and the target translation during training, which also allows us to exploit additional information regarding target words, such as their Part-of-Speech (PoS) tag or their position; (b) use an extended version of CRFs which allows us to locally restrict the set of possible labels to carry out the glossing task. Figure 2 summarises the main ideas behind our approach.

2.1 Aligning lexical glosses with target words

To align the lexical glosses with the target translation, we use the multilingual aligner SimAlign (Jalili Sabet et al., 2020), which relies on the cosine similarity of the source and target unit embeddings. Three heuristics are available to extract the alignments from a similarity matrix; we use the `Match` method in our submission, since it gave the best results in preliminary experiments. This method considers the alignment task as a maximal matching problem in the bipartite weighted graph containing all possible alignment links between lexical glosses and target words. This heuristic notably ensures that all lexical glosses are aligned with a target word.[2]

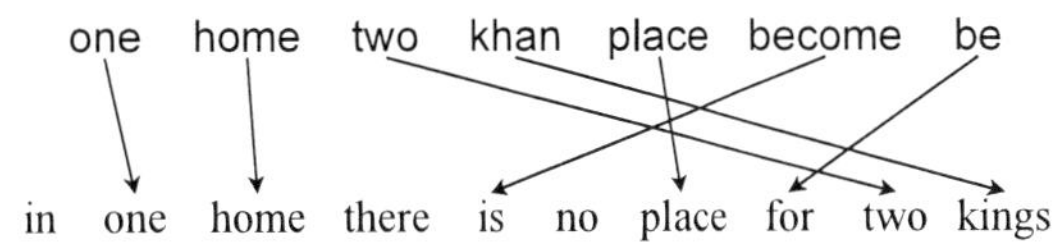

Figure 3: Example of SimAlign alignment between lexical glosses and an English translation (Tsez sentence).

Figure 3 displays an example of alignment computed with the `Match` method. We can note that most alignments are trivial because both units are either identical (e.g. 'one') or have the same lemma (e.g. son/sons). The remaining links are also of great interest in our case. For the alignment pair (khan/'kings'), although the gloss itself is not in the translation, they are synonyms and share valuable properties such as their PoS tag. Besides, the alignment of be with 'for' is obviously wrong and only exists because of the constraint of aligning every lexical gloss. Nevertheless, frequent lemmas such as be occur in multiple sentences, and their possible labels are observed in the training reference annotations.

2.2 Label and label features

Our approach views glossing as a sequence labelling task, meaning that the basic output label for each morpheme is the gloss itself. Our implementation of the CRF model (see below) also enables us to simultaneously predict *label features*, which are arbitrary linguistic properties that can be derived from the label. In our experiments, we chose to incorporate such additional information, which will yield more general, hence more robust, feature functions. In all systems, we thus predict three properties of the label: (a) the actual gloss g, (b) a binary category b about its nature (GRAM for grammatical glosses, or LEX for lexical glosses), and (c) its projected PoS tag p that we collect from the aligned target word.[3]

2.3 Probabilistic sequence labelling model

Our system reuses Lost (Lavergne et al., 2011), a probabilistic model initially devised for statistical machine translation. With Lost, it is possible to label arbitrary segments of a source sentence with

[2]Unless there are more lexical glosses than words in the translation.

[3]As grammatical morphemes have no aligned target words, we use the generic label GRAM for all grammatical glosses.

'phrases' from a large bilingual dictionary and to effectively search for the best possible labelling given a set of trained feature weights. Compared to the original translation task, using Lost for automatic glossing brings several simplifications. In particular, there is no need to consider multiple segmentations of the source as the segmentation in morphemes is observed, nor to consider multiple source reorderings, as the translation is also always observed. We thus only focus below on the features of Lost that are relevant for the glossing task.

Lost uses a discriminative model based on the theory of Conditional Random Fields (Lafferty et al., 2001). In a standard CRF, for a sequence $\boldsymbol{x}$ of T observations, the probability of the corresponding label sequence $\boldsymbol{y} \in \mathcal{Y}^T$ is computed as:

$$p_\theta(\boldsymbol{y}|\boldsymbol{x}) = \frac{1}{Z_\theta(\boldsymbol{x})} \exp\left\{\sum_{k=1}^{K} \theta_k G_k(\boldsymbol{x}, \boldsymbol{y})\right\}, \quad (1)$$

where G_k are the feature functions with associated weights θ_k and $Z_\theta(\boldsymbol{x})$ is the partition function summing over all possible label sequences. In practice, the features usually test local properties (unigram or bigram). Training is performed by maximising the penalised conditional log-likelihood on a set of fully labelled instances.

Implementing this model for machine translation or for our glossing task is challenging. This is because the set of all possible labels is significantly larger than for most sequence labelling tasks, which means that the computational cost of computing $Z_\theta(\boldsymbol{x})$ can get prohibitive, even for sequences of moderate sizes. The implementation we use, Lost (Lavergne et al., 2011), enables us to specify a local (i.e. for a sentence-specific) set of labels, which defines a restricted *search space* both in training and inference: this means that the normaliser in (1) will only consider a restricted number of possible labellings. Using this implementation, the forward-backward computations performed during training remain tractable, even when the number of possible labels gets extremely large. This feature of Lost is also useful here, as we can restrict the set of possible *lexical* glosses by defining a specific search space for each sentence, as we explain below.

2.4 Defining the search space

During training, we define the search space associated with the source $\boldsymbol{x}$ made of T morphemes as comprising all sequences of T labels from either: the set of known grammatical glosses ($\mathcal{G}$), the lemmas of the words in the translation ($\mathcal{T}$), the most frequent lexical glosses associated with the source morphemes in the training set (this can be viewed as a dictionary $\mathcal{D}$), and the gold glosses ($\mathcal{R}$) for reference reachability (Liang et al., 2006). This 'simple' label set comprises two parts: one ($\mathcal{G}$) is common to all sentences, while the remaining labels are defined on a per-sentence basis. In formal terms, the search space is thus $(\mathcal{G} \cup \mathcal{T} \cup \mathcal{D} \cup \mathcal{R})^T$. As explained in Section 2.2, we also consider label features, where the basic labels are augmented with various additional information.

Training the CRF model also requires supervision information, provided here by the reference glosses, from which we readily derive the reference sequence of labels in the search space (an example of reference output labels can be seen on the right-hand part of Figure 4).

During inference, since we have no access to the reference labels, the test search space only comprises the union of the grammatical glosses, the lemmas from the translation, and the labels from the dictionary ($\mathcal{G} \cup \mathcal{T} \cup \mathcal{D}$).[4] Table 1 displays an example output label from each label set for the S1 setting.

set	g	b	p
$\mathcal{G}$	GEN1	GRAM	GRAM
$\mathcal{T}$	king	LEX	NOUN
$\mathcal{D}$	khan	LEX	NOUN
$\mathcal{R}$	khan	LEX	NOUN

Table 1: Example of output labels extracted from each label set (S1 setting), using the example of Figure 3. The reference label set $\mathcal{R}$ is only used during training.

2.5 Feature set

Our two submissions, S1 and S2, use the same model and share most features computed on the source morpheme input. However, the latter extends the former system with additional features.

The input to Lost is the source morpheme s, from which we also deduce the following features: its position p within the word coded as a numerical value (from 0 to n) for complex words, or as 'F' for free morphemes, its length l in characters,

[4]When a lemma is both in the translation and dictionary or repeated in the translation, we still create distinct paths in the search space, as these can be associated with different features (e.g. their PoS and position). The search algorithm will then pick the most likely option.

i	input source morph. m	S1 features position (in word) t	 length l	 first 3 letters d	 last 3 letters e	S2 features copy src cs	 position src ps	outputs reference gloss g	 GRAM or LEX b	 PoS tag p	S2 features copy trg ct	 position trg pt
0	nesi	0	4	nes	esi	0	1/4	he.OBL	LEX	PRON	0	1/4
1	s	1	1	s	s	0	1/4	GEN1	GRAM	GRAM	-1	-2
2	ɬˤono	F	5	ɬˤo	ono	0	2/4	three	LEX	NUM	0	3/4
3	uži	F	3	uži	uži	0	2/4	son	LEX	NOUN	0	4/4
4	zow	0	3	zow	zow	0	3/4	be.NPRS	LEX	VERB	0	2/4
5	n	1	1	n	n	0	4/4	PST.UNW	GRAM	GRAM	-1	-2

Figure 4: Example of input, outputs, and associated features to Lost for the Tsez reference sentence of Figure 1.

and its first and last three letters (d and e respectively). Figure 4 displays an example of input and the associated features.

With all these inputs, we compute unigram and bigram feature functions, detailed in Table 2. On top of the basic unigram and bigram features involving the gloss (top of the table), we also consider the binary category b and PoS tag p to compute more general feature functions (middle of the table). The idea is to capture associations between specific grammatical labels occurring after a given PoS tag (e.g. (VERB, PST.UNW) with the bi-pos-gloss feature).

In the S2 system, we add two more features: first, a binary variable (uni-copy-trg-src), which is True only for lexical glosses that occur letter-for-letter in the source sentence, to account notably for copied words (e.g. proper nouns). Second, we add a categorical feature (uni-pos-src-trg) encoding information about the relative position of the current morpheme with each target word in the translation, to lower the probability of high-distortion source-target associations. This categorical encoding is computed by chunking each sequence into four parts and reporting the chunk numbers: for instance, the value '(1/4, 3/4)' is used when matching a morpheme in the first quarter of the source sentence with a target word in the third quarter of the target sentence. For any unaligned target word, we use -1 as the corresponding position; for grammatical glosses, we assign the value -2 for the corresponding target word.

3 Experimental conditions

3.1 Languages

Our (partial) official submission for S1 considers the following five (out of seven) languages: Tsez (ddo), Gitksan (git), Lezgi (lez), Natugu (ntu; surprise language), and Uspanteko (usp; target translation in Spanish). For our second submission (S2), we could only consider three languages (Tsez, Gitksan, and Lezgi). Since our system relies on the translation to get the lexical glosses, we could not run our models on Nyangbo (nyb), although the corpus has a similar size to other languages we studied. For all submissions, we rely solely on the provided training datasets; no external resource was used.

We have run S2 on Tsez and Uspanteko subsequently and will also report these results below.

3.2 Pre-processing

The PoS tags and lemmas are obtained with spaCy,[5] using the `en_core_web_sm` and `es_core_news_sm` pipelines for English and Spanish translations respectively.

All lemmas from the translation are lowercased except when the associated PoS tag is a proper noun ('PROPN').

3.3 SimAlign settings

Since the glosses and the translation are in the same language, we use the embeddings from the English BERT (bert-base-uncased) (Devlin et al., 2019) when the target language is English and mBERT ('bert-base-multilingual-uncased') when it is in Spanish (for Uspanteko). We can note here that our model is compatible with multiple target languages, SimAlign being an off-the-shelf multilingual (neural) aligner.

Our preliminary experiments showed that the embeddings from the 0-th layer yielded the best alignments, especially compared to the 8-th layer, which seems to work best in most alignment tasks. A plausible explanation is that contextualised embeddings are unnecessary here because lexical glosses do not constitute a standard English sentence (for instance, they do not contain stop words, and their word order reflects the source language word order).

[5] `https://spacy.io/`.

Feature	Test	Example (cf. Figure 4 $i = 5$)
uni-gloss	$\mathbb{1}(g_i = g)$	PST.UNW
bi-gloss	$\mathbb{1}(g_i = g) \wedge \mathbb{1}(g_{i-1} = g')$	(be.NPRS, PST.UNW)
uni-gloss-morph	$\mathbb{1}(g_i = g) \wedge \mathbb{1}(m_i = m)$	(PST.UNW, n)
uni-gloss-position	$\mathbb{1}(g_i = g) \wedge \mathbb{1}(t_i = t)$	(PST.UNW, 1)
uni-gloss-length	$\mathbb{1}(g_i = g) \wedge \mathbb{1}(l_i = l)$	(PST.UNW, 1)
bi-gloss-morph	$\mathbb{1}(g_i = g) \wedge \mathbb{1}(g_{i-1} = g') \wedge \mathbb{1}(m_i = m)$	(be.NPRS, PST.UNW, n)
uni-gloss-start	$\mathbb{1}(g_i = g) \wedge \mathbb{1}(d_i = d)$	(PST.UNW, n)
uni-gloss-end	$\mathbb{1}(g_i = g) \wedge \mathbb{1}(e_i = e)$	(PST.UNW, n)
uni/bi-bin	$\mathbb{1}(b_i = b)\ (\wedge\mathbb{1}(b_{i-1} = b'))$	GRAM ((LEX, GRAM))
uni/bi-pos	$\mathbb{1}(p_i = p)\ (\wedge\mathbb{1}(p_{i-1} = p'))$	GRAM ((VERB, GRAM))
uni-bin-morph/position/length	$\mathbb{1}(b_i = b) \wedge \mathbb{1}(m_i = m)/\mathbb{1}(t_i = t)/\mathbb{1}(l_i = l)$	(GRAM, n) / (GRAM, 1) / (GRAM, 1)
uni-bin-start/end	$\mathbb{1}(b_i = b) \wedge \mathbb{1}(d_i = d)/\mathbb{1}(e_i = e)$	(GRAM, n) / (GRAM, n)
bi-position-bin	$\mathbb{1}(t_i = t) \wedge \mathbb{1}(t_{i-1} = t') \wedge \mathbb{1}(b_i = b)$	(0, 1, GRAM)
bi-bin-gloss	$\mathbb{1}(g_i = g) \wedge \mathbb{1}(b_{i-1} = b')$	(LEX, PST.UNW)
bi-gloss-bin	$\mathbb{1}(b_i = b) \wedge \mathbb{1}(g_{i-1} = g')$	(be.NPRS, GRAM)
uni-pos-morph	$\mathbb{1}(p_i = p) \wedge \mathbb{1}(m_i = m)$	(GRAM, n)
bi-pos-gloss	$\mathbb{1}(g_i = g) \wedge \mathbb{1}(p_{i-1} = p')$	(VERB, PST.UNW)
bi-gloss-pos	$\mathbb{1}(p_i = p) \wedge \mathbb{1}(g_{i-1} = g')$	(be.NPRS, GRAM)
uni-pos-start/end	$\mathbb{1}(p_i = p) \wedge \mathbb{1}(d_i = d)/\mathbb{1}(e_i = e)$	(GRAM, n) / (GRAM, n)
uni-copy-trg	$\mathbb{1}(ct_i = ct)$	-1
uni-copy-trg-src	$\mathbb{1}(ct_i = ct) \wedge \mathbb{1}(cs_i = cs)$	(-1, 0)
uni-posi-ts	$\mathbb{1}(pt_i = pt) \wedge \mathbb{1}(ps_i = ps)$	(-2, 4/4)
uni-gloss-morph-pts	$\mathbb{1}(g_i = g) \wedge \mathbb{1}(pt_i = pt)$ $\wedge\mathbb{1}(m_i = m) \wedge \mathbb{1}(ps_i = ps)$	(PST.UNW, -2, n, 4/4)

Table 2: Unigram and bigram features for our submissions: S1 features about the main gloss label on top, S1 features involving the two other general outputs, and S2 additional features at the bottom.

3.4 Parameter settings

We always use Lost with the default setting, using only the l_1 regularisation penalty $\rho_1 = 0.5$ and keeping the l_2 penalty term to $\rho_2 = 0$. This setting gave the best results on average in our preliminary experiments.

3.5 Metrics

We use the same evaluation metrics as in the Shared Task: morpheme accuracy, word accuracy, BLEU, and differentiated precision, recall, and F1-score for grammatical (gram) and lexical (stem) glosses.

4 Results

Table 3 reports the results for the organiser's baseline[6] and our systems on the development dataset, while Table 4 gives the corresponding test numbers. We only present the word- and morpheme-level (overall) accuracy, which are the two official metrics of the Shared Task results.[7] We also report the results of S2 for Tsez and Uspanteko, which were not available at the time of submission.

model	ddo	git	lez	ntu	usp
baseline	74.2	25.0	32.6	-	75.9
S1	83.6	40.2	84.4	88.2	76.5
S2	84.5*	43.8	85.1	88.5	77.3
baseline	85.0	30.0	50.1	-	81.3
S1	91.0	55.5	87.3	92.1	82.7
S2	91.5*	58.8	88.2	92.4	83.4*

Table 3: Accuracy (overall) at the word (top) and morpheme (bottom) levels for the baseline and our two systems on the *development* dataset. Star-marked values correspond to runs that were not available at the time of submission.

Our systems are consistently better than the baseline, with larger gaps when few training sentences are available (cf. Gitksan or Lezgi). Our second system slightly improves the accuracy on the development set; a similar trend can also be observed on the test set.

Compared to other submitted systems, we reached the best word accuracy for Gitksan and

[6]https://github.com/sigmorphon/2023glossingST/tree/main/baseline.

[7]https://github.com/sigmorphon/2023glossingST/blob/main/results.md.

model	ddo	git	lez	ntu	usp
baseline	75.7	16.4	34.5	41.1	76.6
S1	84.9	28.4	83.4	88.8	76.3
S2	85.5*	31.5	83.0	89.3	76.7*
baseline	85.3	25.3	51.8	49.0	82.5
S1	91.4	50.8	87.2	92.6	82.4
S2	91.8*	51.1	87.0	92.8	82.7*

Table 4: Accuracy (overall) at the word (top) and morpheme (bottom) levels for the baseline and our two systems on the *test* dataset. Star-marked values correspond to runs that were not available at the time of submission.

Natugu and the best morpheme accuracy for Natugu.

5 Discussion

5.1 Impact of training data size

Table 5 displays the evolution of the F1-scores at the morpheme levelCheck this ? broken down by gloss type (lexical and grammatical) for three sizes of the training dataset in Natugu (200, 500, and all 791 sentences). For both settings, the model reaches better scores for grammatical glosses, and, unsurprisingly, lexical glosses benefit more from the increase in training data. While the additional features in S2 were mostly introduced to improve the lexical gloss prediction in the small resource condition, it is noteworthy that they also help improve the prediction of grammatical labels. Similar observations were made for the other test languages.

	S1		S2	
	gram	lex	gram	lex
200	93.3	80.5	93.6	81.3
500	95.3	88.5	95.2	88.3
full	95.7	89.5	95.9	89.6

Table 5: F1-scores for grammatical and lexical glosses with an increasing number of training data in Natugu.

5.2 Number of selected features

Table 6 presents the number of active features (in thousands) selected among all features (in millions) by S1 and S2. We note here that thanks to the l_1-regularisation, most feature weights are set to 0 since less than 1% of the features are actually active. For illustrative purposes, Appendix A lists the features with the largest weight for the Lezgi system.

	ddo	git	lez	ntu	usp
S1	167k (170M)	3k (0.8M)	43k (24M)	60k (39M)	132k (34M)
S2	174k (172M)	3k (0.8M)	46k (24M)	64k (40M)	137k (35M)

Table 6: Number of active features (out of the total number of computed features) for each setting and language.

6 Conclusion

Assuming the lexical glosses can be aligned with words in the target translation, we repurposed a statistical machine translation system based on a globally-normalised model, akin to CRFs, that allows us to dynamically define a local set of labels for the automatic gloss generation task. Using two sets of features, our systems are compatible in low- and very low-resource settings and outperformed the baseline models according to several evaluation metrics.

We plan on further exploring feature functions on both source and target sides. Besides, since our systems rely on automatic alignments, which may contain and project some noise, we will try to remove this dependency modelling alignment as an unobserved variable in a latent variable model. Furthermore, as our submission focused on low-resource data conditions, we did not consider neural methods, which are notably data-intensive; future work would be to integrate word embeddings for better-resourced languages such as Arapaho.

Our code is available at: `https://github.com/shuokabe/gloss_lost`.

Acknowledgements

This work was partly funded by French ANR and German DFG under grant ANR-19-CE38-0015 (CLD 2025). The authors warmly thank Thomas Lavergne for his help and assistance regarding the configuration and exploitation of Lost.

References

Diego Barriga Martínez, Victor Mijangos, and Ximena Gutierrez-Vasques. 2021. Automatic interlinear glossing for Otomi language. In *Proceedings of the First Workshop on Natural Language Processing for Indigenous Languages of the Americas*, pages 34–43, Online. Association for Computational Linguistics.

Balthazar Bickel, Bernard. Comrie, and Martin Haspelmath. 2008. The Leipzig Glossing Rules: Conventions for interlinear morpheme-by-morpheme glosses. Leipzig: Max Planck Institute for Evolutionary Anthropology, Department of Linguistics. https://www.eva.mpg.de/lingua/resources/glossing-rules.php.

Jacob Devlin, Ming-Wei Chang, Kenton Lee, and Kristina Toutanova. 2019. BERT: Pre-training of deep bidirectional transformers for language understanding. In *Proceedings of the 2019 Conference of the North American Chapter of the Association for Computational Linguistics: Human Language Technologies, Volume 1 (Long and Short Papers)*, pages 4171–4186, Minneapolis, Minnesota. Association for Computational Linguistics.

Michael Ginn, Sarah Moeller, Alexis Palmer, Anna Stacey, Garrett Nicolai, Mans Hulden, and Miikka Silfverberg. 2023. Findings of the SIGMORPHON 2023 shared task on interlinear glossing. In *Proceedings of the 20th SIGMORPHON Workshop on Computational Research in Phonetics, Phonology, and Morphology*. Association for Computational Linguistics.

Masoud Jalili Sabet, Philipp Dufter, François Yvon, and Hinrich Schütze. 2020. SimAlign: High quality word alignments without parallel training data using static and contextualized embeddings. In *Findings of the Association for Computational Linguistics: EMNLP 2020*, pages 1627–1643, Online. Association for Computational Linguistics.

John D. Lafferty, Andrew McCallum, and Fernando C. N. Pereira. 2001. Conditional random fields: Probabilistic models for segmenting and labeling sequence data. In *Proceedings of the Eighteenth International Conference on Machine Learning*, ICML '01, page 282–289, San Francisco, CA, USA. Morgan Kaufmann Publishers Inc.

Thomas Lavergne, Alexandre Allauzen, Josep Maria Crego, and François Yvon. 2011. From n-gram-based to CRF-based translation models. In *Proceedings of the Sixth Workshop on Statistical Machine Translation*, pages 542–553, Edinburgh, Scotland. Association for Computational Linguistics.

Percy Liang, Alexandre Bouchard-Côté, Dan Klein, and Ben Taskar. 2006. An end-to-end discriminative approach to machine translation. In *Proceedings of the 21st International Conference on Computational Linguistics and 44th Annual Meeting of the Association for Computational Linguistics*, pages 761–768, Sydney, Australia. Association for Computational Linguistics.

Angelina McMillan-Major. 2020. Automating gloss generation in interlinear glossed text. In *Proceedings of the Society for Computation in Linguistics 2020*, pages 355–366, New York, New York. Association for Computational Linguistics.

Sarah Moeller and Mans Hulden. 2018. Automatic glossing in a low-resource setting for language documentation. In *Proceedings of the Workshop on Computational Modeling of Polysynthetic Languages*, pages 84–93, Santa Fe, New Mexico, USA. Association for Computational Linguistics.

Xingyuan Zhao, Satoru Ozaki, Antonios Anastasopoulos, Graham Neubig, and Lori Levin. 2020. Automatic interlinear glossing for under-resourced languages leveraging translations. In *Proceedings of the 28th International Conference on Computational Linguistics*, pages 5397–5408, Barcelona, Spain (Online). International Committee on Computational Linguistics.

A Feature weights

Type	Feature	Weight
uni-gloss-start	say ∧ луг	3.22
bi-gloss-morph	say ∧ AOR ∧ лагьа	3.22
bi-gloss-morph	talking ∧ AOC ∧ гафарун	2.80
uni-gloss-morph-pts	. ∧ -1 ∧ . ∧ 4/4	2.75
bi-gloss-morph	fortress ∧ OBL ∧ къеле	2.65
uni-gloss-end	now ∧ ила	2.65
uni-gloss-start	dog ∧ киц	2.65
bi-gloss-morph	newspaper ∧ OBL ∧ газет	2.49
uni-gloss-start	girl ∧ руш	2.49
bi-gloss-morph	SBST ∧ PST ∧ ди	2.49

Table 7: Top 10 (positive) features of S2 for Lezgi.

Table 7 displays the features with the largest weight in the S2 system trained on the Lezgi corpus. We can notice here that some (initial or final) character trigram features (uni-gloss-start and uni-gloss-end) are relevant, corresponding to lexemes that either typically occur with an inflexion mark: 'лугьу' and 'лугьун' for 'say', occurring approximately 200 times together or that combine with a prefix, as 'гила' and 'игила' for 'now' (around 20 co-occurrences).

SigMoreFun Submission to the SIGMORPHON Shared Task on Interlinear Glossing

Taiqi He*, Lindia Tjuatja*, Nate Robinson,
Shinji Watanabe, David R. Mortensen, Graham Neubig, Lori Levin
Language Technologies Institute
Carnegie Mellon University
{taiqih,ltjuatja,nrrobins,swatanab,dmortens,gneubig,lsl}@cs.cmu.edu

Abstract

In our submission to the SIGMORPHON 2023 Shared Task on interlinear glossing (IGT), we explore approaches to data augmentation and modeling across seven low-resource languages. For data augmentation, we explore two approaches: creating artificial data from the provided training data and utilizing existing IGT resources in other languages. On the modeling side, we test an enhanced version of the provided token classification baseline as well as a pretrained multilingual seq2seq model. Additionally, we apply post-correction using a dictionary for Gitksan, the language with the smallest amount of data. We find that our token classification models are the best performing, with the highest word-level accuracy for Arapaho and highest morpheme-level accuracy for Gitksan out of all submissions. We also show that data augmentation is an effective strategy, though applying artificial data pretraining has very different effects across both models tested.

1 Introduction

This paper describes the SigMoreFun submission to the SIGMORPHON 2023 Shared Task on interlinear glossing. Given input text in a target language, the task is to predict the corresponding interlinear gloss (using Leipzig glossing conventions). IGT is an important form of linguistic annotation for the morphological analysis of languages, and also serves as an extremely valuable resource for language documentation and education for speakers of low-resource languages.

There were two tracks for this shared task, Track 1 (closed) and Track 2 (open). For Track 1, systems could only be trained on input sentences and glosses; in Track 2, systems could make use of the morphological segmentation of the input as well as any (non-IGT) external resources. Since the Track 2 setting better matches the long-term research goals of our team, we only participate in this open track.

In our submission, we investigate two different approaches. First, we attempt data augmentation by either creating our own artificial gloss data by manipulating the existing training data, or by utilizing existing resources containing IGT in other languages (§2). Second, we explore two different models for gloss generation (§3). The first builds off the token classification baseline, while the second uses a pretrained multilingual seq2seq model.

Finally, we also attempt to post-correct model outputs with a dictionary. We apply this to Gitksan and find that this, combined with our other approaches, results in the highest morpheme-level accuracy for Gitksan in Track 2.

2 Data Augmentation

One major challenge for this shared task is the scale of data provided. All of the languages have less than 40k lines of training data, and all but Arapaho have less than 10k. The smallest dataset (Gitksan) has only 31 lines of data. Thus, one obvious method to try is data augmentation. More specifically, we try pretraining our models on different forms of augmented data before training them on the original target language data.

We explored two forms of data augmentation. First, we generated artificial gloss data in the target language by swapping words in the existing training data. Second, we utilized data from ODIN (Lewis and Xia, 2010; Xia et al., 2014) to see if transfer learning from data in other languages can help improve performance.

2.1 Artificial Data

A challenge our team faced with respect to data augmentation is figuring out how to obtain additional data when we do not have much knowledge of the languages' grammatical systems, along with the fact that these languages are generally from

*These authors contributed equally

Proceedings of the 20th SIGMORPHON workshop on Computational Research in Phonetics, Phonology, and Morphology, pages 209–216
July 14, 2023 ©2023 Association for Computational Linguistics

digitally under-resourced language families. Furthermore, we wanted our solution to be easily implemented and relatively language agnostic due to time constraints and practical usability for researchers working on a variety of languages.

Thus, one avenue of data augmentation we tried was by creating artificial data from the provided training data. This requires no rule-writing or knowledge of the grammar of the language, and thus could be applied quickly and easily to all of the languages in the shared task.

We used a naive word-swapping method to randomly swap morphemes that occur in similar contexts to create new sentences. To do this, for each gloss line, we replace each word stem (that has a gloss label affix) with "STEM" to create a skeleton gloss. We naively determine if a label is a stem by checking if it is in lowercase. We do not do this to words that do not have affixes as (with the exception of Uspanteko) we do not have access to parts of speech, and do not want to swap words that would create an ungrammatical sequence.

We create a dictionary mapping each skeleton word gloss to possible actual glosses, and map each actual gloss to possible surface forms (we make no assumptions that these mappings are one-to-one). We then randomly sample k random skeleton glosses (in this case, we used k equal to roughly three times the amount of training data) and randomly fill in words that match the format of skeleton words present in the line.

(1) to (3) below illustrate an example in this process. We create a skeleton gloss (2) from the Gitksan sentence in (1) by replacing the all word stems that have an affix with "STEM" in both the segmentation and gloss tiers—in this case, only *'witxw-it* applies to this step. Then to create the artificial data in (3), we replace the skeleton word and corresponding gloss with another word from the training data that has the same skeleton form, in this case *hahla'lst-it*.

(1) ii nee-dii-t naa dim 'witxw-it
CCNJ NEG-FOC-3.I who PROSP come-SX

(2) ii nee-dii-t naa dim STEM-it
CCNJ NEG-FOC-3.I who PROSP STEM-SX

(3) ii nee-dii-t naa dim hahla'lst-it
CCNJ NEG-FOC-3.I who PROSP work-SX

While this method may create a somewhat unnatural input surface sequence (as we are unable to capture phonological changes in the surface form and corresponding translations may be nonsensical), this method guarantees that the structure of the gloss is a naturally occurring sequence (as we only use gloss skeletons that are present in the input). However, a limitation of this method is that it does not extend to out-of-vocabulary tokens or unseen gloss structures. Furthermore, as we cannot generate a gold-standard translation for the artificial data, we do not make use of a translation in training.

2.2 ODIN

Another potential avenue for data augmentation is transfer learning from data in other languages, which has been shown to be an effective method to improve performance in low-resource settings (Ruder et al., 2019).

The available resource we utilize is ODIN, or the Online Database for Interlinear Text (Lewis and Xia, 2010; Xia et al., 2014). ODIN contains 158,007 lines of IGT, covering 1,496 languages.

We use the 2.1 version of ODIN data and convert the dataset to the shared task format, and filter out languages with fewer than five glossed sentences. However, there remains significant noise in the dataset that could cause significant alignment issues for the token classification models. Therefore we opt to only train the ByT5 models on ODIN, in the hope that this model is less sensitive to alignment errors. Indeed, we find that the ByT5 model finetuned first on ODIN receives a performance boost when finetuned again on the shared task data.

3 Models

We explore two models for gloss generation. The first one is built upon the token classification baseline with some improvements, and we treat this model as our internal baseline. The second model we deploy tests whether we can achieve competitive performance by finetuning a pretrained character based multilingual and multitask model, ByT5. For this model, we perform minimal preprocessing and use raw segmented morphemes and free translations if available.

3.1 Token Classification Transformer

We use the baseline Track 2 model provided by the organizers as a starting point. The original implementation randomly initializes a transformer model from the default Huggingface RoBERTa base configuration, and uses a token classification objective with cross-entropy loss, where each gloss is treated as a distinct token. The morphemes and free translations are tokenized by space and dashes, with punctuations pre-separated. They are concatenated and separated by the SEP token and are used as the inputs to the model. We modify the original Track 2 baseline model to obtain a better baseline. We use pretrained weights from XLM-RoBERTa base (Conneau et al., 2020), instead of randomly initializing the weights. We also slightly modify the morpheme tokenizer to enforce that the number of morpheme tokens matches the number of output gloss tokens exactly.

Additionally, we introduce the COPY token to replace the gloss if it matches the corresponding morpheme exactly. An example from Natugu is shown in gloss (4):

(4) 67 . mnc-x Mzlo Skul
COPY COPY be-1MINI COPY COPY

We believe this would improve performance by removing the need to memorize glossed code-switching and proper nouns, though it is only effective if the code-switched language is the same as the matrix language (e.g. Arapaho), and would have no effect if the source language uses a different orthography or is code-switched to another language, where the gloss would not matched the morpheme form exactly. This method also compresses all punctuation markers into one token, but the usefulness of this side effect is less clear.

Since we are using pretrained weights, it is then natural to explore integrating the pretrained tokenizer. Since XLM-RoBERTa was not trained on any of the source languages, it makes the most sense to only use the pretrained tokenizer to tokenize free translations, if they are available, and extend the vocabulary to include morphemes.

3.2 Finetuned ByT5

Multi-task and multi-lingual pretrained large language models have been shown to be effective for many tasks. We explore whether such models can be used effectively for glossing. We conduct experiments with both mT5 (Xue et al., 2021) and ByT5 (Xue et al., 2022), but ByT5 is preferred because it takes raw texts (bytes or characters) as inputs and in theory should be more effective for unseen languages. We use a prompt based multilingual sequence to sequence objective for both models. The prompt template is: "Generate interlinear gloss from `[source language]`: `[segmented morphemes]` with its `[matrix language]` translation: `[free translation]` Answer: ". Data from all languages are mixed together and shuffled, with no up or down sampling. After initial experiments, we find ByT5 outperforms mT5 across all languages, and therefore we only conduct subsequent experiments on ByT5 and report those results.

Upon initial experiments, we also find the results for Lezgi to be lower than expected. We hypothesize that the fact that the data are in Cyrillic script causes this deficiency, since ByT5 was trained on far less Cyrillic data than data in the Latin script. Therefore we create an automatic romanization tool, sourced from Wikipedia[1] and integrated in the Epitran package (Mortensen et al., 2018), and convert all Lezgi data to Latin script for ByT5 finetuning.

After inspecting the outputs of the ByT5 models, we find cases where punctuations are attached to the previous glosses, instead of being separated by a space as is standard in the training sets. This is probably due to the fact that the model was pretrained on untokenized data and this behavior is preserved despite finetuning on tokenized data. We therefore use a simple regular expression based tokenizer to fix the inconsistencies. We notice that the procedure only gives performance boost on Gitksan, Lezgi, Uspanteko, and Natugu, and so we only apply the procedure to those languages, leaving the rest of the outputs unchanged.

4 Dictionary Post-correction: Gitksan

One of the key challenges for extremely low resource languages is the integration of structured linguistic data in other forms, such as a dictionary, into machine learning pipelines. We test a simple post-correction method from a pre-existing dictionary on Gitksan only, due to its unique combination of low resource and easily obtainable dictionary in machine readable form. We use the dictionary compiled by Forbes et al. (2021), without consulting the morphological analyzers that they also provided. At inference time, if a morpheme is unseen during training, we search for the exact form in the dictionary. We also expand the search to all sub sequences of morphemes within the enclosing word, plus the previous whole word in cases where a particle is included in the dictionary form. The first

[1] `https://en.wikipedia.org/wiki/Lezgin_alphabets`

matched definition is used as the gloss and if none of the search yields an exact match, we fall back to the model prediction. We only apply this method to the token classification models because the alignment between morphemes and glosses is directly established, whereas the seq2seq models do not guarantee that the number of glosses matches the number of morphemes.

5 Results and Discussion

Tables 1 and 2 show our systems' performance (as well as the original baseline) on the test data with respect to word- and morpheme-level micro-averaged accuracy, respectively. Overall, the token classification model trained first on the artificially generated augmented data perform the best, with the model trained on the shared task data only not far behind. Meanwhile, ByT5 models perform worse, with the model finetuned first on ODIN trailing our best model by a few percentage points, while the model finetuned first on augmented data performs worse than the baseline.

5.1 Data Augmentation

Overall, we find data augmentation to be useful. With artificially generated data, we see the effects are perhaps greatest for the mid-resource languages (ddo, lez, ntu, nyb, usp), while the highest and lowest resourced languages did not receive much benefit from pretraining on the artificial data. We think this is perhaps because there is a "sweet spot" with respect to the amount of data that is required to train a model. If there is enough data already, in the case of Arapaho, then the noisiness of artificial data would out-weight the benefit of training on them. On the other end of the scale, Gitksan perhaps needs more synthetic data for data augmentation to yield meaningful improvements.

For ByT5 models, artificially generated data seem to have the opposite effect, where performance is significantly degraded. A speculation for this effect is the fact the pretrained model is more semantically aware, and since the artificially generated sentences could be nonsensical, the model could become confused. On the other hand, pretraining on ODIN yields improvements for the majority of the languages[2]. This is encouraging since we did not perform much preprocessing for ODIN, and there is definitely still room to make the data cleaner and more internally consistent, which in turn should result in a better model.

5.2 Choice of Hyperparameters

We find the choice of hyperparameters of the token classification models to be necessarily language and dataset specific. Arapaho and Gitksan in particular need special attention, where the number of training epochs need to be adjusted for the very high and low data size. We also developed most of the optimization on the token classification model on Arapaho. However, we did not have time to propagate the changes (using pretrained tokenizer, saving the last model instead of the model with the lowest validation loss) to the rest of languages since initial experiment showed that pretrained tokenizers did not improve on the other languages. However, after the submission deadline is concluded, we ran more experiments and discovered that adding pretrained tokenizers requires more training steps, and the training is better controlled by specifying the training steps instead of epochs. We do not include those latest experiments in this paper, but our token classification models have the potential to perform better with more hyperparameter tuning.

5.3 In- Versus Out-of-Vocabulary Errors

One dimension of error analysis we investigated was what proportion of our systems' errors come from morphemes or words that are either in or out of the training data vocabulary. We count a morpheme or word as in-vocabulary if the surface form and its corresponding gloss co-occur in the provided training data (not including the development data, as our models are only trained on the train set). Note that there is a much larger proportion of OOV words as opposed to morphemes due to the fact that an unseen word can be composed of different combinations of seen morphemes.

Table 3 shows the proportion of morphemes and words that are out-of-vocab (OOV) within the test set. While nearly all the languages have less than 10% of their morphemes classified as OOV, Gitksan notably has a relatively large portion of OOV test data, with $\approx 45\%$ of morphemes and $\approx 78\%$ of words being OOV.

Tables 4 and 5 show our models' performances on in- verses out-of-vocab tokens at the morpheme and word levels, respectively. While we would intuitively expect that word-level OOV accuracy be about the same or worse than morpheme-level OOV

[2] Tsez is the only language that appeared in ODIN (68 sentences). We did not remove it from the corpus but this should have little influence on the performance because the size of the dataset is very small.

Model	arp	ddo	git	lez	ntu	nyb	usp	AVG
xlmr-base	**85.87**	73.77	27.86 / **34.11**[a]	74.15	**82.99**	80.61	73.47	72.14
xlmr-aug	82.92	**80.07**	24.74 / 31.25	**77.77**	78.72	**85.53**	**77.51**	**73.39**
byt5-base	78.86	80.32	14.84	60.72[b]	76.67	76.73	77.21	66.48
byt5-aug	73.27	62.37	4.17	38.60	55.11	69.25	70.85	53.38
byt5-odin	80.56	82.79	20.57	63.77	77.97	82.59	75.72	69.14
baseline	85.44	75.71	16.41	34.54	41.08	84.30	76.55	59.14

[a]We report before / after dictionary based post-correction for Gitksan.
[b]We trained this model without romanizing Lezgi.

Table 1: Word-level accuracy of our submitted systems. Best performance per language in the table is **bolded**. The XLMR baseline is the highest Arapaho accuracy reported out of all shared task submissions.

Model	arp	ddo	git	lez	ntu	nyb	usp	AVG
xlmr-base	**91.36**	84.35	47.47 / **52.82**	80.17	**88.35**	85.84	80.08	80.42
xlmr-aug	89.34	**88.15**	46.89 / 52.39	**82.36**	85.53	**89.49**	**83.08**	**81.48**
byt5-base	78.82	75.77	12.59	44.10	62.40	78.97	74.25	60.99
byt5-aug	72.10	57.93	2.60	26.24	35.62	70.01	67.73	47.46
byt5-odin	80.81	78.24	12.74	50.00	63.39	85.30	73.25	63.39
baseline	91.11	85.34	25.33	51.82	49.03	88.71	82.48	67.69

Table 2: Morpheme-level accuracy of our submitted systems. Best performance per language in the table is **bolded**. The XLMR baseline with artificial pretraining and dictionary post-correction is the highest Gitksan accuracy reported out of all shared task submissions.

	arp	ddo	git	lez	ntu	nyb	usp
Morph	0.043	0.009	0.450	0.056	0.034	0.019	0.070
Word	0.242	0.155	0.781	0.169	0.214	0.084	0.200

Table 3: Proportion of morphemes and words that are OOV within the test set.

accuracy, this is not the case due to the fact that a large portion of out-of-vocab words are formed with in-vocab morphemes. For most languages, with the exception of Gitksan, there appears to be a trade-off between better in-vocab morpheme performance with XLMR and performance out-of-vocab with ByT5.

6 Related Work

There have been a variety of approaches to the problem of (semi-) automatically generating interlinear gloss. Baldridge and Palmer (2009) investigate the efficacy of active learning for the task of interlinear glossing, using annotation time required by expert and non-expert annotators as their metric. The system they use to generate gloss label suggestions is a standard maximum entropy classifier.

A rule-based approach by Snoek et al. (2014) utilizes an FST to generate glosses for Plains Cree, focusing on nouns. Samardžić et al. (2015) view the task of glossing segmented text as a two-step process, first treating it as a standard POS tagging task and then adding lexical glosses from a dictionary. They demonstrate this method on a Chintang corpus of about 1.2 million words.

A number of other works focusing on interlinear glossing utilize conditional random field (CRF) models. Moeller and Hulden (2018) test three different models on a very small Lezgi dataset (< 3000 words): a CRF (that outputs BIO labels with the corresponding gloss per character in the input), a segmentation and labelling pipeline that utilizes a CRF (for BIO labels) and SVM (for gloss labels), and an LSTM seq2seq model. They find that the CRF that jointly produces the BIO labels and tags produced the best results. McMillan-Major (2020) utilizes translations in their training data by creating two CRF models, one that predicts gloss from the segmented input and another than pre-

Model	arp	ddo	git	lez	ntu	nyb	usp
xlmr-base	95.20	85.12	82.89	84.79	90.87	87.46	86.05
	4.97	0.00	16.08	2.60	14.52	0.00	0.82
xlmr-aug	92.98	88.94	84.74	87.10	87.88	91.17	89.31
	7.49	0.00	12.86	2.60	19.35	0.00	0.41
byt5-aug	74.76	58.24	3.42	40.27	36.54	71.27	70.56
	12.31	24.10	1.61	23.54	9.68	3.23	30.20
byt5-odin	83.47	78.55	18.42	62.90	64.38	86.85	75.23
	21.14	43.37	5.79	47.52	35.48	3.23	46.94

Table 4: Morpheme-level accuracy over all tokens of our submitted systems, split by in- versus out-of-vocab. Cells highlighted in gray indicate OOV accuracy.

Model	arp	ddo	git	lez	ntu	nyb	usp
xlmr-base	95.93	78.18	95.23	84.24	93.14	85.85	86.27
	54.44	49.79	17.00	24.67	45.65	23.60	22.41
xlmr-aug	93.72	83.85	94.05	87.64	89.24	90.81	91.11
	49.17	59.51	13.67	29.33	40.00	23.24	28.09
byt5-aug	87.22	68.69	10.71	46.06	65.13	74.59	81.44
	29.69	28.04	2.33	2.00	18.26	11.24	28.63
byt5-odin	91.93	87.66	63.10	73.78	85.93	87.60	83.46
	45.07	56.36	8.67	14.67	48.70	28.09	44.81

Table 5: Word-level accuracy of our submitted systems, split by in- versus out-of-vocab. Cells highlighted in gray indicate OOV accuracy.

dicts from the translation, and then uses heuristics to determine which model to select from for each morpheme. Barriga Martínez et al. (2021) used a CRF model to achieve $> 90\%$ accuracy for glossing Otomi and find that it works better than an RNN, which is computationally more expensive.

Other works, including our systems, have turned to neural methods. Kondratyuk (2019) leverages pretrained multilingual BERT to encode input sentences, then apply additional word-level and character-level LSTM layers before jointly decoding lemmas and morphology tags using simple sequence tagging layers. Furthermore, they show that two-stage training by first training on all languages followed by training on the target language is more effective than training the system on the target language alone. An approach by Zhao et al. (2020), like McMillan-Major (2020), makes use of translations available in parallel corpora, but do so by using a multi-source transformer model. They also incorporate length control and alignment during inference to enhance their model, and test their system on Arapaho, Tsez, and Lezgi.

7 Conclusion

In our shared task submission, we explore data augmentation methods and modeling strategies for the task of interlinear glossing in seven low-resource languages. Our best performing models are token classification models using XLMR. We demonstrate that pretraining on artificial data with XLMR is an effective technique for the mid-resource test languages. Additionally, in our error analysis we find that we may have actually undertrained our token classification models, and thus our systems may have the potential to perform better with additional hyperparameter tuning. While our ByT5 models did not perform as well as our other systems, we show that pretraining on ODIN data is effective, despite this data being very noisy. Finally, we also demonstrate improvements by utilizing a dictionary to post-correct model outputs for Gitksan.

Acknowledgements

This work was supported by NSF CISE RI grant number 2211951, From Acoustic Signal to Morphosyntactic Analysis in one End-to-End Neural System.

References

Jason Baldridge and Alexis Palmer. 2009. How well does active learning *actually* work? Time-based evaluation of cost-reduction strategies for language documentation. In *Proceedings of the 2009 Conference on Empirical Methods in Natural Language Processing*, pages 296–305, Singapore. Association for Computational Linguistics.

Diego Barriga Martínez, Victor Mijangos, and Ximena Gutierrez-Vasques. 2021. Automatic interlinear glossing for Otomi language. In *Proceedings of the First Workshop on Natural Language Processing for Indigenous Languages of the Americas*, pages 34–43, Online. Association for Computational Linguistics.

Alexis Conneau, Kartikay Khandelwal, Naman Goyal, Vishrav Chaudhary, Guillaume Wenzek, Francisco Guzmán, Edouard Grave, Myle Ott, Luke Zettlemoyer, and Veselin Stoyanov. 2020. Unsupervised cross-lingual representation learning at scale.

Clarissa Forbes, Garrett Nicolai, and Miikka Silfverberg. 2021. An FST morphological analyzer for the gitksan language. In *Proceedings of the 18th SIGMORPHON Workshop on Computational Research in Phonetics, Phonology, and Morphology*, pages 188–197, Online. Association for Computational Linguistics.

Dan Kondratyuk. 2019. Cross-lingual lemmatization and morphology tagging with two-stage multilingual BERT fine-tuning. In *Proceedings of the 16th Workshop on Computational Research in Phonetics, Phonology, and Morphology*, pages 12–18, Florence, Italy. Association for Computational Linguistics.

William D. Lewis and Fei Xia. 2010. Developing ODIN: A Multilingual Repository of Annotated Language Data for Hundreds of the World's Languages. *Literary and Linguistic Computing*, 25(3):303–319.

Angelina McMillan-Major. 2020. Automating gloss generation in interlinear glossed text. *Proceedings of the Society for Computation in Linguistics*, 3(1):338–349.

Sarah Moeller and Mans Hulden. 2018. Automatic glossing in a low-resource setting for language documentation. In *Proceedings of the Workshop on Computational Modeling of Polysynthetic Languages*, pages 84–93.

David R. Mortensen, Siddharth Dalmia, and Patrick Littell. 2018. Epitran: Precision G2P for many languages. In *Proceedings of the Eleventh International Conference on Language Resources and Evaluation (LREC 2018)*, Miyazaki, Japan. European Language Resources Association (ELRA).

Sebastian Ruder, Matthew E Peters, Swabha Swayamdipta, and Thomas Wolf. 2019. Transfer learning in natural language processing. In *Proceedings of the 2019 conference of the North American chapter of the association for computational linguistics: Tutorials*, pages 15–18.

Tanja Samardžić, Robert Schikowski, and Sabine Stoll. 2015. Automatic interlinear glossing as two-level sequence classification.

Noam Shazeer and Mitchell Stern. 2018. Adafactor: Adaptive learning rates with sublinear memory cost. In *Proceedings of the 35th International Conference on Machine Learning*, volume 80 of *Proceedings of Machine Learning Research*, pages 4596–4604. PMLR.

Conor Snoek, Dorothy Thunder, Kaidi Lõo, Antti Arppe, Jordan Lachler, Sjur Moshagen, and Trond Trosterud. 2014. Modeling the noun morphology of Plains Cree. In *Proceedings of the 2014 Workshop on the Use of Computational Methods in the Study of Endangered Languages*, pages 34–42, Baltimore, Maryland, USA. Association for Computational Linguistics.

Fei Xia, William Lewis, Michael Wayne Goodman, Joshua Crowgey, and Emily M. Bender. 2014. Enriching ODIN. In *Proceedings of the Ninth International Conference on Language Resources and Evaluation (LREC'14)*, pages 3151–3157, Reykjavik, Iceland. European Language Resources Association (ELRA).

Linting Xue, Aditya Barua, Noah Constant, Rami Al-Rfou, Sharan Narang, Mihir Kale, Adam Roberts, and Colin Raffel. 2022. ByT5: Towards a token-free future with pre-trained byte-to-byte models. *Transactions of the Association for Computational Linguistics*, 10:291–306.

Linting Xue, Noah Constant, Adam Roberts, Mihir Kale, Rami Al-Rfou, Aditya Siddhant, Aditya Barua, and Colin Raffel. 2021. mT5: A massively multilingual pre-trained text-to-text transformer. In *Proceedings of the 2021 Conference of the North American Chapter of the Association for Computational Linguistics: Human Language Technologies*, pages 483–498, Online. Association for Computational Linguistics.

Xingyuan Zhao, Satoru Ozaki, Antonios Anastasopoulos, Graham Neubig, and Lori Levin. 2020. Automatic interlinear glossing for under-resourced languages leveraging translations. In *Proceedings of the 28th International Conference on Computational Linguistics*, pages 5397–5408, Barcelona, Spain (Online). International Committee on Computational Linguistics.

A Hyperparameter Settings

We use Adafactor (Shazeer and Stern, 2018) as the optimizer across all experiments, with the default scheduler from Hugging Face Transformers, a batch size of 32 for RoBERTa based models and a batch size of 4 with a gradient accumulation step of 8 for ByT5 based models. We train the token classification models for 40 epochs except for Arapaho, on which we train 20 epochs, and Gitksan, on which we train 2,000 steps. We train the ByT5 based models for 20 epochs on all of the data mixed together.

An Ensembled Encoder-Decoder System for Interlinear Glossed Text

Edith Coates
Department of Mathematics
University of British Columbia
Vancouver, Canada
icoates1@mail.ubc.ca

Abstract

This paper presents a submission to Track 1 of the 2023 SIGMORPHON shared task on interlinear glossed text (IGT) (Ginn et al., 2023). There are a wide amount of techniques for building and training IGT models (see Moeller and Hulden, 2018; McMillan-Major, 2020; Zhao et al., 2020). We describe the system's ensembled sequence-to-sequence approach, perform experiments, and share the submission's test-set accuracy. We also discuss future areas of research in low-resource token classification methods for IGT.

1 Introduction

This paper is a system demonstration for our submission to the 2023 SIGMORPHON shared task on interlinear glossed text (Ginn et al., 2023). We focused on the closed track of the task, where only the input sentence, output gloss, and translation are provided in training data. This was more restrictive than the open track, in which more information was available, such as morphological segmentations or part-of-speech tags.

1.1 Interlinear Glossed Text

Interlinear glossed text (IGT) is a form of linguistic data annotation which highlights the grammatical properties of a corpus of text. IGT is not standardized and varies from annotator to annotator (Palmer et al., 2009), but typically uses three lines for each sentence of text. The data provided in the shared task follow the Leipzig glossing conventions (Comrie et al., 2008), in which the first line contains a transcription in an "object language," i.e. the language of study; the second line is a morpheme-by-morpheme annoatation of the sentence (called a "gloss"); and the third line is a direct translation.

(1) Ap yukwhl ha'niisgwaa'ytxw.
VER IPFV-CN INS-on-rest
But it was Sunday.

Ex. 1 shows an example in Gitksan from the task's training data. In the gloss, the functional morphemes are referred to as "grams" and the lexical morphemes are "stems," as per Zhao et al. (2020).

1.2 Related Work

Moeller and Hulden (2018) used a character-level system that combined a Support Vector Machine for recognizing grams and stems with a Conditional Random Fields labeller for assigning output grams to input characters, using a BIO-tagging convention (Ramshaw and Marcus, 1995). They also trained a character-level LSTM encoder-decoder on the BIO-tagged data.

McMillan-Major (2020) uses an ensembled system in which two CRF models focus on the source text and gloss, and translation text and gloss, respectively.

Zhao et al. (2020) use a transformer-based encoder-decoder system in which the encoder is multi-sourced: the source text and the translation are encoded separately and then combined in a single attention mechanism.

1.3 Baseline Model

The IGT shared task baseline model (Ginn, 2023) is a transformer-based token classification system. The authors found that a sequence-to-sequence model required more data to converge and performed worse when compared to the token classification approach.

2 Methods

The system was based on an encoder-decoder model using the LSTM architecture (Sutskever et al., 2014). It used ensembling and data augmentation as a method to counteract the relatively lower performance of encoder-decoder models as highlighted in the previous section. The system was implemented with Fairseq (Ott et al., 2019) and trained on a single Nvidia GeForce MX350.

Proceedings of the 20th SIGMORPHON workshop on Computational Research in Phonetics, Phonology, and Morphology, pages 217–221
July 14, 2023 ©2023 Association for Computational Linguistics

Strategy	Input sequence	Output sequence
Character output	h a r i z i _ b o q n o _ ž a	r e q u e s t _ I I I - b e c o m e - T O P _ D E M 1 . S G
Token output	h a r i z i _ b o q n o _ ž a	request III - become - TOP DEM1 . SG
Stem token	h a r i z i _ b o q n o _ ž a	<stem> III - <stem> - TOP DEM1 . SG
Word-level (w=1)	b o q n o _ ž a _ <e>	DEM1 . SG
Stemmer model	t h e _ d r a g o n _ b e g g e d	r e q u e s t _ b e c o m e

Table 1: An example from the shared task's training data in Tsez, showing different preprocessing approaches.

Window size	Stem F1	Morpheme	Word
1	43%	42%	46%
2	46%	50%	**65%**
3	35%	40%	56%
1 and 2	**49%**	**54%**	64%
2 and 3	41%	47%	62%

Table 2: Development-set results for Tsez, comparing different word-level window sizes and ensembling combinations over stem F1-score, morpheme-level, and word-level accuracy. These models all use a token-level output alphabet.

Fairseq has built-in support for transformers as well as LSTMs, but the former requires more resources to train. The GPU used for this project did not have sufficient memory for training a convergent transformer model, and so the LSTM architecture was chosen instead.

2.1 Representing target glosses

The source language text was represented as a sequence of characters, and we experimented with several approaches for representing the gloss as a target alphabet. Initially, the output gloss was also represented as a sequence of characters. Later, we used a token-based output alphabet. See Table 1 for examples.

The shared task dataset includes translated stems in its glosses. We experimented with representing the stems with a special token instead, and a model for generating stems from the translation, but chose to use the token-based output with the original stems in the final results. Development-set results can be found in Table 3.

2.2 Word-level training examples

Instead of giving the system an entire sentence to gloss as one example, the system was trained with word-level examples, which included tokens on either side of the "target" word for added context. Since the output gloss contains the same number of tokens as the input sentence, training and inference can be performed on the word-level, and sentence-level results can be created from a simple concatenation of word-level results. The number of tokens on either side of the "target" became a hyperparameter, and we found that a word-window of two tokens on either side gave the best results for a single model. See Table 2 for results.

Output format	Stem F1	Morph.	Word
Characters	38%	44%	53%
Tokens	**49%**	**44%**	**64%**

Table 3: Development-set results for output formats for Tsez training data. Results for the stemmer and a special stem token are not included. Both systems use an ensemble of window size 1 and 2 word-level models.

2.3 Ensembling and voting

The final form of the system was a combination of a model trained on a window size of one, and another trained on a window size of two. During inference, Fairseq provides a negative log-likelihood (NLL) score for the model's predictions. A final output token was chosen by finding the smallest NLL score for either model's predictions. Figure 1 depicts the ensembling and voting process.

2.4 A model for predicting stems

We experimented with an additional sequence-to-sequence model for generating stems using the gloss and the translation text. The full translation was used as an input sequence, and just the stems from the gloss would be used as an output sequence. The input and output sequences were represented with a character-level alphabet.

The system used a simple technique for adding stems to the final model predictions: During the combination of word-level results into sentence-level outputs, the system replaced the special stem tokens with predictions from the stemmer model in the order that each sentence-level stemmer result was generated. If the model generated too many stems, the rightmost outputs would be left out, and

Word-level accuracy	arp	ddo	git	lez	ntu	nyb	usp	AVG
This submission	56%	74%	7%	66%	71%	77%	67%	60%
Baseline	71%	73%	17%	50%	42%	5%	72%	47%
Best other result (per language)	**79%**	**81%**	**21%**	**79%**	**81%**	**85%**	**73%**	**71%**
Morpheme-level accuracy								
This submission	45%	64%	9%	40%	37%	73%	56%	47%
Baseline	44%	51%	8%	42%	18%	14%	57%	34%
Best other result (per language)	**78%**	**73%**	**12%**	**62%**	**56%**	**87%**	**70%**	**63%**

Table 4: Test-set results of the shared task across all languages.

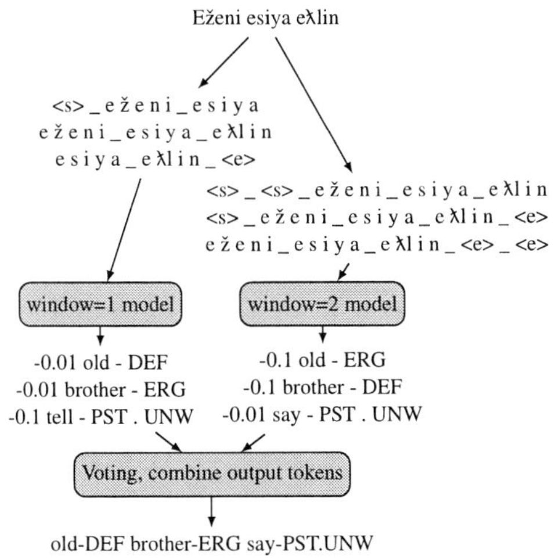

Figure 1: A diagram of the system's approach to word-level training and voting, with an example from Tsez and hypothetical NLL scores and word-level predictions.

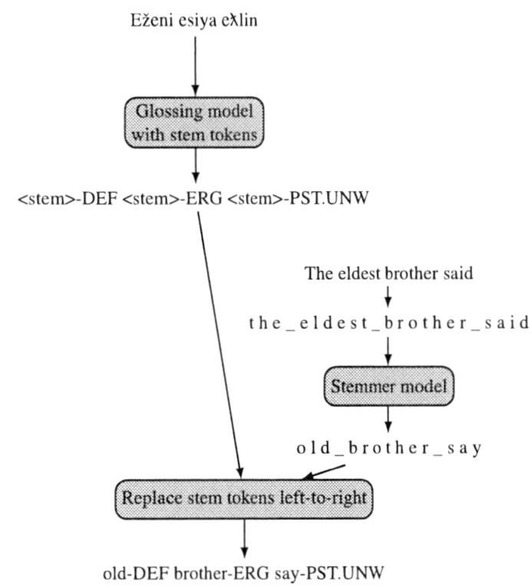

Figure 2: A diagram of the system with a model that uses the translation to predict stem tokens. The glossing model could be a single word-level model or an ensemble like in Figure 1.

if there were too few, at least one special stem token would remain. Figure 2 represents a glossing system working with the stemmer model.

This stemmer model was prototypical and we found that it did not have an effect on overall performance or stem F1 score.

2.5 Evaluation

We used the shared task baseline model's evaluation script, which calculates a variety of metrics, including an overall BLEU score, stem F1, precision, and recall, as well as word- and morpheme-level accuracy.

3 Results

The final system consisted of two word-level sequence-to-sequence models, trained with a word window size of one and two, respectively. The input alphabet consisted of characters and the output alphabet was token-level. The models were trained with an inverse square root learning rate scheduler, early stopping, and the Adam optimizer. Models trained on all languages except for Gitksan used a batch size of 128. Since the Gitksan training dataset was just 31 examples long, it used a batch size of 64 instead.

See Table 4 for results across all languages in the shared task training data.

3.1 Analysis

For most of the languages, the system performed better than the baseline in terms of word-level and morpheme-level accuracy. However, the relative performance varied by language: the system's word-level accuracy for Arapaho is 15% lower than the baseline, while the same metric for Nyangbo is 72% higher.

We hypothesized that these results could have

been caused by differences in morpheme-to-word ratios across the languages. Since the system was trained on word-level examples, a lower ratio would suggest longer sequences for training — Wu et al. (2021) points out that transformer models perform better than RNNs on longer sequences.

For each training dataset, we calculated the average morpheme-to-word ratio and found that Nautugu and Uspanteko have the joint highest ratios of 0.83, while Arapaho and Nyangbo are lower with 0.72 and 0.75, respectively. The language with the lowest ratio was Tsez, at 0.6.

There seems to be a weak trend: The model under-performed or was at par with the baseline for languages with low ratios. For languages with a higher ratios, the model performed better than the baseline, with an exception of Uspanteko.

From this analysis, we conclude that training data size and morpheme-to-word ratio alone cannot explain the model's under-performance for Arapaho and over-performance for Nyangbo.

4 Conclusion

This was a system demonstration of our submission to the 2023 SIGMORPHON shared task on interlinear glossed text. While the system was not the best-performing of all the submissions, it nonetheless performed consistently better than the baseline model in terms of word- and morpheme-level test-set accuracy.

The system was relatively inexpensive to train, as it was built on a single CUDA-enabled laptop. This could be an advantage of the LSTM-based architecture: when Wu et al. (2021) introduced the transformer architecture to character-level transduction tasks, the authors noted that transformer-based performance depended on finely-tuned hyperparameters and longer training times.

However, non-encoder-decoder systems for the ILG task still show lots of promise, especially for small datasets. Further research can be done to examine the effect of ensembling and data augmentation on CRF or LSTM-based token classification systems.

More work can be done on the stem generation system as well: a linguist-created inflectional database like the one described in Oliver et al. (2022) could algorithmically recognize stems and look up translations. Also, an upstream word alignment model, such as one of the IBM models described in Brown et al. (1993), could help with the construction of a stemmer system.

We hope this demonstration will lead to future work on low-resource systems for automatic ILG, in terms of both computation and dataset size.

5 Limitations

Due to time constraints, it was not possible to perform a satisfactory grid search on the large combinations of training hyperparameters, preprocessing techniques, and stem approaches. It is possible that a more optimal system is possible, but we were unable to find it.

6 Acknowledgements

Special thanks to Miikka Silfverberg, Naomi Liu, the organizers of the shared task, and the anonymous reviewers.

References

Peter F Brown, Stephen A Della Pietra, Vincent J Della Pietra, Robert L Mercer, et al. 1993. The mathematics of statistical machine translation: Parameter estimation.

B. Comrie, M. Haspelmath, B. Bickel, and Max Planck Institute for Evolutional Anthropology. 2008. *The Leipzig Glossing Rules: Conventions for Interlinear Morpheme-by-morphene Glosses*. Max Planck Institute for Evolutionary Anthropology.

Michael Ginn. 2023. Sigmorphon 2023 Shared Task of Interlinear Glossing: Baseline Model.

Michael Ginn, Sarah Moeller, Alexis Palmer, Anna Stacey, Garrett Nicolai, Mans Hulden, and Miikka Silfverberg. 2023. Findings of the SIGMORPHON 2023 Shared Task on Interlinear Glossing. In *Proceedings of the 20th SIGMORPHON Workshop on Computational Research in Phonetics, Phonology, and Morphology*. Association for Computational Linguistics.

Angelina McMillan-Major. 2020. Automating Gloss Generation in Interlinear Glossed Text. In *Proceedings of the Society for Computation in Linguistics 2020*, pages 355–366, New York, New York. Association for Computational Linguistics.

Sarah Moeller and Mans Hulden. 2018. Automatic Glossing in a Low-Resource Setting for Language Documentation. In *Proceedings of the Workshop on Computational Modeling of Polysynthetic Languages*, pages 84–93, Santa Fe, New Mexico, USA. Association for Computational Linguistics.

Bruce Oliver, Clarissa Forbes, Changbing Yang, Farhan Samir, Edith Coates, Garrett Nicolai, and Miikka Silfverberg. 2022. An Inflectional Database for Gitksan.

In *Proceedings of the Thirteenth Language Resources and Evaluation Conference*, pages 6597–6606, Marseille, France. European Language Resources Association.

Myle Ott, Sergey Edunov, Alexei Baevski, Angela Fan, Sam Gross, Nathan Ng, David Grangier, and Michael Auli. 2019. fairseq: A Fast, Extensible Toolkit for Sequence Modeling. In *Proceedings of NAACL-HLT 2019: Demonstrations*.

Alexis Palmer, Taesun Moon, and Jason Baldridge. 2009. Evaluating Automation Strategies in Language Documentation. In *Proceedings of the NAACL HLT 2009 Workshop on Active Learning for Natural Language Processing*, pages 36–44, Boulder, Colorado. Association for Computational Linguistics.

Lance Ramshaw and Mitch Marcus. 1995. Text Chunking using Transformation-Based Learning. In *Third Workshop on Very Large Corpora*.

Ilya Sutskever, Oriol Vinyals, and Quoc V. Le. 2014. Sequence to Sequence Learning with Neural Networks.

Shijie Wu, Ryan Cotterell, and Mans Hulden. 2021. Applying the Transformer to Character-level Transduction. In *Proceedings of the 16th Conference of the European Chapter of the Association for Computational Linguistics: Main Volume*, pages 1901–1907, Online. Association for Computational Linguistics.

Xingyuan Zhao, Satoru Ozaki, Antonios Anastasopoulos, Graham Neubig, and Lori Levin. 2020. Automatic Interlinear Glossing for Under-Resourced Languages Leveraging Translations. In *Proceedings of the 28th International Conference on Computational Linguistics*, pages 5397–5408, Barcelona, Spain (Online). International Committee on Computational Linguistics.

Glossy Bytes: Neural Glossing using Subword Encoding

Ziggy Cross[1*] **Michelle Yun**[1*] **Ananya Apparaju**[2] **Jata MacCabe**[2]
Garrett Nicolai[3] **Miikka Silfverberg**[3]
University of British Columbia
[1]{zcross,bibianna}@student.ubc.ca
[2]{ananya.apparaju,jatamaccabe}@gmail.com
[3]{garrett.nicolai,miikka.silfverberg}@ubc.ca

Abstract

This paper presents several subword-modelling-based approaches to interlinear glossing for seven under-resourced languages as a part of the 2023 SIGMORPHON shared task on interlinear glossing (Ginn et al., 2023). In an interlinear glossed text (IGT), each line of the original text is paired with one or more corresponding lines which encode the underlying grammatical structure. While expert annotated glossed text is especially valuable for the study of low-resource languages in both theoretical linguistics and natural language processing, generating high-quality glossed data is expensive and time-consuming. Therefore, approaches which aim to automatically or semi-automatically generate glossed data can be valuable for linguistic research. We experiment with various augmentation and tokenization strategies for both the open and closed tracks of data. We found that while subword models may perform well for greater amounts of data, character-based approaches remain competitive in their performance in lower resource settings.

1 Introduction and Motivation

Subword[1] representations can leverage the compositional nature of input words to model the morphology of a language. Approaches that treat words as atomic units have limitations when handling morphologically rich languages (Ling et al., 2015), where words may be composed of several meaningful morphemes (which, in turn, are composed of characters). Another limitation of the word-level approach is its inability to handle out-of-vocabulary (OOV) words. When data is scarce and many test words are absent from the training set, generic OOV handling (i.e. <UNK> tagging) is especially problematic. Recent strategies for OOV handling in neural machine translation include using pre-trained contextualized word embeddings (Lochter et al., 2020) or exploiting external data (Ngo et al., 2019). However, these methods are often domain-specific and may be unrealistic in a truly low-resource setting.

In such scenarios, models capable of learning relationships between orthographically similar sequences (Ling et al., 2015) may be especially valuable for disambiguating rare and unseen words, as there is often overlap between an OOV word (e.g. *desktop*) and those present in the vocabulary (e.g. *desk, top*). A drawback (Plank et al., 2016) of character-level representations lies in the non-trivial relationship between word forms and their meanings. Subword models may represent a compromise between characters, which are semantically void, and word-level representations. Indeed, byte-pair encoding (BPE) (Sennrich et al., 2016a) can effectively handle rare and unknown words in neural machine translation, particularly when a word-level translation may be derived from the translation of word-internal units.

Throughout this paper, we examine several approaches to neural interlinear glossing, and our contributions are as follows:

1. We implement a *sliding-window* based data augmentation approach, drawing solely from the given training set, to improve results for unsegmented inputs (3).

2. We compare the outputs of input representations at two granularities (subword, character) across various language typologies (6.1.1).

3. We provide a quantitative error analysis of gloss tags generated at the character level (6.1.2).

4. We compare the performance of recursive and transformer models for pre-segmented inputs (6.2).

*The first two authors contributed equally.

[1]Throughout this paper, we use *character* to refer to simple character-level splitting and *subword* to refer to all other subword segmentation

Proceedings of the 20th SIGMORPHON workshop on Computational Research in Phonetics, Phonology, and Morphology, pages 222–229
July 14, 2023 ©2023 Association for Computational Linguistics

Additionally, we propose that sequence-to-sequence (seq2seq) models are a viable approach for automated gloss generation in low-resource scenarios even for the closed-track task, where systems are trained exclusively on unsegmented input sentences and glosses.

2 Related Work

Given the data-hungry nature of neural systems, many approaches for automating *low-resource* IGT generation (Moeller and Hulden, 2018; McMillan-Major, 2020) have been statistical, treating gloss generation as a token classification task where each morphologically segmented source line is mapped to its corresponding morphosyntactic descriptor (MSD). As CRFs cannot encode variable-length sequences, they do not extend to the closed-task setting.

The baseline (Ginn, 2023) for this task uses a BERT-based model to label each whitespace-separated sequence with its corresponding glossed unit. This choice in architecture is motivated by the scarcity of training data and fails to exploit orthographic regularities which lend consistent clues to the internal structures of morphologically rich grammars.

In a recent neural approach to automated gloss generation for Lezgi, Tsez, and Arapaho, Zhao et al. (2020) experimented with both word and byte-pair tokenization. While they noted that the subword model outperformed the word-level model for all languages but Lezgi, they did not systematically analyze each approach.

3 Data

The data for this shared task comes from seven low-resource languages from various language families. Some languages in the set include a large number of training examples, while others contain very few.[2] All languages have original texts (orthographic representations) and gold-standard glosses. Some languages also have translated lines of text (in either English or Spanish). For the open track, all languages except Nyangbo have morphologically segmented lines, and Uspanteko has POS annotations.

The format of the data was as follows for the closed track:

- <t>, the orthographic representation
- <g>, the gold standard gloss
- <l>, the translation (in English or Spanish)

[2] For detailed information on the languages, see Table 1

Original example: Им гатна, лагьана, кӀвализ.
window = 2: Им гатна, гатна, лагьана, лагьана, кӀвализ.
window = 3: Им гатна , лагьана, гатна, лагьана , кӀвализ.

Figure 1: Sliding window augmentation

The format of the data was as follows for the open track:

- <t>, the orthographic representation
- <m>, the morphologically segmented line
- <p>, part of speech tags (Uspanteko only)
- <g>, the gold-standard gloss
- <l>, the translation (in English or Spanish)

3.1 Closed Track Data Augmentation

For the closed track, we used a sliding window augmentation strategy (Figure 1).

Given the training set for a language, we first define a minimum window size $lb = 1$ and a scaling factor $p = 0.5|0.7$. We count the length of each whitespace-segmented target line in the training set and find the average count c. The maximum window size ub is $c * p$. We then generate new source and target examples by segmenting each example in the training set into spans of length $lb...ub$. These spans are added back into the training set as new training instances.

Language	Original	Augmented	Total
Arapaho	39501	370058	409559
Gitksan	31	827	858
Lezgi	701	44517	45218
Natugu	791	53033	53824
Nyangbo	2100	17836	19936
Tsez	3558	238190	241748
Uspanteko	9774	103365	113139

Table 1: Overview of closed track training set

3.2 Open Track Data Representation

For the open track, all sentences were split up into individual words. Each word was represented once for every morpheme it contained, with moving 'morpheme boundaries' for each duplication (we used a <#> tag to represent this boundary). For example, the input *re-connect-ed* would be represented as follows:

```
<#>re <#>connect -ed
re <#>connect <#>ed
re -connect <#>ed<#>
```

Simplifying our input like this allowed us to represent the problem as a series of morpheme classifications, rather than a variable-length sequence output task.

Our final model only used a context size of one word, meaning each word in the input is considered independently. A larger model could allow us to include several words, or even the entire sentence, as context. A larger context could potentially allow the model to learn syntactic patterns, however, we decided this would be too computationally intensive for the shared task, as the improvements would likely be marginal.

Overall, this representation meant that our input data had as many examples as the number of morpheme tokens in given sentences.

Language	# Sents	# Words	# Morphs
Arapaho	39501	139714	251655
Gitksan	31	261	429
Lezgi	701	7029	10497
Natugu	791	10140	16341
Nyangbo	2100	8669	13778
Tsez	3558	37458	74334
Uspanteko	9774	41923	60458

Table 2: Overview of open track training set

4 Model Architecture

4.1 Closed Track

Our closed track model is a standard transformer-based sequence-to-sequence network (Vaswani et al., 2017). We use 3 layers for both the encoder and decoder, as well as 6 attention heads. Dropout is set to 0.25, and the feedforward and embedding dimensions are set to 512 and 300, respectively. The default batch size is set to 32 for both training and inference, adjusted to 8 for Gitksan and 64 for Arapaho to account for differences in the amount of available data. For training, we used PyTorch's implementation of the Adam optimizer[3], with learning rate $\gamma = 10^{-4}$, $\beta_1 = 0.9$, $\beta_2 = 0.98$, and $\epsilon = 10^{-9}$. Each model was trained over 50 epochs. To prevent overfitting, we stopped the training procedure if validation accuracy did not improve for 3 consecutive epochs.

Inputs are segmented into either BPE subwords or characters. During the decoding phase, the decoder auto-regressively generates an output gloss sequence until the `<end>` token is reached; at translation time, the predicted token is selected via a greedy decoding mechanism.

4.2 Open Track

Our open track solution was broken up into two parts, the first being tag prediction, and the second being stem prediction. Example glosses contained a mix of MSDs and stems, and while our models would be capable of predicting both together, we decided that the two tasks should be separated due to their vastly different vocabulary sizes. For example, a language may only contain a few hundred unique tags, but several thousand stems. This separation meant we could greatly reduce the output space of each task, in turn speeding up model learning. To do this, our tag prediction model would obscure all stems by replacing them with a `<STEM>` tag. We could then use a more lightweight prediction model for anything our tag predictor classified as a stem.

4.2.1 Tag prediction - BiLSTM encoder

Our first approach for encoding inputs in the open track task was using a BiLSTM model. Each example was represented as a sequence of characters (or tags in the case of the morpheme boundary <#>), with each character having its own randomly-initialised embedding. Our model would retrieve the embeddings for each character and then sequentially pass them into a bidirectional LSTM network. To get the encoding of our input we took the final hidden states from each LSTM direction and concatenated them into a final context vector.

4.2.2 Tag prediction - ByT5 encoder

To improve on our BiLSTM model, we used the encoder from Google's pre-trained ByT5 model to generate our context vectors. This encoding system is much more powerful than our BiLSTM model, in part due to its higher dimensional layers, but also its pre-trained embeddings and attention

[3]Other implementations of the Adam optimizer may use α to represent the learning rate

mechanisms. When fine-tuning our models we applied multilingual training jointly on all shared task languages before fine-tuning on each individual language. This was done in order to enable some transfer learning, which may be useful for the most low-resource languages. To further this, multilingual training sets could be supplemented with data from high-resource languages to improve results in the multilingual training phase (though that may be outside the spirit of the shared task).

4.2.3 Tag prediction - Feed-forward decoder

After generating context vectors with either the BiLSTM or ByT5 encoder, we then passed the output through a feed-forward network with a single hidden layer to generate a tag prediction. The input size of the network was defined by the size of the encoder's output context vector, and the output size was defined by the vocabulary size of possible output tags observed during training time. The hidden layer size was tuned as a hyperparameter, but always remained above the output dimension.

4.2.4 Stem prediction - Most common vocab

To predict stems we used a vocabulary dictionary to map word forms seen during training with their equivalent glosses. We used a counter to keep track of the most common glosses for each morpheme and used this to replace any forms predicted to be `<STEM>` with their most common gloss. Any forms not seen during training time were replaced with `<UNK>` tags, though they could also be left as the original word form, which might improve performance on noun stems (such as names or places) where the translation and gloss might match.

5 Experiments

5.1 Closed Track - Character-level

For each language-specific model, we built separate source and target vocabularies consisting of the set of unique characters in the transcription (source) and gloss (target) lines of the training data. An early error analysis showed that OOV characters were usually non-alphabetic, so we manually added these characters to both source and target vocabularies.

Each line was split into characters and post-processed. Morpheme separators[4] were re-attached to preceding and following characters. In addition, whitespace was replaced with #. This step prevented the generation of ill-formed glosses with dangling separators such as *'one escape-'*.[5]

For example, the gloss *'one escape-IMPF .'* is tokenized and post-processed as follows, with segments delimited by a pipe character:

1. Original gloss:

```
one escape-IMPF .
```

2. Tokenized:

```
<start>|o|n|e|#|e|s|c|a|p|e|-|I|M|P|F|#|.|<end>
```

3. Post-processed:

```
<start>|o|n|e|#|e|s|c|a|p|e-|-I|M|P|F|#|.|<end>
```

5.2 Closed Track - BPE

We trained separate input and output BPE[6] tokenizers for each dataset, defining the maximum threshold for convergence operations given a set of characters C as $n * |C|$ Although we set $n = 16$ to avoid re-training the tokenizers at different vocabulary sizes, fine-tuning the number of merge operations is likely to yield improved results.

5.3 Open Track - BiLSTM

In our first experiments, we fed the open track data (as modelled in 3.2) into our BiLSTM encoder then feed-forward decoder and most-common-vocab stem prediction model. This performed very well and could be trained within minutes when run locally on a CPU. Our model used early stopping and would keep training only until a drop in the model's accuracy on the development was observed.

5.4 Open Track - ByT5

In our later experiments, we used our ByT5 encoder along with the feed-forward decoder and most-common-vocab stem prediction model. This model took significantly longer to train due to its much more complex architecture. After one week of training, we were unable to get it to perform better than the BiLSTM encoder model, however, we expect that its architecture should theoretically allow for a higher performance ceiling given sufficient training.

[4]Corresponding to the Leipzig Glossing Rules 2 and 4

[5]Whitespace was re-inserted and duplicate separators were removed prior to evaluation

[6]The Hugging Face implementation based on Sennrich et al. (2016b)

To assist multilingual learning, inputs to this model were prepended with a 3-character language tag, which bypassed the byte-level encoding and was treated as a special character with its own embedding. We believe this should help the model distinguish between orthographically similar languages, though further testing would be useful to determine how strong this approach is.

When training this model we used checkpointing to save the weights after each epoch. We then used an evaluation pipeline to assess the results at each checkpoint in order to determine the best model. We began fine-tuning with individual languages after 20 multilingual epochs.

6 Results & Discussion

6.1 Closed track

First, it must be noted that our approach does not appear to extend to the truly low-resource setting given its poor performance on Gitksan. Moreover, improvements in word accuracy are inconsistent, which is unsurprising given the limitations of character-level modelling discussed above. For the remaining languages, our character-level sequence-to-sequence model consistently and noticeably outperforms the baseline model for average morpheme accuracy. The only exception is Lezgi, where there is no significant difference between the morpheme accuracies. This may be due to the size of the Lezgian dataset as well as the structure of the language, but we leave this question for further investigation.

6.1.1 Character vs BPE

Both the character-level and baseline models outperformed the BPE model for all datasets apart from Arapaho; this makes sense since the generalizability of the byte-pair encoding algorithm (w.r.t. identifying rare sequences in the vocabulary) depends on the size and diversity of the training data. As we used a generic approach to training each BPE tokenizer, our results do not necessarily align with a more robust implementation of the byte-pair encoding algorithm. Although we suggest that BPE modelling is likely to be a competitive approach when more training data is available, the hands-off appeal of the character-level approach should not be ignored, especially in the context of the low-resource glossing task. If the dataset is sufficiently large, however, BPE could prove more efficient due to its compactness.

6.1.2 Qualitative Analysis

We analyze examples of predicted glosses for Arapaho (3). In the positive examples (3.1, 3.5), the predicted and target stems are consistent in meaning, while the negative examples (3.3, 3.6) are less coherent. We offer the following observations, with the caveat that we have yet to conduct a systematic analysis:

- There might be a relationship between stem rarity and prediction coherence; that is, the less frequent a stem, the less semantic similarity between predicted and target tags.
- The character-based model might do a better job at predicting semantically related tags for morphologically complex stems.
- Misalignment errors (such as in Table 3.2), where the model fails to generate a gloss tag for each word in the transcription line, occur frequently.

6.1.3 Generalization to unseen stems

The character-level model is able to successfully predict unseen English stems (Table 3.7). When the model encounters an unknown lexeme, it seems to have learned to replicate the stem (or stem-internal constituents) to preserve meaningful elements.

Notably, Arapaho is the only language where the model learns to produce unseen English words. (Liu et al., 2018) report similar results in their character-level seq2seq translator for OOV handling in statistical machine translation: the model learns to produce novel English target words by combining previously seen subwords or transliterating complete sequences. As their system (1) is specifically designed for OOV prediction for moderate-resource languages and (2) leverages external data (bilingual dictionaries, translation tables, there could be a data threshold for stem generation. With a high tag accuracy, this could prove useful for researchers who could prioritize glossing the stems and leverage the model to generate the tags. Orthographic similarity may also play a role: in our data, Arapaho is transcribed in the Latin alphabet while Tsez, the second-largest dataset, is transcribed in the Cyrillic alphabet.

6.2 Open track

We found that the BiLSTM model performed strongest compared to preliminary training on the

Token	Original Sentence	Reference	Prediction
(1) heneenei3oobei'i3i'	Nuhu' tih'eeneti3i' heneenei3oobei'i3i'	IC.tell.the.truth-3PL	IC.true-3PL
(2) Beetbeteeenehk	Beetbeteeenehk wo'uuceh nee'eesoo'	want.to-dance-2S.SUBJ	want.to-dance-SUBJ
(3) te3ou	B Tous te3ou	sandhill.crane	tell.story
(4) ne'koxo'useet	Ne'P ne'koxo'useet	then-walk.slowly-3.S	then-slowly-slowly-3.S
(5) he'ihce'oo'eixootiin	Noh he'ihce'oo'eixootiin	NARRPAST-again-people.assemble	NARRPAST-back-people.are.gathering-0S
(6) hoowuhneniinoo'	'oh hinee 3eboosei3iihi' hoowuhneniinoo' hoowu...	IC.lots.of.things-0S	NEG-too.man-0S
(7) sycamore	nuhu' sycamore huuno-hootin	sycamore	sycamore

Table 3: Error analysis for Arapaho (character level modelling)

	Char			Byte			Baseline		
Language	BLEU	Word	Morph	BLEU	Word	Morph	BLEU	Word	Morph
Arapaho	0.61	0.72	0.74	**0.65**	**0.74**	**0.76**	0.418	0.701	0.519
Gitksan	0.00	0.04	0.06	0.00	0.02	0.09	**0.045**	**0.291**	**0.163**
Lezgi	0.44	0.52	0.48	0.30	0.28	0.32	**0.520**	**0.557**	**0.492**
Nyangbo	0.72	0.79	**0.82**	0.68	0.73	0.76	**0.742**	**0.824**	0.782
Tsez	**0.72**	**0.77**	**0.76**	0.63	0.65	0.65	0.578	0.721	0.529
Uspanteko	**0.63**	**0.71**	**0.70**	0.54	0.63	0.63	0.538	0.703	0.655
Natugu	**0.52**	**0.58**	**0.51**	0.42	0.35	0.38	-	-	-

Table 4: Closed track evaluation results

ByT5 architecture. We believe that additional fine-tuning for individual languages on the ByT5 model would improve performance enough to beat the BiLSTM model results, however, the model's computational complexity meant we didn't have the time required to train the model to this level. Our BiLSTM model was able to outperform the baseline when used on Gitksan, Lezgi, Tsez, and Uspanteko. It was not able to beat the baseline on Arapaho and Nyangbo.[7]

The biggest strength of the BiLSTM model over the ByT5 model was its significantly lower computational complexity. We found that the BiLSTM model could be trained in minutes with a consumer-grade CPU, and the transformer-based ByT5 model took up to several hours to train a single epoch when using a research-grade GPU, which is what likely led to its worse performance in our final results. The BiLSTM architecture is impressively competent for the interlinear glossing task, and its short training time with strong performance shows that this model is a strong contender, even against the vastly more complex transformer model.

6.3 Future Work

Further research could investigate the relationship between morphological attributes (such as morpheme-to-word ratio) and the extent to which neural models can leverage compositional cues in orthographic sequences.

[7] For details on model performance, see Table 5

	BiLSTM			ByT5			Baseline		
Language	BLEU	Word	Morph	BLEU	Word	Morph	BLEU	Word	Morph
Arapaho	0.76	0.84	0.90	0.64	0.76	0.84	**0.792**	**0.854**	**0.911**
Gitksan	0.13	**0.38**	**0.52**	0.07	0.16	0.37	**0.142**	0.250	0.300
Lezgi	**0.71**	**0.83**	**0.87**	0.69	0.82	0.85	0.420	0.326	0.501
Nyangbo	0.60	0.72	0.81	0.23	0.50	0.58	**0.784**	**0.847**	**0.892**
Tsez	**0.75**	**0.79**	**0.88**	0.45	0.56	0.72	0.686	0.742	0.850
Uspanteko	0.64	**0.77**	**0.82**	0.39	0.66	0.69	**0.649**	0.759	0.813
Natugu	**0.84**	**0.89**	**0.93**	0.43	0.76	0.84	-	-	-

Table 5: Open track evaluation results

Additionally, we would like to implement some utilisation of the translation track. For example, this could be used to help resolve unknown ("<UNK>") tokens, by checking which lemmas have already been predicted and selecting the most likely of the rest. In our current approach, this potentially valuable data is left unused.

Another approach we would like to try for resolving unknown tokens is choosing a 'nearest neighbor' vocabulary item to replace any unknown stems. This would help mitigate the impact of misspellings and input noise, which our current stem prediction model (used in the open track models) is not robust to.

When predicting output tags in our open track models, which pair an encoder with a feed-forward decoder, an improved approach could involve feeding previous tag predictions into the model. This would allow us to model some (unidirectional) relationships between words without increasing the context size. This could easily be done by replacing the feed-forward decoder with a recursive decoder, such as a unidirectional LSTM or GRU.

For our BiLSTM model, implementing a patience mechanism into the early stopping might also allow for some improvements in performance and prevent underfitting.

We would also like to train our ByT5 model on a larger transformer architecture. We are currently using Google's ByT5-small model, as implemented on Hugging Face, however, there are several larger models that could easily be swapped in. In addition to this, models could be trained on larger contexts in order to learn inter-token patterns. For example, we could use a context of 3 words (the target word plus one word on either side) instead of only giving the model one word at a time.

For low-resource languages, we would also like to try Good-enough Compositional Augmentation (Andreas, 2020), as well as other data augmentation strategies. We believe this would be beneficial for models with very few training examples, such as Gitksan.

On closed-track tasks, we suggest that using a beam search decoding algorithm may yield better results than the current greedy decoding implementation, which has limited performance, particularly with longer sequences.

7 Conclusion

In this paper, we explored the potential of using subword representations in grammatical gloss-generating models to 'learn' the morphological patterns of a low-resource language. At a byte-pair level, we found this strategy to be competitive but dependent on the amount of training data available. As such, the byte-pair tokenized model performed the best for Arapaho (the dataset with the most tokens). We recognized that there might be more robust ways to implement this tokenization for languages with fewer tokens, and attributed some of the underperformance of the model in other languages to our generic tokenization strategy. We found that at a character level, even with no pre-augmentation and fewer tokens, the model delivered impressive results. We propose that the character level modelling approach excels in terms of both accessibility and performance in this setting.

Acknowledgements

We would like to thank Hariharavarshan Nandakumar and Jayathilaga Ramajayam for their help in early experiments using CRF modelling.

We would like to thank Farhan Samir for his help in preparing the ByT5 model.

This research was supported in part through computational resources and services provided by Advanced Research Computing at the University of British Columbia.

References

Jacob Andreas. 2020. Good-enough compositional data augmentation. In *Proceedings of the 58th Annual Meeting of the Association for Computational Linguistics*, pages 7556–7566, Online. Association for Computational Linguistics.

Michael Ginn. 2023. Sigmorphon 2023 shared task of interlinear glossing: Baseline model.

Michael Ginn, Sarah Moeller, Alexis Palmer, Anna Stacey, Garrett Nicolai, Mans Hulden, and Miikka Silfverberg. 2023. Findings of the SIGMORPHON 2023 shared task on interlinear glossing. In *Proceedings of the 20th SIGMORPHON Workshop on Computational Research in Phonetics, Phonology, and Morphology*. Association for Computational Linguistics.

Wang Ling, Chris Dyer, Alan W Black, Isabel Trancoso, Ramón Fermandez, Silvio Amir, Luís Marujo, and Tiago Luís. 2015. Finding function in form: Compositional character models for open vocabulary word representation. In *Proceedings of the 2015 Conference on Empirical Methods in Natural Language Processing*, pages 1520–1530, Lisbon, Portugal. Association for Computational Linguistics.

Nelson F. Liu, Jonathan May, Michael Pust, and Kevin Knight. 2018. Augmenting statistical machine translation with subword translation of out-of-vocabulary words.

Johannes V. Lochter, Renato M. Silva, and Tiago A. Almeida. 2020. Deep learning models for representing out-of-vocabulary words.

Angelina McMillan-Major. 2020. Automating gloss generation in interlinear glossed text. *Proceedings of the Society for Computation in Linguistics*, 3.

Sarah Moeller and Mans Hulden. 2018. Automatic glossing in a low-resource setting for language documentation. In *Proceedings of the Workshop on Computational Modeling of Polysynthetic Languages*, pages 84–93, Santa Fe, New Mexico, USA. Association for Computational Linguistics.

Thi-Vinh Ngo, Thanh-Le Ha, Phuong-Thai Nguyen, and Le-Minh Nguyen. 2019. Overcoming the rare word problem for low-resource language pairs in neural machine translation. In *Proceedings of the 6th Workshop on Asian Translation*. Association for Computational Linguistics.

Barbara Plank, Anders Søgaard, and Yoav Goldberg. 2016. Multilingual part-of-speech tagging with bidirectional long short-term memory models and auxiliary loss. *arXiv preprint arXiv:1604.05529*.

Rico Sennrich, Barry Haddow, and Alexandra Birch. 2016a. Neural machine translation of rare words with subword units. In *Proceedings of the 54th Annual Meeting of the Association for Computational Linguistics (Volume 1: Long Papers)*, pages 1715–1725, Berlin, Germany. Association for Computational Linguistics.

Rico Sennrich, Barry Haddow, and Alexandra Birch. 2016b. Neural machine translation of rare words with subword units. In *Proceedings of the 54th Annual Meeting of the Association for Computational Linguistics (Volume 1: Long Papers)*, pages 1715–1725.

Ashish Vaswani, Noam Shazeer, Niki Parmar, Jakob Uszkoreit, Llion Jones, Aidan N. Gomez, Lukasz Kaiser, and Illia Polosukhin. 2017. Attention is all you need.

Xingyuan Zhao, Satoru Ozaki, Antonios Anastasopoulos, Graham Neubig, and Lori Levin. 2020. Automatic interlinear glossing for under-resourced languages leveraging translations. In *Proceedings of the 28th International Conference on Computational Linguistics*, pages 5397–5408, Barcelona, Spain (Online). International Committee on Computational Linguistics.

A Hyperparameters

For the model using ByT5 encoding, the output decoder (4.2.3) used one hidden layer of size 1024, which was large enough to encompass the approximately 700 size tag vocabulary.

For the model using BiLSTM encoding, the hidden layer size changed based on the size of the language-specific tag vocabulary (as this model did not use any multilingual training).

No other hyperparameters were optimised for the open track.

All of our model training and prediction code for the shared task can be accessed on GitHub at `https://github.com/michelleyun98/sigmorphon2023-IGT`.

The SIGMORPHON 2022 Shared Task on Cross-lingual and Low-Resource Grapheme-to-Phoneme Conversion

Arya D. McCarthy[♠], Jackson L. Lee, Alexandra DeLucia[♠], Travis Bartley[♡], Milind Agarwal[◇], Lucas F.E. Ashby[♡], Luca Del Signore[♡], Cameron Gibson[♡], Reuben Raff[♡], Winston Wu[♣]

[♠]Johns Hopkins University [♡]City University of New York
[◇]George Mason University [♣]University of Michigan

Abstract

Grapheme-to-phoneme conversion is an important component in many speech technologies, but until recently there were no multilingual benchmarks for this task. The third iteration of the SIGMORPHON shared task on multilingual grapheme-to-phoneme conversion features many improvements from the previous year's task (Ashby et al., 2021), including additional languages, three subtasks varying the amount of available resources, extensive quality assurance procedures, and automated error analyses. Three teams submitted a total of fifteen systems, at best achieving relative reductions of word error rate of 14% in the cross-lingual subtask and 14% in the very-low resource subtask. The generally consistent result is that cross-lingual transfer substantially helps grapheme-to-phoneme modeling, but not to the same degree as in-language examples.

1 Introduction

Many speech technologies demand mappings between written words and their pronunciations. In open-vocabulary systems, as well as certain resource-constrained embedded systems, it is insufficient to simply list all possible pronunciations; these mappings must generalize to rare or unseen words as well. Therefore, the mapping must be expressed as a mapping from a sequence of orthographic characters—*graphemes*—to a sequence of sounds—*phones* or *phonemes*.[1]

Grapheme-to-phoneme (g2p) datasets vary in size across languages (van Esch et al., 2016). In low-resource scenarios, an effective way of "breaking the resource bottleneck" (Hwa et al., 2005) is cross-lingual transfer of information from a high-resource language, either by annotation projection (Yarowsky and Ngai, 2001; Nicolai et al., 2020) or adapting a model to a new language (Zoph et al., 2016; Pino et al., 2019; McCarthy et al., 2019, 2020b; Mueller et al., 2020; Lee et al., 2022). The intent is that either the data or the learned representations and parameters carry across languages. Cross-lingual transfer shows promise for grapheme-to-phoneme conversion (Deri and Knight, 2016). Since this shared task began, *zero-shot* grapheme-to-phoneme procedures have been proposed, using no examples in the language of interest (Li et al., 2022).

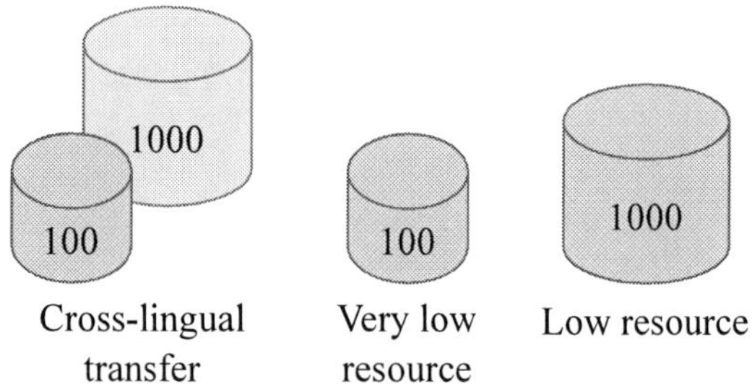

Figure 1: Training grapheme–phoneme pairs in the three subtasks. Transfer language is blue; target language is red. In all cases, the test set was 100 examples in the target language.

SIGMORPHON in 2020 and 2021 hosted shared tasks on grapheme-to-phoneme conversion (Gorman et al., 2020; Ashby et al., 2021). The tasks have drawn wide participation, and in both years the participants outperformed the baseline systems by respectable margins. A major finding of the most recent iteration (Ashby et al., 2021) is that the largest improvements came from data augmentation, rather than alterations of the core model. Consequently, we have proposed a third edition of the shared task that explores data efficiency and language relatedness through cross-linguality.

This year's subtasks are designed so that, by contrasting these two aspects, we can answer two questions about data efficiency:

[1]We note that referring to elements of transcriptions as phonemes implies an ontological commitment which may or may not be justified; see Lee et al., 2020 (fn. 4) for discussion. Therefore, we use the term phone to refer to symbols used to transcribe pronunciations.

Proceedings of the 20th SIGMORPHON workshop on Computational Research in Phonetics, Phonology, and Morphology, pages 230–238
July 14, 2023

1. How much does the transfer language data help?
2. How hard is it to model the language's grapheme-to-phoneme mapping, intrinsically?

This year, we study 10 language pairs, including two **surprise pairs** which were not released to the participants until close to the deadline as a challenge. Each pair of languages shares a script and some other relationship (e.g., phylogeny or hegemony). We investigate three data settings:[2]

Cross-lingual transfer A small amount of data (100 words) in the language of interest (the "target language") and a large amount of data (1000 words) in a nearby language (the "transfer language").

Very-low resource A small amount of data (100 words) in the target language and no data in the transfer language.

Low resource A large amount of data (1000 words) in the target language and no data in the transfer language.

In every case, we use the same 100-word test set, providing only the graphemes to the participants. Because the language pairs are consistent across the subtasks, we can draw meaningful contrasts.

Altogether, 15 systems were submitted, which allow substantial insights into our questions about data efficiency and g2p modelability. This third iteration of the SIGMORPHON shared task on graphme-to-phoneme conversion introduces transfer languages, new target languages, surprise languages, and stringent quality assurance, as the subtask structure which enables comparison.

2 Data

As in the two previous years, all pronunciation data was drawn from WikiPron (Lee et al., 2020), a massively multilingual pronunciation database extracted from the online dictionary Wiktionary. Depending on the language and script, Wiktionary pronunciations are either manually entered by human volunteers working from language-specific pronunciation guidelines or generated from the graphemic form via language-specific server-side scripting. WikiPron scrapes these pronunciations from Wiktionary, optionally applying casefolding to the graphemic form, removing any stress and syllable boundaries, and segmenting the pronunciation—encoded in the International Phonetic Alphabet—using the Python library segments (Moran and Cysouw, 2018). In all, 20 WikiPron languages were selected for the three subtasks. Only four of these were used in the 2021 iteration of the shared task. We give the twenty languages, as 10 target–transfer pairs, in Table 1.

Target language	Transfer language
Swedish	Norwegian Nynorsk
German	Dutch
Italian	Romanian
Ukrainian	Belarusian
Tagalog	Cebuano
Bengali	Assamese
Persian	Pashto
Thai	Eastern Lawa
Irish	Welsh
Burmese	Shan

Table 1: Language pairs used in the shared task. Irish–Welsh and Burmese–Shan were surprise pairs withheld until mid-April.

Morphological information from the UniMorph morphological lexicons (Kirov et al., 2018; McCarthy et al., 2020a) were again provided to participants; however, no participant made use of these, just like last year.

Language selection While the 2021 shared task considered both high-resource and low-resource settings, we did not control for the language itself. It was hard to extrapolate from the scores to claims about the resource requirements and difficulties of particular languages. This year, we use the same languages in all settings. This makes it reasonable and appropriate for the results to be directly compared, answering the two questions from Section 1.

These languages were chosen to avoid particularly pathological languages noted in previous years (English, Croatian) and those with unique and hard-to-predict phenomena, like *stød* in Danish.

Data quality assurance While the WikiPron data (Lee et al., 2020) that we use for the shared task is typically of high quality, some participants reported limitations in the English data. Consequently, we have omitted English data from the task. Beyond this, the data quality assurance pro-

[2]The data are available at https://github.com/sigmorphon/2022G2PST.

cedures are inspired by Ashby et al. (2021).

3 Task Definition

In this task, participants were provided with a collection of words and their pronunciations, and then scored on their ability to predict the pronunciation of a set of unseen words.

3.1 Subtasks

Last year, the task presented high-, medium-, and low-resource scenarios, each in different languages. This hampered cross-setting comparison, muddling whether differences in performance were due to data size, models, or languages.

This year, the same test sets are used across all settings, in the same set of languages. We offer a low-resource subtask, a very low-resource subtask, and a very low-resource subtask with more data available in a related (e.g., phylogenically or hegemonically) language. The relative error rates on each of three subtasks help to answer the research questions from Section 1. The design of these subtasks builds on McCarthy et al. (2019), which introduced the first shared task on cross-lingual transfer of information in morphological inflection.

Cross-lingual transfer This setting is meant to simulate a situation in which few data are available in the language of interest, but more are available in a related language, which can be leveraged. 100 words are given in each of the 10 languages, and an additional 1000 words are given in a related language for each language of interest. Throughout, we use the terms *transfer language* and *target language*, respectively, to refer to these. While it is realistic to have even more data available in a high-resource language, we constrain the size to enable comparison with the third setting.

Very-low resource This setting is designed to be extremely challenging. 100 words are given in each of the 10 languages. Comparing with the cross-lingual transfer setting gives insights about the value of the transfer data, and (indirectly) the similarities of the orthographic and phonetic systems present in the language pairs.

Low resource This setting matches the low resource condition from Ashby et al. (2021). 1000 words are given in each of the 10 languages. Comparing with the very-low resource setting gives insights about the learnability of the task. Comparing with both previous subtasks gives insights about the relevance of in-language data.

3.2 Data preparation

The procedures for sampling and splitting the data are similar to those used in the previous year's shared task; see Gorman et al. (2020, §3) and Ashby et al. (2021, §4.2). For each of the three subtasks, the data for each language are first randomly downsampled according to their frequencies in the Wortschatz (Goldhahn et al., 2012) norms. Words containing less than two Unicode characters or less than two phone segments are excluded, as are words with multiple pronunciations. The resulting data are randomly split into training data, development data, and test data. As in the previous year's shared task, these splits are constrained so that inflectional variants of any given lemma—according to the UniMorph (Kirov et al., 2018; McCarthy et al., 2020a) paradigms— can occur in at most one of the three shards. Training and development data was made available at the start of the task. The test words were also made available at the start of the task; test pronunciations were withheld until the end of the task.

Language-specific decisions The WikiPron data for Welsh has separate files for the North Wales and South Wales dialects. The South Wales dialect was chosen for there being slightly more data. Pashto, Eastern Lawa, and Shan do not have frequency data, so their "freq" file simply has the frequency of 1 for every word.

4 Evaluation

The primary metric for this task was word error rate (WER), the percentage of words for which the hypothesized transcription sequence is not identical to the gold reference transcription. As all three subtasks involve multiple languages, macro-averaged WER was used for system ranking. Participants were provided with two evaluation scripts: one which computes WER for a single language, and one which also computes macro-averaged WER across two or more languages. The 2020 shared task also reported another metric, phone error rate (PER), but this was found in the 2021 shared task to be highly correlated with WER and was not reported.

5 Baseline

The baseline system from 2021, the monotonic hard attention system from CLUZH (Makarov and Clematide, 2020), remained the baseline architecture in 2022. It is is a neural transducer system using an imitation learning paradigm (Makarov and Clematide, 2018).

All models were tuned to minimize per-language development-set WER. We reuse the best hyperparameter settings from last year. Alignments are computed using ten iterations of expectation maximization, and the imitation learning policy is trained for up to sixty epochs (with a patience of twelve) using the AdaDelta optimizer. A beam of size of four is used for prediction. Final predictions are produced by a majority-vote ten-component ensemble. Internal processing uses the decomposed Unicode normalization form (NFD), but predictions are converted back to the composed form (NFC). An implementation of the baseline was provided during the task and participating teams were encouraged to adapt it for their submissions.

In many cases, the baseline's loss did not improve over the course of training. We indicate this with a '-' in Tables 2 to 4.

6 Submissions

The shared task received 15 submissions from 3 teams. Below we provide brief descriptions of sub- missions to the shared task; more detailed descriptions of the first two—as well as various exploratory analyses and post-submission experiments—can be found in the system papers later in this volume.

Tü-G2P Girrbach (2022) evaluated three sequence labeling approaches to grapheme-to-phoneme conversion. In the supervised case, Girrbach trained a BiLSTM model to predict phoneme n-grams. The labels are derived from external alignments calculated by a custom neural aligner. Second, Girrbach trained a Gram-CTC model (Liu et al., 2017) to jointly predict and realign phoneme n-grams. Finally, the main approach is to use a standard BiLSTM sequence labeling model, but predict multiple ($\tau \in \{3,4,5\}$) phoneme unigrams from each grapheme. Girrbach uses standard CTC (Graves et al., 2006) to train the model, which is possible because predicting multiple phonemes from each grapheme causes the number of predicted symbols to always be greater than the number of target phonemes. Note that using CTC avoids relying on external alignments in any way. For the transfer task, Girrbach shares the same grapheme embeddings and BiLSTM encoder between target and transfer language, but uses different prediction layers.

Hammond Hammond (2022) submitted one system. He initially built a Transformer-based system, but because data are so minimal, it performed poorly. He switched to an HMM-based system (Novak et al., 2012).

For the transfer condition, which was his priority, he used the provided transfer data and augmented the system in two ways. First, he used a simplified version of the splicing augmentation scheme developed by Ryan and Hulden (2020) for the core data. Second, for the transfer languages, he only used data where the phonologies overlapped at the bigram level; in other words, he only included transfer training pairs that only included phonetic bigrams that occurred in the target languages.

mSLAM Garrette (2022) prepared a submission based on mSLAM (Bapna et al., 2022), a multilingual encoder model pretrained simultaneously on text from 101 languages and speech from 51 languages. The mSLAM team used the 600M parameter configuration of mSLAM. At fine-tuning time, they combined mSLAM's text encoder, which uses characters as ints input tokens, with an uninitialized RNN-T decoder (Graves, 2012) whose vocabulary was the set of all 384 phonemes appearing in the shared task data. Due to the extremely limited amount of training data for the tasks, the team found that the decoder needed to be very small. They used a single layer, with hidden dimension 8, model dimension of 16, and 4 heads. They also used a dropout rate of 0.3 and a label smoothing of 0.2.

They took an explicitly multilingual approach to modeling the G2P tasks, fine-tuning and evaluating a single model that covered all languages in the task. Having a single model for all languages made it necessary to tell the model, for each input, which language it was generating the pronunciation for, which was accomplished by prefixing each input string with the language's three-letter code (followed by a single space).

NFST Lin (2022) proposed a universal

Language	Baseline	Tü-G2P-1	-2	-3	-4	-5	Hammond	mSLAM
BEN	91.78	82.19	89.04	89.04	83.56	83.56	79.45	-
BUR	-	92.00	90.00	93.00	86.00	86.00	89.00	-
GER	97.00	79.00	74.00	74.00	74.00	74.00	85.00	-
GLE	-	78.00	74.00	80.00	81.00	81.00	85.00	-
ITA	44.00	41.00	41.00	38.00	40.00	40.00	41.00	-
PES	-	80.70	100.00	78.95	82.46	82.46	82.46	-
SWE	80.00	82.00	77.00	80.00	74.00	74.00	81.00	-
TGL	30.00	50.00	40.00	68.00	92.00	92.00	37.00	-
THA	-	91.00	83.00	81.00	94.00	94.00	91.00	-
UKR	96.00	77.00	74.00	76.00	92.00	92.00	86.00	-
Macro-average	83.48	75.29	74.20	75.80	79.90	79.90	75.69	-

Table 2: Results from the cross-lingual transfer subtask.

Language	Baseline	Tü-G2P-1	-2	-3	-4	-5	Hammond	mSLAM
BEN	-	90.41	83.56	83.56	86.30	91.78	91.78	-
BUR	-	90.00	87.00	86.00	87.00	95.00	93.00	-
GER	-	81.00	83.00	84.00	82.00	89.00	90.00	-
GLE	-	78.00	76.00	76.00	79.00	86.00	93.00	-
ITA	51.00	44.00	49.00	51.00	45.00	48.00	50.00	-
PES	-	75.44	80.70	85.96	82.46	80.70	80.70	-
SWE	79.00	84.00	81.00	81.00	81.00	86.00	82.00	-
TGL	29.00	40.00	35.00	37.00	32.00	42.00	24.00	-
THA	-	91.00	84.00	83.00	86.00	96.00	95.00	-
UKR	-	73.00	79.00	80.00	77.00	84.00	96.00	-
Macro-average	85.20	74.68	73.83	74.75	73.78	79.85	79.55	-

Table 3: Results from the very low resource subtask.

Language	Baseline	Tü-G2P-1	-2	-3	-4	-5	Hammond	mSLAM
BEN	67.12	68.49	72.60	69.86	68.49	71.23	71.23	-
BUR	29.00	37.00	31.00	37.00	35.00	51.00	46.00	-
GER	42.00	50.00	50.00	45.00	46.00	47.00	48.00	-
GLE	38.00	33.00	35.00	37.00	36.00	39.00	56.00	-
ITA	15.00	19.00	18.00	18.00	19.00	15.00	29.00	-
PES	59.65	57.89	100.00	57.89	56.14	61.40	59.65	-
SWE	45.00	54.00	53.00	51.00	52.00	51.00	62.00	-
TGL	20.00	15.00	16.00	18.00	15.00	14.00	16.00	-
THA	21.00	39.00	38.00	36.00	35.00	57.00	71.00	-
UKR	32.00	36.00	41.00	39.00	44.00	41.00	53.00	-
Macro-average	36.88	40.94	45.46	40.88	40.66	44.76	51.19	-

Table 4: Results from the low resource subtask.

grapheme-to-phoneme transduction model using neuralized finite-state transducers (NFST; Lin et al., 2019), a generalization of weighted finite-state transducers (WFSTs). The submission was not received by the published deadline. In fairness to other participants, scores are not listed.

7 Results

Overall, teams were able to outperform the baseline in the cross-lingual and very-low resource settings, at best achieving relative reductions of word error rate of 14% in the cross-lingual subtask and 14% in the very-low resource subtask. The best results for each setting are given in Tables 2 to 4. Non-neural approaches like HMMs with data augmentation were particularly successful in regimes where Transformer models often founder, mirroring findings in machine translation and morphological inflection (McCarthy et al., 2019).

7.1 Error analysis

Error analysis can help identify strengths and weaknesses of existing models, suggesting future improvements and guiding the construction of ensemble models. Prior experience using gold crowd-sourced data extracted from Wiktionary suggests that a non-trivial portion of errors made by top systems are due to errors in the gold data itself. For example, Gorman et al. (2019) report that a substantial portion of the prediction errors made by the top two systems in the 2017 CoNLL–SIGMORPHON shared task on morphological reinflection[3] are due to target errors, i.e., errors in the gold data. (These observations led to the development of cleaner data in UniMorph 3.0 (McCarthy et al., 2020a).)

To facilitate ensemble construction and further error analysis, we release all submissions' test set predictions to the research community.[4]

8 Discussion

We once again see an enormous difference in language difficulty. In particular, Hammond (2022) provides examples from the Welsh/Irish language pair to suggest that phylogenic or hegemonic similarity of languages does not entail similarity of orthography and phonology. Moreover, phoneme OOVs were a problem in the very-low resource setting: many phonemes and phenomena were simply not observed in 100 randomly sampled examples. This suggest room for typological information to improve modeling.

As mentioned above, the data here are a mixture of broad and narrow transcriptions. At first glance, this might explain some of the variation in language difficulty; for example, it is easy to imagine that the additional details in narrow transcriptions make them more difficult to predict. However, for many languages, only one of the two levels of transcription is available at scale, and other languages, divergence between broad and narrow transcriptions is impressionistically quite minor, as asserted in Ashby et al. (2021). However, this impression ought to be quantified.

The inclusion of the very-low resource subtask is intended to be a challenging case for participants; however, we did not anticipate the degree to which it would be challenging. In many cases, the baseline and participants' systems achieve a word error rate of zero or one. Clearly, there is room for improvement in minimally supervised grapheme-to-phoneme conversion.

Participants were permitted in all three subtasks to make use of lemmas and morphological tags from UniMorph as additional features. However, no team made use of these resources. Some prior work (e.g., Demberg et al., 2007) has found morphological tags highly useful, and Ashby et al. (2021) suggests this information would make an impact in French.

The results of the shared task suggest several next steps for carrying out a g2p shared task:

1. Split evaluation into frequent and infrequent test sets, as infrequent words may exhibit greater regularity.
2. Evaluate downstream performance for ASR.
3. Provide pointers to linguistic resources detailing phylogenic/hegemonic relationships, etc.

9 Conclusion

The third iteration of the shared task on multilingual grapheme-to-phoneme conversion is structured to provide answers to questions about the value of cross-lingual transfer and data availability.

Three teams submitted fifteen systems, achieving substantial reductions in both absolute and relative error over the baseline in two of three subtasks. We hope the code and data, released under permissive licenses,[5] will be used to benchmark grapheme-to-phoneme conversion and sequence-to-sequence modeling techniques more generally—especially in challenging low-resource scenarios.

[3]https://sigmorphon.github.io/sharedtasks/2017/

[4]https://drive.google.com/drive/folders/1qXKjMqtlgtNtT38o2uSZozLlo-7F_R0w?usp=sharing

[5]https://github.com/sigmorphon/2022G2PST

Acknowledgments

Kyle Gorman served as a consultant in the design of this task. We are grateful for his service. We thank Peter Makarov for discussions relating to the baseline model. We also thank the many Wiktionary contributors whose efforts made this task possible. A.D.M. is supported by an Amazon Fellowship.

References

Lucas F.E. Ashby, Travis M. Bartley, Simon Clematide, Luca Del Signore, Cameron Gibson, Kyle Gorman, Yeonju Lee-Sikka, Peter Makarov, Aidan Malanoski, Sean Miller, Omar Ortiz, Reuben Raff, Arundhati Sengupta, Bora Seo, Yulia Spektor, and Winnie Yan. 2021. Results of the second SIGMORPHON shared task on multilingual grapheme-to-phoneme conversion. In *Proceedings of the 18th SIGMORPHON Workshop on Computational Research in Phonetics, Phonology, and Morphology*, pages 115–125, Online. Association for Computational Linguistics.

Ankur Bapna, Colin Cherry, Yu Zhang, Ye Jia, Melvin Johnson, Yong Cheng, Simran Khanuja, Jason Riesa, and Alexis Conneau. 2022. mslam: Massively multilingual joint pre-training for speech and text.

Vera Demberg, Helmut Schmid, and Gregor Möhler. 2007. Phonological constraints and morphological preprocessing for grapheme-to-phoneme conversion. In *Proceedings of the 45th Annual Meeting of the Association of Computational Linguistics*, pages 96–103, Prague, Czech Republic. Association for Computational Linguistics.

Aliya Deri and Kevin Knight. 2016. Grapheme-to-phoneme models for (almost) any language. In *Proceedings of the 54th Annual Meeting of the Association for Computational Linguistics (Volume 1: Long Papers)*, pages 399–408, Berlin, Germany. Association for Computational Linguistics.

Dan Garrette. 2022. Fine-tuning mSLAM for the SIGMORPHON 2022 shared task on grapheme-to-phoneme conversion. In *Proceedings of the 19th SIGMORPHON Workshop on Computational Research in Phonetics, Phonology, and Morphology*, Seattle, USA. Association for Computational Linguistics. Non-archival; abstract only.

Leander Girrbach. 2022. SIGMORPHON 2022 shared task on grapheme-to-phoneme conversion submission description: Sequence labelling for g2p. In *Proceedings of the 19th SIGMORPHON Workshop on Computational Research in Phonetics, Phonology, and Morphology*, Seattle, USA. Association for Computational Linguistics.

Dirk Goldhahn, Thomas Eckart, and Uwe Quasthoff. 2012. Building large monolingual dictionaries at the Leipzig corpora collection: From 100 to 200 languages. In *Proceedings of the Eighth International Conference on Language Resources and Evaluation (LREC'12)*, pages 759–765, Istanbul, Turkey. European Language Resources Association (ELRA).

Kyle Gorman, Lucas F.E. Ashby, Aaron Goyzueta, Arya McCarthy, Shijie Wu, and Daniel You. 2020. The SIGMORPHON 2020 shared task on multilingual grapheme-to-phoneme conversion. In *Proceedings of the 17th SIGMORPHON Workshop on Computational Research in Phonetics, Phonology, and Morphology*, pages 40–50, Online. Association for Computational Linguistics.

Kyle Gorman, Arya D. McCarthy, Ryan Cotterell, Ekaterina Vylomova, Miikka Silfverberg, and Magdalena Markowska. 2019. Weird inflects but OK: Making sense of morphological generation errors. In *Proceedings of the 23rd Conference on Computational Natural Language Learning (CoNLL)*, pages 140–151, Hong Kong, China. Association for Computational Linguistics.

Alex Graves. 2012. Sequence transduction with recurrent neural networks. *CoRR*, abs/1211.3711.

Alex Graves, Santiago Fernández, Faustino Gomez, and Jürgen Schmidhuber. 2006. Connectionist temporal classification: Labelling unsegmented sequence data with recurrent neural networks. In *Proceedings of the 23rd International Conference on Machine Learning*, ICML '06, page 369–376, New York, NY, USA. Association for Computing Machinery.

Mike Hammond. 2022. Low-resource grapheme-to-phoneme mapping with phonetically-conditioned transfer. In *Proceedings of the 19th SIGMORPHON Workshop on Computational Research in Phonetics, Phonology, and Morphology*, Seattle, USA. Association for Computational Linguistics.

R. Hwa, Philip Resnik, and Amy Weinberg. 2005. Breaking the resource bottleneck for multilingual parsing.

Christo Kirov, Ryan Cotterell, John Sylak-Glassman, Géraldine Walther, Ekaterina Vylomova, Patrick Xia, Manaal Faruqui, Sabrina J. Mielke, Arya McCarthy, Sandra Kübler, David Yarowsky, Jason Eisner, and Mans Hulden. 2018. UniMorph 2.0: Universal Morphology. In *Proceedings of the Eleventh International Conference on Language Resources and Evaluation (LREC 2018)*, Miyazaki, Japan. European Language Resources Association (ELRA).

En-Shiun Lee, Sarubi Thillainathan, Shravan Nayak, Surangika Ranathunga, David Adelani, Ruisi Su, and Arya McCarthy. 2022. Pre-trained multilingual sequence-to-sequence models: A hope for low-resource language translation? In *Findings of the Association for Computational Linguistics: ACL 2022*, pages 58–67, Dublin, Ireland. Association for Computational Linguistics.

Jackson L. Lee, Lucas F.E. Ashby, M. Elizabeth Garza, Yeonju Lee-Sikka, Sean Miller, Alan Wong, Arya D. McCarthy, and Kyle Gorman. 2020. Massively multilingual pronunciation modeling with WikiPron. In *Proceedings of the 12th Language Resources and Evaluation Conference*, pages 4223–4228, Marseille, France. European Language Resources Association.

Xinjian Li, Florian Metze, David Mortensen, Shinji Watanabe, and Alan Black. 2022. Zero-shot learning for grapheme to phoneme conversion with language ensemble. In *Findings of the Association for Computational Linguistics: ACL 2022*, pages 2106–2115, Dublin, Ireland. Association for Computational Linguistics.

Chu-Cheng Lin. 2022. A future for universal grapheme-phoneme transduction modeling with neuralized finite-state transducers. In *Proceedings of the 19th SIGMORPHON Workshop on Computational Research in Phonetics, Phonology, and Morphology*, Seattle, USA. Association for Computational Linguistics. Non-archival; abstract only.

Chu-Cheng Lin, Hao Zhu, Matthew R. Gormley, and Jason Eisner. 2019. Neural finite-state transducers: Beyond rational relations. In *Proceedings of the 2019 Conference of the North American Chapter of the Association for Computational Linguistics: Human Language Technologies, Volume 1 (Long and Short Papers)*, pages 272–283, Minneapolis, Minnesota. Association for Computational Linguistics.

Hairong Liu, Zhenyao Zhu, Xiangang Li, and Sanjeev Satheesh. 2017. Gram-CTC: Automatic unit selection and target decomposition for sequence labelling. In *Proceedings of the 34th International Conference on Machine Learning - Volume 70*, ICML'17, page 2188–2197. JMLR.org.

Peter Makarov and Simon Clematide. 2018. Imitation learning for neural morphological string transduction. In *Proceedings of the 2018 Conference on Empirical Methods in Natural Language Processing*, pages 2877–2882, Brussels, Belgium. Association for Computational Linguistics.

Peter Makarov and Simon Clematide. 2020. CLUZH at SIGMORPHON 2020 shared task on multilingual grapheme-to-phoneme conversion. In *Proceedings of the 17th SIGMORPHON Workshop on Computational Research in Phonetics, Phonology, and Morphology*, pages 171–176, Online. Association for Computational Linguistics.

Arya D. McCarthy, Christo Kirov, Matteo Grella, Amrit Nidhi, Patrick Xia, Kyle Gorman, Ekaterina Vylomova, Sabrina J. Mielke, Garrett Nicolai, Miikka Silfverberg, Timofey Arkhangelskiy, Nataly Krizhanovsky, Andrew Krizhanovsky, Elena Klyachko, Alexey Sorokin, John Mansfield, Valts Ernštreits, Yuval Pinter, Cassandra L. Jacobs, Ryan Cotterell, Mans Hulden, and David Yarowsky. 2020a. UniMorph 3.0: Universal Morphology. In *Proceedings of the 12th Language Resources and Evaluation Conference*, pages 3922–3931, Marseille, France. European Language Resources Association.

Arya D. McCarthy, Xian Li, Jiatao Gu, and Ning Dong. 2020b. Addressing posterior collapse with mutual information for improved variational neural machine translation. In *Proceedings of the 58th Annual Meeting of the Association for Computational Linguistics*, pages 8512–8525, Online. Association for Computational Linguistics.

Arya D. McCarthy, Ekaterina Vylomova, Shijie Wu, Chaitanya Malaviya, Lawrence Wolf-Sonkin, Garrett Nicolai, Christo Kirov, Miikka Silfverberg, Sabrina J. Mielke, Jeffrey Heinz, Ryan Cotterell, and Mans Hulden. 2019. The SIGMORPHON 2019 shared task: Morphological analysis in context and cross-lingual transfer for inflection. In *Proceedings of the 16th Workshop on Computational Research in Phonetics, Phonology, and Morphology*, pages 229–244, Florence, Italy. Association for Computational Linguistics.

Steven Moran and Michael Cysouw. 2018. *The Unicode Cookbook for Linguists: Managing writing systems using orthography profiles*. Language Science Press.

Aaron Mueller, Garrett Nicolai, Arya D. McCarthy, Dylan Lewis, Winston Wu, and David Yarowsky. 2020. An analysis of massively multilingual neural machine translation for low-resource languages. In *Proceedings of the 12th Language Resources and Evaluation Conference*, pages 3710–3718, Marseille, France. European Language Resources Association.

Garrett Nicolai, Dylan Lewis, Arya D. McCarthy, Aaron Mueller, Winston Wu, and David Yarowsky. 2020. Fine-grained morphosyntactic analysis and generation tools for more than one thousand languages. In *Proceedings of the 12th Language Resources and Evaluation Conference*, pages 3963–3972, Marseille, France. European Language Resources Association.

Josef R. Novak, Nobuaki Minematsu, and Keikichi Hirose. 2012. WFST-based grapheme-to-phoneme conversion: Open source tools for alignment, model-building and decoding. In *Proceedings of the 10th International Workshop on Finite State Methods and Natural Language Processing*, pages 45–49, Donostia–San Sebastián. Association for Computational Linguistics.

Juan Pino, Liezl Puzon, Jiatao Gu, Xutai Ma, Arya D. McCarthy, and Deepak Gopinath. 2019. Harnessing indirect training data for end-to-end automatic speech translation: Tricks of the trade. In *Proceedings of the 16th International Conference on Spoken Language Translation*, Hong Kong. Association for Computational Linguistics.

Zach Ryan and Mans Hulden. 2020. Data augmentation for transformer-based G2P. In *Proceedings of the 17th SIGMORPHON Workshop on Computational Research in Phonetics, Phonology, and Morphology*, pages 184–188, Online. Association for Computational Linguistics.

Daan van Esch, Mason Chua, and Kanishka Rao. 2016. Predicting pronunciations with syllabification and stress with recurrent neural networks. In *Interspeech 2016, 17th Annual Conference of the International Speech Communication Association, San Francisco, CA, USA, September 8-12, 2016*, pages 2841–2845. ISCA.

David Yarowsky and Grace Ngai. 2001. Inducing multilingual POS taggers and NP bracketers via robust projection across aligned corpora. In *Second Meeting of the North American Chapter of the Association for Computational Linguistics*.

Barret Zoph, Deniz Yuret, Jonathan May, and Kevin Knight. 2016. Transfer learning for low-resource neural machine translation. In *Proceedings of the 2016 Conference on Empirical Methods in Natural Language Processing*, pages 1568–1575, Austin, Texas. Association for Computational Linguistics.

SIGMORPHON 2022 Shared Task on Grapheme-to-Phoneme Conversion Submission Description: Sequence Labelling for G2P

Leander Girrbach
University of Tübingen, Germany
leander.girrbach@student.uni-tuebingen.de

Abstract

This paper describes our participation in the Third SIGMORPHON Shared Task on Grapheme-to-Phoneme Conversion (Low-Resource and Cross-Lingual) (McCarthy et al., 2022). Our models rely on different sequence labelling methods. The main model predicts multiple phonemes from each grapheme and is trained using CTC loss (Graves et al., 2006). We find that sequence labelling methods yield worse performance than the baseline when enough data is available, but can still be used when very little data is available. Furthermore, we demonstrate that alignments learned by the sequence labelling models can be easily inspected.

1 Introduction

This paper describes our participation in the Third SIGMORPHON Shared Task on Grapheme-to-Phoneme Conversion (Low-Resource and Cross-Lingual) (McCarthy et al., 2022). We evaluate 3 sequence labelling methods for grapheme-to-phoneme conversion (henceforth: g2p). We approach the challenge of different lengths of grapheme and phoneme sequences by allowing to predict multiple phonemes from each grapheme.

The shared task consists of 3 tracks and includes 10 languages. The 3 tracks are high resource, low resource, and transfer. For the high resource track, grapheme-phoneme pairs are given for 1000 words. For the low resource track, grapheme-phoneme pairs are given for 100 words. For the transfer track, grapheme-phoneme pairs are given for 100 words in the target language and additionally grapheme-phoneme pairs are given for 1000 words in a transfer language (that is related to the target language, e.g. Dutch → German). The test set is the same for each track and contains 100 words of the target language. Additionally, a development set is provided for each target language. The development set also is the same for each track. All of our models are applicable to all languages and tracks.

Sequence labelling approaches can claim several advantages over the main alternative, namely (neural) encoder-decoder approaches: Sequence labelling does not require beam search for inference, may allow for smaller models, and defines a direct alignment between the input and predictions. The latter property may make models more interpretable and help with error analysis. However, sequence labelling is less flexible than encoder-decoder approaches and requires special handling of cases where the input and target sequences are of different length.

2 Related Work

Common approaches to g2p are joint-ngram models (Galescu and Allen, 2001; Novak et al., 2016), encoder-decoder models (Wu et al., 2021; Makarov and Clematide, 2018a,b; Clematide and Makarov, 2021), and sequence labelling (Jiampojamarn et al., 2007; Rosca and Breuel, 2016; Schnober et al., 2016; Ribeiro et al., 2018). In previous iterations of this shared task on g2p, encoder-decoder models were dominant both in terms of performance and in terms of number of submissions (Gorman et al., 2020; Ashby et al., 2021).

While this shows that neural encoder-decoder models yield superior performance compared to joint-ngram models, little work has been done to evaluate the performance of neural sequence labelling models. Therefore, two of our three proposed methods (explained in Section 3) directly use or build on existing approaches, namely work by Jiampojamarn et al. (2007) and Liu et al. (2017). Our third method has so far, to our knowledge, not been proposed for string transduction. It is however close to the approaches by Rosca and Breuel (2016) and Ribeiro et al. (2018): Both propose to augment the grapheme sequence by extra symbols, so that phoneme sequences that are longer than the grapheme sequence can be predicted. We propose to turn their approach upside-down and allow each

Proceedings of the 20th SIGMORPHON workshop on Computational Research in Phonetics, Phonology, and Morphology, pages 239–244

grapheme to predict multiple phonemes, instead of optionally deleting unnecessarily added input symbols.

However, in our current implementation, we predict a constant number of phonemes (which includes blank symbols) from each grapheme which is less flexible than the method proposed by Ribeiro et al. (2018), but avoids error propagation due to incorrectly predicted number of insertions. Generally, no pure sequence labelling method can achieve the same flexibility as sequence-to-sequence models, but for some problems with strong local relationship between the input sequence and the target sequence, like g2p, sequence labelling may be sufficient.

3 Method

We propose and evaluate 3 different sequence labelling methods. To refer to the different methods, we term them by their main inspiration: "Supervised" (cf. Jiampojamarn et al. (2007); Novak et al. (2016)), "Gram-CTC" (cf. Liu et al. (2017)), and "Inverse-Scatter-CTC" (cf. Ribeiro et al. (2018); Rosca and Breuel (2016)). The main challenge when applying sequence labelling methods to sequence transduction problems is finding a way to handle different lengths of the grapheme sequence and the phoneme sequence. The solution common to all our proposed methods is allowing to predict phoneme ngrams from grapheme unigrams and allowing to delete graphemes. Since in g2p the length of phoneme sequences cannot differ arbitrarily from the respective grapheme sequences, predicting ngrams, which imposes a strict bound on the length of the predicted phoneme sequence, is still a realistic approach. In the following, we describe each method in more detail.

3.1 Supervised Sequence Labelling

The supervised method is a pipeline consisting of aligning grapheme ngrams to phoneme ngrams and then training a sequence labelling model to predict phoneme ngrams from a sequence of graphemes (cf. Jiampojamarn et al. (2007)). We make the following design choices:

Our aligner is a neuralisation of the EM many-to-many aligner proposed by Jiampojamarn et al. (2007). The aligner calculates grapheme (unigram) and phoneme (unigram) embeddings from 1d convolutions applied to the grapheme sequence and phoneme sequence. Alignment scores of grapheme unigrams and phoneme unigrams are the dot-product between their embeddings. The aligner is trained by normalising the resulting alignment score matrix and maximising the alignment probability of the grapheme sequence and phoneme sequence, which can be efficiently calculated by dynamic programming. Alignments are obtained by calculating the Viterbi path through the alignment matrix. Note that this approach generalises unigram alignment scores to ngram alignments and therefore does not support deletion of graphemes, insertion of phonemes, or alignments of types other than 1-to-many and many-to-1 (which includes 1-to-1). Furthermore, the length of aligned ngrams is learned automatically and does not have to be set as hyperparameter.

Having obtained such alignments, any sequence labelling model can be trained to predict phoneme ngrams from graphemes. However, different from Jiampojamarn et al. (2007), we want to avoid training a chunker to deal with the many-to-1 case. We convert the many-to-1 case to 1-to-1 cases in the following way: Assign the aligned phoneme as label to the first grapheme in the grapheme ngram and assign deletion as label to all following graphemes in the grapheme ngram.

3.2 Gram-CTC Sequence Labelling

Gram-CTC as proposed by Liu et al. (2017) works as follows: Given a whitelist of allowed ngrams, decompose the target sequence (here: the phonemes) into all possible decompositions only containing ngrams in the whitelist. Then, for each symbol in the input sequence (here: the graphemes), calculate prediction probabilities for all ngrams in the whitelist. Also, prediction of a special blank token is possible (cf. Graves et al. (2006)). Finally, the model is trained by maximising the prediction probability of the target sequence, which is the sum of prediction probabilities of all decompositions. This sum can be efficiently computed by dynamic programming.

As whitelist, we use all phoneme ngrams that appear in alignments calculated for the supervised method (see Section 3.1). Compared to the main modus operandi described by Liu et al. (2017), who propose to use all ngrams up to a certain length, restricting the whitelist in this way stabilises and speeds up training.

Compared to the supervised method described in Section 3.1, Gram-CTC is not directly dependent on explicit grapheme-phoneme alignments, but learns such grapheme-phoneme alignments from scratch. Therefore, Gram-CTC can correct errors made by the aligner that would otherwise directly propagate to the sequence labelling model.

3.3 Inverse-Scatter-CTC Sequence Labelling

Inverse-Scatter-CTC works as follows: For each grapheme, predict τ phoneme unigrams. Thereby, the length of the predicted phoneme sequence is increased and, given a suitable τ, so that the number of predicted phonemes is always strictly greater than the number of target phonemes, we can use standard CTC (Graves et al., 2006) to train the model. We find $\tau \geq 3$ to work for all languages in the shared task except for Persian, where only $\tau \geq 4$ works. Therefore, we evaluate $\tau \in \{3, 4, 5\}$.

Compared to the supervised approach (see Section 3.1) and Gram-CTC (see Section 3.2), Inverse-Scatter-CTC has the advantage of only using phoneme unigrams as labels, thereby reducing the number of labels and allowing for more flexible alignments. Furthermore, Inverse-Scatter-CTC is not affected by an external aligner in any way.

4 Models

For sequence labelling, we always use a plain 1-layer BiLSTM model. Models are trained using the different approaches described in Section 3. For the transfer track, we do not entirely mix the target language and the transfer language, but we share the same embeddings and LSTM encoder for both languages and use separate classification layers, since we found this to yield better performance. Our intuition is that transfer data stabilises training and mitigates overfitting of embeddings and the LSTM encoder, but the target phonemes differ to a degree that makes separate decoding necessary.

For each language and track, we train 10 models and keep the best 5 performing models in terms of WER on the development set. We use these 5 models to compute word-level majority-voted ensemble predictions. We resolve ties by choosing the prediction from the model with lowest WER on the development set among all predictions with most votes.

The different approaches also require different hyperparameters. However, common to all setups are embedding size 64, no dropout or weight decay, vanilla SGD optimizer with one-cycle learning rate scheduler (Smith and Topin, 2019), and only keeping the best checkpoint from each training run based on WER on development set evaluated after every epoch. Hyperparameters that differ are training for 100 epochs with batch size 2, max. learning rate 0.01, clipping gradients with absolute value greater than 1 and the LSTM encoder having 128 hidden units for supervised and Gram-CTC, whereas Inverse-Scatter-CTC models are trained for 80 epochs with batch size 16, max. learning rate 0.1, no gradient clipping, and 256 hidden units for the LSTM encoder. All models and training routines are implemented in PyTorch (Paszke et al., 2019).

5 Results

In Table 1, we report test set word error rates (WER) of supervised and Gram-CTC models for all languages and tasks. These are the official results made available by the organisers. For the high and low resource scenarios, Gram-CTC improves upon supervised training for 6 out of 10 languages, and the macro-average WER is around 4 points lower. The most pronounced difference is for Thai in the high resource setting. This suggests that it is indeed helpful to allow learning to realign phoneme ngrams, as is done by Gram-CTC.

However, for the transfer task, we make different observations: While Gram-CTC performs worse in the transfer setting than in the low resource setting, supervised training is able to use the additional transfer data in order to improve upon its performance in the low resource setting. The improvement amounts to approximately 7 points in WER (macro-average). Therefore, transfer data can indeed be very helpful when used with the right kind of model.

This being said, Gram-CTC still outperforms supervised training in 6 out of 10 languages (transfer track). The fact that the macro-average WER of the supervised model is eventually lower is mainly due to the much better performance of supervised training on Tagalog (24 vs 50). If we ignore Tagalog when calculating macro-average scores, Gram-CTC (both low and transfer tracks) and supervised training (transfer track) perform almost equally well, with a slight advantage for Gram-CTC in transfer setting.

In Table 2, we report WER for Inverse-Scatter-CTC. In the high resource setting, we observe that greater τ (more outputs predicted from each grapheme) is beneficial. While there does not seem

	high		low		transfer	
	gram-ctc	supervised	gram-ctc	supervised	gram-ctc	supervised
ben	68.49	71.23	90.41	91.78	82.19	80.82
bur	37.00	51.00	90.00	95.00	92.00	94.00
ger	50.00	47.00	81.00	89.00	79.00	80.00
gle	33.00	39.00	78.00	86.00	78.00	82.00
ita	19.00	15.00	44.00	48.00	41.00	36.00
per	57.89	61.40	75.44	80.70	80.70	82.46
swe	54.00	51.00	84.00	86.00	82.00	74.00
tgl	15.00	14.00	40.00	42.00	50.00	24.00
tha	39.00	57.00	91.00	96.00	91.00	95.00
ukr	36.00	41.00	73.00	84.00	77.00	81.00
Avg.	40.94	44.76	74.68	79.85	75.29	72.93

Table 1: Word error rates (WER) for supervised and Gram-CTC models. Avg is macro-average over languages.

to be a visible trend for the low resource track, greater τ seems harmful in terms of macro-average WER for the transfer track.

Depending on τ, performance of Inverse-Scatter-CTC can be slightly better than performance of Gram-CTC, but we do not observe any decisive advantages. We demonstrate this in Figure 1: The numbers in the heatmap show for how many languages the model on the x-axis achieves strictly lower WER than the model on the y-axis. Despite having the lowest macro-average, supervised training actually is not superior to any model for more than 50% of the languages. Contrarily, Inverse-Scatter-CTC with τ=4 achieves better performance than most models for more than 50% of the languages, but has second-worst macro-averaged WER. Overall, Figure 1 shows that which model is best is language dependent and there is no clear winner among the models evaluated in this paper. Similar results can be found also for the high and the low resource tracks.

Compared to the baseline[1], our models generally perform worse in the high-resource tack, but better in the low resource and transfer tracks. This suggests that sequence-to-sequence models may be superior to sequence labelling models when enough data is available, while it is still possible to train neural (sequence labelling) models in the ultra-low resource settings.

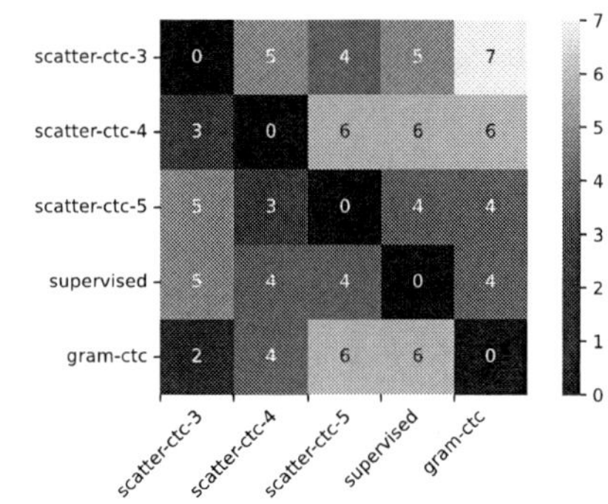

Figure 1: Heatmap showing for how many languages (out of 10) the model on the y-axis achieves strictly lower test set WER than the model on the x-axis. Results are shown for the transfer track.

6 Model Inspection

In the introduction, we claim that one advantage of sequence labelling methods is that they define a direct alignment between graphemes and phonemes, which can be inspected. Therefore, in Table 3, we give the 10 most frequent graphemes appearing in the German development set and their respective phonemes as predicted by the best trained German Inverse-Scatter-CTC model (τ=5). From Table 3, we can see that most alignments are reasonable (of course one would also have to look at the context). This means that the Inverse-Scatter-CTC indeed learns useful alignments of graphemes to phonemes. However, there are also some problems: While the German model seems to handle deletions (e.g. "sch" $\rightarrow$ "ʃ") rather well, it struggles with predicting multiple phonemes from one grapheme.

[1]Results taken from `https://github.com/sigmorphon/2022G2PST#baseline`

τ	high 3	high 4	high 5	low 3	low 4	low 5	transfer 3	transfer 4	transfer 5
ben	72.6	69.86	68.49	83.56	83.56	86.30	89.04	89.04	83.56
bur	31.0	37.00	35.00	87.00	86.00	87.00	90.00	93.00	86.00
ger	50.0	45.00	46.00	83.00	84.00	82.00	74.00	74.00	74.00
gle	35.0	37.00	36.00	76.00	76.00	79.00	74.00	80.00	81.00
ita	18.0	18.00	19.00	49.00	51.00	45.00	41.00	38.00	40.00
per	100.0	57.89	56.14	80.70	85.96	82.46	100.00	78.95	82.46
swe	53.0	51.00	52.00	81.00	81.00	81.00	77.00	80.00	74.00
tgl	16.0	18.00	15.00	35.00	37.00	32.00	40.00	68.00	92.00
tha	38.0	36.00	35.00	84.00	83.00	86.00	83.00	81.00	94.00
ukr	41.0	39.00	44.00	79.00	80.00	77.00	74.00	76.00	92.00
Avg.	45.46	40.88	40.66	73.83	74.75	73.78	74.20	75.80	79.90

Table 2: Word error rates (WER) for Inverse-Scatter-CTC models. τ is the number of outputs predicted from each grapheme. Avg is macro-average over languages.

Grapheme	Predicted Phonemes
e	ə, ␣, a, ɛ, eː, ʔ a, ɔ, ʔ ɛ, n̩
n	n, ␣, ŋ
r	ʁ, ɐ, ɐ̯, r
t	t, ␣
a	a, aː
i	ɪ, ɪ̯, iː, i, ʔ iː
s	ʃ, s, z, ␣, t͡s
h	␣, h
l	l, ␣
u	ʊ, u, ɪ̯, uː, ʊ̯

Table 3: Phoneme predictions of the 10 most frequent graphemes in the development set. Both graphemes and phonemes are sorted by frequency in descending order. "␣" denotes deletion.

In German, this is a rather rare phenomenon, occurring only for the grapheme "x", which is pronounced as "k s", and also for the glottal stop ʔ when words start with a vowel. For example, the pronunciation of German "axt" (English: "axe, ax") is predicted as "a k t", while "a k s t" is correct.

One possibility of how to make use of these direct alignments is using predefined mappings of graphemes to phonemes to restrict which phonemes may be predicted. Another advantage, of course, is error analysis. For the German model, for example, we would recommend adding more examples containing "x" to the training set. In fact, there is only one such example in the high resource training data, namely "existieren" (English: "to exist").

7 Conclusion

We presented and evaluated 3 sequence labelling methods for g2p: Supervised, Gram-CTC, and Inverse-Scatter-CTC. We show that all 3 methods can be applied to all 3 tracks, but no method seems clearly superior to the other methods. In the high resource setting, the baseline sequence-to-sequence model seems to yield better performance than sequence labelling methods. However, sequence labelling methods seem to perform better in the very low resource settings. Finally, we show that Inverse-Scatter-CTC models learn reasonable alignments of graphemes and phonemes, thereby validating the claim that sequence labelling models allow for comparatively easy model inspection.

Acknowledgements

We thank Çağrı Çöltekin for helpful discussions and providing access to computation resources. We thank the organisers for organising this shared task.

References

Lucas F.E. Ashby, Travis M. Bartley, Simon Clematide, Luca Del Signore, Cameron Gibson, Kyle Gorman, Yeonju Lee-Sikka, Peter Makarov, Aidan Malanoski, Sean Miller, Omar Ortiz, Reuben Raff, Arundhati Sengupta, Bora Seo, Yulia Spektor, and Winnie Yan. 2021. Results of the second SIGMORPHON shared task on multilingual grapheme-to-phoneme conversion. In *Proceedings of the 18th SIGMORPHON Workshop on Computational Research in Phonetics, Phonology, and Morphology*, pages 115–125, Online. Association for Computational Linguistics.

Simon Clematide and Peter Makarov. 2021. CLUZH at SIGMORPHON 2021 shared task on multilingual grapheme-to-phoneme conversion: Variations on a baseline. In *Proceedings of the 18th SIGMORPHON Workshop on Computational Research in Phonetics, Phonology, and Morphology*, pages 148–153, Online. Association for Computational Linguistics.

Lucian Galescu and James F. Allen. 2001. Bi-directional conversion between graphemes and phonemes using a joint n-gram model. In *4th ITRW on Speech Synthesis, Perthshire, Scotland, UK, August 29 - September 1, 2001*, page 131. ISCA.

Kyle Gorman, Lucas F.E. Ashby, Aaron Goyzueta, Arya McCarthy, Shijie Wu, and Daniel You. 2020. The SIGMORPHON 2020 shared task on multilingual grapheme-to-phoneme conversion. In *Proceedings of the 17th SIGMORPHON Workshop on Computational Research in Phonetics, Phonology, and Morphology*, pages 40–50, Online. Association for Computational Linguistics.

Alex Graves, Santiago Fernández, Faustino J. Gomez, and Jürgen Schmidhuber. 2006. Connectionist temporal classification: labelling unsegmented sequence data with recurrent neural networks. In *Machine Learning, Proceedings of the Twenty-Third International Conference (ICML 2006), Pittsburgh, Pennsylvania, USA, June 25-29, 2006*, volume 148 of *ACM International Conference Proceeding Series*, pages 369–376. ACM.

Sittichai Jiampojamarn, Grzegorz Kondrak, and Tarek Sherif. 2007. Applying many-to-many alignments and hidden Markov models to letter-to-phoneme conversion. In *Human Language Technologies 2007: The Conference of the North American Chapter of the Association for Computational Linguistics; Proceedings of the Main Conference*, pages 372–379, Rochester, New York. Association for Computational Linguistics.

Hairong Liu, Zhenyao Zhu, Xiangang Li, and Sanjeev Satheesh. 2017. Gram-CTC: Automatic unit selection and target decomposition for sequence labelling. In *Proceedings of the 34th International Conference on Machine Learning, ICML 2017, Sydney, NSW, Australia, 6-11 August 2017*, volume 70 of *Proceedings of Machine Learning Research*, pages 2188–2197. PMLR.

Peter Makarov and Simon Clematide. 2018a. Imitation learning for neural morphological string transduction. In *Proceedings of the 2018 Conference on Empirical Methods in Natural Language Processing*, pages 2877–2882, Brussels, Belgium. Association for Computational Linguistics.

Peter Makarov and Simon Clematide. 2018b. Neural transition-based string transduction for limited-resource setting in morphology. In *Proceedings of the 27th International Conference on Computational Linguistics*, pages 83–93, Santa Fe, New Mexico, USA. Association for Computational Linguistics.

Arya D. McCarthy, Jackson L. Lee, Alexandra DeLucia, Winston Wu, Travis M. Bartley, Milind Agarwal, Lucas F.E. Ashby, Luca Del Signore, and Cameron Gibson. 2022. Results of the third SIGMORPHON shared task on cross-lingual and low-resource grapheme-to-phoneme conversion. In *Proceedings of the 19th SIGMORPHON Workshop on Computational Research in Phonetics, Phonology, and Morphology*, Seattle, USA. Association for Computational Linguistics.

Josef R. Novak, Nobuaki Minematsu, and Keikichi Hirose. 2016. Phonetisaurus: Exploring grapheme-to-phoneme conversion with joint n-gram models in the WFST framework. *Nat. Lang. Eng.*, 22(6):907–938.

Adam Paszke, Sam Gross, Francisco Massa, Adam Lerer, James Bradbury, Gregory Chanan, Trevor Killeen, Zeming Lin, Natalia Gimelshein, Luca Antiga, Alban Desmaison, Andreas Kopf, Edward Yang, Zachary DeVito, Martin Raison, Alykhan Tejani, Sasank Chilamkurthy, Benoit Steiner, Lu Fang, Junjie Bai, and Soumith Chintala. 2019. Pytorch: An imperative style, high-performance deep learning library. In H. Wallach, H. Larochelle, A. Beygelzimer, F. d'Alché-Buc, E. Fox, and R. Garnett, editors, *Advances in Neural Information Processing Systems 32*, pages 8024–8035. Curran Associates, Inc.

Joana Ribeiro, Shashi Narayan, Shay B. Cohen, and Xavier Carreras. 2018. Local string transduction as sequence labeling. In *Proceedings of the 27th International Conference on Computational Linguistics*, pages 1360–1371, Santa Fe, New Mexico, USA. Association for Computational Linguistics.

Mihaela Rosca and Thomas M. Breuel. 2016. Sequence-to-sequence neural network models for transliteration. *CoRR*, abs/1610.09565.

Carsten Schnober, Steffen Eger, Erik-Lân Do Dinh, and Iryna Gurevych. 2016. Still not there? comparing traditional sequence-to-sequence models to encoder-decoder neural networks on monotone string translation tasks. In *Proceedings of COLING 2016, the 26th International Conference on Computational Linguistics: Technical Papers*, pages 1703–1714, Osaka, Japan. The COLING 2016 Organizing Committee.

Leslie N. Smith and Nicholay Topin. 2019. Super-convergence: very fast training of neural networks using large learning rates. In *Artificial Intelligence and Machine Learning for Multi-Domain Operations Applications*, volume 11006 of *Society of Photo-Optical Instrumentation Engineers (SPIE) Conference Series*, page 1100612.

Shijie Wu, Ryan Cotterell, and Mans Hulden. 2021. Applying the transformer to character-level transduction. In *Proceedings of the 16th Conference of the European Chapter of the Association for Computational Linguistics: Main Volume*, pages 1901–1907, Online. Association for Computational Linguistics.

Low-resource grapheme-to-phoneme mapping with phonetically-conditioned transfer

Michael Hammond
Dept. of Linguistics
U. of Arizona
Tucson, AZ, USA
hammond@u.arizona.edu

Abstract

In this paper we explore a very simple non-neural approach to mapping orthography to phonetic transcription in a low-resource context with transfer data from a related language. We start from a baseline system and focus our efforts on data augmentation. We make three principal moves. First, we start with an HMM-based system (Novak et al., 2012). Second, we augment our basic system by recombining legal substrings in restricted fashion (Ryan and Hulden, 2020). Finally, we limit our transfer data by only using training pairs where the phonetic form shares all bigrams with the target language.

1 Introduction

This paper describes the submission by our team to the 2022 version of the SIGMORPHON grapheme-to-phoneme conversion challenge (McCarthy et al., 2022). Here we describe our efforts to improve grapheme-to-phoneme mapping for low-resource languages in a non-neural context using only data augmentation techniques.

The problem in the low-resource condition was to map from graphemes to phonetic segments with extremely limited data. Specifically, there were 10 languages with 100 training pairs and 100 development pairs. Each pair was a word in its orthographic representation and a phonetic transcription of that word. In addition, for each language, there were up to 1000 additional training pairs in a "related" language. Systems were then tested on 100 additional pairs for each language. The 10 languages are given in Table 1 along with their codes and the number of additional training pairs.

In addition, there was a higher-resource condition where each language had 1000 pairs without transfer data; our focus was the low-resource condition.

2 Initial neural approaches

We started with a fairly generic transformer system inspired by one of the 2020 baseline systems (Gorman et al., 2020). The system we used is adapted from the OpenNMT base (Klein et al., 2017) and is similar to the one used by Hammond (2021) in the 2021 challenge. There is a 512-element embedding layer in both encoder and decoder. There are six layers in both encoder and decoder and each layer also has 512 nodes. The systems are connected by a 8-head attention mechanism (Luong et al., 2015). Training proceeds in 1,000 steps and the decay method is Noam. Optimization is Adam, the batch size is 8, and the dropout rate is 0.1.[1]

Using this system and running 1000 steps, performance on validation data is terrible as seen in Table 2. In column 1 we give the language codes; column 2 has performance for the 100-pair condition; column 3 gives the results for the 1000-pair condition; and column 4 gives the results with transfer data included.

To get a sense of how much data might be required to get decent performance, we ran a similar transformer configuration over subsets of the CMU pronouncing dictionary (Weide, 1998) for 5 epochs and got the performance in Table 3. The point of this chart is that 100 data pairs is orders of magnitude less than what is needed.

3 An HMM-based approach

Based on how poorly our neural approaches performed with such limited data, we went back to classical HMM-based approaches, specifically selecting the *Phonetisaurus* system (Novak et al., 2012).

This system is based on OpenFST and uses weighted finite-state transducers and expectation-

[1] Full configuration files for this and the experiments below are available at https://github.com/hammondm/g2p2022.

Proceedings of the 20th SIGMORPHON workshop on Computational Research in Phonetics, Phonology, and Morphology, pages 245–248

Target language	Code	Transfer language	Code	Number
Bengali	ben	Assamese	asm	1000
Burmese	bur	Shan	shn	841
German	ger	Dutch	dut	1000
Irish	gle	Welsh	wel	1000
Italian	ita	Romanian	rum	1000
Persian	per	Pashto	pus	721
Swedish	swe	Norwegian Nynorsk	nno	1000
Tagalog	tgl	Cebuano	ceb	126
Thai	tha	Eastern Lawa	lwl	253
Ukrainian	ukr	Belarusian	bel	1000

Table 1: Languages, codes, and the number of additional training pairs in the transfer language

Lang	100	1000	all
ben	100.00	93.15	98.63
ger	99.00	93.00	98.00
ita	99.00	92.00	97.00
per	98.21	94.64	100.00
swe	100.00	93.00	92.00
tgl	99.00	92.00	98.00
tha	98.00	78.00	99.00
ukr	100.00	91.00	100.00
gle	100.00	94.00	100.00
bur	100.00	81.00	99.00
mean	99.32	90.17	98.16

Table 2: Validation WER for all languages with encoder-decoder after 1000 steps

Data	WER
1000	100.00
5000	100.00
10000	83.00
20000	69.00
30000	65.00
133802	53.55

Table 3: Validation WER for CMU with a transformer for 5 epochs with different amounts of data

Lang	100/2	100/3	1000/2	1000/3
ben	91.78	91.78	65.75	68.49
ger	88.00	86.00	57.00	61.00
ita	54.00	54.00	33.00	25.00
per	87.50	89.29	76.79	67.86
swe	83.00	82.00	65.00	55.00
tgl	34.00	34.00	19.00	18.00
tha	97.00	95.00	74.00	72.00
ukr	86.00	89.00	57.00	50.00
gle	93.00	95.00	57.00	51.00
bur	98.00	98.00	49.00	48.00
mean	81.22	81.4	55.35	51.63

Table 4: Validation WER for Phonetisaurus without augmentation

maximization to compute the best many-to-many alignment of letters and phonetic symbols. The system offers a number of different options for alignment and decoding, but we ran it in its most "generic" form.

In Table 4 we give WER for 100 pairs and for 1000 pairs. We can use bigrams or trigrams for the alignment and both are given. The point is that, out of the box, the HMM system performs much better than the neural systems. Compare Table 4 with Table 2.

4 Augmentation steps

We tried several kinds of augmentations. The first was the substring approach developed by Ryan and Hulden (2020). In this approach plausible alignments from the beginnings and ends of words are recombined. In the original approach, techniques were used to increase the likelihood that the alignment point occurred at a plausible C-V or V-C juncture. We found that this did not work for all languages in our test set, presumably due to how limited the data were. We therefore disabled this feature.

The other augmentation we used applied to the transfer data. If one looks at the training pairs, it's apparent that in a number of cases, the languages are not terribly similar.

For example, Irish and Welsh are indeed related and the diligent linguist can easily find cognates. For example, the Welsh word for 'book' is *llyfr* [ɬɨvɨr] and the Irish word is *leabhar* [lʲəurˠ]. The Welsh word for 'man' is *dyn* [dɨːn]; the Irish word for 'person' is *duine* [dˠɪnʲə]. There are also similar grammatical features. For example, both languages use initial consonant mutation as a grammatical mechanism, both have VSO word order, and both have inflected prepositions.

On the other hand, the orthographic conventions of the two languages are extremely divergent, as are the phonetic inventories. For example, Irish has a contrast between palatalized and plain consonants that is completely absent in Welsh. This contrast is reflected in the orthography where adjacent front vowel letters *i* and *e* indicate that a consonant is palatalized. This orthographic practice applies on both sides of a consonant. Thus, if a consonant is intervocalic and palatalized, it will have front vowels on both sides; if it's not palatalized, it will have back vowels. On the other hand, unlike Irish, Welsh strikingly can use *w* and *y* as vowels giving rise to words that seem quite unpronouncable, e.g. *tywydd* [tʰəwɨð] 'weather' or *gŵr* [guːr] 'husband'.

With this in mind, we tried approaches that would limit the transfer data to just those pairs that were most like the target language.

We tried three approaches in this vein. First, we only took pairs where the phonetic segments of the transfer language were in the inventory of the target language. Second, we further restricted the pairs to only those where the phonetic bigrams of the transfer language all occurred in the target language. Finally, we only included pairs where all orthographic characters in the transfer language occurred in the target language.

Different combinations of these options appear in Table 5. The second column gives validation WER for all 100 training pairs plus all transfer data (all). In the third column we have results when only transfer pairs with shared phonetic elements are included (phon). In column 4, we only include transfer pairs where the phonetic and orthographic elements are shared with the target language (phonorth). In column 5, we further restrict that so all phonetic bigrams must be shared (phorth+bg). In column 6, we leave the orthographic relationship unrestricted, but require shared phonetic bigrams (phbg). Finally, in column 7, we have shared bigrams and we add 1900 forms created with shared legal prefixes and suffixes from the target language (phbg+1900).

Looking at Table 5, we see that adding all transfer data diminishes performance. If we restrict the phonetic relationship between the transfer data and the target language, we get some improvement. We also get improvement if we restrict the relationship further with either phonetic bigrams or orthographic overlap, but curiously those two criteria do not help simultaneously. Finally, we see that we get still further improvement with the substring recombination technique.

Performance on the test data of course varies slightly from what we saw with the validation data so we give those results in Table 6 for the full 1000 pairs, the small 100-pair set, and our final system with phonetically-restricted transfer data (using phonetic bigrams) plus substring recombined forms.

5 Conclusion

In conclusion, we've seen several effects. First, a simple encoder-decoder or transformer does not perform well with so few data. Second, an HMM-based approach does better, and does better still when we restrict the kind of transfer data that is used. Specifically, transfer data should be restricted based on how similar it is to the target language. Similarity in terms of phonetics is clearly beneficial, but similarity in terms of orthography seems to help as well. Finally, we saw that the substring recombination technique of Ryan and Hulden (2020) can be added on top of these moves for an additional benefit.

Acknowledgments

Thanks to Sayed Issa and Diane Ohala for useful discussion. All errors are my own.

References

Kyle Gorman, Lucas F.E. Ashby, Aaron Goyzueta, Arya McCarthy, Shijie Wu, and Daniel You. 2020. The SIGMORPHON 2020 shared task on multilingual grapheme-to-phoneme conversion. In *Proceedings*

Lang	all	phon	phonorth	phorth+bg	phbg	phbg+1900
ben	80.82	79.45	83.56	84.93	84.93	86.30
ger	92.00	85.00	85.00	80.00	80.00	81.00
ita	38.00	38.00	35.00	38.00	38.00	36.00
per	94.64	91.07	91.07	89.29	89.29	89.29
swe	78.00	74.00	71.00	69.00	68.00	71.00
tgl	66.00	37.00	37.00	35.00	35.00	47.00
tha	96.00	93.00	93.00	95.00	95.00	96.00
ukr	96.00	88.00	88.00	95.00	94.00	80.00
gle	98.00	97.00	97.00	96.00	96.00	87.00
bur	97.00	98.00	98.00	98.00	98.00	93.00
mean	83.64	78.05	77.86	78.02	77.82	76.65

Table 5: Validation WER for target + transfer data: a) all data, b) overlapping phonetic segments, c) overlapping and orthographic segments, d) overlapping orthographic segments and phonetic bigrams, e) phonetic bigrams, f) phonetic bigrams and recombined substrings

Lang	1000	100	100+transfer
ben	71.23	91.78	79.45
ger	48.00	90.00	85.00
ita	29.00	50.00	41.00
per	59.65	80.70	82.46
swe	62.00	82.00	81.00
tgl	16.00	24.00	37.00
tha	71.00	95.00	91.00
ukr	53.00	96.00	86.00
gle	56.00	93.00	85.00
bur	46.00	93.00	89.00
mean	51.19	79.55	75.69

Table 6: Test WER for for the full 1000 pairs, the small 100-pair set, and our final system with phonetically-restricted transfer data (using phonetic bigrams) plus substring recombined forms

of the 17th SIGMORPHON Workshop on Computational Research in Phonetics, Phonology, and Morphology, pages 40–50. Association for Computational Linguistics.

Michael Hammond. 2021. Data augmentation for low-resource grapheme-to-phoneme mapping. In *Proceedings of the 18th SIGMORPHON Workshop on Computational Research in Phonetics, Phonology, and Morphology*, pages 126–130. Association for Computational Linguistics.

G. Klein, Y. Kim, Y. Y. Deng, J. Senellart, and A.M. Rush. 2017. OpenNMT: Open-source toolkit for neural machine translation. *ArXiv e-prints*. 1701.02810.

Minh-Thang Luong, Hieu Pham, and Christopher D. Manning. 2015. Effective approaches to attention-based neural machine translation. In *Proceedings of the 2015 Conference on Empirical Methods in Natural Language Processing*, pages 1412–1421.

Arya D. McCarthy, Jackson L. Lee, Alexandra DeLucia, Winston Wu, Travis M. Bartley, Milind Agarwal, Lucas F.E. Ashby, Luca Del Signore, and Cameron Gibson. 2022. Results of the third SIGMORPHON shared task on cross-lingual and low-resource grapheme-to-phoneme conversion. In *Proceedings of the 19th SIGMORPHON Workshop on Computational Research in Phonetics, Phonology, and Morphology*, Seattle, USA. Association for Computational Linguistics.

Josef R Novak, Nobuaki Minematsu, and Keikichi Hirose. 2012. WFST-based grapheme-to-phoneme conversion: Open source tools for alignment, model-building and decoding. In *Proceedings of the 10th International Workshop on Finite State Methods and Natural Language Processing*, pages 45–49.

Zach Ryan and Mans Hulden. 2020. Data augmentation for transformer-based G2P. In *Proceedings of the 17th SIGMORPHON Workshop on Computational Research in Phonetics, Phonology, and Morphology*, pages 184–188. Association for Computational Linguistics.

Robert L. Weide. 1998. The CMU pronouncing dictionary. `http://www.speech.cs.cmu.edu/cgi-bin/cmudict`.

A future for universal grapheme-phoneme transduction modeling with neuralized finite-state transducers

Chu-Cheng Lin
Johns Hopkins University
kitsing@cs.jhu.edu

Abstract

We propose a universal grapheme-phoneme transduction model using neuralized finite-state transducers.

Many computational models of grapheme-phoneme transduction nowadays are based on the (autoregressive) sequence-to-sequence string transduction paradigm. While such models have achieved state-of-the-art performance, they suffer from theoretical limitations of autoregressive models. On the other hand, neuralized finite-state transducers (NFSTs) have shown promising results on various string transduction tasks. NFSTs can be seen as a generalization of weighted finite-state transducers (WFSTs), and can be seen as pairs of a featurized finite-state machine ('marked finite-state transducer' or MFST in NFST terminology), and a string scoring function. Instead of taking a product of local contextual feature weights on FST arcs, NFSTs can employ arbitrary scoring functions to weight global contextual features of a string transduction, and therefore break the Markov property. Furthermore, NFSTs can be formally shown to be more expressive than (autoregressive) seq2seq models. Empirically, joint grapheme-phoneme transduction NFSTs have consistently outperformed vanilla seq2seq models on grapheme-to-phoneme and phoneme-to-grapheme transduction tasks for English. Furthermore, they provide interpretable aligned string transductions, thanks to their finite-state machine component.

In this talk, we propose a multilingual extension of the joint grapheme-phoneme NFST. We achieve this goal by modeling typological and phylogenetic features of languages and scripts as optional latent variables using a finite-state machine. The result is a versatile grapheme-phoneme transduction model: in addition to standard monolingual and multilingual transduction, the proposed multilingual NFST can also be used in various controlled generation scenarios, such as phoneme-to-grapheme transduction of an unseen language-script pair. We also plan to release an NFST software package.

Proceedings of the 20th SIGMORPHON workshop on Computational Research in Phonetics, Phonology, and Morphology, pages 249–249
July 14, 2023

Fine-tuning mSLAM for the SIGMORPHON 2022 Shared Task on Grapheme-to-Phoneme Conversion

Dan Garrette
Google Research
dhgarrette@google.com

Abstract

Grapheme-to-phoneme (G2P) conversion is a task that is inherently related to both written and spoken language. Therefore, our submission to the G2P shared task builds off of mSLAM (Bapna et al., 2022), a 600M parameter encoder model pretrained simultaneously on text from 101 languages and speech from 51 languages. For fine-tuning a G2P model, we combined mSLAM's text encoder, which uses characters as its input tokens, with an uninitialized single-layer RNN-T decoder (Graves, 2012) whose vocabulary is the set of all 381 phonemes appearing in the shared task data. We took an explicitly multilingual approach to modeling the G2P tasks, fine-tuning and evaluating a single model that covered all the languages in each task, and adding language codes as prefixes to the input strings as a means of specifying the language of each example.

Our models perform well in the shared task's "high" setting (in which they were trained on 1,000 words from each language), though they do poorly in the "low" task setting (training on only 100 words from each language). Our models also perform reasonably in the "mixed" setting (training on 100 words in the target language and 1000 words in a related language), hinting that mSLAM's multilingual pretraining may be enabling useful cross-lingual sharing.

References

Ankur Bapna, Colin Cherry, Yu Zhang, Ye Jia, Melvin Johnson, Yong Cheng, Simran Khanuja, Jason Riesa, and Alexis Conneau. 2022. mSLAM: Massively multilingual joint pre-training for speech and text. *arXiv preprint arXiv:2202.01374*.

Alex Graves. 2012. Sequence transduction with recurrent neural networks. *arXiv preprint arXiv:1211.3711*.

Proceedings of the 20th SIGMORPHON workshop on Computational Research in Phonetics, Phonology, and Morphology, pages 250–250
July 14, 2023

Author Index

Association for Computational Linguistics
209 N. Eighth Street
Stroudsburg, Pennsylvania 18360

ISBN 978-1-7138-8180-3

CURRAN ASSOCIATES INC.
proceedings.com